FROMMER'S
DOLLARWISE GUIDE TO FRANCE

by Stanley Haggart and
Darwin Porter

1981-1982 Edition

Published by Frommer/Pasmantier Publishers
A Simon & Schuster Division of
Gulf & Western Corporation
1230 Avenue of the Americas
New York, New York 10020

ISBN 0-671-41425-9

Manufactured in the United States of America

*Although every effort was made to insure the accuracy
of price information appearing in this book,
it should be kept in mind that prices
can and do fluctuate in the course of time.*

CONTENTS

MAPS

For their work in the research and editorial preparation of this book, we are deeply indebted to Mr. and Mrs. Pierre Français and Margaret Foresman.

INFLATION ALERT!!!

In the wave of inflation that has battered Europe, France has been hard hit. The authors of this guide have spent laborious hours of research, trying to insure the accuracy of the prices appearing in this book. As we go to press, we believe we have obtained the most reliable data available. However, in a system that in 1980 saw one restaurauteur in the Loire Valley raise the price of his salmon three times in one summer, we can't offer guarantees for the tariffs quoted. In the lifetime of this edition—particularly in its second year (1982)—the wise traveler will add *at least* 20 percent to the prices quoted.

THE FRANC AND THE DOLLAR: The franc, like all world currencies, is currently fluctuating on the world market. That means that the franc-to-dollar conversions appearing in parentheses throughout these chapters may or may not be exact. There is no way to predict what the rate of exchange will be when you visit France. Check with your bank to determine the up-to-date figure. And refer to the Appendix of this book for franc-to-dollar conversions at the time of this printing.

DOLLARWISE GUIDE TO FRANCE

The Reason Why

FRANCE IS A NATION of contrasts, united by love of country . . . and a loaf of bread. Wherever you go, from the streets of Marseille to the fishing hamlets of Brittany, from the provincial capitals to the "capital of capitals," you'll see the French, the matronly and the chic, carrying home their daily bread.

Of course, even this time-honored ritual is changing. Many modern homemakers in France buy their bread at supermarkets wrapped in waxpaper. Gaul is not entirely trapped by its traditions. You may find some elderly wives of fishermen in Britanny wearing the starched lace headdresses their grandmothers' mothers did before them. But at the next table you might meet their daughters, exquisitely attired in the latest Parisian fashions, discussing the state of the theater in New York.

Some things in France never change, though. Priests still walk the streets of provincial towns greeting aging women in black; lovers with their arms wrapped around each other still stroll along the banks of the Seine; and Left Bank students still spend an evening arguing philosophy over a bottle of wine. The *agent pivot* still directs traffic with a white baton, waving speeding motorists through the Arc de Triomphe; French people still spend hours in their favorite cafés; and little old winemakers practice the same basic techniques they have for generations. The nation, then, is a land rich in tradition, and it is that quality we'll search for as we explore—

THE BEST OF FRANCE: We have set ourselves the formidable task of seeking out France at its finest and condensing that between the covers of this book. The best towns, villages, cities, and sightseeing attractions; the best hotels, restaurants, bars, cafés, and night spots.

But the best need not be the most expensive. Our ultimate aim—beyond that of familiarizing you with the offerings of France—is to stretch your dollar power . . . to reveal to you that you need not always pay scalper's prices for charm, top-grade comfort, and gourmet-level food.

In this guide, we'll devote a great deal of attention to those old tourist meccas—Paris, Cannes, Monaco, Biarritz—focusing on both their obvious and hidden treasures. But they are not the full reason why of this book. Important as they are, they simply do not reflect fully the widely diverse and complicated country that France is. To discover that, you must venture deep into the provinces.

DOLLARWISE—WHAT IT MEANS: In brief, this is a guidebook giving specific details, including prices, about French hotels, restaurants, bars, cafés, sightseeing attractions, nightlife, and tours. Establishments in many price ranges have been documented and described, though mainly we are searching for bargains such as the Hostellerie Gargantua, a family-style inn named after Rabelais' amiable giant, Gargantua, in the charming village of Chinon in the château country. It charges 85F ($19.41) per person for a double room with bath, with a continental breakfast with homemade croissants.

In all cases, establishments have been judged by a strict yardstick of value. If they measured up, they were included.

Now, more than ever, one needs an accurate guidebook including tips for saving money. By careful planning and selecting from our listings, you'll find the true French experience while remaining within your budget. This applies to independent travelers as well as those who visit France on a package tour. Even though you've obtained your flight ticket, and are offered a hotel for a few days, you'll still need helpful tips on restaurants, nightlife, and sightseeing attractions. If you're given a car, then you'll be in the market for suggestions in the country, or at least outside of Paris.

Some Words of Explanation

No restaurant, inn, hotel, nightclub, or café paid to be mentioned in this book. What you read are entirely personal recommendations; in many cases, the proprietors never knew their establishments were being visited or investigated for inclusion in a travel guide.

Unfortunately, although we have made every effort to be as accurate as possible, prices change, and they rarely go downward, at least in France. The country has only limited government regulation of its hotel tariffs, unlike Spain and Italy, but more supervision than England or Scandinavia.

Always, when checking in, inquire about the rate—and agree on it. That policy can save much embarrassment and disappointment when it comes time to settle the tab. If the prices quoted are not the same as those mentioned in this book, remember that our prices reflect those in effect at the time this edition was researched. As we said, prices change.

This guide is revised cover to cover every other year. But even in a book that appears with such frequency, it may happen that that cozy little bistro of a year ago has changed its stripes, blossoming out with cut-velvet walls, crystal chandeliers, and dining tabs that include the decorator's fee and the owner's villa at Deauville. It may further develop that some of the people or settings we've described are no longer there or have been changed.

THE $15-A-DAY TRAVEL CLUB: In just a few paragraphs, you'll begin your exploration of France. But before you do, you may want to learn about a device for saving money on all your trips and travels; we refer to the now widely known $15-a-Day Travel Club, which has gone into its 18th successful year of operation.

The Club was formed at the urging of readers of the $15-a-Day Books and the Dollarwise Guides, many of whom felt that such an organization could bring financial benefits, continuing travel information, and a sense of community to economy-minded travelers in all parts of the world. We thought—and

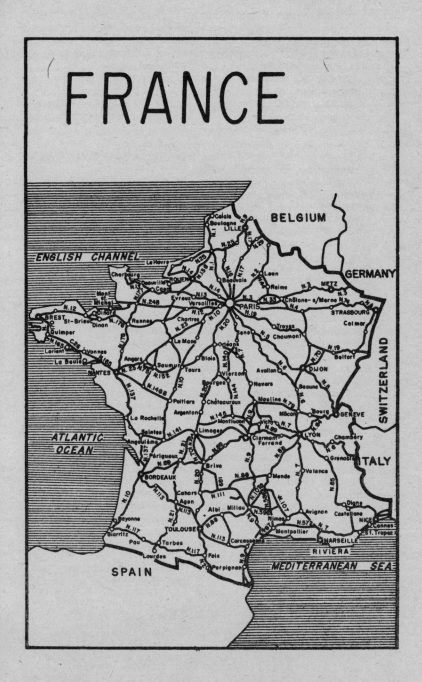

FRANCE

have since learned—that the idea had merit. For by combining the purchasing power of thousands of our readers, we've been able to obtain a wide range of exciting travel benefits—including occasional discounts to members from auto rental agencies, restaurants, sightseeing operators, hotels, and other purveyors of tourist services throughout the United States and abroad.

In keeping with the budget concept, the membership fee is low and is immediately exceeded by the value of your benefits. Upon receipt of U.S. $12 (U.S., Canadian, and Mexican residents), or $14 (other foreign residents) to cover one year's membership, we will send all new members by return mail (book rate) the following items:

(1) The latest edition of any *two* of the following books (please designate in your letter which two books you wish to receive).

Europe on $20 a Day
Australia on $15 & $20 a Day
England and Scotland on $20 a Day
Greece and Yugoslavia on $15 & $20 a Day
Hawaii on $25 a Day
Ireland on $25 a Day
Israel on $20 a Day
Mexico and Guatemala on $15 & $20 a Day
New Zealand on $15 & $20 a Day
Scandinavia on $25 a Day
South America on $15 & $20 a Day
Spain and Morocco (plus the Canary Is.) on $20 a Day
Washington, D.C. on $25 a Day

Dollarwise Guide to the Caribbean (including Bermuda and the Bahamas)
Dollarwise Guide to Canada
Dollarwise Guide to Egypt
Dollarwise Guide to England and Scotland
Dollarwise Guide to France
Dollarwise Guide to Germany
Dollarwise Guide to Italy
Dollarwise Guide to Portugal (plus Madeira and the Azores)
Dollarwise Guide to California and Las Vegas
Dollarwise Guide to New England
Dollarwise Guide to the Southeast and New Orleans
(Dollarwise Guides discuss accommodations and facilities in all price ranges, with emphasis on the medium-priced.)

The Caribbean Bargain Book
(A one-of-a-kind guide to the "off-season" Caribbean—mid-April to mid-December—and the fabulous resorts that slash their rates from 20% to 60%; includes almost every island group in the Caribbean, and the Bahamas too.)

Frommer's Guide to China
(A unique guide to the latest opportunities for group, individual, and business travel to and around China; includes hotels, restaurants, sights, and shopping; history and culture plus a substantial phrase book section.)

How to Live in Florida on $10,000 a Year
(For the resident or anyone contemplating the move, this book provides all the information needed to live economically but well in the Sunshine State.)

Where to Stay USA
(By the Council on International Educational Exchange, this extraordinary guide is the first to list accommodations in all 50 states that cost anywhere from $2 to $20 per night.)

(2) A copy of **Arthur Frommer's Guide to New York,** a newly revised pocket-size guide to hotels, restaurants, nightspots, and sightseeing attractions in all price ranges throughout the New York area.

(3) A one-year subscription to the quarterly Club newsletter—**The Wonderful World of Budget Travel** (about which more below)—which keeps members up-to-date on fast-breaking developments in low-cost travel to all areas of the world.

(4) A voucher entitling you to a $5 discount on any Arthur Frommer International, Inc. tour booked by you through travel agents in the United States and Canada.

(5) Your personal membership card, which, once received, entitles you to purchase through the Club all Arthur Frommer publications for a third to a half off their regular retail prices during the term of your membership.

Those are the immediate and definite benefits which we can assure to members of the Club at this time. Further benefits, which it has been our continuing aim to achieve for members, are announced to members in *The Wonderful World of Budget Travel (WWBT)*. An eight-page, full-size newspaper, *WWBT* carries such continuing features as "The Traveler's Directory" (a list of members all over the world who are willing to provide hospitality to other members as they pass through their home cities) and "Share-a-Trip" (offers and requests from members for travel companions who can share costs); worldwide travel news and feature stories by our acclaimed expert travel writers; plus tips and articles on specific plans and methods for travel savings.

If you would like to join this hardy band of international budgeteers and participate in its exchange of travel information and hospitality, simply send your name and address, together with your membership fee of $12 (U.S., Canadian, and Mexican residents), or $14 (other foreign residents) in U.S. currency to: $15-a-Day Travel Club, Inc., Frommer/Pasmantier Publishers, 1230 Avenue of the Americas, New York, NY 10020. Remember to specify which *two* books in section (1) above you wish to receive in your initial package of members' benefits. Or, if you prefer, use the last page of this book, simply checking off the two books you want and enclosing $12 or $14 in U.S. currency.

Chapter I

GETTING THERE

1. Plane Economics
2. Traveling Within France

A HOLIDAY IN FRANCE, for the readers of this book, must first begin with a transatlantic trip *to* France. That requires a brief examination of the available transportation—especially the question of air transportation.

1. Plane Economics

A popular new formula in budget travel, **Air France Vacances,** offers summer flights between New York and Paris for the round-trip fare of $512 (subject to change). The four-times-weekly service (Monday, Friday, Saturday, and Sunday) is aboard a one-class, 500-seat B747 reserved to Vacances passengers and featuring confirmed reservations and simplified inflight service. There are no group, advance purchase, standby, or other restrictions. The only requirements are full payment at the time of the ticketing and a minimum stay of 14 days and a maximum time of 60 days abroad.

On the **Vacances Youth Fare,** passengers from ages 12 through 22 can stay up to one full year. For an additional $50, they can even leave with an open return ticket and make return reservations in Europe.

Air France Midweeker: Out of Chicago, Houston, and Los Angeles, Air France features Midweeker fares on its nonstop B747's to Paris. These fares apply on weekdays only and are governed by the same rules and regulations as Vacances out of New York.

Round-trip Midweeker fares to Paris are:

Chicago	$620
Houston	755
Los Angeles	820

Midweeker Youth Fare: The same provisions here are in effect as for the Vacances Youth Fare. Midweeker rates apply to passengers who range in age from 12 through 22.

THE CHOICE OF AIRLINE: In choosing an airline for your trip to France, your thoughts will immediately turn to **Air France.** The French national carrier operates more daily transatlantic flights to Paris—as many as eight a day—from more cities in North America than any other carrier: New York, Washington, D.C., Houston, Chicago, Los Angeles, Anchorage, Montreal,

Toronto, and Mexico City. The Air France network covers 395,383 miles and serves 150 cities in 75 countries.

Both for the regular transatlantic business commuter and the first-time aviation enthusiast, the **Air France Concorde,** the world's first and only supersonic air transport, has established a new lifestyle in air travel. Concorde, which cuts U.S.-to-Europe flying times in half and virtually eliminates jet fatigue, flies daily between New York and Paris plus several times weekly to Paris from Washington, Dallas, and Mexico City.

Upon arrival in Paris, you'll find Air France and Air Inter have scheduled convenient ongoing flights to Nice, Lyon, Marseille, Bordeaux, Corsica, and other destinations. The French airline is also well equipped to provide advance trip information.

Air France has 23 district offices across the U.S., staffed by personnel who are constantly being briefed on travel facilities, accommodations, and what's new abroad. As you would expect, Air France is the airline that knows France best.

Also available are some very helpful travel brochures: "Paris à Pied" (a walking guide), the "Business Travelers' Guide to Paris," "Jewish Life in France," and the "Inexpensive Paris Restaurants." All three are chock-full of addresses, tips, and information to make a stay in the French capital easy and enjoyable. Write Air France, P.O. Box 10-747, Long Island City, NY 11101 for copies.

And remember, only Air France puts you in France from the moment you check in. Your Gallic adventure begins with a welcoming "Bonjour!" from a charming bilingual hostess and continues right through a gourmet lunch or dinner, featuring fine food and wines.

2. Traveling Within France

TRAINS: In a few hours, trains link Paris with all parts of France—the fastest way to go, except for travel by air on some long distances. On the network of the S.N.C.F. (French National Railroads), there are 24,000 miles of track, about 5000 stations. Completely safe, the express trains go as fast as 125 miles per hour, their timekeeping fabled throughout the world. You can travel either first or second class by day or in couchette or sleeper by night. Many long-distance trains in France carry dining cars which serve airline-type meals up to five-course dinners.

French National Railroads features an economical rail pass called **France Vacances** which reduces the total cost of train travel considerably. Available for 7, 15, or 30 days in both first and second class, it entitles the holder to unlimited rail transportation throughout France as well as to free bus and subway travel in Paris, free transfer to and from the Paris airports via Orly-Rail or Roissy-Rail, free admission to the Pompidou Center, plus reductions on French Railroads-operated bus excursions and, for those carrying a first-class ticket, a one-day free car rental with 100 kilometers free allowance per ticket in 25 cities in France (two days with a 30-day ticket).

This French equivalent to Eurailpass is available to nonresidents of France. It may be purchased at French National Railroads, 610 Fifth Ave., New York, NY 10020, or through your local travel agency. Submit your passport number and country of residence. France Vacances travel is within France only.

For information in Paris, go to the Gare de l'Est, the Gare du Nord, the Gare Saint-Lazare, the Gare Montparnasse, the Gare d'Austerlitz, and the Gare de Lyon, as well as the **French National Railways Tourist Office** at 127 Av. Champs-Élysées (tel. 225-12-80).

Some of the most popular sleepers in France are the *Train Bleu,* which leaves Paris-Lyon every night at 9:46 serving Cannes and Nice, where it arrives at 7:55 the next morning; *L'Occiten,* which leaves Paris-Austerlitz at 11 p.m. and gets into Toulouse at 7:10 a.m.; and *La Palombe Bleu,* which leaves Paris-Austerlitz at 10:50 p.m. and arrives in Tarbes at 8:18 a.m. Of course, the *Mistral,* which leaves Paris-Lyon station at 1:15 p.m. and reaches Nice at 10:28 p.m., remains one of the standard-bearers, and so is *L'Aquitaine,* which leaves Paris-Austerlitz at 5:50 p.m. to reach Bordeaux at 9:40 p.m.

If you have questions about this method of transportation, you can have them answered before leaving North America by getting in touch with the **French National Railroads** at 610 Fifth Ave., New York, NY 10020; 360 Post St., San Francisco, CA 94108; 11 East Adams St., Chicago, IL 60603; 9465 Wilshire Blvd., Los Angeles, CA 90212; 2121 Ponce de Leon Blvd., Coral Gables, FL 33134; 1500 Stanley St., Montreal, Quebec; or at 409 Granville St., Vancouver, B.C.

Eurailpass

Many in-the-know travelers have for years been taking advantage of one of the greatest travel bargains in Europe—the Eurailpass, which permits unlimited first-class rail travel in any country in Western Europe except the British Isles and Finland. Passes are purchased for periods as short as 15 days or as long as three months and are strictly nontransferable.

Here's how it works: The pass is sold only in North America. Vacationers taking the 14-day low-cost air excursion to Europe may purchase a 15-day Eurailpass for $210; otherwise, a 21-day pass costs $260; a one-month pass, $320; two months, $430; three months, $530. Children under 4 may travel free, and children under 10 pay only half fare.

The advantages are tempting. No tickets, no supplements (simply show the pass to the ticket collector, then settle back to enjoy the European scenery). Seat reservations are required. Some trains have couchettes (sleeping cars), for which an additional fee is charged.

Obviously, the two- or three-month visitor gets the greatest economical advantages; he or she can visit all of France's major sights, from the Alps to Brittany, then end the vacation in Norway—all on the same ticket! Eurailpass holders are entitled to considerable reductions on ferry steamers and some buses. For example, certain Europabus runs, such as between Paris and Brussels, offer 50% reductions. You can take Europabus Bus 241 between Paris and Nice at no extra charge.

If you're under 26, you can purchase a **Eurail Youthpass,** entitling you to unlimited second-class travel for two months at a cost of $290.

The Eurailpass is available from all travel agents and at the offices of CIT Travel Service, the French National Railroads, the German Federal Railroads, and the Swiss Federal Railways.

PLANES—THE FRANCE PASS: Air Inter, the domestic airline of France, serves 30 cities within the country frequently, efficiently, and, of course, quickly. Perhaps the most convincing reason to try its services is the France Pass. This is a one- or two-week carte blanche air ticket which allows purchasers unlimited access to all Air Inter routes; there is no restriction whatsoever to the number of flights you can take or the stopovers you can make.

Valid year round, the France Pass costs $177 for one week, $275 for two weeks. It is available to citizens or residents of the U.S., Canada, and Japan, where it may be purchased at Air France offices and through travel agents. It may also be purchased in France within seven days of arrival in that country (provided you hold a return ticket to the U.S., Canada, or Japan), through any Air Inter office.

Holders of the France Pass must obtain tickets (at no extra charge) from Air Inter for the flights they desire, and advance reservations are possible for most of them. Some weekend and commuter flights are not available to pass holders.

Possession of a France Pass also entitles you to a special "French Connection" room rate offered by the Hilton International at Orly, which allows you to stay overnight for $40 single, $49 double. To book this "French Connection" contact the Hilton International Reservations Service or your travel agent.

Visit France

The cost of domestic air travel for U.S. travelers in France has been cut dramatically, thanks to the new Visit France air fares. Sold only to non-French nationals in conjunction with Air France transatlantic flights, Visit France rates save 40% to 50% off regular economy fares. For example, the round-trip saving on a trip from Paris to Nice and return is $117 (subject to change), the difference between the Visit France fare of $141 and the normal round-trip fare of $258.

Air France Flex-Plan

A shopper's delight of budget tour options in Paris and throughout France is included in this plan. Options range from discount car rentals to a prepaid selection of a hotel, restaurant, or sightseeing tour. For more details, get in touch with Air France, your travel agent, or Tower Travel, 380 Madison Ave., New York, NY 10017 (tel. 212/687-7900).

CAR RENTALS: You'll need a car to get close to the heart of rural France, visiting its out-of-the-way châteaux, those country inns run by creative chefs, or the newly built art museums tucked away in the villages perched above the Riviera coastline. You can rent a car upon your arrival in France, either on a daily, weekly, or monthly basis, with a charge per kilometer, or else on an unlimited-mileage basis. There are many classes of cars available; the cheapest class usually includes something on the order of a Fiat 127, seating two with fair comfort, more with less.

But first a word about taxes: most European countries tax car rentals, the tax varying greatly from border to border (Holland, 12%; Germany, 11%; Belgium, 7%; Switzerland, nothing). France charges the highest tax, a stunning 23%. Therefore, you might consider picking up your car outside France, in a city at the border, perhaps. Many companies do not charge extra if you pick up a car in one country and return it in another. For example, a Swiss car can be picked up in Geneva, then returned in Paris (in some cases brought from Geneva to Paris for a nominal fee).

SETTLING INTO PARIS

PARIS IS THE MOST fabled city of Europe, romanticized beyond reality but somehow always managing to live up to its image. It is discovered anew by each young man or woman who walks along the quays of the Seine, slowly and uniquely making the city his or her own. It is a capital to be savored, like the *ne plus ultra* of claret, a bottle of Château Lafitte-Rothschild.

In the 1920s it was Ernest Hemingway who was to find Paris a "moveable feast." "There is never any ending to Paris," he wrote, "and the memory of each person who has lived in it differs from that of any other."

One reason that memories differ so is that there are so many faces of Paris—districts that live in ignorance or else indifference to other sectors. Paris, after all, is a city of *quartiers* or *arrondissements,* 20 in all. Deciding which quarter most appeals to you—the sector you want to make your living headquarters—will be your first task. Do you like the Left Bank or the Champs-Élysées? The city is split by the winding Seine, the river that knows what has been called the mystery of continuity. The north of the river is the Right Bank or Rive Droite, the lower part the Left Bank or Rive Gauche. You may be fickle, as we are, not wanting to adopt any arrondissement but to walk from quarter to quarter, learning the secrets of all of them.

Novelist Romain Gary put it this way: "The kid will come from Nebraska or Heidelberg, from Poland or Senegal, and Paris will be born again—new, brand-new and unexpected, and the Arch of Triumph will rise again, and the Seine will flow for the first time, and there will be new areas, unknown and unexplored, called Montmartre and Montparnasse . . . and it will all be for the first time, a completely new city, built suddenly for you and you alone."

1. Getting Around

People walk and search in Paris, as did the American composer Ned Rorem, "looking for love where it can't be found—waiting for love where it will not come." Other more fortunate strollers are in love *in* Paris and *with* Paris.

If you don't want to walk, a more mundane but altogether practical method of transport is:

THE MÉTRO: At the turn of the century, pedestrians went "underground." To lure Parisians into its subway, the city posted at street levels flowery wrought-iron entryways. The Museum of Modern Art in New York has elevated these art nouveau creations to the pinnacle of artistic statements; museums in Europe are following suit. At the most prestigious stops, some of these reminders of a more gracious era remain to delight underground travelers of the future.

Le Métro is your most efficient and fastest means of transportation in the traffic-clogged Paris of today. Unlike the lunatic-designed subway system of New York, which often baffles the natives, even more so foreign visitors, Le Métro was laid out so that people might actually use it with some assurance as to where they were going. At the entrance to most stations is a map giving the routes of the various lines, which often criss-cross. You can trace your own route (chances are you'll have to make only one change, if that, although some tricky routes require three). Many of the bigger stations have pushbutton indicators that do the work for you, lighting up automatically when you press the button of your destination. Once you know your goal, follow the line to the end of its run, then take that *direction.* Where you change lines is known as *correspondances,* that is, the converging points of trains. Some of these Métro terminals tend to require long walks (the stop at Châtelet is the most notorious).

To ride to any point on one of the urban lines requires the same fare, the only difference being whether you prefer first or second class. You pay 3F (68¢) for a first-class ride, 2F (46¢) for a second-class fare. Actually, there isn't much difference in the level of comfort between the cars, except at rush hour. In first class, you may be only mildly pushed, shoved, and stepped on. In second class, death by smothering is likely!

Instead of buying individual tickets, it's a better bargain to purchase a *carnet* (pronounced "car-nay")—that is, a booklet of 10 tickets at a reduced cost. In second class, a booklet costs 15F ($3.42), 25F ($5.71) in first class. A *carnet* may be purchased at any Métro ticket counter. A rider in the first-class compartments is often subjected to a ticket inspection (in second class, almost never)—so hold onto your stub. Trains begin their runs at 5:30 a.m., leaving their frontier stations at 12:30 a.m. for the ride back to the "corral."

TAXIS: A mixed blessing. It's impossible to secure one at rush hour—so don't even try. Taxi drivers are strongly organized into an effective lobby to keep their number limited to 14,300. Many riders—and not just the foreign ones—complain that the meters are concealed from view. When boarding a taxi, check out the meter to make sure you don't pay the previous passenger's fare.

In Zone A, inside Paris, from 6:30 a.m. to 10 p.m. the flag goes down at 7F ($1.60), and the meter ticks away at 1.50F (34¢) per kilometer. Another rate applies when you stray outside the 20 arrondissements. However, you do not have to pay the driver's return fare if he takes you either to Orly Airport or the new Charles de Gaulle Airport. At night you can expect an increase of about 30% of the fare.

You pay an extra franc when leaving or arriving at railway stations. You are allowed several small pieces of luggage inside free, providing that none of them weighs more than five kilos (about 11 lbs.). Any suitcase weighing more is usually put in the trunk at the rate of 1F (23¢) per piece.

"Vulture" cabbies often are parked outside the doors to nightclubs catering to big spenders. They wait for their prey, such as a thoroughly inebriated Yankee. Most of these hacks are unmetered, and they charge what the market will bear—and then whatever else they can get. Agree on the price in advance, then have your attorney draw up an ironbound contract. Otherwise, get the doorman to hail you a legitimate taxi.

Incidentally, a taxi can be called in advance (usually your hotel will arrange this the night before—say, if you have an early plane to catch). Tips average around 15% of the fare. One longtime resident of Paris, Herbert R. Lottman, who views taxi drivers with a jaundiced eye, said, "Your Paris chauffeur hardly needs the tip after everything else that he's got from you."

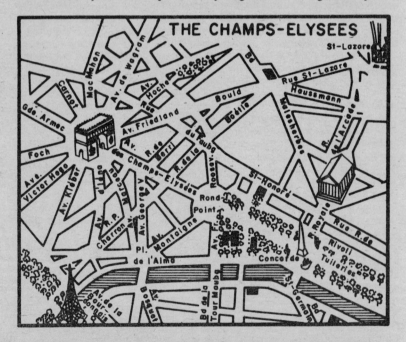

BUSES: Often buses are preferred by some visitors for the sights along the route. Of course, buses are necessarily slow, owing to the traffic congestion. At designated stops are signs listing the number of buses servicing that point as well as the destinations of each (usually north to south, east to west). Most stops along the way are also posted on the sides of the buses.

The vehicles run from 6:30 a.m. until 9:15 p.m. (a few operate until 12:30 a.m., and a handful traverse the city during the early morning hours). The service is greatly curtailed on Sundays and holidays. At rush hours, you may have to draw a ticket from a dispensing machine, indicating your position in the line.

Most bus rides require one ticket, but there are other destinations calling for two. For bus riders, it's more economical to purchase a previously recommended *carnet*—the same one used on the Métro.

If you stay a week or a month, you can also buy a special "Go As You Please" tourist ticket valid for two, four, or seven days on all the RATP networks or a *carte orange* valid for two, three, four, or five zones in the Paris area.

If you intend to do any serious bus riding, pick up an RATP bus map at the office on the Place de la Madeleine or at the tourist offices at RATP headquarters, 53 quai Grands Augustins, Paris (6e). You can also write to the RATP to obtain maps of the transportation systems operated by this authority and other information and pamphlets on the networks. When in Paris, you can also telephone the inquiry center (tel. 346-14-14) to get precise details on the fares, routes, and schedules concerning buses as well as the Métro.

You may also want to use the bus system for excursions outside Paris. Many different trips are offered from Easter to the beginning of October during weekends at reasonable prices to off-the-beaten-path places. You can, of course, go to such standard attractions as Chartres, even Mont Saint-Michel. Also, you can visit various châteaux in the Loire Valley. To get more details on the prices and on the sightseeing tours, you can write to the RATP at its headquarters (address above). When in Paris, you can also have the details and book space by going to the office at the Place de la Madeleine. It is open from 8:30 a.m. to noon and from 1:45 p.m. to 2:15 p.m. weekdays only.

2. The Super-Deluxe

These hotels are among the world's most celebrated and charge corresponding tariffs. Some, such as the Ritz, are legends in themselves. Their suites are far removed from the patronage of the average French person or the middle-class foreign visitor. Still, some of them ask prices in their more standard rooms that are comparable to some of Paris's leading first-class hotels. If you'd like to know how Edward VII and Lillie Langtry lived when they came to Paris, then check into one of the following selections.

The Ritz, 15 Place Vendôme (1er) (tel. 260-38-30), is more than ever the greatest hotel in any European city. Opened in 1898, it is a continuing legend. The "little shepherd boy from Niederwald," César Ritz, converted the Lauzun Mansion—on one of the most beautiful and historic squares in Paris—into a hotel whose name was to become synonymous with elegance and chic. Teamed with that culinary master Escoffier, he created a miracle of luxury living. In the years to come, they would play hosts to some of the great names of the world, including Edward VII of England.

The Ritz broke precedent by providing a bath with every guest room. The drawing rooms, salons, three gardens, and courtyards were kept intact. Two town houses were eventually annexed, joined by a long arcade lined with miniature display cases representing 125 of the leading boutiques of Paris. The salons were furnished with museum-caliber antiques: gilt pieces, ornate mirrors, furniture from the periods of Louis XV and Louis XVI, handwoven tapestries, 10-foot-high bronze torchères.

The regular bedrooms of the Ritz are among the finest in Paris. Elaborate bathrooms with every kind of little and big convenience have been installed. Artisans were brought in to give every room that French look, employing color coordination, tasteful fabrics, rich woods, lustrous marbles, antique chests, desks with bronze hardware, and crystal lighting. Singles range from 520F ($118.72) to 600F ($136.98); doubles, 650F ($148.40) to 830F ($189.50), plus 15% for service.

Le Bristol, 112 rue du Faubourg St.-Honoré (8e) (tel. 266-91-45), is a palace in every sense of the word. Not too large or too small, it is just the right size for the personalized old-world service that it rigidly and meticulously maintains. The location is on the shopping street that runs parallel to the Champs-Élysées and near the Palais de l'Élysée, the state residence of the French president.

The tone is set by the classic 18th-century Parisian façade, with a glass and wrought-iron entryway, under which attendants liveried in green and red await arriving guests. The man behind the high-fashion style and elegance is Pierre Jammet, the latest scion of a line of hoteliers which has brought taste and distinction to the profession. His father, Hippolyte Jammet, founded the Bristol back in 1924, installing a wealth of near-priceless antiques and furnishings.

Everywhere you turn are valuable pieces, many signed, from the Louis XV and Louis XVI periods. All the bedrooms are luxuriously and opulently furnished—either with showcase antiques or skillfully made reproductions, inlaid woods, bronze and crystal, Oriental rugs, and original oil paintings. Even the bathrooms are sumptuously marbled, with separate stall showers, plenty of large towels, and such amenities as a lighted magnifying mirror for makeup or shaving. Singles start at 670F ($152.96), going up to 800F ($182.64). The least expensive double is 750F ($171.23), and some twin-bedded rooms cost as much as 1200F ($273.96).

Raphael, 17 Avenue Kléber (16e) (tel. 502-16-00). When you face the cashier, you'll notice a large gold-and-orange painting on your right. It's an original Turner, and a fine one. As you gaze around at the main reception hall and the salons that open off it, you'll be stepping back into the luxury of romantic France. For example, the main hallway has lustrous dark-paneled walnut walls, with ornate bronze torchères and gilt-framed oil paintings. The music salon is also richly wood paneled, with fine carving, a marble fireplace, and turkey-red carpeting. A favorite with celebrities is the drinking lounge, also ornately paneled and furnished with claret velour sofas, carved oak chairs, and fluted columns.

A mahogany-and-brass elevator takes you to the many floors of impressive bedrooms. Each chamber is large enough to seem like a wing of a suite or a palace room, replete with silk draperies, gilt- and brass-trimmed chests, tables, inlaid woods, and armoires. All important furniture periods are represented: Directoire, Louis XVI, Regency.

A single room with private bath rents from 400F ($91.32); a moderate double room with private bath costs from 450F ($102.74); and a medium-grade double room is priced from 520F ($118.72). Rates include taxes, service, and continental breakfast.

The **Crillon,** 10 Place de la Concorde (8e) (tel. 265-24-10), is unquestionably one of the great hotels of Paris. First of all, the setting is unparalleled: right on the Place de la Concorde, across from the American Embassy. The building itself—designed by Gabriel—is more than 200 years old. Once the palace of the Duke of Crillon, it housed and entertained some of the major names in French history for two centuries. Since 1905 it's been a hotel, its most famous guest none other than Woodrow Wilson during his stay in Paris.

Behind its colonnaded exterior, with its classic fluted columns, the palace-like hotel envelops a large formal courtyard, favored for drinks or tea. Silently attended by two statues, tables and red parasols are set around a reflecting pool and a border of flowers.

The interior is 18th century, with well-preserved architectural details and authentic and tasteful antique decorations. Throughout the parquet-floored salons are paneled walls with large scenic murals, gilt- and brocade-covered furniture, glittering chandeliers, niches with fine sculpture, inlaid desks, Louis XVI chests and chairs.

The bedrooms are classically furnished as well, the accommodations generously proportioned and equipped with handsome bathrooms. Singles rent for 660F ($150.68); doubles, 800F ($182.64), plus 15% for service.

George V, 31 Avenue George V (8e) (tel. 723-54-00). J. Paul Getty used to feel at home here. So did Darryl Zanuck.

So do many visiting New York and Beverly Hills "simple folk." On a tree-lined avenue between the Champs-Élysées and the Seine, the hotel offers grandiose luxury in a semimodern building—almost like a smaller French version of the Waldorf Astoria.

The George V tends to rise and fall in popularity with the fickle chic. At present, it seems to be enjoying a renaissance with many former clients who had deserted it for quieter hotels offering less "show biz." One of the legends of the George V is that it keeps a mysterious file of the preferences of its most favored habitués. How detailed it is or how far the hotel goes to meet those preferences, we simply don't know—except to say that the George V is matched by few hotels in Europe in service. The staff is not only large but attentive. Every guest has virtually his or her own personal servant. The pampering begins the moment you sit at the Empire reception desk to be registered and welcomed.

The public rooms are imbued with a museum air, with rich old tapestries, impressive paintings from the 18th and 19th centuries, even Pompeian inlaid marble walls. In good weather, luncheons are served in the roomy inner courtyard—haute cuisine meals spread under red parasols. Hopefully, you'll get a room or suite overlooking this courtyard, for many of these select accommodations have terrace balconies with summer furniture plus urns and boxes overflowing with red geraniums and other bright summer flowers. A single rents for 590F ($134.70); a double, 780F ($178.07), plus 15% service.

Plaza Athénée, 25 Avenue Montaigne (8e) (tel. 225-43-30). In the old days, Mata Hari used to drop in. Nowadays, you'll more likely encounter a Venezuelan oil baron whispering confidential information in the Scottish tartan English Bar. The hotel doesn't exactly hide its luxuries. First, its location is auspicious, in an embassy area, halfway between the Champs-Élysées and the Seine, on an avenue graced with towering shade trees.

The tone is set when a taxi (or limousine) delivers you to the formal entrance, with its striking awnings. A liveried attendant stands below a glass shelter to welcome you. The architectural details are in the pre-World War I style: arched windows and ornate balconies.

When you check in, you're seated in front of a Louis XVI marquetry desk, facing a rare Flemish tapestry. The hotel is built palace style, the pinnacle achieved by the Regency Salon, paneled in rich grained wood and dominated by a marble fireplace. The better bedrooms overlook a courtyard, with awnings and parasol-shaded tables. Vines climb over inner balconies, and there are formal flowerbeds—in all, a choice spot for breakfast or lunch.

The bedrooms themselves are priced according to their view, quietness, and size. The rooms draw a mixed reaction. One New York woman found them "sterile and lacking in soul." A married couple from the Midwest was rhapsodic about "the antiques—one of the Louis periods, the woven carpets, and the bronze hardware." All of the rooms have private baths, some especially large and fine, with double basins and showers included. Singles range in price from 650F ($148.40) to 780F ($178.07); doubles, 860F ($196.34) to 1400F ($319.62), the latter tariff including a sitting room.

Meals are an occasion, as the food is superb (not always the case in deluxe hotels). The preferred choice for dining is **La Régence-Plaza,** a room of handsome handcarved oak paneling, its large curvy-topped windows fronting Avenue Montaigne. It is known for its lobster soufflé. With its bright colors and decoration, the **Grill Relais Plaza** draws a young, attractive crowd at lunch, and is also ideal for late-night snacks, as it stays open until 2 a.m.

Hôtel Meurice, 228 rue de Rivoli (1er) (tel. 260-38-60). The expression "fit for a king" could have been coined to describe this hotel. Directors in the past were judged on the basis of how discreetly they could slip royal "favorites" in and out of the boudoir. Kings not being as plentiful as they were, you're more likely nowadays to run into diplomats, industrialists, and successful authors. The self-proclaimed "mad genius" Salvador Dali makes the Meurice his headquarters, occupying Suite 108 which was once used by the deposed and exiled king of Spain, Alfonso XIII.

The Meurice is an unmarred, romanticized 18th-century way of life, with a totally French aura. It's a world of gilt-edged paneled walls, monumental crystal chandeliers, ornate tapestries, and furnishings from the periods of Louis XIV, XV, and XVI. The location is impressive, just off the rue de Rivoli and the Tuileries Gardens, within walking distance of the Louvre.

The formal drive-in entrance begs for a Mercedes—a plea that's usually granted. Once inside, a look at the garden evokes life in a country château. In the lounge you stand under a circular "star"-studded ceiling. The bedrooms are richly furnished with some period and modern pieces—each containing a bed-sitting salon and a private bath. One person pays 520F ($118.72); two persons, from 600F ($136.98), plus 15% for service. Quick meals are served in the modern **Copper Grill.**

Hôtel Inter-Continental, 3 rue de Castiglione (1er) (tel. 260-37-80), is a miraculous mixture of French tradition, Gallic know-how, and 20th-century modernity and ingenuity. The result: the largest and splashiest deluxe hotel in Paris. The position is stunning, along the rue de Rivoli and across from the Tuileries Gardens. When it originally opened in 1878, it was known as "The Continental." In 1883 Victor Hugo was fêted at a luncheon. The belle époque hotel has always enjoyed an elite position in Paris, sheltering such guests as the Empress Eugénie of France and Jean Giraudoux. Inter-Continental Hotels, a subsidiary of Pan American Airways, purchased the hotel in 1968, almost totally rebuilding it and refurbishing it at the cost of $8 million.

The alterations were drastic, the improvements dramatic. It just isn't the old Continental anymore, although the unusual and distinguished among the architectural features have been preserved. The great inner courtyard, known as "La Cour d'Honneur," is paved with white marble on several levels, with a circular splashing fountain and an 1864 statue by Cunny. In fair weather, luncheon, tea, or drinks are served alfresco here, under a gold and white canopy.

The public rooms have flair and style. The main lounge, for example, is carpeted in raspberry with period furnishings, bronze sconces, and marble cocktail tables. The colonnaded front entrance, carpeted in red, has a pair of bronze candelabra secured from a palace in Leningrad. The bedrooms and suites are among the finest in Paris. Although there are many antiques, the 520 bedrooms are tastefully and knowingly decorated in the classic French style, with reproductions of Louis XVI pieces. Each chamber has its own paneled walls, matching draperies and bedcovers, and a one-color theme to each room that creates that salon effect—enhanced by a discreet use of crystal, fine fruitwoods, bronze hardware, and inlaid consoles, desks, and tables. Every room is air-conditioned, with direct-dial phones, plus 24-hour room service and same-day valet. Single rooms range in price from 400F ($91.32) to 620F ($141.55); twins, from 500F ($114.15) to 800F ($182.64), plus tax and service.

There is no main dining room as a survey indicated that guests prefer more intimate character rooms. That theory works successfully here. The most popular dining spot is the **Rôtisserie Rivoli**, a theatricalized tavern, with a rustic setting on several levels. On a lower level, **Le Bistro** is set for meals and drinks, providing a background for changing exhibitions of one-person art shows.

l'Hôtel, 13 rue des Beaux-Arts (6e) (tel. 325-27-22). If you were either unkind or blunt, you would have called the 19th-century Hôtel d'Alsace a "fleabag." It was, but it had some style, attracting down-and-out artists—many drawn there because of its reputation as the building in which Oscar Wilde died. A broken man, the Victorian author scrawled his last letter at the Alsace, beseeching Frank Harris to send him "the money you owe me." Nowadays, the clientele—Leopold Rothschild, Mia Farrow, Julie Christie, Jack Lemmon, Ava Gardner, and Natalie Wood—is hardly in such straits.

Called simply l'Hôtel, and on the Left Bank (out-of-bounds for most deluxe Parisian hotels), it was the love child of one of France's favorite actors—Guy-Louis Duboucheron, who wanted to establish an intimate, super-sophisticated place of jewel-box proportions and character, where guests would be pampered and pay the price. ("I wanted it to be like raiding the icebox at home in the middle of the night.") l'Hôtel drew upon the creative energies of a Texas architect, Robin Westbrook, who also aided with the interior furnishings. He gutted the core of the old hotel to make a miniature circular courtyard similar to the interior of the Tower of Pisa.

The smallest rooms rent for 350F ($79.91). Four large doubles, two with fireplaces, opening onto the garden, go for 600F ($136.98). Most doubles fronting the street cost 480F ($109.58).

Two rooms are conversation pieces. One, facing the garden rear, is where Wilde died. The other holds the original furnishings and memorabilia of Mistinguette, France's legendary stage star. Her pedestal bed is set in the middle of the room; and all her furnishings, including the bed, are covered with mirrors! But regardless of the room you get or price you pay, you receive the same ingratiating service.

Drinks are served in a vaulted stone cellar, where fine antiques are set in nooks and crannies. The enclosed courtyard is a true delight: travertine bistro tables with bentwood chairs, glistening silver serving dishes on a mahogany pedestal, even caged monkeys and pigeons, brass street lanterns, lush plants and flowers, and paintings by French actor Jean Marais.

In the petite reception salon, furnished with 18th- and 19th-century charm, and in a lusher, richer drinking lounge, you'll find more paintings by Jean Marais. Be warned that informality reigns: at any moment, a pet duck may waddle in from the courtyard, seeking your attention and upstaging many a super-star in the midst of an elaborate story.

3. The "New-Old" Hotels

Paris is going through a hotel renaissance. You hear more about the new all-glass modern hotels being built than you do about a handful of small restored accommodations that remain comparatively unknown. Just as there are new chef-run restaurants representative of creative cookery, so there are hotels of great character, bearing the vivid imprint of their owners.

Old and dilapidated buildings have been rescued and restored with imagination and taste. Rugged stone walls have been bared; 16th-century beams exposed; worn tiled floors cleaned and repaired; fireplaces made to work; fabrics coordinated with wall colors; modern plumbing discreetly installed—a country or town house feeling established.

In this special category, for those seeking atmosphere and charm, we'll lead off with our discoveries, beginning with the most expensive, then descending the price scale.

Hôtel de l'Université, 22 rue de l'Université (7e) (tel. 261-09-39), is one of the most engaging little hotels of Paris. It's on the Left Bank, near the Seine, within walking distance of the Boulevard Saint-Germain. A remake of a 300-year-old town house, it has only 28 rooms, some looking over the miniature courtyard where you can have your own morning coffee and croissants. The hotel is the creation of Monsieur and Madame Bergmann, who reconstructed the interior to preserve the best of the original architectural features while installing modern conveniences. The bedrooms, many with antiques, are one of a kind, furnished in a personalized and tasteful manner. Both the decor and the colors used are sophisticated. A favorite is Room 54, in which rattan is mixed with period pieces, the bath is marble, and the color Gainsborough blue. The price you pay depends on the plumbing you require; singles range from 112F ($25.57) to 175F ($39.95); doubles, from 250F ($57.08) to 375F ($85.61), all prices including tax and service. There's an additional charge of 17F ($3.88) for breakfast. In the late afternoon and evening, guests gather in the bar and in the 16th-century cellars for a light dinner, drinks, and conversation. Métro: Bac.

Hôtel de l'Abbaye, 10 rue Cassette (6e) (tel. 544-38-11), is a stylish remake of a 17th-century abbey, restored by Monsieur and Madame Lafortune. Fifteen-foot street doors lead to an open paved courtyard and an entry lounge with marble floors and 18th-century antiques. The lower-level lounges have informal dignity, opening onto a rear courtyard with summer furniture. Behind the central living room is a winter salon, with green-and-white floral paper, white wicker furniture, and plants. In the patio beyond, garden furniture is set against a backdrop of shrubbery.

The smallish bedrooms, each with a private bath, are reached by elevator. Madame Lafortune's decor has a tasteful originality, with beds, chairs, and tables made out of simulated bamboo. Her choice of decorative accessories blends with uninhibited color schemes and fabrics. Doubles range from 280F ($63.92) to 340F ($77.62), taxes, service, and a continental breakfast included. The staff extends the hospitality of the owners. Métro: St.-Sulpice.

Grand Hôtel de l'Univers, 6 rue Grégoire-de-Tours (6e) (tel. 033-52-31), wins on many counts. Its owner, Monsieur Beck, gutted the ugly latter-day overlay of this 15th-century inn, exposing the old beams and the rugged stone walls. Skillfully he slipped in private baths and central heating. Each bedroom was furnished distinctively. Your room, for example, might have a provincial theme, perhaps be outfitted in tropical white wicker, even in Danish modern. It's potluck. However, all rooms have tiled baths, TV, background music, and even a small bar stocked with drinks. The color schemes are dramatically attractive. Singles to for 155F ($35.39) to 240F ($54.79); doubles, 260F ($59.36) to 280F ($63.92). The location is bull's-eye center of the Left Bank, just a minute off the Boulevard St.-Germain. Métro: Odéon or Mabillon.

Hôtel de Fleurie, 32 rue Grégoire-de-Tours (6e) (tel. 329-59-81), just about 70 feet off the Boulevard Saint-Germain on this colorful little Left Bank street, is one of the best of the "new" old hotels. Restored to its former glory, the facade is studded with statuary which is spotlit at night, recapturing its 17th-century elegance. The stone walls have been exposed in the reception salon, with its refectory desk where guests check in. A spiral staircase leads to a small TV and breakfast room. The lobby contains a collection of 19th-century antiques and "brown-gravy" paintings. An elevator takes you to the well-furnished, modernized bedrooms, where a double with a complete bath rents for 120F ($47.94), that tariff rising to 250F ($57.08) in a twin-bedded room with bath. A continental breakfast and the service charge are included in the rates quoted. Métro: Odéon.

Hôtel des Deux-Îles, 59 rue St.-Louis-en-l'Île (4e) (tel. 326-13-35), is the newest hotel adventure of the interior decorator Roland Buffat. On the same street, he has restored both the Hôtel St.-Louis and Hôtel de Lutèce. This restored 17th-century building is larger, providing more space for his glamorous setting, a reflection of his impeccable taste. The lounge, with its refectory-table reception area at the door, has a central garden of plants and flowers. Monsieur Buffat has utilized an eclectic collection of furnishings, mostly bamboo and reed blended with period pieces. He shows his charm and sense of whimsy by an occasional touch such as a cage of white doves or else an antique painting. On a lower level is a rustic building-length tavern with an open fireplace, a cozy retreat at which to meet new or old friends. The bedrooms reflect somewhat the same decorative theme as the public lounges, with much use made of bamboo and reed. Unusual paintings abound, and the colors are harmoniously blended. A double with bath costs 250F ($57.08), dropping to 210F ($47.94) in a single with shower. Tax and service are included. Métro: Pont-Marie.

Hôtel de Lutèce, 65 rue St.-Louis-en-l'Île (4e) (tel. 326-23-52). When you open the front door, you'll think you're in a country house in Brittany. Reflected everywhere is the good, restrained taste of Roland Buffat. At the Lutèce, the single, all-purpose lounge is graciously furnished with sofas and armchairs facing an old fireplace with spicy contemporary paintings. The country antiques and the original tiled floors make the hotel mellow and ingratiating. Many famous people, such as the Duke and Duchess of Bedford, use it as their Parisian home base. Conversation in the lounge tends to be a fascinating grab bag. Monsieur Buffat has given each of the bedrooms its own individual stamp. He hasn't been sparing with antiques, either. Each room comes equipped with private bath. Either singles or doubles rent for 230F ($52.51) to 260F ($59.36), taxes and service included. Breakfast is another 15F ($3.42) per person. Métro: Pont-Marie.

Odéon-Hôtel, 3 rue de l'Odéon (6e) (tel. 325-90-67), will convince you you're spending the night in a colorful country inn in Normandy. The renovation uncovered old beams, rough stone walls, and high crooked ceilings. After modern plumbing was installed, rooms were designed and furnished, each with a character of its own. Furnishings have successfully blended the old with modern, ranging from oak and bookbinder wallpaper to bright, contemporary fabrics. All accommodations are doubles, renting for anywhere from 200F ($45.66) to 240F ($54.79), a continental breakfast, tax, and service included. Rooms are equipped with either private baths or showers. The guest lounge is dominated by an old Parisian tapestry, an amusingly beamed and mirrored ceiling, and white plastic furnishings. The hotel is one minute from the Théâtre de l'Odéon and Boulevard St.-Germain. Métro: Odéon.

Hôtel Saint-Louis, 75 rue St.-Louis-en-l'Île (4e) (tel. 634-04-80), is a small hotel fashionably and romantically positioned on the historic Île St.-Louis. Roland Buffat, a Parisian interior decorator, discovered this hotel and has done a good job of converting its 25 rooms. Pleasant decorative accessories adorn the rooms—M. Buffat has saved the antiques for the small reception lounge. Prices are 65F ($14.84) in a single with running water, 115F ($26.25) in a single with shower. A double with shower rents for 180F ($41.09); a double with complete bath, 200F ($45.66). Breakfast is an additional 14F ($3.20). Métro: Pont-Marie.

4. 8th Arrondissement

CHAMPS-ÉLYSÉES/MADELEINE: The Champs-Élysées dominates the 8th Arrondissement. Restaurants such as Maxim's have made it famous. It is the domain of such well-known hotels as the Crillon, the George V, and the Plaza-Athénée. But a notch down from these palaces are lesser-known establishments, such as the Lancaster (which many film stars consider the finest hotel in Paris). Converted town houses have been turned into fine hotels. All of the above are far beyond the average budget. However, you do have your choice of medium-priced selections—but don't come here for low-budget hotels.

Deluxe Hotels

Hôtel Lancaster, 7 rue de Berri (8e) (tel. 359-90-43), was once an exquisite town house off the Champs-Élysées, with an open forecourt and stables. Some years ago it was acquired by Monsieur and Madame Wolf, who transformed the stables into an almost regal dining room. They took in "paying guests," and their salon became known among artists and writers.

As patrons of the arts, the Wolfs acquired many of the paintings of their guests, and throughout the living room these works graced the walls, virtually a private museum. Their most important artist guest was the Russian Pastouhoff. In 1970, the Wolfs, feeling they had made their statement, sold to London's Savoy Hotels who have made excellent improvements in the hotel's physical plant. Nowadays, it is likely to attract movie stars, everybody from Gregory Peck to Peter Ustinov.

A single ranges in price from 450F ($102.74) to 600F ($136.98); a double, from 700F ($159.81) to 800F ($182.64). The more expensive rooms are larger and better positioned, usually opening onto a quiet and restful courtyard. The average chamber is richly furnished in a traditional manner—containing paneled walls, brocaded Louis XVI-style furniture, gilt mirrors, and tasteful accessories. The baths are commodious, having their own special style.

Prince de Galles, 35 Avenue George V (8e) (tel. 723-55-11), is an old hotel mansion that's been fitted with all those 20th-century improvements and renovations required by modern life. Its clientele is international and wide ranging —everybody from airline crews to the members of "le tout Paris," which Ned Rorem described as the "inapproachable innermost snob-life of Paris." The Prince de Galles Hotel is a stone's throw from the Champs-Élysées in the heart of the business and leisure areas of Paris.

The "Prince of Wales" is built around an open courtyard, with a fountain and plants. The most desirable bedrooms contain balconies opening onto an

Andalusian-style patio. There are extensive traditional lounges and a much-frequented restaurant, **Panache,** everything set off effectively by the first-rate facilities. An air of up-to-date efficiency permeates, a curious combination of New York bustle and French leisure and gentility.

The bedrooms, some of them quite large, have been treated in the traditional French manner—many with Louis XVI-style furnishings, others with turn-of-the-century brass beds and contemporary furnishings placed about skillfully. The baths are good size, with a liberal use of highly polished marble and plenty of large towels. A single costs from 400F ($91.32) to 490F ($111.86), and twins and doubles go from 600F ($136.98), plus taxes and service.

Royal Monceau, 35-39 Avenue Hoche (8e) (tel. 561-98-00), is stately and dignified. This classic and traditional French hotel is on a tree-lined boulevard, only two minutes from the Arc de Triomphe—almost in its shadow. Most of its bedrooms turn toward a parklike formal courtyard, with a grassy lawn, lamp lights, urns of flowers, a pool, plus garden tables set under parasols.

Throughout, the style level is sound and authentic. The grand staircase with a Roman bust in a niche and a rare tapestry on the landing suggests the tone. In furnishings, there is a healthy respect for the old—Empire chairs, Directoire chests, desks, and beds, plus an occasional Persian carpet, as well as bronze and crystal lighting fixtures enriching the decor. In the tavern-style cocktail lounge, you encounter an assortment of "quiet" international guests.

Most of the bedrooms were created when space was not at a premium. The rates charged depend on the placement of the room and its size. Singles range from 420F ($95.89) to 550F ($125.57), and doubles go from 520F ($118.72) to 700F ($159.81).

Upper Bracket Hotels

Until 1922, the **San Régis,** 12 rue Jean-Goujon (8e) (tel. 359-11-90), was a fashionable town house. These days it stands in the midst of embassies and exclusive boutiques (Christian Dior is across the street), enjoying, in a quiet and modest way, its position as one of the best hotels in Paris. It is right off the Champs-Élysées, only a short walk from the Seine.

San Régis belongs to Madame Bataille. Many of her guests find it much like a private club. There is a small but attentive staff who quickly learn your whims and fancies and make you feel at home.

Each room is unique (our personal favorite is Room 6), decorated with discretion and taste, lavishly sprinkled with antiques. A few have separate sitting rooms, and many overlook a quiet side garden. The price for one person in a room with bath ranges from 300F ($68.49) to 340F ($77.62); doubles go for anywhere from 400F ($91.32) to 500F ($114.15). A continental breakfast is extra. Métro: Alma-Marceau or FDR.

Royal Alma, 35 rue Jean-Goujon (8e) (tel. 225-83-30), is a well-positioned and modern hotel, just a whisper from the Seine and an eight-minute walk from the Champs-Élysées. Everything's small scale, even the lounge, which opens onto the garden in the rear. The bedrooms too are compact, yet each has its own tiled bath, with either a tub or shower (or both).

A room with a large or twin bed goes for 300F ($68.49), including service, tax, and a continental breakfast. These rooms are absolutely adequate, with simple and contemporary built-in furnishings. A single costs 240F ($54.79). Everything is well-tailored and manicured. The Royal Alma is a favorite with airline crews, who appreciate staying in a good neighborhood at comparatively reasonable rates. Métro: Alma-Marceau.

The Middle Bracket

Schweizerhof-L'Horset, 11 rue Balzac (tel. 359-86-93) is run by the L'Horset chain. If you weren't just two tiny streets from the Champs-Élysées and the Arc de Triomphe, you'd think you were in a small town in Switzerland. Once a private villa, in a posh district of Paris, this is one of the few little hotels with a flower garden in front. Under a chestnut tree, several tables are set out on the flagstoned terrace.

The owners of the "Swiss House" have added antiques wherever possible, and each room is different, particularly as to size. The hotel is not cheap, but the price represents good value to clients. The best bargains are the bathless doubles at 200F ($45.66). However, doubles with shower or complete baths range in price from 260F ($59.36) to 320F ($73.06). A continental breakfast is included.

Lord Byron, 5 rue de Chateaubriand (8e) (tel. 359-89-98), is a select little hotel you can be proud to stay in and recommend to your friends. On a quiet, gently curving street of distinguished buildings, it is just off the Champs-Élysées. The owner, Madame François Coisne, who migrated to Paris from the Île de France, has put her imprint everywhere. Each room has a personalized, tasteful concept, revealing an authoritative woman's touch. The furnishings are usually good reproductions of antiques or else restrained, likable modern. Placed throughout are framed prints of butterflies and historic French scenes.

Prices include taxes, service, and an especially good breakfast (no other meals are provided). Breakfast is served either in your room, in a petit salon, or in a shaded inner garden. A large-bedded room for two with a private bath rents for 210F ($47.94). Available also are a few apartments with two beds for 300F ($68.49). The bathrooms are as functional as they are attractively decorated. Métro: George-V.

The Budget Range

Madeleine-Plaza, 33 Place de la Madeleine (8e) (tel. 265-20-63), couldn't be more Right Bank central, unless you slept in Madeleine church itself. Just on the plaza, it offers many consolidated and streamlined bedrooms, with a view of the church. A renovation program produced many more private baths and showers. Compact doubles with shower begin at 180F ($41.09), going up to 200F ($45.66) with private bath. The bedrooms are not overly spacious. For those who do not want their breakfast in bed, a breakfast room overlooks the church, serving a morning meal for 16F ($3.65). Métro: Madeleine, of course.

5. 16th and 17th Arrondissements

ÉTOILE/CHAILLOT/BOIS DE BOULOGNE: This is one of our favorite districts of Paris. Hemmed in by the Seine and the elegant park, the Bois de Boulogne, the 16th Arrondissement is largely a residential area of old town houses. In addition to the super-deluxe Raphael, the district also contains some of the finest hotels of Paris, including the Majestic and the Résidence du Bois—both especially known to well-heeled, discriminating travelers. Other selections, much preferred, are in the 17th Arrondissement, embracing the Parc Monceau.

A Deluxe Choice

Majestic, 29 rue Dumont-d'Urville (16e) (tel. 500-83-70), is in a league by itself. It consists only of apartment-suites, where you can live in a homelike manner, providing your way of life normally includes Louis XV-style furnishings and the like. If your fancy dictates, you can even dine "at home." The owner has carefully furnished the apartments with especially interesting and attractive antiques, as well as some fine paintings (don't miss the still life by Giovanni Trimboli in the lounge).

The relatively secluded position of the Majestic is ideal for many diplomats who stay here—just minutes from the Arc de Triomphe. The hotel is also a favorite of visiting opera stars. Two petite, but antique-filled, salons are suitable for receiving your guests, although most of the clients prefer to entertain in their own apartments.

If you stay at least a week, the management will furnish the kitchen completely. For two persons, a suite, including a foyer, bedroom, living room, dressing room, kitchenette, and bath, costs 700F ($159.81) daily. There is no charge for a third person sleeping in the living room. A few smaller and less expensive studios are available, with combination sitting- and bedrooms, a dressing salon, a kitchenette, and bath, going for 430F ($98.17) daily for two to three persons. Included in the quotations are taxes, service, and a continental breakfast.

The Upper Bracket

Méridien, 81 Boulevard Gouvion-Saint-Cyr (17e) (tel. 758-12-30), is the largest hotel in France. Under Air France's aegis, the 1023-room, air-conditioned hotel is a first of its kind in Paris. It caters to groups as well as to individuals, and it is big enough to accommodate a separate check-in counter for the former. The location is opposite the Air Terminal and two steps from the Champs-Élysées Avenue. It's at Porte Maillot, on the Neuilly-Vincennes Métro line. A lot of Air France know-how has gone into the design and furnishings—so you're offered rather pampered living. For example, a closed-circuit TV channel shows the same films seen on Air France planes, and a flashing light on your telephone indicates you have a message.

The setting is contemporary French, and the dramatic, overscale lobby chandelier—all glittery with tubular plastic rods hanging like stalactites—is an immediate eye-catcher. The bedrooms are designed to provide attractiveness, convenience, and comfort, plus good views of a great city. Featured are lots of slick built-in pieces, textured and handsomely colored fabrics, TV, direct-dial telephones, and partitioned bathrooms. Doubles cost from 460F ($105.02) to 510F ($116.43), and singles range in price from 440F ($100.45) to 480F ($109.58). All tariffs include taxes and service.

There are four restaurants, featuring everything from traditional French cuisine (Le Clos Longchamp) to Japanese specialties. For the lazy shopper, there is a cluster of boutiques and shops. A bar called Le Patio offers a musical ambience, and from 6 to 10 p.m. you hear piano music. An international jazz band plays from 10 p.m. to 2 a.m., or, if you prefer, you can visit a Parisian night club, L'Écume des Nuits.

La Résidence du Bois, 16 rue Chalgrin (16e) (tel. 500-50-59), is an exquisite little villa—all shiny white with a mansard roof—tucked away in a shady lane off the parklike Avenue Foch, only two minutes from the Arc de Triomphe. Go here only if you like quiet luxury. Monsieur and Madame Desponts bought this 300-year-old mansion from the Comte de Bomeau in 1964 and turned it into a retreat for discriminating guests. When they finished their careful restoration, they brought in their vast collection of antiques (mostly Louis XVI), gilt-edged paintings, crystal chandeliers, bronzes, sculpture, brocaded and silk draperies—making each room a charming world unto itself.

Although the rooms evoke the 17th and 18th centuries, with classic patterns of silk fabric on the walls, the bathrooms are super-modern. Depending on the plumbing, doubles range in price from 420F ($95.89) to 650F ($148.40).

A favorite spot in cooler months is an intimate drinking lounge, with huge armchairs positioned around a fireplace. In the cellar is a historic room where the mansion's first owner, an eminent physician, performed operations. A small front garden is screened from the lane by a stone wall and a wrought-iron fence, a few aged trees lending it a country feeling. In the rear garden are tables for breakfast.

The Middle Bracket

Résidence Foch, 10 rue Marbeau (16e) (tel. 500-46-50), is a gracious and artistic hotel run by Madame Jackie Carton. Off the Avenue Foch, it's only a few minutes from the Arc de Triomphe and a short walk from the Bois de Boulogne. Popular with the diplomatic corps, the hotel is well decorated. The bedrooms are one of a kind, furnished with a good many antiques and custom-upholstered chairs and sofas. Louis XV and Regency furnishings are intermixed with more provincial pieces, against a backdrop of strong colors. All rooms contain private baths.

The regular doubles rent for 280F ($63.92), the singles for 220F ($50.23). Prices quoted include tax and service, although breakfast is extra. Guests drop in for afternoon drinks in the front bar-lounge, enjoying its warm, quiet atmosphere. Métro: Place Dauphine.

Regent's Garden Hotel, 6 rue Pierre-Demours (17e) (tel. 754-39-40), has not one but two gardens, one with ivy-covered walls and umbrella tables—an inviting place to meet fellow guests for a cooling apéritif. And it is three minutes from the Arc de Triomphe. The owners, Mr. and Mrs. Teil, who treat guests with friendly simplicity, are proud of the heritage of the hotel: Napoleon III built the stately château for his physician. Today, the interior is like a country house, with a classic touch. The entry has fluted columns, the living room a casual mixture of family-style furniture—neither too studied nor too impressive, always comfortable.

The bedrooms are cheerfully done, featuring French flower prints on the walls and beds and tall French windows graced by soft filmy curtains. Some modern pieces have been added here and there, but most rooms are traditionally furnished; some even have draped canopy beds. The prices, including taxes, service, and continental breakfast, are 255F ($58.22) for a single with bath, 450F ($102.74) for a double with bath. Métro: Ternes.

La Régence Étoile, 24 Avenue Carnot (17e) (tel. 380-75-60), is only two minutes from the Arc de Triomphe, on a shady tree-lined street. The hotel occupies an attractive building of white stone with white shutters and trim. Inside, a tiny reception area and three small salons are furnished with several antiques, augmented by murals of Paris.

A miniature elevator takes you to the especially nice bedrooms, furnished with reproductions of good French furniture. All the rooms have tiled baths, including a bidet and often a shower as well as a tub. Two sets of prices are charged for the double rooms, the higher rate for the larger ones: 225F ($51.38) to 250F ($57.08), including taxes, service, and a continental breakfast. Singles go from 163F ($37.21) to 194F ($44.29). There's a garage near. Métro: Charles-de-Gaulle (Étoile).

Hôtel Frémiet, 6 Avenue Frémiet (16e) (tel. 524-52-06). Lean out a front bedroom window and you'll see the Seine, its silent parade of barges and boats, perhaps even the spot where the late Anaïs Nin moored her houseboat. Across the river from the Eiffel Tower, the second house down from the Avenue du President Kennedy, which borders the Seine, Frémiet stands in an exclusive residential district, one of only a few hotels here.

It's been owned by the same English-speaking Fourmond family for 14 years. Each year the owners have done renovations, installing new bathrooms with stall showers, even an automatic elevator. That French look is achieved with a generous use of Louis XVI-style furniture. All the freshly decorated bedrooms contain private baths. TV is available on request in the rooms, and each unit has a direct-dial phone. Doubles range in price from 230F ($52.52) to 260F ($59.36); singles, from 180F ($41.09) to 230F ($52.52). The reception lobby is just that, nothing more, although there is a small antique-filled salon for guests. Métro: Passy.

Tivoli-Étoile, 7 rue Brey (17e) (tel. 380-31-22). Many visitors to Paris like to stay right off the Champs-Élysées, in the vicinity of the Arc de Triomphe, yet find the hotels in this district beyond their limited means. The rue Brey is a side street branching off the Avenue de Wagram, one of the spokelike avenues from the Étoile. Although this street has a number of moderately priced hotels (all of which seem to be full all year), the Tivoli-Étoile is the best one. It's been entirely redecorated, and all of its 30 small rooms contain a private bath, radio, TV, and up-to-date furnishings, along with such conveniences as radios. For this midtown location, you pay 275F ($62.78) for two persons, this tariff including a continental breakfast. The hotel has a pleasant contemporary lobby with a mural, and a restful inner patio. Métro: Place Charles-de-Gaulle (Étoile).

The Budget Range

Des Deux Acacias ("The Hotel of the Two Locust Trees"), 28 rue de l'Arc-de-Triomphe (17e) (tel. 380-01-85), is a good bargain if your tastes are simple. A neat, semimodern little hotel, with a white marble facade, it is only a block from the Arc de Triomphe. Actually, it's in a district of budget hotels popular with foreign and provincial visitors who prefer more sedate living than that offered by the Left Bank hotels, which attract a younger crowd.

The emphasis is stricly on the rooms, as the hotel has only a small public lounge. All rooms have private showers or baths and toilets. Singles range from 91F ($20.78) to 121F ($27.63); doubles are 132F ($30.14) to 142F ($32.42), these tariffs including a continental breakfast. Des Deux Acacias is recommended for its cleanliness and certainly its stellar position. Métro: Place Charles-de-Gaulle (Étoile).

READERS' HOTEL SELECTIONS: "The Hôtel Palma, 46 rue Brunel (17e) (tel. 380-29-93), is near the Arc de Triomphe and just two short blocks from the Métro station Argentine. We spent three wonderful days there for 100F ($22.83) per day, including a continental breakfast. We had a large twin-bedded room with sink and bidet. For 150F ($34.26), a large double or twin-bedded room with shower and toilet is available, with breakfast. The management spoke English and was most helpful in giving directions to any place in the city and on how to use the Métro, and in recommending good and economical places to eat. It was clean and neat and very French. We loved it" (Mr. and Mrs. Douglas Cameron, Bellevue, Wash.).

6. 1st Arrondissement

PALAIS ROYAL/PLACE VENDÔME: This is the heart of Paris, rich in hotels appealing to traditional tastes (the deluxe Ritz, Meurice, and Inter-Continental). But you need not pay celestial tariffs for accommodations often furnished sumptuously with antiques. Housed in a room in the 1st Arrondissement, you'll be in the midst of the haut-monde sector of Paris, close to the Louvre, the Tuileries, and luxury boutiques.

The Upper Bracket

Hôtel Lotti, 7 & 9 rue Castiglione (1er) (tel. 260-37-34), has been called a "junior Ritz." Just off the historic Place Vendôme, it costs less than some of its swankier neighbors. Of course, it's not as voluptuous, although nevertheless very French in the best meaning of that expression when applied to decor. True to the tradition of most quietly elegant French hotels, its drawing room is generously endowed with a number of fine old tapestries, marble and gilt tables, plus the inevitable sparkling crystal.

Wide ranging, the bedrooms have that personalized styling of the 19th century. In furnishings, the era of the three Louises is often evoked. Mahogany desks, rosewood chests, gilt chairs, silk damask draperies, tufted slipper chairs, and tambour desks make for a rich and inviting ambience. There are 130 apartments in all, each with a private bath.

The different price levels depend on the location, size, and decor of the room. Singles range in price from 370F ($84.47) to 440F ($100.45); doubles, from 510F ($116.43) to 640F ($146.11), plus 15% for service.

Hôtel Regina, 2 Place des Pyramides (also 192 rue du Rivoli) (1er) (tel. 260-31-10). Sitting in the flagstoned courtyard of this old-fashioned, truly French hotel, you'd never think you were so close to the Tuileries, the Place Vendôme, the Opéra, or the Louvre. Water spurts from the dolphin fountain, and there are large pots of summer flowers, planters with geraniums, and white wrought-iron furniture to complete the rural scene.

Breakfast is pleasant in the morning room, overlooking the garden. The public rooms are gracious, too, utilizing furnishings from many eras, including the Louis XV and Louis XVI periods. Spacious drawing rooms and salons open off the long corridor lounge, with its islands of furniture arranged on rich Oriental rugs. Throughout are good touches: bronze statues, 18th-century paintings, bowls of fresh seasonal flowers, inlaid marquetry desks and tables.

If a private bath is required, the price for one is 260F ($59.36), 300F ($68.49) to 350F ($79.91) for two persons. These quotations include taxes, service, and a continental breakfast.

Vendôme, 1 Place Vendôme (1er) (tel. 260-32-84), couldn't be more chic or more popular. In the old days, you could see Adlai Stevenson rushing through the lobby with a briefcase, or perhaps Noel Coward dropping in for a drink from his nearby apartment. Its fame continues unabated. Surely, its address—1 Place Vendôme—is among the choicest in Paris, on the plaza designed by Mansart for Louis XIV. Behind its grand-siècle architectural façade, the atmosphere is discreet and ingratiating. The Vendôme isn't grandiose—in fact, compared to the neighboring Ritz, it is homelike and informal. Most often the bedrooms are paneled, containing marble fireplaces, brass beds, and Second Empire antiques and reproductions that are not ostentatious. Some of the pieces would make the former empress Eugénie feel at home.

Singles cost from 280F ($63.92); doubles, 350F ($79.91) to 380F ($86.75), including taxes, service, and a continental breakfast.

Hôtel de France et Choiseul, 239-241 rue St.-Honoré (1er) (tel. 261-54-60), is a remake of a gracious 1720 town house, just off the glamorous Place Vendôme. Actually it's been a hotel since the 1870s and became a fashionable oasis in fin-de-siècle Paris. Now, more than a century later, it has been completely remodeled. The bedrooms—most of which open onto the inner courtyard—were entirely gutted, then turned into tiny bandbox-size accommodations that are, nevertheless, attractively decorated. All sorts of conveniences are offered as compensation for the lost belle-époque glamor: a refrigerator, television, radio, a dressing table, plus a decorative tiled bath with all the latest gadgets. All is color coordinated and every room has its token Louis XVI-style chair "to set the right tone." A few minisuites have been installed on the top floor under the mansard roof, with a rustic staircase leading up to twin beds on a balcony. Singles go for 300F ($68.49); doubles, for 415F ($94.74), including taxes and service. There is a small Pullman-style dining room for guests and a charming restaurant, Le Lafayette, opening onto the inner courtyard and consisting of the historic salon where Lafayette received the subsidies to participate in the American War for Independence. Métro: Concorde, Tuileries, Opéra, or Madeleine.

The Middle Bracket

Hôtel de Castille, 37 rue Cambon (1er) (tel. 261-55-20), is a pleasant old hotel between the Paris headquarters of Chanel and the Chase Manhattan Bank, across the street from the Ritz. It provides excellent facilities: a provincial-style dining room with ivory-paneled walls, an open red-brick fireplace, a small salon with Louis XVI-style chairs, and—best of all—a large paved open garden, with a wall of climbing ivy, a vine-covered trellis, pots of flowers, and furniture set out under scalloped parasols.

Quiet for a hotel so close to major shops, museums, and busy boulevards, it is only a few minutes' walk from the Place Vendôme, la Concorde, or la Madeleine. The rooms are traditionally furnished; they have an old-fashioned spaciousness, and they're well tended—most pleasant for a stay in Paris. All come with private bath.

Singles go for 170F ($38.81) and up; doubles, 240F ($54.79) to 290F ($66.21).

Des Tuileries, 10 rue St.-Hyacinthe (1er) (tel. 261-04-17). Count yourself lucky if you get a room at this miniature (28 rooms) gem of a hotel. It proudly and lovingly owned by Madame Monique Poulle-Vidal, a blond-haired woman who has turned what was once a dull side-street hotel into an oasis of good taste and comfort. She refurbished the entire interior, guiding craftsmen so that Des Tuileries would become a reflection of her own taste. She wanted fine living not only for herself, but for her guests.

Each room has its own distinct personality—perhaps a unified color scheme, with matching draperies and bedspread, perhaps Directoire, Louis XV, Louis XVI, even Empire styling. Although not overly large, the rooms are comfortable, and each has its own attractive and efficient bath, plus a TV set. Madame charges 280F ($63.92) nightly for two persons, this rate including taxes, service, and a very French breakfast. For a single, the fee is 240F ($54.79).

Breakfast is likely to be served in the little rear salon—in fact, it's her own living room, where during the evening she welcomes guests who drop in to chat or watch television. Her reception lounge sets the pace, with gold velvet walls,

Louis XVI-style furniture, and 18th-century mirrors. Leading to the rooms is an open spiral staircase, with the original wooden steps preserved—but you can also take an elevator. Last, but not least, is the fortunate position of the hotel: next to the Tuileries, off the Place Vendôme, a few minutes' walk from either the Louvre or the Opéra. Métro: Pyramides or Tuileries.

The Budget Range

Montpensier, 12 rue de Richelieu (1er) (tel. 742-54-34), has many advantages and a few drawbacks. It is convenient, next to the Palais Royal, a few minutes' walk from the Louvre; but it is on a noisy street, so the bedrooms opening onto the inner courtyard are more desirable. The hotel has a rich heritage: three centuries ago it was the private palace of one of the most celebrated ladies of 17th-century France, the Duchess of Montpensier, known as "La Grande Mademoiselle." She was said to have been secretly married—against the wishes of Louis XIV—to the Duc de Lauzun, popularly known as Don Juan.

But long since, the building was adapted for hotel purposes, rooms being carved out in every size and description—and price tab. The better doubles with private baths rent for 178F ($40.63), the cheaper doubles with shower for 166F ($37.91). A few singles with toilets cost only 65F ($14.84). These tariffs include breakfast, taxes, and service. A group of three can ask for the best bargains: a room with a private bath for 195F ($44.56).

Don't expect furnishings evoking the grandeur of the heyday of the duchess—rather, a workable combination of traditional pieces, with a few antique and modern ones tossed in. Métro: Palais-Royal.

Saint-Roch Hôtel, 25 rue St.-Roch (1er) (tel. 260-17-91), has been totally renovated and decorated by its gracious woman owner. You enter behind a marble and glass façade, ascending an exquisite miniature spiral staircase. By elevator you go to one of the tastefully furnished bedrooms, perhaps on the seventh floor where, from some chambers, you can look at the chic shops along rue St.-Honoré. The floors have been carpeted, the walls papered in tasteful designs. The most expensive double with full bath rents for 200F ($45.66), although with a shower instead of a tub the charge is only 175F ($39.95). A single with shower or toilet rents from 135F ($30.82). The street-floor lounge has a little salon separated from the hallway by exposed oak beams. The decor theme is French provincial. The hostess speaks some English, and is rightly proud of her standard of cleanliness, comfort, and decoration. Métro: Opéra, Pyramides.

l'Hôtel Saint-Romain, 5-7 rue St.-Roch (1er) (tel. 260-31-70), has a few gracious touches of the Louis XVI period, yet doesn't overlook such modern conveniences as an elevator, too often missing in budget Paris hotels. The reception parlor has a sparkling crystal chandelier, and salon chairs are gathered around galleried mahogany coffee tables. Art objects such as period paintings give the downstairs ambience a French provincial touch. However, the rooms have been modernized, and are quite comfortable, although modest in appeal. A double with full bath goes for 155F ($35.39), which is quite a bargain considering the chic location, off the Tuileries, right near the fashionable shops of rue St.-Honoré. A twin-bedded room with full bath is more expensive—160F ($36.53), although doubles with shower go for just 135F ($30.82). Métro: Opéra, Pyramides.

READER'S BUDGET HOTEL SELECTION: "Hôtel le Loiret, 5 rue des Bons-Enfants (1er) (tel. 261-47-31), charges 70F ($15.98) to 110F ($25.11) in a single, 80F ($18.26) to

120F ($27.40) in a double, a continental breakfast included. The hotel is convenient to the Opéra, Comédie Française, and the Louvre" (Andrea Frey, Riverdale, N.Y.).

7. 2nd and 9th Arrondissements

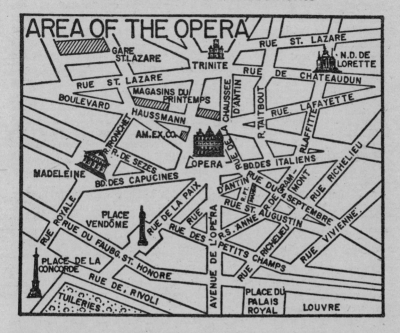

OPÉRA/GRANDS BOULEVARDS: These are two of the most international districts of Paris, especially the 2nd Arrondissement. The 9th stretches all the way to Pigalle, where Maurice Chevalier, as he confessed to an American TV audience, had his first affair. The Grands Boulevards are legendary, though the pinnacle of fashion they once enjoyed has now largely passed. The streets are crowded, the cafés bustling . . . no one ever said this was the quietest district of Paris. You can walk along rue de la Paix, go to the Opéra or the Opéra-Comique, and end up eventually at the infamous "Pig Alley" of World War II without ever leaving these arrondissements. Go to these quarters for lower-cost Right Bank living.

The Middle Bracket

Métropole Opéra, 2 rue de Gramont (2e) (tel. 269-91-03), is a super-French hotel, just a five-minute walk from the Opéra. On a quiet street off the main thoroughfare, it is perfect for travelers who want to be in the heart of the shopping district, near American Express and the Grands Boulevards. This well-run hotel went through a gigantic rebuilding and refurbishing program in 1968. What emerged was a fine hotel, showing equal reverence for good decoration and good plumbing.

There has been a generous use of reproductions of Directoire furnishings, creating a tasteful ambience in the reception lounges and in the bedrooms as well. There are four price levels, based on size, placement, and plumbing.

Singles with bath rent for 160F ($36.53) to 195F ($44.52); doubles with bath, for 250F ($57.08), including service and taxes. Breakfast is extra. Métro: Opéra, Bourse, or 4-Septembre.

Hôtel Richmond, 11 rue du Helder (9e) (tel. 824-75-27), is a substantial, three-star hotel, just a short walk from the Opéra—a superb location, as it lies near the American Express, the Café de la Paix, and many fine shops. The hotel itself has been much improved in recent years. Lying behind an attractive façade, it invites you to its pleasantly decorated lounge. Groups of sofas are conveniently placed for conversation. There are also marble columns, even a water fountain, Roman style—all tasteful, everything evoking an old-world mood. The rooms have comfort and convenience. The cost is 240F ($54.79) in a double, and a high 200F ($45.66) in a single. Métro: Opéra.

London Palace, 32 Boulevard des Italiens (9e) (tel. 824-54-64), is a bit of contemporary France in a superb central location, just a block from the Opéra departure point of tours. Within walking distance of many of Paris's fine restaurants and department stores, it has been renovated and overhauled and given a new lease on life. Occupying the upper floors of a classic building, with a row of dormers across the top, it fronts one of the Grand Boulevards, the haunt of 19th-century society.

Behind its classic façade modernity blazes with joyful colors and modern furnishings. White and vivid oranges are the color theme. The main lounge has a country-home look with picture windows opening onto a busy scene. The 50 bedrooms are equally well styled, again using for the most part contrasting white and orange. Most of the rooms contain private baths. A single with basin and toilet is 133F ($30.36), rising to 167F ($38.14) with shower, or 195F ($44.52) with full bath. Again, depending on the plumbing, double rooms go from 164F ($37.45) to 243F ($55.48). Taxes, service, and a continental breakfast are included in these tariffs. Most important, in July and August discount rates are granted visitors.

Hôtel Opéra d'Antin-L'Horset, 18-20 rue d'Antin (2e) (tel. 073-13-01), near the American Express and the Opéra, is run by the L'Horset chain. Antiques and reproductions give it a traditional look. The service is polite and friendly, and the price is right: 240F ($54.79) for a double with private bath or shower. Economy tip: Book a double with hot and cold running water only at 160F ($36.53) nightly. Singles range in price from 110F ($25.11) without bath to 200F ($45.66) with a private bath or shower. Tariffs include a continental breakfast, service, and tax. Métro: Opéra.

Hôtels de France, 22 rue d'Antin (2e) (tel. 742-19-12), are a pair of small adjoining hotels, just off the Avenue de l'Opéra. In a modernized building, with a wedge-shaped reception lounge, they are furnished in semimodern style, offering good bedrooms at slightly lower prices than most of their neighbors. The rate for a double with private bath or shower is from 160F ($36.53) to 220F ($50.24) nightly. A single room with a toilet only goes for 70F ($15.98), these tariffs including a continental breakfast, service, and taxes.

The real advantage of these hotels is their location: just a few minutes' walk from the Opéra, the Place Vendôme, the Louvre, and some of France's leading department stores. Métro: Opéra.

Hôtel de Sèze, 16 de Sèze (9e) (tel. 742-69-12), is a rather good buy, considering its central location—right off the Avenue de l'Opéra, within sight of the Madeleine. There's an elegant but tiny lobby, with wood paneling, chunky brass hardware, and some Louis XVI-style furniture. The 25 bedrooms, with all kinds of plumbing, have a curious hit-or-miss quality, but whether they're furnished with well-chosen antiques or plain old modern, they're serviceable and practical.

The cheapest doubles go for 110F ($25.11), including hot and cold running water and a bidet, plus use of the corridor bath and toilets. For a room with basin, bidet, and shower, two persons pay 140F ($31.96). For a room with private bath and toilet, the tariff is 195F ($44.52) for two. Taxes, service, and breakfast are included. English is spoken quite well. Métro: Madeleine.

The Budget Range

Hôtel du Nil, 10 rue du Helder (9e) (tel. 770-80-24), has to be valued for its location and price, not its lounge and entryway. Although it resembles many small hotels of Paris, its situation is prime, right near the Opéra and just a short walk from the Boulevards Haussmann and des Italiens. There are no salons, but you can always meet a friend at the Café de la Paix for a coffee. The cheapest rooms are those with showers (no private toilets, although there is adequate plumbing in the hallways on the same floors as the bedchambers). Cost for one person is 85F ($19.41), rising to 95F ($21.69) for two guests. In rooms with two big beds or one big bed and one small bed, the charges begin at 143F ($32.64) for one, 151F ($34.49) for two, and 155F ($35.39) for three occupants. Métro: Opéra.

8. 5th Arrondissement

LATIN QUARTER: Now we cross over to the Left Bank, into the Quartier Latin, that traditional intellectual and artistic center of Paris. Through its narrow streets and on its wide, café-studded boulevards throng students and visitors from every corner of the world. The hotels are plentiful, and, if not always inexpensive, at least moderately priced.

The colleges of the Sorbonne dominate the area. This section of Paris appeals more to the young and adventurous than to older readers. If you take the Métro to the Place St.-Michel, you will then emerge onto the Boulevard St.-Michel (called "Boul Mich"), the heart of the university sector of Paris. In this district, the rue des Ecoles is the most concentrated section for budget hotels, but we'll have many selections on little side streets branching off from it.

The Middle Bracket

Hôtel Le Colbert, 7 rue de l'Hôtel-Colbert (5e) (tel. 385-85-65). How can you miss by staying at this little, centuries-old, 40-room inn? It's not only on the Left Bank, a minute from the Seine, but it provides a fine view of Notre-Dame from many of its rooms. There's even a small front courtyard, setting the hotel apart from the bustle of Left Bank life.

True, the reception lounges are at a minimum, but the rooms themselves are well designed and tailored, furnished with good pieces. Most of them provide comfortable chairs and space for a breakfast area. The baths (one for every room) are semimodernized; the beds are comfortable, and such amenities as a telephone, a bell to ring for your breakfast, plenty of towels, and efficient maid service add that extra touch.

The doubles go for 240F ($54.79) per night. Actually, all the rooms are suitable for two, although a few with large double beds are rented to one person for 156F ($35.62). Breakfast is an extra 13F ($2.97). Most of the rooms are quiet. This hotel is well recommended—and a five-minute walk from the front door will take you to some of the finest restaurants in Paris, at any price level!

The Budget Range

Grand Hôtel du Mont-Blanc, 28 rue de la Huchette (5e) (tel. 033-49-44). Who has ever written a guide to Paris without including this little inn on the famous street of the Latin Quarter? The "grand" in its name is a pretension, of course. It's really modest. Behind its ivory-white façade and beckoning coach lamps, simple but clean and comfortable bedrooms are offered at 190F ($43.38) in a double with a complete private bath. Without bath, two persons can stay here for 115F ($26.25). Those filled with a nostalgia for the Paris of yesteryear recall the hotel's associations with Hemingway. And, of course, Elliot Paul, the novelist and friend of Gertrude Stein (she called Paul "the New England Saracen") and author of *The Last Time I Saw Paris,* stayed at the Mont-Blanc.

Hôtel Claude Bernard, 43 rue des Écoles (5e) (tel. 326-32-52). If you enjoy living among swarms of students in the heart of the Latin Quarter, then this hotel may be for you. Alive with its own particular joie de vivre, the Claude Bernard is just off an old tree-shaded square. The location is handy for exploring or just sampling the life along the Boulevard Saint-Michel, perhaps visiting some of the student nightclubs or restaurants. English is spoken fluently.

The public rooms are at a minimum. The breakfast room is cell-like, so you may want to have your morning meal upstairs—especially if you are fortunate enough to have snared a room with a view of the quarter. A continental breakfast, incidentally, is included in the rates quoted. For a single, no bath, the tariff is 79F ($18.04). The least expensive doubles (those with shower, no toilets) cost 158F ($36.07), rising all the way to 208F ($47.49) in a twin-bedded chamber with complete private bath; these tariffs including not only the breakfast but taxes and service as well.

Hôtel de Sully, 31 rue des Écoles (5e) (tel. 326-56-02), has been skillfully redecorated and modernized, with a sparkling, up-to-date lounge. It's mostly modern except for traditional touches, such as a large copper cash register and a sedan chair used as a telephone booth. The bedrooms are done in a country style, with provincial furniture. Television sets are placed near the ceiling so as not to intrude on the decor of the rooms. Most beds contain chintz-padded headboards. A double with full bath rents for 200F ($45.66), 151F ($34.49) with a shower. If you're saving francs, ask for one of the doubles with a shower (but no toilet) at 108F ($24.65). A continental breakfast is brought to your room for 11.50F ($2.62), and there is an elevator. Métro: Maubert-Mutualité.

Hôtel Elysa, 6 rue Gay-Lussac (5e) (tel. 325-31-74), is a traditional hotel, featuring the atmosphere of Brittany, and standing in one of the oldest parts of Paris. The furnishings are in the provincial style, making use of strong colors and wallpaper. There are only 36 bedrooms offered, and these are occasionally booked by teachers or else the families of students going to the Sorbonne, in Paris to visit with their offspring. Most of the bedrooms are attractively furnished, with a full bath, shower, or phone. A double peaks at 185F ($42.24), though a few doubles with shower (no tub) cost only 135F ($30.82). Breakfast and taxes are included. Métro: Luxembourg.

Select, 1 Place de la Sorbonne (5e) (tel. 354-29-01), is the only hotel in the Latin Quarter that stands directly on this famous square dominated by the Church of the Sorbonne, built between 1635 and 1642 by Le Mercier. Try to get a room overlooking this plaza which has been replanted with trees and had a fountain and benches added. Although the square is quiet and dignified, it opens onto the busy "Boul Mich," where you can enjoy café sitting. The interior has been modernized, and all the comfortably furnished bedrooms

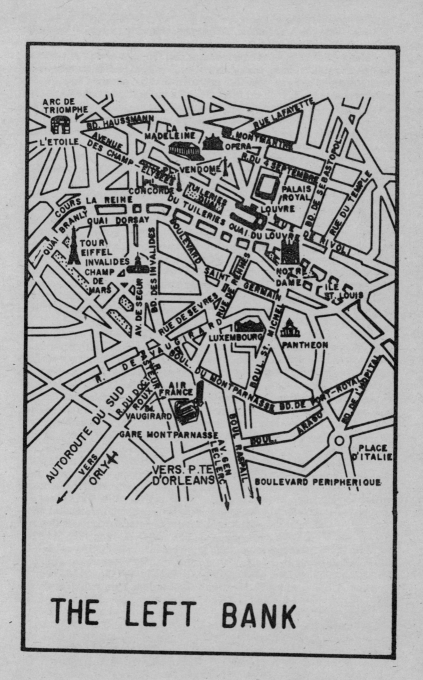

THE LEFT BANK

contain private baths, a double renting for 200F ($45.66), a single for 170F ($38.81), these tariffs including a continental breakfast, service, and taxes. Métro: St.-Michel.

Hôtel du Levant, 18 rue de la Harpe (5e) (tel. 033-42-61), caters to art, theater, and concert buffs, among others. The walls of its lounges are covered with posters advertising concerts, openings, and art shows. On a street of budget restaurants, right in the heart of the St.-Michel district, the hotel stands apart from the teeming life. Its wide front windows are filled with ferns. Those who want to be in the Latin Quarter will find moderately comfortable doubles with full bath renting for 135F ($30.82), that tariff falling to 125F ($28.54) in a double with shower. Doubles with less plumbing rent for even cheaper rates—from 95F ($21.69) to 110F ($25.11), the latter containing a shower but no toilet. Breakfast is an additional 11F ($2.51) per person. Happily, there's an elevator. Métro: St.-Michel.

Hôtel d'Albe, 1 rue de la Harpe, off the Place St.-Michel (5e) (tel. 634-09-70), is right in the center of one of the most teeming streets of the Latin Quarter, and, as such, is preferred by those who like to be in the whirlwind of Left Bank life. The d'Albe is a six-story corner building which has recently been modernized. The lounge is inviting, with a breakfast salon where you can order your morning coffee and croissants. An elevator takes you to the rooms on the upper floors. All the bedrooms are comfortably furnished and well kept. Doubles with water basins rent for 109F ($24.88), rising to 180F ($41.09) with shower or complete bath. Singles with bath or shower cost 159F ($35.30), but only 99F ($22.60) if bathless. Tax is included, but a continental breakfast is an additional 11F ($2.51) per person. English is spoken. Métro: St.-Michel.

Hôtel du Brésil, 10 rue Le Goff (5e) (tel. 033-76-11). Hemingway used to stroll by here after having killed a fat pigeon in the Luxembourg Gardens for his dinner (he wheeled the dead bird in a baby carriage). Between the years 1885 and 1886, Sigmund Freud lived here. In spite of some famous associations, the hotel is relatively unknown, appearing in no guide books that we know of. However, it may become better known, as it is being completely modernized, and, hopefully, these recent renovations will make it a more attractive Latin Quarter choice for visitors. Depending on the plumbing, double rooms cost anywhere from 110F ($25.11) to 160F ($36.53). Breakfast is extra. Métro: Luxembourg.

Grand Hôtel St.-Michel, 19 rue Cujas (5e) (tel. 354-47-98), with its old-fashioned furnishings, reflects the graciousness of its owner, Madame Salvage. Her little salon has elegance and is *très intime.* A large crystal-and-bronze chandelier, a grand piano that is seldom if ever played, period furnishings—an eclectic collection—fill the room. The bedrooms are simply furnished and a little antiquated, as is customary in the Latin Quarter. A double room with shower and water basin costs 60F ($13.70) a night, but only 50F ($11.42) if bathless. A twin-bedded room with shower and water basin goes for 70F ($15.98) a night. A few apartments are also available—two rooms with four beds and a complete bath, costing from 120F ($27.40) to 140F ($31.96) a night. In addition, there are some studios with three or four beds, as well as shower baths, rented out at a cost of 35F ($7.99) per person nightly. Métro: St.-Michel or Odéon.

Plaisant, 50 rue des Bernardins (5e) (tel. 354-74-57), is set back in a cul-de-sac, facing the Square Monge. In summer its façade is peppered with flower boxes of red geraniums, a pleasant sight. The hotel is an excellent one, mainly because of the reception and friendliness of the management. The woman manager speaks English. The rooms are well furnished, although some, frankly, are far better than others. Preferred, of course, are the twins with complete private bath, costing 195F ($44.52). However, doubles with shower rent for only 150F ($34.26), certainly a fine bargain. In the more modest doubles, without much plumbing, the rate is just 95F ($21.69) for two. You can order breakfast in your room, or else take it in a combination TV lounge and dining salon. Métro: Maubert-Mutualité, Jussieu, or Cardinal-Lemoine.

Welcome, 5 impasse Royer-Collard (5e) (tel. 354-09-63), on a quiet cul-de-sac, lies behind a rather ornate façade peppered with balconies. It's an attractive, older, period-style hotel with a polished marble floor in its entrance and ornate brass hat racks. Rooms are pleasant—carpeted and painted with muted color schemes. If you take a room at the top, you'll literally be sleeping under the eaves. Doubles with complete bath rent for 122F ($27.85); with a shower only, 102F ($23.29). Without a bath, some basic, simply furnished doubles (you use the corridor bath) rent for only 70F ($15.98). A continental breakfast is served in a rather sunny room, equipped with Scandinavian-style furnishings. Métro: Luxembourg.

Hôtel St.-Jacques, 35 rue des Écoles (5e) (tel. 326-82-53), is a skillfully decorated hotel in the heart of the Quartier Latin. Its lounges and breakfast rooms are prettily furnished with provincial reproductions. A few antiques are added to give it more charm. There's even a *Mona Lisa* reproduction in the hallway staring enigmatically at every guest. An elevator leads to the slightly old-fashioned rooms, where the most expensive double, with full bath, costs 178F ($40.63), but only 152F ($34.72) in a double with shower. Some doubles without such plumbing rent for as little as 85F ($19.41). These tariffs include a continental breakfast, service, and taxes. Métro: Maubert-Mutualité.

READER'S HOTEL SELECTION: "We stayed at the **Hôtel du Square Monge,** 42 rue des Bernardins (5e), between the rue des Écoles and rue Monge. Doubles come with a wide range of plumbing, costing from 120F ($27.40) to 140F ($31.96), and a three-bedded room with bath and toilet goes for 183F ($41.77). The hotel is clean and comfortable, nicely furnished. The manager, Monsieur Baur, is friendly and speaks English. The location is in the Latin Quarter east of Boulevard St.-Michel and just south of Boulevard St.-Germain, a short distance to the Maubert-Mutualité Métro stop and near at least one of every kind of food shop as well as the open-air fruit and vegetable market at Place Maubert (open Tuesdays, Thursdays, and Fridays)" (Patricia Hagan, New Haven, Conn.).

9. 6th Arrondissement

ST.-GERMAIN-DES-PRÉS/ODÉON: The 6th Arrondissement embraces the most interesting quartier of the Left Bank—St.-Germain-des-Prés and the Luxembourg Gardens with its magnificent grounds. Although the student population of the Sorbonne has invaded, there is, as well, an elegant residential quarter.

For the budget hotel shopper, there are more quality choices here than in the 5th Arrondissement, just previewed. Somehow the hotels of St.-Germain-des-Prés seem to have more style and character than those around the Sorbonne, although you may disagree.

In the 6th Arrondissement, art galleries, studios, restaurants, and celebrated cafés (such as Flore and Deux Magots) abound.

Many of our recommendations in this sector center around the Place de l'Odéon, a square dominated by the Théâtre de France, one of the three state-run theaters of Paris.

If you're searching for a room with some of the color and charm that you traditionally associate with Left Bank Paris, then you've come to the right quarter. Happy hunting!

The Middle Bracket

Aviatic, 105 rue de Vaugirard (6e) (tel. 544-38-21), maintains tradition down in Montparnasse, wherein are those legendary cafés. Guests are likely to include everybody from unpublished novelists to jazz musicians. It's totally Gallic, with a simple inner courtyard and an ivy-covered lattice on its walls. The entrance is impressive, too, with its marble columns, ornate brass chandeliers, and old-style furniture. In a little salon you can meet your friends. Each bedroom has its own distinct style, as well as numerous conveniences, likely to include a wide range of plumbing and an automatic telephone. Singles cost from 240F ($54.79); doubles, 280F ($63.92); tax, service, and a continental breakfast included. Métro: Montparnasse-Bienvenue.

Hôtel du Pas de Calais, 59 rue des Saints-Pères (6e) (tel. 548-78-74). Many famous people have stayed here: Maurice Béjart, the dancer-choreographer-stage designer; even Sartre, along with a host of lesser-known singers, actors, and writers. The building itself dates from the 17th century. Chateaubriand (who lived here between 1811 and 1814) began the long parade of artistic and literary visitors to its doorstep. In 1815 the town house was converted into a hotel.

Du Pas de Calais was redecorated and modernized in 1969 with varying results. The rooms, although clean and well kept, rely heavily on bentwood pieces, blond woods, and plastic coverings. In the more expensive rooms with private baths, the rate is 210F ($47.94) for two. Singles are charged 178F ($40.64). Included in the tariffs are taxes, service, and breakfast. Guests are invited for afternoon drinks or breakfast on the small patio. Métro: St.-Germain-des-Prés.

Hôtel d'Angleterre, 44 rue Jacob (6e) (tel. 260-34-72). No matter how hard other hotels try to create an old-world atmosphere of gentility and simplicity, they are amateurs compared to this mellowed charmer, built in 1650. In a district of antique shops and private art galleries, d'Angleterre once sheltered the British Embassy. Since 1910 it has been managed by the Berthier family. Shut off from street traffic, most of its rooms open onto an exposed courtyard, planted with grass, climbing ivy, and spring or summer flowers. Many of the clients prefer to take their breakfast at one of the little tables set up on the edge of the courtyard in a Rive Gauche atmosphere.

Picture a small old-fashioned salon which hasn't succumbed to a decorator's touch, with a grand piano, an antique writing desk, comfortable chairs—and you can understand why d'Angleterre has long been favored by such illustrious guests as Anne Morrow Lindbergh, who doesn't seem to mind the antiquated plumbing. Hemingway stayed here and was ill, but Madame Berthier took care of him, as related in his son's book. The tariffs include taxes, service, and a continental breakfast, and the accommodations contain private baths with either tubs or showers and a toilet. For a single, the rate is 180F ($41.09) nightly; for a double, 230F ($52.51). Métro: Colonel-Fabien.

Hôtel d'Isly, 29 rue Jacob (6e) (tel. 329-59-96), is a renovated corner hotel, on the street where Richard Wagner lived from 1841 to 1842 (look over the Bar Vert at No. 14). A good base from which to explore Left Bank art galleries, bookstores, and antique shops, d'Isly appears as white as vanilla ice cream. The hotel is entered from a busy street but many of its rooms overlook a quiet, inner courtyard which, although minuscule, evidences the owner's green thumb.

There is a small contemporary lounge in cocoa-brown and chalk-white, and the living room, where you can take your morning meal on a bentwood chair, evokes a bistro ambience. But the Hôtel d'Isly puts most of its care and concern into its bedrooms, which have that French feminine look—many with lacy flowered paper on the ceilings and walls. The overall effect is restful and comfortable. Most of the rooms have private baths, in which the color-coordinated wallpaper scheme carries over.

The all-inclusive cost (continental breakfast, service, and taxes) for a single room with a large bed and a private bath is 160F ($36.53), but only 100F ($22.83) for a single with water basin. A double room with bath or shower goes for 210F ($47.94). Colonel-Fabien.

Hôtel des Saints-Pères, 65 rue des Saints-Pères (6e) (tel. 544-50-00). The best recommendation for this time-tested favorite is the long list of habitués who swear by it. Others who have passed through and judged it more superficially haven't always been as enthusiastic. Just a minute off Boulevard St.-Germain, it offers 40 bedrooms facing an inner courtyard. It has a welcoming entrance with all-glass doors, potted trees, and coach lights. All the rooms have been modernized and come complete with private bath. The rates include service, taxes, and a continental breakfast. A double costs from 200F ($45.66) to 250F ($57.08); single occupancy ranges from 145F ($33.10) to 220F ($51.15). While the rather modern furnishings may not be imaginatively selected, they are comfortable. It's recommended you order breakfast in the courtyard, weather permitting, as the pots of flowers can cheer your expeditions for the day. Métro: St.-Germain-des-Prés or Sèvres-Babylone.

Hôtel de Seine, 52 rue de Seine (6e) (tel. 634-22-80), is one of the best of the little three-star hotels in St.-Germain-des-Prés. The entrance is impressive, through 17-foot bronze-studded oak doors. The reception salon has a château look, although the hotel itself is actually intimate, lying off a small plaza with a splashing global fountain. The hotel is kept in tiptop condition, and it's marvelously located right near some of the most interesting and esoteric Left Bank shops of Paris. The rooms are simply but tastefully decorated. One person pays from 120F ($27.40) for a chamber with shower (no toilet), up to 200F ($45.66) for a complete bath. Doubles with shower (no toilet) cost 160F ($36.53), rising to 240F ($54.79) with complete bath. All these tariffs include a *petit déjeuner.* Métro: Mabillon.

The Budget Range

Regent's Hôtel, 44 rue Madame (6e) (tel. 548-02-81), is deep in the Left Bank district, one short block from the Luxembourg Gardens. On a relatively quiet street, it offers 36 rooms. Perhaps its best feature is a little paved patio with beds of flowers, shrubbery, and white wrought-iron furniture. Breakfast is leisurely in this secluded spot.

The bedroom furnishings are a mixture of modified modern, antiques, and reproductions. In all cases, the rooms are comfortable, the beds large and soft. The Jacques and Cretey families offer some doubles and twins with private bath for 196F ($44.75). Doubles with hot and cold running water are 120F ($27.40). These rates include a continental breakfast and taxes. You can meet with friends (or make new ones) in the petit salon, highlighted by Louis XV-style furniture. Métro: St.-Sulpice.

Deux-Continents, 25 rue Jacob (6e) (tel. 326-72-46), is the domain of Madame Chresteil, who inherited these "two continents." She is a host with that rare combination of sense and candor, good humor, and kindliness. She's furnished the bedrooms in modern and not so modern, installed telephones, and ensured that there are reading lights over the beds. Cleanliness prevails.

The prices include taxes, service, and a breakfast tray brought to the room. All the accommodations have shower or bath costing 152F ($43.82) to 220F ($50.23) in twins or doubles, 130F ($29.68) to 190F ($43.38) in a single.

The two buildings are so connected that there are myriads of corridors, little staircases, and courtyards.

Michelet-Odéon, 6 Place de l'Odéon (6e) (tel. 634-27-80), is a mansard-roofed corner building right on the 18th-century Place de l'Odéon, itself dominated by the Greek- and Roman-style Théâtre de France. The classic columns of the hotel's reception hall seem appropriate to the setting, and because of its proximity to the state-run theater, it is often home base for many performing artists.

Although there's a homey little lounge for meeting one's friends, the hotel is recommended mainly for its comfortable and fairly priced bedrooms. The rate for a double with shower and toilet is 160F ($36.53); with a complete bath, it increases to 175F ($39.95). The furnishings are adequate and pleasant but not distinguished. Métro: Odéon.

Hôtel du Lys, 23 rue Serpente (6e) (tel. 326-97-57), is a well-restored 17th-century, six-floor town house. It's the Latin Quarter creation of Monsieur Steffen, who has made the Lys an attractive and stylish hotel. It's on a quiet little street just off the Boulevard St.-Germain, a minute's walk from the Seine.

Even the façade is inviting, the upper floors set back behind a narrow terrace. The wide stone entrance is graceful, with glass doors and brass fleur-de-lis handles. Wherever aesthetically appropriate, stone walls and beams have been exposed, antiques placed here and there. The bedrooms vary in comfort and size—as do the furnishings. Many are modest; others richly adorned. The cost for a single with shower is 106F ($24.20) to 120F ($27.40). For a double with shower, the tab is 125F ($28.54) to 155F ($35.39). Reservations are imperative if you wish to stay here in summer. Métro: St.-Michel or Odéon.

St.-André-des-Arts, 66 rue Saint-André-des-Arts (6e) (tel. 326-96-16), is old, rambling, and little, the atmosphere casual, friendly, and appealing to youthful travelers. The owner brought a treasured grandfather clock from his family attic for the hallway, a tavern table from his hometown village for his tiny combination reception lounge and breakfast room. Just off St.-Germain-des-Prés, this modest Left Bank establishment is easy to spot: the façade is deep red and its name is in gold letters. It's right in the center of a district of dozens of small galleries and antique specialists.

The bedrooms are furnished helter-skelter, but they do offer a wide choice of plumbing facilities. With shower, a double costs 140F ($31.96); a single with shower is 120F ($27.40), rising to 130F ($29.68) in a single with bath. Prices include taxes, service, and a continental breakfast. Métro: St.-Michel.

Hôtel du Vieux Paris, 9 rue Gît-le-Coeur (6e) (tel. 033-41-66), is one of those hard-to-find little hotels just off the Seine. But this one is a winner, tucked away in a building with a chocolate-brown façade. Many artists and writers have stayed here, arising the next morning to contemplate the view of Notre-Dame after a short walk along the river. The rooms have been given decorator touches, such as large patterned wallpaper on the ceilings. The owner, Madame Odillard, runs a fine little hotel, charging 162F ($36.99) in a double with private bath, but only 115F ($26.25) in a double without bath. These tariffs include a continental breakfast. Métro: St.-Michel.

Hôtel Racine, 23 rue Racine (6e) (tel. 326-00-60), is a little hotel made by joining two buildings, lying just a few feet from the Place de l'Odéon with its marble Théâtre de France. Its entry suggests that it's a well-cared-for hotel.

A splashy use is made of the red colors, and there's even a classic bust of Racine on a pedestal. In a small covered patio, a continental breakfast is served to guests, and the reception is from helpful students. Many of the rooms have much character, although the less expensive ones are more bone-bare. A double with full bath goes for 205F ($46.80), but only 180F ($41.09) with a shower. A decent single without bath is priced at 98F ($22.37). Included in these tariffs are a continental breakfast and tax. Métro: Odéon.

Grand Hôtel des Balcons, 3 rue Casimir-Delavigne (6e) (tel. 325-99-89), is perhaps the best buy on this little street off the Odéon, if you're willing to play down the importance of a lounge and lobby, which are nonexistent. Only a one-star hotel, it once sheltered Endre Ady (1877–1919), Hungary's greatest lyric poet, who died a victim of alcoholism. His Paris years were characterized as his "angry young man" period, when he became the target of violent attacks. At the hotel today, the minuscule reception has a small modern desk, plastic-and-chrome chairs and tables. But the bedrooms are better, costing 140F ($31.96) in a double with full bath, 120F ($27.40) with shower, and only 90F ($20.55) if you'd be happy with a water basin. A continental breakfast and service are included. Métro: Odéon.

Welcome Hôtel, 66 rue de Seine (6e) (tel. 634-24-80), is a successful restoration of a 17th-century house. A second-floor reception lounge is furnished skillfully, with tapestries between old beams, chandeliers, and comfortable armchairs. A continental breakfast is served on a long oak refectory table. The bedrooms, for the most part, are oddly shaped and furnished with French provincial pieces. Twin-bedded rooms with a complete bath go for 165F ($37.68); with a shower, 159F ($36.30). A single with private shower and toilet rents for 135F ($37.68). There is an additional charge of 12F ($2.74) for breakfast. The location is memorable, just off the Boulevard Saint-Germain, next to a colorful open-air market filled with booths and vendors selling fruit and vegetables from all over France. Hopefully, you'll be there the morning the fresh strawberries come in. You can buy some to go with your breakfast. Métro: Odéon or Mabillon.

La Résidence du Globe, 15 rue des Quatre-Vents (6e) (tel. 633-62-69), after extensive remodeling and restoration, recaptures some of the character of a 17th-century town house. The renovation revealed rugged stone walls and twisted old oak beams, and modern decorators added a touch of sophistication by bringing in an eclectic collection, including ornate wrought-iron gates, an old chest, a bishop's chair, ornate gilt mirrors, and a bronze chandelier. Close to interesting shops, the hotel lies right off the Carrefour de l'Odéon. Its rooms are simply furnished and well kept, costing 185F ($42.24) in a double with complete bath, but only 135F ($30.82) in a double with shower. There are no twins, only doubles. Métro: Odéon.

Hôtel du Danemark, 21 rue Vavin (6e) (tel. 326-93-78), seems to have been a rendezvous for painters and writers for decades. What makes it such a compelling choice is that it is located right in the heart of Montparnasse, near the cafés that enjoyed such a vogue in the 1920s—the Dôme, la Coupole, the Select, and la Rotonde. To make it extra nice, the Jardin du Luxembourg is only a short stroll away. The five-floor hotel is admittedly modest, as are its prices. A double with bath costs only 145F ($33.10), and this rate drops to 96F ($21.92) in a double room with water basin. Breakfast is an additional 11F ($2.51). The management is friendly and helpful, and if you stay here you'll be near some of the most interesting and characteristic restaurants of Paris. Métro: Vavin.

10. 7th and 15th Arrondissements

EIFFEL TOWER/INVALIDES: This is largely a middle-class residential sector on the Left Bank, embracing the Eiffel Tower and the Champ de Mars, plus a military school which Madame de Pompadour founded and Napoleon attended. The 15th Arrondissement was hardly considered a hotel district—until the Hilton opened its doors. The 7th Arrondissement, however, has long been noted for its few select hotels. These Left Bank districts are characterized by tree-lined boulevards and large open squares, ranging around Les Invalides (founded by Louis XIV).

In the 15th Arrondissement, not far from the Eiffel Tower, a *front de Seine* development of highrise modern buildings has gone up. One critic said that it looks like "a little bit of New York's East Side or Chicago's Lake Shore Drive."

First-Class Hotels

Paris Hilton, 18 Avenue de Suffren (15e) (tel. 273-92-00). At first the Parisians were skeptical. After all, Hilton was synonymous with America's extreme and sterile modernity. As a further break with tradition, the hotel sprouted up on the Left Bank, shattering the Right Bank deluxe monopoly. Nowadays, many of the more progressive French accept the fact that the Hilton may be around for some time.

The management shrugged off the initial indifference, citing the case of the Eiffel Tower at the Hilton's doorstep. It didn't get a warm reception when it was built, either. Now take any night, especially Saturday, and try to get into Hilton's Le Western, where mouth-watering Texas steaks and roast beef are flown in fresh daily from the United States. Chances are you'll have to wait in line. The French have beat you to the tables (they even know what a "Cowboy Cut" is!).

Built in the true Hilton formula, the 11-floor, 492-room hotel consists of window walls of glass, streamlined throughout with contemporary gadgets. Not since the inauguration of the George V in the 1930s had Paris had a new luxury hotel when the Hilton was first opened. The emphasis is on personal service and amenities: ice cubes, babysitting, an underground garage, major airline desks on the premises, same-day laundry and cleaning.

The bedrooms are priced according to the view. Those facing the Eiffel Tower and the Seine are the most expensive, of course. A single starts at 425F ($97.03), going up to 500F ($114.15). Doubles are in the top 600F ($136.98) to 750F ($171.23) bracket. To all these tariffs you must add 7% for tax and 15% for service. The accommodations have a decorator look, a harmonious blending of contemporary furnishings combined with modified French period styles (95% Hilton, 5% Louis XV). The color themes are refreshing. Your all-tiled bath has such niceties as slippers and dressing robes.

For an *experience extraordinaire,* you can dine at "Le Toit de Paris," the Hilton's rooftop restaurant and cocktail lounge. Its tables are set in front of wide windows, allowing an unmarred view of the city's skyline. Le Coffee Shop offers a different national cuisine for each day of the week. The decor is ultra chic and modern, with stainless-steel floors (a first for us) and metallic walls, contrasting with the Louisiana plantation furniture.

The Middle Bracket

Hôtel de Bourgogne et Montana, 3 rue de Bourgogne (7e) (tel. 551-20-22), is in a quiet, dignified sector of Paris, in the Place du Palais-Bourbon, opposite the mansion housing the president of the National Assembly. The hotel is two blocks from the Seine and directly across the river from the Place de la Concorde. The interior of this six-story, 35-room building is suitable for homey comfort. The main-floor reception, with its intimate circular writing room and classic columns, adjoins a cozy salon. A small elevator takes you to your bedroom, which is likely to be decorated with floral chintz and comfortable beds and armchairs. Doubles begin at 200F ($45.66) and go up to 375F ($85.61). Singles are from 200F ($45.66) to 350F ($79.91), a continental breakfast, service, and taxes included. Métro: Invalides or Chambre des Députés.

St.-Thomas-d'Aquin, 3 rue du Pré-aux-Clercs (7e) (tel. 261-01-22), has been entirely renovated and redecorated, offering one a chance to live in a refined, traditional ambience. Behind a cream-colored façade with shutters and balconies, it stands on a relatively traffic-free street between the busy Boulevard St.-Germain and the rue de l'Université. The reception hall and small lounge are modestly and traditionally furnished, with flocked paper and paneled woodwork. The ceiling is also paneled, and there are bronze chandeliers casting soft light. The bedrooms are good for the price. Many contain provincial reproductions, and some have tester beds set in oaken alcoves. Most of the rooms are adorned with flowery French wallpaper, and all have phones. For a twin with a complete bath, you'll pay 200F ($45.66). Métro: Bac or St.-Germain-des-Prés.

The Hôtel du Quai Voltaire, 19 Quai Voltaire (7e) (tel. 261-50-91), doesn't depend on its namesake for its reputation but rather on Oscar Wilde, Baudelaire, and Richard Wagner, who occupied rooms 47, 56, and 55 respectively. Most of the rooms of this charming if modest inn directly overlook the bookstalls and boats of the Seine.

The manager, Madame Trollat, likes to keep the atmosphere of the place. Staircase and corridors are decorated with blue paper walls and white doors. The bar and the little salon with its fine tapestry allow the guests to meet over drinks. A double with bath costs 240F ($54.80); a single with bath, 170F ($38.81). A bathless single goes for from 85F ($19.41) to 120F ($27.40). All tariffs include taxes, service, and a continental breakfast. Métro: Bac.

The Budget Range

St.-Simon, 14 rue de St.-Simon (7e) (tel. 548-35-66). In the heart of the Left Bank, the inn is a mainstay of old-world charm. It's a small villa, really, with a garden in front and out back, the indulgence of Monsieur Lindqvist. His list of guests, many of whom have become his friends, includes ambassadors, noted writers, playwrights such as Edward Albee, painters, and sculptors. The 34 highly individualized rooms are in great demand. In the central hallway is a desk piled high with letters requesting reservations and a large hand-lettered cardboard chart programming occupancy for weeks in advance.

The rooms vary greatly in size, comfort, and price, but in every one is sure to be a treasured antique. The units have charm—a lived-in look—and good beds; decorative objects are scattered everywhere. Double rooms, all with private baths, range in price from 200F ($45.66) to 250F ($57.08), including service and taxes, with a continental breakfast costing another 15F ($3.42).

In the lower lounge, decidedly informal, guests gather for long talks and drinks. Two ground-floor salons are jewels of taste and style.

Lindbergh, 5 rue Chomel (7e) (tel. 548-35-53), honors the late American aviator whose nonstop solo flight across the Atlantic electrified Paris in 1927.

Not so long ago this formerly insignificant establishment looked as if nothing had changed since that day. However, it's happily entered the 1980s, becoming modern. On a somewhat hidden-away Left Bank street, it is next to one of our little surprise budget restaurants, off the Boulevard Raspail. The pint-size reception lounge is inviting. The bedrooms have been given a new look, with plumbing added. A single with shower goes for 100F ($22.83); the price is 120F ($27.40) for an equivalent double. The doubles with complete bath, and that means a toilet as well, cost from 130F ($29.68) to 160F ($36.53). Métro: Sèvres-Babylone.

11. 14th Arrondissement

Rapidly undergoing massive renovation, the 14th Arrondissement of Paris has been given a tremendous push in its bid for the tourist dollar with the opening of the following hotels.

THE UPPER BRACKET: PLM St.-Jacques, 17 Boulevard St.-Jacques (14e) (tel. 589-89-80), is one of the latest ventures of Baron and Baronne Elie de Rothschild. This 812-room, 14-story glass-and-steel hotel is refreshingly stylish and very French—red, white, and blue everywhere. Not only are the public rooms attention-getting, but the bedrooms as well have strong textures and primitive colors, contrasting with bone-white in effective combinations. The rooms come complete with refrigerators, direct-dial telephones, televisions, radios, and individually controlled air conditioning. Tiled bathrooms have both showers and tubs, plus a separate toilet area. All year, singles rent for 440F ($100.45); doubles, for 500F ($114.15), including service, tax, and a continental breakfast.

The Rothschilds do not skimp on facilities for their guests. The most winning of the public rooms is a bistro called Le Café Français, a recreation of a turn-of-the-century brasserie, with bentwood chairs, 1890s posters, potted palms, and belle époque lighting fixtures. A meal here would run about 150F ($34.26). In addition, you might want to patronize Le Patio. Drinks are served in both a garden bar and a Polynesian bar. And, on the lower level, is a maze of little boutiques, including, of course, a Banque Rothschild. Métro: Denfert-Rochereau.

Paris-Sheraton, 19 rue Commandant-Mouchotte (14e) (tel. 260-35-11), is the largest hotel on the Left Bank, its skyscraper tower dominating Montparnasse. Encased in the 32-story tower are 1000 rooms. Singles range in price from 425F ($97.03) to 485F ($110.73), and doubles go from 485F ($110.73) to 550F ($125.57), tax included. Rooms are color coordinated, containing color TVs, tiny bars, radios, sofas, and armchairs, plus direct-dial telephones.

Most hotels have inadequate arrival space, but at the Sheraton there is a wide driveway leading to the core of the hotel, and it is surrounded by an acre of terraces, its bars and restaurants opening onto a sunken garden.

The gourmet restaurant, Montparnasse 25, serves a high-level French cuisine. With potted palms, black lacquered chairs and tables, and a fine art exhibition, it takes its theme from the Montparnasse period of 1925. Some of the art reproductions are by artists who once lived in the quarter, including Modigliani and Van Dongen, and large-scale photos of famous theatrical personalities of the era are also used. Of course, the vista of Paris is always alluring.

An adjoining place for predinner drinks is Le Corail, with an oceanic theme using both coral and futuristic driftwood. A streamlined coffeeshop, La Ruche, with its beehive theme, provides quick meals; and La Pampa is the clubroom-style main restaurant. Adjoining the hotel is a rink for ice skating and curling, plus a bowling alley, shopping center, and a parking lot for 2500 cars. The subway stop, Montparnasse-Bienvenue, is across the street, and Gaité, exactly underground, connects directly to the Champs-Élysées (six stops).

12. 4th Arrondissement

LE MARAIS: Once the heart of aristocratic Paris, le Marais dipped into decay for centuries, but now its mansions are being restored, and some private apartments here are renting at prices higher than nearly anywhere else in Paris. However, le Marais remains a bastion of inexpensive hotels and restaurants. If you go now, you can take full advantage of the low tariffs charged at the following recommended hotels.

The Budget Range

Hôtel du Grand Turenne, 6 rue de Turenne (4e) (tel. 278-43-25). The façade is a brown-and-white canopy with potted plants placed about. Inside this little two-star hotel you'll find unqualified respectability. It's one of the more expensive hotels in the Marais, as it has been considerably upgraded in recent years, with many comforts and modern conveniences added. The breakfast room and reception area are quite attractive. A well-furnished double with complete bath or shower goes for 145F ($33.10), but is only 118F ($26.93) with a water basin. The management speaks English. Métro: St.-Paul-le-Marais.

Hôtel du Parc Royal, 25 rue de Turenne (4e) (tel. 887-86-77), is, despite its fancy name, modesty itself; but that may be just what you're looking for, as the tariffs are low. The hotel lies only a short walk from the Place des Vosges, right in the middle of an artisan district where many of the crafts of the Middle Ages are being revived. The hotel probably takes its name from the days of the Place Royale, which was a meeting place of Paris society in the early 17th century. Here there are no luxury touches. Instead, the rooms are simple and clean, and the friendliness of the management also compensates. There are four floors of rooms behind the old stone façade, and a neatly decorated entryway. The hotel has undergone much restoration. Doubles without bath rent for 110F ($25.11), rising to anywhere from 130F ($29.68) to 150F ($34.26) with complete bath. Métro: Bastille or Saint-Paul.

Hôtel des Célestins, 1 rue Charles V (4e) (tel. 887-87-04), within walking distance of the Bastille, stands on a seldom-used, narrow street. One reader called it "a jewel among Parisian hotels." After an extensive modernization program, the hotel has emerged as most appealing. Guests are welcomed into a reception lounge area, decorated, like the private rooms, in the style of the Marais. The bedchambers themselves are handsomely furnished and immaculately kept. Two persons occupying a room without bath pay 60F ($13.70) a night, the cost rising to 130F ($29.68) if they desire a complete bath. A continental breakfast is an additional 11F ($2.41). Métro: Bastille or Sully-Morland.

Hôtel Stella, 14 rue Neuve St.-Pierre (4e) (tel. 272-23-66), is perhaps one of the least-known hotels of Paris, lying deep in the Marais off the Place des Vosges, near the Métro stop at the Place de la Bastille. The government grants it only one star, and it is admittedly a very modest selection, but it is clean, friendly, and provides routine comfort. A corner building, it offers bathless accommodations only. A double costs 80F ($18.26), and this is the most expensive accommodation! Breakfast is another 13F ($2.97), as are the baths.

The lounge is in the provincial style, with comfortable armchairs where guests sit watching TV. Reader Gale Glazer, of Cambridge, Mass., wrote: "For very satisfying meals, we would buy the component parts along the rue de St. Antoine which is loaded with pastry, wine, cheese, and meat shops. Our meals were supplemented by deliciously fresh fruits from one of the many street vendors who lined both sides of the avenue."

13. 18th Arrondissement

MONTMARTRE: The 18th Arrondissement, which takes in Montmartre, is not the most recommendable place for hotels. Of course, finding a hotel around Pigalle and Place Clichy that isn't a "hot bed" candidate takes some talent, although such hotels do exist. However, the steep hill of Montmartre has a particular appeal all its own for certain readers, so we've included the following recommendations which are safe havens in an otherwise rough district.

The Budget Range

Hôtel de Flore, 108 rue Lamarck (18e) (tel. 606-31-15), is a good little two-star choice for those tourists who want to be in proximity to Sacré-Coeur, Pigalle, and la Place Clichy. It's not everybody's glass of vin rouge, but then the tastes of Paris visitors are wide ranging. Even though the hotel has been modernized, it still appeals to the ones nostalgic for La Butte. A short walk will take you to Lapin Agile, which was once patronized by Picasso and Utrillo. And it was on St.-Vincent Street that little Rose de Bruant was murdered. Of course, some of the displaced families who occupy de Flore couldn't care less that the heroine of *La Dame aux Camélias* or Madame Récamier, the legendary beauty, were buried in the Cemetery of Montmartre. The rooms at de Flore are quiet and moderately comfortable in this turn-of-the-century town house with its little balconies from which you can peer down at the street below. Try to get one of the upper rooms, as they are sunnier. Singles begin at 85F ($19.41), going up to 180F ($41.09) in a double. Métro: Lamarck.

Paradis Hôtel, 11 Place Émile-Goudeau (18e) (tel. 255-74-79), stands next to the Bateau-Lavoir, which burnt down but is being reconstructed by the City of Paris. This "Boat Washhouse" has been called the cradle of Cubism. Picasso once lived there. A two-star choice, the Paradis rents out 63 old-fashioned rooms which open onto this most characteristic square of Old Montmartre. Gertrude Stein crossed the square, heading for the Bateau-Lavoir and a Picasso waiting to paint her celebrated portrait, *The Third Rose*. Modigliani, Henri Rousseau, and Braque had studios nearby. The best rooms at the Paradis rent for only 160F ($26.53), and this is the rate for two persons in a unit with shower and toilet; a continental breakfast is included. Of course, if you'll settle for less plumbing and space, you'll be quoted lower tariffs. The furnishings are often worn, and antimacassars cover the chairs in the parlor. But then, you wouldn't expect too much modernity here. Métro: Abbesses.

14. Neuilly-sur-Seine

Club Méditerranée, 58 Boulevard Victor-Hugo, Neuilly (tel. 758-11-00), is a modern, resort-style hotel, the Paris headquarters of this worldwide chain of unique holiday hotels. At the edge of Paris, it is reached by taking the Métro to the Anatole France stop on the Levallois-Gallieni line.

The Club Méditerranée is more an adventure than just a place to lay your head—and youth reigns supreme. You're met at the door by a brace of young men. A hostess will check you in at the reception table, and someone will help you with your luggage, but after that you're pretty much on your own.

The bedrooms, 340 in all, have a contemporary style, with an uninhibited use of sun colors. Everything is built in, from desks to minibars. The main lounge is a modern art gallery, and from here you can go straight out to the rear garden and join the other guests for drinks, sunbathing, and conversation. For a fixed price, you can help yourself to hors d'oeuvres in the main dining room, although you'll be served your hot course and dessert at your table.

A double room with complete private bath costs 430F ($98.17). Taxes and service are included, although there's a 28F ($6.39) supplement for breakfast.

15. For Students and Senior Citizens

FOR STUDENTS: Armed with a student identification card in Paris, you can enjoy many bonuses, including savings of 20% to 30% on transportation or meals at certain establishments. You'll need proof of full-time student status, best obtained by requesting an **International Student Identity Card** (which costs $3) from the **Council on International Educational Exchange**, 205 East 42nd St., New York, NY 10017; or 49 rue Pierre Charron, Paris 75008. Write first for the application form, which, properly filled out and submitted with payment and required documentation, will expedite your receiving the card. Two types of cards are issued, one for college and university students, the other for high school students.

A good base for students is the **Foyer Jacques de Rufz de Lavison**, 18 rue Jean-Jacques-Rousseau (1er) (tel. 508-02-10), which receives both male and female students from April 1 to October 1, charging them 36F ($8.22) in double or single rooms, including a continental breakfast, taxes, service, and showers. Meals are generally available. Métro: Les Halles, Palais-Royal, or Louvre.

Year-round temporary housing (44 beds) for students, male and female, is available at the **Association des Étudiants Protestants de Paris**, 46 rue de Vaugirard (6e) (tel. 354-31-49), on the Left Bank. Rates, including a continental breakfast, are 34F ($7.76) for dormitories, 38F ($8.68) for double rooms, and 40F ($9.13) for singles. Métro: St.-Sulpice, St.-Germain, or Odéon.

FOR SENIOR CITIZENS: For those who reach what the French call "the third age," there are a number of discounts. At any railway station in France, a senior citizen (that means 60 for women and 65 for men) can obtain a **Carte Vermeil** (Vermilion Card), for a cost of 35F ($7.99). With this card, a person gets a reduction of 30% on train fares in both first- and second-class compartments. Further discounts include a 10% reduction on all rail excursions and 10% reduction on the Europabus running from Paris to Nice. The catch is that these discounts do not apply at certain peak periods of travel, including runs on express trains and on Paris commuter lines.

The French domestic airline, Air Inter, honors "third agers" by giving them 25% reductions on its regular, nonexcursion tariffs. Again, certain flights are not included, mainly the one from Paris to Nice.

Finally, half-price admission to state-owned museums is yet another concession the French make to those aging. Detailed information is available at the French Government Tourist Office, 610 Fifth Ave., New York, NY 10020 (tel. 212/757-1125).

THE RESTAURANTS OF PARIS .

IN A CITY OFTEN CONSIDERED the gastronomic capital of the world, and one with more than 12,000 restaurants, it is a difficult task to pick out the very best. As you may imagine, a rather ghastly degree of elimination proved necessary.

We don't pretend to have surveyed all the good restaurants of Paris. What we have done is list our personal favorites in all price ranges. Some of our choices are fabled throughout the world; others are relatively unknown bistros. The selection is varied enough to keep you well fed for a weekend . . . or a decade.

Is Paris the gastronomic capital of the world? Many restaurants, such as Lassere, are truly among the finest. Others, however, take advantage of the city's culinary reputation and trap tourists with shoddy cooking. We shall not answer the question we posed. Instead, we shall offer two thoughts: do not overrate the restaurants of Paris, and do not hesitate to sing the praise of well-prepared French food.

We do not share the snobbish attitude that "no one" goes to the great restaurants of Paris, such as La Tour d'Argent or Maxim's. Both of these establishments offer such uniquely Parisian experiences that they number, along with the Eiffel Tower, among the top "sights." Still, for the best food and to keep your budget intact, we'll recommend far less expensive establishments.

1. The Haute Cuisine

Lassere, 17 Avenue Franklin-D.-Roosevelt (8e) (tel. 359-53-43), is perhaps the greatest citadel of the haute cuisine in Paris. Much to the chagrin of its more tradition-laden competitors, it continues its lead position year after year. Its success revolves around Monsieur Lassere, who combines his flairs for drama and for food in both the cooking and the presentation.

Before World War II, what is now the restaurant was just a bistro and a rendezvous for chauffeurs. When Monsieur Lassere purchased the dilapidated, two-story building, he began on the long road toward creating a miniature culinary paradise. Behind a pair of gleaming white front doors are two private ground-floor dining rooms with a "disappearing wall," plus a reception lounge, keynoted by Louis XVI furnishings and brocaded walls. You ascend to the second landing via a petite elevator lined with brocaded silk. The main dining room is elegantly appointed and designed—two stories high, with a mezzanine on two sides. Tall, arched windows are draped softly with silk. On a Louis XV salon chair, you sit down to an exquisite table set with the finest of porcelain, gold-edged crystal glasses, a silver bird, a ceramic dove, and a silver candelabrum.

Monsieur Lassere contracted a painter to decorate the ceiling with a blue sky and fleecy-white clouds; but in fair weather he slides back the roof to let in the real sky or the moonlight in the evening. He's been known to bring in a flock of white doves from his country place to release in the main dining room, with raffle numbers attached to their feet.

No matter what you select, it'll have its own decorative drama. Garnish vegetables become flowers in the hands of the artists back in the kitchen. To begin your repast, we'd suggest a specialty, the pâté d'anguille aux fines herbes, an eel pâté, at 85F ($19.41). Of the fish dishes, many are on their way toward becoming house specialties, they are so well conceived. Try especially the filets de sole Lassere en casserole, 85F ($19.41). Incidentally, the proprietor is often called "the king of casseroles," his position reconfirmed by the fact that the "Club de la Casserole" dines here.

Especially recommendable is the ris de veau braisé Grand Palais, the finest we've ever had anywhere, 90F ($20.55). Of the poultry offerings, the star selection is the canard (duckling) à l'orange, at 90F ($20.55). In addition, Lassere presents two dozen gloriously fattening desserts. Try the pannequet soufflé flambé at 48F ($10.96). The cellar of some 180,000 bottles is among the most remarkable in Paris, the red wine decanted into silver pitchers or ornate crystal.

Reservations are imperative. Wanting to be certain to have a table, one wealthy Californian wrote six months in advance. Closed in August and on Sundays and Mondays.

Maxim's, 3 rue Royale (8e) (tel. 265-27-94). Edward VII, then the Prince of Wales, used to revel in its atmosphere, enjoying his freedom away from his stern mother, Queen Victoria. Perhaps the single most legendary restaurant in the world, Maxim's is a belle époque bonanza. Gowned women who dine here are made to feel like precious jewels in a velvet-lined Cartier box. The whole aura suggests the Opéra Comique of the Gay '90s, where elegant cocottes, beplumed with ostrich feathers, sat in their boxes flashing smiles and diamonds.

Today, Maxim's remains the choice of the affluent, fashionable, and globe-trotting set. The "greats" of another era are still here, too, but in caricature form on the walls.

Maxim's was the setting for *The Merry Widow* in which silent-screen stars Mae Murray and John Gilbert "dipped and swayed," and the orchestra is still fond of playing the famous waltz, reminiscent of the days when dark, almond-eyed men waited in vain to meet a wealthy widow. Louis Jourdan took Leslie Caron to Maxim's "the night they invented champagne" in *Gigi*.

The present owners, Monsieur and Madame Louis Vaudable, inherited this fin-de-siècle showcase from his father, who had obtained it in the early 1930s. They bring impeccable taste and a refined sense of drama to this time-mellowed institution. A skilled and most intuitive maître d', Roger, is the host. He seldom (if ever!) makes a mistake in seating his guests—somehow he just knows when not to seat a person near the wrong party. There are several dining rooms, and the intricacy of which table is best escapes most first-time diners, who wouldn't get it anyway. The background is art nouveau, with paneled walls, gilt and colored vines, leafy cut-out overlays, and a stained-glass ceiling.

Then there's the question of what to order. At Maxim's you can almost forget about the cuisine, so dazzling is the atmosphere. But the chef is backed up by some of the finest young cooks in France, who train at Maxim's before heading back to the provinces to open their own bistros.

For appetizers, the "Billi-By" soup is the time-tested favorite. Topped with whipped cream and grated parmesan cheese, it is made with mussels, coarsely ground pepper, white wine, cream, chopped onions, celery, and parsley. Anyone who knows anything about Maxim's has tried sole Albert (named after the famous, now-deceased maître d'). It is flavored not only with bread crumbs and chopped fine herbs but a large glass of vermouth. Bon vivants favor two other dishes as well—coquilles Saint-Jacques (scallops flavored with saffron) and poularde de vendée aux concombres (pullet with cucumbers). For dessert, we'd recommend either the crêpes veuve joyeuse or the tarte tantin, made with thick slices of Reinette apples and a pâté brisée dough. What to drink? Everybody—just everybody—orders champagne at Maxim's, although the cellar is stocked with other fine wines.

Maxim's is open all year, daily except Sundays. After-theater suppers are served to musical accompaniment (with dancing), and orders are taken until midnight. Reservations are imperative. A full meal will cost from 450F ($102.74) to 550F ($125.57) per person.

La Tour d'Argent, 15 Quai de la Tournelle (5e) (tel. 354-23-31), is the great-granddaddy of Parisian restaurants. Actually a restaurant in some form or another has stood on this spot since 1582, although an amusing "family tree" mural in the before-dinner drinking lounge traces the beginning back to Adam and Eve! Illustrations highlight culinary coups, such as the 1870 dinner—the Christmas during the war with Prussia—when the chef served elephant soup, antelope chops, camel hump, bear steaks, even wolves, cats, and side dishes of rats!

Now this fabled restaurant is under the eagle eye of Claude Terrail, a debonair gentleman who was once called "the playboy of the Western world." Celebrities he's used to—Truman, Eisenhower, and Churchill have all dined here. The restaurant grew in fame when it was owned by Frédéric Delair, who purchased the wine cellar of the legendary Café Anglais on its demise and started the custom of issuing certificates to diners who order the house specialty, pressed duck (caneton)—the birds are numbered.

A modern structure surrounds and absorbs the original building, which has been turned into a gastronomic museum. On the Left Bank, directly on the

Seine, the restaurant seats its guests on the top floor, where all-glass walls provide a panoramic view of the 17th-century houses along the quays of the Ile St.-Louis. As darkness approaches, the flying buttresses of Notre-Dame are illuminated, partially at the expense of La Tour d'Argent.

So many well-heeled Americans flock here for "that French culinary experience" that, quite honestly, there are times when no French accents are heard except those of the staff.

The cookery is brilliant, the food immaculately served on Dresden china. Most first-timers seem to order the duck, and it's sensational. Incidentally, a quarter of the menu is taken up with various ways you can order the celebrated bird. If you don't like the duck, you'll find a host of other selections, including filets de sole cardinal or filet Tour d'Argent. For a beginning, the potage Cladius Burdel is made with sorrel, egg yolks, fresh cream, chicken broth, and butter whipped together. For dessert, the pêches flambées is everything you'd expect it to be. The restaurant is closed on Mondays, but otherwise receives orders until 10 p.m. Reserve, reserve, and expect to pay from 350F ($79.91) to 550F ($125.57) for a complete meal.

Grand Véfour, 17 rue de Beaujolais (1er) (tel. 296-56-27), is by now a national monument. Founded in 1760 during the reign of Louis XV, it was once known as the Café de Chartres, attracting such habitués as Napoleon and Danton. In the postwar years it became a haven for such artists as Colette and Jean Cocteau, both tenants of the Palais Royal, which the restaurant faces. Cocteau, in fact, designed the menu cover in 1953. Nowdays, you're likely to run into, say, Princess Grace and Prince Rainier.

You can't talk about Grand Véfour for long without mentioning Raymond Oliver. Originally from Bordeaux, he is today one of the most successful restaurateurs in France—perhaps best known for his television appearances. One enthusiastic fan called him "the John Barrymore of chefs," although the comparison seems far-fetched. He is the author of two dozen cookbooks, including *La Cuisine*, which sold 100,000 copies in the United States at $30 a volume.

The past has left a dramatic imprint on the two dining rooms. The food? Superb! We recommend, as an example, the rognons de veau aux trois moutardes. This is veal kidneys with three mustards. The cost is 80F ($18.26). A special dish ordered at the beginning of a repast is salade quimperloise, with bits of lobster laced with cognac, costing 80F also. From April to July, gourmets come here to order lampreys à la bordelaise. These river eels go for 92F ($21) per serving. Stuffed pigeon named after Prince Rainier is another main-dish selection, 80F ($18.26). All the desserts are winning, especially the poire Grand Véfour at 45F ($10.27). The restaurant is closed Saturday night and all day Sunday and in August.

Lucas-Carton, 9 Place de la Madeleine (8e) (tel. 265-22-90). Now that belle époque is back in style, this fabulous turn-of-the-century restaurant might first appear to be a recreation. But it's the real thing—created in the era of Edward VII by an Englishman named Lucas and a talented French chef, Francis Carton.

The interior is happily preserved, glistening with half a century of loving care. Many prefer to dine in the front on red velvet banquettes, backed by great mirrors framed in the wood paneling and set off effectively with art nouveau bronze and wood decorations. Bowls of roses and fine stemware grace each table. But the very setting of the restaurant is dramatic enough without all that: right on the corner of the Madeleine.

There are many main dishes to recommend—délices de sole Lucas, le rognon (kidney) flambé, duckling in the style of Rouen, and half poulet de grain étuvé au porto mousse des prairies. For an exciting dessert, order the crêpes flambées au Grand Marnier, and, for a gala opening, perhaps you'll try the terrine de bécasse (woodcock). The wine cellar at Lucas-Carton is one of the best in Paris. A full dinner will cost about 300F ($68.49). The restaurant is open daily for lunch and dinner. No orders are taken after 10:30 p.m. Telephone for reservations. English is spoken.

Ledoyen, Carré des Champs-Élysées (8e) (tel. 266-54-77). Take someone here for a passionate proposal. It's that glamorous: the most romantic garden restaurant in Paris. A classic structure, it is right in the gardens of the Champs-Élysées, surrounded by weeping willows, splashing fountains, and flower gardens. With its spacious entrance hall decorated with Louis XV and Directoire furnishings, it suggests a royal summer palace.

Inside, there's an aura of a stage setting, evoking *La Dame aux Camélias.* Luncheon tastes all the better when your table opens onto the garden, the wide windows permitting an unobstructed view. At dinner, when your companion wears her diamonds and satin, the character mood is transformed. You notice the elegant handmade lacy mantles with ruffled edging covering the carnation-pink cloths, the silk-brocaded armchairs, the low bowls of pink flowers, the red candles flickering in the Louis XVI candelabra, the silver tablewear, the opera-red velvet, the geometrically designed beams and posts, the creamy chiffon ceiling, and the glittering chandeliers.

The director, Monsieur Lejeune, presents a superb cuisine and might recommend the foie gras frais de canard (duckling) with four spices. Main courses include such selections as la marmite Dieppoise, la sole soufflé à l'Armoricaine, and les rognons (kidneys) flambés. Personally, we prefer the "grande spécialité," which is young guinea hen with peaches. The desserts, if you can manage them, are regal—especially La surprise Ledoyen and crêpe soufflé flambée au Cointreau. Expect to pay around 220F ($50.23) per person for a complete meal. The restaurant is closed on Sundays and for most of August.

2. La Nouvelle Cuisine

The revolution is on! Down with Escoffier!

Unlike another revolution, the battle between the haute cuisine and La Nouvelle Cuisine didn't begin in Paris. Romantically, one would like to think it started when Michel Guérard's beautiful, mysterious Christine murmured in his ear, *"Vous savez,* Michel, if you would lose some weight, you'd look GREAT."

For a man who loved food as much as Guérard, that was a formidable challenge. But he set to work and, ultimately, invented the cuisine minceur, which is a way to cook delicious French food without the calories. The world now makes its way to Guérard's restaurant, at Eugénie-les-Bains in the Landes, just east of the Basque country. His *Cuisine Minceur* became a bestseller in North America, and Gael Greene, the food critic, hailed Guérard as "the brilliant man who is France's most creative chef."

The cuisine minceur is more of a diet cuisine than La Nouvelle Cuisine. You will not necessarily lose weight by eating at any of the following recommendations. However, the "new cuisine," like cuisine minceur, represents a major break with haute cuisine, yet it is still based on the classic principles of French cookery. Rich sauces, for example, are eliminated. Cooking times which can destroy the best of fresh ingredients are considerably shortened. The aim is to release the natural flavor of food without covering it with heavy layers

of butter and cream. New flavor combinations in this widely expanding repertoire are often inspired.

What follows are some—by no means all—centers in Paris where the
revolution of La Nouvelle Cuisine has struck.

l'Archestrate, 84 rue de Varenne (7e) (tel. 551-47-33), is the restaurant
most in vogue in Paris at the moment. Its young owner, Alain Senderens, has
been called the most creative chef in Paris today. He is one of the masters of
the new French cuisine. He also shows discerning taste as a decorator; he chose
for his restaurant not the fancy furnishings of the Louis XV period but the
subdued understatement of the Louis XIII era, with many Oriental touches
indicating his passion for the East.

Although only in his 30s, Senderens has trained at such citadels of haute
cuisine as La Tour d'Argent and Lucas-Carton. Here, across from the Rodin
Museum, he has indeed earned his reputation for creativity. In search of "new"
recipes, he has adapted many 15th-century dishes to contemporary tastes.

If they're in season, order the navets farcis (stuffed turnips), a delight.
Another of his specialties is turbot in fennel sauce. Among the endless temptations at the beginning of the menu, the terrine of sole and crayfish—delicate
as a mousse—is particularly recommendable. Wanting to lose weight himself,
Senderens began to experiment with La Nouvelle Cuisine, and has added many
dishes to this rapidly expanding repertoire—an asparagus and sweetbread
salad; aiguillettes de canard (duck) au vinaigre; scallops marinated with a corn
salad; boned and cut-up pigeon, meltingly tender, served with a thick conserve
of leeks; lobster with cucumber, and a crackling apple tart bonne femme baked
to order for two, or else a pear charlotte with a chiffonlike mantel of fresh
raspberries.

Set menus are offered at 260F ($59.36) and 320F ($73.06). However, if you
order à la carte, expect to pay from 350F ($79.91) to 450F ($102.74) per person,
depending on your selection of wine. Some specialties we recently enjoyed on
the à la carte menu include lobster in a mango salad, a fricassée of seafood with
asparagus and basil, and roast pigeon with fresh peas. Reserve at least three
to six days in advance. No meals are served on Saturdays and Sundays. The
annual vacation is in August.

La Ciboulette, 141 rue St. Martin (3e) (tel. 271-72-34). The Pompidou
Museum is just across the way, so this would make a perfect choice for lunch,
providing you can get a table. The restaurant is the creation of the amazing
Jean-Pierre Coffe, who has had many professions—actor, press attaché, and
gastronome. Paris society discovered him at his small bistro at Les Halles, and
at first they didn't take his credentials as a chef too seriously. He was considered
a dilettante among more dedicated restaurateurs. But in time he broke through
the early veneer of skepticism, tempting diners' palates with a different type of
repertoire from his theatrical one, forming his own style and language with
food.

Monsieur Coffe managed to acquire a beautiful 16th-century house on the
Plateau de Beaubourg. There, with the aid of his talented chef Claude Segal,
he formed an unusual cuisine that blends some of the best of French regional
cookery with La Nouvelle Cuisine. The ham from Landes is a special feature,
as is the raw foie gras de canard (duck). His pot-au-feu de poissons au corail
d'oursins is unique, and we'd recommend this dish above all others if we hadn't
tasted his salade de cresson (watercress) aux goujonnettes de poissons et crus-
tacés, made with five different types of fish. We're also fond of his lapin (rabbit)
confit à l'oseille à la purée d'echallotes (a shallot purée). For dessert, we'd
recommend a stuffed pear with pistachio ice cream, covered with a cold choco-

late sauce. Ordering à la carte, expect to pay from 180F ($41.09) to 220F ($50.23) for a complete dinner.

No lunch is offered on Monday, and the restaurant is closed on Saturday and Sunday. Métro: Rambuteau.

Dodin Bouffant, 25 rue Frédéric-Sauton (5e) (tel. 325-25-14). On the Place Maubert, in a former rehabilitation center for the type of Parisian described so vividly in George Orwell's first book, *Down and Out in Paris and London,* that well-known creative chef Jacques Manière has opened this modern restaurant dedicated to La Nouvelle Cuisine. He named it Dodin Bouffant after a fictional character in 19th-century gastronomic lore. Frankly, we consider it one of the best dollarwise, upper-class restaurants of Paris.

Sidewalk tables are placed behind hedges in fair weather, and the interior has been done in a contemporary chic, not terribly successful. But, then, you don't come here for the decor.

Manière's shellfish dishes are superb. You might begin with a savory mussel soup at 20F ($4.57). All the main dishes seem to reflect a personalized and imaginative touch, set off effectively by his fine wine cellar. Try, for example, le ris de veau (sweetbreads) à ma façon at 65F ($14.84), or else filets de sole courtine at 55F ($12.56). He can take ordinary ingredients and turn them into extraordinary dishes, as reflected by his haddock de lotte beurre à la vierge at 40F ($9.13). Nearly all his dishes can be recommended, especially the canard (duck) poêlé au bitter at 50F ($11.42). Desserts are also excellent creations, as exemplified by his soufflé glacé à l'orange at 25F ($5.71), or even a tart made with the fresh fruits of the season, also 25F. The restaurant is closed on Saturday and Sunday. Expect to pay from 160F ($36.53) to 220F ($50.23) for a complete meal. Incidentally, reservations are imperative. Métro: Maubert-Mutualité.

Le Duc, 242 Boulevard Raspail (14e) (tel. 320-96-30), is, in its own words, "the Greatest Fish Restaurant in France." It's run by two brothers, Paul and Jean Minchelli. Jean is the manager; Paul, the chef. Paul has come a long way from his days in Marseille, and he honors his heritage by turning out superb seafood dishes, probably better than any you'll find in his home port. Proof of that is the flock of discerning gourmets who come here from all over Paris, even the Île de France.

The restaurant serves remarkable shellfish dishes, although by no means is the Minchelli repertoire limited to that. The menu is subject to change, depending on the harvest of the ocean. The crab cocktail is generally featured, as is a savory fish soup. The Mediterranean loup or sea bass comes swaddled in seaweed and is priced according to weight. Surely the subtlety of the lobster soufflé is unequaled anywhere in Paris. Many diners prefer to begin with half a dozen oysters. Also good are the sauteed clams in a sauce subtly seasoned with thyme. Dishes that appeal to both eye and palate include tartare of salmon and escalopes de dorade (sea bream). Luscious pastries are baked right on the premises. The wine list is carefully chosen. The restaurant is closed on weekends *and* Monday, too. Expect to spend from 250F ($57.08) to 300F ($68.49) for a meal. Métro: Raspail.

Faugeron, 52 rue de Longchamp (16e) (tel. 727-95-02), in the Trocadero district. Young Henri Faugeron is an inspired chef. We've followed his career since we first heard of him at Les Belles Gourmandes on the Left Bank, and were delighted there with his mastery of French cooking in the classic style. In fact, we'd heard him quoted as making disparaging remarks about La Nouvelle Cuisine. Now, in a dramatic about-face, he's a rival of the more celebrated Guérard. Today the handsome young chef, along with his beautiful Austrian wife Gerlindé, entertain a faithful list of gourmets: artists, diplomats, and business executives. Faugeron has created a restaurant that is elegant yet not an obtrusive backdrop for his superb cuisine. Among his specialties are eggs stuffed with a truffle purée, l'escalope de foie gras aux oignons, and a soufflé aux oranges confites. He does a well-prepared and spicy lamb curry for two at 184F ($42.01), and a ragoût de truffes au foie gras, surely his pièce de résistance —expensive, but a dish you'll long remember. For a memorable meal for two, including poached turbot in a cream of leek sauce, wild filet of duck in lemon sauce, and a soufflé aux oranges Grand Marnier, expect to pay from 550F ($125.57). Mr. Jambon, the wine steward, will guide you carefully in your choice. Closed for Saturday lunch and all day on Sundays. Métro: Iéna.

Le Relais Louis XIII, 8 Grands-Augustins (6e) (tel. 326-75-96). This little air-conditioned corner restaurant, hidden on a narrow street a minute's walk from the left bank of the Seine, serves some of the finest meals in Paris.

Let's go back many years, when an exceptional woman named Odette Delanoy discovered in a dilapidated building an inn of basic beauty and rich historical associations. In what was once a convent on this site, Marie de Medici, mother of Louis XIII, was named regent of France following the assassination of Henri IV.

When Mme. Delanoy realized what a treasure she had found, she set out to recreate the bygone era. She went to auctions, private châteaux, even the flea markets, seeking authentic period furnishings. Rough stone walls and old beams were uncovered, wrought-iron chandeliers brought in, Louis XIII candlesticks placed on the tables, a wooden 16th-century stairway rescued from the Île de France, and portraits discovered of Louis XIII, Anne of Austria, and Marie de Medici.

Among the most recommendable appetizers are fonds d'artichaut frais à la Moëlle, or else a terrine chaude of scallops. Preferred among the fish courses are the filet de rouget (red mullet) au Bouzy Rouge and saumon à l'osielle (sorrel) with cucumbers cut julienne style. In the meat department, we'd suggest a grenadin de veau with fresh basil or noisettes of lamb flavored with fresh tarragon. The desserts are delicious, especially the tarte tatin (cold) or the charlotte à l'ananas frais. A complete dinner is likely to cost from 120F ($27.40) to 175F ($39.95). The inn is closed on Sundays and in August. Métro: Odéon.

Au Petit Montmorency, 26 rue Rabelais (8e) (tel. 225-11-19), was created as the dream of Daniel Bouché and his wife Nicole.

Before opening his own place just north of the Champs-Élysées, Bouché trained at a number of restaurants, including Maxim's in Chicago. But he seems to have discarded most of what he learned, preferring to chart his own course in the turbulent waters of La Nouvelle Cuisine. Paintings, engravings, and hanging lanterns give a decidedly old-fashioned touch to his restaurant, the ambience heightened by candlelight and the profusion of fresh flowers.

All on his own, Bouché turns out a delicate and subtle cuisine—daube with calf's feet, sweetbreads with kidneys and morels, a chausson au roquefort (a sort of cheese turnover), stuffed turbot with vegetables, and a delicious gourmandise aux légumes, a charlotte made with seven vegetables. If you can afford it, we'd suggest a caramelized foie gras of duck to begin your meal. Expect to pay from 175F ($39.95) to 225F ($51.38) per person for a complete meal. The French wines are well selected, including some choice but little publicized ones. The restaurant is closed on weekends and in August. Métro: F.-D. Roosevelt.

Les Semailles, 3 rue Steinlen (18e) (tel. 606-37-05). In the former atelier of Bonnard, Jean-Jacques Jouteux is the finest chef cooking in Montmartre today. Near the legendary Montmartre cemetery, where so many famous people are buried, the bistro looks as if it might have existed at the turn of the century. But in fact Les Semailles is a center of La Nouvelle Cuisine, and one of the best ones at that. Small, charming, and intimate, the fashionable bistro has only a few tables, so you don't stand a chance of snaring one unless you call ahead for a reservation (two or three days are preferable). However, we've been able to arrive unannounced for lunch and have always been accepted. After all, there are few recommendable places to eat in the 18th Arrondissement.

Normandy-born, the young chef is tall and slender; he speaks only a few words of English, but he is ingratiating and justly proud of the original dishes in his repertoire. He is one of the most exciting and talented of the young chefs of Paris today, and has totally broken from the cookery tradition in which he was born. "It's always cream and Calvados in Normandy," he says.

Prepare yourself for some dishes you may never have been served before— boudin au homard Perce Pierre, râble de lièvre (hare) sauté, and a composite de poissons (fish) that is a work of artistry. To begin, you might request the assiette gourmande, or else chèvre crottins marinés, a kind of marinated goat cheese, which might sound terrible but is anything but. The restaurant closes on Sundays and Mondays and charges from 220F ($50.23) to 350F ($79.91) for a complete meal. The annual closing is from January 25 to February 15. The nearest Métro stop is at Clichy, so it's best to take a taxi unless you want to walk up by the graveyard, which might not be a bad idea at that.

Chiberta, 3 rue Arsène-Houssaye (8e) (tel. 563-77-90), right near the Étoile, has a young chef who has stunned the gastronomic world, Jean-Michel Bedier. He once worked with the equally well-known Monsieur Delaveyne at Bougival's Le Camelia. In an elegantly modern setting, Bedier turns out inventive dishes, and is himself adding a chapter to La Nouvelle Cuisine.

Try, for example, his courgettes farcies aux moules, zucchini stuffed with mussels. Among his heavenly main dishes, we'd suggest a crayfish ragoût with quenelles and truffles, or else rouget barbets, and expecially his delicate veal kidneys with mushrooms. For an exciting opener, we'd recommend a terrine of haddock with pears. A medley of sorbets with fresh fruits provides a spectacular finish. Expect to pay 220F ($50.23) and up for a complete meal. The restaurant is closed on Saturday and Sunday and in August. Métro: Place Charles-de-Gaulle (Étoile).

Île de France, Quai Debilly (16e) (tel. 723-60-21), is a stylized and glorified "riverboat" permanently moored on the right bank of the Seine, opposite the Eiffel Tower. The two levels of tables in the inner salon allow for unobstructed views of river life and, of course, that landmark. Some of the trappings, such as the brass-rimmed portholes, seem to have been salvaged from the junked *Île de France.* Complementing the picture are bronze lights with frosted globes, and tufted banquettes. The bar is in the belle-époque style.

François Benoist, a celebrated restaurateur in Paris, is the captain. He has turned the boat into an imaginative setting for La Nouvelle Cuisine. A dinner on board might begin with a salade de confit de canard (duck) aux noix, or else a terrine de ris de veau (sweetbreads). We're especially fond of the sauté de rognon de veau in raspberry vinegar sauce and the wild duck filet with peppercorns. One of the zesty fish specialties is suprême de barbue (brill) braisé aux perles de légumes. An unusual dessert is oranges à l'orange; another fine one is a salade à l'orange with Cointreau. Expect to pay around 250F ($57.08) per person for a complete meal. A 15% service charge is added to everything. The restaurant is closed for Saturday lunch and all day on Sundays. Métro: Iéna.

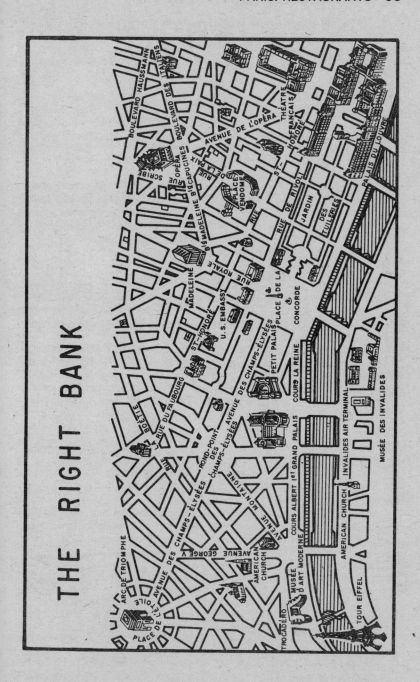

3. 1st and 2nd Arrondissements

Les Halles, the Bourse, the Opéra, the Palais Royal, the rue Montmartre, the Place Vendôme, the Île de la Cité, and the rue St.-Honoré are found within these two arrondissements, as are many fine restaurants.

THE UPPER BRACKET: Drouant, Place Gaillon (2e) (tel. 742-56-61). Jean Drouant's world-famous restaurant was founded in 1880 by his grandfather, Charles, who wanted to open a gourmet restaurant in the fashionable heyday of the Grands Boulevards and the Opéra. Family recipes and culinary secrets have been passed down from generation to generation; so, too, has an almost fanatical fastidiousness about the standard of the cuisine. Small wonder that the dishes are so classic and so consistently fine.

Upon his retirement, Monsieur Drouant turned his celebrated restaurant over to Monsieur Pascal, who continues the fine tradition, although adding his own creative touches.

The Drouant is located attractively on a small plaza. Besides the two major dining roms, there are several private dining rooms, including a special salon reserved monthly for the gatherings of the Académie Goncourt, France's great literary society (the prize its jury awards yearly is one of the most prestigious a novelist can receive). At the grill on your left (upon entering) meals are served with greater speed and the tariffs are slightly lower. The restaurant on your right is for those who favor more leisurely dining in a restrained, somewhat luxurious background. One kitchen, one chef serve both rooms, and the food is excellent in either. Reservations are suggested, especially if you want special dishes prepared (English is spoken).

For a beginning we'd suggest six stuffed mussels at 35F ($7.99). Monsieur Pascal specializes in seafood—notably filets de sole at 68F ($15.52). A plate of fruits de mer at 92F ($21) is yet another specialty, as is the rognon d'agneau grillé au bacon at 60F ($13.70). In the grill the specialty is loup flambé with fennel at 81F ($18.49). The new chef, Michel Moreau, offers some very creative dishes, including la farandole gourmande, a large plate with four specialties, costing 78F ($17.81); escalope de bar gratinée at 75F ($17.12); blanc de tourbot à la crême d'oseille, 95F ($21.69), and steak de canard au poivre vert, 60F ($13.70). The wine cellar is renowned, the judgment of the sommelier above reproach. The restaurant is open daily from noon to 2 a.m. (last orders at 1 a.m.). Métro: 4 Septembre.

Prunier, 9 rue Duphot (1er) (tel. 260-36-04), is one of the great fish restaurants of the world. The restaurant, which has a branch at 16 Avenue Victor-Hugo, is owned by Aldo Funaro. The decoration and style of this long-established favorite has been renewed. The owner has renovated the downstairs bar and widened the small first-floor salon to make a large dining room, with faded blue tapestry on the walls and round tables. He has maintained the traditional fish plates, but in addition, with the help of Gilbert and Maguy Le Coze, has added a zest of La Nouvelle Cuisine, as reflected in the cooking of the vegetables and the lightening of the sauces.

The clams of Brittany make a good appetizer, and the marmite Dieppoise, one specialty we've particularly enjoyed over the years, is still there. The latter is similar to bouillabaisse, cooked in white wine, and it is served on Wednesdays and Fridays only. Also exceptional is the filet de turbot Vérilhac, served with lobster tails and boned at the table. Many of the accompanying wines are surprisingly inexpensive.

Other main dishes of the deep—in "la tradition Prunier"—include merlan Colbert, filets de sole Prunier, and lotte au poivre vert. For dessert you may order a soufflé au Grand Marnier or ask for a chance at the large bowl of chopped fresh fruit (left at your table for seconds), studded with strawberries and flakes of almonds. Expect to spend from 250F ($57.08) to 350F ($79.91) per person. Prunier is now open on Sundays but closed Mondays.

Escargot-Montorgueil, 38 rue Montorgueil (1er) (tel. 236-83-51). No wonder the divine Sarah took many of her meals here, virtually adopting the kitchen as her own. That mural of those chubby cherub chefs on the ceiling is said to have come from her summer home on an island off the southern coast of Brittany. Mlle. Bernhardt is gone, of course, and fashion is fickle; but the Escargot (Snail) of Les Halles still reigns supreme. Ms. Kouikette Terrail, sister of the famous Mr. Terrail of La Tour d'Argent, has taken over the place, improving the style without disturbing the atmosphere.

The building is said to date from the time of Henri II and Catherine de Medici, and the restaurant itself opened back in the 1830s. The original Louis Philippe decor is carefully preserved; two dining rooms on the ground floor have starched Breton lace curtains and (electrified) gaslight fixtures on sepia walls. An open spiral staircase leads to a formal paneled dining room upstairs.

First-timers always seem to order the snails—they are delicious. We'd recommend the pieds de porcs and the feathery turbot soufflé. For dessert the specialty is strawberry beignets. Your complete meal is likely to run from 200F ($45.66) to 350F ($79.91) per person with wine, plus a 15% service charge. Closed Saturday mornings and Mondays. Reservations are imperative. Métro: Les Halles.

THE MEDIUM-PRICED RANGE: Lyonnais, 32 rue St.-Marc (2e) (tel. 742-65-59), offers the finest Lyonnaise cuisine in Paris. And the cooking of Lyon is considered the best in France—especially the pork dishes. (The menu at Lyonnais proclaims that in Lyon "le cochon est roi"—pig is king.)

Nearly half the tables are booked in advance by habitués—many from the nearby stock exchange—and there's no trouble in filling up the rest. The atmosphere is set by frosted globe chandeliers, floral tiled dado, and stuffed deer and boar heads. A dining room is also open on the second floor.

We invariably start things off with la salade verte au lard avec de saucisson chaud (a green salad with bacon and hot sausage). And in the meat and poultry department, chicken in a velvety-smooth cream sauce with tarragon and mushrooms is a classic. Crayfish in a cognac sauce is almost an obligatory choice, however. For dessert, try the cake of the house with burnt almonds. The owner, Mrs. Schoulder, offers a set menu at 85F ($19.41); otherwise, expect to pay from 150F ($34.26) to 225F ($51.38). Add 15% for service. Beaujolais is the wine of Lyon and very much the specialty here.

The restaurant is just off the Boulevard des Italiens, about a five-minute stroll from the Opéra. Closed from mid-July until September. Métro: Richelieu-Dronot.

Auberge de France, 1 rue du Mont-Thabor (1er) (tel. 073-60-26), was a coachman's inn in the 16th century. But today it's owned and run by Mr. and Mrs. Martin. They believe that dining out should encourage and enable guests to sample dishes they'd never get at home. Specialties include fresh French foie gras, snails baked in a garlic sauce, filet Limousin (filet mignon with a red wine sauce), canard à l'orange (duck with orange sauce), and canard au poivre vert (duck with a green pepper sauce). By all means try a side order of purée de haricots verts (mashed green beans with cream). Expect to pay 125F ($28.54) for a complete meal. The restaurant is open daily until 11:30 p.m. Métro: Place de la Concorde and Tuileries.

Louis XIV, 1 bis Place des Victoires (1er) (tel. 261-39-44). In spite of its location—on one of the most historic squares in Paris—this old-style bistro seems more like the leading restaurant in a proud town. Yet in fact it's an easy walk from the Palais Royal.

A handful of sidewalk tables puts a diner smack into the local scene—but Parisian journalists and stockbrokers always seem to get there first. Inside, you can dine in the ground-floor restaurant, complete with old-fashioned bar, oil paintings, and revolving turn-of-the-century fan; or else ascend an open wrought-iron staircase to the second-floor room. Notice an intriguing aroma? It's dandelion leaves in hot bacon sauce!

A set meal, not including wine, is offered for 70F ($15.98). One of the most characteristic—and one of the best—dishes to order here is escargots pur beurre, 38F ($8.68). Gastronomes come here for onglet, 42F ($9.59), one of the choicest parts of the beef. The chef bakes his cakes and pastries fresh daily, utilizing especially good fruit. The average price for a tarte maison is 16F ($3.65). The restaurant is closed all day Sundays, Saturday nights, and in August. It's likely to be crowded at lunch, so it's better to go in the evening if possible. Métro: Palais-Royal.

Pharamond, 24 rue de la Grande-Truanderie (1er) (tel. 233-06-72), a timbered neo-Norman structure founded in 1832, sits on a street in the Les Halles sector once frequented by the famous vagabonds of Paris. The dish to order here is tripes à la mode de Caen served over a charcoal burner. Tripe admittedly isn't popular with North Americans, but if you're at all experimental you'll find no better introduction to this really good dish than at Pharamond.

A more common and frankly more delicious offering is the turbot au champagne. For a good beginning, try half a dozen of the Breton oysters, served between October and April. Other main-dish specialties include grillade du feu de bois for two persons, as well as filets de sole Normande. Your bill will range from 100F ($22.83) to 130F ($29.68). Closed Sundays and in July. Métro: Les Halles.

Le Soufflé, 36 rue du Mont-Thabor (1er) (tel. 260-27-19). What Paris needs, decided André Faure when he arrived from Cahors, is a good soufflé. So he set up shop near the Tuileries and the Place Vendôme, and he's been dispensing "cloud puffs" ever since, along with the deeply colored red wine from his region. Soufflés come in all shapes and sizes here, and you can go through the entire menu, from appetizers to desserts, ordering nothing but. For variety, however, you might elect to begin your meal with fond d'artichaut gourmande at 14F ($3.20), an artichoke served with fresh mushrooms and freshly made mayonnaise. The cheese soufflé at 25F ($5.71) is justly praised. An especially good main dish is the poule sautée à l'estragon (sauteed chicken in a cream-laced white wine sauce that's been flavored with tarragon), 36F ($8.22). The raspberry soufflé at 22F ($5.02) is spectacular, although you may prefer chocolate or hazelnut. Closed Sundays. Métro: Tuileries.

Restaurant Lescure, 7 rue de Mondovi (1er) (tel. 260-18-91). Finding a reasonably priced restaurant near the Place de la Concorde is no easy task. Hence, this miniature bistro is a discovery. Off the rue de Rivoli, it's right around the corner from the 18th-century mansion where Talleyrand died. The tables on the sidewalk are tiny, and there isn't much elbow room inside either. What it does have is rustic charm. The kitchen is exposed to view, and round about are hung drying bay leaves, salami, and garlic pigtails. Don't expect anybody to speak English either. The patron is a very down-to-earth man who calls his food "cuisine bourgeoise." For example, you might begin with a pâté en croûte at 16F ($3.65), or (in season only) coquilles St. Jacques at 35F ($7.99). Main-course house specialties include le confit de canard, also 35F, and that select onglet cut of beef in a béarnaise sauce at 42F ($9.59). Try also the cochon de lait roasted with sautéed potatoes, going for 41F ($9.36). Our favorite dessert is one of the chef's fruit tarts, costing 16F ($3.65). The restaurant is closed Sundays and in August.

Au Pied de Cochon, 6 rue Coquillière (1er) (tel. 236-11-75), near the contemporary buildings which have replaced Les Halles market in the center of Paris and also close to the famous 16th-century church St. Eustache, has succeeded in keeping the tradition of good food. On the ground floor, which is in the cheerful Parisian brasserie style, as well as on the first or second floors with their quiet, elegant dining rooms, you can enjoy such offerings as pigs' feet grilled with béarnaise sauce or stuffed with goose liver and mustard sauce. Another specialty is the suckling pig St. Eustache (sliced pork filet and chops, roasted and cooked with mustard sauce). The famous onion soup is a standard of the house to start your meal, or try one of the delicious trays of shellfish. Oysters, clams, mussels, and sea urchins are brought every day from the sea directly to the Pied de Cochon. For a dessert, we'd suggest La Vie en Rose. A set menu will cost 100F ($22.83); or if you choose from the à la carte offering, your bill is likely to average about 120F ($27.40). The restaurant is one of the last in Paris to be open day and night all year. Métro: Les Halles.

La Rose de France, 24 Place Dauphine (1er) (tel. 354-10-12), enjoys a setting worthy of an operetta, complete with candlelit tables, in the old section of the Île de la Cité near Notre-Dame. You can dine with a sophisticated crowd of young Parisians who know they can get good and reasonably priced meals here. In fair weather, the sidewalk tables overlooking the Palace of Justice are favored. The restaurant's just around the corner from the old Pont Neuf.

A typical dinner might include hors d'oeuvres, 25F ($5.71) to 38F ($8.68). Try, for example, oeufs (eggs) cocotte à la crème. Most fish and meat dishes go for 35F ($7.99) to 40F ($9.13). Desserts range from 15F ($3.42) to 20F ($4.57). It's closed Wednesdays, Thursday noon, and all of July. Métro: Pont-Neuf.

Joe Allen, 30 rue Pierre Lescot (1er) (tel. 236-70-13), long ago invaded Les Halles with his American hamburger. Even though the New York restaurateur admits "it's a silly idea," it works. First there was the money needed, but backers appeared in the form of such as Lauren Bacall and Roy Scheider. Then he had to get the tablecloths, those little red-checked ones you associate with Paris bistros. Not finding them in the French capital, he had to import them from New York. Likewise, the green awning outside. The brick walls, the pine floors, the movie stills, even the blackboard menu—all evoke a saloon atmosphere. Most of the work, however, went into creating the American burger, which is easily the best in Paris. Joe concedes, however, that it's not as good as the ones dispensed at P. J. Clarke's in New York. While listening to Garland or Streisand on the jukebox, you can order such delights as black bean soup, chili, a sirloin steak, barbecued spareribs, and apple pie. By all means try the spinach salad with a creamy roquefort dressing and little crunchy bits of bacon and fresh mushrooms.

Joe claims his saloon is the only place in Paris which serves an authentic New York cheesecake or a real pecan pie. The pecans are flown in from the United States. Further, Joe had to import English muffins for the popular eggs Benedict. But, thanks to French chocolate, Joe claims that his brownies are even better than those made in the States. Your final bill is likely to range from 100F ($22.83) to 120F ($27.40). The waiters speak American. Hours are daily from noon to 2 a.m. Unless you're prepared to wait 30 minutes at the New York bar (not a bad idea!), you should call ahead and reserve a table for dinner.

THE BUDGET RANGE: Caveau Montpensier, 15 rue de Montpensier (1er) (tel. 742-82-96), is a family affair, combining the talents of Papa Maurice (who comes from the gastronomic heart of France, Lyon) and those of his wife, Evonne, a native of Anjou, known in Paris among discriminating diners for her hors d'oeuvres. Now a daughter and her husband and a brother and his wife have pitched in. Employing young students as waiters, the "Cave" is both informal and likeable. Most important, it is inexpensive.

In 1965 the family took over this cellar in a building dating from 1640 (formerly it was a stable for Philippe-Égalité, across from the Palais Royal). With old beams, bright reds and yellows, suit of armor, a Breton cupboard, glistening copper pots and pans, and crude country ceramics, they created the pleasant aura of a rustic inn.

You might begin with the soup of the day, depending on what went in the big pot at the back of the stove. Kidneys with three mustards and the omelet campagnarde are specialties. You can finish with a cheese from a heavily laden tray or else a delicious pastry made with fresh fruit. If you wish to dine here and enjoy the house dishes, expect to pay from 60F ($13.70) to 90F ($20.55). Closed Sundays. Métro: Palais-Royal.

La Moisanderie, 52 rue de Richelieu (1er), is a relatively unknown bistro of high quality and low prices. It's conveniently located—just off the Palais Royal arcades, opening onto a passageway leading to the 18th-century Théâtre du Palais Royal. (Diderot, the editor of the great 28-volume *Encyclopédie,* died at No. 39 on this street on July 31, 1781, and Molière lived and died, in 1673, at No. 40.)

The tiny restaurant is the domain of Monsieur Baesch, a kindly, grayhaired gentleman who seats everyone himself, keeping a sharp eye out to see that every guest is served properly. His place is simple and small, the tables big enough for sparrows—but somehow everything goes smoothly. The bistro has a pleasant, homey, rustic French decor: wood paneling covered with 16th-century tapestries, a brick fireplace, red cloths, a basket of crusty bread, a counter of mouth-watering homemade pastries.

A set meal is offered for only 45F ($10.27), plus 15% service. For some fancier dishes, such as steak with cognac or orange duck, a supplement ranging from 5.50F ($1.25) to 7F ($1.60) is asked. For openers you are offered eight different hors d'oeuvres, a soup (the vegetable soup with cream is excellent), or marinated herring. Next comes a meat or fowl course: stuffed chicken, pork with mushrooms, grilled liver, perhaps a veal cutlet in a cream sauce with mushrooms. For dessert you help yourself from a large glass bowl of fresh fruit salad, unless you prefer a wedge of green apple tart. Half a bottle of wine is in the 13F ($2.97) to 18F ($4.11) range. Lunch orders are taken between noon and 2 p.m., dinner orders between 7 and 9 p.m. Closed Sundays and in August. It's crowded, so go early. Métro: Palais-Royal.

Le Drouot, 103 rue Richelieu (2e), is one of the best budget restaurants in this arrondissement. A curving stairway leads to this second-floor dining hall. Under high ceilings, rows of tables have been covered with plastic, awaiting hungry diners who gravitate to this friendly, informal atmosphere. At mealtimes, between 11 a.m. and 3 p.m. and 6 and 9:30 p.m., it is usually packed with economy-minded Parisians who know they can get well-prepared food at low cost.

Almost in the tradition of the famous *bouillons* at the turn of the century in Paris, a breadman comes around to see that your plate is kept full. For an appetizer, you might select ham from the Ardennes or perhaps asparagus vinaigrette. Among the main courses offered, we'd recommend the veal kidneys in a Bordelaise sauce, although you might like the couscous or even the sauerkraut which comes with a number of pork products. Chocolate mousse is the favored dessert. Expect to pay from 50F ($11.42) to 70F ($15.98) per person for a meal. Métro: 4-Septembre.

La Vigne, 30 rue de l'Arbre-Sec (1er) (tel. 260-13-55), is a tiny refuge set apart from the bustle of the Les Halles area. Owned by André and Lucie Verger, La Vigne is a bistro-style restaurant where great care is given to both the food and the service. Mme. Verger is from Turin, Italy, and Monsieur Verger was the headwaiter for 14 years at the celebrated Lassere restaurant.

Their chef offers an exciting classic cuisine. To begin a meal, you can order a terrine du chef at 16F ($3.65). Recommendable second courses are the Basque-style pipérade (an omelet with ham, pimiento, tomatoes, and garlic), 16F also, and the filets de sole du chef, 42F ($9.59). Our favorite meat offering is tender roast loin of lamb flavored with tarragon and served with braised endives, 80F ($18.26) for two. The dessert specialty, always pleasing if you've got the appetite, is the soufflé au Grand Marnier, 18F ($4.11); it's at least five inches high, softly browned, and fluffy. Expect to pay an additional 15% for service. Closed Sundays and Mondays and from late July through August. Métro: Louvre or Pont-Neuf.

André Faure, 40 rue du Mont-Thabor (1er) (tel. 073-39-15), has a great virtue: modesty. Totally unheralded, Monsieur Faure's Right Bank establishment, decorated with paintings, serves simple French cooking— but of a fine standard. A special five-course dinner is featured nightly except Sunday at 48F ($10.96). Likely offerings are le poulet en cocotte grand'mère, lapin (rabbit) sauté, and coq au vin. The tables are crowded, especially at lunch with local business people attracted by the 30F ($6.85) set luncheon, which is not only a fine bargain but well prepared. Service is slapdash in the grand tradition of the French bistro. Closed Sundays. Métro: Tuileries. The restaurant is good for sightseers in the area, as it lies only a short block from the Place Vendôme and within an easy walk of the Place de la Concorde.

Restaurant Paul, 15 Place Dauphine (1er) (tel. 354-21-48). When the century was young, this address was to be dispensed with strictest confidence to first-time visitors to Paris. Over the decades it has become a virtual cliché for the hidden little bistro. The only secret today is that it's still here, still serving the same good food, and that madame is still behind the cash register. On the historic Place Dauphine, that triangular square on the Île de la Cité, Chez Paul has another entrance bordering the Seine on the Quai des Orfèvres.

Find a seat in its narrow confines, then relax and enjoy the escalope papillotte, veal cooked in parchment, for 40F ($9.13). For a beginning, why not the quenelles de brochet à la Nantua, 35F ($7.99)? The dessert specialty is baba à la confiture flambé au rhum, 20F ($4.57). It's closed Mondays, Tuesdays, and in August. Métro: Pont-Neuf.

Au Grand Comptoir, 4 rue Pierre-Lescot (1er) (tel. 233-56-30). The opening of Les Halles Forum has given a new lease on life to this restaurant, a reminder of the "ventre de Paris." At this *grand comptoir* (grand, long bar) the last century has hardly mattered. In the dining room beyond, the decor hasn't been changed in more than 50 years. The restaurant itself has been functioning since 1868. It's still in a prime position, offering you a chance to sample food long savored by the merchants from the central markets, even the porters who used to line the long bar. A lot of Limousin specialties are offered, in addition to other dishes. Try the haddock with fondue butter, or perhaps the coq au vin. Most meals begin with an order of rillettes. This is diced meat, generally pork brisket, pounded and preserved in pots. The most typical salad is made with lentils. Of course, the century-old specialty, and it never changes, is grilled pigs feet. If you arrive in the right season, you can order oysters on a bed of seaweed and crushed ice. The restaurant serves a lightly chilled Sancerre and a good Beaujolais, among other wines. For dessert, we'd recommend the chocolate caramel parfait. A good, healthy meal of typically popular French food will cost from 90F ($20.55) to 110F ($25.11) here. Closed Sundays.

Crêperie Pommier-La Prugne, 5 rue Berger (1er), is the best place to go for crêpes at Les Halles. It's an old-fashioned place, with art deco posters and a painted dado. Collette Maraguinsky is the chef, and she invites you for some delicious cookery in her tiny restaurant. For 6.50F ($1.48) you can order a green salad, and if you're feeling luxurious you can ask for the smoked salmon at 20F ($4.57). But most people come here for her crêpes, costing around 16F ($3.65) each. A specialty is her crêpe printanière, a garden salad wrapped in a delicately thin crêpe. You can order wine, of course, but for a change we'd suggest the Normandy cider. For dessert, you have a wide choice. Especially good are the banana crêpe at 8.50F ($1.94) and the chocolate crêpe at 8.50F also. Service is friendly and polite in this homey atmosphere. Métro: Les Halles.

4. 8th Arrondissement

Highlights of the 8th Arrondissement are the Champs-Élysées, the George V, the Place de la Concorde, the Madeleine, the Saint Lazare, the Faubourg Saint-Honoré, and the Place de l'Alma. Got your bearings? Then let's go dining.

THE UPPER BRACKET: Taillevent, 15 rue Lamennais (8e) (tel. 565-39-94), is named after a famous 14th-century chef, author of one of the earliest French books on cookery. The town-house restaurant off the Champs-Élysées is managed by Monsieur Vrinat, who has quietly and wisely created a rich ambience true to the decorative tradition of Louis XV. A meal here links you to the world of another century, and pleasantly so.

Monsieur Vrinat greets you as if you were a guest in his own home. When you order, consider the specialties, all conceived and prepared in the classic tradition. For a beginning, try the cervelas de fruits de mer aux truffes et aux pistaches, 136F ($31.05) for two persons. For a main course, we'd suggest the escalopes de ris de veau au coulis de homard, 78F ($17.81). The selle d'agneau en rognonnade, 162F ($36.98) for two persons, is another house specialty. For a finale, les fromages des provinces, 30F ($6.85) are fitting and good. Reservations are imperative at lunch, preferred in the evenings. The restaurant is closed Saturdays, Sundays, and for part of August. Métro: George-V.

Restaurant Copenhague and Flora Danica, 142 Avenue Champs-Élysées (8e) (tel. 359-20-42), is the "Maison du Danemark," one of the finest eating establishments along the Champs-Élysées. The good-tasting food of Denmark is served with considerable style and flair. In summer you can dine outside on the rear terrace, an idyllic spot.

If you want to go Danish all the way, you'll order an apéritif of aquavit and ignore the wine list in favor of Carlsberg or Tuborg, the two most famous beers of Denmark. For a starter, you might prefer crème d'oignons à la bière at 25F ($5.71) or the even better pâté de poisson (fish) Copenhague at 46F ($10.50). If you want to order the house specialty, it's called délices scandinaves, costing 250F ($57.08) for two persons—"a platter of joy" of foods the Danes do exceptionally well. The crêpes confitures de fraise (strawberries) is a fine finish, 36F ($8.22). It's open Sundays.

At the Boutique Flora Danica facing the Champs-Élysées you can have a small snack from noon until midnight. Open-faced sandwiches, Danish "smørrebrød," with beer go for around 60F ($13.70). Sandwiches, pastries, beer, and aquavit are available in the small delicatessen. Métro: George-V.

THE MEDIUM-PRICED RANGE: Les Tres Limousins, 8 rue Berri (8e) (tel.

256-35-97), is a Parisian showcase for the food of Limousin province, another section of France of high gastronomic repute. The cattle of Limousin are famous, and so are its pigs (many fine pork products come from this region). Under the aegis of Baron Hubert de Blomac, the wealthy landowners of Limousin decided to open this restaurant many years ago to focus attention on their region. Outside, a window display of mounted cowheads greets you. Go here for some of the finest beef in the capital. The price of your main dish determines the cost of your meal. Included also are an appetizer, a salad, cheese, pastries or sorbet, even coffee and wine in a carafe, as well as the 15% service charge. With each meat dish comes a baked potato served with heavy cream and fines herbes. For the popular T-bone, you'll pay 180F ($41.09). The rib of beef for two costs 320F ($73.06). By the way, steak tartare is called "cannibale maison" here, and it's delicious at 146F ($33.33). Closed Sundays. Métro: George-V.

Les Tres Moutons, 63 Avenue Franklin-D.-Roosevelt (8e) (tel. 225-26-95), has much the same formula as the recommendation above—except it is a showcase for the mutton from Limousin. In this case the mutton is really four-month-old lamb nourished on milk and flour, which make the meat tender. The lamb is then allowed to graze one month on herbs and grasses to flavor the meat. Les Tres Moutons has an attractively contemporary decor. Because of the restaurant's popularity, reservations are essential. Although not pleasing to everybody, the most prized hors d'oeuvres here are lamb's testicles. French chefs have such uncanny ability they can make anything taste good. For your main dish, we'd suggest the "epigramme," 150F ($34.26). This is breast of lamb

with a sauce diable. An amusing choice is Le Guidon at 165F ($37.68); these
are two hefty chops attached to the main bone—the whole thing resembling
the handlebars of a bicycle. A baked potato with heavy cream and herbs is
served as an accompaniment. Wine from Cahors, salad, and dessert are included in the main-dish price. Closed Sundays. Métro: F.-D. Roosevelt.

   Moulin de Village, 25 rue Royale in the Cité Berryer (8e) (tel. 265-08-47),
fills a great gap by providing reasonably priced food along the gold-paved rue
Royale in the high-priced Madeleine district. Gérard Coustal is the talented
young chef, and he got his training at Maxim's, around the corner. The "moulin" isn't on the rue Royale—rather, in a busy alleyway right off it. Try to visit
it on a Tuesday or Friday when the street market is busy, vendors hawking their
wares right in front of you if you are lucky enough to get an outside table.
   Otherwise, you can go inside, and if you're alone you might be offered a
perch at the tiny bar on the left. Owner Chuch Scupham, an American, gives
Monsieur Coustal free reign in the kitchen, and he turns out some original and
often very imaginative dishes. We recently enjoyed his heart of lettuce stuffed
with crayfish. Crayfish is also used ingeniously in a delicious soup. A salad of
firm, fresh artichokes can also be yours. There is always an interesting plat du
jour and such standbys as braised sole, which is really well prepared, not bland
at all as it so often is. Try the tart for dessert. It's made right on the premises.
If you order a soup of mussels, or else the heart of lettuce stuffed with mussels,
followed by a fricassée of sole and a tart, expect to pay from 110F ($25.11) to
140F ($31.96), including a carafe of the house wine.
   One of the owners is Stephen Spurrier, an Englishman who seems to know
more about wine than most of the French. Thus, he offers some well-selected
wines, many very reasonably priced. Reservations are imperative, as the meager
number of tables are filled quickly. Métro: Concorde.
   Au Vieux Berlin, 32 Avenue George V (8e) (tel. 720-88-96). Good German cooking—with a French accent—is what you get in "Old Berlin." The
setting is stylish, and so is the address, across from the George V hotel. The
front windows with their changing display suggest the high fashion level of the
interior. You dine in armchairs set against a modish background. The visiting
celebrities prefer the dining room in the rear on a lower level.
   Paris has precious few German restaurants, a fact which makes the outstanding specialties here that much more appealing. You are served such classic
à la carte dishes as wienerschnitzel at 58F ($13.24), followed by a typical
apfelstrudel at 19F ($4.34). Another interesting specialty the chef does well is
filet de porc cooked in beer, 50F ($11.42). Closed Sundays. Métro: George-V.
   Mignonnette du Caviar, 13 rue du Colisée (8e) (tel. 225-30-35), serves
more than just caviar, although it offers two different kinds of that. But since
most people can't afford it, you can order instead a very good-tasting borscht
or a plate of herring. A popular main-dish specialty is the chef's beef Stroganoff,
and there are blinis with cream. Ever had a fruit salad with vodka? Depending
on the amount and class of caviar-tasting you want to do, the cost is from 60F
($13.70). Otherwise, a Russian dinner here will hit the 120F ($27.40) mark. The
restaurant is closed for Saturday lunch and all day Sunday, but open otherwise
from noon to 2:30 p.m. and from 7 to 11 p.m. Métro: F.-D. Roosevelt.
   Chez "Tante Louise," 41 rue Boissy-d'Anglais (8e) (tel. 265-06-85), is an
intimate little place with a tiny mezzanine, just off the Madeleine and the Place
de la Concorde. An oil painting on the wall and a bronze plaque on the brown
marble façade pay homage to the restaurant's originator, "Aunt Louise," who
reigned from the mid-1920s to the mid-1950s, retiring eventually to a small
château in the Loire Valley. Before she retired, however, she turned over her
culinary mysteries to the husband-and-wife team of Monsieur and Madame

Salles. Consider the foie gras d'oie de Landes, suprême de turbot, or coq à la Juraissienne. A good dessert would be the strawberry tart. A complete meal with wine will cost from 175F ($39.95) to 225F ($51.38) per person. Closed on Sundays and in August. Métro: Madeleine.

Androuet, 41 rue d'Amsterdam (8e) (tel. 874-26-93), is one of the most unusual restaurants in the world, if only because cheese is the basic ingredient in most of the dishes. It all began in World War I when the founder, Monsieur Androuet, started inviting favored guests down to his cellar to sample cheese and good wine. The idea caught on, and at one time it was considered one of the most fashionable things to do in Paris. Nowadays, Androuet isn't merely chic: it's an institution.

Cheese experts, of course, flock here; we heard one claim that he could tell what the goat ate by the cheese made from its milk. If you're not an expert but would like to be, order "la dégustation unique de tous les fromages," 82F ($18.72). One man at one sitting allegedly sampled 120 varieties before being carried out. Some items you're familiar with: certainly the Welsh rarebit, 18F ($4.11), and the quiche Lorraine, also 18F. Main-dish specialties include the côte de veau (veal) savoyarde and the rognons de veau Beauge, 64F ($14.61). It's closed Sundays. It's best to reserve for lunch and dinner. Métro: St.-Lazare.

THE BUDGET RANGE: Fauchon, 26 Place de la Madeleine (8e). For epicures, this store has always been the "haut grocery of Paris." In fact, it's such a symbol of the Establishment that French Maoists once launched what the press called "a daring caviar and foie gras heist in broad daylight" at this exclusive store, the Fortnum & Mason of Paris.

What many people don't know about Fauchon is that it offers a very reasonably priced cafeteria-style lunch. First, tell the waitress at the counter what you are going to order (difficult if you don't maneuver well in French), pay at the cashier's desk, and receive a ticket which you give to the clerk behind the counter. You may order a delicious Fauchon's omelet for 9.50F ($2.17), a shrimp salad for 18F ($4.11), or even a club sandwich, 15F ($3.42). A "coupe" of ice cream makes a soothing dessert at 9F ($2.05). Only hitch is that you stand at a counter while you eat. In the afternoon, Fauchon's cakes and pastries make tea a delight. Métro: Madeleine.

La Boutique à Sandwiches, 12 rue du Colisée (8e) (tel. 359-56-69), is a well-adjusted marriage of American and French tastes. Run by two Alsatian brothers, Hubert and Claude Schick, it's an inexpensive place at which to order absolutely delectable sandwiches in many unusual and imaginative varieties. A quarter of a block from the Champs-Élysées, it is upstairs, with bare wooden tables and colored mats—quite informal. There are at least two dozen different sandwich concoctions on the menu, as well as light snacks or "plate meals," some with distinctly Swiss and Alsatian overtones. Special hot plates include pickelfleisch (Alsatian corned beef), 30F ($6.85). An unusual dish is la raclette valaisanne à gogo, 35F ($7.99): a wheel of cheese—part of it melted—is taken to your table and scraped right onto your plate; accompanying it are pickles and boiled potatoes, the latter resting in a pot with a crocheted hat. A sweet conclusion to your meal might be in the apple strudel, 10F ($2.28). Service is 15% extra. It's closed Sundays and in August. Métro: F.-D. Roosevelt.

Goldenberg's, 69 Avenue de Wagram (8e) (tel. 227-34-79), is the best place to go in the Champs-Élysées area for Jewish-deli food. The "doyen of Jewish restaurateurs in Paris," Albert Goldenberg opened his first delicatessen in Montmartre in 1936. He's been going strong ever since, tempting Parisians with such dishes as cabbage borscht at 14F ($3.20); blinis at 12F ($2.74) for two;

stuffed carp at 30F ($6.85); and pastrami at 33F ($7.53). Naturally, Jewish rye bread comes with almost everything. The front half of the deli is reserved for a specialty takeout section, the rear half for proper in-house dining. The menu even offers Israeli wines. Métro: Place Charles-de-Gaulle (Étoile).

5. 5th and 6th Arrondissements

These two quarters are the most popular from the tourist point of view and the most densely populated districts on the Left Bank. The largest quantity of restaurants (but not necessarily those of the highest quality) are centered in the teeming Latin Quarter. This area embraces parts of Montparnasse, the Quai des Grands Augustins, the Quai de la Tournelle, the Panthéon, St. Michel, the Sorbonne, St.-Germain-des-Prés, and Odéon.

THE MEDIUM-PRICED RANGE: Au Pactole, 44 Boulevard St.-Germain (5e) (tel. 633-31-31), is a Left Bank restaurant offering creatively prepared food that reaches gourmet levels. There's no time-tired menu here; changing daily specialties are the thing.

The restaurant has two dining areas, the inner one with oak-paneled wainscoting and original still-life paintings. An armoire against a brick wall, antlers, and potted palms add a country-inn touch. However, the glass-enclosed section on the boulevard places you smack into Left Bank life.

The food platters are first brought to a central carving table. They are likely to include a terrine of avocados with kiwi fruit or filet of duck in raspberry vinegar sauce. Expect to pay around 175F ($39.95) to 222F ($50.68) per person, depending on the wine, if you order à la carte. Otherwise, you can select the 100F ($22.83) set meal, receiving, for example, a fricassée of lamb in mint sauce. Add 15% for service. Reservations are important. Closed on Saturdays and in August. Métro: Maubert-Mutualité.

André Allard, 41 rue St.-André-des-Arts (6e) (tel. 326-48-23). The street outside was the setting for George du Maurier's *Trilby,* but inside it is simply an unpretentious Left Bank bistro. In a down-to-earth atmosphere of sawdust-littered floors and old-fashioned marble-topped tables, Monsieur Allard welcomes you—and BB, and Delon, and Gabin, etc. His wife, an honored chef (some say among the country's finest), directs the kitchen staff with an eye for detail and an instinctive concern for culinary excellence.

The bistro earned its original reputation under Allard's father, who opened it in 1930. The building (or more especially the cellar) is from the days of Louis XIII and his domineering mother, Marie de Medici. The family makes yearly trips to Burgundy to select their own wine, and they bottle it themselves. Two rooms are found here, the front one with a zinc bar and low ceilings. In either you may order the house specialty, duckling with olives, 105F ($23.97) for two. Also good is the filet of turbot, 75F ($17.12), prepared in smooth white butter (beurre blanc). To commence your meal, try the terrine de canard (duckling) at 28F ($6.39), and to end it, perhaps a tart made with fresh strawberries, 28F also. Closed Saturdays and Sundays and in August. Reservations are always necessary. Métro: St.-Michel.

La Méditerranée, 2 Place de l'Odéon (6e) (tel. 326-46-75), was acknowledged by Paris's *Metro* magazine as one of the most romantic restaurants in Paris. To quote the magazine, "The outdoor terrace and small upstairs salon have witnessed many a chablis inspired proposal. Only Jean-Yves, one of the most conscientious young maîtres d'hôtel in Paris, knows for certain how many of these loves have been requited, and wisely he's not saying." Jean Cocteau

designed the menu way back when, and lent a hand to stage designers Claude
Bérard and Vertès in the decorations.

The square on which the canopied restaurant stands is handsome in the
18th-century style. Across the street is the state-owned Théâtre de France.

La Méditerranée comes close to duplicating the dishes you might be served
at one of the best-known waterfront restaurants of Marseille. The restaurant,
to our knowledge, is unique among those in Paris in that it sends a truck daily
to the Normandy coast to buy the freshest seafood products. The savory
bouillabaisse is always our favorite. If you like the taste of garlic, you can order
two characteristic Provençal dishes: either the frog legs (imported) or the
coquilles St.-Jacques (scallops). Another specialty is the turbot in champagne
sauce, for two persons. With your appetite's permission, the crêpes suzette will
be yours for dessert. One person will pay from 140F ($31.96) to 170F ($38.81)
for a complete meal with wine. The restaurant is now open all year. Métro:
Odéon.

Dominique, 19 rue Bréa (6e) (tel. 327-08-80). Shades of imperial Russia
in Montparnasse. But don't be carried away by the turn-of-the-century St.
Petersburg aura in the upstairs room; you might order a "tin" of Sevruga
Iranian caviar before you know it. You'll still see some of the lost colony of
Russian aristocracy here—or, more accurately, their offspring—as they know
they'll get some of the best Russian food in the city.

All the familiar dishes are offered: borscht at 26F ($5.94); blinis with
cream, 25F ($5.71); a Russian salad, 18F ($4.11). For a main course we recommend côtelette de volaille (poultry) Dominique, 62F ($14.15); and for dessert,
the house specialty, kasha gourieff flambé, 25F ($5.71). Of course, no Russian
repast is complete without vodka (try a glass of Zubrovka, imported from
Poland and made with a special herb). If you have too much vodka, Léon, the
manager, will send you back in an ambulance! But do stay awake to hear the
gypsy music. Downstairs, where there is a counter and prices are slightly
cheaper, delicacies are sold to take out. The place is open daily; try to get there
before 10 p.m. Closed in July.

Roger à la Grenouille (Roger the Frog), 26-28 rue des Grands Augustins
(6e) (tel. 326-10-55), is an oddball little Left Bank restaurant, belonging to
Monsieur and Madame Frog. Their near-surrealist bistro is an experience
you're not likely to forget easily. The first clue is the tiny display window on
the narrow street, filled with every kind of frog object imaginable—stuffed
cotton, metal, whatever. The hidden entrance to this bizarre and almost ribald
eatery is through a small courtyard.

As you enter, Monsieur or Madame Frog will greet you (he's the traffic
director, cop, social director, or bouncer). If he's in the mood, he might kiss
your wife and throw you out! There are two narrow (and crowded) dining
rooms, with a blackboard menu at each end. You'll be given a pair of binoculars
for menu decisions. Dressed in pre-Revolutionary revealing frocks, the waitresses are saucy. Many a guest they've slapped or kissed, depending on his
actions and their mood.

The turn-of-the-century decor could hardly be more cluttered. Every inch
of the ceiling and walls contains something either fascinating or incongruous:
an airplane propeller or a rusty street sign.

Main dishes include duckling in orange sauce and beef bourguignonne.
Other dishes include frog legs and salads. First-timers are usually more tempted
by the plate the waitress offers for a kiss: suggestively shaped coffee ice cream
with two halves of peach covered with crushed raspberries and smothered with
whipped cream. A meal here will average around 120F ($27.40) per person. In
this permissive atmosphere tables are freely shared, and you may find yourself

making new friends and waving farewells to the fellow revelers at other tables. Closed Saturday and Sunday. Métro: St.-Michel.

THE BUDGET RANGE: Le Procope, 13 rue l'Ancienne-Comédie (6e) (tel. 326-99-20), is the oldest café in Paris. Originally created back in 1686 by a Sicilian, Francesco Procopio dei Coltelli, who is said to have popularized the art of drinking coffee among Parisians, the café is now a restaurant, lush with gilt-framed old mirrors, time-aged portraits of former guests, crystal chandeliers, red-leather banquettes, and strawberry-pink tablecloths.

Few restaurants can name-drop with such aplomb as Le Procope: La Fontaine, Voltaire, Benjamin Franklin, Rousseau, Anatole France, Robespierre, Danton, Marat, Desmoulins, even the young Bonaparte. Balzac drank one cup of coffee after another here, Victor Hugo taking it a little easier, Verlaine preferring absinthe.

Many of today's guests prefer the quiet, more spacious second-floor restaurant, with its provincial furnishings and drinking lounge, although the ground floor (in the words of one habitué) has more immediacy.

For 75F ($17.12) plus 15% for service, you might enjoy the following repast: daurade Niçosie, followed by a plate of beef Stroganoff, then a cheese selection, plus a stuffed plum with a rum-based filling. From the à la carte menu, you may prefer grilled andouillette at 30F ($6.85); caille (quails) in grapes, 30F also; or pintade (guinea fowl) au choux, a classic dish at 32F ($7.31). It's open daily but closed in July. Métro: Odéon.

Au Beaujolais, 19 Quai Tournelle (5e) (tel. 033-67-74), stands in the shadow of the world-famed Tour d'Argent across the street. On the Seine, this restaurant specializes in a cuisine "du Beaujolais et du Mâconnaise." When you see the name à la Mâconnaise, it generally refers to meat dishes flavored with red wine. The cooking is hearty and satisfying—nothing unusual, but everything well prepared and politely served. On an à la carte menu, we'd recommend cochonnailles du Beaujolais et beurre. This is the same as a charcuterie, a selection of pork cold cuts, served with bread and butter. As a main course, the house specialty is entrecôte Bercy for two. The coq au vin is another good choice. The bill can range from a reasonable 80F ($18.26) to a high of 130F ($29.68), depending on the plates and wine selected. Service is 15% extra. The restaurant, also called "Chez Charles," is at the Pont de la Tournelle. Closed Mondays and in August. Métro: Pont-Marie.

La Cabane d'Aubergne, 44 rue Grégoire-de-Tours (6e) (tel. 325-14-75). This self-proclaimed "rabbit hutch" is like a rustic Breton tavern, where under beamed ceilings typical regional meals are served on bare plank tables with provincial stools. The stone and wood-paneled walls are decorated with farm and country implements: wooden shoes, a hayfork, copper bed-warming pans, coach lanterns, a tall grandfather's clock. A cozy entrance bar is so crowded that friendships are instant.

One waitress handles the always-filled eight tables. The owner, Gilbert Guibert, wears a wide-brimmed black hat and red sash, hovers between the bar and the dining room, and keeps bright, breezy chitchat going.

The chef specializes in terrines. One is made from marcassin (young boar), another from fricandeau (larded veal loin), yet another from caneton (duckling). You can enjoy a complete meal here for as little as 40F ($9.13), although many tabs climb beyond the 70F ($15.98) mark. Métro: Odéon.

La Cafetière, 21 rue Mazarine (6e) (tel. 633-76-90), in the heart of the Odéon district, is a tiny neighborhood bistro that serves remarkably good cookery at reasonable prices. Because of the limited space, it is imperative that you reserve a table. Dining is on two levels, and the restaurant serves both lunches and dinners daily, including Sundays when many other bistros nearby are closed. A coffee-pot theme forms the decor downstairs, and service is polite and friendly. The wine selection is limited but good. A set meal—unavailable after 8 p.m.—is offered for 58F ($13.24), including service but not your drink.

Among the à la carte selections, you might begin with an endive salad or a salad of lentils with freshly chopped shallots. A terrine de canard (duck) is also good. Among the recommendable main courses are a côte de veau au citron and a peppersteak flambé, even a steak tartare. To finish, you might prefer a plate of French cheese or else a fresh fruit tart. The chocolate mousse is generously served from a large bowl. Ordering à la carte is likely to run your bill up to 90F ($20.55). Métro: Odéon.

Au Cochon de Lait, 7 rue Corneille (6e) (tel. 326-03-65), feeds you heartily, elegantly, and well, giving you a selection of classic French dishes ranging in price from 35F ($7.99) to 60F ($13.70). The house specialty is cochon de lait rôti à la broche (roast suckling pig with sauce). We enthusiastically endorse the stuffed mussels (either marinière or in a cream sauce). In addition, the least expensive way to dine here is to order the set dinner at 50F ($11.42), including an appetizer, main course, dessert, or cheese. Your drink is extra. Red curtains and stained glass make the "Suckling Pig" all the more appetizing. It's open from 11:30 to 2:30 and from 6:30 to 10:30. Métro: Odéon.

Aux Charpentiers, 10 rue Mabillon (6e) (tel. 326-30-05). Once it was the rendezvous of the master carpenters, whose guild was next door. Nowadays it's where the young men of St.-Germain-des-Prés take their dates for inexpensive meals in a pleasant atmosphere. Presided over by motherly Frenchwomen, Aux Charpentiers keeps alive the fast-disappearing tradition of the neighborhood family dining room—it's like Paris of 30 years ago.

The restaurant takes up two floors; the street level is more animated, the lower level quieter, better for conversation. Although not especially imaginative, the food is well cooked in the best tradition of the Left Bank bistro. Appetizing appetizers include regal d'Auvergne. Especially recommendable as a main course is the roast duck with olives. Each day of the week a different plat du jour is offered, with traditional French home cooking: petit salé aux lentilles, pot au feu, boeuf à la mode are among the main dishes on the menu. Desserts always include a homemade fruit tart. A service charge is added to all tabs. There is a large choice of Bordeaux wines direct from the château. For example, you may have Château Gaussens. A set menu costs only 25F ($5.71). However, if you order à la carte, count on spending from 50F ($11.42) to 60F ($13.70). Closed Sundays. Métro: Mabillon.

Restaurant des Beaux-Arts, 11 rue Bonaparte (6e) (tel. 326-92-64), near the École des Beaux-Arts, is a virtual legend among local artists and students, and has been so since the 1920s. Old paintings of student life decorate the walls. The menu never changes from year to year, but the price does—still, the management charges only 30F ($6.85) for a complete meal, with wine and service included, a remarkable buy. Traditionally you get the potage of the day, followed by sauté de boeuf, then a dessert (most limited selection here). We'd suggest, as an alternative, the bleu de Bresse cheese. If you want more freedom in your selection, you'll probably spend from 40F ($9.13) to 60F ($13.70) ordering à la carte. Expect the restaurant to be noisy and crowded, and if you're a lone diner you'll have to share your table. Nostalgia note: Oscar Wilde, who died at the old fleabag Hôtel d'Alsace (now the chic l'Hôtel), used to take his meals here. Occasionally you'll spot someone who remembers the old St.-Germain-des-Prés, but most of today's clientele consider Juliette Greco ancient. Closed Mondays and in August. Métro: St.-Germain-des-Prés.

Crémerie-Restaurant Polidor, 41 rue Monsieur-le-Prince (6e) (tel. 326-95-34), is the most characteristic bistro in the Odéon area, serving the "cuisine familiale." You might call it a "vieille maison très sympathique." It still uses the word *crémerie* in its title, an appellation dating back to the early part of this century when it specialized in frosted cream desserts.

In time it became one of the Left Bank's oldest and most established literary bistros. In fact, it was André Gide's favorite. But many famous people have dined here, including Hemingway, Paul Valéry, Artaud, Charles Boyer, even Jack Kerouac.

The atmosphere is one of lace curtains, polished brass hat racks, and drawers in the back where repeat customers lock up their cloth napkins. Frequented in large part by students and artists, who always seem to head for the rear, the present restaurant was founded in 1930 and it's been little changed since then. The art deco ceiling fixtures are still there, and pottery pitchers of water are placed on the tables, which are most often shared.

Overworked but smiling waitresses serve such dishes as a terrine du chef at 10F ($2.88) or else Greek-style mushrooms at 12F ($2.74) for an appetizer. Main dishes include such hearty fare as canard (duck) Barbarie at 21F ($4.79) or côtes d'agneau (lamb) at 23F ($5.25). You might finish with a fruit tart at 10F ($2.28). The restaurant is closed on Sundays. Métro: Odéon.

Zéro de Conduite, 64 rue Monsieur-le-Prince (6e) (tel. 033-50-79), is named after the French film classic, and perpetuates that cinematic theme by using photographs of movie stars on the walls. The cuisine is decidedly French, though with a Greek overtone. Set above the sidewalk, Zéro de Conduite is large and rambling, decorated in a rustic style with rock walls and wooden partitions. The place is really like an inn, and the cooking is homey. Everyone feels comfortable and among friends here. The big attraction is the low-cost set meal at 25F ($5.71). For that low figure, we recently enjoyed a fresh tomato salad, followed by chicken curry, then ice cream for dessert, plus a pitcher of vin rouge. On the à la carte menu, you can sample Russian-style eggs at 6F ($1.37); brochette paysanne (skewers of meat roasted over an oven pit and served with rice), 30F ($6.85); and a luscious tarte bonne femme at 13F ($2.97). Métro: Odéon.

READER'S RESTAURANT SELECTION: "Don't miss **La Cambuse** restaurant, 8 rue Casimir-Delavigne (6e) (tel. 326-48-84), just a block or two from Place de l'Odéon. It's very small—seats only 30 people— but a real find. Madame cooks, serves, and cashiers, and does it all well. Prices are right, too: 90F ($20.55) for a full meal for the two of us, including a bottle of excellent wine, onion soup, potatoes, carrots, and peppersteak. Madame does it up right" (Joseph McCann, Gladwyne, Pa.).

6. 3rd and 4th Arrondissements

Now we head toward the Bastille, the Île de Cité, the Place des Vosges, the Île Saint-Louis—good sightseeing, good dining. (We don't mean to confuse you, but two of our recommendations, on the triangular Place Dauphine on the Île de la Cité, are technically within the First Arrondissement.)

THE UPPER BRACKET: Marc Annibal de Coconnas, 2 bis Place des Vosges (entrance on the rue de Birague) (4e) (tel. 278-58-16). The restaurant, in the Louis XIII style, could have been called the Bistrot de Henri II (who lost his life on the Place des Vosges). It could have been called the Victor Hugo restaurant (the novelist lived in an apartment, now a museum, on this square of the grand siècle). Instead it's called Marc Annibal de Coconnas, honoring some esoteric figure of the 16th century. But what's in a name? Concentrate instead on the delicious cuisine, courtesy of Claude Terrail, who also owns La Tour d'Argent.

A complete fixed-price meal, including drink and service, is 120F ($27.40) and might include a tartare of salmon with lemon juice, a pot-au-feu, followed by a sorbet to finish—a good bargain. We recommend that you phone for a table, as the place gets quite crowded. Closed Tuesdays. Métro: Chemin-Vert.

THE MEDIUM-PRICED RANGE: La Falcatule, 14 rue Charles V (4e) (tel. 277-98-97), attracts gourmets to the Marais district. Near the Bastille, the restaurant looks like it's one for the memory book, but chef Jean Aulibé performs a winning cuisine. The fill of fare is original. On one recent occasion, we began our meal with mousse de gibier (game). This was followed with a timbale de queues d'écrevisses—crayfish tails in a perfectly seasoned cream sauce. Our dining partner one evening enjoyed a mousse de canard à l'orange, an imaginative and delicious duckling pâté on a bitter-orange gelatin. Another specialty which we enthusiastically endorse is calf's liver. One final dish, also heartily recommendable, is ris de veau Périgueux; this is a cassoulette of sweetbreads. For a spectacular finish we'd suggest the crêpes soufflés Grand Marnier. This formidable bastion of grand cuisine is closed in August, for Saturday lunch, and all day Sunday. Expect to pay between 150F ($34.26) and 200F ($45.66), depending on the wine. Métro: Sully-Morland.

La Colombe, 4 rue de la Colombe (4e) (tel. 633-37-08), is on the Île de la Cité. The rue de la Colombe runs into the Quai aux Fleurs, one of the smallest in Paris, behind Notre-Dame. The house of La Colombe (the dove) is an idyllic setting for a meal. It dates from 1275. Ludwig Bemelmans owned the building at one time, and his paintings still adorn one of the dining rooms. The owner today, Michel Valette, a movie actor, often receives the customers. While drinking your coffee, you might ask him to tell you the old legend of the doves and the story of the tavern over seven centuries.

In the small patio a Virginia creeper creeps, and behind the sienna façade we've enjoyed many a set menu costing 125F ($28.54), wine and tip included. The set meal includes some of the chef's specialties.

À la carte items include such dishes as roast duckling with peaches at 55F ($12.56) and le tournedos en croûte sauce Perigueux, 64F ($14.61). Also fine is médaillon Sarah Bernhardt, 48F ($10.96). The wine list presents a prestigious choice of French wines beginning at 32F ($7.31) per bottle. All the prices are *prix nets,* meaning service included. The restaurant closes in mid-August for ten days and for three weeks in February. Otherwise, it offers lunch from 12:30 to 2:30 p.m. and dinners and late suppers from 7:30 p.m. to midnight. Métro: Cité.

Hostellerie Nicolas Flamel, 51 rue de Montmorency (3e) (tel. 272-07-11). First-time visitors to Paris never fail to fall in love with this one. It is, after all, a national monument (the second oldest house in Paris, built in 1407), and it does serve good and imaginative food. Once it was owned by a fascinating medieval character, Nicolas Flamel, who charitably turned it into a free kitchen for the poor. A plaque on the façade mentions that Pernelle, the alchemist, lived here at one time.

Restored in 1900, this ancient inn offers two set menus, with a different specialty featured daily, for a flat 75F ($17.12) to 90F ($20.55), and those tabs include both your wine and service charge. On one of our most recent expeditions here, we enjoyed as a main course a rôti d'agneau (roast lamb) with "secret herbs."

The setting is medieval, there's a time-aged bar on your right, and the furnishings are in the tradition of a provincial auberge. Closed Sundays and Mondays. The staff vacations from mid-July to August 22. Go before 10 p.m. for dinner. Métro: Rambuteau.

L'Ambassade d'Auvergne, 22-24 rue de Grenier St.-Lazare (3e) (tel. 272-34-90). In an obscure district of Paris, this rustic tavern not only oozes with charm but dispenses the hearty cuisine bourgeoise of Auvergne, the heartland of France. You enter through a busy bar, with heavy oak beams, hanging hams, and ceramic plates. At the entrance is a display of the chef's specialties: jellied meats and fowls, pâté cakes, plus an assortment of regional cheese and fresh fruit of the season. Rough wheat bread is stacked in baskets, rush-seated ladderback chairs are placed at tables covered with orange cloths. Stem glassware, mills to grind your own salt and pepper, a jug of mustard bedeck each table.

The chef, Emmanuel Moulier, has introduced among the more classical dishes some nouvelle cuisine plates, including kidneys with spinach and a compote of volaille (poultry) with garden vegetables. A complete meal with regional wine will cost from 120F ($27.40) to 150F ($34.26) per person. The tavern, open for dinner only, is closed Sundays. Métro: Arts et Métiers.

Bofinger, 5 rue de la Bastille (4e) (tel. 272-87-82), is the oldest Alsatian brasserie in Paris, tracing its origins back to 1864. It successfully retains the palace style of that era: lots of leaded glass, creamy macramé curtains, lampshades shaped like tulips, antique mirrors, mahogany pieces, dark-gray benches, a revolving main door, and a central dome of stained glass. At night many members of the Parisian slumming chic venture into the Bastille district for beer and sauerkraut at Bofinger.

The brasserie is run by Monsieur and Madame Urtizvéréa, who offer not only excellent Alsatian fare but hearty portions and friendly service by waiters in floor-length white aprons. The chef prepares a different main dish every day of the week; on a recent Wednesday a savory stew in casserole (le cassoulet Toulousain) was offered.

But, slumming or not, most guests order the choucroûte formidable (sauerkraut) complete with sausages, smoked bacon, and pork chops. Dessert? Frankly, we've never had room for it at Bofinger, although the apple tart always looks good, as do the fresh berries of spring. For a supper here, expect to pay from 175F ($39.95) per person. It's open all year. Métro: Bastille.

THE BUDGET RANGE: Au Gourmet de l'Isle, 12 rue St.-Louis-en-l'Île (4e) (tel. 326-79-27). A good restaurant is hard to find on the Île St.-Louis; many just look good. So does this one—the flickering candlelight at its tables, heavy dark beams overhead—but it also serves a fine meal.

A sign "A.A.A.A.A." is posted outside. That signifies that the restaurant is a meeting ground for a society of gastronomes, the friendly association of amateur devotees of the authentic andouillette. Andouillettes, chitterling sausages grilled on a low fire, are to the French what clam chowder is to a Cape Cod resident, chili con carne to a Texan, and a Nathan's hot dog to a New Yorker. Accompanied by mashed potatoes and costing 35F ($7.99), they're delicious. Another well-recommended dish is la charbonnée de l'Île, also 35F, a savory pork dish.

Personally, we visit the "isle" just to taste Mme. Bourdeau's stuffed mussels in shallot butter at 12F ($2.74). Try one of her sorbets made with fresh fruit at 11F ($2.51). Your palate will fare as well as your wallet if you order the 55F

($12.56) fixed-price menu. Closed Thursdays and in August. Only dinners are
served on Mondays. Métro: Pont-Marie.

La Taverne du Sergent Recruteur, 41 rue St.-Louis en l'Île (4e) (tel.
356-75-42). Take a hitherto insatiable appetite to this 17th-century setting on
the principal street of the Île St.-Louis. For 80F ($18.26) plus service you'll get
enough to eat to last you through the next day. Note the Romanesque arches
above on your way to the tables in the rear. The dining room itself is beamed
and narrow, with leaded-glass windows, placemats that are reproductions of
old French engravings, and ladderback country chairs. Pronged iron racks
suspended from the ceiling hold everything from round loaves of crusty bread
to pigtails of garlic, a horse collar, and oil lamps.

But back to the meal. First, the makings of a salad are placed before you:
carrots, radishes (red and black), fennel, celery, cucumbers, green peppers, and
hard-boiled eggs. Next comes a huge basket of sausages—you slice off as much
as you wish. A bottomless carafe of wine (rosé, red, or white) is set on your
table, along with a crock of homemade pâté. Then the waiter asks you for your
selection of a main dish—steak, chicken, veal, whatever. A big cheese board
follows, but that's not the end of it; a basket of fresh fruit marks the finale. The
restaurant is open from 7:30 p.m. to 2 a.m. Métro: Pont-Marie.

A GASTRONOMIC TOUR: One street in the 4th Arrondissement is a virtual
neighborhood gastronomic tour, the **rue des Rosiers.** Before the war the
Marais sector was filled with many fine Jewish restaurants. In the Middle Ages
this was the ghetto. The street still retains the air of a little village town.
However, the neighborhood has changed considerably with the arrival of many
North African Jews, specifically from Tunisia, Morocco, and Algeria. John
Russell once wrote, "The rue des Rosiers is the last sanctuary of certain ways
of life; what you see there, in miniature, is Warsaw before the ghetto was razed
. . . Samarkand before the Soviet authorities brought it into line."

If you're in the market for pastrami, corned beef, dill pickles, schmaltz,
herring, chopped chicken livers, and matzoh balls, then go here. It's best viewed
on Sunday morning when much of Paris is asleep. Actually, you don't have to
enter a restaurant. You can wander up and down, eating as you go. Perhaps
an apple strudel will tempt you, certainly a pastrami on Jewish rye bread, even
smoked salmon, pickled lemons, perhaps the smoked sausages of Algeria
known as *merguez.* Of course, a thick chunk of Jewish cheesecake is always a
temptation.

On this "Street of the Rose Bushes" the best-known restaurant is **Goldenberg,** 4 rue des Rosiers. The doyen of Jewish restaurateurs in Paris, Albert
Goldenberg, has moved to another restaurant, in chicer surroundings, at 69
Avenue de Wagram (8e) in the Champs-Élysées area. But his brother Joseph
has remained at the original establishment. The original Goldenberg delicatessen was opened in Montmartre in 1936. (The brothers Goldenberg were born
in Constantinople. Their father was Russian.)

On the rue des Rosiers, the carpe farcie (stuffed carp) is a preferred
selection, although you may choose the beef goulash. We also like the eggplant
moussaka. The pastrami is one of the most popular items. For the truly patriotic, the menu offers Israeli wines at 24F, but Mr. Goldenberg admits they are
not as good as French wines. A complete meal here will range in price from
40F ($9.13) to 55F ($12.56).

For strictly kosher food, head for **À la Bonne Bouchée,** 1 rue des Hos-
pitalières St.-Gervais, off the rue des Rosiers (4e). Two set dinners are offered
here, one costing 40F ($9.13), another 55F ($12.56). On the à la carte menu,

we'd recommend the stuffed kiszke (kishke) and the roast duck. With either of these specialties plus two other courses, your bill should be no higher than 60F ($13.70). You can, in our opinion, get better couscous—the tender, staple cereal of North Africa—in Paris than you can in Morocco or Algeria. On this ethnic street, we'd suggest **Tunisien,** 5 bis rue des Rosiers (4e). Here, the semolina-based North African specialty is well prepared and served in large portions. For an hors d'oeuvre, we prefer the brochette of lamb at 7.50F ($1.71). To be traditional, finish the meal with mint tea. You can enjoy a meal here for a low of 35F ($7.99) or a top of 40F ($9.13), depending on your choice of a main dish.

READERS' RESTAURANT SELECTIONS: "In the Marais part of the 4th Arrondissement, just across the narrow street from the old Église des Blancs-Manteaux, lies **Les Blancs-Manteaux chez Suzon,** 17 rue des Blancs-Manteaux (Métro: Rambuteau or, easier, Hôtel-de-Ville then a little walk). From the street, it does not look very much like a restaurant, with its wooden door, arched doorway, and overhanging lantern. Once inside, you are on a little landing from which you can catch a glimpse of the small kitchen. The stairs lead down to a beautiful ancient vault consisting of two rooms connected by a small archway. The meals are served in the second room. The three-course meal consists of entrée—an appetizer to be chosen from pâté, pâté de campagne, saucisson, various salads or crudités, depending on the season; plat du jour—chosen from two or three traditional French dishes such as pot au feu (boiled beef with various vegetables); cheese or dessert—a good choice of French cheeses or a choice of desserts generally including tarts, various other cakes, fruit salad, fromage blanc (cream cheese), sometimes crème de marron (chestnut cream), and fruits. With a quarter-liter of decent wine, this costs 45F ($10.27), including the 15% tip. The cooking, done by Suzon, is entirely unpretentious and of a high standard. Portions are always generous, often enormous. From a strict food viewpoint, a meal at Suzon's is a relishable experience. On top of that, Suzon herself is a fascinating character: a middle-aged, rather stout woman of remarkable charm, kindness, and warm-heartedness, and the kind of distinction to make her at ease with everybody. She can meet a duke or the local drunkard and behave adequately with either. When properly requested, she may sing a number of oldish songs known here as *populaire* or, rather, *réaliste,* mostly popular songs dating between 1870 and 1940. She sings with the utmost sincerity and a remarkable sense of pathos, in a vibrant though controlled contralto voice which stresses the poignancy in these songs. As you may see from the description, it is better to go there with plenty of time and spend the whole evening. With respect to language problems, I should think Suzon's English, although perhaps sketchy, should be sufficient to help people find their way through the menu" (Marie-Françoise Audollent, Paris, France).

"One of the real bargains in Paris eating is in the Marais, just a few steps from the Hôtel De Rohan at the intersection of rue Vieille-du-Temple and rue des Francs Bourgeois (4e). It's the cheery and spotless **Au Vieux Paris,** featuring a 25F ($5.71) dinner, including service. Wine is extra at 5F ($1.14). The food is terrific, and the service is in the best French tradition" (Murray Burns and Cynthia Benson, Hollywood, Calif.). . . . "Two fine budget restaurants can be found in the area of the Opéra. These are **Chez Stella** and the **Medova.** Both are small establishments (seating 20-50), and offer good, but not overly elaborate, dishes. Chez Stella, rue Thérèse (1er) (closed weekends and August), offers a three-course fixed-price meal (service included, but drink extra) for an average of 30F ($6.85) to 45F ($10.27). The Medova, rue l'Échelle (1er), offers a large variety on its menu for anywhere from 30F ($6.85) to 45F ($10.27), including drink and service. Unfortunately, the Medova is closed Sundays and in August. We ate at each of these restaurants several times, and were always satisfied" (Mr. and Mrs. J. R. Le Blanc, Charlottesville, Va.).

7. 7th Arrondissement

The 7th Arrondissement includes such attractions as the Eiffel Tower, the Military School, the Invalides, and the Boulevard St.-Germain—plus some especially good restaurants.

THE UPPER BRACKET: Chez les Anges, 54 Boulevard de Latour-Maubourg (7e) (tel. 705-89-86). The encyclopedia *Larousse Gastronomique* reported that "Burgundy is undoubtedly the region of France where the best foods and the best wines are to be had." Well, whether or not that's true, the "House of Angels" does serve some of the finest Burgundian meals in Paris.

On the Left Bank, almost opposite the Invalides, Les Anges is worth the trek. It is directed by François Benoist. The ambience is that of a bistro, and although there's a praiseworthy collection of contemporary paintings, the emphasis is placed where it should be: on the food. Before dinner, try a refreshing apéritif, "le badule," made with champagne spiked with fresh raspberry juice.

As a starter, les oeufs en meurette (poached eggs in a red wine sauce) are recommended. Another favorite is le pâté que faisait ma grandmère (his grandmother's pheasant pâté). Another exciting hors d'oeuvres is a salad of scallops with crayfish tails. Among the main dishes, the most reliable are the sauté de boeuf bourguignonne and the coq au vin. The most expensive specialty is la tranche épaisse de foie de veau (thickly sliced calf's liver) cooked very rare, for two. Be sure to order a fluffy light gratin dauphinois, an excellent accompaniment to most dishes.

For dessert, you may choose from what is certainly the widest assortment of goat cheese in a Parisian restaurant. Not in the mood? Perhaps a fresh strawberry sorbet with the esteemed Cassis liqueur (made with black currants) from Dijon will tempt you. The Burgundy wines in the cellar are above reproach. The average bill is likely to be around 225F ($51.38) per person. Closed Sunday nights and Mondays, and from August 15 to September 15. Métro: Latour-Maubers.

THE MEDIUM-PRICED RANGE: Le Bistrot de Paris, 33 rue de Lille (7e) (tel. 261-16-83). What is that magic element that makes discriminating diners zero in on a little place? Whatever it is, Michel Oliver knows the secret. He's the son of Raymond Oliver, one of the great restaurateurs of France, the owner of the Grand Véfour in the Palais Royal. Known for his appearances on French television, the young Oliver is the author of a unique cookbook for children, *La Cuisine est un Jeu d'Enfants*, with an introduction by the late Jean Cocteau. His magnificent kiddie book even includes a recipe for quiche Lorraine.

His Left Bank restaurant is timely and sophisticated, set in the midst of art galleries and antique shops. The decor is belle époque, tastefully executed. Two dining areas comprise the bistro, the front part with clusters of brass and frosted globes for lighting. On a raised platform in the rear are a few favored tables and a great old wooden bar, a wall of blue Spanish tiles, and a glass roof with a jungle of growing plants and vines.

The cooking is as excellent as it is straightforward—Monsieur Oliver doesn't need to put on airs. Specialties include oeuf poché (poached egg) feuilleté, mignonettes de canard (duckling) au poivre vert, fresh duck liver, and sauté of lamb in ginger. To finish your meal, why not the orange soufflé for two persons? An average meal (in cost, not in quality) goes for around 175F ($39.95) per person. The bistro is closed Saturday noon, Sunday, and in August. Orders are taken until 11 p.m.

Au Quai d'Orsay, 49 Quai d'Orsay (7e) (tel. 551-58-58). Go here for stuffed duck neck. Yes, stuffed duck neck. It's a superb specialty, rarely found. Served at the beginning of your meal, it is a concoction whereby the skin has been stuffed with a blend of pork and chopped duck, flavored with several seasonings including pistachios. The effect is somewhat like a crude pâté. Another heartily recommendable beginning is pleurotes de peupliers, wild mushrooms, meaty and firm, served in a cream sauce. Among the bourgeois dishes is calf's head ravigote. Known in the heyday of Les Halles, this dish is tender and tasty. Expect to pay around 175F ($39.95) to 225F ($51.38) per person with wine included. However, the budget-minded visitor will stick to the 65F ($14.84) set menu. On the banks of Seine, the restaurant is crowded and popular, so reservations are important. The dining rooms are old-fashioned. Friday is the busiest night, and the restaurant closes on Saturday nights, Sundays, and in August.

THE BUDGET RANGE: l'Auberge Basque, 51 rue de Verneuil (7e) (tel. 548-51-98), offers excellently prepared food. The à la carte menu depends on what the day's shopping expedition turned up.

Monsieur Rourre, the owner, comes from the Basque country near the Spanish border—hence, his meals reflect the wonderful cooking of that district. Before he came to Paris, he opened a restaurant for artists in Cannes, where he began to collect paintings (among them drawings by Max Ernst). Backed by the tremendous moral support he gathered on the Riviera, Rourre finally ventured to Paris.

In a tavern setting with a beamed ceiling, you're likely to receive, say, a pâté, veal in a cream sauce with noodles, a lettuce and endive salad, a selection of cheese, and such desserts as tarts and sorbets. The wines are simple, a full bottle of Cahors costing 40F ($9.13). Expect to pay around 75F ($17.12) to 90F ($20.55) for a complete meal. Guitarists play for you in the evenings. Closed in August. Métro: Bac.

La Cigale, 11 bis rue Chomel (7e) (tel. 548-87-87), means "cicada" in French, a name that has absolutely nothing to do with the restaurant. However, it does serve one of the most remarkably good low-cost meals on the Left Bank. Monsieur and Madame Pierre Grocat have teamed up with a Burgundian chef, Georges Louchin, to provide a most recommendable set dinner at 45F ($10.27). In a simple and unpretentious setting you can select hors d'oeuvres, then proceed to your main dish, enjoying a dessert or cheese at the end. On the à la carte menu, favorite dishes include pâté aux morilles, les filets de sole à la crème, and l'escalope Normande, the latter in a tasty cream sauce. Ordering à la carte will likely mean a tab in the neighborhood of 55F ($12.56) to 70F ($15.98). The atmosphere is congenial but crowded. You'll probably have to wait a bit, but it's worth your time. Closed Saturdays and Sundays. Rue Chomel is a tiny street a minute from the Sèvres-Babylone Métro stop.

READER'S RESTAURANT SELECTION: "La Petite Chaise, 36-38 rue de Grenelle (7e) (tel. BAB 13-35), just off Boulevard Raspail (7e), claims to be the oldest restaurant in Paris. We found the prices very reasonable, the French onion soup the best we have ever eaten. A complete meal goes for 55F ($12.56), wine included. We returned the second night in a row, the food was so good. Métro stops Bac or Sèvres-Babylone" (Mrs. Dayne L. Davis Jr., Flint, Mich.).

8. 9th and 10th Arrondissements

These two arrondissements go from the elegance of the Opéra district to the honky-tonk of Pigalle and Clichy. Within these confines are some of the worst restaurants in Paris . . . plus some good ones outlined below.

THE UPPER BRACKET: Julien, 16 rue du Faubourg, St.-Denis (10e) (tel. 770-12-06), offers you an opportunity to dine in one of the most sumptuous belle époque interiors in Paris. It stands in an area once known to Mistinguette and Maurice Chevalier, not too far from Les Halles.

The interior has been carefully restored—the 15-foot-high murals, the peacock-shaped coathooks, the brass railing, the twisted rococo pillars, the glass panels painted by lovers of marshmallow, and the paintings of odalisques. At the turn of the century Julien was an elegant place, and it remained so until right after the war. Then it declined, becoming a cheap restaurant, although the decor remained. At least no one bothered to modernize it.

Now returned to its former splendor, it serves excellently prepared food. A feature is its soups, including "Bilibi" (a creamy mussel soup, as good as the one served at Maxim's), soupe au pistou, and vichyssoise, at around 18F ($4.11) a plate. Main courses are likely to be a filet de boeuf en croûte at 65F ($14.84); roast suckling pig at 53F ($12.10); chevreuil (roebuck) in season at 65F ($14.84); or dorade (sea bream) at 53F ($12.10). The price of your main dish includes an appetizer. Sorbets are in the 15F ($3.42) to 18F ($4.11) range. The restaurant is closed on Sundays and in July. Métro: Strasbourg-St.-Denis.

Nicolas, 12 rue de la Fidélité (10e) (tel. 770-10-72), is owned and operated by Monsieur Julien François, the president of the National Union of Restaurant Owners. Considering his position, he wouldn't dare run a bad place, even though his old, long-established restaurant, founded in 1919, is in one of the unfashionable parts of Paris, right near the Gare de l'Est. The cookery is classic and exemplary. You might begin with a savory mussel soup. The seafood salad is even better. The chef does superb seafood dishes, as exemplified by les coquilles St.-Jacques with a béarnaise sauce. This dish of scallops is available from October to April only. Among the well-prepared main dishes usually featured, we're especially fond of le civet de lièvre (jugged hare) or le perdreau (young partridge) rôti. For dessert, we'd suggest an orange salad with Cointreau. A complete meal begins at around 120F ($27.40), although wine costs extra. The restaurant is closed on Saturday but open on Sunday when most other Parisian restaurants aren't. It also shuts down in August. Métro: Gare de l'Est.

THE MEDIUM-PRICED RANGE: Brasserie Flo, 7 Cour des Petites-Écuries (10e) (tel. 770-13-59). Fin-de-siècle Paris lives on. The area is remote, hard to find. You walk through passageway after passageway, perhaps being solicited along the way. Then Flo emerges. In what might be a slum in any other city, chauffeurs open the doors for their clients, who often look like Lord Alfred Douglas with a spotted Dalmatian on the rein. You expect high prices, but you're wrong.

Inside, the leather banquettes, the brass-studded chairs, the old mahogany bar—everything is right, including the beer mugs. The house specialty, la formidable choucroûte, is served for two persons—a heaping mound of sauerkraut surrounded by boiled ham, bacon, and sausage. Another good main dish is pintadeau (guinea hen) with lentils. The onion soup is the traditional opener. The average dinner will cost about 125F ($28.54) per person. Closed Sundays and from mid-July to September 1. Métro: Château d'Eau.

Haynes, 3 rue Clauzel (9e) (tel. 878-40-63). When a late-night jazz musician drops into Haynes and orders oysters, he doesn't mean those fancy *belons* that come from Brittany. Rather, he's referring to Kentucky oysters—and to soul-food devotees that means chitterlings, served with rice and gravy. Big, burly Haynes—straight from the Deep South, U.S.A.—is the proprietor, general watchdog, emissary of goodwill, confidant of the down-and-out, and a most remarkable man.

One night—clad in a T-shirt—he emerged from the kitchen, all 240 pounds of him, to bounce a drunken Frenchman. The scene could have been from the Keystone Kops. Haynes did it with such warmth and style that the Frenchman—out on the street—put his arms around him and kissed him.

His little bit of Louisiana bayou country holds forth deep in Paris (within walking distance of the Place Pigalle). It's a homing point for many a homesick Yank, jazz artist, or visiting movie company. Even French people, with their versatile and adventurous palates, are hooked on "le soul food." The setting is incongruous: mud-daub plaster walls, Moorish columns, alcoves on low mezzanines, a bar with stools, and signed photographs of visitors: Elizabeth Taylor, Warren Beatty, and Rod Steiger.

Haynes does the cooking himself: southern fried chicken, his own original cole slaw, barbecued spareribs, a hell-hot Mexican chili, corn on the cob, and an old-fashioned homemade apple pie. You can dine here for as little as 35F ($7.99), or, if you're more extravagant, 60F ($13.70). Open from 7 p.m. till 1 a.m. Closed Sundays. Métro: Notre-Dame-de-Lorette.

THE BUDGET RANGE: Le Grand Zinc, 3 Faubourg Montmartre (9e) (tel. 770-77-85). True, the quarter is unfashionable. But the Paris of the 1880s survives here, as exemplified by the spirit lamps hanging inside. You make your way into the restaurant, passing baskets of seafood. You can inspect the *belons* of brown-fleshed oysters from Brittany. A traditional favorite and available year round, these oysters may be purchased inside, half a dozen costing from 70F ($15.98) to 110F ($25.11), depending on the size and the type. The atmosphere is bustling in the tradition of a brasserie. A full meal goes for only 45F ($10.27). Our latest repast began with a selection of crudités (raw vegetables), and was followed by rognons sauté (fried kidneys), then a coupe de glace, an ice cream dessert. Included also was a quarter of a carafe of vin rouge. Métro: Bonne-Nouvelle.

9. 14th Arrondissement

Most tourists come to Montparnasse, where Hemingway and Stein once walked, to find those straight-out-of-the-'20s bars. One restaurant here evokes the same nostalgia.

THE UPPER BRACKET: Closerie des Lilas ("Pleasure Garden of the Lilacs"), 171 Boulevard Montparnasse (14e) (tel. 326-70-50). Hemingway wasn't kind when he wrote of meeting with Ford Maddox Ford at this early-19th-century café: "I have always avoided looking at Ford when I could and I always held my breath when I was near him in a closed room. . . ."

The number of legendary people who have sat in the Closerie, watching the falling leaves blow along the streets of Montparnasse, are almost endless: Gertrude Stein, Ingres, Henry James, Chateaubriand, Apollinaire, Lenin and Trotsky at the chess board, Proust, André Gide, Sartre, Simone de Beauvoir, Verlaine, Braque, Valéry, and James Abbot McNeill Whistler, who would sit here expounding the "gentle art" of making enemies. We come here for the memories and the food.

To get a seat in what they call the "bateau" section of the restaurant, following in the footsteps of the prewar celebrities, is hard. However, you may enjoy waiting for a seat at the bar and ordering the best champagne julep in the world, prepared by Claude the barman. In the "bateau," you can order such rustic dishes as poached haddock or beef with a salad, even steak tartare. In the chic restaurant inside the Closerie, the cooking remains more classic.

Try the escargots façon Closerie for openers. Of the main-course selections, highly recommended are the rognons de veau à la moutarde (veal kidneys with mustard) and ribs of veal in a cider sauce. A 15% service charge is added. Expect to pay around 55F ($12.56) to 100F ($22.83) per person in the "bateau," about 130F ($29.68) in the restaurant. The Closerie is open daily all year.

10. 15th Arrondissement

Down in the 15th Arrondissement you'll find one of the better-tasting bargain meals in Paris today.

THE BUDGET RANGE: Le Bistro de la Gare, 59 Boulevard du Montparnasse (15e), is the lovechild of the now famous Michel Oliver, son of the even more famous Raymond Oliver of the three-star Grand Véfour. The younger Oliver is experimental, usually ahead of most restaurateurs. His concept is to feature a very limited menu of his own creation for only 60F ($13.70), including service and wine. He wanted to cut down on long, wasteful menus and utilize fresh ingredients. Here at the Bistro de la Gare he offers a first course that might include a delicious and original vegetable terrine, which is several purées layered in an attractive way. The second course might be a pork stew with olives, accompanied by delicately slender pommes frites. Coffes is extra. There are more than a dozen imaginatively prepared desserts from which to choose, including a "floating island."

The big surprise is not only the tasty, superior food, but the breathcatching interior. Oliver has taken over a turn-of-the-century meat market, skillfully adapting it to his present-day needs. To reproduce it completely would cost a fortune, but he has retained the intricately carved wood and mirroring, the walls of ornate ceramics and decorative wood, and the artnouveau ceiling with floral designs. One can almost imagine petticoated ladies with parasols and picture hats selecting their meat cuts in the late 1890s. The bistro is a big success with Parisians who don't mind waiting 10 to 15 minutes for a table (reservations aren't accepted). The bistro is open daily.

(At the moment, Monsieur Oliver has another Bistro de la Gare at 73 Avenue des Champs-Élysées. In addition, he has three Les Assiettes au Boeuf, with similar decor and menus, at the following addresses: 9 Boulevard des Italiens, near the Opéra; 73 Avenue des Champs-Élysées, and Place St.-Germain-des-Prés. His own specialty restaurant, with much higher dining tabs, is called Bistrot de Paris and stands at 33 rue de Lille. It's recommended separately in this chapter.)

11. 16th Arrondissement

La Grande Cascade, Bois de Boulogne (16e) (tel. 772-66-00), stands opposite the Longchamp racecourse and serves, incidentally, the best food in this fashionable park. Named after the waterfall of the Bois de Boulogne, the restaurant is a belle époque shrine, the perfect spot for a long, lingering afternoon lunch or a fashionable tea. This indoor-outdoor restaurant was a hunting lodge for Napoleon III, but its fame as a restaurant dates from the early part of this century. Once it was attended by the theatrical chic, Mistinguette always making her entrance in a wide hat as she emerged from a grand carriage.

If the sun is shining, most guests ask for a table on the front terrace with its view. Otherwise, on a foggy day, the interior looks more inviting—made all

the more so with its gilt and crystal and glass roof. Selecting La Grande
Cascade is also a good idea at dinner, as it's more romantic then. Guests dine
to the soft sounds of the nearby cascade, and the tall frosted lamps cast a soft,
forgiving light.

The restaurant presents such à la carte selections as foie gras de canard
(duckling) at 64F ($14.61) and délices de sole Grande Cascade, 64F also. Two
persons can order a most delicious côte de boeuf à la moelle, at 150F ($34.26).
A spectacular finish is provided by the crêpes soufflées à l'orange, 35F ($7.99).
Service is extra. The restaurant is reached by car or taxi only and serves dinner
only from October 15 to May 15 (closed from mid-December to mid-January).

Le Pré Catelan, Bois de Boulogne (16e) (tel. 524-55-58). In a lovely park
setting, you can dine in a classic château, built in the grand manner at the turn
of the century by Nestor Roqueplan. Make it a special occasion—and try to
avoid weekends when receptions, weddings, conventions, whatever, seemingly
reign supreme. Reached by taxi, the restaurant has a definite belle époque style.

Under Colette and Gaston Lenôtre, the restaurant has been totally refurbished. On a spring or summer day, the flowers in the surrounding garden invite
guests to linger long. When you make your entrance, you're seated in a luxuriously appointed dining room, its tall, wide windows opening onto a vista of
greenery.

In addition to the fine à la carte menu, a set meal is offered at 280F
($63.92). Ordering independently, you might dine on a terrine of Mediter-
ranean sea bass with cucumbers, "flower eggs" with caviar, smoked fresh
salmon, and a tomato fondue. However, your tab is likely to run in the neighborhood of 320F ($74.09) to 380F ($86.75) if you should get carried away and
order the lobster roasted with herb butter, climaxed by a pâtisserie Lenôtre.
Always reserve a table. The restaurant is closed on Sunday nights and on
Mondays.

12. 17th Arrondissement

Our lone entry in the Tèrnes-Pereire area is followed by a reader's suggestion:

THE MEDIUM-PRICED RANGE: Mère Michel, 5 rue Rennequin (17e)
(tel. 924-59-80). This is a tiny Paris citadel of beurre blanc. White butter? Well,
not really—it's a frothy sauce made with freshly ground pepper and fish stock,
combined with wine vinegar and minced shallots. You can order it with one
of the fish dishes, such as brochet (pike), turbot, bar (sea bass), or barbue (brill)
at a cost of 68F ($15.52). Wine is simple here, a muscadet usually accompany-
ing the fish.

If you can manage a second course, try the poulet Mère Michel at 52F
($11.87). The armagnac-flamed specialty with a fresh tarragon filling is roasted
for a long time in butter; cream and madeira are added at the end to make the
sauce richer and smoother. Another fine specialty is rognons de veau madère
(veal kidneys with madeira) at 68F ($15.52). Two excellent openers are the fish
soup at 30F ($6.85) and a smooth and rich-tasting terrine maison au foies de
volailles, 35F ($7.99). To cap your meal, try the omelette soufflé au Grand
Marnier for two at 40F ($9.13).

The setting is simple, with only eight tables—so reservations as far ahead
as possible are imperative. The busiest night is Friday, when the chic go out
to dine. It's an informal, homelike, and memorable place. Mère Michel is closed
Saturdays, Sundays, and in August. Métro: Tèrnes.

READER'S RESTAURANT SELECTION: "At 13 rue Brey (17e) is L'Étoile Verte (tel. 380-69-34), a bustling, friendly restaurant where the staff serves an excellent 22F ($5.02) prix-fixe dinner, wine and tip included. Huge plates of tomatoes or mushroom vinaigrette, as well as other appetizer choices, were followed by such dishes as coq au vin, steak au poivre, and steak in wine sauce—all in ample portions with roast potatoes or vegetable. A wide choice of desserts is also included" (Prof. S. Frienland, Brooklyn, N.Y.).

13. 18th and 19th Arrondissements

Old Montmartre has its share of tourist-trap restaurants, but there's one outstanding exception, described in "The Medium-Priced Range" below. Our other recommendation, our first listing, is in the area of the La Villette slaughterhouses.

THE UPPER BRACKET: Cochon d'Or (Golden Pig), 192 Avenue Jean-Jaures (19e) (tel. 607-23-13). The slumming chic come here for some of the best beef in the city, even if they do have to journey out to the remote Porte de Pantin in the 19th Arrondissement. This temple of beef faces the slaughterhouses of La Villette, and its history goes back to the turn of the century when it was created as a bistro for butchers in skullcaps. Nowadays, it's run by Monsieur Ayral, who extends personal greetings.

You get hefty portions at sky-high prices, but good value nonetheless, considering the quality of the produce and the concern that goes into the preparation. The one dish that we'd assume you'd make the trip for is the charcoal-grilled côte de boeuf with a moelle (marrow) sauce for two. It is usually accompanied by a delicious potato soufflé. Known mainly by gastronomes, an especially satisfying choice is the onglet grillé, one of the best beef cuts we've ever sampled in Paris. An expenditure of 170F ($38.81) to 250F ($57.08) per person is to be expected. The Golden Pig is open all year, every day. You must arrive before 9:30 p.m.

THE MEDIUM-PRICED RANGE: Relais de la Butte, 12 rue Ravignan (18e) (tel. 606-16-18). Most restaurants in Montmartre claim to be this good; the Relais, as it is known, is one of the few that is. Across from the Hôtel Paradis, the inn stands on one of the most famous (and one of the steepest) streets in Montmartre. At the adjacent Place Émile-Goudeau lived Picasso, Modigliani, Douanier Rousseau, and the poet Max Jacob. But the restaurant holds out against all the gimmicky, arty associations so popular here, although it is very much in keeping with the Montmartre atmosphere of colorful tablecloths, red-and-white checked gingham curtains, and the like. The works of local artists grace the walls.

The tone, the cooking, the welcome—everything stems from the Relais' patron, Michel Jouan, and his wife, Rose. From the restaurant's 65F ($14.84), prix-fixe menu, you can begin with a fine soupe à l'ail gratinée (garlic soup with cheese), with just enough garlic to make it eminently edible, followed by a canard à l'orange (duck with orange sauce). Many have praised the game dishes, such as quail and partridge. A more expensive selection on the à la carte menu is lobster Newburg, beautifully prepared and priced from 75F ($17.12) to 100F ($22.83), depending on the size and daily market rate. For a regal finish, order oranges flambées Grand Marnier, 25F ($5.71), followed by a 30-year-old Calvados after your coffee. The inn is open daily except Thursdays, from noon to 2:30 p.m. and from 7:30 to 10:30 p.m. The restaurant is closed Thursdays, at lunch Fridays, and in August. Métro: Abbesses.

Chapter IV

DISCOVERING PARIS

**1. Nine Top Sights
2. Other Major Sights
3. More Museums
4. More Churches
5. The Gardens of Paris
6. The Markets of Paris
7. A Sightseeing Miscellany
8. In the Environs
9. Shopping in Paris**

IF IT'S YOUR FIRST visit to Paris, you are lucky. If it's your second, third, fourth, or your fifieth, you're even more fortunate. Like any good lover, Paris doesn't reveal all her charms and subtleties at once. The full impact of her beauty takes years to understand.

Paris is an old city, yet very much in the present, trying at times—almost hysterically—to be the style-setter of the world. Fads come and go with such rapidity that only New York and London could harbor so much fickleness. Somehow the old has learned to adapt to the new, and vice versa.

We'll spend a lot of time discussing monuments and art in this chapter, fashionable promenades and beautiful gardens. But even though we glorify monumental Paris, remember that its main attraction is and has always been the Parisians themselves. They're a unique breed, as even the most cursory visitor to the French capital finds out. Even the French from the provinces regard Parisians with interest, detachment, sometimes outright jealousy.

ORGANIZED TOURS: Before plunging into more detailed sightseeing on your own, you might like to take the most popular get-acquainted tour in Paris. It's called **Cityrama,** 4 Place des Pyramides (tel. 260-30-14) (Métro:Tuileries). On a double-decker bus with enough windows for the Palace of Versailles, you're taken on a nice and lazy three-hour ride through the city's streets. You don't actually go inside specific attractions—rather, settle for a look at the outside of such places as Notre-Dame, the Eiffel Tower, and the studios of Montmartre.

The language barrier is overcome as individual earphones are distributed, with a canned commentary in nine different languages. In comfortable armchair seats you sit back as Paris unfolds before you. Costing 80F ($18.26), tours depart on the hour (except noon) from 9 a.m. to 4 p.m. Leaving at 10 p.m. is another Cityrama offering, a tour of the nighttime illuminations, for 60F ($13.70), from May to October only.

1. Nine Top Sights
We shall now proceed to detail our itinerary listed above.

THE LOUVRE: From far and wide they come—from North Dakota to Pakistan, from Nova Scotia to Japan—all bent on seeing the wonders of the legendary Louvre. Those on one of those "Paris-in-a-day" tours try to break track records to get a glimpse of the two most famous ladies of the Louvre: the *Mona Lisa* and the armless *Venus de Milo.* Those with an extra five minutes to spare go in pursuit of *Winged Victory,* that headless statue discovered at Samothrace and dating from about 200 B.C. You might as well appraise the considerable charms of these ageless favorites before making a big decision: which of the other 200,000 works would you like to see?

The Louvre suffers from an embarrassment of riches. Hence, masterpieces are often ignored by the casual visitor—there is just too much of a good thing. It is the world's largest palace and the world's largest museum (some say greatest). As a palace, it leaves us cold, except for its old section, the Cour Carrée. As a museum, it's one of the great artistic heritages of the human race.

Marie Antoinette's head had rolled less than a month before the Revolutionary Committee decided that the king's collection of paintings and sculpture would be opened to the public. Between the Seine and the rue de Rivoli (Métro to the Palais Royal or the Louvre, the latter the most elegant subway stop in the world), the Palace of the Louvre stretches for almost half a mile. In the days of Charles V it was a fortress, but François I, a patron of Leonardo da Vinci, had it torn down and rebuilt as a royal residence. At the lowest point in its history, in the 18th century, it was home for anybody who wanted to set up housekeeping. Laundry hung out the windows; corners were literally pig pens, and each family built a fire somewhere to cook a meal during the long Paris winter. Napoleon changed all that, chasing out the inhabitants and launching the restoration of the palace. In fact, the Louvre became the site of his wedding to Marie-Louise.

The collections are divided into six departments: Egyptian, Oriental, and Greek and Roman antiquities; sculpture; painting; and furniture and art objects. For an admission of 7F ($1.60) (free on Sundays), you can view the collections any day except Tuesday from 9:45 a.m. to 8 p.m. If you don't have to "do" Paris in a day, perhaps you can return to the Louvre for several visits, concentrating on different collections or schools of painting. Those with little time should go on one of the guided tours (in English) that leave daily except Sunday and Tuesday at 10:30 a.m. and 3 p.m.; for a well-spent additional 7F ($1.60), you can cover the highlights with a well-informed guide. The vast museum has several entrances; most notable are the Porte Denon and the Barbet de Jouy on the Seine.

The Louvre's most important collections are in the wings devoted to painting and Greek and Roman sculpture. What to see after you've seen the "big three" *(Winged Victory, Venus de Milo, Mona Lisa)?* We'll give you a rough idea of some of the Louvre's masterpieces in the painting collection. After that you're on your own—it would take a book to describe the Louvre in any detail (many have been written).

Da Vinci's much traveled *La Gioconda* was acquired by François I. Note the guard and the bullet-proof glass: it was stolen in the summer of 1911, found in Florence in the winter of 1913. Less well known (but to many even more enchanting) are Da Vinci's *Virgin and Child with St. Anne* and the *Virgin of the Rocks.* For Americans, at least, there's a picture which must rank No. 4 (in interest) among the ladies of the Louvre: *Whistler's Mother.* The palace must certainly be big to house this stern woman under the same roof as those voluptuous naked women painted by such artists as Rubens.

Incidentally, one gallery displays 21 paintings by Rubens—done for Marie de Medici for her Luxembourg Palace in only two years. The Louvre stacks masterpiece upon masterpiece: Ingres's *The Turkish Bath;* David's portrait of Madame Récamier lounging on her familiar sofa; the Botticelli frescoes from the Villa Lemmi; Raphael's *La Belle Jardinière;* Giorgione's *Open Air Concert;* a 1460 *Pietà* from Avignon; Dürer's self-portrait; Anthony Van Dyck's portrait of Charles I of England; Lucas Cranach's curious *Venus;* Fra Angelico's *Coronation of the Virgin;* Hans Memling's *Portrait of an Old Woman;* Jan Van Eyck's *Madonna with Chancellor Rolin;* Correggio's *The Mystic Marriage of St. Catherine;* Hans Holbein's (the Younger) *Portrait of Erasmus of Rotterdam;* Mantegna's *Calvary;* Ribera's *Clubfoot;* Rubens's portrait of Helena Fourment (his second wife) with her children; Vermeer's *Lacemaker;* Delacroix's bare-breasted *Liberty Leading the People;* and Titian's portraits of Protestant-burning François I and his exquisite *Man with a Glove.* Usually no visit is complete without a look at some "fluff": Boucher's *Diana Resting after Her Bath* and Fragonard's *Bathers.*

You ask, where did all these paintings come from? The kings of France, notably art patrons François I and Louis XIV, acquired many of them. Others have been willed to or purchased by the state. Many that Napoleon contributed were taken from reluctant donors (the church a heavy and unwilling giver). Much of Napoleon's plunder had to be returned, although France hasn't seen its way clear to giving back all the booty!

Of the Greek and Roman antiquities, the most notable collections, aside from the *Venus de Milo* and *Winged Victory,* are fragments of the frieze from the Parthenon. In Renaissance sculpture, two slaves by Michelangelo were originally intended for the tomb of Julius II but were sold into other bondage. Combine all that wealth of art with Sumerian and Babylonian treasures, Assyrian winged bulls and Persian friezes, bronze Egyptian queens and a world-renowned *Squatting Scribe,* Cellini's *Nymph of Fontainebleau,* Marie Antoinette furniture, and 18th-century snuffboxes—and you've got a busy three days . . . at least!

The Jeu de Paume Museum of Impressionism

The Louvre didn't want them, and only "the crazy Americans" were buying these "weird" works for a while. Although often hungry and always ridiculed, the Impressionists of the late 19th century continued to paint. Today, they warrant a separate gallery—the Galerie du Jeu de Paume—of the Louvre, and remain one of the most enduring and popular attractions in all of Paris. At the Place de la Concorde (Métro: Concorde), the museum is open daily except Tuesday from 9:45 a.m. to 5:15 p.m., for an admission of 7F ($1.60) (half-price on Sundays).

The Jeu de Paume does not house a school of painting. If nothing else, the Impressionists were independent, though unified in opposition to the dictatorial Académie des Beaux-Arts. For their subject matter they chose the world about them, and insisted on bathing their canvases in light, ignoring ecclesiastical or mythological scenes. They painted the Seine, Parisians strolling in the Tuileries, even railway stations such as the Gare St. Lazare (some critics considered

Monet's choice of the latter unforgiveable vulgarity). The Impressionists were the first to paint the most characteristic feature of Parisian life: the sidewalk café, especially those in what was then the artists' quarter of Montmartre.

Perhaps the most famous painting displayed is Manet's *The Picnic on the Grass,* which when it was first exhibited was decried as *"au grand scandale des gens de bien."* Painted in 1863, it depicts a forest setting with a nude woman and two fully clothed men. Two years later, his *Olympia* created another scandal, showing a woman lounging on her bed and wearing nothing but a flower in her hair and high-heeled shoes. Attending her is a black maid. Zola called Manet "a man among eunuchs."

One of Renoir's brightest, most joyous paintings is here—the *Moulin de la Galette,* painted in 1876. That mill is still standing in the Paris of today. Of course, there is always Degas with his racecourses and dancer series. His 1876 *Absinthe*—again, rejected when it was first shown—remains one of his most reproduced works, and *The Laundresses,* painted much later, is celebrated as well. Paris-born Claude Monet was fascinated by the changing light effects on Rouen Cathedral, and in a series of five paintings he makes the old landmark live as never before.

Other works (not all Impressionistic) are by the American Mary Cassatt, with her familiar *Mother and Child* theme; Paul Cézanne (a forerunner of Cubism); Fantin-Latour (note his *Studio at Batignolles*); Gauguin's *Tahitian Women;* Pissarro's sleepy village scenes; Henri Rousseau's *The Snake Charmer;* Seurat's *The Circus,* painted in 1891 but never finished because of his death; the modest Sisley, who was actually English although he lived and painted his dreamy scenes in France all his life; the incomparable Toulouse-Lautrec; and Van Gogh, who wins new friends with each generation by such works as *The Restaurant de la Sirène, Room at Arles,* and the *Church of Auvers.*

ÎLE DE LA CITÉ:
Medieval Paris, that architectural blending of grotesquerie and Gothic beauty, began on this island in the Seine. The venerated island ever since has been known as "the candle" of the city. Actually, the river formed a protective moat around it. Sauval once observed: "The island of the City is shaped like a great ship, sunk in the mud, lengthwise in the stream, in about the middle of the Seine."

Few have written more movingly about 15th-century Paris than Victor Hugo, who invited the reader "to observe the fantastic display of lights against the darkness of that gloomy labyrinth of buildings; cast upon it a ray of moonlight, showing the city in glimmering vagueness, with its towers lifting their great heads from that foggy sea."

Medieval Paris was a city of legends and lovers, none more notable than Abélard, who was emasculated because of his love for Héloise (afterward, he became a monk, she a nun), of blood-curdling tortures and brutalities. Explore as much of it as you can, but even if you're in a hurry, try to visit Notre-Dame, Sainte Chapelle, and the Conciergerie.

Notre-Dame de Paris

Notre-Dame is regarded as the venerable heart of Paris, even of France itself. For example, distances from Paris to all parts of France are calculated from its precincts.

Although many may disagree, Notre-Dame is, in our opinion, more interesting from the outside than in. Hence, you'll want to walk around the entire structure to appreciate this "vast symphony of stone" more fully. Better yet, cross over the bridge to the Left Bank and view it from the quay.

The history of Paris and that of Notre-Dame are inseparable. Many came here to pray before going off to lose their lives in the Crusades. Napoleon was crowned emperor here, taking the crown from Pius VII and placing it on his own head. Before that event, "Our Lady of Paris" had been sacked by revolutionaries, who destroyed the Galerie des Rois. But wars of religion, carelessness, vandalism, and "embellishments" had destroyed much that previously existed.

The cathedral was once scheduled for demolition, but, partly because of the Victor Hugo classic and the revival of interest in the Gothic, a movement mushroomed to restore the cathedral to its original glory. The task was completed under Viollet-le-Duc, an architectural genius.

The setting has always been memorable: on the banks of the Seine on the Île de la Cité. Founded in the 12th century by Maurice de Sully, bishop of Paris, Notre-Dame grew and grew. Over the years, the cathedral has changed as Paris has—often falling victim to fads in decorative taste. Its flying buttresses were rebuilt in 1330.

Once the houses of old Paris crowded in on the structure, but Haussmann ordered them torn down to show off the edifice to its best advantage from the square known as Parvis. From that vantage point, you can view the trio of 13th-century sculptured portals. On the left, the portal of the Virgin depicts the signs of the Zodiac and the coronation of the Virgin. The association of the Virgin and the Cosmos is to be found in dozens of earlier and later medieval churches.

The restored central portal of the Last Judgment is divided into three levels: the first shows Vices and Virtues; the second, Christ and his Apostles; and above that, Christ in triumph after the Resurrection. The portal is a close illustration of the Gospel according to Matthew.

Finally, the portal of St. Anne is on the right, depicting such scenes as the Virgin enthroned with Child. It is the best preserved and probably the most perfect piece of sculpture in Notre-Dame. Over the central portal is a remarkable rose window, 31 feet in diameter, forming a showcase for a statute of the Virgin and Child.

Equally interesting (although often missed by the scurrying visitor) is the portal of the cloisters (around on the left), with its dour-faced 13th-century Virgin, a unique survivor of the many that originally adorned the façade. Unfortunately, the Child figure she is holding is decapitated. Finally, the portal of St. Stephen on the Seine side traces the martyrdom of that saint.

If possible, see the interior of Notre-Dame at sunset. Of the three giant medallions that warm the austere cathedral, the north rose window in the transept, dating from the mid-13th century, is best. The interior itself is in the typically Gothic style, with slender, graceful columns. The stone-carved choir screen from the early 14th century depicts such biblical scenes as the Last Supper. Near the altar stands the famous 14th-century Virgin and Child, highly venerated among the more faithful of Paris.

It costs 3F (68¢) to visit the Treasury, with its display of vestments and gold objects, including crowns, behind glass. Exhibited are a cross presented to Haile Selassie, the former Emperor of Ethiopia, and a reliquary offered to Napoleon. Notre-Dame is especially proud of its relics of the True Cross, said to include the Crown of Thorns.

Finally, to visit those grimy gargoyles immortalized by Hugo, you have to scale steps leading to the twin square towers, flat on top, rising to a height of 225 feet. If you're sturdy-limbed and will spend 6F ($1.37), you can do so any day except Tuesday from 10 a.m. to 4:45 p.m. (closes an hour earlier off-season). On Sundays, the charge is only 3F (68¢). Once there, you can closely inspect those devils (some sticking out their tongues), hobgoblins, and birds of prey. You expect to see the imaginary character of Quasimodo in one of his celluloid hunchback interpretations (Charles Laughton or Lon Chaney, depending on which version you saw).

Approached through a garden behind Notre-Dame is the **Memorial to the Deportation,** jutting out on the very tip of the Île de la Cité. Birds chirp nowadays, the Seine flows gently by—but the memories are far from pleasant. It is a memorial to French martyrs of W.W. II, who were deported to camps like Auschwitz and Buchenwald. In blood-red are the words: "Forgive, but don't forget." It may be visited from 10 a.m. to noon and from 2 to 7 p.m.; no admission charge.

Métro to Notre-Dame: Cité.

Sainte Chapelle

It is customary to call this tiny chapel a jewel box. That hardly suffices— nor does such a contemporary expression as a "light show." Go when the sun is shining, and you'll need no one else's words to describe the remarkable effects of natural light in Sainte Chapelle.

Approach Sainte Chapelle from the Boulevard du Palais (Métro: Cité) and enter through the Cour du Mai (Courtyard of May) of the Palace of Justice. If it weren't for the chapel's 247-foot spire, the law courts here would almost swallow it up.

Built in only two or three years, beginning in 1246, the chapel has two levels. It was constructed to house relics of the True Cross, including the Crown of Thorns acquired by St. Louis (the Crusader king, Louis IX) from the Emperor of Constantinople. In those days, cathedrals throughout Europe were busy acquiring relics for their treasuries, regardless of authenticity. It was a seller's—perhaps a sucker's—market. Louis IX is said to have paid heavily for his precious relics, raising the money through unscrupulous means. He died of the plague on a Crusade and was canonized in 1297.

You enter through the lower chapel, supported by flying buttresses and ornamented with fleur-de-lis designs. The lower chapel was used by the servants of the palace, the upper chamber by the king and his courtiers. The latter is reached by ascending narrow spiral stairs.

Viewed on a bright day, the 15 stained-glass windows seem to glow with ruby red and Chartres blue. They vividly depict scenes from the Bible. The walls consist almost entirely of the glass which had to be removed for safekeeping during the Revolution and again during both world wars.

In them are embodied the hopes, dreams, even the pretensions of the kings who ordered their construction.

The chapel, closed Tuesdays, is open otherwise from 10 a.m. till noon and from 1:30 till 5 p.m. Admission is 6F ($1.37), but you can visit it for half price on Sundays and holidays.

The Conciergerie

London has its Tower of London, Paris its Conciergerie. Although it had a long and regal history before the Revolution, it is visited today chiefly by those wishing to bask in the horrors of the Reign of Terror. The Conciergerie lives on as a symbol of infamy, recalling the days when carts pulled up daily to haul off the fresh supply of bodies to the guillotine.

On the Seine, at 1 Quai de l'Horloge, it is approached through its landmark twin towers, the Tour d'Argent and the Tour de César. The 14th-century vaulted Guard Room, which remains from the days when the Capets made the Palace of the Cité a royal residence, is the actual entrance to the chilling building. Also dating from the 14th century, and even more interesting, is the vast, dark, and foreboding Gothic Salle des Gens d'Armes (People at Arms), totally changed from the days when the king used it as a banqueting hall.

Architecture, however, plays a secondary role to the list of famous prisoners who spent their last miserable days on earth at the Conciergerie. Few in its history endured the tortures of Ravaillac, who assassinated Henry IV in 1610. He got the full treatment—pincers in the flesh, hot lead and boiling oil poured on him like bath water.

During the Revolution, the Conciergerie became more than a symbol of terror to the nobility or the "enemies of the State." Meeting just a short walk from the prison, the Revolutionary Tribunal dispensed "justice" in a hurry. And the guillotine fell faster. If it's any consolation, these "freedom-loving" jurors did not believe in torturing their victims—only decapitating them.

In failing health and shocked beyond grief, Marie Antoinette was brought here to await her trial. Only a small screen (and sometimes not even that) protected her modesty from the glare of the guards stationed in her cell. The Affair of the Carnation failed in its attempt to abduct her and secure her freedom. In retrospect, one can, perhaps, feel sympathy for the broken and widowed queen. By accounts of that day, she was shy and stupid, although the evidence is that upon her death she attained the nobility of a true queen. Further, historians deny she uttered the famous quotation attributed to her: "Let them eat cake," when told the peasants had no bread. It was shortly before noon on the morning of October 16, 1793, when her executioners came for her, grabbing her and cutting her hair, as was the custom for victims marked for the guillotine.

Today you can see lithographs and paintings depicting scenes from the Revolution, including a model of the dreaded guillotine. Also displayed is a facsimile of the final touching letter, or "testament," written by Marie Antoinette to Madame Elizabeth, sister of Louis XVI.

Later the Conciergerie housed yet more noted prisoners, including Madame Elizabeth herself; Madame du Barry, mistress of Louis XV; Mme. Roland ("O Liberty! Liberty! What crimes are committed in thy name!"), and Charlotte Corday, who killed Marat with a kitchen knife while he was taking a sulfur bath. In time, the Revolution turned on its own leaders, such as Danton and Robespierre. Finally, even one of the most hated men in Paris, the public prosecutor Fouquier-Tinville, faced the same guillotine to which he'd sent so many others.

The Conciergerie is open from 10 to 11:25 a.m. and from 1 till 4:25 p.m., except Tuesdays. The admission is 6F ($1.37) on weekdays, 3F (68¢) on Sundays.

Pont Neuf

After leaving the Conciergerie, turn left and stroll along the Seine past medievalesque towers till you reach the Pont Neuf or "New Bridge." The span isn't new, of course—actually, it's the oldest bridge in Paris, erected in 1604. In its day, the bridge had two unique features: it was not flanked with houses and shops, and it was paved.

At the Hôtel Carnavalet, a museum in the Marais section (see below), is a painting, *Spectacle of Buffons*, showing what the bridge was like between

1665 and 1669. Duels were fought on the structure; great coaches belonging to the nobility crossed it; peddlers sold their wares; and, as there were no public facilities, men defecated right on the bridge, as depicted in the painting. With all those crowds, it attracted entertainers, such as Tabarin, who sought a few coins from the gawkers. The Pont Neuf is decorated with corbels, a mélange of grotesquerie.

Square du Vert Galant

Finally, continue on to the "prow" of the island, the Square du Vert Galant, pausing first to look at the equestrian statue of the beloved Henri IV, killed by an assassin. A true king of the people, Henri was (to judge from accounts) also regal in the boudoir. Hence the nickname "Vert Galant," or gay old spark. Gabrielle d'Estrées and Henriette d'Entragues were his best-known mistresses, but they had to share him with countless others—some of whom would casually catch his eye as he was riding along the streets of Paris.

In fond memory of the king, the little triangular park continues to attract lovers. If at first it appears to be a sunken garden, that's because it remains at its natural level; the rest of the Cité has been built up during the centuries.

THE GRANDE PROMENADE: In 1891 that "Innocent Abroad" Mark Twain called the Champs-Élysées "the liveliest street in the world," designed for the favorite pastime of Parisians, promenading. It is rather too innocent to rank walking as a Parisian's number-one pastime, but surely it comes in second. Nowadays, tourists invariably take up that highly respectable custom of the 19th century. Visitors from Minnesota who normally would get into their automobiles to drive half a block to the drugstore are seen doing the sprint from Place Charles-de-Gaulle (Étoile) to Place de la Concorde. That walk is surely a grand promenade, and you won't know Paris till you've traversed it.

Arc de Triomphe

At the western end, the Arc de Triomphe (Métro: Place Charles-de-Gaulle) suggests one of those ancient Roman arches—only it's larger. Actually, it's the biggest triumphal arch in the world, about 163 feet high and 147 feet wide. To reach it, don't try to cross the square, the busiest traffic hub in Paris (death is certain!). Take the underground passage and live longer. With one dozen streets radiating from the "Star," the roundabout was called by one writer "vehicular roulette with more balls than numbers."

After the death of Charles de Gaulle, the French government—despite protests from anti-Gaullists—voted to change the name of the heretofore Place de l'Étoile to the Place Charles-de-Gaulle.

The arch has witnessed some of France's proudest moments—and some of its more shameful and humiliating defeats, notably those of 1871 and 1940. The memory of German troops marching under the arch that had come to symbolize France's glory and prestige is still painful to the French. And who could ever forget the 1940 newsreel of the Frenchman standing on the Champs-Élysées openly weeping as the haughty Nazi stormtroopers goose-stepped through Paris?

Commissioned by Napoleon in 1806 to commemorate his victories, the arch wasn't ready for the entrance of his new empress, Marie Louise, in 1810. It served anyway; in fact, it wasn't completed until 1836, under the reign of Louis-Philippe. Four years later the remains of Napoleon—brought from his grave at St. Helena—passed under the arch on the journey to his tomb at the

Invalides. Since that time it has become the focal point for state funerals. It is also the site of the permanent tomb of the unknown soldier.

The greatest state funeral was that of Victor Hugo in 1885; his coffin was placed under the center of the arch, and much of Paris turned out to pay tribute to the author. Another notable funeral was the one in 1929 of Ferdinand Foch, the supreme commander of the Allied forces in World War I. Perhaps the happiest moment occurred in 1944, when the Liberation of Paris parade passed through. That same year Eisenhower paid a visit to the tomb of France's unknown soldier, a new tradition among leaders of state and important figures. An eternal flame is kept burning.

Of the sculpture on the monument, the best known is Rude's *Marseillaise*, also called *The Departure of the Volunteers. The Triumph of Napoleon in 1810*, by J. P. Cortot, and the *Resistance of 1814* and the *Peace of 1815*, both by Etex, also adorn the façade. The monument is engraved with the names of hundreds of generals (those underlined died in battle) who commanded French troops in Napoleonic victories.

From 10 a.m. to 5 p.m. you can take an elevator to the top for 7F ($1.60) or scale the steps. Up there is an exhibition hall, with lithographs and photos depicting the arch throughout its history. From the observation deck, you have the finest view of the Champs-Élysées as well as such landmarks as the Louvre, the Eiffel Tower, and Sacré-Coeur.

Champs-Élysées

The greatest boulevard in Paris, perhaps in the world, has a two-faced character. Part is a drive through a chestnut-lined park, the other a commercial avenue of sidewalk cafés, automobile showrooms, airline offices, cinemas, lingerie stores, even a Wimpy. The dividing point between the park and the commercial sections is Rond-Point des Champs-Élysées. Close to that is a philatelist's delight, the best-known open-air stamp market in Europe, held Sundays and Thursdays. To chronicle the people who have walked this broad avenue would be to tell the history of Paris through the last few centuries. Ever since the days of Thomas Jefferson and Benjamin Franklin, Americans have gravitated here (some of the business establishments report 75% patronage by Yankees). The Champs-Élysées has, of course, lost the fin-de-siècle elegance described by Proust in *The Remembrance of Things Past*. For one thing, not all the kids playing in the park today are rich. Puppet shows, carousels, and other amusements entertain the present brood.

A slight detour from the Champs-Élysées takes you to—

Palais de l'Élysée

The French "White House" is called Palais de l'Élysée, and it occupies a block along fashionable Faubourg St.-Honoré. It is now occupied by President Valéry Giscard d'Estaing and cannot be visited by the public without an invitation.

Built in 1718 for the Count d'Evreux, the palace had many owners before it was purchased by the Republic in 1873. Once it was owned by Madame de Pompadour. When she "had the supreme delicacy to die discreetly at the age of 43," she bequeathed it to the king. The world premiere of the Voltaire play *The Chinese Orphan* was presented there. After her divorce from Napoleon, Josephine also lived there. Napoleon III also lived at l'Élysée when he was president, beginning in 1848. When he became emperor in 1852, he moved to the Tuileries. Such celebrated English visitors as Queen Victoria and Wellington have spent their nights there as well.

Included among the palace's works of art are tapestries made at Beauvais in the 18th century, Raphael and Leonardo da Vinci paintings, and Louis XVI furnishings. A grand dining hall was built for Napoleon III, as well as an orangerie for the Duchesse du Berry (now converted into a winter garden).

Place de la Concorde

In the east, the Champs-Élysées begins at Place de la Concorde, an octagonal traffic hub ordered built in 1757 to honor Louis XV. The statue of the king was torn down in 1792 and the name of the square changed to Place de la Revolution. Floodlit at night, it is dominated nowadays by an Egyptian obelisk from Luxor, considered the oldest man-made object in Paris. It was carved circa 1200 B.C. and presented to France in 1829 by the Viceroy of Egypt.

In the Reign of Terror, the dreaded guillotine was erected on this spot, and claimed the lives of thousands—everybody from Louis XVI, who died bravely, to Madame du Barry, who went screaming and kicking all the way. Before the leering crowds, Marie Antoinette, Robespierre, Danton, Mme. Roland, and Charlotte Corday rolled away. (You can still lose your life on the Place de la Concorde; all you have to do is chance the traffic and cross over.)

For a spectacular sight, look down the Champs-Élysées—the view is framed by the Marly horses. On the opposite side, the gateway to the Tuileries is flanked by the winged horses of Coysevox.

On each side of the obelisk are two fountains with bronze-tailed mermaids and bare-breasted sea nymphs. Gray-beige statues ring the square, honoring the cities of France. To symbolize the city's fall to Germany in 1871, the statue of Strasbourg was covered with a black drape which wasn't lifted until the end of World War I. Two of the palaces on Place de la Concorde are, today, the Ministry of the Marine and the deluxe Crillon Hotel. They were designed in the 1760s by Ange-Jacques Gabriel.

Tuileries

Bordering the Place de la Concorde, the Tuileries are as much a part of the Paris scene as the Seine. These statue-studded gardens were designed by Le Nôtre, the gardener to Louis XIV, who planned the grounds of Versailles.

About 100 years before that, a palace was ordered built by Catherine de Medici. Connected to the Louvre, it was occupied by Louis XVI after he left Versailles. Napoleon I called it home. Twice attacked by the people of Paris, it was finally burnt to the ground in 1871 and never rebuilt. The gardens, however, remain.

Like the orderly French mind, the trees are arranged according to designs. Even the paths are straight, as opposed to winding English gardens. To break the sense of order and formality are bubbling fountains. (Two museums in the Tuileries—the Jeu de Paume and the Orangerie—were discussed above.)

The neoclassic statuary is often insipid and is occasionally desecrated by rebellious "art critics." Seemingly half of Paris is found in the Tuileries on a warm spring day, listening to the chirping birds and watching the daffodils and red tulips bloom. Fountains bubble, and mothers roll their carriages over the grounds where 18th-century revolutionaries killed the king's Swiss guards.

At the end of your walking tour of the Tuileries—two miles from Place Charles-de-Gaulle (Étoile)—you'll be at the **Arc de Triomphe du Carrousel**, at the Cour du Carrousel. Pierced with three walkways and supported by marble columns, the monument honors the "grande armée," celebrating Napoleon's victory at Austerlitz on December 5, 1805. The arch is surmounted by statuary, a chariot, and four bronze horses. "Paris needs more monuments," Napoleon once shouted. He got his wish.

THE EIFFEL TOWER: Everyone visits the landmark that has become the symbol of Paris itself. For maximum enjoyment, however, don't just rush to it right at once. Approach it gradually. Take the Métro to Place du Trocadéro, dominated by a statue of Marshal Foch. Once you've surfaced from the underground, you'll be at the gateway to the—

Palais de Chaillot

Replacing the 1878 Palais du Trocadéro, the new palace was built in 1937 for the International Exhibition. If you have time, try to visit at least two of the three important museums lodged in the building: one a maritime showcase, another a gallery of reproductions of many of the monuments of France, a third devoted to people (see our museum section below for more detailed descriptions).

From the palace terrace (one writer called it "Mussolinian"), you have a panoramic view across the Seine to the Eiffel Tower. The **Jardins du Palais de Chaillot** in back sweep down to the Seine. They are noted for their fountain displays. From April to October, the gardens are a babel of international tongues. In a simulated grotto, an **Aquarium** has been installed. Conger eels swim by, children scream, and the admission costs 2.70F (62¢). The Aquarium is open from 10 a.m. to 5:30 p.m.

The Tower

Cross the Pont d'Iéna and you'll reach your goal, the incomparable Eiffel Tower. Except for perhaps the Leaning Tower of Pisa, it is the single most recognizable structure in the world. Weighing 7000 tons but exerting about the same pressure on the ground as an average-size person sitting in a chair, the tower was never meant to be permanent. It was built for the Exhibition of 1889 by Gustave Alexandre Eiffel, the French engineer whose fame rested mainly on his iron bridges, such as the one built in Porto, Portugal. (Incidentally, one of the lesser-known aspects of his career is his designing of the framework for the Statue of Liberty.)

The tower, including its 55-foot television antenna, is 1056 feet high. On a clear day, you can see it from some 40 miles away. An open-framework construction, the tower ushered in the almost unlimited possibilities of steel construction, paving the way for the skyscrapers of the 20th century.

Skeptics said it couldn't be built, and Eiffel actually wanted to make it soar higher than it did. For years, it remained the tallest man-made structure on earth, until such skyscrapers as the Empire State Building usurped that record.

Artists and writers vehemently denounced it, although later generations sang its praise. People were fond of calling it names: "a giraffe," "the world's greatest lamppost," "the iron monster," "suicide bait." Others suggested, "Let's keep art nouveau grounded." Nature lovers feared it would interfere with the flights of birds over Paris.

The Prince of Wales, later King Edward VII of England, was the first person to ascend the Eiffel Tower. In 1909 it was almost torn down, but the advent of "the wireless" gave it a new lease on life.

You can visit the tower in two stages, but few settle for the 5F ($1.14) green ticket that gets them to the first landing, with its view over the rooftops of Paris. The white ticket, costing 11F ($2.51), gets you by elevator to the second stage—and that is quite sufficient for many. The view from there is spectacular. The third and final stage cannot be visited as of this writing. On the first and second stages are restaurants. You can visit the tower from 10:30 a.m. to 5:30 p.m. and from 6:30 p.m. to 11 p.m.

Champ-de-Mars and École Militaire

With time remaining, explore the Champ-de-Mars, the gardens between the Eiffel Tower and the Military School. Traditionally, these gardens, laid out around 1770, were the World's Fair grounds of Paris, the scene of many a military parade.

Thanks in part to one of France's best-known mistresses, Madame de Pompadour, the École Militaire (Military School) was established; the plans drawn up by J. A. Gabriel. This classical school was founded in 1751 for about 500 young men who wanted a military career.

Napoleon entered in 1784, the year his father died of cancer. He was graduated a year later as a lieutenant, aged 16. According to accounts, he wasn't popular with his classmates, many of whom openly made fun of him. One wrote, "All boots, no man." Pity those creatures when their names came up for promotions years later. Another French general, Charles de Gaulle, also studied at the school. Special permission is needed to go inside.

Behind the military school is the **UNESCO Building**, a Y-shaped structure fronting the Place de Fontenoy. On the piazza may be seen Alexander Calder's mobile, standing out like a sentinel against a travertine wall; the big *Reclining Figure* by Henry Moore, and two perpendicular walls covered with ceramic designed by Miró and executed by Arigaz. Inside the conference hall Picasso has brushed a panel 10 by 9 meters; a large mural by Tamayo, *Prometheus Bringing Fire to Man,* and a Roman mosaic made in Carthage in 200 B.C. may also be seen. On the eastern façade is a garden arranged by Noguchi according to the rules of ancient Japan, in which may be seen a statuette of an angel, a survivor of the holocaust of Nagasaki in 1945. A mosaic of Bazaine forms the background of this garden, joining it to the ancestral inspiration of certain Western paintings. In spite of the ethnic diversity of its authors, the headquarters building is a creation of unity. The different architects and artists, with their respective nationalities and concepts working on one enterprise, have permitted UNESCO to express the finest symbol of its universal mission.

The UNESCO building is open from 9 a.m. to 6 p.m. daily except Saturday and Sunday. Information programs on UNESCO and its activities are provided free for visitors and should be requested in advance.

HÔTEL DES INVALIDES: The glory of the French military lives on here. Actually, it was the Sun King himself who decided to build the "hotel" to house soldiers who'd been disabled. It wasn't entirely a benevolent gesture, since these veterans had been injured, crippled, or blinded while fighting his battles. Louvois was ordered in 1670 to launch this massive building program. When it was completed—and Louis was long dead—the corridors stretched for miles. Eventually the building was crowned by a gilded dome designed by Mansart.

The Invalides is best approached by walking from the Right Bank across the turn-of-the-century Alexander III Bridge. Of this span, critic Ian Nairn wrote, "The whole thing is carried to the limit of mock pomposity, like Offenbach satirizing a romantic situation yet at the same time providing a beautifully tender melody for lovers." In the building's cobblestoned forecourt is a display of massive cannons—a formidable welcome.

Before rushing on to Napoleon's tomb, you may want to take the time to visit the greatest **Army Museum** in the world. In 1794, a French inspector started collecting all these weapons, uniforms, and equipment.

With the continued accumulation of war material over the centuries, the museum has become a horrifying documentary of man's self-destruction. Viking swords, Burgundian bacinets, blunderbusses from the 14th century, Balkan khandjars, American Browning machine guns, war pitchforks, salamander-engraved Renaissance serpentines, "Haute Époque" armor, a 1528 Griffon, musketoons, grenadiers . . . if it could kill, it's enshrined in a place of honor here. As a sardonic touch, there's even the wooden leg of General Daumesnil.

The museum was looted by the Germans in 1940.

Among the outstanding acquisitions are in the suits of armor worn by the kings of France, including Louis XIV. The best-known one—the "armor suit of the lion"—was made for François I. Henri II ordered his suit engraved with the monogram of his mistress, Diane de Poitiers, and (perhaps reluctantly) that of his wife, Catherine de Medici. The showcases of swords are reputedly among the finest in the world.

The mementos of World War I, including those of American and Canadian soldiers, are especially interesting. Included is the Armistice Bugle which sounded the cease-fire on November 11, 1918.

Much attention is focused on that Corsican general who became France's greatest soldier. A plaster death mask by Antommarchi is one of the most notable pieces on display. So, too, an oil by Delaroche, painted at the time of Napoleon's first banishment (April 1814), which depicted him as he probably looked, paunch and all.

In the rooms relating to the First Empire are displayed the field bed of Napoleon with his tent. In the room devoted to the Restoration, the 100 Days, and Waterloo, you can see the reconstituted bedroom of Napoleon at the time of his death at St. Helena. On the more personal side, you can view Vizir, a stuffed horse he owned, as well as a saddle used mainly for state ceremonies. The Turenne Salon contains other souvenirs of Napoleon, including the hat he wore at Eylau, his sword from his victory at Austerlitz, and his "Flag of Farewell" which he kissed before departing for Elba.

The new Salle Orientale in the west wing shows arms for the eastern world, including Asia and the Muslim countires of the Mideast, from the 16th to the 19th centuries. Turkish armor and weapons and Chinese and Japanese armor and swords are on display.

A walk across the Court of Honor delivers you to the **Church of the Dome,** designed by Mansart for Louis XIV. The great architect began work on the church in 1677, although he died before its completion. The dome is the second-tallest monument in Paris. In the Napoleon Chapel is the hearse used at the emperor's funeral on May 9, 1821.

To accommodate the **Tomb of Napoleon,** the architect Visconti had to redesign the high altar in 1842. First buried at St. Helena, Napoleon's remains were returned to Paris in 1840. Louis-Philippe had demanded that of England. The triumphal funeral procession passed under the Arc de Triomphe, down the Champs-Élysées, en route to the Invalides. Snow whirled through the air.

The tomb itself is made of red Finnish porphyry, the base from green granite. Napoleon's remains were locked away inside six coffins. Surrounding the tomb are a dozen amazonlike figures representing his victories. Almost lampooning the smallness of the man, everything is made large, big, awesome. You'd think a real giant was buried here, not a symbolic one. In his coronation robes, the statue of Napoleon stands 8½ feet high. The grave of Napoleon's son, "the King of Rome," lies at his feet.

Napoleon's tomb is surrounded by that of his brother, Joseph Bonaparte; the great Vauban; Foch, the Allied commander in World War I; Turenne, and La Tour d'Auvergne, the first grenadier of the Republic (actually, only his heart is entombed here).

The Army Museum is open every day from 10 a.m. to 6 p.m. from April 1 to September 30; from 10 to 5, October 1 to March 31. It is closed January 1, May 1, November 1, and December 25. The entrance price of 8F ($1.83) includes the Army Museum, the Tomb, and the **Museum of Plans and Reliefs** in a top-floor gallery. Métro: La Tour-Maubourg, École Militaire, Varenne, Invalides.

A **son et lumière** program—titled "Shades of Glory"—is presented nightly (at 9 and 11 p.m. in English) at the Invalides. The entrance is at the Esplanade des Invalides, and the admission price is 18F ($4.11) for adults, 14F ($3.20) for children. It is presented from April 1 through October 31 (at 11 p.m. only during June and July). The pageant makes for a fascinating evening.

MONTMARTRE: Soft-white three-story houses, slender, barren trees sticking up from the ground like giant toothpicks—that's how Utrillo, befogged by absinthe, saw Montmartre. On the other side of the canvas, Toulouse-Lautrec brush-stroked it as a district of cabarets, circus performers, and prostitutes. Today, Montmartre remains truer to the dwarfish artist's conception than it does to that of Utrillo.

From the 1880s to the years preceding World War I, Montmartre enjoyed its golden age as the world's best-known art colony. *La vie de bohème* reigned supreme. At one time, the artistic battle in La Butte was the talk of the art world. There was, for one, the bold Matisse, and his band of followers known as "The Savage Beasts." Following World War I, the pseudo-artists flocked to Montmartre in droves, with camera-snapping tourists hot on their heels. The real artists had long gone, perhaps to Montparnasse.

Before its discovery and subsequent chic, Montmartre was a sleepy farming community, with windmills dotting the landscape. The name has always been the subject of disagreement, some maintaining that it originated from the "mount of Mars," a Roman temple that crowned the hill; others asserting it means "mount of martyrs." The latter is a reference to the martyrdom of St. Denis, patron saint of Paris, who was beheaded on the mountain along with his fellow-saints Rusticus and Eleutherius.

Up to Sacré-Coeur

The simplest way to reach Montmartre is to take the Métro line to the Anvers station, then walk up the rue Steinkerque in the direction of the funicular. Funiculars run every day from 6 a.m. till 11 p.m., costing 2F (46¢) for a round-trip ticket. You will be delivered to the precincts of Sacré-Coeur. Another, and preferable, way is to take the Métro to Place Pigalle, from which you proceed down the Boulevard de Clichy, turning right at the Cirque Médrano and beginning your climb up the rue des Martyrs. (On your left, at No. 75, is Madame Arthur, a club known throughout Europe for its female impersonators.) Turn left on the rue Abbesses, then go right along the steep rue Ravignan.

At No. 12 is one of the best restaurants in Montmartre, the Relais de la Butte (see the previous chapter).

Eventually, you arrive at the **Place Émile-Goudeau,** a tree-studded square in the middle of the rue Ravignan. At No. 13, across from the Hôtel Paradis, stood **Bateau-Lavoir** ("Boat Washhouse"), called the cradle of Cubism. Fire gutted it in 1970. Picasso once lived here, painting, in the winter of 1905-06, one of the world's most famous portraits, *The Third Rose* (Gertrude Stein). Other residents have included Kees Van Dongen and Juan Gris. Modigliani had his studio nearby, as did Henri Rousseau and Braque.

A sign at the Place Jean-Baptiste-Clément points the way to the **Musée de Cire,** the waxworks of Montmartre, at 11 rue Poulbot. Charging 8F ($1.83) for adults, 4F (91¢) for children, the museum documents historical Montmartre. In wax tableaux, the exhibit depicts the days that used to be: one, for example, is devoted to a café as it might have been in the 19th century. Captured in wax are such figures as George Sand, Delacroix, Toulouse-Lautrec (his studio has been recreated), Liszt, Chopin, Berlioz, Renoir, and Utrillo. St. Denis is relegated to stained glass, where he's been frozen walking head in hand! The museum is open daily from 10 a.m. to noon and from 2 to 6 p.m.

Poulbot crosses the tiny **Place du Calvaire,** which offers a panoramic view of Paris. On this square (a plaque marks the house) lived Maurice Neumont (1868-1930), the artist, painter, and lithographer. From here, follow the sounds of an oompah band to the **Place du Tertre,** the old town square of Montmartre. Its cafés are overflowing, its art galleries (in and out of doors) always crowded. Some of the artists still wear berets, and the cafés bear such names as La Bohême—you get the point. Everything is so loaded with local color—applied as heavily as on a Seurat canvas—it gets a little redundant. If you must dine here, the best restaurant is La Mere Catherine.

Right off the square fronting the rue du Mont Cenis is the **Church of St. Pierre.** It has played many roles: a Temple of Reason during the Revolution, a food depot, a clothing store, even a munitions factory. Nowadays it's back to being a church, although originally, during the reign of Louis VI, it was a Benedictine abbey. In 1147 the present church was consecrated, which makes it one of the oldest in Paris. Two of the columns in the choir stall are the remains of a Roman temple. Among the sculptured works is one depicting a nun with the head of a pig, the symbol of sensual vice.

Finally, we reach the crowning achievement of the butte, the **Basilica of Sacré-Coeur.** Next to the Eiffel Tower, it is the most characteristic landmark of the Parisian scene. Like the tower, it has always been—and still is—the subject of much controversy. One Parisian called it "a lunatic's confectionery dream." An offended Zola declared it to be "the basilica of the ridiculous."

Sacré-Coeur has had warm supporters as well, including Max Jacob, the Jewish poet, and the artist Maurice Utrillo. Utrillo never tired of drawing and painting it, and he and Jacob came here regularly to pray.

In gleaming white, it towers over Paris—its five bulbous domes suggesting some Byzantine church of the 12th century, and its campanile inspired by Roman-Byzantine art. But it's not that old. After France's defeat by the Prussians in 1870, the basilica was planned as a votive offering to cure France's misfortunes. Rich and poor alike contributed money to build it. The National Assembly approved its construction in 1873. The church was not consecrated until 1919.

It costs 9F ($2.05) to visit the dome and the crypt, which are open from 9:30 a.m. to noon and from 2 to 5:30 p.m. On a clear day, the vista from the dome can extend for 35 miles. You can also walk around the inner dome of the church, peering down like a pigeon (one is likely to be keeping you company).

Even if you have only 24 hours in Paris and can't explore most of the sights recommended in this chapter, try to make it to Sacré-Coeur at dusk. There, as you sit on the top steps, the church at your back, the Square Willette in front of you, nighttime Paris begins to come alive. First, a twinkle like a firefly; then all of the lights go on. One young American got carried away with it all: "Here, away from the whirling taxis, concierges, crazy elevators, and tipping problems, the sound of Paris permeates by osmosis." Try to see it.

The Cemetery of Montmartre

Second only in frame to Père-Lachaise, the Montmartre Cemetery is the resting place of many famous personages. The burial ground lies west of the "Butte," north of the Boulevard de Clichy. Opened in 1795, the cemetery was the final call for such composers as Berlioz (died 1869) and Offenbach (died 1880). The poet Heinrich Heine was forced to leave Germany in 1848 because of his political convictions. The author of the *Lorelei,* who was born Jewish but converted to Christianity, was buried in Montmartre in 1856. The great Stendhal was buried here, as were the Goncourt brothers, and poets such as Alfred de Vigny and Théophile Gautier. But when we're in the area, we like to pay our respects at the tomb of Alphonsine Plessis, the heroine of *La Dame aux Camélias,* and Madame Récamier, who taught the world how to lounge. Métro: Clichy.

On to the Moulin Rouge

The **Museum of Old Montmartre,** 17 rue St.-Vincent, is in the charming 17th-century house of Roze de Rosimond, a member of the acting troupe of Molière's "Illustre Théâtre." Utrillo once lived in the building. With its wide collection of Vieux Montmartre, it makes for an interesting visit that needn't take too long. Charging a 6F ($1.37) admission, it is open daily from 2:30 to 7:30 p.m. (from 11 a.m. to 7:30 p.m. on Sunday).

Nearby, at 4 rue des Saules, is the vine-covered **Lapin Agile** ("Agile Rabbit"), an old inn that once attracted Utrillo, Picasso, and a host of other artists (see our nightlife recommendations). If you take the winding rue Lepic (ordered built by Napoleon III) in the direction of Place Blanche, you will pass along the way the **Moulin de la Galette** (1 Avenue Junot), immortalized in the Renoir painting at the Jeu de Paume Museum. In 1886, Van Gogh lived at 54 rue Lepic with Guillaumin. The interesting old house is still standing today, although in dire need of repair.

At the Place Blanche stands an even better known windmill, the **Moulin Rouge,** one of the most famous nightclubs in the world, immortalized by Toulouse-Lautrec.

Down to Pigalle

From Place Blanche, you can begin a descent down **Boulevard de Clichy,** fighting off the pornographers and hustlers trying to lure you into tawdry striptease joints. With some rare exceptions—notably the citadels of the chansonniers—Boulevard de Clichy is one gigantic tourist trap. Still, as Times Square is to New York, Boulevard de Clichy is to Paris: anyone who comes to Paris invariably winds up there.

The boulevard strips and peels its way down to **Place Pigalle,** the nudity center of Paris. Ironically, the square is named after a French sculptor, Pigalle, whose closest association with nudity was a depiction of Voltaire in the buff. Place Pigalle, of course, was the notorious "Pig Alley" of World War II. Toulouse-Lautrec had his studio right off Pigalle at 5 Avenue Frochot. In the days when she was lonely and hungry, Edith Piaf (the "little sparrow") sang in the alleyways off Pigalle, hoping to earn a few francs for the night.

At Cirque Médrano, the boulevard changes its name and becomes **Boulevard de Rochechouart.** Seurat maintained his studio at No. 128 on this wide thoroughfare, much frequented today by prostitutes of both sexes.

LE MARAIS: When Paris began to overflow the confines of Île de la Cité in the 13th century, the citizenry settled in le Marais, the marsh that used to be flooded regularly by the high-rising Seine. By the 17th century, le Marais had reached the pinnacle of fashion, becoming the center of aristocratic Paris. At that time, many of its great mansions—now in decay—were built by the finest craftsmen in France.

In the 18th and 19th centuries, fashion deserted le Marais for the expanding Faubourg St.-Germain and Faubourg St.-Honoré. Industry eventually took over the quarter, and the once-elegant hotels were turned into tenements. There was talk of demolishing this seriously blighted sector, but in 1962 the alarmed Comité de Sauvegarde du Marais banded together and saved the historic district.

Today, the 17th-century mansions are being restored, and many artisans are moving in. The *Herald-Tribune* called it the latest refuge of the Paris artisan fleeing from the tourist-trampled St.-Germain-des-Prés. The "marsh" sprawls across the 3rd and 4th Arrondissements, bounded by the Grands Boulevards, the rue du Temple, the Place des Vosges, and the Seine.

A good place to start your exploration of le Marais is at—

Place de la Bastille

Here, on July 14, 1789, a mob of people attacked the Bastille and so began the French Revolution. Here? In all this traffic? Precisely, for nothing remains of the historic Bastille, built in 1369. It was completely torn down. A symbol of despotism, it once contained eight towers, rising 100 feet high. Many prisoners—some sentenced by Louis XIV for "witchcraft"—were kept within its walls, the best-known being "The Man in the Iron Mask." And yet, when the fortress was stormed by the revolutionary mob, only seven prisoners were discovered. The Marquis de Sade had been transferred to the madhouse 10 days earlier. The authorities had discussed razing it anyway. So in itself the attack meant nothing. What it symbolized, however, and what it started will never be forgotten. Bastille Day is celebrated with great festivity each July 14.

It was much easier to storm the Bastille, we think, than it is to skip by the speeding cars to the center, where the **Colonne de Juillet** (July Column) doesn't commemorate the Revolution at all. It honors instead the victims of the July Revolution of 1830, which put Louis-Philippe on the throne. The tower is crowned by a winged nude, the God of Liberty, a star emerging from his head. Because the monument is in a bad state, it is dangerous to climb its 238 steps. Therefore, it has been closed to the public until it is restored.

Incidentally, on this square you can dine at La Tour d'Argent, but not *the* Tour d'Argent, as you'll quickly discover by looking at the prices.

From Place de la Bastille, walk up the rue St.-Antoine, turn right on rue des Tournelles, and note the statue (1895) honoring the 18th-century dramatist Beaumarchais *(The Barber of Seville* and *The Marriage of Figaro).* Cut left again, on the colorful and typical rue Pas-de-la-Mule ("Footsteps of the Mule"), and you'll soon note by the posters and graffiti that you're in a hotbed of left-wing French politics. Then, suddenly, you've entered the enchanted—

Place des Vosges

It is the oldest square in Paris and was once the most fashionable. Right in the heart of Marais, it was called the Palais Royal in the days of Henri IV. The king planned to live here, but his assassin, Ravaillac, had other intentions for him. Henry II was killed while jousting on the square in 1559, in the shadow of the Hôtel des Tournelles. His widow, Catherine de Medici, had the place torn down.

Place des Vosges, once the major dueling ground of Europe, is considered one of the first truly planned squares in Europe. Its grand-siècle rosy-red brick houses are ornamented with white stone. The covered arcades allowed people to shop at all times, even in the rain—quite an innovation at the time. In the 18th century, chestnut trees were added, sparking a controversy that continues to this day: critics say that the addition spoils the perspective.

Over the years, such personages as Descartes, Pascal, Cardinal Richelieu, the courtesan Marion Delorme, Gautier, Daudet, and the most famous letter-writer of all time, Madame de Sévigné, lived there. Its best-known occupant was Victor Hugo (his home, now a museum, is the only house that can be visited without a private invitation). The great writer could be seen rushing under the arcades of the square to a rendezvous with his mistress. In the center of the square is a statue of Louis XIII on horseback. An excellent but expensive restaurant facing the square is the Coconnas (see the restaurant chapter).

Victor Hugo Museum

Appraisals of Hugo have been varied. Some have called him a genius. Cocteau said he was a madman, and an American composer discovered that in the folly of his dotage he carved furniture—with his teeth! From 1832 to 1848, the novelist and poet lived on the second floor at 6 Place des Vosges, in the old Hôtel Rohan Guéménée, itself built in 1610 on what was then the Place Royale. His maison is owned by the City of Paris, which has taken over two additional floors.

A leading figure in the French Romantic movement, Hugo is known for such novels as *The Hunchback of Notre Dame* and *Les Misérables*. The museum owns some of Hugo's furniture as well as pieces that once belonged to Juliette Drouet, the mistress with whom he lived in exile on Guernsey, one of the Channel Islands.

Worth the visit are Hugo's drawings, more than 450, illustrating scenes from his own works. See, in particular, his *Le Serpent*. Mementos of the great writer abound: samples of his handwriting, his inkwell, first editions of his works, and the death mask in his bedroom. A painting of his funeral procession at the Arc de Triomphe in 1885 is on display. Portraits and souvenirs of Hugo's family are also plentiful. Of the furnishings, especially interesting is a chinoiserie salon. The collection even contains Daumier caricatures and a bust of Hugo by David d'Angers, which—when compared to Rodin's—looks saccharine.

The maison is open daily, except Mondays and legal holidays, from 10 a.m. to 5:40 p.m.; 3F (68¢) admission, free on Sundays.

From the Place des Vosges, the rue des Francs-Bourgeois leads to the—

Hôtel Carnavalet and Musée de la Chasse

At this museum, the history of Paris comes alive in intimately personal terms—right down to the chessmen Louis XVI used to distract his mind in the days before he went to the guillotine. A renowned Renaissance palace, it was built in 1544 by Pierre Lescot and Jean Goujon; later it was acquired by Madame de Carnavalet. The great François Mansart transformed it between the years 1655 and 1661.

But its best-known memories concern one of history's most famous letter-writers, Madame de Sévigné, who moved into the house in 1677, losing her dear friend La Rochefoucauld two years later. Fanatically devoted to her daughter (until she had to live with her), she poured out nearly every detail of her life in letters, virtually ignoring her son. A native of the Marais district, she died at her daughter's château in 1696. It wasn't until 1866 that the City of Paris acquired the mansion, eventually turning it into a museum.

You enter at 23 rue de Sévigné, any time between 10 a.m. and 5:30 p.m., and pay a 5F ($1.14) admission (free on Sundays). Closed Monday.

Many salons depict events related to the Revolution: a bust of Marat, a portrait of Danton, and a replica of the Bastille (one painting shows its demolition). Another salon is devoted exclusively to the story of the captivity of the royal family at the Temple, including the bed in which Madame Elizabeth slept. The exercise book of the Dauphin is there—the pathetic legacy he left the world before his mysterious disappearance.

There is much to see: the Bouvier collection on the first floor, façades of old apothecary shops, extensive wrought-iron works, a bust of Napoleon by Charles-Louis Corbet, a Cazals portrait of Paul Verlaine that makes him look like Lenin, Jean Beraud's parade of 19th-century opulence, and Baron François Gerard's painting of Madame Récamier—lounging, of course.

You end your tour in the immaculate courtyard in front of a statue of Louis XIV (which Coysevox originally did for l'Hôtel de Ville).

Nearby, François Mansart also built the Hôtel Guénégaud, which the Sommer Foundation has restored and turned into the **Musée de la Chasse et de la Nature** at 60 rue des Archives (Métro: Rambuteau). It is open daily except Tuesdays from 10 a.m. to 5 p.m.; 7F ($1.60) admission fee. Photographs at the entrance depict the shocking state of the building's decay before its subsequent restoration.

Mounted heads are plentiful, ranging from the antelope to the elephant, from the bushbuck to the waterbuck, from the moose to the hideous "bush pig." Rembrandt's sketch of a lion is here, along with a collection of wild-animal portraits by Desportes (1661-1743). The hunt tapestries are outstanding and often amusing—one a cannibalistic romp, another showing a helmeted man standing eye to eye with a bear he is stabbing to death. The rifles, some inlaid with pearls, others engraved with ivory, are exceptional, many dating from the 17th century.

A short walk from the hunting museum deposits you at a Paris landmark steeped in French history:

The National Archives

On Napoleon's orders, the Palais Soubise was made the official records repository of France. But the building itself—designed by the much-underrated Delamair—is as fascinating as, or even more so than, the exhibits contained within. Apartments once belonging to the Prince and Princess de Soubise have been turned into the **Musée de l'Histoire de France**, open 2 to 5 p.m. daily except Tuesdays; 4F (91¢) admission, 2F (46¢) on Sundays. The entrance is at

60 rue des Francs-Bourgeois. You enter into the colonnaded Court of Honor. Before going inside, walk around the corner to 58 rue des Archives to see the medieval turreted gateway to the original Clisson mansion.

The Clisson mansion gave way to the residence of the Dukes of Guise, who owned the property until it was purchased by the Soubise family. The Princess Soubise was once the mistress of Louis XIV, and apparently the Sun King was very generous, giving her the funds to remodel and redesign the palace.

The museum contains documents that go back to Charlemagne and even earlier. The letter collection is highly valued, exhibiting the penmanship of not only Joan of Arc, Marie Antoinette (a farewell letter), Louis XVI (his will), Danton, Robespierre, and Napoleon I, but of Franklin and Washington as well. The museum possesses the only known sketch made of the maid from Orléans while she was still alive. Even the jailer's keys to the old Bastille are found here. For a much later Princess de Soubise, Germain Boffrand in 1735 designed a Salon Ovale, with "parfaites (faultless) expressions." Adding to the lush decor, the gilt, and the crystal are paintings by Van Loo, Boucher, and Natoire.

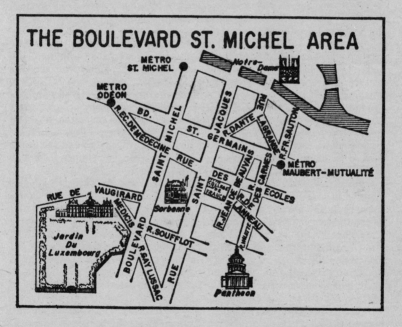

From the Hôtel de Rohan to the Hôtel de Sully

Within the same precincts (entrance is at 87 rue Vieille-du-Temple) is Delamair's **Hôtel de Rohan,** once occupied by the cardinal of the "diamond necklace scandal," which implicated Marie Antoinette. That was the fourth Cardinal de Rohan. The first, the original occupant of the hôtel, was reputed to be the son of Louis XIV.

The interior is open to the public only for guided visits on Mondays, Wednesdays, and Fridays at 3:30 p.m. The main attraction is the amusing Salon des Singes (Monkey Room) of the 18th century. In the courtyard (open working days 9 a.m. to 6 p.m.) you can see a stunning bas-relief depicting a nude Apollo and four horses against a background exploding with sunbursts.

Also on rue Vieille-du-Temple, at No. 47, is the **Hôtel des Ambassadeurs de Hollande**, where Beaumarchais wrote *The Marriage of Figaro*. It is one of the most splendid mansions in le Marais—and it was never occupied by the Dutch Embassy. You cannot go inside.

From rue Vieille-du-Temple, turn onto **rue des Rosiers** ("Street of Rosebushes"). Again the name misleads. Actually, it's one of the most colorful and typical streets remaining from the old Jewish quarter. The Star of David shines here; Hebrew letters flash (in neon, no less); couscous is sold from the shops run by Moroccan or Algerian Jews; bearded old men sit in the doorway watching time pass them by; restaurants serve strictly kosher meats, and signs appeal for the liberation of the Jews of Russia.

Whatever you're in the market for—goose sausage stuffed in a goose neck, roots of black horseradish, pickled lemons—you'll find it here.

Although the courtyard at the 17th-century **Hôtel de Beauvais**, 68 rue François Miron, is badly damaged, it remains one of the most charming in Paris. A plaque commemorates the fact that Mozart inhabited the maison in 1763. Although he was only seven years old, he played at the court of Versailles. Louis XIV presented the mansion to Madame Beauvais, who reportedly had the honor of introducing young Louis, then 16, to the facts of life.

Nearby, the **Hôtel de Sens**, a Paris landmark at 1 rue du Figuier, was built between the 1470s and 1519 for the archbishops of Sens. Along with the Cluny on the Left Bank, it is the only domestic architecture remaining from the 15th century. Long after the archbishops had departed, 1605 to be exact, it was inhabited by the scandalous Queen Margot, wife of Henri IV. Her new lover—"younger and more virile"—slew the discarded one while she looked on in great amusement. The restoration of the Hôtel de Sens was, as usual, the subject of great controversy; nonetheless, today it houses the **Forney Library**. Leaded-glass windows and turrets characterize the façade; you can go into the courtyard to see more of the ornate stone decoration—the gate is open from 1:30 to 8 p.m., except on Sundays and Mondays.

Finally, the **Hôtel de Sully**, 62 rue St.-Antoine. Work began on this mansion in 1625, on the orders of Jean Androuet de Cerceau. In 1634 it was acquired by the Duc de Sully, who had been Henri IV's minister of finance before the king was assassinated in 1610. After a straight-laced life as "the accountant of France," Sully broke loose in his declining years, adorning himself with diamonds and garish rings . . . and a young bride. Noted for her indiscretion, the young bride told not only her confidantes but her husband as well of her preference for "very young" men, whom she openly invited to their home. Sully, incidentally, was 74 years old when he moved to the Marais address with her. He died seven years later.

The Hôtel de Sully was acquired by Paris just after World War II. Recently restored, the relief-studded façade is especially appealing. Unless you want to go to a lot of trouble making special arrangements for a visit, you have to settle for a look at the courtyard. The ideal way is to attend a June concert during the Festival du Marais.

THE LATIN QUARTER: This is the precinct of the University of Paris (often called the Sorbonne), lying on the Left Bank in the 5th Arrondissement—where students meet and fall in love over coffee and croissants. Rabelais called it the "Quartier Latin," because of the students and professors who spoke Latin in the classroom and on the streets. The sector teems with belly dancers, exotic restaurants (from Vietnamese to Balkan), sidewalk cafés, bookstalls, *caveaux*, and the *clochards* and *chiffonniers* (the bums and ragpickers).

A good starting point for your tour might be **Place St.-Michel,** where Balzac used to get water from the fountain when he was a youth. This center was the scene of much Resistance fighting in the summer of 1944. The quarter centers around **Boulevard St.-Michel,** to the south (the students call it "Boul Mich").

From the "place," your back to the Seine, you can cut left down **rue de la Huchette,** the setting of Elliot Paul's *The Last Time I Saw Paris.* Paul first wandered into this typical street "on a soft summer evening, and entirely by chance," in 1923. Although much has changed since his time, some of the buildings are so old they often have to be propped up by timbers. Paul captured the spirit of the street more evocatively than anyone, writing of "the delivery wagons, makeshift vehicles propelled by pedaling boys, pushcarts of itinerant vendors, knife-grinders, umbrella menders, a herd of milch goats, and the neighborhood pedestrians." The local bordello has closed, however.

Branching off from Huchette is **rue du Chat Qui Pêche** (the "Street of the Cat Who Fishes"), said to be the shortest, narrowest street in the world, containing not one door and only one window. It is usually filled with garbage or lovers . . . or both.

Now, down rue de la Harpe to rue St.-Séverin and—

The Church of St.-Séverin

This flamboyant Gothic building, just a short walk from the Seine, hardly recaptures the lifestyle of its namesake, the ascetic recluse of the sixth century. An act of Henri I in the 11th century gave the church to Paris, and by the end of the 15th century it was imitating some of the arhictectural features of Notre-Dame across the river. At one point in its long history, Mlle. de Montpensier (La Grande Mademoiselle) was one of its parishioners and certainly its heaviest financial contributor.

Before entering, walk around the church to see its gargoyles, birds of prey, and reptilian monsters projecting from the top. To the right, facing the church, is the "garden of ossuaries" of the 15th century. The entrance on the rue des Prêtres (Métro: St.-Michel or Maubert-Mutualité) leads to the wide interior. Inside, the stained glass is its most obvious adornment—in cobalt, burgundy, amber, magenta, white-gold, royal-blue, indigo, oyster-pink, ruby-red.

The present church was built from 1210 to 1230, then reconstructed in 1458. The tower was completed in 1487, the chapels between 1498 and 1520. Hardouin-Mansart designed the Chapel of the Communion in 1673 when he was 27 years old.

Across rue St.-Jacques lies the—

Church of St.-Julien-le-Pauvre

This church, at 1 rue St.-Julien-le-Pauvre, occupies a virtual oasis in Paris. Stand first at the gateway and look at the beginning of rue Galande, especially the old houses with the steeples of St. Séverin rising across the way—one of the most characteristic and most painted scenes on the Left Bank. You enter through a courtyard, listening to chirping birds, walking into a slice of medieval Paris, isolated and aloof. The garden to the left of the entrance offers the best view of Notre-Dame.

The church is like a country chapel, and everybody from Rabelais to Thomas Aquinas has passed through its doors. Before the sixth century, a chapel stood on this spot. The present structure goes back to the Longpont monks, who began work on it in 1170, which makes it the oldest existing church in Paris. In 1655, it was given to the Hôtel Dieu, and in time became a small warehouse for salt. In 1889, however, it was turned over to the followers of the Melchite Greek rite, an eastern branch of the Byzantine church.

Do stop by—then head for the major attractions on the Left Bank:

The Cluny Museum

You stand in the cobblestoned Court of Honor, admiring the flamboyant Gothic building with its clinging vines, turreted walls, gargoyles, and dormers with seashell motifs. Along with the Hôtel de Sens in Le Marais, the Hôtel de Cluny is all that remains of domestic medieval architecture in Paris. Originally, the Cluny was the mansion—built over the ruins of a Roman bath—of a rich 15th-century abbot.

By 1515, it was the residence of Mary Tudor, teenage widow of Louis XII and daughter of Henry VII of England and Elizabeth of York.

Seized during the Revolution, the Cluny was rented in 1833 to Alexandre du Sommerard, who adorned it with his collection of medieval works of art. Upon his death, both the building and the collection were bought back by the government.

The present-day collection of arts and crafts of the Middle Ages is considered the finest in the world. Most people come primarily to see the Unicorn Tapestries, viewed by critics (and we heartily concur) as the most outstanding tapestries in the world. A beautiful princess and her handmaiden, beasts of prey, and just plain pets—all the romance of the age of chivalry lives on in these remarkable yet mysterious tapestries. They were discovered only a century ago in the Château de Boussac in Auvergne. Five seem to deal with the five senses (one, for example, depicts a unicorn looking into a mirror held up by a dour-faced maiden). The sixth shows a woman under an elaborate tent with jewels, her pet dog resting on an embroidered cushion beside her. The lovable unicorn and his friendly companion, a lion, hold back the flaps. The background in red and green forms a rich carpet of spring flowers, fruit-laden trees, birds, rabbits, donkeys, dogs, goats, lambs, and monkeys.

The other exhibitions are wide ranging, including a grille from the cloisters of the 16th-century church of Augerolles; a 16th-century retable—*The Passion* —from Anvers; a 15th-century Florentine (lifesize) John the Baptist; 14th-century French consoles; four statues—Saint Barthelmy sans head—from Sainte Chapelle, dating from 1243-1248; 13th-century crosses, studded with gems; golden chalices, manuscripts, ivory carvings, vestments, leather work, jewelry, coins, a 13th-century Adam, and heads and fragments of statues from Notre-Dame de Paris recently discovered. In the fan-vaulted medieval chapel hang tapestries depicting scenes from the life of St. Stephen.

Downstairs are the ruins of the Roman baths, dating supposedly from around 200 A.D. You wander through a display of Gallic and Roman sculptures and an interesting marble bathtub engraved with lions. A collection of altars dates from the days of Tiberius. Both the museum and baths are open daily except Tuesdays from 9:45 a.m. to noon and from 2 to 5:15 p.m. 7F ($1.60) for admission, only 3.50F (80¢) on Sundays. The museum is at 6 Place Paul-Painlevé. Métro: Odéon or St.-Michel.

Head down the Boul Mich, and shortly you'll arrive at—

The Sorbonne

The University of Paris—everybody calls it the Sorbonne—is one of the most famous institutions in the world. Founded in the 13th century, it had become the most prestigious university in the West by the 14th century, drawing such professors as Thomas Aquinas. Reorganized by Napoleon in 1806, the Sorbonne is today the premier university of France.

At first glance from Place de la Sorbonne, it seems architecturally undistinguished. In truth, it was rather indiscriminately reconstructed at the turn of the century. Not so the **Church of the Sorbonne,** built in 1635 by Le Mercier which contains the marble tomb of Cardinal Richelieu, a work by Girardon based on a design by Le Brun. At his feet, the statue *Science in Tears* is remarkable.

At the end of rue Soufflot stands—

The Panthéon

Some of the most famous men in the history of France (Victor Hugo, for one) are buried here, in austere grandeur, on the crest of the mount of St. Geneviève. In 1744, Louis XV made a vow that if he recovered from a mysterious illness, he would build a church to replace the decayed Abbey of St. Geneviève. He recovered. Madame de Pompadour's brother hired Soufflot for the job. He designed the church in 1764, in the form of a Greek cross, with a dome reminiscent of that of St. Paul's Cathedral in London. Soufflot died, and the work was carried out by his pupil Rondelet, who completed the structure nine years after his master's death.

Came the Revolution, and the church was converted into a "Temple of Fame"—ultimately a pantheon for the great men of France. The body of Mirabeau was buried here, although his remains were later removed. Likewise, Marat was only a temporary tenant. However, Voltaire's body was exhumed and placed here—and allowed to remain.

In the 19th century, the building changed roles so many times—first a church, then a pantheon, then a church—that it was hard to keep its function straight. After Victor Hugo was buried here, it became a pantheon once more. Other notable men entombed within include Jean-Jacques Rousseau, Soufflot himself, Émile Zola, and Louis Braille.

The finest frescoes—the Puvis de Chavannes—are found at the end of the left wall before you enter the crypt. One illustrates St. Geneviève bringing supplies to relieve the victims of the famine. The very best fresco depicts her white-draped head looking out over moonlit medieval Paris, the city whose patroness she became.

Charging 6F ($1.37), 3F (68¢) on Sundays, the Panthéon is open daily except Tuesdays from 10 a.m. to 4:30 p.m. Métro: St.-Michel.

ALONG THE SEINE: A stroll along the banks and quays of the noble Seine is for many visitors the most memorable walk in Paris. Some of the city's most important monuments, such as Notre-Dame on the Île de la Cité, are best viewed from the riverbank. Many of them, such as the mighty façade of the Louvre, take on even more interest at night when they are floodlit.

Famous bridges, such as **Pont Neuf,** the oldest in Paris, recall the Middle Ages. (In those days, you came to the bridge to have your tooth pulled.) The best-known footbridge in Paris is **Pont des Arts,** its old-fashioned lampposts bearing yellow and orange lights. One observer wrote, "The effect is like that of a moving palette, with swirls of mixed hues dramatizing the Seine."

Between the Louvre and the Institut de France, the Pont des Arts was the first cast-iron bridge built in Paris. It is said that Napoleon rode across it on horseback, surveyed the view, and quietly but emphatically proclaimed, "Everything shall remain as it is." Strolling musicians frequented it in the 19th century, and the bridge became a great favorite with the promenade crowd. Because it was planted with boxed trees, it was known as the garden over the Seine.

Seven other crossings lie between the Invalides and the Île de la Cité, but those are open to vehicular traffic.

The Seine is called the loveliest avenue in Paris. You walk past flower vendors, seed merchants, pet shops, sellers of caged birds (parakeets, finches, fantail pigeons, pheasants, and parrots), perhaps stopping at one of the *bouquinistes* or booksellers which line the parapets. Postcards, stamps, souvenirs, reproductions of paintings . . . the *bouquinistes* sell more than books. Suitable for framing are the prints and drawings of Vieux Paris. Incidentally, along the way you'll pass fishermen called by one writer "the most patient in the world."

If you should fall in love with the Seine, you can always moor your houseboat here, as did the writer Anaïs Nin, recording her experience in a memorable short story, "Houseboat."

You may also want to ride on the Seine. The glass-topped **Bateaux Mouches** offer tours leaving from the Right Bank at the Pont de l'Alma (Métro: Alma Marceau). Two popular observers of the Parisian scene have called these boats "big sharks with their pointed Plexiglas snouts." Boats begin running at 10 a.m. Afternoon departures are from 2 to 6 p.m. The fare is 12F ($2.74), increasing to 18F ($4.11) at night. It's possible to take a luncheon cruise on the weekends, leaving at 1 p.m. and costing 100F ($22.83). The evening dinner cruise leaves at 8:30, the set meal going for 225F ($51.88).

Another company running boat rides on the Seine, with commentary in English, is **Les Vedettes,** operating streamlined, glass-enclosed cruisers. Costing 15F ($3.42), these hour-long tours are operated from 9:30 a.m. to noon and from 1:30 to 6:30 p.m. They depart every 20 minutes. The floodlit glory of Paris is revealed on their "Illuminations Cruise," May 10 to September 20. Boats leave at 9 p.m. and again at 10 p.m. All these luxury cruises leave from the Pont d'Iéna (the subject of the Gauguin painting).

2. Other Major Sights

Those with more time can plunge deeper into the soul of Paris, beginning at the—

ÎLE SAINT-LOUIS: As you walk across the little iron footbridge from the rear of Notre-Dame, you descend into a world of tree-shaded quays, aristocratic town houses and courtyards, restaurants, and antique shops.

The sister island of the Île de la Cité is primarily residential; its denizens fiercely guard their heritage, privileges, and special position. If you meet a resident on the Riviera and ask him where he lives, he doesn't answer just "Paris," he'll say perhaps "Île Saint-Louis," or, more defiantly, "Île."

Saint-Louis was originally two "islets," one named "Island of the Heifers." It was popular as a dueling ground, prompting one foreigner to write home, "There isn't a Frenchman worth his salt who has not slain a man in a duel." The two islands were ordered joined by Louis XIII.

The number of famous people who have occupied these patrician mansions is now a legend. Plaques on the façades make it easier to identify them. Madame Curie, for example, lived at 36 Quai de Bethune, near Ponte de la Tournelle, from 1912 until her death in 1934.

The most exciting mansion (and there is almost universal agreement on that) is the **Hôtel de Lauzun,** built in 1657. It is surely one of the most elegant town houses of Paris. It is owned by the city, and permission to visit it requires bureaucratic red tape. At 17 Quai d'Anjou, it is named after the 17th-century rogue the Duc de Lauzun, famous lover and on-again-off-again favorite of Louis XIV (he once hid under the Sun King's bed while the monarch made love to his mistress of the moment). At the hôtel, the French courtier was secretly married to "La Grande Mademoiselle" (the Duchess of Montpensier), much to the dislike of Louis XIV, who dealt with the matter by hustling him off to the Bastille.

That "Flower of Evil" Charles Baudelaire, French poet of the 19th century, lived at Lauzun with his "Black Venus," Jeanne Duval. At the same time that he was squandering the family fortune, Baudelaire was working on poems that celebrated the erotic. Though he had high hopes for them, they were dismissed by many as "obscene, vulgar, perverse, and decadent." (It was only in 1949 that the French court lifted the ban on all the works.) Baudelaire attracted such artists as Delacroix and Courbet to his apartment, which was often filled with the aroma of hashish. Occupying another apartment was 19th-century novelist Théophile Gautier ("art for art's sake"), who is remembered today chiefly for his *Mademoiselle de Maupin*.

Voltaire lived at 2 Quai d'Anjou, in the **Hôtel Lambert,** with his mistress Emilie de Breteuil, the Marquise du Châteley, who had an "understanding" husband. The couple's quarrels at the Hôtel Lambert were known all over Europe (Emilie did not believe in confining her charms, once described as "nutmeg-grater skin" and "bad teeth," to her husband or her lover.) But not even Frederick, king of Prussia, could permanently break up her liaison with Voltaire.

The mansion was built by Louis Le Vau in 1645 for Nicolas Lambert de Thorigny, the president of the Chambre des Comptes. For a century, the hôtel was the home of the royal family of Poland, the Czartoryskis, who entertained Chopin, among others.

Further along, at No. 9, stands the house where Honoré Daumier, the painter, sculptor, and lithographer, lived between 1846 and 1863. From that house he satirized the petite bourgeoisie of his day. In hundreds upon hundreds of lithographs he attacked corruption in the French government. His caricature of Louis-Philippe netted him a six-month jail sentence.

THE PALAIS ROYAL: At the demolished Café Foy in the Palais Royal, Camille Desmoulins jumped up on a table and shouted for the mob "to fight to the death." The date was July 13, 1789. The French Revolution had begun. But the renown of the Palais Royal goes back much further. Facing the Louvre, the gardens were planted in 1634 for Cardinal Richelieu, who presented them to Louis XIII. As a child, the future Louis XIV played around the fountain, once nearly drowning. Children frolic here to this day.

In time the property became the residence of the dukes of Orléans. Philippe-Égalité, a cousin of Louis XVI, built his apartments on the grounds, and subsequently rented them to prostitutes. By the 20th century those same apartments were rented by such artists as Colette and Cocteau. Of the gardens Colette wrote, "It is as though I were living in the provinces under the shadow of the parish church! I go into the temple en passant." (A plaque at 9 rue Beaujolais marks the entrance to her apartment, which she inhabited until her death in 1954.)

New York-born American actor and playwright John Howard Payne wrote *Home, Sweet Home* while living in one of the apartments.

Let us turn the clock back again: Napoleon Bonaparte, then an 18-year-old lieutenant, met his first prostitute in the Palais Royal. Robespierre and Danton dined here. An actress, Mlle. Montansier, "knew" many of them, including the Corsican. Charlotte Corday came this way, looking for a dagger with which to kill Marat. During the Directoire, when gambling dens flourished at the Palais Royal, foreigners reported seeing Frenchmen leaving the salons without their silk breeches—they had literally lost their trousers at the tables!

Today, a sleepy provincial air remains. It's hard to imagine its former life. From the Place Colette, you enter the Court of Honor, colonnaded on three sides. The palace is the headquarters of the Councils of State these days, and the Court of Honor is a parking lot during the day. In the center of the Palais Royal is the Galerie d'Orléans, with two fountains and many a colonnade. You can stroll through the gardens or down the Galerie Montpensier, filled with little shops no one but stamp collectors ever seem to patronize.

Everything seems sadly neglected, though it has a physical location that could make it the most elegant boutique district of Paris.

Métro: Palais-Royal.

PLACE VENDÔME: Always aristocratic, sometimes royal, Place Vendôme enjoyed its golden age in the heyday of the Second Empire. Dress designers—the great ones, such as Worth—introduced the crinoline there. Louis Napoleon lived here, wooing his future empress, Eugénie de Montijo, at his address at Hôtel du Rhin. In its halcyon days, the waltzes of Strauss echoed across the plaza. But in time they were replaced by cannon fire.

Today the most prestigious tenant on the plaza is the Ritz. Banks and offices abound. Still, the Place Vendôme is considered one of the most harmonious squares in France, evoking the Paris of le grand siècle—that is, the age of Louis XIV.

The square is dominated today by a column crowned by Napoleon. The plaza was originally planned by Mansart to honor Louis XIV—so it's a good thing he died earlier. There was a statue of the Sun King here until the Revolution, when it was replaced briefly by "Liberty."

Then came Napoleon, who ordered that a sort of Trajan's Column be erected in honor of the victor at Austerlitz. The Napoleon himself won the battle was "incidental." The column was made of bronze melted from captured Russian and Austrian cannons.

After Napoleon's downfall, the statue was replaced with one of Henri IV, everybody's favorite king and every woman's favorite man. Later Napoleon surmounted it once again, this time in uniform and without the pose of a Caesar.

The Communards of 1871, who detested royalty and the false promises of emperors, pulled down the statue. The artist Courbet is said to have led the raid. For his part in the drama, he was jailed and fined the cost of restoring the statue. He couldn't pay it, of course, and was forced into exile in Switzerland. Eventually, the statue of Napoleon, wrapped in a Roman toga, finally won out.

The plaza is one of the best known in Paris. It has attracted tenants such as Chopin, who lived at No. 12 until his death in 1849. Who was Vendôme, you ask? He was the son (delicate writers refer to him as "the natural son") of the roving Henri IV and his best-known mistress, Gabrielle d'Estrées. Métro: Opéra.

AROUND THE HÔTEL DE VILLE: Back in the good old days, you could stroll down to the Hôtel de Ville for an evening's amusement. If it was a good day, you could see Robespierre being hauled off to the guillotine, Foulon getting lynched on a lamppost, or revelers tossing cats into a bonfire.

You can still visit the district, but the entertainment isn't what it used to be. Take the Métro (one of four lines) to **Place du Châtelet**—a theatrical square, dominated by Napoleon's palm fountain, at the foot of which rest four sphinx-like figures.

On one side of the square is the **Théâtre de la Ville,** honoring Sarah Bernhardt; on the other, the **Théâtre Municipal du Châtelet,** the largest in Paris. A fortress once stood on this spot, overlooking the Seine, and in it was imprisoned the highwayman Cartouche. Before he was removed to the Conciergerie, the fashionable ladies of Paris considered it "sport" to peer in at his cell, giggling their little hearts out.

In a satellite square stands the **Tower of St. Jacques,** isolated and alone today. In the flamboyant Gothic style, it was erected between 1508 and 1522, but the church to which it was attached was destroyed by revolutionaries. For some reason, somebody decided to spare the tower, and it remains as an anachronistic landmark at the point where rue de Rivoli meets the Boulevard de Sébastopol. You can't scale it as Pascal did to make experiments, but you can sit in the surrounding park and either watch the cars whiz around you or contemplate the marble statue of Pascal, his robes clustered around him, a curious position for the founder of the modern theory of probability.

From Place du Châtelet, take the Avenue Victoria, named after the English queen, to the **Hôtel de Ville,** at Place de l'Hôtel-de-Ville. In the 1920s two elegantly dressed American visitors arrived demanding rooms. They had seen photographs of the pseudo-Renaissance-style building and had mistakenly assumed that it provided deluxe accommodations. Hôtel de Ville, of course, means town hall in French.

One of the most flamboyant buildings in Paris, the municipal building boasts a façade studded with 136 statue-filled niches honoring such Frenchmen as Pigalle. It is not the original building that stood on this spot. After France's defeat by the Prussians in 1871, the Communards burned down the building. It was rebuilt in the following decade.

Town Hall Square was once the infamous **Place de Grève,** center of public executions. Before cheering crowds, Leonora Galigai, confidante of Marie de Medici, was beheaded following her conviction on a charge of witchcraft. When "the Jack the Ripper of France," Cartouche, was brought to the execution stand, he "squealed" for almost a full day, naming his accomplices. They killed him nonetheless.

The most publicized execution was that of Ravaillac, the mystic who killed Henri IV. As French historian Roger-Armand Weigert put it: "He was tortured with red-hot pincers, burned with 'fire and brimstone,' sprinkled with hot lead, boiling oil, pitch, burning resin, wax and brimstone melted together, and then pulled apart and dismembered by four horses." The year was 1610. Some 60 years later, the Marquise de Brinvilliers was beheaded for being a bad cook. She was. Her arsenic-flavored cuisine killed both her father and two of her brothers.

Behind the Town Hall on the Place St.-Gervais is the **Church of St. Gervais and St. Protais,** named after two Roman martyrs. The façade—the first of the classical style in Paris—incorporates Doric, Ionic, and Corinthian features which have nothing to do with the Gothic interior. The church was begun in 1494, completed in 1657, when much of Paris turned out to see the new and "daring" style.

Inside, the chapels are richly decorated, the art work including a 19th-century sculptured "Christ on the Cross" by Antoine-Auguste. Memorable is the mausoleum of Louis XIV's chancellor, Michel Le Tellier, the work of Pierre Mazeline and Simon Hurtrelle. The oldest chapel, dating from the late 15th century, was dedicated to St. Madeleine. Adjoining it is the Chapel of St. Pierre, finished in 1510.

Many great names in French history have attended the church; Madame de Sévigné was married there. During the Middle Ages, it is said, French justice was dispensed under an elm tree outside.

Head back to the Tower of St. Jacques, walk down rue de Rivoli, then turn left on rue St.-Bon, which turns into steps. A narrow alley leads to rue de la Verrerie and (at No. 76) the **Church of St. Merry,** crowded in by houses (the area is slated for redevelopment). Once this was the liveliest district of Paris, and St. Merry's was known as "the worshipping hole of sluts."

Inside the 16th-century Gothic church are some notable art works, including a painting, *The Blue Virgin,* by Van Loo (to the right of the choir). The large Chapel of the Communion was constructed between 1741 and 1754. It contains a painting, *The Pilgrims d'Emmaüs,* by Charles-Antoine Coypel (1694-1752). Within the church are two haut-reliefs—one a monument to Joan of Arc by Paul-Amboise Slodtz, dated 1743. The attendants close the church around lunchtime every day. After lunch it reopens at 2:30.

LES HALLES: In the 19th century Zola called it "the underbelly of Paris." For eight centuries, Les Halles was the major wholesale fruit, meat, and vegetable market of Paris. The smock-clad vendors, the carcasses of beef, the baskets of what many regarded as the most appetizing fresh vegetables in the world—all that belongs to the past. Today, the action has moved to the steel-and-glass contemporary structure at Rungis, a suburb near Orly Airport. The original edifice, Baltard's old zinc-roofed Second Empire "umbrellas of iron," has been torn down. Part of the newly developing forum at Les Halles consists of luxurious shops and a garden. The ultimate work on the transformation into its new role is scheduled for completion some time in 1982.

Nevertheless, for many tourists a night on the town is still capped by the traditional bowl of onion soup at Les Halles, usually at Au Pied de Cochon ("Pig's Foot") or at Au Chien Qui Fume ("Smoking Dog"), in the wee hours. One of the most classic scenes of Paris was night-owling tourists or elegantly dressed Parisians (many just released from Maxim's) standing at a bar drinking cognac with bloody butchers. Some writers have suggested that one Gérard de Nerval introduced the custom of frequenting Les Halles at such an unearthly hour. (De Nerval was a 19th-century poet whose life was considered "irregular." He hanged himself in 1855.)

A newspaper correspondent described the market scene today this way: "Les Halles is trying to stay alive as one of the few places in Paris where one can eat at any hour of the night."

There is still much to see in the Les Halles district, beginning with the **Church of St.-Eustache,** which, in the opinion of many, is rivaled only by Notre-Dame. In the old days, cabbage vendors came there to pray for their produce. Even before that, it knew the famous and the infamous of its day—everybody from Madame de Pompadour (she was baptized here; so was Richelieu) to Molière, whose funeral was held here in 1673.

In the Gothic-Renaissance style, the church dates from the mid-16th century, though it wasn't completed until 1637. It has been known for its organ recitals ever since Liszt played here in 1866. Inside is the black-marble tomb of Jean Baptiste Colbert, the minister of state under Louis XIV. A marble statue of the statesman rests on top of his tomb, which is flanked by a Coysevox statue of *Abundance* (a horn of flowers) and a J. B. Tuby depiction of *Fidelity*. The main entrance to the church is at 2 rue du Jour (another entrance on rue Rambuteau).

The district around the protective mother church of Les Halles has always had an unsavory reputation. Centuries ago a Parisian was saying how "ideal it was for assassinations." The best-known murder was that of Henri IV ("Vert Galant") in front of No. 11 rue de la Ferronnerie (the street of ironmongers). The assassin was Ravaillac, whose punishment we have described above.

Close at hand, rue des Lombards is worth seeking out. Once it was the banking center of Paris.

ST.-GERMAIN-DES-PRÉS: In the époque of l'aprés-guerre, a long-haired girl in black slacks, black sweater, and black sandals drifted into St.-Germain-des-Prés. Her name was Juliette Greco. She arrived in the heyday of the existentialists, when all the world seemed to revolve around Jean-Paul Sartre, Simone de Beauvoir, and Albert Camus. The Café de Flore, the Brasserie Lipp, and Deux-Magots were the stage settings for the newly arriving postwar bohemians who came there to "existentialize."

In time, Sartre was eulogizing Miss Greco ("She has millions of poems in her throat"); her black outfit was adopted by girls from Paris to California; and eventually she earned the title of "la muse de St.-Germain-des-Prés."

In the 1950s, new names appeared: Françoise Sagan, Gore Vidal, James Baldwin. By the time the 1960s had arrived, the tourists were as firmly entrenched at the Café de Flore and Deux-Magots. The old days are gone, but St.-Germaine-des-Prés remains an interesting quarter of nightclubs in "caves," publishing houses, bookshops, art galleries, Left Bank bistros, and coffeehouses —as well as two historic churches.

St.-Germain-des-Prés Church

Outside it's an early 17th-century town house, a handsome one at that. But beneath that covering, it's one of the oldest churches in Paris, going back to the sixth century, when a Benedictine abbey was founded on the site by Childebert, son of Clovis, the "creator of France." Unfortunately, the marble columns in the triforium are all that remain from that period. At one time, the abbey was a pantheon for Merovingian kings.

Its Romanesque tower, topped by a 19th-century spire, is the most enduring landmark in the village of St.-Germain-des-Prés. Its church bells, however, are hardly noticed by the patrons of Deux-Magots across the way.

The Normans were fond of destroying the abbey, and did so at least four times. The present building, the work of four centuries, has a Romanesque-style nave and a Gothic-style choir with fine capitals. Among the people interred at the church are Descartes and Jean-Casimer, the king of Poland who abdicated his throne.

Church of St. Sulpice

Pause first on the 18th-century **Place St.-Sulpice** (Métro: St.-Sulpice). On the 1844 fountain by Visconti are sculptured likenesses of four 18th-century bishops: Fenelon, Massillon, Bossuet, and Flechier. Napoleon, then a general, was given a stag dinner there in 1799. He liked the banquet but not the square.

When he was promoted he changed it. One of the two towers of the church was never completed.

Work originally began on the church in 1646; the façade, "bastardized classic," was completed in 1745. Many architects, including Le Vau, worked on the building. Some were summarily fired; others, such as the Florentine Servandoni, were discredited.

One of the most notable treasures inside the 360-foot-long church is Servandoni's rococo Chapel of the Madonna, with a marble statue of the Virgin by Pigalle. One critic wrote that you'd have to go to Versailles to find a peer of that chapel. The church contains one of the world's largest organs, with more than 6500 pipes. The Sunday mass concerts—made known by Charles Widor —draw many visitors. Chalgrin designed the organ case in the 18th century.

One of the largest and most prestigious churches in Paris, St. Sulpice was sacked during the Revolution and converted into the Temple of Victory. Camille Desmoulins, the revolutionary who sparked the raiding of the Bastille, was married here.

But the real reason you come to St. Sulpice is to see the Delacroix frescoes in the Chapel of the Angels (first on your right as you enter). Seek out his muscular Jacob wrestling (or is he dancing?) with an effete angel. On the ceiling St. Michael is having his own troubles with the Devil, and yet another mural depicts Heliodorus being driven from the temple. Painted in the final years of his life, the frescoes were a high point in the career of the baffling, romantic Delacroix.

If you are impressed by Delacroix, you can pay him a belated tribute by visiting the—

National Museum of Eugène Delacroix

To art historians, Delacroix is something of an enigma. Even his parentage is a mystery. Many believed that Talleyrand had the privilege of fathering him. The Frank Anderson Trapp biography saw him "as an isolated and atypical individualist—one who respected traditional values, yet emerged as the embodiment of Romantic revolt." By visiting his atelier, you will see one of the most charming squares on the Left Bank and also the romantic garden of the museum.

The apartment is at 6 Place de Fürstenberg (Métro: St.-Germain-des-Prés). You reach the studio through a large arch on a stone courtyard. The house may be visited from 9:45 a.m. to 5:15 p.m. for an admission of 2F (46¢). In spring and summer, a special exhibition takes place in the museum, each year on a different theme about Delacroix. Special price, 5F ($1.14).

Delacroix died in this apartment on August 13, 1863. Lithographs, watercolors, oils, and reproductions fill the house where the artist sat up into the late hours writing his memorable and penetrating journals.

In the Louvre is a portrait of Delacroix as a handsome, strong, mustachioed man with a hairdo that would be au courant today. You'll also have to go to the Louvre to see some of the artist's best-known paintings, such as *Liberty Leading the People.*

A short walk away is the **rue Visconti,** a street obviously designed for pushcarts. At No. 17 is the maison where Balzac established his printing press in 1825. The venture ended in bankruptcy—which forced the author back to his writing desk. In the 17th century, the French dramatist Jean Baptiste Racine lived across the street. Such celebrated actresses as Champmeslé and Clairon were also in residence.

MONTPARNASSE: For the lost generation, life centered around the literary cafés of Montparnasse. Hangouts such as Dôme, Coupole, Rotonde, and the Select became legendary. Artists, especially American expatriates, turned their backs on Montmartre, dismissing it as "too touristy." Picasso, Modigliani, and Man Ray came this way, and Hemingway was a popular figure. So was Fitzgerald when he was poor (when he was in the chips, you'd find him at the Ritz). William Faulkner, Archibald MacLeish, Isadora Duncan, Miró, James Joyce, Ford Madox Ford, even Trotsky—all were here. Except Gertrude Stein, who would not frequent the cafés. To see her, you would have to wait for an invitation to her salon at 27 rue de Fleurus. She bestowed her favor on Sherwood Anderson, Elliot Paul, and, for a time, Hemingway. However, Papa found that there wasn't "much future in men being friends with great women." John Malcolm Brinnin wrote in *The Third Rose:* "To have paid respects to Gertrude and to have sat with Alice [Alice B. Toklas] was to have been admitted into the charmed circle of those whose pretenses, at least, were interesting and fashionable."

When not receiving, Miss Stein was busy buying paintings—works by Cézanne, Renoir, Matisse, and Picasso. One writer said that her salon was engaged in an international conspiracy to promote modern art. At her Saturday evening gatherings you might meet Braque.

The life of Montparnasse still centers around its cafés and exotic nightclubs, many of them only a shadow of what they used to be. Its heart is at the crossroads of the Boulevard Raspail and the Boulevard du Montparnasse, one of the settings of *The Sun Also Rises.* Hemingway wrote that "the Boulevard Raspail always made dull riding." Rodin's controversial statue of Balzac swathed in a large cape stands guard over the prostitutes who cluster around the pedestal. Balzac seems to be the only one in Montparnasse who doesn't feel the impact of time and change.

Stretching 58 stories into the sky over Montparnasse today is the **Maine-Montparnasse Tower,** a semi-oval structure made of smoked glass and steel. The tower, at 33 Avenue du Maine, was completed in 1973 on the site of the former railway station. The Maine-Montparnasse block shelters a commercial center and 80 shops, including Galeries Lafayette. The incredibly fast elevators whisk you to the observation area on the 56th floor in only 38 seconds. From this vantage point, a panoramic view of all of Paris is yours. With the aid of maps, telescopes, and spoken commentaries available in six languages, you can pick out monuments and sights up to 25 miles away.

Nearby is the **Belvedere** bar-café, good for lunch or a quick snack. Also on the 56th floor is **Le Ciel de Paris,** the highest restaurant in the city, open daily from 11 a.m. to 2 a.m. and serving fine French cuisine. For bookings at the restaurant, telephone 538-52-35. The observation tower is open daily from April 1 to September 30 from 9:30 a.m. to 11:30 p.m., and from 10 a.m. to 10 p.m. during the rest of the year. Admission is 10F ($2.28) for adults and 6F ($1.37) for children under 10 years. At this price you'll be admitted to the 56th floor. It will cost another 2.40F (55¢) per person for access to the 58th floor.

THE GRANDS BOULEVARDS: Once there was nothing more fashionable than dining at a restaurant along these boulevards. Their chic began in the mid-18th century, reaching a pinnacle with the carriage trade, which later abandoned them for the Champs-Élysées. Stretching from the Madeleine to Baron Haussmann's Place de la République, the boulevards are lined today with many fine department stores and shops.

The Madeleine Church

The promenade begins at the Madeleine, one of the most imposing Grecian-inspired temples in the world. The Madeleine church stands right in the heart of the Right Bank on the landmark Place de la Madeleine. Actually, the "Madeleine" is a nickname—the church is dedicated to St. Mary Magdalene. Construction begin in 1764, but the original architect was replaced with another who wanted to turn the structure into a building "that would shame the Parthenon."

In Napoleon's heyday, the church was torn down and reconstructed as "the Temple of Glory," honoring the Grand Army. In 1816 it was made into a church again, although it didn't officially open until 1842. And it almost became the first railway station in Paris.

The temple is ringed with a Corinthian colonnade, its columns holding up an encircling frieze (one of the pediments depicts the Last Judgment). Bas-reliefs on the bronze door represent the Ten Commandments, and in niches along the façade are statues of saints. From the portal you have a panoramic vista down the rue Royale to the Egyptian obelisk on the Place de la Concorde, where Madame Tussaud collected heads. Inside the church, a trio of skylit domes illuminate the central nave, the gilded globe lanterns, and the inlaid marble floor.

Concerts are staged here at least once a month (tel. 265-86-32 for information). Métro: Madeleine.

Boulevard de la Madeleine

The Boulevard de la Madeleine is the most fashionable part of the Grands Boulevards in this era. At No. 11, La Marquise de Sévigné, called "La dame aux camélias," died of consumption. Nowadays, the ground-floor is a tea salon and chocolate shop. On the right side, you can purchase boxes of chocolate; on the left, order tea and mouth-watering, calorie-loaded pastries served by waitresses in black uniforms and stiffly starched white aprons.

Boulevard des Capucines

The Boulevard de la Madeleine leads to the Boulevard des Capucines, where, at No. 14, now the Hôtel Scribe, a plaque honors those "pioneers of the cinema" the Lumière brothers, who launched their films on December 28, 1895.

Across the street is the **Museum Cognacq-Jay,** 25 Boulevard des Capucines—like a specimen of the past preserved under a bell jar. This somewhat esoteric collection was gathered by the late Ernest Cognacq, founder of the Samiritaine department store.

In a town house, the museum is a world of gilt, paintings, tapestries, porcelain, statuary, fat cherubs—and various renditions of maidens in their bath. Of the French works, those of Boucher, Fragonard, Watteau, and Greuze are the most important. But there are also portraits by English artists, such as Francis Cotes, Joshua Reynolds, Sir Thomas Lawrence, and others. Tiepolo's *Banquet of Cleopatra* and Rembrandt's *L'Ânesse du Prophète Balaam* (painted when he was only 20) represent the old masters of Europe.

A good collection of furniture and decorative objects of the 18th century assembled by Cognacq and Louise Jay have been tastefully arranged in the museum.

Diagonally across the street from the Café de la Paix, the museum is open daily except Mondays from 10 a.m. to 5:40 p.m., admission 7F ($1.60).

Place de l'Opéra

The Place de l'Opéra is dominated by the Opéra house, described in the following chapter. Also opening onto that square is one of the best-known cafés in Europe, the Café de la Paix, described in the next chapter.

What we will describe in this chapter is the **Opéra Museum,** entered from a side entrance of the Opéra itself. All is nostalgia here: the sets, the sketches, the costumes, the performances from the Opéra's memorable past. Simulated stage sets of famous operas produced since 1669 are only part of the attractions. On display are Léger's sketch of *Bolivar,* Utrillo's *Louise,* a portrait of Carlotta Zambelli, one of Wagner by Renoir, and many sketches by Boucher. Fans, masks, busts by Carpeaux, the piano of Massenet, memorabilia of Pavlova and Nijinsky, even a scale model of the Opéra itself—nothing is forgotten. Both the museum and the more-than-200,000-volume library are open daily except Sundays from 10 a.m. to 5 p.m. for 1F (23¢) admission.

GEORGES POMPIDOU NATIONAL CENTER FOR ART AND CULTURE: In 1969, Georges Pompidou, then president of France, decided to create a large cultural center including every form of 20th-century art. The center was finally opened in 1977 on the Plateau Beaubourg, in the midst of a huge, car-free pedestrian district east of the Boulevard de Sébastopol (4e). The structure, towering over a festive plaza, is the subject of much controversy. Parisians refer to the radical exoskeletal design as "the refinery." The Tinker-toy-like array of pipes and tubes surrounding the transparent shell are actually functional, serving as casings for the heating, air conditioning, electrical, and telephone systems for the center. The great wormlike tubes crawling at angles up the side of the building contain the escalators which transport visitors from one floor to the next. Inside, no interior walls block one's view. Each floor is one vast room, divided as necessary by movable partitions.

The unique structure has already proved a favorite attraction for Parisian and foreign visitors alike, drawing more viewers each year than Paris's former top sight, the Eiffel Tower. From the top of the center, you can also enjoy one of the best views of the city. The center itself is made up of four separate attractions:

The **National Museum of Modern Art** is the most important part of the center for the sightseer. Its collection of paintings and sculpture is a history of art in this century. Braque and Picasso are represented alongside minor Cubists. The museum has acquired its first Mondrian, and there is a token representation of German painting. American art, surprisingly, looms largest in the museum. The permanent collection, moved from the old museum, includes works ranging from the Fauves to Icelandic conceptual art.

Featured are such artists as Max Ernst (a sculpture, *The Imbecile*), Kandinsky, Vuillard, Bonnard, Utrillo, Chagall, Dufy, Juan Gris, Léger, Pollock, as well as sketches by Le Corbusier and stained glass by Rouault. Modern sculpture includes works by Alexander Calder, Henry Moore, and Jacob Epstein. A gallery of contemporary artists demonstrates the trends in artistic activity today. Special exhibitions and demonstrations are constantly being staged to acquaint the public with the significant works of the 20th century.

The Center also houses the **Public Information Library,** where, for the first time in Paris's history, the public has free access to one million French and foreign books, periodicals, films, records, slides, and microfilms in nearly every area of knowledge.

The **Center for Industrial Design,** covering some 40,000 square feet of space, emphasizes the contributions made in the fields of architecture, visual communications, publishing, and community planning.

The **Institute for Research and Coordination of Acoustics/Music** brings together musicians and composers interested in furthering the cause of music, both contemporary and traditional. Concerts, workshops, and seminars are frequently open to the public.

In addition to its four main departments, the center also offers a children's workshop and library and a "cinémathèque," which tells the history of motion pictures.

The Pompidou Center is open daily except Tuesdays. Hours are from noon to 10 p.m. on weekdays and from 10 a.m. to 10 p.m. on Saturdays and Sundays. A day pass, costing 14F ($3.20), grants visitors access to any part of the center, although special exhibits may require an additional admission fee. The Museum of Modern Art, visited separately, costs 7F ($1.60), with free admission on Sundays. Persons under 18 or more than 65 years of age are admitted free.

3. More Museums

The greatest museum of Paris, the Louvre, and other important ones such as the Cluny have already been previewed. Here are some others, the first of which is one of the most interesting in Paris.

THE RODIN MUSEUM (HÔTEL BIRON): These days Rodin is acclaimed as the father of modern sculpture, but in a different era his work was labeled obscene. The world's artistic taste changed, and in due course the government of France purchased the gray-stone 18th-century luxury residence in Faubourg St.-Germain. The mansion was the studio of Rodin from 1910 till his death in 1917. The rose gardens were restored to their 18th-century splendor, a perfect setting for Rodin's most memorable works.

In the courtyard are three world-famous creations: *The Gate of Hell, The Thinker,* and *The Burghers of Calais.* Rodin's first major public commission, *The Burghers* commemorated the heroism of six burghers of Calais who, in 1347, offered themselves as hostages to Edward III in return for his ending the siege of their port. Perhaps the single best-known work, *The Thinker* in Rodin's own words "thinks with every muscle of his arms, back, and legs, with his clenched fist and gripping toes." Not yet completed at Rodin's death, *The Gate of Hell,* as he put it, is "where I lived for a whole year in Dante's Inferno."

Inside the building, the sculpture, plaster casts, reproductions, originals, and sketches reveal the freshness and vitality of that remarkable man. Many of his works appear to be emerging from marble into life. Everybody is attracted to *The Kiss* (of which one critic wrote, "the passion is timeless"). Upstairs are two different versions of the celebrated and condemned nude of Balzac, his bulky torso rising from a tree trunk (Albert E. Elsen commented on the "glorious bulging" stomach). Included are many versions of his *Monument to Balzac* (a large one stands in the garden), which was Rodin's last major work and which caused a furor when it was first exhibited.

Other significant sculpture includes Rodin's *Prodigal Son* (it literally soars); *The Crouching Woman* (called the "embodiment of despair"); and his *The Age of Bronze,* an 1876 study of a nude man, modeled by a Belgian soldier. (Rodin was accused—falsely—of making a cast from a living model.)

At 77 rue de Varenne, the museum (Métro: Varenne) is open daily except Tuesdays from 10 a.m. to 5 p.m. (6 p.m. from April 1 to September 30); 7F ($1.60) admission, only 3.50F (80¢) on Sundays.

Digression: At the Hôtel Biron, you'll be on the threshold of what was the most elegant residential district of Paris in the 18th century, the **Faubourg St.-Germain.** If you don't have to rush immediately to Napoleon's Tomb, try to explore some of that once-aristocratic district, lying roughly between the Invalides and St.-Germain-des-Prés. At one time or another, some of the most celebrated names in France have lived there: Mme. Récamier, Lafayette, Chateubriand, Turgot, Queen Hortense, Mme. de Montespan, André Gide, Ingres, Corot, Baudelaire, and Guillaume Apollinaire.

Deserted by fickle fashion, the former mansions are now occupied by foreign embassies or ministries such as the French Ministry of National Education. At 138 rue de Grenelle, Marshall Foch, the supreme Allied commander in World War I, died on March 20, 1929. On the same street, at 59 rue de Grenelle, Alfred de Musset lived from 1824 to 1839, before George Sand lured him away on an amorous adventure. The façade at the poet's residence is the most elegant on the street—note the *Fountain of the Four Seasons,* designed by Bouchardon in 1739. A woman, signifying the City of Paris, is seated on a throne of lions, dominating the figures of the Seine and the Marne at her feet. In niches to each side of her—favorite roosts of Parisian pigeons—are bas-reliefs depicting the four seasons. Autumn is illustrated with cherubs harvesting the grapes from the vineyards.

MARMOTTAN MUSEUM: A town-house mansion with all the trappings of the First Empire, the Marmottan Museum is one of the many private family collections on display in Paris. Occasionally a lone art historian would venture to 2 rue Louis-Boilly (Métro: La Muette), on the edge of the Bois de Boulogne, to see what Paul Marmottan donated to the Académie des Beaux-Arts. Hardly anybody else did . . . until 1966, when Michel Monet, son of Claude Monet, died in a car crash, leaving a bequest of his father's art—valued at $10 million—to the little museum. The Académie des Beaux-Arts suddenly found itself heir to more than 130 paintings, watercolors, pastels, and drawings—and a whole lot of Monet-lovers, who can, in one place, trace the evolution of the great man's work.

The gallery owns more than 30 pictures of his house at Giverny, and many of water lilies, his everlasting intrigue. The bequest included his famous *Willow,* painted in 1918, his *Houses of Parliament,* from 1905, even a portrait Renoir did of Monet when he was 32. The collection has been hailed "one of the great art treasures of the world," and that it is. Ironically, the museum had always owned Monet's *Impression,* from which the movement got its name.

Paul Marmottan's original collection includes fig-leafed nudes, First Empire antiques, assorted objets d'art, bucolic paintings, and crystal chandeliers. Many of the tapestries date from the Renaissance.

The museum is open daily except Monday from 10 a.m. to 6 p.m.; 10F ($2.28) admission.

MUSEUM OF THE MONUMENTS OF FRANCE: At the Palais de Chaillot, Place du Trocadéro (Métro: Trocadéro), this museum houses mouldings of the *grandes oeuvres* of French sculpture, including entire façades and portals, as well as reproductions of the most significant mural paintings up to the 16th century. Reproduced in detail are such landmarks in art as the southern

façade of Chartres Cathedral (1220-1225) as well as the western one (1145-60).
The Romanesque and Gothic sculptures can be examined from an intimate
perspective; in the original, much of the intricacy is lost or the sculpture too
elevated to be appreciated.

Not only will you see some of the sculpture of such cathedrals as Notre-
Dame and Reims, but such sights as the 16th-century southern door of the
transept of Beauvais Cathedral; that decorative masterpiece, the tomb of
François II and of Marguerite de Foix at Nantes; the door to the chapter house
of Bourges Cathedral; the 1560 north door of the transept in Rouen's Church
of St. Maclou, and the 1535 Hôtel de Bernuy (school for boys) at Toulouse.
Notable are the reproductions of the painted pillars at St.-Savin-sur-Gartempe
at Vienne.

Many of the Romanesque and Gothic mural paintings are reproduced
right down to their faded glory (see, for example, the 14th-century dome of the
Cathedral of Cahors, the town that was the ancient capital of Quercy). Perhaps
the most ghoulish work is from La Brigue Chapel, the most humorous the
fork-tailed monsters devouring flesh from the château de Villeneuve-Lembron,
Puy-le-Dôme (1515-1517). The monuments museum is open daily except Tuesdays from 9:45 a.m. to 12:30 p.m. and from 2 to 5:15 p.m., charging an
admission of 6F ($1.37), half-price on Sundays.

MUSÉE DE L'HOMME: Venus de Milo may draw them to the Louvre, but
the Hottentot Venus is the star of this museum of man at the Palais de Chaillot,
Place du Trocadéro. One can hardly compare the two, of course. The former
is an idealization of beauty, the latter truth as beauty—a molding executed
from the body of Sarah Bartman, a native of South Africa who died in Paris
in 1816 at the age of 38.

In the first gallery as you enter is a case containing the second most
important exhibit, the Cro-Magnon "Menton man," discovered in 1872 in the
Grimaldi grottos on the French Riviera. Among the replicas, perhaps the most
intriguing are the primitive cave drawings. One long gallery traces Primitive
Africa, including prehistoric art and cave drawings (such as those discovered
in the 1935 expedition by Française du Hoggar into the desert of Libya). There
is modern African art as well; on one recent occasion a Nigerian pop painting
entitled *Blue Lady* demonstrated originality in the contemporary idiom.

One wing is turned over to temporary exhibitions from anywhere in the
world. Another section is devoted to France's more immediate neighbors in
Europe: "suits of light" from Spain, peasant dress from Old Bohemia, and the
like.

The upstairs galleries are filled with artifacts from Asia, Oceania, the
Americas; masks from Greenland; ivory sculpture carved by the Eskimos;
costumes from Siberia; the weaving of Afghanistán; rifles from Tibet; fans from
Japan; sculpture from the Philippines and New Guinea; pre-Columbian art,
and Mayan monuments. Open daily except Tuesdays the museum may be
visited from 10 a.m. to 6 p.m. in summer (from April to September); from 10
a.m. to 5 p.m. in winter (from October to March), for a 6F ($1.37) fee.

MARINE MUSEUM: This museum occupies the same address as the two
above—Palais de Chaillot, Place du Trocadéro et du 11 Novembre (Métro:
Trocadéro). A lot of it is pomp: gilded galleys and busts of stiff-necked admi-
rals. There's a great number of old ship models, including, for instance, the big
galley *La Réale*, the *Royal-Louis*, the rich ivory model *Ville de Dieppe*, the

gorgeous *Valmy.* A barge constructed in 1811 for Napoleon I was used to carry another Napoleon (the Third) and his queen, Eugénie, on their first visit to the port of Brest in about 1858. The imperial crown is held up by winged cherubs.

Models of World Wars I and II warships strike a more ominous note, and there are many documents and artifacts concerning merchant fishing and pleasure fleets, oceanography, hydrography, with films illustrating the subjects. Then there are the personal mementos, such as a vamplike photograph of Virginia Heriot, showing her yacht, *l'Ailée,* and a map tracing her journey (1930-32) from Egypt to Scandinavia. Among the paintings, the most important ones are by Joseph Vernet, a series of 13 canvases of the ports of France, including those at Dieppe, Rochefort, Bordeaux, Bayonne, Toulon, and Marseille, among others. The museum is open daily except Tuesdays from 10 a.m. to 6 p.m.; admission is 5F ($1.14).

While visiting the museum in the Palais de Chaillot, you can always take a cool break by walking into the gardens, where there is a small **aquarium.** Built on the style of the Vincennes zoo structures, it resembles a rough-walled rock underground cave. The exhibits aren't exceptional; they represent the river fishes of France. The aquarium is open daily from 10 a.m. to 6 p.m.

PALAIS DE TOKYO: This imposing building was erected on the site of an establishment which used to turn out the Savonnerie carpets. The present structure is a palace constructed for a 1937 exhibition. It is not, as its name suggests, a museum of Japanese art. At 13 Avenue du Président Wilson, the Palais de Tokyo used to house the Museum of Modern Art before its transfer to the Pompidou Centre.

The Palais is affiliated with the Musée d'Art et d'Essai, which features temporary expositions on various themes and presents works lent by the Louvre and other museums. The Palais contains one of the finest collections of Post-Impressionists in Paris. See, for example, Seurat's famous *The Circus,* painted in 1891 but never finished because of his death. There is a large collection of paintings by Vuillard, as well as quite a few by Bonnard, plus one entire salon devoted to the works of the artists from the School of Pont-Aven. It is open from 9:45 a.m. to 5:15 p.m. daily except Tuesdays, charging 7F ($1.60) admission, but only half-price on Sundays. Métro: Iéna.

MUSÉE D'ART MODERNE DE LA VILLE DE PARIS: Right next door to the Palais de Tokyo, at 11 Avenue du Président Wilson, this interesting museum displays a permanent collection of paintings and sculpture owned by the City of Paris. In addition, the city's modern art museum presents ever-changing temporary exhibitions on individual artists from all over the world or on international art trends. Bordering the Seine, the salons display works by such artists as Chagall, Matisse, Léger, Braque, Picasso, Dufy, Utrillo, Delaunay, Rouault, and Modigliani. See, in particular, Pierre Tal Coat's *Portrait of Gertrude Stein.* Picasso wasn't the only artist to tackle this difficult subject. Other sections in the museum are **ARC,** which shows work of young artists and new trends in contemporary art, and the **Musée des Enfants,** which has exhibitions and shows for children. The Modern is open from 10 a.m. to 5:40 p.m. daily except Monday, charging 6F ($1.37) admission, half-price for children and students. It's free on Sundays. Métro: Iéna and Alma.

GUIMET MUSEUM: The Guimet was given the Far East collections from the overstuffed Louvre, making it one of the world's richest museums of its genre. Named after its founder and established originally at Lyon, it was transferred to Paris in the late 19th century. Like Topsy, it just grew, and today it is more popular than ever.

The art ranges from Tibet to Japan to Afghanistan to Nepal to Java to India to China. There are even sculptures from Vietnam. The most interesting —certainly the most grotesque—displays are on the ground floor, the exhibits encompassing bronze Buddhas, heads of serpentine monsters, funereal figurines. See, for example, a ten-armed bronze from Java, plus lots of antiquities from Khmer. The Jacques Bacot salon is devoted to Tibetan art: fascinating scenes of the Grand Lamas entwined with serpents and demons.

On the first floor is the Indian section with the remarkable Mathura Serpent-King (second century A.D.), the Amaravati reliefs. René Grousset, a French art historian, was impressed with the "simple paganism, the innocent pleasure in the nude form." Of a harem group from that school (third century), he found its sensuality "refined," its freshness "agreeable." On the same floor, the Rousset collection is to be seen.

On the top floor, the Michel Calmann collection is devoted to jade vases, statuettes, porcelain, ceramics, and pottery, including the Grandidier collection, that run the gamut of Chinese dynasties—going back six or seven centuries before the birth of Christ and forward to the Ts'ing Dynasty (1644-1911).

Across from the Museum of Modern Art (above), the Guimet is open daily except Tuesdays from 9:45 a.m. till noon and from 1:30 till 5:15 p.m.; 7F ($1.60) admission.

MUSEUM OF DECORATIVE ARTS: What draws most people to this museum is its diverse collection of furniture and objets d'art from the Middle Ages to the present, plus its prestigious collection of the works of Jean Dubuffet, donated by the artist himself. A prodigious painter whose style fluctuated amazingly from period to period, Dubuffet once wrote, "I feel a need that every work of art should in the highest degree lift one out of context, provoking a surprise and shock." In that, he succeeds!

By our emphasis on Dubuffet, we don't mean to slight the contents of the Decorative Arts Museum itself—in fact, its exhibitions are among the finest in Europe, the world for that matter. Salon after salon reveals the scope and depth of the French style: a 15th-century four-poster, a sword or rifle, 16th-century musical instruments, exquisite enamelware, Norman glassware, clocks on the backs of hippopotamuses, a Regency console, decorative woodwork, and lots of gilt, plus some of Josephine's and Madame de Pompadour's silverware.

The museum is particularly rich in furnishings and objets d'art from the Louis XV and Louis XVI periods. Perhaps most elegant are the salons from the First and Second Empire. From the Watteau sketches, we gain a nostalgic look at the France of yesteryear. The top floor is turned over mainly to ceramics, faïence, and porcelain, including collections from the Far East. The ground floor usually houses temporary exhibitions, such as the recent display of modern sports cars and paintings.

The museum (Métro: Palais-Royal) is at 107 rue de Rivoli, in the northwest wing of the Louvre's Pavillon de Marsan. It is open daily except Mondays and Tuesdays from 10 a.m. to noon and 2 to 5 p.m. Exhibitions are open from noon to 6 p.m. Depending on the exhibit, admission ranges from 6F ($1.37) to 10F ($2.28).

PETIT PALAIS: Built by architect Charles Girault, the small palace faces the Grand Palais (housing special exhibitions)—both erected for the 1900 Exhibition.

The Petit Palais contains works of art belonging to the City of Paris. Most prominent are the Dutuit and Tuck collections. In the Dutuit collection are Egyptian bronzes, Roman copies of Greek statuary, Etruscan bronzes, ivory carvings, a 16th-century St. George slaying the dragon, 11th-century Byzantine designs, 14th-century hand-lettered and painted books, 16th-century Limoges ware, 17th- and 18th-century Flemish paintings, even a torso by Rodin.

Important paintings include Mary Cassatt's *The Bath;* Brueghel's *The Wedding Pageant;* works by Corot, Daumier, Manet, Lucas Cranach, Renoir, Bonnard, Edouard Vuillard, and especially Courbet. Also represented are Cézanne, Gauguin, Toulouse-Lautrec, and Degas (a self-portrait). The exhibit is rewarding for those desiring to see works of the Impressionists before many of them had perfected, or rather matured in, their style. In the Tuck collection are tapestries, antique furnishings (much gilt), wood-paneled salons, and porcelain, among other displays.

On the Avenue Winston-Churchill (Métro: Champs-Élysées), the museum is open daily except Mondays and Tuesdays from 10 a.m. to 5:40 p.m.; 6F ($1.37) admission unless there's a special exhibition, free on Sundays.

JACQUEMART-ANDRÉ MUSEUM: This late 19th-century town house was built by Edouard André, who later married Nélie Jacquemart, an artist. Together they formed a collection of rare French 18th-century decorative art and Italian Renaissance works. Mme. André, who died shortly before World War I, willed the building and its contents to the Institut de France. At 158 Boulevard Haussmann, 8e, it is perhaps the best of the little decorative art museums of Paris. The collection can be viewed any day except Mondays and Tuesdays from 1:30 to 5:30 p.m. for 8F ($1.83) admission (Métro: Miromesnil or St. Philippe-du-Roule). Closed in August.

You enter through an arcade leading into an enclosed courtyard. Two white lions guard the doorway. Inside are Gobelin tapestries, Houdon busts, Savonnerie carpets—and a rich art collection, including Rembrandt's *The Pilgrim of Emmaüs.* Represented are paintings by Van Dyck, Tiepolo, Rubens, Watteau, Boucher, Capaccio, and Mantegna *(Virgin and Child).* Donatello torchères, statuary (including a wingless victory), Slodtz busts, Della Robbia terracottas (Ganymede with the eagle), and antiques round out the collection. The salons drip with gilt, and the winding stairway to the top floor is elegant.

MUSÉE CERNUSCHI: Bordering the Parc Monceau, this small museum is devoted to the arts of China. It's another one of those mansions whose owners stuffed them with an art collection, then bequeathed them to the City of Paris. The address—7 Avenue Velasquez—was quite an exclusive one when the town house was built in 1895.

Inside, there is, of course, a bust of Cernuschi himself—and that is as it should be, a self-perpetuating memorial to a man whose generosity and interest in the East was legend in his day. The collections include a fine assortment of Neolithic potteries, as well as bronzes from the 14th century B.C. The jades, ceramics, and funereal figures are exceptional, as are the pieces of Buddhist sculpture. Most admirable is a Bodhisattva originating from Yun-kang (sixth century). Rounding out the exhibits are some ancient paintings, the best known of which is *Horses with Grooms,* attributed to Han Kan (eighth century, T'ang dynasty). The museum also houses a good collection of contemporary Chinese painting. The museum (Métro: Monceau) may be visited any day except Monday from 10 a.m. to 5:30 p.m.; 4F (91¢) admission, free on Sundays except for exhibitions.

NISSIM DE CAMONDO MUSEUM: At 63 rue de Monceau, near the Musée Cernuschi, this museum is a jewel box of elegance and refinement, evoking the days of Louis XVI and Marie Antoinette. The pre-World War I town house was donated to the Museum of Decorative Arts by Comte Moïse de Camondo (1860-1935) in memory of his son, Nissim, a French aviator killed in combat in World War I.

Entered through a courtyard, the museum is like the private home of an aristocrat of two centuries ago—richly furnished with needlepoint chairs, tapestries (many from Beauvais or Aubusson), antiques, paintings (the inevitable Guardi scenes of Venice), bas-reliefs, silver, Chinese vases, crystal chandeliers, Sèvres porcelain, and Savonnerie carpets. And, of course, a Houdon bust (in an upstairs bedroom). The Blue Salon, overlooking the Parc Monceau, is impressive. You can wander without a guide through the gilt and oyster-gray salons.

Open all year, the museum may be visited from 10 a.m. to noon and from 2 to 5 p.m. for a 6F ($1.37) admission fee. Closed Mondays and Tuesdays. Métro: Villiers.

BALZAC MUSEUM: At 47 rue Raynouard, in the residential district of Passy near the Bois de Boulogne, sits a modest house. Here the great Balzac (or, to hear his mother-in-law tell it, "the Gascon hound") lived for seven years beginning in 1840. Fleeing there after his possessions and furnishings were seized, Balzac cloaked himself in secrecy (you had to know a password to be ushered into his presence). Should a creditor knock on the Raynouard door, Balzac could always escape through the rue Berton exit.

The museum's most notable memento is the Limoges coffee pot (the novelist's initials are in mulberry pink) that his "screech-owl" kept hot throughout the night as he wrote *La Comédie Humaine* to stall his creditors. Also enshrined here is a cast of Balzac's hands, described by Gautier as the hands of a true prelate.

Although unfurnished, the little house is filled with reproductions of caricatures of Balzac. (A French biographer once wrote: "With his bulky baboon silhouette, his blue suit with gold buttons, his famous cane like a golden crowbar, and his abundant, disheveled hair, Balzac was a sight for caricature.")

The house is built on the slope of a hill, with a small courtyard and garden. The museum is open daily except Mondays and Tuesdays from 10 a.m. to 5:45 p.m.; 4F (91¢) admission. Métro: Passy or La-Muette.

GRÉVIN MUSEUM: The desire to compare this museum at 10 Boulevard Montmartre to Madame Tussaud's of London is almost irresistible. Grévin is the number-one waxworks of Paris. It isn't all blood and gore, and doesn't shock some as Tussaud's might. Presenting a panorama of French history from Charlemagne to the mistress-collecting Napoleon III, it shows memorable moments in a series of tableaux.

Depicted are the consecration of Charles VII in 1429 in the Cathedral of Reims (Joan of Arc, dressed in armor and carrying her standard, stands behind the king); Marguerite de Valois, first wife of Henri IV, meeting on a secret stairway with La Molle, who was soon to be decapitated; Catherine de Medici with the Florentine alchemist Ruggieri; Louis XV and Mozart at the home of the Marquise de Pompadour; and Napoleon on a rock at St. Helena, reviewing his victories and defeats.

Two shows are staged frequently throughout the day. The first, called the "Palais des Mirages," starts off as a sort of Temple of Brahma, and, through magically distorting mirrors, changes into an enchanted forest, then a fête at the Alhambra at Granada. A magician is the star of the second show, "Le Cabinet Fantastique"; he entertains children of all ages.

The museum (Métro: Montmartre) is open from 2 to 7 p.m. weekdays, from 1 to 8 p.m. Sundays and holidays. It charges adults 18F ($4.11); children under 15 pay 12F ($2.74).

Grevin Museum has opened a subsidiary, **Serelor,** at Forum des Halles, the new "heart" of Paris. This is a sound-and-light show with 130 personages and automates, devoted to La Belle Époque, between 1885 and 1900. The show (Métro: Les Halles) is open from 11 a.m. to 10 p.m. weekdays, from 1 to 8 p.m. Sundays and holidays. Entrance fees are 18F ($4.11) between 1 and 6 p.m., 15F ($3.42) from 11 a.m. to 1 p.m. and after 6 p.m.

SÈVRES MUSEUM: Madame de Pompadour loved Sèvres porcelain. She urged Louis XV to order more and more of it, thus ensuring its position among the fashionable people of the 18th century. Two centuries later, it is still fashionable.

The Sèvres factory, next door to the museum, has been owned by the State of France for more than two centuries. It was founded originally in Vincennes, and moved to Sèvres, a riverside suburb of Paris, in 1756. The factory may be visited on certain occasions, but the museum opens its doors every day except Tuesday from 9:30 a.m. to noon and from 1:30 to 5:15 p.m. for a 7F ($1.60) admission charge, 3.50F (79¢) on Sundays.

Officially called the **Musée National de Ceramique de Sèvres,** it shelters one of the finest collections of faïence and porcelain in the world. Some of it belonged to Madame du Barry, Pompadour's handpicked successor. You can see the Sèvres ware as it looked from the day it was created and as it looks straight from the factory today.

On view, for example, is the "Pompadour rose" (which the English insisted on calling the "rose du Barry"), a style much in vogue in the 1750s and 1760s. The painter Boucher made some of the designs used by the factory, as did the sculptor Pajou (he did the bas-reliefs for the Opéra at Versailles). The factory pioneered what became known in porcelain as the Louis Seize style—it's all here, plus lots more, including works from Meissen (archrival of Sèvres).

Take the Métro to the end of the Pont de Sèvres line, walk across the Seine to the Left Bank, and you'll be there.

4. More Churches

VAL-DE-GRÂCE: According to an old proverb, to understand the French you must like Camembert cheese, Pont Neuf, and the dome of Val-de-Grâce.

After 23 years of a barren marriage to Louis XIII, Anne of Austria gave birth to a boy who would one day be known as the Sun King. In those days, if monarchs wanted to express gratitude, they built a church or monastery. Seven years after his birth, on April 1, 1645, the future Louis XIV himself laid the first stone of the church. At that time, Mansart was the architect. To him we owe the façade in the Jesuit style. Le Duc, however, designed the dome, and the painter Mignard decorated it with frescoes. Other architects included Le Mercier and Le Muet.

The origins of the church go back even further, to 1050, when a Benedictine monastery was founded on the grounds. In 1619, Marguerite Veni d'Arbouze was appointed abbess by Louis XIII. She petitioned Anne of Austria for a new monastery, as the original one was decaying. Then came Louis XIV's church, which in 1793 was turned into a military hospital and in 1850 an army school.

The church may be visited from 9 a.m. to noon and from 2 to 5 p.m. daily, except during services. To reach it, walk up rue du Val-de-Grâce from Boulevard St.-Michel (Métro: Luxembourg).

CHURCH OF ST. STEPHEN-ON-THE-MOUNT: Once there was an abbey on this site, founded by Clovis and later dedicated to Ste. Geneviève, the patroness of Paris. Such was the fame of this popular saint that the abbey proved too small to accommodate the pilgrimage crowds. Now part of the Lycée Henri IV, the **Tower of Clovis** is all that remains from the ancient abbey (you can see the Tower from rue Clovis).

Today, the task of keeping alive the cult of Ste. Geneviève has fallen on the Church of St. Étienne-du-Mont, on Place Ste.-Geneviève, practically adjoining the Panthéon (Métro: St.-Michel, then a long walk). The interior is in the Gothic style, unusual for a 16th-century church. Construction on the present building began in 1492 and lasted until 1626.

Besides the patroness of Paris, such men as Pascal and Racine were entombed in the church. Incidentally, the tomb of the saint was destroyed during the Revolution. However, the stone on which her coffin rested was discovered later, and the relics were gathered for a place of honor at St. Étienne.

The church possesses a remarkable rood screen, built in the first part of the 16th century. Across the nave, it is unique in Paris—uncharitably called spurious by some, although others have hailed it as a masterpiece. Another treasure is a wood-carved pulpit, held up by a seminude Samson who clutches a bone in one hand, having slain the lion at his feet. The fourth chapel on the right (when entering) contains most impressive stained glass from the 16th century.

CHURCH OF ST. GERMAIN L'AUXERROIS: Once it was the church for the Palace of the Louvre, drawing an assortment of courtesans, men of art and of law, artisans from the quartier, even royalty. Sharing the Place du Louvre with Perrault's colonnade, the church contains only the foundation stones of its original belfry built in the 11th century. It was greatly enlarged in the 14th century by the addition of side aisles. The little primitive chapel that had stood on the spot eventually gave way to a great and beautiful church, with 260 feet of stained glass, including some rose windows from the Renaissance.

The saddest moment in its history was on August 24, 1572. The unintentional ringing of its bells signaled the St. Bartholomew Massacre, in which the Protestants suffered a blood bath. The churchwardens' pews are outstanding, with intricate carving, based on designs by Le Brun in the 17th century. Behind the pew is a 15th-century triptych and Flemish retable (so badly lit you can hardly appreciate it). The organ was originally ordered by Louis XVI for Sainte Chapelle. In that architectural mélange, many famous men were entombed, including the sculptor Coysevox and Le Vau, the architect. Around the chancel is an intricate 18th-century grille.

5. The Gardens of Paris

We've already walked through the Tuileries. In this section we explore some other oases, beginning with the—

LUXEMBOURG GARDENS: Hemingway told a friend that the Luxembourg Gardens "kept us from starvation." He related that in his poverty-stricken days in Paris, he wheeled a baby carriage (the vehicle was considered luxurious) and child through the gardens because it was known "for the classiness of its pigeons." When the gendarme went across the street for a glass of wine, the writer would eye his victim, preferably a plump one, then lure him with corn . . . "snatch him, wring his neck," then flip him under Bumby's blanket. "We got a little tired of pigeon that year," he confessed, "but they filled many a void."

Before it became a feeding ground for struggling Montparnasse artists of the 1920s, Luxembourg knew greater days. But it's always been associated with artists, although students from the Sorbonne and children predominate nowadays. Watteau came this way, as did Verlaine. Balzac, however, didn't like the gardens at all. In 1905 Gertrude Stein would cross the gardens to catch the Batignolles-Clichy-Odéon omnibus pulled by three gray mares across Paris, to meet Picasso in his studio at Montmartre, where she sat while he painted her portrait.

The gardens are the best on the Left Bank (some say in all of Paris). Marie de Medici, the much-neglected wife and later widow of the roving Henri IV, ordered a palace built on the site in 1612. She planned to live there with her "witch" friend, Leonora Galigaï. A Florentine by birth, the regent wanted to create another Pitti Palace, or so she ordered the architect, Salomon de Brossee. She wasn't entirely successful, although the overall effect is most often described as Italianate.

The queen didn't get to enjoy the palace for very long after it was finished. She was forced into exile by her son, Louis XIII, after it was discovered she was plotting to overthrow him. Reportedly, she died in Germany in poverty, quite a comedown from that luxury she had once known in the Luxembourg. Incidentally, the 21 paintings she commissioned from Rubens that glorified her life were intended for her palace, though they are now in the Louvre. The palace can't be visited without special permission in advance.

But you don't come to the Luxembourg to visit the palace, not really. The gardens are the attraction. For the most part, they are the classic French tradition: well groomed and formally laid out, the trees planted in designs. A large water basin in the center is encircled with urns and statuary on pedestals —one honoring Ste. Geneviève, the patroness of Paris, depicted with pigtails reaching to her thighs. Another memorial is dedicated to Stendhal.

Crowds throng through the park on May Day, when Parisians carry their traditional lilies of the valley. Birds sing, and all of Paris (those who didn't go to the country) celebrates the rebirth of spring.

BOIS DE BOULOGNE: One of the greatest and most spectacular parks in Europe, le Bois is often called the main lung of Paris. Horse-drawn carriages traverse it, but you can also take your car through. Many of its hidden pathways, however, must be discovered by walking. If you had a week to spare, you could spend it all in the Bois de Boulogne and still not see everything.

Porte Dauphine is the main entrance, though you can take the Métro to Porte Maillot as well. West of Paris, the park was once a forest kept for royal hunts. In the late 19th century it was in vogue. Carriages containing elegantly attired and coiffured Parisian damsels with their foppish escorts rumbled along the Avenue Foch. Nowadays, it's more likely to attract picnickers from the middle class.

When Emperor Napoleon III gave the grounds to the City of Paris in 1852, they were developed by Baron Haussmann. Separating Lac Inférieur from Lac Supérieur is the Carrefour des Cascades (you can stroll under its waterfall). The Lower Lake contains two islands connected by a footbridge. From the east bank, you can take a boat to these idyllically situated grounds, perhaps stopping off at the café-restaurant on one of them.

Restaurants in the Bois are numerous, elegant, and expensive. The Pre-Catelan contains a deluxe restaurant of the same name and a Shakespearean theater in a garden said to have been planted with trees mentioned in the bard's plays.

Two racetracks, Longchamp and the Auteuil, are in the park. The annual Grand Prix is run in June at Longchamp (the site of a medieval abbey). The most fashionable people of Paris turn out, the women gowned in their finest haute couture. Directly to the north of Longchamp is Grand Cascade, the artificial waterfall of the Bois de Boulogne.

The Jardin d'Acclimation is for children, with a small zoo, an amusement park, and a narrow-gauge railway. Its major attraction, however, is pedal cars which the *enfants* can drive, following traffic signals. Unlike in the real world, violators are only reprimanded by a policeman, never ticketed.

In the 60-acre Bagatelle Park, the Comte d'Artois (later Charles X), brother-in-law of Marie Antoinette, made a bet with her—he could erect a small palace in less than three months—and won. If you're in Paris in late April, go to the Bagatelle to look at the tulips, if for no other reason. In late May one of the finest and best-known rose collections in all of Europe is in full bloom.

PARC MONCEAU: One widely known American writer once said that all babies in the Parc Monceau were respectable. Having never known one who wasn't, we can only agree with the pundit. At any rate, babies like Parc Monceau. Or at least their mothers and/or nurses are fond of wheeling their carriages through it. Much of the park (Métro: Monceau or Villiers) is ringed with 18th- and 19th-century mansions, some of them evoking Proust's *Remembrance of Things Past*.

The park was opened to the public in the days of Napoleon III's Second Empire. It was built in 1778 by the Duke of Orléans, or Philippe-Égalité, as he became known. Carmontelle designed the park for the duke, who was considered at the time the richest man in France. "Philip Equality" was noted for his debauchery and his pursuit of pleasure. No ordinary park would do.

Monceau was laid out with an Egyptian-style obelisk, a dungeon of the Middle Ages, a thatched Alpine farmhouse, a Chinese pagoda, a Roman temple, an enchanted grotto, various chinoiseries, and, of course, a waterfall. These fairytale touches have largely disappeared except for a pyramid and an oval-shaped *naumachie* fringed by a colonnade. Many of the former fantasies have been replaced with solid statuary and monuments, one honoring Chopin. In spring, the red tulips and magnolias are worth the air ticket to Paris.

BUTTES-CHAUMONT: In the industrial working-class district of Belleville, immortalized in the songs of Maurice Chevalier, Napoleon III and Baron Haussmann created this park out of a plaster-of-paris quarry. In a sense, they were the harbingers of the ecology movement, as the quarry had been turned into a rubbish dump.

Today, in the northeast of Paris, in the 19th Arrondissement, the 60 acres of parkland center around a rock island and a swan lake. You can take a boat for a tour of the lake, or else climb a mountain. A suspension bridge over the water was once called Suicide Bridge.

Try to avoid the park on Sunday afternoons—unless you love people, lots of them. Métro: Buttes-Chaumont.

6. The Markets of Paris

Paris at times seems a vast open-air market. The most important ones are previewed below, beginning with the—

FLEA MARKET: The French call this world-famed market **Marché aux Puces.** Here, what someone considered junk becomes valuable property in the eyes of others. Some of the merchandise is stolen only the night before. The ragpickers of Paris still come here, although whoever buys their poor merchandise, bits of string and scraps of 1920 cloth, we'll never know. It's estimated that the complex has 2500 to 3000 open stalls and shops spread over a four-square-mile area.

The market is open only on Saturdays, Sundays, and Mondays. To get there by Métro, take the train to Porte de Clignancourt (bus 56 also goes to this point). After leaving the underground station, walk to your left along Boulevard Ney. Monday is the traditional day for bargain hunters. Remember to bargain, and that means not paying the second price asked, or even the third. Steals are rare here, because the best buys have been skimmed by dealers. However, someone occasionally turns up with a masterpiece.

THE VILLAGE SUISSE: This is a vast Left Bank complex of 200 antique shops and boutiques at 78 Avenue de Suffren (15e) and 54 Avenue de la Motte Picquet (15e). Don't go here for bargains. Unlike the Marché aux Puces, everything at the Village Suisse is in an excellent state of repair. Interior decorators of Paris frequent the village's precincts for their wealthy clients, looking for that Louis XVI console. Oil paintings, silver, copper, and pewter plus antique furniture in all major periods and styles are presented. It is open Thursdays through Mondays from 10:30 a.m. to 7 p.m. By Métro, get off at the La Motte Picquet underground station, then walk along Avenue de la Motte Picquet until you reach the entrance at number 54.

THE BIRD MARKET: We don't suggest you buy anything—this market is one of the *curiosités* of Paris. From the Louvre to the Hôtel-de-Ville, long rows of shops are spread along the Seine, selling both wild and tame birds. Like unset gems, these birds in all the colors of the rainbow huddle in cages. Fantail pigeons, parrots, canaries, parakeets, and many rare birds are sold here. (Sometimes, though, there are complaints that the beautiful colored bird becomes a pale yellow canary after his first bath.) Pet fishes and tortoises are also for sale. On Sundays, birds are sold at the Flower Market, previewed below.

THE FLOWER MARKET: Certainly France has no more colorful market. The **Marché aux Fleurs** is a bouquet treat. Walking along enjoying this feast of scent, you'll encounter stall after stall ablaze with color. Most of the flowers are shipped in from the Riviera, having escaped the perfume factories. The market is on the Île de la Cité (4e) at Place Louis-Lépine, along the Seine behind the Tribunal de Commerce. It is open weekdays. Métro: Cité.

THE STAMP MARKET: Avid collectors are drawn to nearly two dozen stalls set up on a permanent basis under shade trees below Rond Point, off the Champs-Élysées. Rare stamps and ordinary ones are sold on Thursday, Saturday, and Sunday (Métro: Champs-Élysées).

COUR AUX ANTIQUARIES: This elegant Right Bank arcade is a complex of miniature shops and art boutiques, each opening onto a courtyard. Nearly two dozen collectors are found here, each one operating independently. Merchandise includes East Indian handicrafts, post-Impressionist 19th-century paintings, Oriental porcelains, silver pill boxes, jade bottles, modern art, circa 1925 jewelry, 18th-century paintings, and Russian icons. The address is 54 Faubourg St.-Honoré (8e). Métro: Place de la Concorde.

7. A Sightseeing Miscellany

From graveyards to sewers, this grab bag of Parisian "extras" is wide ranging, beginning at:

PÈRE-LACHAISE: When it comes to name-dropping, this cemetery knows no peer. Its directory even lists as tenants those lovers of the Middle Ages Héloïse and Abélard, at whose monument Parisian lovers for decades have pledged their fidelity. Everybody from Mme. Bernhardt to Oscar Wilde (his tomb by Epstein) was buried here. So were Balzac, Delacroix, and Bizet. The body of Colette was taken here in 1954, and in time the little sparrow, Piaf, would follow. The lover of George Sand, Alfred de Musset, the poet, was buried under a weeping willow. Napoleon's marshals, Ney and Masséna, were entombed here, as were Chopin and Molière.

Spreading over more than 40 acres, Père-Lachaise was acquired by the City of Paris in 1804. Nineteenth-century French sculpture abounds, each family trying to outdo the other in ornamentation and cherubic ostentation. Some French Socialists still pay tribute at the Mur des Fédérés, the anonymous grave site of the Communards who were executed on May 28, 1871. Frenchmen who died in the Resistance or in Nazi concentration camps are also honored by the monument.

The cemetery is open from 7:30 a.m. to 6 p.m., spring through autumn (from 8:30 to 5 p.m. otherwise). A guide at the entrance may give you a map outlining some of the well-known grave sites. Métro: Père-Lachaise.

LES GOBELINS: The founding father of the dynasty, Jehan Gobelin, came from a family of dyers and clothmakers. In the 15th century, he discovered a scarlet dye that was to make him famous. By 1601, Henry IV had become interested, bringing up 200 weavers from Flanders whose full-time occupation was to make tapestries (many now scattered across the museums and residences, both public and private, of Europe). Oddly enough, until then the

Gobelin family had not made any tapestries, although the name would become synonymous with that art form.

Colbert, the minister of Louis XIV, purchased the works, and under royal patronage the craftsmen set about executing designs by Le Brun. Closed during the Revolution, the industry was reactivated by Napoleon. It is still going strong at 42 Avenue des Gobelins (Métro: Gobelins). You can visit the factory —the studios of the crafts people, called *ateliers*—on Wednesdays, Thursdays, and Fridays from 2 to 3:45 p.m. Some of the ancient high-warp looms are still in use. The crafts people turn out modern tapestries inspired by such artists as Picasso, Léger, Matisse, and Miró.

CITÉ UNIVERSITAIRE: At the border of the Parc Montsouris (Métro: Cité Universitaire) is an international student community founded in 1922. In an idyllic setting, the students live in houses (often designed by famous architects) which suggest those of their native lands. For example, Le Corbusier did the Swiss House in 1933. The Portuguese House was donated by the Gulbenkian Foundation, the estate left by the Armenian oil tycoon. Donated by John D. Rockefeller, Jr., the Maison Internationale is the largest building, complete with a swimming pool and theater. The most interesting walk is along **Avenue Rockefeller,** where in spring the trees are heavily laden with blossoms, and students can be seen returning to their residences with loaves of French bread under their arms.

THE CATACOMBS: Every year an estimated 15,000 tourists explore some 1000 yards of tunnel in these dank Catacombs (tel. 329-58-00) to look at some six million skeletons ghoulishly arranged in artistic skull-and-crossbones fashion. It has been called the empire of the dead. First opened to the public in 1810, the Catacombs are now illuminated with overhead electric lights over their entire length.

In the Middle Ages, the Catacombs were originally quarries, but in 1785 city officials decided to use them as a burial ground. So the bones of several million persons were moved here from their previous resting places—overcrowded cemeteries considered health menaces.

In 1830, the prefect of Paris closed the Catacombs to the viewing public, considering them obscene and indecent. He maintained that he could not understand the morbid curiosity of civilized people who wanted to gaze upon the bones of the dead.

Later, in World War II, the Catacombs were the headquarters of the French Underground. You can visit these underground chambers every Saturday from July to mid-October at 2 p.m. From mid-October to June, you can go only on the first and third Saturdays of each month, also at 2 p.m. The entrance is 2 bis Place Denfert-Rochereau (14e). Admission: 6F ($1.37).

THE SEWERS OF PARIS: Some say Baron Haussmann will be remembered mainly for the vast, complicated network of Paris sewers he erected. The *égouts* of the city are constructed around a quartet of principal tunnels, one extending 18 feet wide and 15 feet high. It's like an underground city, with the street names clearly labeled. Further, each branch pipe bears the number of the building to which it is connected (guides are fond of pointing out Maxim's). These underground passages are truly mammoth, containing pipes bringing in drinking water as well as telephone and telegraph lines.

That these sewers have remained such a popular attraction is something of a curiosity itself. They were made famous by Victor Hugo's *Les Misérables*. "All dripping with slime, his soul filled with a strange light," Jean Valjean in his desperate flight through the sewers of Paris is considered one of the heroes of narrative drama.

Tours begin at Pont de l'Alma on the Left Bank (Métro: Alma-Marceau). A stairway there leads into the bowels of the city. However, you often have to wait in line as much as 2½ hours. Visits are possible on Monday and Wednesday and on the last Saturday of each month, except for holidays. Hours are 2 to 5 p.m. A one-hour visit costs 5F ($1.14). *Warning:* Visiting hours are likely to change from those stated, and times and days of opening should be verified with the tourist office before you go there. Telephone 705-10-29 for more information.

8. In the Environs

In the suburbs of Paris—reachable by either bus or Métro—are more sightseeing targets, beginning with:

THE BASILICA OF ST. DENIS: In the 12th century, Abbot Suger placed an inscription on the bronze doors of St. Denis: "Marvel not at the gold and expense, but at the craftsmanship of the work." The first Gothic building in France that can be dated precisely, St. Denis was the "spiritual defender of the State" during the reign of Louis VI ("The Fat"). The massive façade, with its crenelated parapet on the top similar to the fortifications of a castle, has a rose window. The stained-glass windows, in stunning colors—mauve, purple, blue, and rose—were restored in the 19th century.

St. Denis, the first bishop of Paris, became the patron saint of the French monarchy. Royal burials began here in the sixth century and continued until the Revolution. The sculptures designed for tombs—some two stories high—span the country's artistic development from the Middle Ages to the Renaissance. You are conducted through the crypt on a guided tour (in French only). François I was entombed at St. Denis. His funereal statue is nude, although he demurely covers himself with his hand. Other kings and queens here include Louis XII and Anne of Brittany, as well as Henri II and Catherine de Medici. However, the Revolutionaries stormed through, smashing many marble faces and dumping royal remains in a lime-filled ditch in the garden. Royal remains were reburied under the main altar during the 19th century.

In the dreary industrial suburb of St. Denis, the basilica is on the rue de la République (take the Métro to St. Denis Station). It is open from 10 to 11:30 a.m. and from 2 to 5 p.m. from April through September; off-season, the basilica closes at 4 p.m. The price of admission is 6F ($1.37), half-price on Sundays and holidays.

The next sight can easily be tied in with a visit to St. Denis.

MUSÉE NATIONAL DE LA RENAISSANCE: At a charmingly situated place right outside Paris, heading north on the route to Chantilly, Valery Giscard d'Estaing, the French president, inaugurated this museum devoted to works of the Renaissance. Called Le Château d'Ecouen, the castle in the hamlet of Ecouen was construed between 1538 and 1555 for the high constable, Anne de Montmorency. In 1806 Napoleon assigned the building as a school for daughters of Le Légion d'Honneur. On a promontory in a parklike setting, the château contains an exceptional collection of works from the Renaissance—

tapestries, paintings, and objects of art—which betray a heavy Italian influence. See especially the best-known tapestry, *David and Bathsheba,* 245 feet long. The museum is open daily except Tuesdays from 9:45 a.m. to 12:30 p.m. and from 2 to 5:15 p.m., charging an admission of 7F ($1.60), which is lowered to half-price on Sundays. To reach the château, take the Métro to the Basilique de St.-Denis, then bus 268 to Ezanville, which stops at the imposing museum.

CHÂTEAU DE VINCENNES: It's been called the Versailles of the Middle Ages, and it's had a checkered career. Encircled by the once-great forest the Bois de Vincennes, the château, like Versailles, was originally a hunting lodge. At the south of the town of Vincennes, the castle was founded by Louis VII ("The Young") in 1164, but it has subsequently been rebuilt many times. What you see today is merely a shell of its former self.

St. Louis (Louis IX) was fond of the castle; it is said that he administered justice while sitting under his favorite oak tree in the forest. Inspired by Saint-Chapelle in Paris, Charles V ordered a chapel built in 1379. That "citizen of the world" Mazarin and his mistress (the mother of Louis XIV) directed the completion of two so-called pavilions.

Louis XIV, however, wasn't especially fond of Vincennes, because he had another home in mind. In time, the château was to become a porcelain factory, an arsenal under Napoleon, and a supply depot for the Nazis. Now it is being restored by the government. Its most memorable role was that of a prison or dungeon, the most famous prisoner being Mirabeau, the French revolutionist and statesman.

Vincennes is a suburb, about five miles east of Notre-Dame. Take the Métro to the Château de Vincennes. It is open daily except Tuesdays, with guided tours conducted at 10 and 11 a.m., then again at 1:30 p.m. and every hour thereafter until 5:30 p.m. Admission costs 8F ($1.83), dropping to half that on Sundays and holidays. Telephone 328-15-48 for more information.

ST.-GERMAIN-EN-LAYE: Gourmet cooks know that béarnaise sauce was invented here, although the town has other distinctions. Only 13 miles north-west of Paris by rail, St.-Germain-en-Laye traditionally drew Parisians wishing to escape the summer heat.

Louis XIV lived here, but he was to desert it for Versailles. Still, St.-Germain-en-Laye has been the seat of the royal court. The Métro line from Paris will take you directly to the entrance to the Château Vieux (tel. 451-53-65), standing in the heart of town and dating from the 12th century. Built by François I, the castle is of ugly brick. Once James II stayed here, enjoying French hospitality while hoping to regain the throne of England. However, this Stuart king died here.

Napoleon III ordered that the château—built on a hill on the left bank of the Seine—be turned into a museum, tracing the history of France from the cave dwellers until the Carolingian era. And so it is today: the French Museum of National Antiquities, open daily except Tuesday from 9:45 a.m. to noon and from 1:30 till 5:15 p.m., charging an admission of 6F ($1.37).

Glass cases display tools, stones, even armor and jewelry, used or worn by the early settlers of Gaul. Of special interest is Sainte-Chapelle, built by St. Louis in the 1230s. To visit it, however, you must apply to the custodian.

At the end of the tour, we'd suggest a stroll through Le Nôtre's gardens, open from 7 a.m. till 9:30 p.m. At the world-famed Terrace, a panoramic view of Paris unfolds before you. On this terrace Henri IV built the Château Neuf, stashing his brood of illegitimate children there, at the end of the 16th century. The remains of the castle are now the **Pavillon Henri IV**, 21 rue Thiers, an illustrious hotel now closed for restoration. The Comte d'Artois, the brother of Louis XVI, was granted it as a gift. He planned to demolish it; then along came the Revolution. It was partly rebuilt in 1836 and became a hotel of world renown, favored by such writers as Dumas, who wrote *The Three Musketeers* here. Standing at the edge of the belvedere gardens of the old château, it is still elegantly old-fashioned. In a corner chamber the Sun King played fun and games with Mme. de Montespan. In memory of them, a room has been set aside as a museum.

9. Shopping in Paris

Perfumes in Paris are almost always cheaper than in the States. And that means all the famed brands: Guerlain, Chanel, Schiaparelli, Jean Patou. Cosmetics bearing French names (Dior, Lancôme) also cost less. Gloves are a fine value.

You can take advantage of a special discount offered to foreigners, which simply means you are exempt from French purchase taxes. This entitles you to a 15% discount off list prices, although it does entail some red tape. First, if you're taking your purchases with you, ask if the store allows tourist discounts (most do). Then you must purchase a minimum of 400F ($91.32) total in each shop to be eligible. You pay the full price to the store, and it in turn will give you a receipt in triplicate—one green copy (for your personal records) and two pink ones for the French Customs—and a stamped, self-addressed envelope. When you leave the country you hand the two pink receipts along with the envelope to the Customs official. He mails one back to the store and keeps the other to give the shop tax credit. Eventually, you will receive a check in the mail from the store for the discount due you. And don't worry about it—all good Paris shops follow through.

If you mail your purchases through a store, the discount will be immediately taken off your payment at the cashier's desk. Major department stores have hospitality desks on the street levels to assist in handling tourist discounts and to help you with any other shopping problems.

Further choice: Do your shopping within the city proper or wait until you fly out to make some of your purchases. In the tax-free shops at Orly and Charles de Gaulle Airports, you will get a minimum discount of 20% on all items and up to 50% off on such things as liquors, cigarettes, and watches. Among the stock on sale: crystal and cutlery, French bonbons, luggage, wines and whiskies, pipes and lighters, filmy lingerie, silk scarves, all the name perfumes, knitwear, jewelry, cameras and equipment, French cheeses, and antiques. Remember that what you buy must travel with you, and you are allowed to bring into the States the retail value of $300 in overseas purchases without paying Customs duty.

Shops are open from around 9 a.m. to 7 p.m. Small shops take a two-hour lunch break. Most close on Sundays and Mondays. The flea market and some other street markets are open Saturdays, Sundays, and Mondays. That intriguing sign on shop doors reading *Entrée Libre* means you can browse at will. *Soldes* means "Sale." *Soldes Exceptionel* means they're pushing it a bit.

RIGHT BANK SHOPS: Start at the Havre-Caumartin Métro stop to begin your tour of two "Grands Magasins." On the corner is **Au Printemps** (tel. 285-22-22), the city's largest department store. Actually, it consists of three stores and one supermarket connected by bridges on the second and third floors. Go to Brummel for clothing for men, both sports and dress. Printemps-Havre is mainly for books, furniture, and housewares, while Printemps New-store sells clothes for young people and children (the ground floor is mainly for perfume, cosmetics, gifts, and Paris "handicrafts"). Interpreters stationed at the Welcome Room on the main floor will help you claim your discounts, guide you to departments, and aid you in making purchases.

Another of the great department stores of Paris is the **Galeries Lafayette,** 30 Boulevard Haussmann (tel. 282-34-56). Inside most doorways is a Welcome Service telephone to direct you to the merchandise you're interested in. Of the three buildings comprising this department store, Lafayette offers the most exciting merchandise for visitors. On the ground floor are found the perfumes for which Paris is famous, as well as gifts, books, and records. The third floor has an exceptional collection of dresses for women. Incidentally, the top of Galeries Lafayette is open on sunny days. We suggest you take the elevator up there for an exceptional view of Paris.

After the vastness of these emporiums, you may want to devote your attention to some specialty shops. Up the avenue, at No. 73 Boulevard Hauss-mann, is the century-old **Trousselier.** You'll think at first it's simply a florist shop with some artfully displayed sprays. But look again, or touch—and you'll see that every flower is artificial, shaped in silk and handpainted by crafts people who pursue this famous French craft in the workshops in the rear. And what exquisite work! Everything is lifelike in the extreme. One cluster will bear a bud, a full-blown flower, and then one just past its prime and fading at the edges. The prices are worthy of the quality. This recently renewed store has been in the same family for three generations. Ms. Trousselier is actually there to welcome you.

Then walk back to the rue Tronchet. Before turning down the street, stop in at the corner establishment, **Aux Tortues,** 55 Boulevard Haussmann (tel. 265-56-74), across from Au Printemps. Offbeat and charming, this is one of the most delightful specialty shops of Paris, offering items unique and unusual made in ivory, *écaille* (tortoiseshell), and semiprecious stones. Look especially for the tortoiseshell combs, the ivory miniatures, and the tortoiseshell dressing sets. The prices aren't cheap, but then, you wouldn't expect them to be.

Turning down the street flanked by young boutiques, you'll arrive at the "youngest" shop of them all, the **Soldes Enfantines,** 17 rue Tronchet (8e), specializing in clothing for children.

Along the rue Royale, the street of the legendary Maxim's, you can turn right onto the Faubourg St.-Honoré, that platinum strip of the city where the presidential palace shares space with the haute-couture houses of Lanvin and Courrèges.

Lanvin occupies three buildings at the corner of Faubourg St.-Honoré and the rue Boissy-d'Anglas. The shop at 15 Faubourg St.-Honoré specializes in men's clothing, with a handsome collection of shirts and ties (the shop will also custom-make men's shirts and suits). We think Lanvin is the most elegant shirtmaker in Paris.

Hermès, 24 Faubourg St.-Honoré, is a legend, of course. The shop is especially noted for its scarves, made of silk squares printed with antique motifs. Three well-known Hermès fragrances, two for women and one for men, make excellent gift choices. The gloves sold here are without peer, especially those for men in reindeer hide, doeskin, or supple kid. The leather-goods store at Hermès is the best known in Europe. The crafts people working on the premises turn out the Hermès handbag, an institution that needs no sales pitch on these pages.

Courrèges, 46 Faubourg St.-Honoré (8e), is a bright, modern shop with lots of chicly used vinyl and plastic. It's a great place to drop in, especially if you're out walking your poodle. The workmanship in some of the boutique items is flawless.

Of course, there are others—so many others! You can visit **Christian Dior,** world-famous for its custom-made haute couture, at 26-32 Avenue Montaigne (8e) (tel. 256-74-44), with a wide selection of both women's and men's ready-to-wear, sportswear, and accessories, including separate salons for shoes and leather goods, furs, children's and juniors' clothing, and a variety of gift items, costume jewelry, lighters, pens, among other offerings.

The spirit of **Chanel** lives on, and her shop at 31 rue Cambon, across from the Ritz, is still very much in business.

And **Pierre Cardin** boutiques are popping up in every hotel and on every street corner. You can't miss them.

Emilio Pucci, 4 rue de Castiglione (1er) (tel. 260-89-42), is the Parisian showcase for this talented and temperamental Italian designer. Across the street from the Inter-Continental Hotel, this boutique carries a full line of accessories for women, all created with special flair. Included in the array are scarves, handbags, hats, belts, shoes, even his own perfume. Of course, Pucci enjoys one of the most outstanding reputations in Europe for his blouses and slacks.

Gucci, 350 rue St.-Honoré (1er) (tel. 265-55-60), is yet another showcase for a fabled Italian designer. Gucci, of course, is noted for his leather goods, including shoes and handbags. This boutique also has an excellent collection of scarves and two-piece ensembles. Its sweaters are especially outstanding. Another address is 27 rue du Faubourg St.-Honoré (8e) (same telephone number).

If your tastes are not traditional, you may want to avoid all these deluxe citadels and seek out exotica supreme at **La Factorerie,** 5 Boulevard Malesherbes (8e) (reached by heading up the Boissy d'Anglas from the Faubourg St.-Honoré). This is one of the most unusual and offbeat boutiques on the Right Bank, with a selection of items from Sumatra, the Philippines, Tibet, Ethiopia, and Singapore, to name only a few faraway sources.

Here's a round-up of other Right Bank shopping establishments you might want to take a peek at:

For Books

W. H. Smith & Son, 248 rue de Rivoli (1er) (tel. 260-37-97), is the English bookshop in Paris. A wide selection of books, magazines, and newspapers published in the English-speaking world are available. You can even get *The Times* of London. There's a fine selection of maps if you plan to do much touring. Across from the Tuileries Gardens, W. H. Smith also has a combined tearoom and restaurant.

For Unusual Engravings

Carnavalette, 2 rue des Francs-Bourgeois, off the Place des Vosges (4e) in the Marais sector, sells unusual one-of-a-kind engravings, plus illustrations from old magazines—some dating from the turn of the century. You can also obtain copies of *L'Indiscret,* which sold for 20 centimes in 1903.

For Perfumes

Freddy of Paris, 10 rue Auber (9e), near the American Express and the Opéra, offers moderate rates on all name-brand scents, top-fashion handbags, scarves, ties, French umbrellas, Limoges, crystalware, and costume jewelry. His shop is open daily except Sundays from 9 a.m. to 6 p.m.

Cathy Laferriere, 10 rue St.-Florentin (8e), is also good for perfumes. It's a small shop near the Place de la Concorde and is well stocked with all the familiar brands advertised in top-fashion magazines, including Lanvin, Nina Ricci, and St. Laurent.

For Antiques

Le Louvre des Antiquaires, Place Palais Royal (1er), is the largest antique center in Europe, attracting collectors, browsers, and those interested in Art Nouveau and Deco objects. For Americans, the Art Noveau and Deco objects are the best buys. The center stands across the street from the Louvre. Housing some 240 antique dealers, the showrooms are spread across 2½ acres of well-lit modern salons. The building, a former department store, was erected in 1852 according to Napoleon's plans for the rue de Rivoli. Arranged on three levels, the widely varied showrooms are a happy mélange, including everything from antiques to secondhand clothing items, from tapestries to books and stamps. Hours are Tuesday through Saturday from 11 a.m. to 7 p.m.

China and Crystal

Au Grand Siècle, 31 rue La Boetie (8e), is an elegant shop presenting the final word on antiques and reproduction furniture, silver, and crystal, especially Lalique. A small place, it is nevertheless filled to the brim with every imaginable item, including a splendid collection of lamps and small gifts. No low-priced items are offered, but it is a memorable experience in exquisite taste. It is open Tuesdays through Saturdays from 9:30 a.m. to 6:30 p.m.

Haute Coiffure

Molinario Coiffures, 1 rue Scribe (9e), is one of Paris's most complete and prestigious beauty complexes, a name famous in the world of haute coiffure. This luxurious salon is a favorite of women around the world who demand the ultimate in style and service. In addition to tending to the faces and tresses of women, Molinario offers a wide selection of wigs and other items. Men aren't neglected, either. **Molinario for Men** styles your hair, and will also help you if you are interested in a hairpiece or want to know more about hair weaving. Arrange for a consultation.

Operated in conjunction with the hair-styling salon is a boutique, offering a full range of small gifts, perfumes, and stylish hairpieces (tel. 742-39-35).

Gifts for Children

Au Nain Bleu, 406 rue St.-Honoré (8e). Any child you love is expecting a present from Paris, and at the "Blue Dwarf" you'll be bedazzled by the choice. Nor can any adult withstand the temptation to browse through this paradise of playthings. It's a world of toy soldiers, stuffed animals, games, model airplanes, technical toys, model cars, even a "Flower Drum Kit." Puppets come in all shapes, sizes, and costumes.

Men's Wear

Olden, 189 rue St.-Honoré (8e) on the corner of the rue des Pyramides, offers the discriminating shopper the maximum choice in menswear and accessories. The man who likes style will find high-fashion shirts, designer silk ties, sweaters, suits, sports jackets, sports shirts, belts, swimsuits, plus all manner of suede and leather.

Lenzo, 78 Avenue Champs-Élysées (8e). In the Lido Arcade, this outstanding shop for men's apparel caters to a large number of international stage and screen personalities (ask to see the customer scrapbook). The décor—Florentine wood paneling, marble tables, crystal chandeliers—is reflective of the kind of taste you'll find here. Ties, shirts, sweaters, shoes, coats, and hats in the latest styles are offered. Lenzo also does custom tailoring.

Cerruti, with a men's boutique at 27 rue Royale (8e) and one for women at 15 Place de la Madeleine (8e) (tel. 265-68-72), is also a good tailor for men—and has been since 1881.

Gifts

Innovation, 104 Avenue Champs-Élysées (8e). There are two floors to entice here, containing many items of exquisite taste. You can browse through the immense selection of purses, umbrellas, clocks, unique chess sets, leather luggage, toys, and wallets.

Eiffel Shopping, 9 Avenue de Suffren (7e) (tel. 566-55-30), offers you a free glass of cognac while you browse through the designer collection (Dior, St. Laurent, Lanvin, Chanel, to name just a few) of handbags, ties, scarves, watches, sunglasses, jewelry, perfumes, Lalique crystal, and much more. This tax-free shopping center, only one block from the Eiffel Tower, offers top-quality merchandise at discount prices, and all the salespeople are bilingual. It is open daily from 9:15 a.m. to 8 p.m. and on Sundays from 11 a.m. to 8 p.m. A second shop is at the Paris Convention Center, Porte Maillot, Boulevard Gouvion St.-Cyr (17e) (tel. 758-24-09), two floors above the Air Terminal, close to Concorde Lafayette and Meridien Hotels.

CUT-RATE SHOPPING: Paris no longer caters just to the well-heeled in its boutiques. Several shops have opened which offer leftover merchandise from some of the better-known fashion houses. Many items are sold 20% to 50% less than their original prices when they were displayed in a store along the Champs-Élysées. Of course, the famous labels have been cut out, but it's still the same clothing.

Perhaps the best known of the cut-rate boutiques is **Le Mouton à Cinq Pattes,** 48 rue St.-Placide (6e) (Métro: St.-Placide), which is down in the Montparnasse area. Here you can find the creations of such well-known designers as Daniel Hechter and Sonia Rykiel selling at one-third of their original price. Two similar shops, **La Braderie** and **Credule,** are on the same street, so check them out, too.

Another shop that seems to have a "permanent sale" is **La Trouvailles,** 43 rue de la Convention (15e) (Métro: Javel). Here outfits sell at about one-fourth of their original price.

At last Paris has a hand-me-down shop, although the merchandise hardly qualifies for "Second-hand Rose." It's **Maxipuces,** 18 rue Cortampert (16e) (Métro: La Muette). Some of the wealthiest women in Paris, and some of the most chicly dressed, bring their high-fashion clothing to this shop. How does an André Courrèges hand-stitched evening gown which originally sold for some $2000 strike you with a price tag of $225? Your friends back home may be dazzled when you appear at a party in a Saint Laurent original.

LEFT BANK SHOPS: Start your Left Bank shopping tour at the historic Place de l'Odéon. On a street branching off from here is **Lorenzi Frères,** 19 rue Racine (6e) (tel. 326-38-68), containing some of the most interesting sculpture reproductions, decorative accessories, and *moulages* (castings or moldings) *d'art* on the Left Bank. The house has been in business since 1871. You can also visit the studio of the talented craftsmen-owners (in the rear, but wait for an invitation).

Right nearby is **Rigodon,** 15 rue Racine (6e) (tel. 633-79-98). This is a puppet-and-doll world for every child, even those who are children only at heart. Hanging from its ceiling is one of the most varied and sophisticated collections of puppets in Paris. They come in all characters, sizes, and prices. It seems like a dreamland of unlimited imagination—donkey-headed women, Madame Pompadour, ducks, long-beaked birds, angels, Balinese dancers, skeletons, white-hatted chefs, witches on broomsticks, batwomen with feather wings, even Mistinguette with a cluster of feathers in her hair.

Back at the Place de l'Odéon, you can strike out again—this time down the rue de l'Odéon, which contains the kinds of item you might pick up at the Flea Market. Especially notable is a collection of jugs and pitchers, as well as turn-of-the-century bric-a-brac, even a sword collection. On the same street, at 22 rue de l'Odéon, stands *Seraphine,* which features framed embroideries and primitive artifacts.

At the end of the street, at the Car. de l'Odéon, you can turn onto the rue St.-Sulpice, and there you'll find **Art Investigation,** 38 rue St.-Sulpice (6e). You enter the building through huge wooden doors leading into a courtyard. Proceed to the first floor, where a beautiful collection of woodcarvings, silkscreens, and lithographs is on display. Most of the work shown here is by contemporary international artists, with the emphasis on graphics.

From here, you can walk to the rue de Tournon (6e), one of the most interesting streets for shopping on the Left Bank. At 13 rue de Tournon is a fashion complex, featuring that Vogue look at **Tan Giudicelli** and stylish boutique items for both men and women at **Micmac St. Tropez.**

After walking back along the rue de Tournon for a while, you can cut onto the rue de Seine (6e), where art-nouveau posters are sold cheek-by-jowl with genuine old masters. You pass along the **Buci street market,** where you can gather the makings of an unforgettable picnic under the shrill guidance of vendors.

Turning left onto the rue de Seine, you can stop next at **Jane Pradier,** 78 rue de Seine (6e), which has a collection of items from Japan, including flatware in primary colors, kitchenware, table accessories, wood cutting boards, wicker hat boxes, and bamboo coat hangers, among other things.

Nearby **François Girand,** 76 rue de Seine (6e), has extensive shelves of old books and stacks of prints, including colored prints of automobiles (1910 Fords, 1919 Renaults) and railway engines.

The **Galerie Documents,** 53 rue de Seine, contains one of the most original poster collections in Paris. Many of them are inexpensive, although you could easily pay 600F ($136.98) for an original. Your poster selection will be mailed back home in a tube.

Check the **Galerie Raymond Duncan,** 31 rue de Seine (6e), a rather culty shrine to Isadora's brother, with an interesting exhibition of the looms he developed and the unique tapestrylike artwork he produced.

Further along is **Robert Proute,** 12 rue de Seine (tel. 326-93-22), which was founded in 1894 and has been offering ancient and modern prints ever since, at bargain prices.

Autographs, 14 rue de Seine (6e), is a ten-foot-wide shop, owned by a bright-eyed collector of rare autographs, letters, and documents with famous connections. Often for very little money you can pick up some famed signature (of course, you'll pay far more if that person happens to be, say, Anne d'Autriche). He's collected all the fun people, including Henry Miller, Clemenceau, Rodin, Somerset Maugham, Marguerite de Navarre, and Picasso.

If you want a photograph of any Paris scene, old or new, apply at **H. Roger Viollet,** 6 rue de Seine (at the foot of the street). Every inch of wall space is lined with green looseleaf notebooks containing archives of photographs, some seven million in all, from every country in the world. The shop has been stockpiling photos since 1880.

At the end of the rue de Seine you can walk along the quais for galleries filled with graphics. On the river side of the street open stalls dispense tourist prints, postcards, second-hand books, and funky antique postcards—but few real bargains or finds.

And **Le Monde en Marche,** 34 rue Dauphine (6e) (tel. 326-66-53), has a large assortment of creative playthings for children at reasonable prices.

LES HALLES: Now that Les Halles is going through a rebirth, the produce market having moved elsewhere, a growing number of fashionable boutiques have moved in, opening on the side streets. The following is a random selection of the first of these avant-garde boutiques:

Mauve, 3 rue des Precheurs (1er), is the discovery of the year—that is, if you're seeking sophisticated second-hand finery. Typical is a second-hand dress by Jean Patou or a wedding gown from circa 1880. Lanvin and Chanel are heavily represented, as is Mistinguette, the late French actress. And, of course, where can you find beaded Napoleon III hosiery on the spur of the moment? In addition, a large collection of delightful white nightdresses, sumptuously embroidered, is featured. They are from 50 to 150 years old. Other items include a good collection of famous-name reading lamps and decorator's vases (Daum, Gallée), as well as ancient boxes, flasks, and perfume bottles.

Maurice Brocante, 4 rue des Prêcheurs (1er), is a miniature flea market with soda siphons, decanters, coffee mills, flat irons, glass curtain rings, porcelain, clocks, jewelry, and art deco lighting fixtures.

Campagnie des Mers du Sud, 3 rue des Prêcheurs (1er), is a miniature bazaar, with Moroccan capes, toys, a wicker basket of assorted spices, wall hangings, and vegetable colorings.

Sara Shelburne, 10 rue du Cygne (1er) (tel. 231-74-40), is what happens when a law student graduates but switches to couture. This is a ready-made boutique for women, with colorful dresses, separates, hostess gowns, hats from the 1920s, coats, sportswear, knits, and well-styled evening wear. An interesting detail: Sara designs and makes all her fabrics. She will make "on measure" for the same price as ready-to-wear. However, you must allow her a few days.

Antiques, 18 rue de la Grande Truanderie (1er), within full sight of the old market at Les Halles and set back about 200 feet off rue Pierre-Lescot, displays a tiny but unusually imaginative collection of belle-époque figurines, busts, and lamp statues.

Chapter V

PARIS AFTER DARK

1. Cafés, Bars, and Pubs
2. Spectacles and Striptease
3. Folk Songs and Chansonniers
4. A Supper Club
5. Jazz and Discos
6. Opera, Theater, and Music Halls

IN PARIS, YOU CAN DO almost anything after dark; you can even have the Arc de Triomphe lit just for you. The entertainment is varied, not just at the Lido and the Folies Bergère, where everybody goes, but at little offbeat places, such as the *caveaux* of the Left Bank. Visitors are constantly seeking the unusual.

Whether it's a splashy Las Vegas spectacle, "crazy" striptease, Juliette Greco in a supper club, a walk along the Seine, a cellar disco, or a smoky jazz club—Paris offers it.

1. Cafés, Bars, and Pubs

CAFÉS: The hour of the apéritif is a firmly entrenched ritual in Paris. Below, some of the more interesting cafés for your initiation into this custom.

Brasserie Lipp, 151 Boulevard St.-Germain (6e) (tel. 548-53-91), has been called the "rendezvous for le tout Paris," the city's unofficial Social Register. Picasso and Charles de Gaulle used to patronize this St.-Germain-des-Prés landmark, as did Max Ernst, Sartre, André Gide, Man Ray, Simone de Beauvoir, James Joyce, and James Baldwin. The owner, Roger Cazes, said Hemingway was the first man he saw at the 1944 Liberation. Nowadays, sitting on the moleskin banquettes, their faces reflected in the "hall of mirrors," are, perhaps, Françoise Sagan and Simone Signoret.

The Lipp doesn't serve Coca-Cola, but it does offer good-tasting Alsatian beer. Right after the Franco-Prussian war of 1870-71, an Alsatian, Lippman, opened the café, preferring "not to live in Germany."

A restaurant is inside, including an upstairs dining room that never enjoys quite the same chic as the back room. At the rush hours it's always difficult to get a seat, unless you're known by the management.

Many prefer to visit for breakfast, even as early as 8:30 a.m., ordering the traditional black coffee and croissants. At lunch or dinner, the house specialty is choucroûte (sauerkraut), served with pork accompaniments, 50F ($11.42). Some say Lipp serves the best sauerkraut in Paris; others ask, "Who cares?"

About three or four plats du jour are offered, costing from 52F ($11.87) to 60F ($13.70). The soup goes for 12F ($2.74), the Alsatian tarte maison for 22F ($5.02). Food is served until 1 a.m. (it's most fashionable to arrive late at night). The café is closed on Mondays and in July.

In black jackets and white aprons, the waiters keep alive the tradition of fin-de-siècle Paris. May it live forever!

Café de Flore, 173 Boulevard St.-Germain (6e) (tel. 548-55-26). In his *A Memoir in the Form of a Novel (Two Sisters),* Gore Vidal introduces his two main characters thus: "I first saw them at the Café de Flore in the summer of 1948. They were seated side by side at the center of the first row of sidewalk tables, quite outshining Sartre and de Beauvoir, who were holding court nearby."

Sartre, the granddaddy of existentialism, was often here during the war years. A key figure in the Resistance, he sat at his table clad in a leather jacket and wearing a beret. He was writing a trilogy: *Les Chemins de la Liberté* ("The Roads to Freedom"). Other famous faces who have frequented the Flore include Camus, Picasso, and Apollinaire.

An espresso costs 5F ($1.14); domestic beer, 6F ($1.37). Go any time before 2 in the morning.

Deux Magots, 170 Boulevard St.-Germain (6e) (tel. 548-55-25). Piquant blonds smoke long cigarettes. Women in black leather stroll in looking as if they've stepped right out of 1933 Berlin. An assortment of male clients resemble extras from *Irma la Douce.* Just blink your eyes for a moment and you will have missed a scene. The Deux Magots is now legendary, of course, drawing not only the most sophisticated of the St.-Germain-des-Prés set but an abundance of tourists in summer, the latter virtually monopolizing the limited number of sidewalk tables. Waiters rush about, seemingly oblivious to your waiting to place your order or pay the bill.

Inside are two large Oriental statues that give the café its name. Once known as the gathering place of the intellectual elite, Deux Magots drew such illustrious figures as Sartre, Simone de Beauvoir, and Jean Giraudoux. The crystal chandeliers are too brightly lit, but the regular clients are used to the glare. After all, some of them even read newspapers there. Off-season, it's not a lonesome café, as the habitués quickly learn who's who. A coffee costs 5F ($1.14), and domestic beer begins at 6F ($1.37). Deux Magots is closed in August.

Café de la Paix, Place de l'Opéra (9e) (tel. 260-33-50), is an institution, staked out as an American enclave ever since the Yankee troops marched down the street in their victory parade after World War I. It is still the most popular café in Paris with U.S. visitors, many of whom sit there reading their mail from the nearby American Express. Legend has it that if your next-door neighbors from Omaha are in Paris, you'll find them if you sit under the familiar green canopy at a sidewalk table long enough. To entertain you in the meantime, there's that stunning view of the Opéra.

The ghosts of the great are here: Émile Zola, Oscar Wilde, Edward VII, de Maupassant, Dali, Chevalier, Caruso, Chagall. No one can remember Charles de Gaulle dining here, but a messenger arrived and ordered a "tinned" ham for the general's first supper when he returned to Paris in 1944 at the Liberation. Even Nixon has had a coffee at the Café de la Paix.

You can get the drink your fancy dictates: a whiskey for 15F ($3.42) to 20F ($4.57), a Coca-Cola, for 5F ($1.14), or café espresso for 7F ($1.60). Add 15% for service. It's open from 10 a.m. to 1:30 a.m. all year.

La Coupole, 102 Boulevard Montparnasse (14e) (tel. 320-14-20). So well known is this Montparnasse café that some visitors stop off here with suitcases for a beer or coffee before beginning the search for a hotel. The clientele is mixed, ranging from Orson Welles to attractive artists' models to young men dressed like Rasputin. In 1928, Fraux and Lafon—two waiters at the Café du Dôme—opened La Coupole. At first, the Montparnasse regulars resented it, but it is now more of a landmark than any other café. Many of the Dôme's faithful customers were lured away, including Kiki, the prostitute who wrote a memoir with a foreword by Hemingway. The pillars running down the middle of the large room were decorated by artists between the two world wars.

Open till 2 a.m., La Coupole is a big, bold, and brassy brasserie. At one of its sidewalk tables you can sit and watch the passing scene, ordering a coffee for 5F ($1.14), a cognac VSOP for 19F ($4.34). Actually, you wouldn't think it to look at the place (the dining room resembles that of a railway station), but the food is quite good. Try, for example, such main dishes as sole meunière at 43F ($9.82). Especially popular are the fresh *belons* (oysters) in season. The tables on the right have the white tablecloths and the corresponding higher tabs.

Couples frequent the basement where a band plays for dancing. The "tea dance" is from 4:30 till 7 p.m., the soirée from 9:30 p.m. to 2 a.m. Your minimum is achieved by ordering a drink at 40F ($9.13). Métro: Vavin.

La Rotonde, 105 Boulevard du Montparnasse (6e). It's only a memory drawn from the pages of *The Sun Also Rises.* Once patronized by Hemingway, the original Rotonde has faded into history. The new one shares the once-hallowed site with a motion-picture theater. Papa wrote, "No matter what café in Montparnasse you ask a taxi-driver to bring you to from the right bank of the river, they always take you to the Rotonde." At an outside table, a coffee costs 3.50F (79¢). Food is served in the restaurant upstairs.

Le Select, 99 Boulevard du Montparnasse (6e), was also in *The Sun Also Rises.* Hemingway's hero walked past the "sad tables" of the Rotonde to the Select. Physically, the Select is somewhat as it was when it was favored by Jean Cocteau. Le Select basks in its former glory as a literary café; but it continues to flourish. It is beyond fads, seemingly outliving change, based on the eternal truth that a person needs a drink and drinking companions. A beer goes for 5F ($1.14) to 20F ($4.57), coffee for 4F (91¢). Hard-boiled eggs are still placed on the bar counter, with a shaker of salt.

Le Dôme, 108 Boulevard du Montparnasse (14e), has made a comeback. Redecorated in the belle époque style, it has never been more glamorous. All that remains of Le Dôme of times past are the pictures on the walls. Everybody showed up here at one time or another; today you get a healthy quota of tourists. A regular beer goes from 6F ($1.37) to 8F ($1.83); espresso, 4F (91¢). The food is adequate, including a potage du jour at 9F ($2.05) or sauerkraut garni at 30F ($6.85). A raspberry sorbet makes a good finish at 12F ($2.74). Métro: Vavin.

Rosebud, 11 bis rue Delambre (14e) (tel. 326-95-28), perpetuates the memory of Orson Welles's great movie *Citizen Kane.* It also refers to an Otto Preminger movie, *Rosebud,* which marked the screen debut of John Lindsay. An all-night eatery and bar, open till 3 a.m., it draws such drinkers as Marguerite Duras, Simone de Beauvoir, and Eugene Ionesco. Some of the clients appear dressed '20s-style, with headbands and cloches. Others could have modeled for Toulouse-Lautrec! The Rosebud is a combined coffeehouse, bar, and social center. Wine bottles line the walls, the tables are packed tightly together, and you're allowed just to "be"—screened off from the street viewers by discreetly drawn shades. Everybody seemingly knows everybody else.

The prices of drinks include service: 13F ($2.97) for beer. Popular with the late-night set is a bowl of homemade chili con carne, 22F ($5.02), although you can order a steak tartare for 31F ($7.08).

Le Henri IV, 13 Place du Pont-Neuf (1er). Try to drop in at sunset, ordering an apéritif at this dramatic location—in a 17th-century building opposite the statue of the "Vert Galant" at Pont-Neuf. Your patron, Monsieur Cointepas, bottles his own wines, listing some of his prize drinks on a blackboard menu. For example, you may order a special Beaujolais at 3.20F (73¢), or perhaps a glass of Chinon, 3.20F also, but "tasting more of the earth." He calls Le Henri IV a "bistro à vin." The snacks are good here, too, especially the sandwiches at 6.90F ($1.58) to 9.20F ($2.09). A special "farmer's lunch" is offered for 23F ($5.25). The place is closed Saturday and Sunday and in August, but open otherwise from 10 a.m. to 9 p.m. Métro: Pont-Neuf.

Ma Bourgogne, 19 Place des Vosges (4e) (tel. 278-44-64). As you sit under the arcades here, you'll think you're in an Italian town, perhaps Bologna. The café is most exciting at festival time in the Marais district, but otherwise it slumbers quietly, little changed since the days of Victor Hugo, who used to live on the square. An espresso costs 3F (68¢); a small admission price to pay for the mood and the view. For 9F ($2.05) you can have a glass of Châteauneuf-du-Pape. In summer select one of the rattan tables outside. In winter you may have to hover under the beamed ceiling inside.

BARS AND PUBS: Surpassed by the sidewalk cafés, the bars nevertheless enjoy a unique position in Parisian life. The pubs, on the other hand, are currently more in vogue than the cafés—especially if they are in the belle époque style.

Harry's New York Bar, 5 rue Daunou (5e) (tel. 261-71-14). The management instructs you how to get here: tell the cab driver, "Sank roo Doe Noo." Otherwise, take the Métro to the Opéra and walk down.

No bar in Europe is better known (a host of imitators was inspired). No bar in Paris is more popular with Americans, Harry's having been made famous by such men as Fitzgerald, William Faulkner, and John Steinbeck. In the 1920s and 1930s, it was patronized by Elliot Paul *(The Last Time I Saw Paris)*, Gertrude Stein, Ford Madox Ford, and Ring Lardner. It was also an oasis for American newspapermen in Paris and the birthplace of the Bloody Mary and the Sidecar.

Opened on Thanksgiving Day, 1911, it was operated by the original Harry until his death in 1958. Nowadays, the atmosphere of polished wood is kept suitably subdued by a Scot, Andy McElhone, the son of the founder. In 1932, J. H. Cochrane set the world's drinking-speed record here, downing 4.4 pints in 11 seconds. Primo Carnera hung up his gloves at Harry's in 1929, after losing the world's heavyweight championship; they are still there, dangling from a wooden monkey. Perhaps the greatest tribute to Harry's today comes from the fact that the IBF, the International Bar Flies, meets here regularly. A dry martini costs 18F ($4.11), and whiskeys range from 21F ($4.79) to 29F ($6.62).

Le Salamandre, 54 rue Pierre-Charron (8e) (tel. 359-35-07), between the Champs-Élysées and Avenue George V, was created by Jean Marais, the French actor and friend of the late Jean Cocteau, in an off moment. He was inspired by the sets of the movie *Beauty and the Beast.* This bar and restaurant shelters in the Château Frontenac, in an area of boutiques and high-fashion designers, and only an elegant place would do here. You drink under antler-like chandeliers and dine by candlelight, while soft piano music is heard in the background. The colors are Christmas green and red. One of the most "elegant" drinks that Frenchpeople order here is Scotch with a bottle of Perrier, 32F ($7.31). With the plat du jour at 76F ($17.35) go a free salad and wine as well as dessert.

La Factorerie, 5 Boulevard Malesherbes (8e) (tel. 265-96-86). Cancel your African safari and settle for a drink in this second-floor jungle, where you sip a planter's punch while a roving tiger considers whether you'd be suitable for dinner (a giant sheet of glass restrains him).

You climb a crude, curving staircase, hang your coat on a jungle branch or vine, climb through a simulated forest to find yourself a squatting spot on a black, shaggy, fur-coated seat. Everywhere are chattering, rude monkeys, exotic and extravangantly colored birds. It does seem a bit mad when you realize you're seeing portions of the Pantheon of Paris out a window past a prowling panther! Things like this usually happen in California—not in the Madeleine. Equally exotic are the habitués. Everyone is a production. The taped music of Duke Ellington or Louis Armstrong often provides the background mood.

The drinks are the third bit of exoticism. Try, for example, a Tigre (made with orange juice, Cointreau, Grenadine) or a Cobra (ginger ale, ginger beer, orange, and Angostura bitters). Most of the exotic concoctions from the bar cost 22F ($5.02) with alcohol, 19F ($4.34) without. A limited selection of food is offered. Service is an additional 15%.

La Factorerie is lodged on a tree trunk over a far-out boutique, under the same management, that offers a wide assortment of unusual gifts and apparel from Africa and Asia. It is open nightly till 11:30; closed on weekends. Métro: Medeleine.

Sir Winston Churchill, 5 rue de Presbourg (16e) (tel. 500-75-35). A corner of "ye olde" England in Paris. Actually, it's "merely the mock," but the reproduction is good. If the cut-glass mirrors, the Edwardian decor, the plush banquettes, and the dark wood do not convince, the tea from Fortnum & Mason surely will. Preferred drinks are Winston Red Barrel and Churchill Brown Ale on draught. Ale goes from 9F ($2.05) a half pint. You can even get "the real English breakfast," with orange juice, porridge, eggs, bacon, grilled tomato, toast, butter, and marmalade, plus tea, for 35F ($7.99). A set meal at 34F ($7.76) is served from noon to 2:30 p.m. and from 7 to 9:30 p.m. Métro: Place Charles-de-Gaulle (Étoile).

Pub Renault, 53 Avenue des Champs-Élysées (8e). Although it borrows the word "pub" from the English, there is no resemblance to that familiar institution. This is a decidedly offbeat place, where, to get to your seat in the back, you have to walk through an exhibition hall of Renault cars. While munching a hamburger, you can order the latest vehicle. In addition, there are gifts and gadgets, a boutique of records, and a car-rental office. At the charming café, you sit in a "horseless carriage," ordering a simple set meal for 35F ($7.99) to 45F ($10.27), served from noon to 2:30 p.m. and from 7 to 9 p.m., or just have a drink.

Pub St. Germain des Prés, 17 rue de l'Ancienne Comédie (6e) (tel. 329-38-70), pulls out all the stops to create a turn-of-the-century English setting. It's the biggest pub in France, and is the only pub in the country that offers 15 draught beers and 250 international beers. Rows of booths are set on a raised platform screened by a railing. Tufted black-leather banquettes, plate-glass mirrors, hanging converted kerosene lamps, and polished mahogany complete the picture. Glory hallelujah, it's open all night. You can order beverages of every description, including ales, lager, and beer, plus soda-fountain items as well. Drinks begin at 4.60F ($1.05), and menus start at 45F ($10.27).

Le Village Bar, 7 rue Gozlin (6e) (tel. 326-80-19), used to be a favorite haunt of James Joyce, and for those who would never be seen sitting out at a café table at the Deux Magots or the Flore it remains an oasis. The crowd's a little older, but the pace is not as frenetic as at the rivals in St. Germain-des-Prés, including the Brasserie Lipp. Interesting paintings hang over the bar; art posters are pasted about; recorded music plays softly; the service is smooth and polite, the company nice. A Scotch whiskey goes for 18F ($4.11), one of Copenhagen's Carlsberg beers for 10F ($2.28). In the back full meals are served. On the à la carte menu you can enjoy such dishes as a dozen escargots or sauerkraut garni, a complete meal costing from 85F ($19.41). Métro: St.-Germain-des-Prés.

Le Bar, 10 rue de l'Odéon (6e), right off the Place de l'Odéon, is one of the most popular Left Bank hangouts for students. It is permanently packed in the evenings with university students who order drinks which range in price from 8F ($1.83) to 15F ($3.42). The walls are decorated with posters, and a jukebox makes the joint jump. If you speak French, it might help if you're seeking contacts. But, as one Frenchman remarked, "Everybody at the Odéon speaks English." Métro: Odéon.

Bar Belge, 75 Avenue de Saint-Ouen (17e) (tel. 627-41-01), enjoys a certain vogue, which is why the denizens of Paris are willing to venture here to the hinterlands of Clichy (Métro: Guy Moquet)—anything for fashion. At least at the Bar Belge you'll be given some of the best beer in Paris, from Belgium. Your beer is served in special glasses, some a foot high. Try, for example, Radieuse Royale at 14F ($3.20) or "Triple Blonde" at 11F ($2.51).

The habitués stand at the bar, while those more romantically inclined take one of the tiny tables. The wife of the proprietor, Monsieur Forêt, sits behind the counter. The decor includes pictures of the Belgian royal family. All in all, the place looks as if it were lifted from the songs of Jacques Brel. You can order sandwich plates from 5.50F ($1.25) to 20F ($4.57). Closed Mondays.

Les Drug Stores

In a class by themselves, these so-called Drug Stores are pacesetters of what has become an international craze. Combined are a coffeehouse, ice-cream soda fountain (serving champagne and caviar, no less), snackbar, cocktail lounge, newsstand, and boutiques offering everything from baby oil to jewelry. When first created, they were denounced by the traditional French as American "vulgarisms," but they are, in fact, uniquely Parisian—totally unrelated to the drugstore usually found in the United States. Sophisticated, stylish, glitteringly avant garde, they offer frenzied activity approaching a world's fair exposition.

The exteriors of the Drug Stores are architecturally traditional, but inside they're another story. The St.-Germain-des-Prés branch—the most popular—is imaginatively decorated with huge bronze molds of the lips of Moreau, Marlene, Marilyn, Greco, Bardot, and Sagan—each one seen by the "eyes" of Picasso and Camus. Next door to the Brasserie Lipp, at 149 Boulevard St.-Germain-des-Prés (Métro: St.-Germain-des-Prés), Le Drug Stores's boutiques sell everything from mustache cups to hearts of palm. They are open daily till 2 a.m., even on Sunday.

A set menu, served all day, costs 35F ($7.99), including drink and service. The most popular item, seemingly, is a hamburger on a toasted bun, 10F ($2.28); a club sandwich is 15.50F ($3.53); a banana split or a Coca-Cola float, 10.50F ($2.39). Some of the desserts are smothered in enough whipped cream to make them immoral.

Other Drug Stores in Paris, quite similar to the one at St.-Germain, are at Publicis Champs-Élysées, 133 Avenue des Champs-Élysées (Métro: Étoile); Publicis Matignon, Rond-Point des Champs-Élysées (Métro: F.-D. Roosevelt); and Publicis Défense, Centre Commercial (Métro: R.E.R. Défense).

TIME OUT FOR TEA: For those who don't like wine at cafés or hard liquor at bars, the **Boulangerie,** 73 Avenue Franklin-Roosevelt (8e), continues the tradition of the "grandes pâtisseries" of Paris. This café specializes in brioches, chocolates, croissants, and all sorts of confectionery. The tarts average 8F ($1.83) a serving and are among the best you're likely to have in the city. The pastry chef is especially proud of his macaroons with almonds. A regular sandwich begins at 4F (91¢).

2. Spectacles and Striptease

According to legend, the first G.I. to reach Paris at the Liberation in 1944 asked for directions to the **Folies Bergère,** 32 Rue Richer (9e) (tel. 246-77-11). His son does the same today. Even the old man comes back for a second look.

A roving-eyed Frenchman would have to be in his second century to remember when the Folies Bergère began. Apparently, it's here to stay, like Sacré-Coeur and the Eiffel Tower. The affection of Parisians for it has long turned into indifference (but try to get a seat on a July night). Some, however, recall it with sentimentality. Take, for example, the night the "toast of Paris," Josephine Baker, descended the celebrated staircase, tossing bananas into the audience.

Ever since 1914, the Folies Bergère has stood as the symbol of unadorned female anatomy. Fresh off the boat, Edwardians—starved for a glimpse of even an ankle—flocked to the Folies Bergère to get a look at much more. Yet the Folies also dresses its girls (at least 1600 costumes at the last revue we saw) in those fabulous showgirl outfits you associate with Hollywood musicals of the 1930s.

The spectacle is the creation of Michel Gyarmathy, who surely must have inspected more navels than General Eisenhower did troops. Every Folies girl, house rules seemingly dictate, must wear at least eight bushy tails and a nest of towering head plumes.

The big musical revue begins nightly, except Monday, at 8:45. You can go to the box office at any time between 11 a.m. and 6:30 p.m. for tickets. The orchestra or balcony loge seats are likely to run you around 200F ($45.66), with the "galerie" going for 100F ($22.83). For the first and second balcony tiers, you'll pay from 130F ($29.68). A scale model at the box office shows you locations.

New Lido Cabaret Normandie, 116 bis Avenue des Champs-Élysées (8e) (tel. 563-11-61), is housed in a new panoramic room with 1200 seats, with excellent visibility. This palatial nitery puts on an avalanche of glamor and talent, combined with enough showmanship to make the late Mr. Barnum look like an amateur. The permanent attraction is the Bluebell Girls, a fabulous precision ensemble of long-legged international beauties. The rest of the program changes, but the bill we last saw included an artful juggler, a couple on ice skates, the best antipodists in the world, a ventriloquist, a troupe of dancing waiters, and a real waterfall. And that's only one show.

The dinner-dance at 8:30 nightly costs 255F ($73.52), including half a bottle of champagne. However, you can go solely for "la Revue" (at either 10:45 p.m. or 1 a.m.) and pay a minimum of 170F ($38.81), which also includes the half bottle of champagne, taxes, and service. And if you perch at the bar, you can get two glasses of champagne for 120F ($27.40). If you're a lone man you'll run into thirsty companions at the bar.

Go at least once in a lifetime! Métro: George-V.

Moulin Rouge, Place Blanche (18e) (tel. 606-00-19). Sometimes the show-girls are dressed (but not always) in feathers befitting a bird of paradise. At a recent opening a critic put it aptly: "The show must have cost a bundle." Seemingly, no expense is spared in this would-be wicked, spectacularly stunning revue. A question arises, "Is it any different from the Lido?" Frankly, not that much; it's even owned by the same management although supposedly a down-to-the-buff competitor. However, that truth admittedly won't stop hordes of visiting firemen from going to both of them.

For the festivities, the minimum charge is 190F ($43.38) per person, that tab including half a bottle of champagne. Should you desire both dinner and the obligatory champagne, the charge is 285F ($65.06) per person, the quotation including service. The food? Newspaperman Wolf Kaufman put it thus: "The groceries are well served and decently cooked." If you drop in and station yourself at the bar, drinks average around 85F ($19.41) each. Dinner begins at 8 p.m., the show at 10 p.m.

Hollywood studios of yore notwithstanding, the French cancan is danced best here. Renoir and Toulouse-Lautrec, especially the latter, immortalized "The Red Windmill." In his billboards Toulouse-Lautrec captured the dancers as no artist ever did, before or after.

If you're not interested in women displaying their wares, perhaps you'll be titillated by handsome young men in lamé loincloths (considered daring before the age of show-everything). On one recent occasion a nude couple dove into a tank for underwater love. You may be less fortunate and see a ballet, more naughty than Esther Williams—but a ballet, nevertheless.

Footnote: Appearing with Madame de Morny is a mime drama, *The Dream of Egypt,* Colette once performed a prolonged kiss—much to the righteous indignation of the first-nighters. The affair became known as the "Scandal of the Moulin Rouge."

Métro: Place Blanche.

Crazy Horse Saloon, 12 Avenue George V (8e) (tel. 723-32-32). Arthur Sainer wrote a review of the Sam Shepard play *Shaved Splits* that would have been appropriate as a description of the show at "Crazy." He called it (the play, that is): "frantic, wondrous, surly, delicious, expansive, cryptic, blatant, elegiac, fatiguing, corrupting, virginal, metaphorical, literal, stupefying, messy, giggly, two-dimensional, corrosive, counter-erotic, spaced out, rhetorical, convulsive, metallic, grubby, pricky, convivial, gyrational, overheated, popeyed, flat-eyed, wide-eyed, and funky."

That should tell you that Alain Bernardin's stripteasery is no ordinary cabaret. Gypsy Rose Lee told Bernardin, "You have gone beyond Minsky!" It's a French parody of a Far West saloon, which became the first emporium in France where the strippers tossed their G-strings to the winds, throwing up their hands for the big "revelation."

The management invites you to "Be cool! Do it yourself! We dig English like Crazy!" The out-of-towners are crowded in tighter than a powwow at Crazy Horse's tent. Between striptease acts, which make use of rear-screen projections, there are vaudeville-type skits and dancing on the minisize floor. The first show goes on at 9 p.m., the second at 11:30 p.m. At the bar, drinks cost 135F ($30.82) for two, increasing to 210F ($47.94) for two drinks at the tables.

The **Tour Eiffel,** Champ-de-Mars (15e) (tel. 550-32-70), offers a spectacle in a setting that competes with the show. The establishment is on the second floor of the Eiffel Tower. International headliners are featured. You can see it all for 200F ($45.66), including dinner but not the 15% service charge. The club is open nightly, and dinners begin at 8 p.m., the show following.

Le Milliardaire, 69 rue Pierre-Charron (8e) (tel. 225-25-17). The French have a hard-to-translate word for it: *bruit.* Call it almost anything you like: roar, zip, snap, clatter, bang, crack, ping, rattle, tramp, tread, blare. Regardless, we fully guarantee you'll hear all of these sounds by spending one *soir* at the Milliardaire.

Right off the Champs-Élysées, this glamor nook is entered by walking down an arcade and through a saloon-like door. Inside, at 10:30 p.m. and 12:30 a.m., the girls take it all off, a treat for students of anatomy. The "skin game" is played with professional skill. A rival of the Crazy Horse Saloon, Le Milliardaire boasts a bevy of beauties.

Two drinks at the tables cost 170F ($38.81) per person. At the bar, drinks go for the standard 70F ($15.98). If you're a lone male, expect some Dry Gulch Gerties to move in to help you share your thirst. Closed Sundays.

3. Folk Songs and Chansonniers

FOLK SONGS: In a class by themselves, the following recommendations are sentimental favorites and decidedly offbeat.

Au Lapin Agile, 22 rue des Saules (18e) (tel. 606-85-87), is a quaint little cottage near the top of Montmartre. Once known as the Café des Assassins, it was patronized by Picasso and Utrillo. Amateurs and established artists have painted it (see, in particular, *Le Lapin Agile* by Utrillo at the National Museum of Modern Art in Paris).

For decades, it has been the heartbeat of French folk music. Although the writers, poets, and artists have seemingly vanished to be replaced by tourists, the poetry reading, folk songs, and sing-alongs continue. Every night except Mondays talented performers entertain in a humble atmosphere, with tables and crude banquettes set around the walls.

The price of admission and your first drink ranges from 36F ($8.22) to 41F ($9.36). The second drink is half the price. Evening performances begin at 9:15, ending at 2 a.m. An hour at Au Lapin Agile is a glimpse into the soul of Old Montmartre. Métro: Lamarck.

Au Caveau de la Bolée, 25 rue de l'Hirondelle (6e) (tel. 633-33-64 before 7 p.m.; afterward, 354-62-20). This is a cabaret managed by the elegant and beautiful Renée Devainegie. The action takes place in a cellar built in 1317 as part of the historic Abbey of St.-André. In time it was a prison, a breeding ground for the Revolution, and a literary club, drawing such absinthe drinkers as Paul Verlaine and Oscar Wilde.

After descending a staircase, you search for a seat in one of the niches of the vaulted cellar—and then the spell begins. Balladeers, poets, and what one observer called "wittytellers, realistic and fancy fellows" are the performers. Often the audience joins in; it's especially popular with Left Bank students who know the "dirty old French songs." The performances begin at 9:15 and 10:30 p.m. Wednesday, Thursday, and Friday; at 10 p.m. and again at 12:45 a.m. on Saturdays. Dinner, served from 9 p.m., costs 110F ($25.11), everything included. Drinks are in the 20F ($4.57) to 30F ($6.85) range. Closed Sunday through Tuesday and in August. Métro: St.-Michel.

Caveau des Oubliettes: You enter through a church close, which hardly puts you in the mood for what you're about to see. The address is 1 rue St.-Julien-le-Pauvre (5e) (tel. 354-94-97), in the Latin Quarter, across from Notre-Dame (Métro: St.-Michel). Founded in 1920 by Marcel François, the *caveau* is one of the most popular attractions on the after-dark tourist circuit of Paris. It's sheltered in a 14th-century prison, the word *oubliette* meaning a dungeon with a trap door at the top as its only opening: victims were pushed through portholes into the Seine to drown. In costumes of different epochs, singers present *chansons* (love songs)—sentimental or bawdy—of France from the 11th to the 14th centuries. After the show, a guide will conduct you through the museum exhibiting a chastity belt, arms and armor, and thumbscrews. Drinks begin at 45F ($10.27), including service.

CHANSONNIERS: The chansonnier (literally "songwriter") is a Parisian institution. *Chansonner* means to lampoon, which gives you some idea of what to expect. The theaters of the chansonniers, especially those on the otherwise tawdry Boulevard de Clichy, provide a nostalgic link with the past. Nightly songs are not only sung but are often created on the spot, depending for their inspiration on "the disaster of the day."

The commentary on the day's events is loaded with satire, as parody holds hands with burlesque in this time-honored Gallic amusement. Wit and ridicule, fanciful and fantastic, make for an extravagant, bombastic revue. At the pinnacle of his power and glory, Charles de Gaulle was the number-one target of the barbs of these pundits, who irreverently pictured him as *le roi soleil* (sun king). Hear the comments of the chansonniers on the "oldest profession," many of whose devotees slink by outside their doors at Clichy.

Our favorite places include **Des Deux Ânes,** 100 Boulevard de Clichy (18e) (tel. 606-10-26). A sign, "Leave your chewing gum at the door," sets the tone. Down from the Moulin Rouge (Métro: Blanche), the theater charges 70F ($15.98) to 75F ($17.12) for its seats. Performances begin nightly at 9. Closed Wednesdays. The box office is open from 11 a.m. to 7 p.m.

We hope these revues survive forever; society needs them.

4. A Supper Club

Villa d'Este, 4 rue Arsène-Houssaye (8e) (tel. 359-78-44), is a sentimental favorite of ours. That's where we first met and photographed Juliette Greco. "You have made me beautiful," she said upon seeing the photographs. Frankly, in her case that task wasn't difficult. Amália Rodrigues, the great *fadista* of Lisbon, has also appeared there. You get the point: a showcase of some of the finest vocal artists in Europe. Of course, don't go expecting legendary talent such as the women named—but if they were appearing in Paris, the Villa d'Este is likely to be where you'd go to see them.

Right off the Champs-Élysées, this elegant supper club offers—in addition to entertainment—a smooth orchestra for dancing. A four-course dinner (typical nightclub cookery) is yours for 120F ($27.40), plus 20% for service, increasing to 150F ($34.26) on weekends. The minimum for drinks is 60F ($13.70). Closed in July and August.

5. Jazz and Discos

JAZZ: Paris is the leading jazz center of Europe. From the *caveaux* of the Left Bank to the clubs on the Right, you'll hear that Dixieland or Chicago rhythm. Many of the establishments recommended below combine jazz with rock.

Club St.-Germain, 13 rue St.-Benoît (6e) (tel. 222-51-09), may have enjoyed the peak of its fame during the existentialist heyday, but it's still around, offering some of the best jazz in Paris. The film *Paris Blues* was shot here. It is right in the throbbing heart of St.-Germain-des-Prés. You have a choice of going upstairs to **Le Bilboquet** (tel. 548-81-84), where a trio usually entertains for guests who want to drink and dine. For more than a dozen years, Robert Martin, the Gallic vocalist, has been singing here. Alcoholic beverages are priced high, because the drinks must pay for the entertainment. A bottle of beer costs from 28F ($6.39) to 40F ($9.13), depending on when you arrive. In addition, a service charge of 12% is added to the bill. You're admitted after ringing a bell and getting a peephole onceover, as in Chicago speakeasy days. Downstairs is the jazz cellar where drinks are more expensive. You pay about 60F ($13.70) for your first libation and about 30F ($6.85) thereafter. But, to compensate, there is no admission charge.

Le Patio, Hotel Méridien, 81 Boulevard Gouvion-St.-Cyr (17e) (tel. 758-12-30), may look like the Palm Court at the Plaza Hotel in New York. But it's a good jazz center, located in the largest hotel in the country, at Porte Maillot. A good jazz band plays here against a backdrop of fountains from 10 p.m. to 2 a.m. At intermission, you're treated to smooth piano playing. Just enter from the street, heading for the courtyard in the heart of the hotel. You will be charged no cover, and there isn't even a minimum. However, drinks begin at about 40F ($9.13).

La Chat qui Pêche, 4 rue de la Huchette (5e) (tel. 326-23-06), is a popular restaurant/bar/disco/*caveau.* Although the jazz at "The Fishing Cat" is not quite what it used to be, it's still played. You can also dine and dance to recorded music. Set meals go from 30F ($6.85) to 50F ($11.42). Couscous, the typical dish of Algeria and Morocco, is available. If you go just for dancing, you'll find whiskey costing 25F ($5.71) weekdays, rising to 30F ($6.85) on the weekends.

Le Riverbop, 67 rue St.-André-des-Arts (6e). Have you ever wondered where the jazz musicians themselves go after they finish work in those Right Bank clubs? Quite a few jammers head for a spot called "Le Riverbop" in the Latin Quarter. At first you'll think you've arrived at a deserted storefront. But it's the right address. After you're hit with an entrance fee of 20F ($4.57), you're shown down a stone stairway (watch your head!) into a dank "cave." But once you've arrived in these lower depths, the sounds are as cool as the climate. A beer costs 15F ($3.42), and the audience—mostly in their late 20s or early 30s—shows a respect for jazz bordering on reverence. Seating is on hard benches. The club is closed Sundays and Mondays and in August. Métro: St.-Michel.

Caveau de la Huchette, 5 rue de la Huchette (5e) (tel. 326-65-05), is also popular, especially with a young crowd and jazz lovers, although it was once known by Robespierre and Marat. French jazz musicians reign supreme here, joined sometimes by international and American greats, such as Lionel Hampton, Art Blakey, Wild Bill Davis, and others. Providing you are 18 years of age, you descend a winding stone staircase into a real cellar where you can listen to jazz and jive. The entrance fee is 35F ($7.99), although students pay only 30F ($6.85). With that ticket, beer is only 5F ($1.14). The caveau is open till

3:30 a.m. Saturdays. Hours other days are 9:30 p.m. to 2:30 a.m. The Caveau de la Huchette is open daily.

Les Trois Mailletz, 56 rue Galande (5e) (tel. 354-00-79), is a Left Bank jazz temple, visited by many overseas disciples. Devotees of black jazz get their fill here. Usually Memphis Slim is the headliner with a saxophone, or perhaps Bill Coleman on trumpet.

Your first drink costs 50F ($11.42), and there is no entrance fee. The music starts at 10 nightly, but the stride isn't reached until midnight. If you don't object to the cramped floor, you can dance. Closed Sundays and Mondays. Métro: Maubert-Mutualité.

Slow Club, 130 rue de Rivoli (1er) (tel. 233-84-30), really isn't. Offering New Orleans Dixieland jazz, it is one of the most popular Right Bank clubs, near the Louvre. Most often billed is the Michel Attenoux jazz group. From Tuesday to Friday two bands play, showcasing the famous Claude Luter, who played for 10 years with the late Sidney Bechet. The regular entrance fee is 40F ($9.13). The club is open every night except Sundays and Mondays from 9:30 p.m. till 2 a.m. Drinks begin at 5F ($1.14).

Other Right Bank favorites include the Living Room, 25 rue du Colissée, right off the Champs-Élysées (8e) (tel. 359-25-29). The Alice Darr Trio, one of the best groups in the city, appears here regularly. Go any time after midnight. The entrance fee is 30F ($6.85), and drinks begin at 18F ($4.11).

Perhaps the most authentic jazz club in the city is La Cigale, 124 Boulevard Rochehouart (9e) (tel. 606-59-29), 200 meters from Place Pigalle. Jazz and soul—imported from New Orleans—are featured nightly. American black groups often appear here. Whiskey costs 32F ($7.31); beer, 15F ($3.42).

Caméléon, 57 rue St.-André-des-Arts (6e) (tel. 326-64-40). Your host is Mr. Fang, but not the one made famous by Phyllis Diller. You're invited to the downstairs cellar, a combined disco/jazz center specializing in "cave dancing." Weekdays, there's a 25F ($5.71) entrance charge; 30F ($6.85) on weekends. A whiskey costs upward of 25F ($5.71). Look for the neon-lit chameleon outside. Métro: Odéon.

THE DISCOS: The French gave the world the discothèque, but that term is likely to mean anything today, as the recommendations set forth below will reveal.

Le Palace, 8 rue du Faubourg Montmartre (8e) (tel. 246-02-56), is the leading disco of Europe. Right in the heart of the Boulevards, it was once a theater, and many of the old trappings still remain. The main hallway is decorated in light brown with large mirrors, and the former foyer on the left (as you enter) is a bar, drawing fashionable Parisians who often finish the evening here after a premiere at a Right Bank theater.

From the bar you can climb to the balcony which is now filled with tables and chairs. Or from the main entrance you can join the disco dancing in the hall, the scene reflected in a wide mirror at the end. There you'll find another bar, this one with bartenders dressed as "punk angels" in psychedelic orange coveralls.

The music is quite loud but of good quality, and you will likely be listening to everybody from Diana Ross to Paul McCartney, from Grace Jones to Pink Floyd. Colored light rays flash around you, and an illuminated mobile rises and falls. A curtain rises, revealing erotic but humorous posters, along with pictures of the great Hollywood film stars. Most of the crowd is young, but all ages patronize the place. The entrance fee, including your first drink, is 70F

($15.98). After that you pay 25F ($5.71) for each drink. The disco temple is closed on Monday and Tuesday.

The **Barbary Coast Saloon,** 11 rue Jules-Chaplain (6e) (tel. 033-68-87). It's in the best of the speakeasy tradition. Incongruous for Paris, it thrives apparently for that reason. The decor was once described in the French press as a "pseudo-Texas saloon deep in the heart of Montparnasse." Ring the bell if you want to be admitted (we've never seen anyone turned away). People put it down, but we like it at certain times.

At 7 p.m. the house features what it calls a "minispectacle," with an orchestra, one or two usually talented vocalists, and, of course, the man at the keyboard. The regular dinner costs from 50F ($11.42) to 80F ($18.26). Incidentally, you can dine until dawn breaks over Paris.

From 9 p.m. on (and we mean *on*), there's disco dancing. The entrance fee, including your first drink, ranges in price from 25F ($5.71) to 50F ($11.42), depending on the day of the week. Métro: Vavin.

Wonder Club, 38 rue du Dragon (6e) (tel. 548-90-32), is one of the most frequented discos in teeming St.-Germain-des-Prés. The lighting is amorous, the customers young, the passports international, and the friends easy to meet. The recorded music is pop, with occasional deviations.

The doors open nightly at 9 (but we've never seen anybody there at that hour). On week nights, you pay a minimum of 25F ($5.71), which includes both your entrance fee and your first drink, as well as service. However, on the busy, crowded weekend nights that tariff goes up to 30F ($6.85). On Saturdays and Sundays, the matinees are popular as well, beginning at 3 p.m. and finishing just in time for dinner. When the doors reopen, they remain so until daybreak. Should you become ravenously hungry after all that frenetic dancing, the Wonder Club boasts a grill room offering emergency provisions.

Riverside Club, 7 rue Grégoire-de-Tours (6e) (tel. 354-01-72), is the typical Left Bank cellar disco. Usually this one has a line at the door, an international crowd attracted here not so much by what's happening inside as by the interesting clients likely to show up. It opens at 9 nightly, with matinees at 3 on Sundays. The entrance fee is 30F ($6.85) from Sunday to Thursday, increasing to 35F ($7.99) on Friday and Saturday nights.

LATIN MUSIC: Currently, rue Monsieur-le-Prince in St.-Germain-des-Prés (6e) is one of the most popular nightlife streets on the Left Bank. Activity reaches a frenzied pitch on Friday and Saturday nights, when automobiles are parked on the sidewalk and laughter and singing go on until dawn.

A standout on the street is **l'Escale,** 15 rue Monsieur-le-Prince (6e), which is small and dark, a cozy, intimate ambience enhanced by Latin murals. Latin rhythm is featured. The sound of the gaucho pierces the air. Your first drink costs anywhere from 45F ($10.27), but you can nurse it as long as you like. The club also has a "cave" where you can dance to a Cuban combo. Métro: Odéon.

FEMALE IMPERSONATORS: **Madame Arthur,** 75 bis rue des Martyrs (18e) (tel. 264-48-27). Behind the splashy façade, right off the Place Pigalle, Madame Arthur is no lady. His/her robust, blatant innuendo and humor, with no holds barred, either stuns or amuses.

For years now, this club has been one of the leading female-impersonator cabarets in Paris—in the world, really. You can dine here, although most tourists purchase only drinks. At the bar, your first libation will cost 45F ($10.27), increasing to 70F ($15.98) at a table. Every night Madame Arthur is receiving at 10, although it's better to call after 11 p.m. The cabaret shuts down at 3 a.m. Métro: Pigalle.

6. Opera, Theater, and Music Halls

THE OPÉRA: Dominating that frenetic traffic hub the Place de l'Opéra, the Paris Opéra is the largest in the world. Although it consumes more land area than any other theater, it doesn't have as many seats as the theater at Châtelet. The building itself was designed by a young architect who entered a contest in 1860 in the heyday of Napoleon III's Second Empire. He adorned the façade with marble and sculptures, including *The Dance* by Carpeaux.

At one time or another, most of the great, glittering personages of Europe —Henry James, the Divine Sarah—have descended the wide marble steps of the Grand Staircase. In red and gold, the theater or auditorium is sheltered under a dome adorned by Chagall in 1964, the subject of a controversy that continues to this day. Between acts, gravitate to the Grand Foyer, decorated with paintings, sculpture, chandeliers. Any fabulously wealthy king or monarch would feel at home there.

You have to attend a performance to see the inside of this neobaroque splendor. Tickets usually go on sale about one week before the actual performance. The box office is open from 11 a.m. to 6:30 p.m. Tickets range in price from 5F ($1.14) for the cheapest seats—*stalles de côté*—to 200F ($45.66), depending on the type of performance, in the orchestra and "first balcony." The Opéra is closed in August and on Sunday nights. Métro: Opéra.

For light-opera productions, go to the **Opéra-Comique,** 5 rue Favart (2e) (tel. 296-12-20). The most expensive seats cost about 80F ($18.26), although many good ones are offered for 50F ($11.42). The Opéra-Comique is closed in summer, but the box office is open otherwise from 11 a.m. to 6:30 p.m. one week before a performance is scheduled. Métro: Richelieu-Drouot.

THEATERS: Paris has five national theaters, including its opera house. Of course, the problem for most visitors is the language. However, for those who speak even high-school French, the theater can be a sparkling attraction in Paris. Perhaps you'll want to spend one night at the **Comédie-Française,** Place du Théâtre-Français (1er) (tel. 296-10-20), the First Theater in Paris. The French classics, including works by Racine and Molière, are performed here at prices that begin as low as 12F ($2.74), ranging upward to 56F ($12.78). Métro: Palais-Royal.

Ballet and opera are performed at the **Théâtre des Champs-Élysées,** 15 Avenue Montaigne (8e) (tel. 359-36-88). The National Orchestra, incidentally, appears here. The box office is open daily except Sunday from 11 a.m. to 5:30 p.m. Tickets cost from 10F ($2.28) to 200F ($45.66).

MUSIC HALLS: Still going strong in Paris! Offering popular family entertainment at its best, the **Olympia,** 28 Boulevard des Capucines (2e) (tel. 742-25-49), has seen the greats, including Piaf. It still books top entertainers, often venturing into Broadway-type shows. At widely varying prices, 2000 seats are available in the huge hall, ranging from 50F ($11.42) to 100F ($22.83) if Charles Aznavour is performing. Expect lots of vaudeville, much of it corny. There are usually two shows nightly at 7:30 and 9:30. Métro: Opéra.

THE ÎLE DE FRANCE

FIRST, VERSAILLES, then Fontainebleau and the Cathedral of Chartres. Those are the places known to international tourists, and those are the meccas that draw the tour buses. Indeed, they are the principal stars in the galaxy of the Île de France—and rightly so. They need no selling from us, but the lesser-known spots in this green belt surrounding Paris do.

Everything recommended in the chapter that follows lies within a one-day trip from Paris. You can, for example, wander through the archaeological garden of medieval Senlis in the morning, thrill to the Château of Chantilly in the afternoon, and enjoy the showgirls at the Moulin Rouge in Paris that evening.

Much of the "Island of France" is known to us through the paintings of such artists as Corot, Renoir, Sisley, Degas, Monet, and Cézanne. This ancient land through which Caesar's armies marched is often called the heart of France. Seemingly, it is the dream of every Parisian to have a little rustic cottage or farmhouse in this province. Romanesque ruins, Gothic cathedrals, castles left over from the age of feudalism, châteaux evoking the splendor of the 18th century, great forests such as Fontainebleau or Chantilly, sleepy villages, even an African game reserve—you'll find all of these and more.

Besides the attractions, small regional restaurants will introduce you to the provincial cooking of France.

We'll begin our exploration at one of the top-ranking sights in the world—

1. Versailles

Back in *le grand siècle,* all you needed was a sword, a hat, and a bribe for the guard at the gate. Providing you didn't look as if you had smallpox, you'd be admitted to the inner precincts of the palace, there to stroll through glittering salon after dazzling chamber—watching the Sun King at his banqueting table, or else doing something more personal. Louis XIV was indeed the State, and was accorded about as much privacy as an institution.

In 50 years, Versailles went from the simple hunting lodge of Louis XIII to a lavish palace, a monument to the age of absolutism. What you see today has been called the greatest living museum of a vanished life on the face of our planet. Conceived in 1661, the construction involved anywhere from 32,000 to 45,000 workmen, some of whom had to drain marshes—often at the cost of their lives—and move forests.

Enraged with jealousy that his finance minister, Fouquet, could live better than he did at Fontainebleau, Louis XIV set out to create a palace that would be the awe of Europe. He entrusted Louis Le Vau with the architecture, although Hardouin-Mansart was to play a great role later on. Le Brun decorated the interior. Together these men created grandeur and elegance that were to be copied but never duplicated all over Europe. Versailles became a symbol of pomp, ceremony, and opulence.

To keep an eye on them (and with good reason), Louis XIV summoned the nobles of France to live at his court. There he amused them with constant entertainment and lavish banquets. To some he awarded such tasks as holding his ermine-lined robe. While the French aristocrats played away their lives, often in silly intrigues, the peasants back on the estates were sowing more than grain. They were planting the seeds of the Revolution.

When the Sun King shone no more in 1715, he was succeeded by his great-grandson, Louis XV, who continued the outrageous pomp, although he is said to have predicted the outcome: *"Apres moi, le déluge"* ("After me, the deluge"). His wife, Marie Leczinska, was shocked at the morality, or lack of it, at Versailles. When her husband tired of her, she lived as a nun, while the king's attention wandered to Madame de Pompadour, who was accused of running up a debt for her country far beyond that of a full-scale war. On her death, Madame du Barry replaced her.

Louis XVI, however, found his grandfather's behavior scandalous—in fact, he ordered that the "stairway of indiscretion" be removed. This rather dull, weak king and his queen, Marie Antoinette, were at Versailles when they were notified, on October 6, 1789, that mobs were marching on the palace. As predicted, "le déluge" had arrived.

Napoleon stayed at Versailles, but he never seemed overly fond of it. Perhaps the image of the Sun King burned too strongly in his mind. The Citizen King, Louis-Philippe, who reigned from 1830 to 1848, prevented the destruction of Versailles by converting it into a museum dedicated to the glory of France. To do that, he had to surrender some of his own not-so-hard-earned currency. John D. Rockefeller contributed heavily toward the restoration of Versailles, and work continues to this day.

The six magnificent **Grands Apartments** are in the Louis Quatorze style, taking their names from the allegorical ceiling paintings. The best-known is the Salon of Hercules, painted by François Le Moyne, using Pompadour red and depicting the club-carrying strongman riding in a chariot. Beginning in 1733, the artist worked on that ceiling for three years, completing it in time for his suicide. Louis XV was delighted (by the painting, not the suicide). In one of these apartments, the Salon of Mercury, Louis XIV died in 1715 after one of the longest reigns in history, lasting 72 years.

Visitors pass through the Salon of War, wherein a bas-relief by Coysevox depicting a triumphant Sun King on horseback trampling on his enemies (or victims). Finally, they arrive at the most famous room at Versailles: the **Hall of Mirrors,** 236 feet long. Begun by Mansart in 1678 in the Louis-XIV style, it was decorated by Le Brun with 17 large windows matched with corresponding reflecting mirrors. On June 28, 1919, the treaty ending World War I was signed in this corridor. Ironically, the German Empire was also proclaimed there in 1871.

The royal apartments were for show, but Louix XV and Louis XVI retired to the **Petits Apartments** to escape the demands of court etiquette. Louis XV died in his bedchamber in 1774, the victim of smallpox. In a second-floor apartment, which can be visited only with a guide, he stashed away Mme. du Barry and earlier Mme. de Pompadour. Also shown is the apartment of Mme. de Maintenon, who was first the mistress of Louis XIV, later his wife. Attempts are being made, as far as possible, to return the **Queen's Apartments** to their original setting as in the days of Marie Antoinette, when she played her harpsichord in front of specially invited guests.

Her king, Louis XVI, had an impressive **Library,** designed by Gabriel, which was sumptuous enough; but, library or no, the monarch remained dim-witted. Its panels are delicately carved, and the room has been restored and refurnished. The Clock Room contains Passement's astronomical clock, encased in gilded bronze. Twenty years in the making, it was completed in 1753. The clock is supposed to keep time until the year 9999. At the age of seven Mozart played in this room for the court.

Gabriel designed the **Opéra** for Louis XV in 1748, although it wasn't completed until 1770. The bas-reliefs are by Pajou, and bearskin rugs once covered the floor. In its heyday, it took 3000 powerful candles to light the place. The final restoration of the theater was carried out in 1957, replacing Louis Philippe's attempt at refurbishing.

With gold and white harmony, Hardouin-Mansart built the **Royal Chapel** in 1699, dying before its completion. Louis XVI, when still the dauphin, married Marie Antoinette there. Both were teenagers.

Spread across 250 acres, the **Gardens of Versailles** were laid out by the great landscape artist André le Nôtre. At the peak of their glory, 1400 fountains spewed forth (a limited fountain display is now staged on the first and third Sundays of each month from June through September—but consult the Tourist Bureau). *The Buffet* is an exceptional one, having been designed by Mansart. One fountain depicts Apollo in his chariot pulled by four horses, surrounded by tritons emerging from the water to light the world.

Le Nôtre created a Garden of Eden in the Île de France, using ornamental lakes and canals, geometrically designed flower beds, and avenues bordered with statuary. On the mile-long "Grand Canal" Louis XV—imagining he was in Venice—used to take gondola rides with his "favorite," whoever that was.

A long walk across the park will take you to the **Grand Trianon,** in pink-and-white marble, designed by Hardouin-Mansart for Louis XIV in 1687. Traditionally, it's been a place where France has lodged important guests, although De Gaulle wanted to turn it into a weekend retreat for himself. Nixon slept there in the room where Madame de Pompadour died. Queen Victoria did not, failing to show up for an expected visit. Madame de Maintenon—once called "a devil in the guise of a woman"—also slept there, as did Napoleon I. The original furnishings are gone, of course, with mostly Empire pieces there today.

Gabriel, the designer of the Place de la Concorde in Paris, built the **Petit Trianon** in 1768 for Louis XV. Actually, its construction was inspired by Madame de Pompadour, who died before it was readied. So Louis used it for his trysts with Madame du Barry. In time, Marie Antoinette adopted it as her favorite residence. There she could escape the rigid life back at the main palace. Many of the current furnishings, including a few in her rather modest bedroom, belonged to the ill-fated queen. Napoleon I once presented it to his sister, Pauline Borghese, but the emperor ungallantly took it back and gave it instead to his new bride, Marie-Louise.

Behind the Petit Trianon is the **Hamlet,** that collection of little thatched farmhouses—complete with a water mill—where Marie Antoinette could pretend she was a shepherdess, tending to her perfumed lambs. Lost in a bucolic world, she was there on the morning the news came from Paris that the Revolution was launched. Nearby is the **Temple of Love,** built in 1775 by Richard Mique, the queen's favorite architect. In the center of its Corinthian colonnade is a reproduction of Bouchardon's Cupid shaping a bow from the club of Hercules.

Between the Grand and the Petit Trianons is the entrance to the **Carriage Museum,** housing coaches from the 18th to the 19th centuries—among them one used at the coronation of Charles X, another used at the wedding of Napoleon I to Marie-Louise. One sleigh rests on tortoise runners. (Your ticket to the Petit Trianon will also admit you to see these *voitures*).

The Grand Apartments, the Royal Chapel, and the Hall of Mirrors can be visited without a guide any time between 9:45 a.m. and 5:30 p.m., costing 9F ($2.05) for admission, but only half price on Sundays. Other sections of the château may be visited only at specific hours. For example, the apartments of Mme. de Pompadour and Mme. du Barry are open at 2:45 p.m., the Opéra at 11:30 a.m. The same ticket to the Grand Apartments will also admit you to the Museum of the History of France, open daily from 2 to 5 p.m. Some of these sections are closed temporarily as they undergo restoration. The palace is closed Mondays and holidays.

The Grand Trianon is open daily from 9:45 a.m. to 6 p.m. from April 1 to September 30, and until 5 p.m. otherwise. Entrance costs 7F ($1.60), that tab reduced to half on Sundays. The Petit Trianon is open daily except Mondays from 2 to 6 p.m., charging 4F ($91¢) weekdays, 2F (46¢) on Sundays. The Museum of Carriages is closed as of this writing because of restoration. Son et lumière programs are staged in summer (consult the Tourist Bureau).

GETTING THERE: Versailles lies only 13 miles southwest of Paris. If you're driving down (Route N10), you can park your car on the Place des Armes in front of the palace. To reach Versailles, it's not necessary to take a guided tour. Take the Métro to the Pont de Sèvres exit and switch onto bus 171. The trip to Versailles, costing 7.50F ($1.71), lasts 15 minutes. If you pay with three Métro tickets from your carnet packet of 10, the cost is only 4F ($91¢). You'll be let off right near the gates of the palace. It's also possible to travel to Versailles on one of the commuter trains leaving every 15 minutes from Paris. The station is connected to the Invalides Métro stop. Go all the way to the Versailles-Rive Gauche station, turning right when you come out. Eurailpass holders travel free; otherwise, the cost is 3.60F (82¢) one way.

THE LEADING HOTEL: Trianon-Palace, 1 Boulevard de la Reine (tel. 950-34-12), is almost like living at the Grand Trianon. It's a classically designed palace, set in its own five-acre garden bordering those of the Trianons of the Château de Versailles. Its stately old-world charm, its quietness near where Marie Antoinette romped with her "perfumed" sheep, are persuasive.

In 1919 the hotel was the headquarters of the Versailles Peace Conference. Gathered in the salon were Woodrow Wilson, Lloyd George, and Clemenceau, plus other national leaders from Italy and Belgium. Today the Trianon-Palace graciously serves many tourists who make it their base for exploring Paris, as it's only 25 minutes by car from the Champs-Élysées to the peace of the countryside. The dignified rooms are decorated traditionally, with subdued colors—all harmonious, aided by the discreet use of antiques and many fine reproductions. Many of the bedchambers are decidedly old-fashioned, although a few of them have been renewed in a modernization program. In a single room the rate is 215F ($49.08), rising to 340F ($77.62) in a double.

For years, the hotel's restaurant has been the classic dining choice in Versailles. The dining room is dramatic, with fluted columns, crystal chandeliers, and cane-backed Louis XVI-style chairs. The set menus are quite extensive, at 85F ($19.41) and 115F ($26.25), plus 15% service. The food embraces most of the classic French dishes. On one recent occasion, we began with an avocado vinaigrette, followed by coquille St.-Jacques Bordelaise, lamb chops with a risotto studded with bits of chicken liver, then a selection from the cheese board, and, finally, crêpes suzette. A banquet really! If you order à la carte, expect to pay from 200F ($45.66) to 250F ($57.08) per person.

If you're staying over, consider the **Hotel Richaud,** 16 rue Richaud (tel. 950-10-42), on a small street opposite the Versailles Hospital, which was built during Louis XIV's reign. This hotel has been completely redecorated, with modernized rooms and plumbing. The floors are carpeted, and the decorations are classic but nicely assorted. The furniture has no particular style, but it's comfortable. Prices start at 92F ($21) for a double room with shower, rising to 150F ($34.26) for a room with bath and toilet. A continental breakfast is 12F ($2.74) extra. Some of the accommodations have television sets.

RESTAURANTS: Chances are, you'll be dining at Versailles. The town is well equipped, offering restaurants in all price ranges, of which we shall survey three.

The Top Choices

Les Trois Marches, 3 rue Colbert (tel. 950-13-21), Gérard Vié is, it is generally conceded, the most talented and creative chef entertaining visitors to Versailles these days. He has brought a remarkable culinary experience to his restaurant, and, because of that, attracts a discerning clientele who don't mind paying from 200F ($45.66) to 250F ($57.08) for a complete meal. The food is subtle, often daringly inventive and conceived, the service smooth. Don't go with any preconceived notions about food here, because Monsieur Vié is likely to break down your reserves. In air-conditioned comfort, you can order his specialty, which is canard (duck) de Challans with cider vinegar and honey. For those who want to be more experimental, we'd suggest, if featured, a raw haddock with pepper, even steak with oysters. From September to May he offers a cold flan made with foie gras and oysters which is heavenly, smooth and delicious. Another seasonal specialty in the spring is a crayfish salad with crisp vegetables. For closing times, phone the number given above.

La Boule d'Or, 25 rue du Maréchal Foch (tel. 950-22-97), is the oldest inn in Versailles (1696). Diners are transported back through the centuries. There are two floors, the upper one more formal, with an antique grandfather clock, paneled windows, ceramic-stove fireplaces, damask cloths, Louis XIII-style chairs, a glass case with books of Louis XIII, Louis XIV, and Louis XV, plus pictures by Hobéma, Mignard, and Sorg. The chef specializes in many dishes native to Franche-Comté, a mountainous district south of Alsace, and also in the 17th- and 18th-century style of cooking, which is very important in Versailles.

Among the à la carte selections, a well-recommended specialty is le carré d'agneau (loin of lamb) with gratin dauphinois (potatoes thinly sliced and baked with a creamy cheese mixture), costing 70F ($15.98) per person (a minimum of two must order it). For dessert, try perhaps a sorbet covered with raspberry liqueur, 28F ($6.39). For a complete meal, expect to spend at least 150F ($34.26). Closed Mondays.

The Budget Range

Du Dragon, 30 bis rue des Réservoirs (tel. 950-70-02), is an old-style corner restaurant not far from the heart of Versailles. In a tab-happy town, it is a refreshing change of pace for overburdened budgets. Brown-red cloths drape the tables in the glassed-in sidewalk café, although the inside is the magnet in the cooler months.

There are two price levels for lunch: the cheaper costs 35F ($7.99); wine and service are extra. For that, you are given an appetizer, a meat or fish course, then a dessert. The more elaborate 49F ($11.19) menu includes five courses. Two of the à la carte specialties are Burgundy-style snails, 28F ($6.39), and frog legs à la Provençale, also 28F. Du Dragon is open every day except Tuesday.

2. Fontainebleau

Napoleon called the Palace of Fontainebleau the house of the centuries. Much of French history has taken place within its walls, perhaps no moment more memorable than when Napoleon I stood on the horseshoe-shaped stairway and bade a loving farewell to his army before his departure to Elba and exile. That scene has been the subject of seemingly countless paintings, including Vernet's *Les Adieux* of the emperor.

Napoleon's affection for Fontainebleau (perhaps Versailles carried to many memories of Louis XIV) was understandable. He was following the pattern of a grand parade of French kings in the pre-Versailles days who used Fontainebleau as a resort, hunting in its magnificent forest. Under François I the hunting lodge became a royal palace, much in the Italian Renaissance style that the king so admired and wanted to imitate. The style got botched up, but many artists, including Benvenuto Cellini, came from Italy to work for the French monarch.

Under the patronage of François I, the School of Fontainebleau—led by the painters Rosso Fiorentino and Primaticcio—grew in prestige. These two artists adorned one of the most outstanding rooms at Fontainebleau: the **Gallery of François I,** 210 feet long. (The restorers under Louis-Philippe did not completely succeed in ruining it.) Surrounded by pomp, François I walked the length of his gallery while artisans tried to tempt him with their wares, job-seekers asked favors, and heavily scented courtesans tried to lure him away from the Duchess d'Étampes. The stucco-framed panels depict such scenes as Jupiter (portrayed as a bull) carrying off Europa, the *Nymph of Fontainebleau*

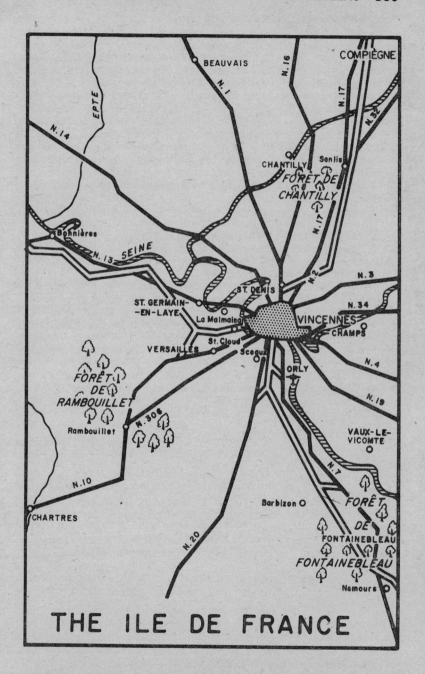

THE ILE DE FRANCE

(with a lecherous dog appearing through the reeds), and the monarch himself holding a pomegranate, a symbol of unity. However, the frames compete with the pictures. Everywhere is the salamander, symbol of the Chevalier King.

If it is true that François I built Fontainebleau for his mistress, then Henri II, his successor, left a fitting memorial to the woman he loved, Diane de Poitiers. Sometimes called the Gallery of Henri II, the **Ballroom** is in the mannerist style, the second splendid interior of the château. The monograms H & D are interlaced in the decoration. The king didn't believe in keeping his affection for his mistress a secret. At one end of the room is a monumental fireplace supported by two bronze satyrs, made in 1966 (the original ones were melted down in the Revolution). At the opposite side is the salon of the musicians, with sculptured garlands. The ceiling contains octagonal coffering adorned with rosettes. Above the wainscoting is a series of frescoes, painted between 1550 and 1558, depicting such mythological subjects as *The Feast of Bacchus*.

An architectural curiosity is the **Louis XV Staircase**, richly and elegantly adorned. Originally, the ceiling was decorated by Primaticcio for the bedroom of the Duchess d'Étampes. When an architect was designing the stairway, he simply ripped out her floor and used the bedroom ceiling to cover the stairway. Of the Italian frescoes that were preserved, one depicts the Queen of the Amazons climbing into Alexander's bed.

When Louis XIV ascended to the throne, Fontainebleau was virtually neglected because of his preoccupation with Versailles. However, he wasn't opposed to using the palace for house guests—specifically such unwanted ones as Queen Christina, who had abdicated the throne of Sweden. Apparently thinking she still had "divine right," she ordered one of the most brutal royal murders on record—that of her lover, Monaldeschi, who had ceased to please her.

Although in the main neglected by Louis XIV and his heirs, Fontainebleau found renewed glory—and shame—under Napoleon I. You can wander around much of the palace on your own, but most of the **Napoleonic Rooms** are accessible by guided tour only. Impressive are his throne room and his bedroom (look for his symbol, a bee). You can also see where the emperor signed his abdication (the document exhibited is a copy). The furnishings in the Empress Josephine's apartments and the grand apartments of Napoléon evoke the Imperial heyday.

Minor apartments include those once occupied by Mme. de Maintenon, the much-neglected wife of Louis XIV. Another was occupied by Pope Pius VII, who was kept a virtual prisoner by Napoleon; still another by Marie Antoinette. A bed she ordered didn't arrive on time, although the Empress Eugénie, wife of Napoleon III, later slept in it.

The apartments are open daily except Tuesday from 10 a.m. to 12:30 p.m. and from 1 to 5 p.m., charging an admission weekdays of 6F ($1.37), 3F (68¢) on Sundays.

After your long trek through the palace, a visit to the gardens and especially the carp pond is in order, but the gardens are only a prelude to the Forest of Fontainebleau.

GETTING THERE: Fontainebleau is reached by frequent train service from the Gare de Lyon in Paris, a 37-mile journey. Depending on which train you take, the trip lasts from 35 minutes to one hour. The round-trip fare in economy class is 35F ($7.99). The train station of Fontainebleau is just outside the town in Avon, a suburb of Paris. For the two-mile trip to the château, you can take the town bus, which makes a round trip every 10 to 15 minutes on weekdays (every 30 minutes on Sundays); the one-way fare is only 3F (68¢).

HOTELS AND RESTAURANTS: You need not venture far from the château for either a room or a meal.

Hôtel de l'Aigle Noir ("The Black Eagle"), 27 Place Napoléon Bonaparte (tel. 422-20-27), directly opposite the château, has its own share of dignity and glamor. Once the private home of the Cardinal de Retz, it was built with a formal entrance to its courtyard, through the high dark-green iron grill and pillars crowned by the namesake black eagles.

The interior is splendid, as exemplified by the *campagne* bar in honor of Napoleon, decorated with a red-and-white-striped canopied ceiling, swords, and helmets. The main salon jealously retains its original high stone fireplace, glistening marble floors, and Directoire furnishings with silk coverings and polished woods.

The private mansion was converted into a hotel in 1720. The hotel was entirely renovated in 1976, but the atmosphere has remained unchanged or, rather, has been reinforced. The 25 bedrooms and four suites have bathrooms and toilets, television, radio, minibar, direct-line telephone, double windows, and electric heating. They are all furnished with antiques, and each room has its individual decoration.

Rates range from 288F ($65.75) to 360F ($82.19) for double rooms, and suites are quoted at 432F ($98.63), service and taxes included. A set meal will cost 108F ($24.66), and à la carte meals somewhere from 144F ($32.88) to 180F ($41.09).

Napoléon, 9 rue Grande (tel. 422-20-39), is a classically designed, rather formal hotel directly opposite the château. A coaching inn a century ago, it has turned its rear carriage yard into a miniature garden, with a flagstone walk, urns of flowers and shrubbery, statues, and lounge chairs arranged so guests can relax and sunbathe. The inn is operated by the Verne family.

The main lounge is lit naturally through its glass roof. Opening off it in the Roman fashion are small recessed salons. The bedrooms are furnished in blond reproductions of antiques, the attention centering around the padded flowered headboards. A double with private bath rents for 170F ($38.81) to 200F ($45.66) nightly; it's only 105F ($23.97) to 130F ($29.68) in a room that has only a water basin and a bidet. Singles with bath go for 140F ($31.96), 95F ($21.69) without. All tariffs include service, taxes, and a continental breakfast.

Since the Napoléon is so convenient to the château, many visitors come to the attractive dining room for a luncheon. A choice of two set meals is offered for 60F ($13.70) and 90F ($20.55). You can also order à la carte, spending around 100F ($22.83) per person.

Le Filet de Sole, 5-7 rue du Coq-Gris (tel. 422-25-05), is a well-honored little restaurant, just a few minutes' walk from the château. Its neo-Norman façade is difficult to spot on a narrow street deep in the heart of town, but it's well worth the search. A four-course set menu is offered for 80F ($18.26), including service, although you pay extra for wine. To begin, you can choose between a homemade pâté or half a dozen escargots, followed by your main dish, usually the namesake of the restaurant: filets de sole with a lobster sauce. The 110F ($25.11) menu gastronomique is more elaborate, of course, and also includes service.

The specialties are filet de sole, lobster bisque, and carré d'agneau (loin of lamb) with parsley, served only for two persons. A mouth-watering crêpe suzette—quite a concoction—is the preferred dessert, again just for two. The set meals are served from noon to 2 p.m. and from 7 to 8:30 p.m. An à la carte menu is offered until 11 nightly. The restaurant is closed Tuesday for dinner, all day Wednesday, and during July.

Chez Arrighi, 53 rue de France (tel. 422-29-43), offers a friendly mood, decor, and setting. The main dining room is dominated by a wide oak sideboard, provincial chairs, and helter-skelter decorations, with curious touches of art nouveau. On one wall is a mural of the homeland of the Corsican patron, Monsieur Arrighi.

True to his traditions, his cuisine is Corsican, interspersed, of course, with classic French dishes. The price of your meal depends on the number of courses you order, as in a Chinese restaurant. For example, a three-course meal goes for 60F ($13.70), rising to 75F ($17.12) for four courses, a peak 125F ($28.54) for five courses. The latter meal is definitely not for dainty appetites. The Corsican vin du patron is another 30F ($6.85). Most of the hors d'oeuvres are of Corsican origin, including a dry country ham. The restaurant is closed for Sunday dinner, all day on Monday, and during the entire month of January.

3. Vaux-le-Vicomte

Just north of the Forest of Fontainebleau, the **Château Vaux-le-Vicomte** was built in 1656 by Nicolas Fouquet, Louis XIV's ill-fated minister of finance. After mismanaging the French treasury and accumulating a large personal fortune, Fouquet had the gall to invite Louis to a banquet at the château. Louis, offended by the minister's ostentatious behavior and entertainments, brought Fouquet to trial, but not before he hired the same artists and architects who had built the château to begin work on the grand task of building Versailles. Visitors today can see the striking similarities between the two monuments to *le grand siècle.*

The view of the château from the main gate gives one an idea of the splendor of 17th-century France. The French columns and pillars echo grandeur. On the south side, a majestic staircase sweeps toward the formal gardens, designed by Le Nôtre. Lined by a border of trees and statues, the gardens are dominated by a copy of the *Farnese Hercules.* The grand canal, flanked by cascading waterfalls, divides the lush greenery.

The interior of the château, now a private residence, is completely furnished and decorated in 17th-century pieces. The great entrance hall leads to 12 state rooms among which is the famous oval rotunda. Many of the rooms are hung with Gobelin tapestries and decorated with painted ceiling and wall panels by Le Brun with sculpture by Giradon. A tour of the interior also includes the huge basement with its wine cellar, the servants' dining room, and the copper-filled kitchen. Both the château and the gardens are open to the public daily from March through the end of October from 10 a.m. to noon and from 2 to 5:30 p.m. Admission is 14F ($3.20).

After a tour of the château, you can enjoy an excellent repast at **Au Moulin** (tel. 431-67-89) in nearby Flagy, just outside Montereau-Faut-Yonne. You'll dine in a 13th-century mill, where a complete meal is served for about 80F ($18.26). The restaurant is closed from January 20 to March 1, and also on Tuesday nights and Wednesdays.

4. Barbizon

In the 19th century, the Barbizon School of painting gained world renown. On the edge of the Forest of Fontainebleau, some 35 miles southeast of Paris, the village was a haven and a refuge for such artists as Théodore Rousseau, J.

F. Millet, and Corot. Many of these painters could not find acceptance in the conservative salons of Paris.

In Barbizon, they turned to nature for inspiration and painted pastoral scenes as they saw them—that is, without nude nymphs and dancing fauns. These artists attracted a school of lesser painters, including Charles Daubigny and Diaz. Charles Jacques, Decamps, Paul Huet, Ziem, Troyon, and many others would follow. Although recognition was delayed, it finally arrived. The School of Barbizon enjoyed the last laugh: the paintings of its adherents hang in the great museums of the world.

Today Barbizon's chic is known far and wide, attracting some of the most fashionable Parisians with its celebrated inns, such as Bas-Bréau, that flank the main street. Some dismiss the village as affected, complaining about its outrageous prices. Like the artists in the past, others bask in Barbizon's sunshine and enjoy its forest-filtered air. Because of the high level of innkeeping, it is popular for gourmet weekends.

Along the street you can visit the ateliers of some of the more noted painters such as Millet. Inside his studio, now an art gallery, is an etching of *The Man with the Hoe,* as well as some of his original furnishings. Born of a peasant family in Normandy, Millet used to take his sketch pad into the fields during the day. He returned in the late afternoon to add the finishing touches in his studio, which is open daily except Tuesdays till 6 p.m., charging no admission. You can also visit the vine-covered second-floor atelier of Rousseau on the same street, next door to a little chapel.

Finally, **l'Auberge du Père Gannes,** an ancient inn, has been turned into a gallery open to the public. In its heyday, Millet, Charles Jacques, Corot, Rousseau, Rosa Bonheur, even Delacroix and Ingres used to drop in. The management didn't discriminate: writers, too, were welcomed. Verlaine came this way, as did Robert Louis Stevenson and George Sand with here effete lover, the poet Alfred de Musset.

FOOD AND LODGING: Among the inns, the best value is found at the following:

The Upper Bracket

Bas-Bréau (6e) (tel. 066-40-05) is one of the great old inns of France. Starting in the 1830s, it sheltered many famous artists when it was known as Monsieur Siron's auberge. Robert Louis Stevenson stayed here, writing his *Forest Notes* in one of the bedrooms. When Napoleon III and his empress stopped by for a day in 1868, purchasing some paintings from the Barbizon School, the inn became known as the Hôtel de l'Exposition.

Right in the center of the village, the hotel itself is rambling, with vistas of shade trees opening onto courtyards. It's furnished in rich, lustrous provincial antiques or else fool-the-eye reproductions. In cooler months, life centers around an open brick fireplace in the living room, with its heavy overhead beams and decorative objects such as a copper lavabo, wooden wine-press tables, and bright chintz-covered furniture.

The bedrooms are furnished in part with antiques—many of them collector's pieces. Often clients prefer the rooms in the rear building which open directly onto semiprivate sun terraces laden with red chairs and parasols along with long flower boxes profusely planted with red geraniums.

The prices are extremely high, but worth it for those who can afford it. A twin- or double-bedded room peaks at 500F ($114.15). If rented as a single, the charge is 450F ($102.74). Accommodating two to three persons, suites are available at rates going from 700F ($159.81) to 900F ($205.47).

Meals in the old-world dining room or in the courtyard range in price from 160F ($36.53) to 220F ($51.15). Specialties include sole braisée aux fleurs de safran, pâtés fraîches, noisettes de Marcassin aux quatre garnitures, and soufflé chaud aux praslines de Montargis. The inn shuts down in early January, reopening in mid-February.

The Middle Bracket

Les Charmettes (tel. 066-40-21) is an informal chatelet-style inn in the center of Barbizon. Enclosed on three sides, its courtyard contains a graveled area for tables (very French) and towering old trees facing the main street. Vines crawl over the rustic inn, sprawling over the front stone-and-iron grill.

Simple though it may be, it was the 1948 honeymoon rendezvous of the then Princess Elizabeth and Prince Philip. The 19th-century painter J.K. Bodner also lived here.

The interior rooms are styled like a hunting lodge: beamed walls and ceiling, stuffed moose heads, plus the additional warming touches of lots of paintings and sketches left by artist guests. No one has ever tried to create a chic setting, preferring to keep it homelike.

The tariffs for rooms depend on their size and the plumbing. A double with bath costs 200F ($45.66), although two persons pay only 115F ($26.25) in the cheaper rooms. Singles without bath go for 92F ($21). Breakfast is an additional 12F ($2.74).

If you're just stopping by for a meal, you might try, for a starter, ballotine de caneton aux pistaches (a roll of duckling with an elaborate stuffing accompanied by pistachios). Those two classic dishes coq au vin and pepper steak are done superbly, but the specialty is roast duckling with peaches. Among fish courses, grilled freshwater salmon with anchovy butter is delicious. Pineapple with kirsch makes a proper finish.

If you order à la carte, expect to spend from 70F ($15.98) to 90F ($20.55) per person.

The Budget Range

Le Relais, 2 Avenue Charles-de-Gaulle (tel. 066-40-28), is seemingly incongruous for ultra-chic Barbizon. But it has its own style—in fact, it is so personal and down-to-earth comfortable that many prefer it to the more prestigious inns. The Relais is a corner tavern, with a provincial dining room centering around a small fireplace. In sunny weather, tables are set out on the rear yard, with a trellis, an arbor, and trees. Two set meals are offered, their tabs including service but not your beverage. The most popular meal costs 60F ($13.70), and is simple, delicious, and filling, although served on weekdays only. The 75F ($17.12) menu offers a wider selection, including, on one recent occasion, some superbly delicate scallops, followed by a steak tartare, plus a homemade dessert.

Like a true inn, the Relais offers six simple but adequately furnished bedrooms. The rooms alone go for 50F ($11.42) in a double. There are two corridor showers. Closed Wednesdays and from mid-January to mid-February.

5. Milly-la-Forêt

Jean Cocteau believed that religion and artistic freedom did not necessarily conflict. As if to prove his point, he decorated the interior of the little stone

12th-century **Chapel of St. Blaise** right outside this little village 12 miles from Fontainebleau. Painted in the closing years of his life (he died in 1963), the chapel formed his own memorial, and his tomb was placed there. The man who flavored the pre-World War II decades in France with his imaginative and daring unconventionality, who traveled far (he once went around the world in three months), made for himself a peaceful, even sleepy resting place.

Inside, the frescoes are secular. One, for example, depicts a wide-eyed and bewhiskered cat, his tail curving upward toward his head, looking haplessly at a beanstalklike giant flower. Another shows an almond-eyed Christlike figure wearing a crown of thorns, his mouth a snarl.

In his day Cocteau was considered immoral, but by 1955, following his election to the Académie Française, his reputation was assured. In his *White Paper* he has written candidly about his homosexuality, making the point that he did not want mere toleration. The poet, who was considered avant-garde in the 1920s, got his wish. By today's standards, the opium-smoking *enfant terrible* of another era appears tame.

6. Rambouillet

Pompidou used to go there "for the hunt," as did Louis XVI. Thirty-four miles southwest of Paris, Rambouillet was also visited by Charles de Gaulle, although his grandson actually got more use out of it than did the general. Dating from 1375, the château is surrounded by a park and a great forest. Once it was occupied by the Marquise de Rambouillet, before it became a royal abode. It is said that she taught the haut monde of Paris how to talk. To her home she brought a string of poets, painters, and cultured ladies and gentlemen.

François I, the Chevalier King, died at Rambouillet in 1547, having been stricken with a fever at the age of 52. When it was later occupied by the Count of Toulouse, Rambouillet was often visited by Louis XV, who was amused by the nobleman's witty and high-spirited wife. Louis XVI acquired the château for the state, but his wife, Marie Antoinette, was bored with the whole place, calling it "the toad." In her surprisingly modest boudoir are four panels representing the seasons.

Marie-Louise came here in 1814, after leaving Napoleon. She was on her way to Vienna with "the king of Rome." A sad Napoleon himself slept there shortly before leaving on the long voyage to exile at St. Helena.

In 1830 Charles X, the brother of Louis XVI, abdicated after the July Revolution. After that, Rambouillet became privately owned. At one time it was a fashionable restaurant, attracting Parisians, who could also go for rides in gondolas. Napoleon III, however, returned it to the crown. In 1897 it was designed as a residence for the presidents of the Republic. Superb woodwork is used throughout, although the furnishings are unprepossessing. The walls are adorned with tapestries, many dating from the era of Louis XV.

The château charges 4F (91¢) admission on weekdays, lowering it to only 2F (46¢) on Sundays. From April 1 to September 30 it is open from 10 a.m. to noon and from 2 to 6 p.m. (closes at 5 p.m. off-season). It is closed all day Tuesdays and when the president is in residence.

WHERE TO DINE: While in Rambouillet, you may want to consider the **Auberge Joyeux Louvetier,** 2 kilometers north on the N306 (tel. 041-03-19), which is a restaurant on the outskirts. Inside, it's furnished with dignity and taste. In all, this is a gracious and not-too-expensive place to dine. A set meal of excellently prepared dishes is offered for 75F ($17.12). The restaurant is closed on Tuesday nights, Wednesdays, and from mid-July to mid-August, the latter unfortunate because it occurs at the peak of the tourist season.

READER'S RESTAURANT SUGGESTION: "A superior, and modestly priced, restaurant we discovered by accident was in the village of **Gazeran**, just a few kilometers west of Rambouillet, between Chartres and Paris. It's the **Villa Marinette** (tel. 483-19-01), on the main road through Gazeran. This is primarily a restaurant, but there are six simple yet spotlessly clean and very comfortable rooms on the second floor. The food was the best we encountered in all of France. The owner/chef has won numerous culinary awards, and, in our opinion, they were well deserved. The owner's wife manages the dining room/hotel, and a son is the waiter" (Harold W. Baird, Eau Claire, Wisc.). *Editor's Note:* The hotel is closed from September 1 to 20, and the restaurant is closed Tuesday nights and Wednesdays year round. Meals range from 60F ($13.70). A room with a continental breakfast is about 50F ($11.42) per person.

7. Chartres

Many observers have felt that the building aspirations of medieval man in France reached their highest expression in the **Cathedral of Chartres.** Down through the centuries, it has been known as the "Stone Testament of the Middle Ages." Go there to see its architecture, its sculpture, and—perhaps most importantly—its stained glass, which gave the world a new and unique color, Chartres blue.

The town of Chartres lies 60 miles southwest from Paris by car, reached by N10. From Paris's Gare Montparnasse, trains run directly to Chartres, the trip taking less than an hour, passing through the sea of wheatfields that characterize Beauce, the granary of France. Suddenly, the massive bulk of Our Lady of Chartres, with its two dissimilar towers, appears above the small gabled houses.

Before entering, stand in awe in front of the royal portal. Reportedly, Rodin sat for hours on the edge of the sidewalk, drinking in the Romanesque sculpture. His opinion: Chartres is the French Acropolis. When a shower descended, a friendly soul offered him an umbrella—which he declined, so transfixed was he by the magic of his precursors.

First, how did it begin? The origins are uncertain; some have suggested that the cathedral grew up over an ancient Druid site, which had later become a Roman temple. As early as the fourth century, it was a Christian basilica. A fire in 1194 destroyed most of what had then become a Romanesque cathedral, but it spared the western façade. The cathedral that you see today dates principally from the 13th century, when it was built with the combined efforts and contributions of kings, princes, churchmen, and pilgrims from all over Europe.

One of the greatest of the world's High Gothic cathedrals, it was the first to use flying buttresses. In size, it ranks third in the world, bowing only to St. Peter's in Rome and the Cathedral of Canterbury in Kent, England.

The **Old Tower** (Clocher Vieux) with its 350-foot-high steeple dates from the 12th century. The so-called **New Tower** (Clocher Neuf) is from 1134, although the elaborate ornamental tower was added in 1506 by Jehan de Beauce, following one of the many fires that have swept over the cathedral.

French sculpture in the 12th century broke into full bloom when the western façade or **Royal Portal** was added. A landmark in Romanesque art, the sculptured bodies are elongated, often formalized beyond reality, in their long, flowing robes. But the faces are amazingly (for the time) lifelike, occasionally betraying *Mona Lisa* smiles. In the central tympanum, Christ is shown at the Second Coming, while his descent is depicted on the right, his ascent on the left. Before entering, you should walk around to both the north and south portals, each dating from the 13th century. The bays depict such biblical scenes as the expulsion of Adam and Eve from the Garden of Eden.

Inside is a celebrated **choir screen**; work on it began in the 16th century and lasted until 1714. The niches, 40 in all, contain statues illustrating scenes from the life of the Madonna and Christ—everything from the massacre of the innocents to the coronation of the Virgin.

But few of the rushed visitors ever notice the screen: they're too transfixed by the light from the **stained glass.** Covering a distance of more than 3000 square yards, the glass is without peer in the world and is truly mystical. It was spared in both world wars because of a decision to remove it painstakingly piece by piece.

See the windows in the morning, at noonday, at sunset—whenever and as often as you can. Like a kaleidoscope, they are never the same. Most of the stained glass dates from the 12th and 13th centuries.

It is difficult to single out one panel or window of special merit; however, an exceptional one is the 12th century "Vierge de la Belle Verrière" ("Our Lady of the Beautiful Window") on the south side. Of course, there are three fiery rose windows, but you couldn't miss those even if you tried.

The nave—the widest in France—still contains its ancient maze. The wooden *Virgin of the Pillar,* to the left of the choir, dates from the 14th century. The crypt was built over a period of two centuries, beginning in the ninth. Enshrined within is *Our Lady of the Crypt,* a 19th-century Madonna that replaces one destroyed during the French Revolution. You can visit the crypt from 10:30 to 11:30 a.m. and from 2:30 to 5:30 p.m. for an admission of 2F (46¢). Apply at the Maison des Clercs, 18 Cloître Notre-Dame (the south portal).

After your visit, you can stroll through the episcopal gardens, enjoying yet another view of this most remarkable of French cathedrals. If time remains, you may want to explore the cobbled medieval streets of the **Old Town** (Vieux Quartiers). At the foothill of the cathedral, the lanes contain gabled medieval houses that close in like sheets in the wind. Humped bridges span the Eure River. From the Bouju Bridge, you will see the lofty spires in the background. Try, in particular, to find your way to the rue Chantault, with its colorful façades, often timbered, one dwelling eight centuries old.

READER'S TIP: "Please tell your readers not to miss the English-language 'visits' of the cathedral given by Malcolm Miller, a marvelous Englishman who has spent more than 20 years studying the cathedral and giving the English visits. His rare blend of solid scholarship, an informative and engaging lecture style, wit, enthusiasm, and humor are a great aid to understanding and appreciating the cathedral. Besides the 'what' of history, architecture, stained glass, and sculpture, he provides insight into the 'why'—the purpose and organizing plan of the glass and sculpture. After listening to Malcolm Miller, you will not soon forget the marvel that is Chartres Cathedral" (Patricia Hagan, New Haven, Conn.).

HOTELS: Many visitors like Chartres so much they want to stay over. If such is your wish, the following recommendations are suitable.

Grand Monarque, 22 Place des Epars (tel. 21-00-72), is the leading hotel of this cathedral city. A classic building enclosing an inner courtyard; it provides quiet, comfortable bedrooms. Recent renovation has improved it considerably, and it still attracts a handsome clientele that enjoys its old-world charm—such as an art nouveau stained-glass skylight or the Louis XV-style chairs in the dining room.

The bedrooms offer reproductions of antiques, and most of them have space enough for a sitting area. A double with private bath goes for 205F ($46.80), but only 165F ($37.68) with shower. The breakfast is an extra 16F ($3.65). Even if you don't stay here, you may want to drop in to dine. A 75F ($17.12) luncheon or dinner is offered, as are more elaborate ones. The chef, Monsieur Jallerat, proposes as his specialties filets de sole homardine, canard col vert aux baies de genièvre (wild duck with gingerberries), and fricassée de rognons (kidneys) et de ris de veau (sweetbreads) aux girolles.

Pâté de Chartres is another delight, as is the boneless rib of lamb. If you order à la carte, expect to spend from 90F ($20.55) to 150F ($34.26) per person.

Hôtel de France, 10 Place des Epars (tel. 21-00-07), sits right on the main square, with a front canopy covering sidewalk tables. Its dormered roof is steep, its windows overlooking the square shuttered. Inside, the wood-paneled dining room is the core of the social life of Chartres.

The bedrooms contain traditional Gallic trappings, with floral wallpaper and "matching suites" of furniture. Doubles with private baths cost 140F ($31.96). Two persons who'll settle for a room with water basin need pay only 90F ($20.55). Singles range in price from 75F ($17.12) to 90F ($20.55), depending on the plumbing. Taxes and service are included, but breakfast is 11F ($2.51) extra.

If you wish to dine at the hotel, two set meals are offered: a four-course one for 40F ($9.13) and a five-courser for 85F ($19.41).

READER'S HOTEL SELECTION: "Hôtel à la Barrière Verte, 18 rue du Dr. Manoury (tel. 21-05-59), is owned by a gracious couple, M. and Mme. Bernard Riboust. They run a restaurant and bar on the premises. A double room and continental breakfast for two was the best bargain we found in France—86F ($19.63). The four-course dinner menu starts at 35F ($7.99), including wine and service. The Ribousts' son can translate for non-French-speaking guests, although M. Riboust's enthusiasm and friendliness alone can bridge most gaps" (Beryl E. Wauson, Sunset Beach, Calif.).

WHERE TO DINE: Henri IV, 31 rue du Soleil d'Or (tel. 36-01-55), is ruled by a well-known cuisinier, Monsieur Maurice Cazalis. His restaurant—the finest dining room in Chartres—occupies the second floor of a small building, about a five-minute walk from the cathedral. Inside, it is modern, with a slight provincial overtone of beamed ceilings, paneled walls, and bay windows with pink geraniums.

You can order à la carte at an average cost of 150F ($34.26), or else you can request the set menu of 78F ($17.81), including, on one recent occasion, onion soup gratinée, filets de sole meunière, accompanied by a fluffy potato soufflé, a fresh garden salad, a selection from the cheese board, plus a home-made dessert. On the à la carte menu, specialties include pâté de Chartres au perdreau (young partridge) and homard rôti (roast lobster) et flambé sauce aux truffés. The chef also prepares an excellent ris de veau (sweetbreads) des Carnutes. From the cellar, wine is available at any price you want to pay, including an 1893 bottle of champagne. The restaurant is closed in mid-July, mid-January to mid-February, and Monday nights and Tuesdays.

Normand, 24 Place des Epars (tel. 21-04-38), is a Norman-style restaurant on the main square of Chartres, about a 10-minute walk from the cathedral. Owned by Madame Normand, it offers a highly individualized cuisine and an inviting decor of wooden timbers, plaster walls, heavy beams, wrought-iron lamps, stained-glass windows, and murals depicting scenes from Normandy. Specialties on Madame's à la carte menu include pâté en croûte, 15F ($3.42);

escalope Normande, 36F ($8.22); and pepper steak, 40F ($9.13). A pear melba costs 12F ($2.74). The restaurant is closed Mondays, except for holidays.

8. Illiers

On the outskirts of this small town, 15 miles from Chartres, the Syndicat d'Initiative has posted a sign: "Illiers, Le Combray de Marcel Proust." Illiers is a real town, but Marcel Proust in his imagination made it world famous as Combray in *A la recherche du temps perdu.*

The taste of a madeleine launched Proust on his immortal recollection. To this day hundreds of his readers from all over the world flock to Illiers to taste a madeleine dipped in limeflower tea in one of the many pastry shops which sell them.

Following the Proustian labyrinth, you can explore the gardens, streets, and houses which he so richly wrote about. Young Proust visited Illiers more or less regularly until he was 13 years old. The town is epitomized by its Church of St. Jacques, where Proust as a boy placed hawthorn on the altar.

Some members of the Proust family have lived at Illiers for centuries. Proust's grandfather, François Proust, was born there on the rue de Cheval-Blanc. At 11 Place du Marché, just opposite the church, he ran a small shop where he made candles. His daughter, Elisabeth, married Jules Amiot, who ran another shop, this one at 14 Place du Marché. Down from Paris, young Marcel would visit his aunt at 4 rue du Saint-Esprit, which has now been renamed rue du Docteur-Proust, honoring Marcel's grandfather.

The **Amiot House** is now a museum, charging a 4F (91¢) entrance fee. In the novel this was the house of "Aunt Léonie." Filled with antimacassars, it is typical of the solid bourgeois comfort of its day. Upstairs you can visit the bedroom where the young Marcel stayed, and today it contains souvenirs of key episodes in the novel. In addition, you can see the room where his aunt spent many years before dying of an illness.

In the center of town, a sign will guide you to sights which have connections with the great writer. The only drawback is this: you can't sample a madeleine in the pâtisserie which young Marcel loved so much. It's now a florist's shop.

9. Provins

Feudal Provins, the "city of roses," lies about 50 miles southeast of Paris. It is one of the most interesting tourist destinations in the Île de France. To wander through its medieval streets is to experience France of long ago. Historic, romantic, and beautiful, Provins is a town that soared to the pinnacle of its power and prosperity in the Middle Ages, then fell into a slumber after its ruin in the Hundred Years' War. Because of its proximity to Paris, it is surprising that it remains so little known by foreigners.

Once it was the third town of France, after Paris and Rouen, and its famous Fair of Champagne rivaled those of Troyes. The city is also known for its "Damask Rose," brought back from the Crusades by Thibault IV. The Duke of Lancaster through marriage became the Count of Provins, including the rose in his coat-of-arms. A century and a half later the red rose of Lancaster confronted the white rose of York in the "War of the Roses."

The upper town—*ville-haute*—is perched on a promontory, and the lower town—*ville-basse*—is crossed by two rivers, the Durteint and the Voulzie, an affluent of the Seine.

With its towers and bastions, Provins was surrounded by ramparts in the 13th century, protecting it from the vast plains of Brie. From the Porte St.-Jean, you can tour the **ramparts** which are well preserved.

In the upper town, **Caesar's Tower,** erected on the site of a Roman fort, can be visited from 9 a.m. to noon and from 2 to 6 p.m. for a 3F (68¢) admission. This dungeon is full of hidden chambers and undergrounds, and some of its passageways have graffiti evoking those of Pompeii. Its tower is a belfry to the **Church of St. Quiriace,** built in the 12th and 13th centuries. The church contains a majestic Gothic primitive choir and a modern dome. Joan of Arc stopped off here on her way to Orléans.

A short walk away takes you to **Grange-aux-Dîmes,** containing three 12th-century rooms, one above the other, housing an archaeological museum with some precious stones.

WHERE TO DINE: If you're on a tour, we'd suggest lunch at **Le Berri,** 17 rue Hugues-le-Grand (tel. 400-03-86), where Monsieur Tournefier will welcome you to his pleasant auberge, featuring an agreeable menu for 32F ($7.31), or more elaborate repasts for 38F ($8.68) and 70F ($15.98). You can also order à la carte at a cost of about 110F ($25.11). The food is in the typical regional style—duck pâté, lamb cooked with green beans, a selection of local cheese, or a tart of the house made with fresh fruit. On the à la carte menu, you can select from more elegant fare, such as tournedos Rossini, even roebuck in season, and quenelles of pike covered with a crayfish sauce. The service is friendly. The restaurant is closed in July and for the first two weeks in January. It is always closed on Mondays. Incidentally, the set menus are not featured on Sundays.

READER'S RESTAURANT SELECTION: "I suggest **Le Vieux Chatel,** 1 Place Honoré-de-Balzac (tel. 400-02-27), where one may dine in a beautiful room overlooking the square. With a variety of menus offered, I selected the one for 48F ($10.96), and feasted on pâté de foie gras, escargots served sizzling in garlic butter, steak, vegetables, cheese, and dessert, all presented in the elegant manner for which the French are famous" (Barry Gleen, Cedarhurst, N.Y.).

10. Malmaison

This old house has had its moments. From his campaign in Egypt, Napoleon wrote to the woman who "called forth from me the basic forces of nature, impetuosity as volcanic as thunder." The recipient of the letter was Joséphine de Beauharnais, his wife. She wasn't exactly mourning his absence—rather, she was locked in the arms of her lover, Hippolyte Charles. Apparently, however, she changed her mind about "the beast" she'd married, rushing to meet him on his return from Paris. He kept her waiting outside his locked door for four hours, finally accepting his adulterous spouse back into the good graces of his bedchamber.

Of course, Napoleon wasn't exactly a faithful husband. When he was writing her the letter from Egypt, he was with a mistress. Further, at Malmaison he once entertained Marie Walewska, the sensual wife of an aging Polish count; she bore the emperor his first son in 1810.

The château—really a country residence far removed from the grandeur of the Tuileries or Compiègne (other Napoleonic residences)—was built in the 17th century, but was subsequently enlarged by Joséphine at the dawn of the 19th century. In 1622 it was a sanitorium for lepers—hence the name *malmaison,* or bad house. Today, it is filled with mementos and Empire furnishings.

One bedroom was obviously inspired by Napoleon's tent from his military campaigns. His study and desk are exhibited in his library (downstairs was the kitchen, and the smells used to drift up, much to his annoyance). Marie-Louise, his second wife, took Napoleon's books with her when she left France. They were eventually purchased by an American banker, who returned them to their rightful place at Malmaison.

Some of the furnishings were used by the deposed emperor at Elba. He always attached a sentimental importance to Malmaison, spending the night there before his departure for St. Helena.

In 1809, following her divorce because of childlessness, Joséphine retired there. She was passionately devoted to her roses until her death in 1814 at the age of 51. The roses in the garden, where swans glide gracefully by, form a fitting memorial to Napoleon's "sweet and incomparable love of my life." A towering tree on the premises is said to have been planted by the deposed empress.

The bed in which Joséphine died is exhibited, and even her toilet kit with such practical items as a toothbrush. The guide will tell you how she got water from a cistern on the roof for her baths. A Gerard portrait flatters her. In fact, many of the portraits and sculpture immortalize a Napoleonic deity. See, for example, David's famous equestrian portrait of the emperor.

The château, about 10 miles west of Paris (three miles northwest of St. Cloud), can be visited from 10 a.m. to noon and from 1:30 to 5:30 p.m. (closes at 4:30 p.m. off-season) for an admission of 6F ($1.37), 3.50F (79¢) on Sundays. To reach Malmaison by public transportation from Paris, take the Métro line from Place Charles-de-Gaulle (Étoile) to the La Défense stop. There board bus 158A for a six-mile run to the country house. You can also catch a train at the Gare St.-Lazare in Paris, which stops at Rueil, less than two miles from Malmaison.

11. Senlis

An ancient Roman township surrounded by forests, Senlis slumbers quietly today. Barbarians no longer threaten its walls, as they did in the third century. Royalty is gone, too, though all the kings of France from Clovis to Louis XIV have either passed through or taken up temporary residence here.

A visit to the northern French town can be tied in with a trek to nearby Chantilly (Paris is 32 miles to the south). Today, the core of Vieux Senlis is an archaeological garden, attracting visitors from all over the world. But the first target on everybody's list is the journey across cobblestoned streets to:

THE CATHEDRAL: Its graceful and elegant 13th-century spire—towering 256 feet—dominates the countryside for miles around. The façade is a study in contrasts: the western side almost severe, the southern portal in the flamboyant Gothic style. A fire swept over the building in 1504, and much rebuilding followed—so the original effect is lost. A 19th-century decorative overlay was applied to the original Gothic structure, which was begun in 1153 to honor Notre-Dame.

Before entering the cathedral, walk around to the western porch to see the sculptures, which enjoy a landmark position in French art. Depicted in stone is an unusual calendar of the seasons, along with scenes showing the ascension of the Virgin and the entombment. The builders of the main portal imitated the work at Chartres.

Inside, the light, airy feeling of Gothic echoes the words of a critic who said it was "designed so that man might realize that he was related to the infinite and the eternal." In the forecourt are memorials to Joan of Arc and Marshal Foch.

A short walk from the cathedral delivers you to the doorway of the:

CHÂTEAU ROYAL: Built on the ruins of a Roman palace, the castle followed the outline of the Gallo-Roman walls, some of the most important in France owing to their state of preservation. Once inhabited by such monarchs as Henri II and Catherine de Medici, the château—now in ruins—encloses a complex of buildings. It is open every day except Tuesdays and Wednesday mornings, from 10 a.m. to noon and from 2 to 6 p.m., April 1 to September 30 (otherwise, it closes at 5 p.m.). Entrance fee for Château Royal gardens is 2F (46¢), and to the unique **Museum of the Veneri** ("Hunting") it is 3F (68¢). Of the 28 towers originally built, only 16 remain, some well preserved. One ruin houses the King's Chamber, the boudoir of French monarchs since the time of Clovis. Nowadays, it's in bad need of restoration, and hopefully funds can be found. Within the complex is the Priory of St. Mauritius, resting under a wooden sloped roof. It not only honors a saint but was founded by one, the French king Louis IX.

FOOD AND LODGING: An economical choice is **Le Chalet de Sylvie,** 1 Place de Verdun (tel. 453-00-87). A mock-timbered and stucco structure at a busy intersection, this popular restaurant is across from the **Hôtel du Nord,** 66 rue de la République (tel. 453-01-16). A modest establishment, the hotel nevertheless is the finest in town for anyone staying over, renting its clean and comfortable bathless double rooms for 100F ($22.83), 130F ($29.68) with bath.

Le Chalet itself attracts those seeking drinks (both an American Bar and a Salon de Thé are on the premises). For either luncheon or dinner it draws the budget-conscious with its set meal at 45F ($10.27), which might begin with quiche Lorraine or a terrine de lapin (rabbit), then follow with a grilled entrecôte. Service and drink are extra.

12. Compiègne

The most famous dance step of all time was photographed in a forest about four miles from the center of town: Hitler's "jig of joy" on June 22, 1940, not only heralded the ultimate humiliation of France but shocked much of the world. At the peak of his power, the Nazi dictator forced the vanquished French to capitulate in the same railway coach where German plenipotentiaries signed the Armistice on November 11, 1918.

The coach itself was transported to Berlin, where it was exhibited, but an Allied bomb in 1943 destroyed it. What you see today is a reproduction in exact detail of the original coach of Marshal Foch, the supreme Allied commander in World War I. It can be visited from 8:30 a.m. to noon and from 1 p.m. to 6:30 p.m. Three-dimensional slides are projected on the screen, showing scenes from "The Great War." **The Glade,** as it is known, is on the Soissons Road.

But you don't go to Compiègne—which the French call *la ville de l'armistice*—just for memories of war. In the town's heyday, before it became an unwilling host to the Germans in 1870, again in World War I, and finally in 1940, royalty and the two Bonaparte emperors flocked there.

Life at Compiègne centered around **the Palace.** It wasn't always a place of pomp. Louis XIV once said: "In Versailles, I live in the style befitting a

monarch. In Fontainebleau, more like a prince. At Compiègne, like a peasant."
But the Sun King returned again and again.

His successor, Louis XV, set about rebuilding the château, based on plans
drawn up by Gabriel. The king died before work was completed, but Louis XVI
and Marie Antoinette continued the expansion program. The palace always
had special memories for them. Both were teenagers when they first met there
on a spring day in 1770. An up-and-coming dauphin, the future king was so
embarrassed by the encounter that, it is said, he never once dared look into her
face—rather, kept gazing at her feet.

As if Austrian princesses hadn't learned a lesson, another teenage girl,
Marie-Louise, arrived at Compiègne to marry a French emperor, Napoleon I.
In a dining room visited on a guided tour, Marie-Louis had her first meal with
the mighty ruler. Accounts maintain that she was paralyzed with fear of this
older man (Napoleon was in his 40s at the time). After dinner, he seduced her,
an act that is said to have only increased her fears.

It wasn't until the Second Empire that Compiègne reached its pinnacle of
social success. Under Napoleon III and his empress, Eugénie, the autumnal
hunting season was the occasion for gala balls and parties—some, according
to accounts, lasting 10 days without a break. It was the "golden age": women
arrived in Worth-designed crinolines and danced to the waltzes of Strauss.
Light operas of Offenbach echoed through the chambers and salons. Eugénie
fancied herself an actress, performing in the palace theater for her guests.

In the gold and scarlet Empire room, Napoleon I spent many a troubled
night. His library, known for its "secret door," the ceiling designed by Girodet,
is also on the guided tour. In the Queen's Chamber, the "horn of plenty" bed
was used by Marie-Louise. The furniture is by Jacob, the saccharine nude on
the ceiling by Girodet.

Dubois decorated the charming Salon of Flowers. The largest room, the
Ball Gallery, was adorned by Girodet, the work symbolizing the battles of
Napoleon I (sculpture fancifully depicts the emperor and his mother in flowing
Grecian robes.).

In the park, Napoleon I ordered the gardeners to create a green bower to
remind his new queen, Marie-Louise, of the one at Schönbrün.

The château is open daily except Tuesdays from 9:45 a.m. to noon and
from 1:30 to 5:30 p.m., March 1 to October 31; otherwise it is open in the
afternoons till 4:15 p.m. Admission is 6F ($1.37) weekdays, 3F (68¢) Sundays.

One wing of the palace houses the **National Automobile and Touristic
Museum,** exhibiting about 150 vehicles: everything from chariots familiar to
Ben Hur to bicycles to a Citroën "chain-track" vehicle. Open the same times
as the château, it charges 7F ($1.60) for admission, 3.50F (79¢) on Sundays.

Also to be seen in Compiègne are the **Musée du Second-Empire,** with its
collection of paintings, sculpture, and furniture from that period, including
works by Carpeaux; and **Musée de l'Impératrice,** with its souvenirs from the
imperial family.

The *picatins* strike the hours at the **Hôtel de Ville,** erected in the early
16th century with a landmark belfry. Inside is a **Museum of Historical Figurines,** a unique collection of about 100,000 tin soldiers: everything from a Louis
XVI trumpeter to an 1808 *chasseur* of the guard. The Battle of Waterloo is
depicted. It can be visited from 8 a.m. to noon and from 2 to 6 p.m. (closes
earlier off-season). Admission is 4F (91¢). At the town square stands a statue
of Joan of Arc, who was taken prisoner at Compiègne by the Burgundians on
May 23, 1430, before she was turned over to the English.

GETTING THERE: The journey from Paris to this Oise River valley town takes 50 minutes by rail. By car, it's reached on the northern Paris-Lille motorway (E3), a distance of 50 miles. A visit to Compiègne is traditionally tied in with an excursion to Senlis.

FOOD AND LODGING: The best spot is **L'Hostellerie au Royal-Lieu,** 9 rue de Senlis (tel. 420-10-24), on the Paris road more than a mile from the palace. On a spring day you can sit out on the terrace watching the tulips grow, ordering meals that range in price from 90F ($20.55) to 130F ($29.68).

One dish has earned the restaurant acclaim: a cassolette d'escargots à l'anis (anise-laced snails browned with crumbs in a casserole). Specialties include mignon de veau Dominique and biscuit de brochet à l'oseille du jardin. A superb dessert is pêche soufflée belle Compiegnoise. The roadside hostelry dispenses its wares behind a mock-timbered façade with a Louis XIII-style interior.

The leading choice in the center of town is the **Rôtisserie du Chat Qui Tourne,** holding forth under the roof of the **Hôtel de France,** 17 rue Eugène-Floquet (tel. 440-02-74). Madame Robert, the proprietor, believes in judicious cooking and careful seasoning, and she prices her table d'hôte menus to appeal to a wide range of budgets.

For example, you can order a complete dinner for 36F ($8.22), 65F ($14.84), or 100F ($22.83). The latter tariff, of course, is for the menù gastronomique, and is likely to begin with a terrine de canard (duck), follow with a trout meunière, proceed to le poulet rôti (roast chicken) à la broche, and end with dessert. Service and taxes are included, but you must add the cost of your drinks.

The old name, "Inn of the Cat that Turns the Spit," dates from 1665. Downstairs is a bar as well as a dining room in the traditional country-inn style.

If you're staying over in Compiègne, the Hôtel de France provides the finest accommodations in town, renting its best double rooms for 100F ($22.83) to 160F ($36.53), a continental breakfast and service included.

READERS' HOTEL SELECTION: "We stayed at the **Hôtel du Nord,** Place de la Gare (tel. 440-04-73), right by the railroad station. The rooms are clean and spacious and very inexpensive: 70F ($15.98) for a double without bath; 100F ($22.83) for a double with shower; 130F ($29.68) for a double with full bath" (Mr. and Mrs. James Reardon, APO, N.Y.).

13. Chantilly

Parisians use this town, 26 miles north of the capital, as a resort retreat from big-city living. Known for its frothy whipped cream and its black lace, it draws the crowds mainly because of its racetrack and its château. The first two Sundays in June are the highlight of the turf season, bringing out such a fashionable crowd that many women go just to see who's wearing what.

The grand château—once the seat of the Condé—is idyllically situated on an artificial lake. You approach it along the same forested drive that Louis XIV, along with hundreds of guests, rode for a banquet prepared by Vatel, one of the best-known of French chefs. One day, when the fish didn't arrive on time, Vatel committed suicide. The effect of the château is decidedly French Renaissance, with gables and domed towers, but a part of it was rebuilt in the 19th century. It is skirted by a romantic, mysterious-looking forest once filled with stag and boar.

In 1886 the owner of the château, the Duc d'Aumale, left the park and palace to the Institute of France, along with his fabulous art collection and library. Aside from the sumptuous furnishings, the château is a museum, housing works by artists such as Memling, Van Dyck, Botticelli, Poussin, Watteau, Ingres, Delacroix, Corot, Rubens, and Vernet. See especially Raphael's *Madonna of Lorette, Virgin of the House d'Orléans,* and his *Three Graces* (sometimes called the *Three Ages of Woman*). The foremost French painter of the 15th century, Jean Fouquet did a series of about 40 miniatures, and the museum is also rich in Clouet portraits, such as one of Marguerite de France as an *enfant.* In the jewel collection shines the rose diamond which received worldwide attention when it was stolen in 1926. Of the Condé library acquisitions, one is celebrated: an illuminated manuscript from the 15th century illustrating the months of the year, *Les Très Riches Heures du Duc de Berri.*

The petit château was built by Jean Bullant in about 1560 for one of the members of the Montmorency family, a man named Anne. The stables, a hallmark in French 18th-century architecture, were built to house 250 horses and about 400 hounds. If time remains, try to wander in the garden laid out by Le Nôtre. In the park are a hamlet of rustic cottages and the **House of Sylvie,** rebuilt by Mansart, open only on Saturdays and Sundays.

The château is open from 10:30 a.m. to 5:30 p.m., charging 10F ($2.28) for admission. Closed on Tuesdays. Trains leave the Gare du Nord station in Paris, the trip taking about an hour.

A LEADING INN: Hôtel d'Angleterre, 5 Place Omer-Vallon (tel. 457-00-59), is a typical village inn. Unpretentious, it is not without charm if you accept it for what it is. The simple bedrooms are immaculately kept and modestly priced. Depending on the plumbing, singles range from a low of 55F ($12.56) to a high of 115F ($26.25), and doubles begin at 75F ($17.12) going up to 125F ($28.54). You can dine either inside or, on fair-weather days, in the tiny courtyard. The cuisine is good home-cooking. A set meal costs 55F ($12.56), plus the cost of your beverage. Try the country terrine and the beef bourguignonne. Closed between January 5 and February 15.

THE BEST RESTAURANTS: Tipperary, 4 Avenue Joffre (tel. 457-00-48), is one of the leading restaurants. On the ground floor of an old town house, it offers outside café tables resting under a red canopy. The ambience is traditional, with old-fashioned curtains at the windows. To begin your repast, try the chef's specialty, a terrine de perdreau (young partridge). Other delicious specialties include the chef's omelet and chicken curry. Expect to spend at least 60F ($13.70) for a really good meal. Closed Tuesday evenings in winter, Thursdays, and in February.

Chantilly Bar (Chez Jean), 9 Avenue du Général Leclerc (tel. 457-04-65), is a tiny, family-owned, modest bistrot which has been gaining a surprising vogue among visitors to Chantilly. Its habitués are not only the local people but in-the-know visitors who find their way there—less than a mile from the center of Chantilly, on the N16 road.

A 40F ($9.13) menu, planned by the patron, features good simple cooking that is, in a word, delicious. For example, on our most recent rounds, we sampled a big salad of tomatoes and cucumbers, followed by a large piece of grilled pork with creamy, light mashed potatoes, then ice cream shaped like a pineapple slice. On Sundays, the price rises to 50F ($11.42). Closed Fridays and in August.

ON THE OUTSKIRTS: If you'd like to stay within easy driving distance of Chantilly, you'll find far better accommodations, atmosphere, and food outside of town at the following recommendations:

Coye-la-Forêt

Château du Regard, 5 Chemin Écureuils (tel. 458-60-16), five miles south-east from Chantilly by way of N16 and D118, lies right in the heart of the Chantilly Forest, in a 17-acre, beautifully maintained parkland setting. The small château, built on lands once granted by Napoleon Bonaparte, is in the turn-of-the-century style, with large windows allowing you to soak up that view. Lawn furniture is placed out on the grass in fair weather, so you can sit ordering drinks and listening to the birds sing in the trees.

Monsieur Pillot welcomes you, offering an indoor riding circle and a swimming pool which is heated; and, of course, there are plenty of chances for leisurely strolls in the forest.

As the hotel is particularly popular with Parisians on the weekends, it is recommended that you reserve well in advance. The bedrooms, 18 in all, are decorated with originality and flair, costing from 100F ($22.83) to 190F ($43.38). You can stay here on the half-pension plan for 170F ($38.81) to 150F ($34.26). If you are visiting, a complete meal can be ordered for 150F ($34.26). The hotel is closed in August and does not serve dinner on Sunday nights.

An alternate possibility is at—

Chaumontel (Luzarches)

Château de Chaumontel, at Chaumontel, just northeast of Luzarches, 6½ miles from Chantilly (tel. 471-00-30), dates from the latter part of the 16th century. Although it has had many aristocratic owners in its long history, it was once the hunting lodge of the Prince de Condé, whose domain was at Chantilly.

But by 1960 it had been turned into a hotel, offering 19 bedrooms furnished with a restrained taste, although all are most comfortable. The least expensive chambers (with a toilet only) rent for 86F ($19.63); the cost rises to anywhere from 150F ($34.26) to 180F ($41.09) in a double with complete bath. A few apartments are available, costing two persons a peak 320F ($73.60).

The dining room is done in the rustic style, and you almost feel as if you're an invited guest at a private country estate rather than a room number. The food is excellent, including a number of specialties such as roast lamb and poached turbot. A meal costs from 85F ($19.41).

There are many strolls you can take on the château's parklike grounds. It is closed from mid-July until the end of August and from mid-December to January 5.

14. Beauvais

Beauvais, where Victor Hugo "spent mellow hours," has always been at the crossroads between such points as Paris, Rouen, Reims, and Amiens. Because of that, it has known the ravages of war inflicted by the Normans, the English, the Burgundians, and the Germans. In the 1472 seige by the Burgundians, a girl named Jeanne Hachette (Hatchet) seized the enemy standard by axing its bearer and became the local heroine. In 1918 Marshal Foch directed operations from Beauvais.

The last attack was by the Nazis in June of 1940. However, the town has risen from that disaster, having been rebuilt according to the original plan.

Before the war, Beauvais was known for its tapestries, the manufacture of which was started by Colbert in 1664. The looms and the artists are now at Gobelins in Paris. The town lies 46 miles northwest from Paris, 50 miles east of Rouen.

Spared from the 1940 bombardments was the:

CATHEDRAL OF ST. PIERRE: In the words of Viollet-le-Duc, this cathedral was "the Parthenon of France." Still uncompleted, it is a masterpiece of Gothic architecture, dating from 1247 when it incorporated part of a Carolingian church. It is said to have the highest Gothic choir in the world, 158 feet under the vault. In fact, the pillars were so tall that the vaulting fell in 1284. After this inauspicious beginning, a stone bell tower was erected which soared more than 500 feet high, the tallest in the world at that time. However, it collapsed in 1573, just four years after it was built.

So many wars and structural collapses did the Beauvais cathedral suffer that only the transept, choir, and a single bay of the nave, plus seven apse-chapels, were ever completed. It has been said that the nave of Amiens, the portal at Reims, the towers of Chartres, and the choir at Beauvais would make the greatest cathedral in the world.

The collection of tapestries inside is remarkable, especially the *Acts of the Apostles,* based on original designs by Raphael and woven at Beauvais by 17th-century artisans. Some of the stained glass dates from the 13th century and from the 16th-century School of Le Prince. On the north portal is a remarkable carving, *The Man in the Wheelbarrow.* In the Treasury is a collection of liturgical vestments and goldsmiths' work, and the cloisters are from the 14th century.

The curiosity of the cathedral is an astronomical clock, built in 1865 by August Vérité and said to be the largest in the world. It was based on another celebrated clock, the one at Strasbourg. At certain times of the day it presents a scene from the Last Judgment.

CHURCH OF ST. ÉTIENNE: If time remains, try to visit this nearby church that represents a marriage of Romanesque (nave) and Gothic (choir). Somehow the union manages to come off harmoniously. The bombs of 1940 badly damaged the choir, though it has subsequently been repaired. Of the 16th-century stained glass, the most outstanding is the *Tree of Jesus* by Angrand-le-Prince. Goering wanted to own the bearded statue of St. Wilgeforte in the nave, dating from the 16th century. On the façade is a *roue de la fortune* (wheel of fortune) in the rose window of the north transept.

WHERE TO DINE: La Côtelette, 8 rue Jacobins (tel. 445-04-42). The chef de cuisine, Roland Luck, is always filled with surprises. He takes many of the standard French dishes and prepares them with an original touch. He's always got something to tempt you as an opener, perhaps his succulent escargots maison. The specialties include filet de boeuf au poivre vert and gratin de turbot. You might like to precede your main platter with quenelles de homard (lobster). The fresh fruit sorbets are unbeatable. Expect to spend from 80F ($18.26) to 130F ($29.68) per person here for a complete meal. The centrally located restaurant offers a pleasant ambience, with the decorative touches of a country inn. Closed Tuesdays and in July.

Crémaillère, 1 rue Gui-Patin (tel. 445-03-13). This family-run restaurant, in a charming, rustic-style house, offers excellently prepared regional specialties. Jean-Louis Leménager is the talented chef, and he maintains a consistent quality in the *bonne tradition familiale*. He is assisted by his son, who seems every bit the professional chef his father is. Especially recommendable are their young guinea hen (or rabbit) served with prunes and their tripe braised in cider. To finish your meal, we'd suggest a cow-milk cheese of the region known as "rollot." Alternatively, you might try tarte aux pommes chaude, a hot apple tart which has been flambeed with old Calvados and served with a crème fraîche. If you order à la carte, your tab is likely to be 100F ($22.83). The restaurant shuts down on Wednesdays.

15. Château de Thoiry

What do you do if you're sitting out a storm in a 16th-century château playing Chopin's piano (a gift of his mistress, George Sand) and raindrops keep falling on your head? Well, the Count de la Panouse decided it was time to open his castle to the public and raise some funds to fix the roof.

In they trekked that year (1966), asking to see not only the piano but the original manuscripts of two unpublished Chopin waltzes that the American pianist Byron Janis discovered in a broom closet. Much to the count's disappointment, however, the antique furniture, more than 43 handwritten letters of French kings, and the original financial records of France from 1745 to 1750 just didn't lure enough customers.

Then the count's son, Paul, came up with an idea that turned the Château de Thoiry into a tourist attraction which in one year drew more tourists than either the Louvre or Versailles.

He turned the grounds into a wild game reserve, populated with elephants, giraffes, zebras, monkeys, rhinoceroses, alligators, hyenas, lions, tigers, kangaroos, bears, and wolves. More than 1000 animals and birds roam at liberty. The reserve and park cover 300 acres, although the estate itself is on 1200 acres.

The park has extensive possibilities for promenades on foot. In the French gardens you can see Asian deer, llamas, Asian sheep, and many types of birds, including flamingos and cranes. In the tiger park a promenade has been designed above the tiger cages. The monkey park also has pleasant walks, and visitors can touch the animals. In addition, in the *caveau* of the château is a vivarium. More gardens may be opened in the near future.

To see the animal farm, you take a minibus from the parking lot of the château, or else drive your own automobile, providing it isn't a convertible. Is there any danger? Perhaps, although it is slight. Anticipating troubles, the owners carry thousands upon thousands of francs' worth of insurance. However, all that is likely to happen to you is that an elephant might stick his trunk in your window if you leave it open.

The park is most crowded on weekends, but if you want to avoid the crush at these times, visit on Saturday or Sunday mornings. The grounds are open daily from 9:30 a.m. to 6:30 p.m. (Sundays and holidays from 9 a.m.). Closed in January. The comprehensive entrance ticket, admitting you to all the attractions, cost 30F ($6.85) for adults, 16F ($3.65) for children over four years old. On the grounds is a cafeteria offering homemade foods, a standard menu going for 40F ($9.13). You can take a food basket and have a picnic among the gentler animals.

Telephone 487-40-91 for more information.

GETTING THERE: Drivers should take the Autoroute de l'Ouest toward Dreux, turning at Le Pontel onto Route D1·1. Tourist-bus passengers enjoy a special group price to and from Thoiry, including visits to the park and château and other attractions, at a cost of 65F ($14.84). On Saturdays such buses leave Porte Maillot at 8:45 a.m. and Porte St.-Cloud at 8:55 a.m. On Sundays departures are from Porte Maillot at 1:15 p.m. and from Porte St.-Cloud at 1:25 p.m. You may call 460-19-94 for more information about the bus schedule.

16. Giverny

The house and gardens where Claude Monet lived for 43 years have been restored and opened to the public. Born in 1840, Monet, the French impressionist painter, was a brilliant innovator, excelling in representing the effects of light at different times of the day. He is most known, of course, for his series of paintings of the Rouen Cathedral and of water lilies.

Leaving Poissy, Monet came to Giverny in 1883. He took a small railway linking Vetheuil to Vernon, discovering the village at a point where the Epte stream joined the nearby Seine. To his home, **Le Pressoir**, many celebrities came to visit and enjoy the company and the good cooking, among them Clemenceau, Cézanne, Rodin, Renoir, Degas, and Sisley.

At the death of Monet in 1926, his son, Michel, inherited the house but left it abandoned until it decayed in ruins. The gardens became almost a jungle, inhabited by river rats. In 1966 Michel Monet died, leaving the house to the Beaux Arts Academy.

It wasn't until 1977 that Gerald Van der Kemp, who restored Versailles, decided to work on Giverny. Mostly it was restored with gifts from American benefactors, especially Mrs. Lila Acheson Wallace, head of *Reader's Digest,* who contributed $1 million.

Guests can stroll through the garden with its thousands of flowers, including the famous nympheas. You cross a Japanese bridge hung with wisteria to a dreamy setting of weeping willows and rhododendrons. Monet's studio barge was installed on the pond.

In the house itself every detail has been painstakingly restored, including the artist's salon and dining room, as well as the kitchen with its copper and brass equipment. Monet collected Japanese prints, also left to the Academy by Michel Monet, and the house once again is filled with them.

The best way to go to Giverny is to rent a car, taking the Autoroute de l'Ouest (Pont de St. Cloud) toward Rouen. You leave the autoroute at Bonnières, then cross the Seine on the Bonnières Bridge. From there, a direct road with signs will bring you to Giverny. Expect about an hour of driving, and try to avoid weekends.

The museum is open every day except Monday from April 1 to October 31, charging an admission of 25F ($5.71).

THE CHÂTEAU COUNTRY

THE VAL DE LOIRE is called "The Garden of France." Bordered by vineyards, the winding Loire Valley cuts through the soft contours of the land of castles deep in the heart of France. Along the way are *levées* (dikes), some dating from centuries ago, built to hold back the lazy Loire should it become the turbulent Loire.

Many Crusaders returning to their medieval dungeonlike quarters brought with them the news of the elegance and opulence of the East. Soon enough, they began to rethink their surroundings. Later, word came across the Alps from neighboring Italy of a great artistic flowering, of artists such as Leonardo da

Vinci and Michelangelo. And so, in the days of the French Renaissance, when the kings of France built châteaux throughout this valley, the emphasis was on sumptuousness. An era of pomp and circumstance was to reign here until Henri IV moved the court to Paris, marking the decline of the Loire.

The Valley of the Loire has played a major part in the national consciousness. Joan of Arc, the maid of Orléans, came this way looking for her dauphin, finding him at Chinon. Carried around from castle to castle were mistresses, the list now lengendary, ranging from Agnès Sorel (the mistress of Charles VII) to Diane du Poitiers (the mistress of Henri II). In his heyday, the Chevalier King brought Leonardo da Vinci from Florence, installing him at Amboise. Catherine de Medici and her "flying squadron" of beauties, Henry III and his handsome minions—the people and the events make a rich tapestry. The Loire has a tale to tell, as even the most cursory visitor to its châteaux discovers.

Its sights and curiosities are multifarious, ranging from Renaissance, medieval, and classical châteaux to residences where Balzac wrote or Rabelais lived, to Romanesque and Gothic churches, to Roman ramparts, to such art treasures as the Apocalypse Tapestries. There's even the castle that inspired the fairytale "Sleeping Beauty."

The best way to see the Loire is in your own car, free from tour buses and guides herding you in and out of castles. Attempts to explore the valley in two to three days are doomed. If your schedule can accommodate it, allow at least a week.

If you wish, you can stay in one of the big towns, such as Tours, with their wide range of accommodations. But you may prefer to seek out a central yet seemingly isolated village with an old inn where the pace is less frenetic, the food worthy of the finest tables in the Loire, and the price the kind you don't mind paying.

Gastronomy would be a good enough reason for going to the Loire even if it didn't have châteaux. From Nantes to Orléans, the specialties are many, including, for example, shad cooked with sorrel, Loire salmon, chitterling sausage, lark pâté, goats'-milk cheese, partridge, rillettes (shredded and potted pork), herb-flavored black pudding, plus good Loire wines, including rosés.

Autumn or spring is ideal, though most of the intriguing son-et-lumière (sound-and-light) programs take place in summer when the châteaux are floodlit. First performed on the banks of the Loire, these pageants have become one of the main attractions of France.

Proceeding directly from Paris via Chartres, the first stopover is at:

1. Châteaudun

Twenty-seven miles south of the cathedral city of Chartres, your first château in the Loire Valley emerges. Austere, foreboding, it rises on a stone-bound table above a tributary of the Loire. Looking like an impregnable fortress, it isn't the most "warm-hearted" gateway to the château country, but it's imposing and interesting.

Originally, it was erected as an important fortress to protect the surrounding countryside from its jealous and restless neighbors. In 911, the Normans went on a rampage in this area and succeeded in burning much of the castle.

The famous comrade in arms of Joan of Arc Jean Dunois, called the Bastard of Orléans rebuilt the chapel and the façade in the 15th century. The donjon, a huge round tower 150 feet high, had been reconstructed in the 12th century. The façade on the right, elaborately ornamented, was the result of a 16th-century restoration.

Although begun in the Middle Ages, the château is a mixture of medieval and Renaissance architecture. The roof is pierced with towering chimneys and large dormers. After a great fire swept over Châteaudun in the 18th century, Hardouin, an architect of Louis XV, directed what was almost an entire reconstruction of the town, indiscreetly turning over the castle to the homeless, who stripped it of its finery. By 1935, the State had acquired the fortress and a major restoration program was launched. Even today it's not richly furnished, but a collection of tapestries depicting such scenes as the worship of the golden calf now cover the walls. The most admirable architectural features are the two carved staircases.

Inside the Sainte-Chapelle, a keep dating from the Middle Ages, is a collection of more than a dozen 15th-century robed statues, including a woman with a sword standing on a man's head.

Châteaudun may be visited daily from Palm Sunday to October 1 between 9:30 and 11:15 a.m. and from 2 to 6 p.m. for a 5F ($1.14) admission (half-price on Sundays). Otherwise, it is open daily except Tuesdays, closing at 4:45 p.m.

WHERE TO DINE: Caveau des Fouleurs, 56 rue Fouleries (tel. 45-23-72), is what is known as a troglodytic cave, a rough-hewn "caveau" bordering the Loire, complete with a flower garden and a stereo club. The service is friendly and efficient, and the food is the best at Châteaudun. The price is reasonable, too, an excellently prepared set meal going for just 50F ($11.42), a more elaborate one for 64F ($14.61). If you dine à la carte expect to pay 110F ($25.11) and up.

In air-conditioned comfort you can select such classic dishes as coq au vin and roast lamb. The crab soup here has lots of fresh crab in it, and trout is served with a frothy sauce known as "white butter" (made with freshly ground pepper and fish stock, combined with wine vinegar and minced shallots). The chef specializes in pigeon cooked in an earthenware casserole. The cave makes a fine luncheon stopover if you're driving down from Paris en route to the Loire Valley. The restaurant is closed August 15-30 and February 1-15, as well as on Sunday nights and Mondays.

READERS' HOTEL SELECTION: "We stayed at the Hôtel de Beauce, 50 rue de Jallans (tel. 45-14-75), a short street to the left as you enter town if you are driving south. It is modern and very clean. The owner speaks excellent English. A double with private bath goes for 135F ($30.82). Breakfast, the only meal served, costs an additional 9.50F ($2.16)" (Dorman and Evie Combest, West Hollywood, Calif.).

2. Tours

Although without a major château itself, the industrial and residential city of Tours is the traditional center for exploring the Loire Valley. At the junction of the Loire and Cher rivers, it was one of the great pilgrimage sites of Europe in the Middle Ages. The devout en route to Santiago de Compostela in northwest Spain stopped off at Tours to pay homage at the tomb of St. Martin, the Apostle of Gaul, who had been bishop of Tours in the fourth century. One of the most significant conflicts in world history, the Battle of Tours in 732 checked the Arab advance into Gaul.

The townspeople are fond of pointing out that Tours, not Paris, is the logical site for the capital of France. It virtually *was* the capital in June of 1940, when Churchill flew there to meet with Paul Reynaud.

The **Cathedral of St. Gatien,** the chief attraction of Tours, honors an evangelist of the third century. Its façade is in the flamboyant Gothic style, flanked by two towers the bases of which date from the 12th century, although the lanterns are Renaissance. The choir was built in the 13th century, and each century up to and including the 16th produced new additions. Sheltered inside is the handsome 16th-century tomb of the children of Charles VIII. Some of the stained-glass windows, the building's glory, date from the 13th century.

The **Musée des Beaux-Arts de Tours,** an archbishop's palace of the 17th and 18th centuries complete with Louis XVI woodwork and Tours silk-damask hangings, provides the background for this museum of art. Among the foreign acquisitions the most outstanding paintings are Mantegna's *Christ in the Garden of Olives* and *The Resurrection.* Other foreign works are an early Rembrandt (*Flight into Egypt*), plus canvases by Rubens, Luca Giordano, and Matthäus Günther.

The French school is represented by Le Sueur, Fouquet, Boucher, Vernet, Vuillard, David, Ingres, Degas (*Calvary*), Delacroix (*Comedians and Buffoons*), and Monet. The most important sculpture is by Houdon and Lemoyne. Charging 4F (91¢) for admission, the museum, at 18 Place Francois-Sicard, is open daily in summer from 9 a.m. to noon and from 2 to 6 p.m.; in winter, from 9 a.m. to noon and from 2 to 5 p.m. (closed on Tuesdays).

HOTELS: In accommodations, the best choices fall in:

The Middle Bracket

Le Royal, 65 Avenue Grammont (tel. 64-71-78), caters to travelers who want modern facilities without sacrificing tradition. Its lounges as well as its 32 bedrooms are furnished in Louis XV and Louis XVI styles, showing both taste and imagination. Based on size and placement, doubles range in price from 155F ($35.39) to 175F ($39.95), with a continental breakfast costing an additional 16F ($3.65) per person. Although there is no restaurant, a country-style tavern offers alcoholic drinks. Underground parking is available.

Hôtel de l'Univers, 3-5 Boulevard Heurteloup (tel. 05-37-12) on the principal artery, is highly rated, and is, in fact, the oldest place in town. In its gold book of signatures you'll find the names of Thomas Edison, Rudyard Kipling, Ernest Hemingway, John D. Rockefeller, and the former kings of Spain, Portugal, and Romania. Rather large, it offers 100 bedrooms with some form of private plumbing. Singles with shower go for 172F ($39.27), increasing to 204F ($46.57) with private bath. Doubles with shower cost 195F ($44.52), 250F ($57.08) with private bath, these tariffs including a continental breakfast. Each room is different and functional with fully tiled, well-equipped bathrooms and color-coordinated schemes. All the floors in the public rooms are carpeted. The furnishings have been improved, and you'll notice an occasional antique.

In the hotel's main dining room, which has been redecorated, you'll find a set menu beginning at 65F ($14.84). The restaurant is closed on Sundays.

Méridien, 292 Avenue de Grammont (tel. 28-00-80), is a pleasant modern hotel in the style of the *grand siècle.* It might be called "the Inn of the Three Rivers," as it stands on the banks of the Cher between the Indre and the Loire. Built on the prestigious boulevard of Tours, it lies outside the heart of the city, with plenty of its own grounds including a French garden and a swimming pool. It's a curious combination of a 20th-century motel in the style of an 18th-century French country home. In the modernized château it is fully air-conditioned, each of its soundproofed bedrooms containing a private bath. The rooms are appropriately styled and designed for today's traveler, with a discreet use of good modern furnishings blended with antique reproductions.

The colors are bright, and there's a sitting area for breakfast or drinks. In a single the tariff is 190F ($43.38) nightly, increasing to 280F ($63.92) in a double. In addition, six apartments, spacious and well appointed, are rented at far higher tariffs. The reception hall is classic, the effect softened by glittering crystal chandeliers and planters of boxwood to keep conversational groupings apart. At the recessed salons the windows are draped in velvet. A rôtisserie, which is closed on Sundays and from the first of November until April 1, is on the premises, serving a set menu for 78F ($17.81).

Le Central, 21 rue Berthelot (tel. 05-46-44), is a simple, old-fashioned hotel off the main boulevard, within walking distance of the river and cathedral. It provides adequate and comfortable lodgings at reasonable rates. Set back from the street, the aptly named Central has a front and rear garden with lawns and trees. It is owned and operated by the Brault family, who are gradually and pleasantly redecorating the rooms. Those twin-bedded with private baths cost 195F ($44.52) for two persons. Cheaper are the doubles with showers, ranging between 135F ($30.82) and 155F ($35.39). The bargains are the bathless doubles with concealed wash basins and bidets, going for 107F ($24.43). Singles range from 100F ($22.83) to 150F ($34.26). There are two salons, decorated in the French manner with reproductions of 18th-and 19th-century pieces. An enclosed garage is available.

The Budget Range

Hôtel de Châteaudun, 38 rue et Place de la Préfecture (tel. 05-79-94), has only one official star in its crown, but it's a rare find in a bustling city. On a corner of a quiet little square, it is painted white with blue shutters—utterly basic, but attractive in its own way. Inside the miniature hallway is a tiny sitting room filled with family antiques, including a pair of handcarved armoires, Louis XV-style chairs, and old framed prints. Run by the Cartegnie family, the hotel offers a great bargain during its busy summer season. The bedrooms are roomy and modernized, half of them containing private showers. Doubles with shower cost 58F ($13.24), rising to 90F ($20.55) for three persons. The one single room costs 40F ($9.13). A breakfast tray is brought to your room for 10F ($2.28).

Family Hotel, 2 rue Traversière (tel. 05-25-63), a white-shuttered beige-stucco building, lies between the railway station and the cathedral. It has a side entrance through a shady garden, suggesting that it's a quiet and simple place at which to stay. For many years it's been owned by Madame Renaud, who knows how to maintain a small hotel that's sparkling clean as well as friendly in its reception (English spoken).

Reached by a graceful inner staircase, the bedrooms are simply furnished, with hot and cold running water and bidets (you use the corridor baths). Doubles rent for 60F ($13.70) and singles go for 45F ($10.27). You'll pay another 8F ($1.83) for a continental breakfast, plus yet another 7F ($1.60) for a bath or shower.

READERS' HOTEL SELECTION: "We found the best petit hôtel in the city, at 31 rue Origet (tel. 64-45-54). It is run by Monsieur and Madame Dubernard, a charming couple with two sons and a delightful little dog. The hotel, **Le Belvedere,** has been remodeled with Mme. Dubenard, a former interior decorator, at the helm. Her artistic flair and warm and homey touches, such as handmade curtains and quilted bedspreads, beautiful rich wood furniture, and cheerful wall coverings, have made this our favorite hotel. Each of the rooms has hot and cold running water. Showers and toilet facilities are being installed in the rooms in the near future. Rooms rent at about 24F ($5.48) for a single, 50F ($11.42) for the two doubles" (Cheri Senft and Lisa Specter, Sherman Oaks, Calif.).

WHERE TO DINE: Tours offer choices for dining from deluxe to budget:

Deluxe Dining

Charles Barrier, 101 Avenue de la Tranchée (tel. 54-20-39). Across the bridge in the St. Symphorien district, this restaurant is known to all European gastronomes. It's celebrated, in fact. Monsieur Charles Barrier is a great restaurateur who sees to it that the cuisine of the Loire Valley is prepared with consummate skill, that the service is efficient, immaculate, and friendly at the same time, and that his guests are welcomed with open arms (well, almost). In other words, we love it without qualification.

The Touraine is known for its famous chefs. For a showcase of cookery par excellence of that region, we know of no place in the Loire Valley with the standards of this establishment. For the 200F ($45.66) dinner, service and drink extra, you can select from the specialties of the house. For example, you might begin with a terrine d'anguille (eel) de Loire truffé, follow with a crayfish of the country au Vouray, proceed to a tarragon chicken suprême, ending the meal with a soufflé glacé aux fraises (strawberries). Most guests like to order the poached Loire salmon with "beurre blanc" (the famous white butter sauce). Other guests select the fondue de poireaux (leeks) an feuilleté, saumon en papillote aux légumes (vegetables) nouveaux, and filet mignon d'agneau (lamb) à la graine de moutarde (mustard). Guests who order à la carte are likely to spend from 250F ($57.08).

The setting with a patio filled with flowers is elegantly romantic. If you have the money, then by all means partake of its wares. The restaurant usually shuts down during the first two weeks of July.

Upper Bracket Viands

Lyonnais, 46-48 rue Nationale (tel. 05-66-84). One of the best restaurants in the district, this well-run establishment draws not just the tourist traffic but a loyal following who prefer its quiet service, lack of salesmanship in promoting the more expensive wines, and its generally high-level cuisine. The modern setting, with paneling, plants, and climbing vines, is a professional atmosphere for dispensing the smooth wares.

A fixed-price dinner goes for 110F ($25.11). However, you can spend as much as 160F ($36.53) if you order specialties from the à la carte menu. The chef de cuisine, Claude Pinier, is preening-proud of his aiguillette de canard (duckling), sweetbreads "belle époque", sandre (a very white, flaky pike-perch) Val de Loire, terrine d'anguilles (eel) with three sauces, roasted young partridge with pears, and roast pheasant in a Clémentines sauce. Under the direction of Jacqueline Coolen, the restaurant is closed on Sundays and in August.

Budget Dining

La Petite Marmite, 103 Avenue de la Tranchée (tel. 54-03-85), belongs to Monsieur Barrier, a great restaurateur who runs the world-famed Charles Barrier next door. At La Petite, the cooking is less elaborate but extremely good—and a bargain. The dining room is in the simple rustic style. Two set meals are offered, the first costing only 45F ($10.27) and featuring three courses. Most recommendable is the 75F ($17.12) menu, which is likely to include rillettes from Tours, grilled flounder with anchovy butter, coq au vin de Tours, plus a cheese tart. In addition to the rillettes de Tours, the chef also specializes in quenelles de brochet maison and gibellotte de lapin (rabbit) aux petits oignons. The establishment usually is shut during the first two weeks in July.

La Chope, 25 bis Avenue de Grammont (tel. 05-05-90), is a bustling brasserie. In front is a café popular with young people. In the rear is a substantial restaurant decorated with tapestries, mirrors, and brass lighting fixtures. You can dine until 2 a.m. A wide choice of set menus is offered, one at 32F ($7.31), another at 45F ($10.27), and a huge one at 85F ($19.41). On the à la carte menu, you can order stuffed mussels or perhaps lotte à l'américaine. A complete à la carte meal is likely to cost from 45F ($10.27) to 100F ($22.83).

READERS' RESTAURANT SUGGESTION: "Overfed and oversauced from three days at an expensive château-hotel, we waddled along the streets of this lovely, flower-filled city looking for a place for a light lunch. We fell happily into the **Café-Brasserie de l'Univers.** It's in the heart of Tours, at 8 Place Jean-Jaures, directly across the plaza from the impressive Town Hall. Here we had delicious salades Niçoises—tuna, olives, anchovies, tomatoes, and lettuce—for 15F ($3.43) each, complete with bread, and two glasses of white wine for 3.50F (79¢) each. You can get anything here from a full, four-course hot meal, 40F ($9.13), to American-style banana splits and ice-cream sundaes, in the 16F ($3.65) to 22F ($5.02) range. The restaurant is large and casual, with an extensive outdoor café in front" (Jeanne and Paul Pasmantier, West Orange, N.J.).

CHÂTEAU-LIVING IN THE OUTSKIRTS: Château de Beaulieu, Joué-les-
Tours (tel. 28-52-19). Secluded and gracious, this 18th-century country estate 4½ miles southwest of Tours will link you to the lifestyle of another era, even though it has been completely renovated and is now classified as a three-star hotel. You'll be captivated by the formal entrance with its graveled drive encircling a bronze fountain of cherubs and urns of flowers. A double curving stairway leads to the reception hall.

Even if you can't stay here, try at least a visit for a meal; but call in advance, as space is limited. Mr. Jean-Pierre Lozay is the owner of the hotel, and he is also an excellent chef de cuisine. He offers two tourist menus, one at 95F ($21.69) and another at 115F ($26.25). His special feature is his menu gastronomique at 220F ($50.24), which includes foie gras frais maison. The specialties of the house include mousseline de brochet sauce Nantua, ris de veau aux morilles, and giboulée de cerises.

In the beamed-ceilinged dining room classic French windows open onto views of the gardens, complete with two swimming pools and four tennis courts. In summer the hotel has a terrace with a large grill where clients can select from the best cuts of meat or fish and watch the chef prepare them to their liking. The terrace overlooks the garden.

There are only 17 bedrooms, with mahogany and chestnut pieces, paneled recessed window, fireplaces, and good plumbing. The cost of the rooms ranges from 130F ($29.68) with shower and from 250F ($57.08) for the deluxe chambers with private baths and toilets. For a minimum stay of three days, half-pension rates are offered, ranging from 300F ($68.49) to 420F ($95.89) for two persons daily. Beaulieu is open all year long.

The village of Joué-les-Tours is reached by taking D86 from Tours and then the D207 for Beaulieu.

3. Montbazon

The Indre River winds its way below. Cows graze in the fields. All is quiet now. Once, however, the sound of battle was heard between the forces of the warring counts of Anjou and of Blois. In time, Henri III made Montbazon a grand duchy, but the Revolution ended that bit of pomposity.

The ruins of a tenth-century **keep**—built by Foulques Nerra, known as the Black Falcon—can be explored between 9 a.m. and noon and from 2:30 to 7 p.m. from March to October for a 4F (91¢) admission. These ruins have been restored by William Dudley (architect) and Lilian Whitteker (painter).

Nearby you can visit **Montlouis-sur-Loire,** where the castle of **La Bourdaisière** has been rebuilt since its destruction. Only the stables are authentically 17th century. Lilian Whitteker, the American painter born in Cincinnati, Ohio, in 1881, retired there. She is known for her paintings of flowers. The Franco-American Foundation displays a permanent exhibit of paintings on the grounds.

LIFE IN THE CHÂTEAUX: Le Chateau d'Artigny, Montbazon (tel. 26-24-24), is *très grand.* It was built for the perfume king François Coty, who lived and entertained there lavishly. For example, what is now the wine cellar was once a private cold storage for Madame Coty's furs or those of her guests. In the rotunda ballroom an artist did a ceiling painting of the red-caped tycoon and his wife in white surrounded by their family.

The director, Mr. Traversac, will tell you about an unfinished chapel, a pavilion half the size of the one at Versailles, and why the kitchen was installed upstairs. (Monsieur Coty's sense of smell was so acute that he only enjoyed the scent of flowers, and he knew that unpleasant cooking odors ascended.) A favorite room, lined with pink marble, was the onetime pastry room.

Nowadays, the former private mansion is operated as a deluxe hotel for guests who want country-estate holidays where they can live in grandeur and total comfort. Everybody—just everybody—checks in, from Henry Ford II to Elizabeth Taylor.

Against this background weekend soirées are popular, as well as musical evenings featuring perhaps a violinist. In the paneled and gilt dining room an orchestra plays background music. The Caveau-Discothèque Louis XIII is incongruous. The dignified drawing room and corridors are furnished classically, with fine antiques, gilt torchères, Louis XV-style chairs, and bronze statuary.

In true château style, there are many acres of private parkland, as well as a large formal garden at the front entrance with a round reflection pool. Set among the trees is a flagstone-edged swimming pool.

The bedrooms are furnished in various periods, with a generous use of antiques (much Louis XVI and Directoire). The cost for a double room with private bath is 550F ($125.57). Singles begin at 175F ($39.95). It's preferred that you take the full-pension rate, at a cost ranging between 400F ($91.32) and 520F ($118.72) per person.

The superb cuisine is one of the major reasons for staying here. The least expensive set menu begins at 100F ($22.83). Ordering à la carte, expect to pay from 120F ($27.40) to 220F ($50.23) per person. Two specialties are particularly recommended—the noisettes d'agneau (boneless rib of lamb) à la crème d'estragon (tarragon) and the escalope de saumon (salmon) George Sand. Wines? You name it. Certainly Chinon and Montlouis. The hotel is closed from November 20 to January 10. On Route N10, it lies less than a mile outside Montbazon.

Domaine de la Tortinière, Montbazon (tel. 26-00-19), is a picture-postcard château perched high on a hillside overlooking the Vallée de l'Indre. It was built in the belle époque style in 1861, with high peaked towers, baroque gables and windows, and curving exterior balustraded staircases leading from the rolling lawns to the ivy-covered terraces.

It was the ancestral home of Madame Olivereau-Capron. The interior furnishings are modest in comparison with the architecture, although quite adequate. Half-pension is required in season, costing 400F ($91.32) in a single room and from 550F ($125.57) to 850F ($194.06) in a double, the latter the charge for a private apartment with complete bath. Fourteen rooms are offered, costing from 300F ($68.49) in a single, with doubles going for a low of 300F ($68.49) all the way to 475F ($108.44) for the private apartments. Some of the rooms are in an ivy-covered, petite Renaissance-style pavilion in the garden between fir trees.

If you can't stay at the château, perhaps you'll consider a meal in the trellis garden. If you order à la carte, you are likely to pay from 130F ($29.68) to 170F ($38.81), and you can sample such dishes as stuffed sole served with a creamy crayfish sauce, fried filet of duck with a sweet-and-sour sauce and the fresh fruit of the season, and a filet of beef sauté with a very delicate foie-gras-and-pepper sauce, garnished with greens. The "domaine" is open from February 15 to November 15. It lies about one mile off N10 between Tours and Montbazon.

4. Azay-le-Rideau

Its machicolated towers and blue-slate roof pierced with dormers shimmer in the moat, creating a reflection like one in a Monet painting. Then a white swan glides by, rippling the waters. The defensive medieval look is all for show. The Château of Azay was created as a private residence during the Renaissance.

A site was selected at an idyllic spot on the banks of the Indre River, about 13 miles southwest of Tours. A previous château that stood there was in ruins. (In fact, the whole village was known as Azay-le-Brûlé or Azay the Burnt. Passing through with his court in 1418, the dauphin, later Charles VII, was insulted by the Burgundians. A whole garrison was killed for this "outrage," the village and its fortress razed.)

Gilles Berthelot, the financial minister of François I, built the château beginning in 1518. Actually, his big-spending wife, Philippe, supervised its construction. Both of them should have known better. So elegant and harmonious, so imposing was the creation that the Chevalier King grew immensely jealous. In time Berthelot fled, the château reverting to the king. François I didn't live there, however, but started the custom of granting it to "friends of the crown." After a brief residency by Prince Frederick of Prussia in 1870, the château became the property of the state in 1905.

Before entering you can circle the mansion, enjoying its near-perfect proportions. Many critics consider it the crowning achievement of the French Renaissance in Touraine. Architecturally its most fancifully ornate feature is a great bay enclosing a grand stairway with a straight flight of steps. The Renaissance interior is a virtual museum.

The largest room at Azay, the Banqueting Hall, is adorned with four 17th-century Flemish tapestries representing scenes from the life of Constantine (it took a crafts person one year to weave just four square feet). In the kitchen is a collection of utensils, including a wooden mold capable of making 45 different designs on cakes. The corner carvings are most unusual: one, for example, shows a dog biting its own ear.

In the dining room is a trio of 16th-century Flemish tapestries. The fireplace is only a plaster molding of a chimneypiece made by Rodin for the Château of Montal. The fireplace masterpiece, however, is in a ground-floor bedroom containing a 16th-century four-poster. Over the stone fireplace hovers a salamander, the symbol of François I.

From the second-floor Royal Chamber look out at the gardens—the scenery described by Balzac in *The Lily of the Valley*. This bedroom—also called the Green Room—is believed to have sheltered not only François I but Louis XIII and Louis XIV. The adjoining Red Chamber—so named because of its damask—contains a portrait gallery, including a *Lady in Red* (erroneously attributed to Titian) and a scene showing Gabrielle d'Estrées (the favorite of Henri IV) in her bath. An odd 17th-century inlaid cabinet with ivory plates represents *The Woes of War*.

Charging 6F ($1.37) for admission, the château is open from 9 a.m. to noon and from 2 to 6:30 p.m. (closes at 4:30 p.m. off-season). For 8F ($1.83) you can attend a son-et-lumière program there on a summer night at 10 and 11.

A MEDIUM-PRICED INN: Hôtel du Grand Monarque, Place de la République (tel. 43-30-08), is an old ivy-covered coaching inn dedicated to providing the best local cuisine, along with clean and attractive rooms and personalized service. But it's more than that, of course. The inn has been in the hands of the same family for several generations. Today, Monsieur Serge Jacquet runs everything like clockwork.

The guest book tells the story. You'll see everybody from the Duke and Duchess of Kent, the president of Turkey, the Queen Mother of England, and "Harry & Bess" who had a "grand luncheon." Calder liked staying here so much that he contributed a large sketch which hangs in the glass-covered courtyard.

The patio is the hub of life, with its open staircase leading to the antique-furnished bedrooms. A tamed boar runs loose, the rest of the menagerie consisting of a couple of peacocks, two hens, three dogs, three cats, and six chinchillas. Naturally, animals belonging to guests are also welcome.

The food is especially good, so it's easy to comply with the requirement that in season half or full pension is required. For half pension, the tariff ranges from 152F ($34.72) to 250F ($57.08) in a single, from 140F ($31.96) to 180F ($41.09) per person in a double. The higher tariffs are for accommodations with private baths.

A typical meal might include rillettes (highly seasoned ground pork), followed by a fish course such as grilled Loire shad, then a sirloin, plus all the accompaniments. Specialties include côte de boeuf Richelieu for two, carré d'agneau (loin of lamb), and quenelle de brochet. A simple meal here might cost 70F ($15.98), although you could easily spend 120F ($27.40). The complete cellar places emphasis on the wines of the region. The restaurant is closed from November 15 to March 15; the hotel is open all year.

5. Luynes

A stark 15th-century castle rises on the banks of the Loire on an ancient Gallo-Roman site. Underneath the mountain the local vineyard owners use the caves as storage warehouses. The château was originally built by the Maillé family, but its name was changed when it was acquired by Charles d'Albert de Luynes, whom the king made a duke in 1619. His descendants still own the château today and haven't opened it to the public.

LIVING IN A CHÂTEAU: Domaine de Beauvois, Luynes (tel. 55-50-11). Its position is memorable: set up from the Loire in the midst of its own 350 acres of parkland, including a large pond for fishing and canoeing plus a swimming pool. Dating from the 15th century, the hotel reflects the simple, classic château architecture, with its central tower, formal entrance, and a terraced reflection pool. You can climb the tower for a view of the "domaine," taking in the bridle paths, the tennis courts, and the putting green.

The château is owned by a gentleman from Paris, the famous Monsieur Traversac, who also owns the Château d'Artigny as well as Le Mas d'Artigny on the Côte d'Azur. He treats it as an expensive hobby, but it is resident-managed and skillfully run. The most persistent question put to the hosts from prospective American visitors—"Do you have modern plumbing?"—can be answered with an emphatic "Yes."

The drawing room is wood paneled, with a marble fireplace, a chandelier of iron and colored glass, and three tall windows opening onto the reflection pool. The furnishings are eclectic, utilizing both antiques, upholstered pieces, and fabric-covered walls. Depending on one's mood, there are four places at which to dine—an opulent Louis XV room, a rustic Louis XIII room, the more primitive 15th-century tower room with a stone fireplace, and a canopied luncheon terrace.

The chef's specialties include seaman's stuffed pike, roast piglet, baked mushrooms, and pears in Bourgueil wine. If you want to drop in for a meal, a set dinner is featured for 105F ($23.97). Dining à la carte at a price ranging from 200F ($45.66) to 260F ($59.36), you can enjoy such dishes as a mousseline de brochet with crayfish and a gâteau de légumes (vegetables).

The bedrooms are individually decorated in a highly stylized fashion, with matching fabric on the walls coordinated with the draperies and upholstery. Skillfully made reproductions are mixed discreetly with antiques. Room 10 is on a grand-opera scale, with a 10-foot fireplace and an armoire, and Room 26 has overscale pink hydrangea wallpaper, the same motif reflected in the draperies and bedcover.

In high season no reservations are accepted unless a request is made for half pension, although full board is preferred (a minimum of five days is required). For full pension the tariff ranges from 320F ($73.06) to 450F ($102.74) per person. The Château, closed between January 15 and March 15, is 6½ miles from Tours, two miles from Luynes, lying off D49.

6. Villandry

The 16th-century-style gardens of this medieval and Renaissance château are celebrated throughout the Touraine. Forming a trio of superimposed "cloisters," with a water garden on the highest level, they were planned in the 19th century by Dr. Carvallo, founder of La Demeure Historique. The grounds contain 10½ miles of boxwood sculpture, which the gardeners must cut to style in only two weeks in September.

Every square of the gardens seems like a mosaic. The borders represent the many faces of love: tender, tragic (with daggers), or crazy, the latter evoked by a labyrinth in the middle that doesn't get you anywhere. Pink tulips and dahlias suggest sweet love; red, tragic; and yellow, unfaithful. Crazy love is symbolized by the use of all colors. The vine arbors, citrus hedges, shady walks—all this keeps six men busy full time. One garden contains all the common French vegetables except the potato, which wasn't known in France in the 16th century (even as late as 1771 the potato was considered "unfit for human consumption," until its virtues were extolled by Parmentier).

You can visit the gardens alone, arriving finally at a terrace from which you can see not only the gardens but a view of the small village and the 12th-century church of Villandry. If you want to visit the château, you'll need a guide. He'll explain the Spanish paintings in the salons, the furnishings in the dining room and gallery. In addition, you'll see a curious Moorish ceiling with scallop shells.

Originally a feudal castle stood at Villandry, but in 1532 Jean Lebreton, an official of François I, built the present château, its buildings forming a U and surrounded by a two-sided moat. It costs 8F ($1.83) to visit the gardens, another 2F (46¢) supplement for a guided tour of the château. It can be visited daily all year from 9 a.m. till dusk. The château is open only from March 30 to mid-November. Villandry is 20 miles from Chinon, 11 from Tours, and five from Azay-le-Rideau.

7. Loches

Forever linked to the memory of that legendary beauty Agnès Sorel, Loches is the *cité médiévale* of the château country. In the hills on the banks of the Indre River, it is called the city of kings. Known as the acropolis of the Loire, the château and its satellite buildings form a complex called the **Cité Royale.** The House of Anjou, from which the Plantagenets descended, owned the castle from 886 to 1205. The kings of France occupied it from the mid-13th century until the days of Charles IX, the son of Catherine de Medici, who was king from 1560.

The château today is mainly remembered for *la belle des belles* (the beauty of beauties) Agnès Sorel. After much wandering (including a time in Paris) and much abuse, her tomb rests inside the castle today, her velvet cushion guarded by two angels, her feet resting on two rams. In 1777 her tomb was opened, the coffin revealing a set of dentures and some locks of hair, all that remained from what was considered the most dazzling beauty of the 15th century.

She had been the maid of honor to Isabelle de Lorraine, but was singled out by the dauphin (Charles VII) for his "favors." She was to have great influence over the king until the day of her mysterious death. Mlle. Sorel was the first of a long line of royal mistresses living ostentatiously along with the kings at court. Her successors would be women such as Diane de Poitiers and Madame de Pompadour. The future king, Louis XI, wasn't captivated by Mlle. Sorel; he once slapped her in the face and chased her at swordpoint.

Fouquet painted her as the Virgin—one of her breasts completely exposed —but it was a posthumous portrait, its likeness to the actual mistress unknown (the masterpiece is now owned by Antwerp).

The château also contains the oratory of Anne of Brittany, decorated with sculptured ermine tails. One of its most outstanding treasures is a triptych of *The Passion* from the Fouquet School, dating from 1485. Charging 6F ($1.37) for admission, the château is open from 9 a.m. to noon and from 2 till 7 p.m. in summer (closes at 5:30 p.m. and Saturdays in winter).

The ancient **keep** (*donjon*) of the Counts d'Anjou can also be visited. The Round Tower of Louis XI contains rooms formerly used for torture. A favorite method of tormenting the victim was to suspend him in an iron cage. The Cardinal Balue was held that way for more than 10 years. In the 15th century in the Martelet, the Duke of Milan, Ludovico Sforza (Ludovico il Moro), its most famous prisoner, painted frescoes on the walls to pass the time. He died at Loches in 1508. The keep (you're admitted with your château ticket) is open from 9:30 a.m. to 12:30 p.m. and from 2:30 to 7 p.m. (in winter till 5:30 p.m.), and closed on Thursdays. The château and the keep are open between noon and 2 p.m. from July 1 to September 15.

Nearby, the **Collegiate Church of St. Ours** spans the tenth to the 15th centuries and is an interesting example of Romanesque architecture. The portal is richly decorated with sculptured figures, unfortunately damaged by time and renovations but still attractive. Monumental stone pyramids (*dubes*) surmount the nave. The west door reflects exceptional carving.

Finally, you may want to walk the **ramparts,** enjoying the view of the town, including a 15th-century gate and Renaissance inns.

Loches lies 25 miles southeast of Tours.

THE BUDGET INNS: Grand Hôtel de France, 6 rue Picoys (tel. 59-00-32), is charmingly French, with an inner courtyard where you can dine under parasols. Many of its bedrooms overlook this green domestic scene. There is a petite dining room with soft paneling, crystal, bowls of flowers, and crisscross white-organdy curtains—a welcoming atmosphere. Three set meals are offered, the lowest just 32F ($7.31); the next, a 45F ($10.27) meal with six courses; and the most expensive, a 58F ($13.24) meal featuring four of the chef's specialties. The hotel is closed for the month of November 15 to December 15. The accommodations are cheap for the area: from 45F ($10.27) to 100F ($22.83) in double rooms with some plumbing, the top price for a complete bath. Many rooms open onto a courtyard with vine-covered balconies. English is spoken.

Hôtel du Château, 18 rue du Château (tel. 59-07-35), is a simple 15th-century inn with a plain façade on a hillside street, just below the medieval town. The house is U-shaped, with a little courtyard and terrace for breakfasting containing a wide pergola of honeysuckle and yellow roses. A circular stone staircase leads to the rooms.

The bedrooms are modernized, often with tiled baths and provincial reproductions of antiques. Armoires are substituted for closets. Some rooms are tiny; others are large enough for three. For the better doubles with private bath, the rate is 130F ($29.68) nightly. The bathless singles cost 50F ($11.42). Breakfast under the pergola is included in the room rates.

The best feature for last: Madame Robin, the innkeeper, is as natural as homemade bread with stone-ground flour.

The hôtel is closed from mid-January to March.

8. Amboise

On the banks of the Loire, Amboise is in the center of vineyards known as Touraine-Amboise. Leonardo da Vinci spent his last years in this ancient city. Dominating the town is the **Château of Amboise,** the first in France to reflect the impact of the Italian Renaissance.

A combination of both Gothic and Renaissance, this 15th-century château is mainly associated with Charles VIII, who built it on a rocky spur separating the valleys of the Loire and the Amasse. The only son of Louis XI of France and Charlotte of Savoy, the future Charles VIII was born at Amboise on June 30, 1470. At the age of 25, he returned to France after his Italian campaign. With him he brought artists, designers, and architects from "that land of enchantment." In a sense, he was bringing the Italian Renaissance to France.

His workers built the *logis du roi,* the apartments of the king, its façade pierced by large double-mullioned windows and crowned by towering dormers and sculptured canopies. Charles VIII died at Amboise on April 8, 1498, after an accident: he banged his head against the wall; the blow didn't kill him until after he'd witnessed a fête planned that day for his entertainment. At the end of the terrace, near the room of his queen, Anne of Brittany, is a low doorway where it is said the mishap took place.

Later Louise of Savoy and her children lived at Amboise. One of her offspring in 1515 became King François I; the other was Margaret of Navarre. François continued to live at Amboise, making considerable additions to the castle. The château enjoyed its golden hours under the Chevalier King, as he sponsored a number of brilliant festivals, including some that featured contests between wild animals. The most memorable event was the arrival of Charles V in 1539. Preceded by torchbearers, the emperor grandly began to climb up one of the ramps, but a torch ignited a banner in the fabric-draped tower and he was nearly burned alive.

The skyline of Amboise is characterized by two squat towers, the Hurtault and the Minimes, which contain ramps of huge dimensions so that cavaliers on horseback or nobles in horse-drawn chariots could ascend them.

The name Amboise became linked in 1560 with a series of some of the most savage executions in France—executions that followed the Amboise Conspiracy, a Huguenot plot led by a La Renaudie of Brittany. Its aim was to remove François II from the influence of the House of Guise. Decapitations and mass hangings followed, much to the after-dinner amusement of the young François II and his queen, Mary Stuart (later Mary, Queen of Scots).

During the 19th century much of Amboise was destroyed, and it was only partially restored later.

You visit first the flamboyant Gothic Chapel of St. Hubert, built on the ramparts in the late 15th century and distinguished by its lacelike tracery. It allegedly contains the remains of da Vinci. Actually the great artist was buried in the castle's Collegiate Church, which was destroyed between 1806 and 1810. During the Second Empire excavations were undertaken on the site of the church, and bones discovered were "identified" as those of Leonardo.

Today, the walls of the château are hung with tapestries, the rooms furnished in the style of the époque. From the terraces are panoramic views of the town and of the Loire Valley. The château may be visited daily all year from 9 a.m. to noon and from 2 to 7 p.m. (till sunset in winter). Admission is 7F ($1.60).

Finally, you might visit **Clos-Lucé,** a 15th-century manor house of brick and stone. In what had been an oratory for Anne of Brittany, François I installed "the great master in all forms of art and science," Leonardo da Vinci. Loved and venerated by the Chevalier King, da Vinci lived there for three years, dying at the manor in 1519. (Incidentally, those death-bed paintings depicting Leonardo in the arms of François I are probably symbolic; the king was supposedly out of town when the artist died.)

From the window of his bedroom Leonardo liked to look out at the château where François lived. Whenever he was restless, the king would visit Leonardo via an underground tunnel, discovered recently by the Beaux-Arts. Nine days before his death, the artist made a will leaving untold riches of books, drawings, and instruments to his "beloved pupil and faithful companion" Francescoda Metzi. You can visit what is believed to have been the kitchen— the domain of the faithful servant Mathurine, mentioned by da Vinci in his will, to whom he left his cloak of "good black cloth, trimmed with leather."

Inside, the rooms are well furnished, some containing reproductions from the period of the artist. The downstairs is reserved for da Vinci's designs, models, and inventions, including his plans for a turbine engine, an airplane, and a parachute. Clos-Lucé is open daily from 9:30 a.m. to noon and from 2 to 6:30 p.m., charging 6F ($1.37) for admission.

GETTING THERE: Amboise is 15½ miles from Tours, 22 miles from Blois. In summer, regular bus service connects Amboise with such centers as Tours, Blois, and Chenonceaux.

DELUXE CHÂTEAU LIVING: Le Choiseul, 36 Quai Charles Guinot (tel. 57-23-83). Right on the Loire River road, the château is entered through a formal gate. You emerge into a drawing room where French charm and grace captivate. Le Choiseul is built on a historic site. During "La Guerre des Gaules" Julius Caesar chose this place for his military camp. On top of the hill, where a castle now stands, he built wooden houses, a tower with a statue of Mars, and baths. His soldiers burrowed four large underground caves to house food and grain. By stairs you can go from the top of the hill to the land near the river where the Romans created a harbor 60 meters in elevation. The caverns still exist and can be visited.

Centuries later, King Charles VIII gave the land to build a convent, which became known for its library and its beautiful terraces. (In place of the terraces there is now a magnificent dining room overlooking the Loire River and the park.) During his exile the Duke of Choiseul-Amboise added a Louis XV pavilion.

The convent was destroyed during the Revolution. Only the Choiseul pavilion and a part of the House of Pages of Charles VIII still exist. On the site two houses were built in the 18th century; they were converted into a charming home in 1945.

Le Choiseul's 18 rooms and suites overlook the Loire River or the gardens, which have had the same design since the 16th century. The drawing rooms contain lots of gilt, oil paintings, and petit-point-covered Louis XVI-style chairs, sparkling crystal, inlaid tables, and porcelain bowls of fresh flowers brought in from the luxuriant garden. The bedrooms are well furnished in the Louis XV and Louis XVI periods, each with its own delicate color theme—much gilt, embroidered fabric, canopies, marble-topped tables, and richly colored tapestry rugs.

All the rooms contain private baths and are priced according to their size, view, and richness of decor. Demi-pension guests are preferred. A single costs from 200F ($45.66) to 420F ($95.89), a double from 400F ($91.32) to 600F ($136.98), taxes and service included.

The **Château de Pray** (N751) (tel. 57-23-67) provides a genuine introduction to the better half of French life at moderate prices. It is rooted in French history, tracing its origins to Geoffroy de Pray in 1244. Since 1955, however, it has belonged to the Farard family, who have turned it into a paying proposition. The four lovely daughters—Martine, Véronique, Béatrice, and Isabelle—join in the undertaking.

The castle, on a hillside overlooking the Loire, rivals those on the Rhine. It is of a simple but classic design, with tall twin towers on either side and an elaborately formal garden. Antlers and other such hunting trophies hang in the entry hall. The small drawing room is paneled, with a fireplace, fine antiques, old oil paintings, and an adjoining terrace where guests gather for drinks.

The best bargain is half pension, costing from 191F ($43.61) to 210F ($47.94) per person. As only 16 rooms are available, reservations are imperative. Most Americans like No. 16 the best. Called "Sorbiers," it contains a fine antique four-poster bed with twisted columns, as well as a tiled private bath.

The family has engaged a chef whose meals make dining a pleasure and a treat. He offers 82F ($18.72) to 98F ($22.37) menus, the latter including a fish course. A typical dinner would start with a selection of hors d'oeuvres, follow with grilled Loire salmon with beurre blanc, then roast guinea hen, a fresh salad, a selection of cheese, and a homemade pastry. Excellent Loire wines are available. The dining room has a classic ceiling-high, sloped fireplace where logs burn slowly on nippy nights. The chairs are provincial fruitwood, the dishes and linen are patterned, and most importantly, the leaded-glass windows open toward the river. Closed from January till mid-February.

BUDGET INNS: **Lion d'Or** (Golden Lion), 17 Quai Guinot (tel. 57-00-23), is the other leading hostelry of Amboise. Bearing the stamp of a manor, it has steep slate roofs and wide windows providing a view of the Loire. The lounges are less important here, as the emphasis is on the high-ceilinged dining room with its river view.

The owner, Pierre Viot, reigns in the kitchen, and Mme. Viot runs the hotel. The demi-pension rate ranges from 95F ($21.69) to 125F ($28.54). In the dining room, you can choose one of two different meals, the lower priced at 60F ($13.70), the other at 85F ($19.41). We recently sampled the 85F meal, which began with a selection of fresh-tasting hors d'oeuvres, followed by delicious filets of sole garnished with shrimp tails and mushrooms, then sauteed veal cutlets, with a salad of hearts of lettuce, a selection from the cheese board, plus a pineapple melba for dessert. A banquet! Specialties include terrine lapin (rabbit) aux pruneaux, pepper steak flambé, and sorbet St. Michel. Ordering à la carte will cost about 85F ($19.41) to 120F ($27.40) per person. Closed November 25 to February 25; off-season it is closed Wednesday evenings and Thursday noons.

Belle-Vue, 12 Quai Charles-Guinot (tel. 57-02-26), is an efficient inn right at the bridge crossing the Loire. Its façade is uninspired, with lots of functional additions and modernizations, and its interior lounges aren't exactly decorators' dreams. However, the Belle-Vue does open onto a garden area which is not only beautiful but restful. Parasol tables are set out on various flagstone terraces around a free-form swimming pool.

In a double, the full-pension rate ranges from 138F ($31.51) to 160F ($36.53) per person, depending on the plumbing. In a single, the full-pension rate is 146F ($33.33) in a bathless room. All the rooms are furnished in modern, convenient style.

The hotel's river-view restaurant, called **Monseigneur** (tel. 57-07-60), offers three set menus at 45F ($10.27), 60F ($13.70), and 95F ($21.69). On Sundays only a 70F ($15.98) and a 120F ($27.40) menu are featured. The hotel is closed in January and February and on Sunday nights from November to April.

THE LEADING RESTAURANT: The **Auberge du Mail,** 32 Quai Général-de-Gaulle (tel. 57-00-39), is a little riverfront restaurant outside the town on the road to Tours. In the opinion of many discriminating diners, it serves the finest food in Amboise, even if it is more unpretentious than some of the other establishments. You can park your car across the street under the shade trees, where a gypsy family is likely to solicit you.

At the auberge itself, you can select a table under a grape arbor, then decide which of Monsieur Le Coz's set menus you wish to sample. Each one offers tasty fare. The cheapest menu costs 68F ($15.52) and the menu gastronomique goes for 130F ($29.68). Some of the chef's specialties appear on these menus, but you can order à la carte as well, paying around 60F ($13.70) to 120F ($27.40), depending on the specialties you select.

The dish that seems to earn the most praise is the filet de chevreuil sauce grand veneur (roebuck with a chestnut purée and sauce). If you're very hungry, you might want to precede the course with the chef's celestines de fruits de mer or the foie confit (goose liver) au Vouvray. A simple bottle of Loire wine complements most meals. The restaurant is closed from December 1 to March 1, and on Tuesday nights and Wednesdays for lunch.

READER'S HOTEL SELECTION: "Hôtel de la Loire, 7 rue Commire-Entrepont (tel. 57-14-02), is recommended for three main reasons: location, service, and price. It stands on an island in the middle of the river. From one of its windows (only 12 rooms) you can see the whole landscape of Amboise, plus the château sitting majestically on the top of a mountain. The hotel also has small tables and chairs set up by the side of the river so that customers can enjoy the tranquility and serenity of the place. The hotel is run by a family who make sure that everything is in order. There is a little bar and restaurant on the first floor where you can have meals or enjoy a drink. Finally, the price is really very reasonable. A room for two with bath costs 85F ($19.41). Breakfast is 11F ($2.51) each, and the 48F ($10.96) dinner has three or four selections to choose from (the scallops are excellent)" (Anthony V. DeLuca, Huntington Station, N.Y.).

9. Blois

A wound in battle had earned him the name "Balafré" (scarface), but he was quite a ladies' man nonetheless. In fact, on that cold misty morning of December 23, 1588, the Duke of Guise had just left a warm bed and the arms of one of Catherine de Medici's lovely "flying squadron" girls. His archrival, Henri III, had summoned him. As he made his way to the king's chambers perhaps he was dreaming of the day when the effeminate little monarch would be overthrown and he, the champion of the Catholics, would become ruler of France.

The king's minions were about. Nothing unusual—Henri was always surrounded with attractive young men these days. Then it happened. The guards moved menacingly toward him with daggers. Wounded, the duke was still strong enough to knock a few down. He made his way toward the door, where more guards awaited him. Staggering back, he fell to the floor in a pool of his own blood.

Only then did Henri emerge from behind the curtains. "My God," he is reputed to have exclaimed, "he's taller dead than alive!" The body couldn't be shown: the duke was too popular. Quartered, it was burned in a fireplace in the château. Then Henri's mother, Catherine de Medici, had to be told the "good news."

The murder of the Duke of Guise—one of the most famous assassinations in French history—is only one of the memories of this château, which was begun in the 13th century by the counts of Blois. Charles d'Orléans (son of Louis d'Orléans, assassinated by the Burgundians in 1407), the "poet prince," lived at Blois after his release from 25 years of English captivity. He had married Mary of Cleves and had brought a "court of letters" to Blois. In his 70s, Charles became the father of the future Louis XII, who was to marry Anne of Brittany. Blois was launched in its new role as a royal château. In time it was to be called the second capital of France, and Blois itself the city of kings.

However, Blois became a palace of banishment. Louis XIII for a time got rid of his interfering mother, Marie de Medici by sending her there; but this plump matron escaped by sliding into the moat on a coat down a mound of dirt left by the builders. Then in 1626 the king sent his conspiring brother, Gaston d'Orléans, there. He stayed.

If you stand in the courtyard of the great château, you'll find it's like an illustrated storybook of French architecture. The Hall of the Estates-General is a beautiful work from the 13th century; the so-called gallery of Charles d'Orléans was actually built by Louis XII in 1498-1501, as was the Louis XII wing. The François I wing is a masterpiece of the French Renaissance; the Gaston d'Orléans wing was built by François Mansart between 1635 and 1637. Of them all, the most remarkable is the François I wing, containing a spiral staircase with elaborately ornamented balustrades and the king's symbol, the salamander. In the Louis XII wing, seek out paintings by Antoine Caron, court painter to Henri III, depicting the persecution of Thomas More.

Restoration of the interior is continuing, but the royal emblems were destroyed during the Revolution. Note the paneling behind which many people placed secrets, perhaps Catherine de Medici her poisons. The room where the Estates-General met in 1588 is the oldest part of the château, nowadays containing tapestries from the 17th century, some based on cartoons by Rubens, others in the Renaissance style illustrating scenes from the life of Marc Antony.

From March 16 to September 30, the château is open daily from 9 a.m. to noon and from 2 to 6:30 p.m.; from October 1 to January 31, from 9 a.m. to noon and from 2 to 5 p.m.; from February 1 to March 15, from 9 a.m. to noon and 2 to 5:30 p.m. Admission costs 8F ($1.83), 4F (91¢) for students. A son-et-lumière production titled "Ghosts Like It Dark" is presented in English at 10:30 p.m. from March 20 to October 3, costing 8F ($1.83) for admission.

GETTING THERE: Usually visited in conjunction with nearby Chambord, Blois lies 35 miles from Orléans, 37 miles from Tours. On the right bank of the Loire, it is the center of the château district. (In 1429, Joan of Arc launched her expeditionary forces from here to oust the English from Orléans.)

MEDIUM-PRICED INNS: Hostellerie de la Loire, 8 rue de Lattre-de-Tassigny (tel. 74-26-60), is an inn where you can get not only rooms but well-prepared meals. In fact, it's generally conceded that the Loire serves the finest food in Blois. Right on the river, the bedrooms on the lower floor are apt to be noisy—so request, if possible, an upper-floor accommodation. There are 18 rooms in all, a few with private bath renting for 120F ($27.40) for a single, 160F ($36.53) for a double with bath and toilet. A single without bath costs 80F ($18.26). The rooms are basic, but sufficiently comfortable for an overnight stopover.

In the dining room, you're offered meals at various prices. The 50F ($11.42) tourist menu is always generous, and you're not made to feel a criminal for requesting it. A more elaborate meal is featured for 75F ($17.12).

On the à la carte menu, house specialties include a cassolette d'escargots (snails in casserole) à la caulderan and canard (duckling) à l'orange. In season, fresh strawberries from Orléans make a perfect dessert. Try the vin d'orange (an orange wine) as an apéritif. Ordering à la carte is likely to mean a tab ranging from 120F ($27.40) to 170F ($38.81) per person. Closed from mid-January till mid-February and Sunday evenings all year.

Au Grand Cerf, 42 Avenue Wilson (tel. 78-02-16), right on the main road, offers sensible prices and a pleasant ambience. The owner, Madame Colaert, obtained government aid to modernize her three-story building. Logis de France inns of this nature get grants for updating, providing they equip their buildings with good plumbing facilities and offer the regional cuisine.

Comfortable bedrooms contain reproductions of classic French furniture, including tufted headboards (plus plastic slipcovers), and go for 60F ($13.70) to 100F ($22.83). Breakfast is an extra 10.50F ($2.39). Travel agents like to book groups here, as the food is good and the accommodations bring few complaints.

Complete meals are offered, including a simple beverage and service, beginning as low as 35F ($7.99) and ranging upward to 110F ($25.11) for the menu gastronomique. A house specialty is confit d'oie (slices of goose meat in goose fat). In spite of its unappetizing sound in English, this dish enjoys much favor among gastronomes, who consider it a delicacy. Another favorite dish is ris de veau (sweetbreads) Grand Cerf. À la carte orders usually range between 50F ($11.42) and 150F ($34.26) per person. The inn is closed from December 15 to Christmas and on Fridays.

BUDGET MEALS AND LODGINGS: St. Jacques, Place de la Gare (tel. 78-04-15), is a bustling hotel/brasserie right opposite the railway station. It offers 28 bedrooms, with bathless singles going for 45F ($10.27), the most expensive doubles going for 90F ($20.55). But mostly this Logis de France is known as a place where you can get an exceptionally fine low-priced regional meal.

For just 38F ($8.68), you can get the pâté of the district served with crusty bread, then a bouillabaisse in the Provençal style, topped off by fresh strawberries (in season) with sugar. If you're really hungry, ask for the five-course, 70F ($15.98) menu. This included, on one recent occasion, soup, terrine of rabbit, filet of pike with beurre blanc, veal kidneys with cream, and profiteroles glacées for dessert. The brasserie is closed during most of November and takes a long Christmas vacation.

Anne de Bretagne, 31 Avenue J.-Laigret (tel. 78-05-38), is a simple inn a two-minute walk from the railway station, tucked away on a petite plaza. It has a gabled front and a pair of large vines of red roses meeting to form an arch. Little red-and-white tables are set out invitingly. The proprietress, Madame Loyeau, has been putting up guests from all over the world, and on her desk rests a stack of the letters requesting space that she is forever answering.

Her inn is scrubbed and waxed clean—no fussiness, no frills, but good value for your money. There's central heating in the nippy months. Her cheapest doubles with hot and cold running water and a bidet go for only 48F ($10.96). A few doubles with private baths or showers are tabbed at 75F ($17.12). If you require a room for four, she offers that for 95F ($21.69). Breakfast only is served, at 10.50F ($2.39). Closed February 15 to March 15.

READER'S HOTEL SELECTION: "In Blois, the Hôtel Saint-Nicolas, 2 rue du Sermon (tel. 78-05-85), offers singles for only 40F ($9.13), including breakfast. It is only a block from the Loire River and across the square from the fascinating old St. Nicolas Church, about three blocks from the Château Blois" (Robert F. Fera, Orchard Lake, Mich.).

10. Chaumont

On that long-ago morning when Diane de Poitiers crossed the drawbridge, the château of Chaumont looked grim. Its battlements, its pepper-pot turrets crowning the towers—the whole effect resembled a prison. Henri II, her lover, had died. The king had given her Chenonceaux, which she loved, but Catherine de Medici in her widow's weeds had banished her from her favorite château and shipped her off to Chaumont.

Inside, portraits reveal the king's mistress to have truly lived up to her reputation as forever beautiful. Another portrait—that of Catherine de Medici, wife of Henri II, looking like a devout nun—invites unfavorable comparison.

Chaumont ("Burning Mount") was built during the reign of Louis XII by Charles d'Amboise. Looking down at the Loire, it is approached by a long walk up from the village through a tree-studded park. The original fortress had been dismantled by Louis XI. In 1560, it was acquired by Catherine de Medici. At one time Madame de Staël, banished from Paris by Napoleon, resided there. Chaumont was privately owned and inhabited until it was acquired by the state in 1938.

Architecturally, the castle spans the intermediate period between the Middle Ages and the Renaissance. Inside, the prize exhibit is a rare collection of medallions by Nini, an Italian artist. A guest of the château for a while, he made medallion portraits of kings, queens, nobles, even Benjamin Franklin who once visited Chaumont.

In the bedroom occupied by Catherine de Medici is a portrait of a witty-looking cardinal who wanted to become the pope (he bears a striking resemblance to Vincent Price). There is also a rare portrait of Catherine, painted when she was young, wearing many jewels, including a ruby later owned by Mary Queen of Scots.

Catherine was superstitious, always keeping her astrologer, Cosimo Ruggieri, at beck and call. She had him housed in one of the tower bedrooms (a portrait of him remains). It is reported that he foretold the disasters awaiting her sons, including Henri III. In the astrologer's bedroom is a most unusual tapestry depicting Medusa with a flying horse escaping from her head.

Chaumont, 10½ miles from either Amboise or Blois, is open from April 1 to September 30 from 9 to 11:45 a.m. and from 2 to 6:30 p.m., charging 5F ($1.14) for admission, plus an extra 3F (68¢) for the stables. It closes at 5 p.m. in October, at 4 p.m. between November 1 and March 31. The castle is closed Tuesdays.

UPPER-BRACKET LIVING: Hostellerie du Château (tel. 46-98-04) is a rather glamorously styled country inn, a few minutes from the Loire and opposite the entrance gate to the château. Norman in style, with brown timbers and stucco, it is mostly known for its cuisine.

It's owned by Monsieur and Madame Bonnigal, who have brought a semiluxurious standard to this hostellerie. True, you can't see the Loire from the terrace, but when you get an upper-floor bedroom, there is an extensive view. Each of the public rooms has its own country style, achieving a homelike atmosphere with a feeling of privacy. The bar is a favorite, with its whitewashed stone walls, oak beams, chestnut paneling, and provincial chairs. The living room achieves its theme with a brick fireplace, Oriental rugs, old chests, and soft chairs covered in bright fabrics.

The bedrooms are individually designed, with coordinated color themes and antiques or good reproductions. The baths are well tiled in strong colors. The best doubles range in price from 170F ($38.81) to 250F ($57.08).

The main dining room provides its own drama, with a high-timbered ceiling, rustic chairs and accessories, plus a ceiling-high white stone fireplace. A set menu is offered for 75F ($17.12), although you'll pay extra for service. Some of the chef's specialties are a terrine of vegetables, ballotine de caneton (duckling) with hazelnuts, fresh Loire salmon, poularde (pullet) à la Medicis, and Chariot de desserts. Ordering à la carte will mean a tab ranging in price from 120F ($27.40) to 150F ($34.26). The inn is closed from November 15 until March 15 and on Tuesdays all year round.

A MANOR (MEALS ONLY): Manoir du Moutier St.-Martin (tel. 46-98-13) is more of an old priory than an inn. On the river road near a bridge, it is surrounded by gardens with many weeping willows, lilacs, and roses. The reception lounges set the tone: worn paneling, beamed ceilings, high country fireplaces, provincial furniture, and an adjoining loggia overlooking the river garden. A small tower with a winding stairway leads down to a big farmhouse-style dining room with thick walls, black beams, provincial chairs, an open fireplace surrounded by copper and brass bric-a-brac, baskets of fresh fruit, and the day's pastry set out for serving.

The chef-owner, Marcel Picard, is very clever in the kitchen, making the manoir a most recommendable stopover. The gastronomique dinner costs a comparatively modest 85F ($19.41). A large bottle of wine from the nearby vineyards is only 24F ($5.48). The manor is closed Tuesdays and from December 15 to January 15.

11. Chambord

When François I, the Chevalier King, used to say, "Come on up to my place," he meant Chambord, not Fontainebleau or Blois. Construction workers, some 2000 strong, began to piece together "the pile" in 1519. What emerged after 20 years was the pinnacle of the French Renaissance, the largest château in the Loire Valley. It was ready for the visit of Charles V of Germany, who was welcomed by nymphets in transparent veils gently tossing wildflowers —fresh from the encircling forest of Sologne—in the emperor's path.

In the years that ensued, French monarchs—Henri II and Catherine de Medici, Louis XIII, Henri III—came and went from Chambord, but not one of them developed the affection for it held by François I. The brother of Louis XIII, Gaston d'Orléans, restored the château in part. His daughter, "La Grande Mademoiselle" (Mlle. de Montpensier), related in her writings that she used to force her father to run up and down Chambord's famous double spiral staircase after her. Because of its curious structure, he never caught her.

Louis XIV made nine visits there. Molière's *Monsieur de Pourceaugnac* was performed at Chambord for the Sun King. According to a much-repeated theatrical legend, the playwright saved the play by leaping into the orchestra pit, eliciting a hearty roar from the up-to-then stony-faced king. Molière also previewed *Le Bourgeois Gentilhomme* there.

Driven from the throne of Poland, Stanislas Leczinski, the father-in-law of Louis XV, took up residence in 1725, spending eight years at Chambord. Perhaps its most colorful resident, however, was Maurice Saxe, the marshal of France in 1743 and an illegitimate son of Augustus II of Saxony. To Chambord he imported cavalrymen from the West Indies. Ruling with an iron fist (even invoking the death penalty), he apparently applied the standard of brutality to his mistress, Madame Favart. Falling into decay, the château became—at the lowest point in its history—a munitions factory. Or perhaps the lowest point in its saga was its occupation by the Nazis in the last war. The state acquired Chambord in 1932.

The château is set in a park of more than 13,000 acres, enclosed within a wall stretching some 20 miles. Looking out one of the windows from one of the 440 rooms, François I is said to have carved on a pane, with a diamond ring, these words: "A woman is a creature of change; to trust her is to play the fool." On seeing the estate, Chateaubriand said Chambord was like "a lady whose hair has been blown by the wind." Its façade is characterized by four monumental towers. The keep contains a spectacular terrace which the ladies of the court used to stand on to watch the return of their men from the hunt.

From that platform, you can inspect the dormer windows and the richly decorated chimneys, some characterized by winged horses.

The three-story keep also encloses the already mentioned corkscrew staircase—superimposed so that one person may descend at one end and another ascend at the other without ever meeting. The apartments of Louis XIV, including his redecorated bedchamber, are also in the keep. A trio of rooms was restored by the government, but not with the original furnishings, of course.

Eleven miles from Blois, on the banks of the Cosson, Chambord is open daily from 9 to 11:45 a.m. and from 2 till 6:30 p.m. from April 1 to September 30 (closes at 4 or 5 p.m. otherwise). Admission costs 6F ($1.37), 3F (68¢) on Sundays and holidays. It is closed Tuesdays off-season. A son-et-lumière program is staged in June and July at 10 and 11 p.m.; at 9:30 and 10:30 p.m. in August; and at 9 and 10 p.m. in September. Admission is 8F ($1.83). In fact, the first sound-and-light show in France was at Chambord.

A CONVERTED MANOR (BUDGET LIVING): Hôtel du Grand St.-Michel (tel. 46-31-31), is a manor house turned hotel, occupying an enviable position opposite the entrance to Chambord. The front bedrooms, of course, overlook the château, especially handsome when illuminated in the evenings. The character of St.-Michel is that of a country inn geared to overnight visitors —so don't expect personalized service. The decor is provincial. Hopefully you'll take your meals on the terrace under a geranium-red awning.

The rooms are plain, but well kept and comfortable. A double with private bath rents for 170F ($38.81); but many satisfactory doubles with a minimum of plumbing, such as water basins and bidets, are in the 70F ($15.98) range. The full-pension rate is 200F ($45.66) to 230F ($52.51) per person daily, but it is granted for guests staying five days. There is only one set menu, at 65F ($14.84), which at last inspection offered a lot of the chef's specialties, including civet de marcassin and quenelles de brochet. In season a large choice of game is offered. Expect to pay 95F ($21.69) for the set meal on Sundays, which is more elaborate. Closed from November 12 to December 20.

12. Beaugency

The heart of this ancient Loire Valley town is an archaeological garden called the **City of the Lords,** named after the counts who enjoyed great power in the Middle Ages. A major event in the history of medieval Europe took place there: the marriage of Eleanor of Aquitaine and Louis VII was dissolved in 1152. These two monarchs had fallen into a bitter dispute during the Second Crusade, and attempts at a reconciliation had failed.

The tempestuous Eleanor sought a divorce on the grounds of consanguinity—that is, they were cousins in the fourth degree, such relatives being forbidden to marry according to the rules of the day. This remarkable woman later became queen consort of Henry II of England, bringing southwestern France as her dowry. She was also, of course, the mother of Richard the Lion-Hearted. At a much later date, in 1429, Joan of Arc rid Beaugency of the English.

On the right bank of the Loire, the town boasts a bridge dating from the 14th century. It's unusual in that each of its 26 arches is in a different style.

The 15th century **Château Dumois,** floodlit at night, contains a folklore museum of the Orléans district. At the Place Dumois, the collection consists of hairpieces, costumes, waistcoats, and antique furnishings, displayed in various salons. For a 4F (91¢) admission, the château may be visited from 9 to 11:30 a.m. and from 2 to 6 p.m. (till 4 p.m. in winter). A son-et-lumière program is staged there at 9:45 p.m. from mid-May to August 30, costing 5F ($1.14) per person.

Near the château is **St. George's Vault,** a gate of the former castle of the Lords of Beaugency, which opened from the fortress onto the Rû Valley and the lower part of town.

The **Church of Notre-Dame** would have been a good example of Roman-esque art of the 12th century if the Gothic hadn't intruded. Originally it was attached to a Benedictine abbey. Nearby is **St. Firmin's Tower,** all that remains of an old church which once stood on the Place St.-Firmin. A trio of bells is sheltered in this tower, whose spire rises to a height of 180 feet. From the structure a magnificent view of the river valley unfolds before you. In the archaeological garden, the **Hôtel-Dieu** (the old hospital) is one of the oldest buildings in Beaugency, having been erected in the 11th century, its roofing edge in the Romanesque style.

A COACHING INN (BUDGET): Hostellerie de l'Écu de Bretagne, Place du Martroi (tel. 44-67-60), is an oldish, low, sprawling coaching inn, set on a quiet square. There are café tables outside for enjoying beverages, plus an inner courtyard for cars (here horse-drawn coaches used to bring travelers from Paris). You feel the presence of the attentive and proud proprietor, Monsieur Conan, who keeps his keen eye on the kitchen and dining room. Have a predinner drink in the country tavern, with its crude tables and Breton carved paneling.

Dining in the modernized restaurant is the real reason for staying here. There are three set meals, 45F ($10.27), 60F ($13.70), and 80F ($18.26), the latter for the menu gastronomique. Note that the menu is divided into classic and regional dishes. On the à la carte menu, try the following: lentilles en salade, 14F ($3.20), or cul de lapereau (young rabbit) au miel (honey), 45F ($10.27). Especially recommendable is noisette de porc aux pruneaux, 45F also. Homemade fruit tarts cost 15F ($3.42).

A bathless double goes for 60F ($13.70); doubles with bath range from 120F ($27.40) to 150F ($34.26). The room furnishings are modest.

13. Cour-Cheverny

The *haute monde* still comes to the Sologne area for the hunt. It's as if the 17th century never ended. It did, of course, and 20th-century realities such as taxes are *formidable*—hence, the château must open some of its rooms for inspection by paying guests. At least, that keeps the tax collector at bay and the hounds fed in winter.

Unlike most of the Loire châteaux, Cheverny is inhabited, actually lived in by the descendant of the original owners. The sporting Marquis de Vibraye, who loves to be photographed with his hounds leading the chase, traces his lineage back to Henri Hurault, the son of the chancellor of Henri III and Henri IV, who built the first château in 1634.

This particular ancestor married an 11-year-old girl, Françoise Chabot. When that lady grew up, she developed a passion for page boys which lasted until her husband interrupted her nocturnal activities. After killing her fright-ened lover, he offered his spouse two choices: she could either swallow poison or else have his sword plunged into her heart. She elected to swallow from the bitter cup. Perhaps to erase the memory, he had the old castle torn down and a new one—the present château—built for his second wife.

It attracted many fashionable visitors over the centuries, among them the "Grande Mademoiselle," who compared its beauty to "the Alcine Island or the Apolidor Palace." In a sense the château is "pure"—that is, it was constructed in a short period of time and has remained substantially as it was intended. Designed in the classic Louis XIII style, it contains square pavilions flanking the central pile.

Inside, the antique furnishings, tapestries, rich decorations, and objects of art warm things up considerably. A 17th-century French artist, Jean Mosnier, decorated the fireplace with motifs from the legend of Adonis. In the Guards' Room is a collection of medieval armor resting under a painted ceiling. Also displayed is a Gobelins tapestry depicting *The Abduction of Helen of Troy*. In the king's bedchamber, another Gobelins tapestry traces the *Trials of Ulysses*, such as his landing on the island of Circe. Most impressive, however, is a stone stairway of carved fruit and flowers.

Bypassing a kennel of hounds, you reach the **Musée de l'Équipage**, a hunting museum with an outstanding collection of antlers—more than 2000 of them. You needn't spend much time there unless you dig weird headgear. The tree-shaded park of streams and ponds—although offering only a hint of its former glory—is impressive enough.

Floodlit at night, the château is open daily from 9 a.m. to noon and from 2 to 6:30 p.m., charging an admission of 8F ($1.83) for a 30-minute guided tour. Cheverny is easily explored by a side-trip jaunt from Blois, eight miles to the northwest.

TWO PROVINCIAL INNS (BUDGET): Les Trois Marchands, Place de l'Église (tel. 79-96-44). This much-renovated coaching inn has been handed down for generations from father to son, the present proprietor being Jean Bricault. Next to a church with a tall thin spire, the "Three Merchants" is three stories high, with red awnings, a mansard roof, sidewalk tables, and a glassed-in courtyard. Tables are set under brightly colored umbrellas in the shade of linden trees. There diners are courteously served a fine regional cuisine. Meals are also available in a large tavern-style dining room with beamed ceilings and provincial furnishings.

Set meals are offered: 50F ($11.42) and 80F ($18.26). The menu gastronomique at 110F ($25.11) might include a ballotine de canard (duckling) with pistachio nuts, followed by fresh salmon, then quail flambé, plus fresh string beans, a garden salad, a selection from the cheese board, and a homemade pastry. The 50F ($11.42) meal isn't to be ignored either—including, on one recent occasion, a selection of fresh hors d'oeuvres, followed by lapereau (young rabbit) sautéed in a red wine and stock. The cellar offers a good white wine of the house, called Cour-Cheverny.

Madame Bricault is in charge of the rooms and the comfort of the guests. Most of their rooms are traditionally furnished, with padded headboards and provincial chests. Doubles range from 65F ($14.84) to 150F ($34.26), depending on the plumbing: the top price brings a complete bath. The hotel is closed from January 15 to March 1. It is closed on Tuesdays from October 1 until the end of the year.

Saint-Hubert (tel. 79-96-60), about 800 yards from the château, is a roadside inn built in the old provincial style, with bedroom wings opening onto a courtyard. All is kept refreshingly spic and span. The secret of its success lies in the teamwork of its proprietor, Monsieur Charbonnier, and his son-in-law, Jean-Claude Pillaut, the chef de cuisine. They provide not only a restful and pleasant stopover but an especially delicious cuisine.

Three set menus are offered: 55F ($12.56), 85F ($19.41), and 120F ($27.40). For the least expensive tab, we recently dined on la terrine de caille en gelée, followed by sandre (a Loire fish) with "white butter," a selection of cheese, and a homemade fruit tart. The more expensive menus are likely to offer lobster or fresh spring asparagus. Game is featured here in season. When Monsieur Charbonnier can find no more chevreuils (roebuck) in the Sologne area, he goes himself to Alsace for fresh ones, because the cooking of roebuck in particular, and game in general, is his specialty. The inn is closed from December 5 to January 15 and on Wednesdays from October 1 to Easter.

Depending on the plumbing you desire, rooms range in price from 55F ($12.56) to 120F ($27.40), service and tax included.

14. Valençay

One of the handsomest Renaissance buildings in the château country, Valençay was acquired in 1803 by Talleyrand on the orders of Napoleon, who wanted his shrewd minister of foreign affairs to receive dignitaries in great style. During its occupancy by Talleyrand, some of the most important personages in Europe passed under the portal of Valençay. Not all those guests, notably Ferdinand VII of Spain, wanted to visit the château. Driven from his homeland in 1808, the king was housed at Valençay for six years, on orders of Napoleon, as "the guest of Talleyrand."

In 1838, Talleyrand was buried at Valençay, the château passing to his nephew, Louis de Talleyrand-Périgord. Before the Talleyrand ownership, Valençay was built in 1550 by the d'Estampes family on the site of an old feudal castle of the lords of Châlons. The dungeon and the great west tower are of this period, as is the main body of the building; but other wings were added in the 17th and 18th centuries. The effect is grandiose, almost too much so, with domes, chimneys, and turrets.

The interior furnishings are especially rewarding, as the apartments are sumptuously furnished, mostly in the Empire style but with Louis XV and Louis XVI trappings as well. In the main drawing room is a star-footed table, said to have been the one on which the Final Agreement of the Congress of Vienna was signed in June 1815 (Talleyrand represented France).

Charging 9F ($2.05) for admission, Valençay may be visited daily in summer from 9 to 11:45 a.m. and from 2 to 7 p.m. In winter, it is open only on Sundays and public holidays, from 10 a.m. to noon and from 2 to 6:30 p.m.

Facing the château is the **Museum of Talleyrand** (admission is included in the ticket for the castle), put together in 1953 in an orangerie that stood on the grounds. The gallery assembles some historical souvenirs of the prince, including portraits of him as well as one of King Ferdinand VII. Two corner cabinets house the numerous decorations of the French statesman, along with his swords, miniatures, and seals. You'll also see a reconstruction of his Empire bedroom, a gift from the king of Naples. After your visit to the main buildings you can walk through the zoological garden and deer park. On the grounds are many exotic birds, including flamingos.

The village of Valençay lies 35 miles south of Blois.

A COACHING INN (UPPER BRACKET): Hôtel d'Espagne, 8 rue du Château (tel. 00-00-02). When you pass through the wide-arched entrance of this former coaching inn, you'll find yourself in an old compound—a U-shaped building encompassing an open flagstone courtyard with trimmed boxwood shrubbery, plus tubs and planters of bright flowers. It's the tiny kingdom of

Monsieur and Madame Fourré and their family, who provide an old-world ambience combined with comforts and a first-class kitchen. The kinks in the hotel have long ago been smoothed out, as the Fourré family has been there since 1875. One of the sons, Philippe, is in charge of the dining room; another, Maurice, is the chef.

The bedrooms have their own names and individuality. You may, for example, be assigned a chamber decorated in the authentic period of Empire, Louis XV, or Louis XVI. The hotel in reality is a cluster of adjoining buildings, almost like a village in miniature. There are 19 bedrooms, plus half a dozen lusher suites, most of the accommodations containing private baths. The average double or twin-bedded room rents for anywhere between 170F ($38.81) and 340F ($77.62). Breakfast is 22F ($5.02) extra, but taxes and service are included.

Meals are provided in the dining room or gardens. The chef's specialties include both his terrine truffée in gelatin and his special dessert, délicieuse au chocolat. If you are selecting the specialties on the à la carte menu, expect to pay from 180F ($41.09) to 220F ($50.23) per person. The inn is closed from December 1 to March 1 and Tuesdays off-season.

A BUDGET CAFE: If your budget calls for something far less expensive, then your best bet is **Le Chêne Vert** ("The Green Oak"), Route Nationale (N760) (tel. 00-06-54). It's merely a wayside village café, with outdoor tables, where you can order especially good meals for only a few francs. There is a 32F ($7.31) meal which on a typical day might include an appetizer of Westphalian ham, followed with beef bourguignon, accompanied by tomatoes in the Provençale style, and ending with cheese and dessert. A better meal, the menu gastronomique, featuring dishes such as terrine, roebuck with a pepper sauce, braised endive, cheese, and dessert, costs 70F ($15.98). Drinks are extra. You may want to cap your luncheon by ordering a glass of framboise. The inn is closed from June 10 to 25 and from December 10 to January 10, and on Saturday and Sunday nights in the off-season.

15. Chenonceaux

This *chef-d'oeuvre* of the Renaissance has essentially orbited around the series of famous *dames de Chenonceaux* who have occupied it. Originally the château was owned by the Marqués family, but its members were extravagant beyond their means. Deviously, Thomas Bohier, the comptroller-general of finances in Normandy, began buying up land around the château. Finally, the Marqués family was forced to sell to Bohier, who tore down Chenonceaux, preserving only the keep, and building the rest in the emerging Renaissance style. In that undertaking, he was ably assisted by Catherine Briçonnet, the daughter of a wealthy family from Tours. After her husband died in 1524, Catherine lived for only two more years; at her death François I seized the château.

In 1547, Henri II gave Chenonceaux to his mistress, Diane de Poitiers, who was 20 years his senior. For a time this remarkable woman was virtually the queen of France, in spite of Henri's wife, Catherine de Medici. Apparently, Henri's love for Diane continued unabated, even though she was in her 60s when the king died in a jousting tournament in 1559. Critics of Diane de Poitiers accused her of using magic not only to preserve her celebrated beauty but to keep Henri's attentions from waning.

Upon Henri's death, his jealous wife became regent of France. She immediately forced Diane de Poitiers to return the jewelry Henry had given her and to abandon her beloved Chenonceaux in exchange for Chaumont, which she did not want. Catherine added her own touches to the château, building a two-story gallery across the bridge—obviously inspired by her native Florence. The long gallery running along the Cher River contains a black-and-white diamond floor.

It was at Chenonceaux that Catherine received a pair of teenage honeymooners: her son, François II, and his bride, Mary Stuart. Another son, Henri III, sponsored an infamous fête at Chenonceaux. As described by the historian Philippe Erlanger: "Under the trees of this admirable park the King presided over the banquet, dressed as a woman. He wore a gown of pink damask, embroidered with pearls. Emerald, pearl, and diamond pendants distended the lobes of his ears, and diamonds shone in his hair which, like his beard, was dyed with violet powder."

After Henri III was assassinated (by Jacques Clément), Chenonceaux was occupied by his widow, Louise de Lorraine. Even though the king had preferred his "curly-haired minions" to her, she nevertheless mourned his death for the rest of her life, earning the name "La Reine Blanche" ("White Queen").

In the 18th century, Madame Dupin, the grandmother of George Sand, acquired the château. A lady of the aristocracy, she was the wife of the "farmer-general" of France. She is said to have brought the "talents of the époque" to her château, employing Rousseau as a tutor for her sons. However, when the author of *The Social Contract* declared his undying love for her, she asked him not to return. Rousseau is said to have fallen violently ill, "sick with humiliation."

In the 19th century, Madame Pelouse acquired the château and began the difficult task of restoring it to its original splendor. That duty is still being admirably carried out by the present owners, the chocolate-making Menier family.

Many of the walls today are covered with Gobelins tapestries, including one depicting a woman pouring water over the back of an angry dragon, another of a three-headed dog and a seven-headed monster. The chapel contains a delicate marble Virgin and Child, plus portraits of Catherine de Medici in her traditional black and white. There's even a portrait of the stern Catherine in the former bedroom of her rival, Diane de Poitiers. But in the Renaissance-style bedchamber of François I, the most interesting portrait is that of Diane de Poitiers as the huntress Diana, complete with a sling of arrows on her back. *The Three Graces* are by Van Loo.

The château is open daily from 9 a.m. to 7 p.m. from mid-March to mid-September. From then until October 31 it closes at 6 p.m., and in November it shuts down at 5 p.m. From December 1 through January 31, it's open from 9 a.m. to noon and 2 to 4 p.m. From February 1 to mid-March, it closes at 5 p.m. Admission is 8F ($1.83).

The history of Chenonceaux is related in 15 tableaux in the **wax museum,** which charges an additional 4F (91¢) admission. Diane de Poitiers, who, among other accomplishments, introduced the artichoke to France, is depicted in three of the tableaux. One shows her in a familiar setting—in her bedroom with Henri II. Another portrays Catherine de Medici tossing out her husband's mistress.

A son-et-lumière spectacle—"In the Old Days of the Dames of Chenonceaux"—is staged from April 1 to September 30; admission is 8F ($1.83). The village of Chenonceaux is 7½ miles from Amboise, 21 miles from Tours.

FOOD AND LODGINGS: Hôtel du Bon Laboureur et du Château (tel. 29-90-02). Even though it's on the main road of the village, it suggests a remote country house. The façade and tall chimneys are covered with ivy, and the rear garden has a little guest house, plus formally planted roses. Within sight of the Loire, and within walking distance of the château, the inn is run by a kindly, attractive family whose fine taste is apparent everywhere. Louis Jeudi ("Mr. Thursday") is not only the owner but the chef de cuisine; Mme. Jeudi is in charge of the welfare of their guests.

Founded in 1880, the hotel still maintains the flavor of that era, but fortunately many private bathrooms have been added to the well-appointed bedrooms. Doubles, either with private showers or complete baths, range in price from 147F ($33.56) to 180F ($41.09). Singles with bath go for 140F ($31.96). A continental breakfast is another 15F ($3.42).

If weather permits, you can request a table in the courtyard, under a maple tree (hopefully the pink hydrangeas will be in bloom and the red roses clinging to the high stone wall). Inside, the beamed dining room is properly old-world, with a tall grandfather's clock, high-backed ladder chairs, and an open cupboard with pewter bottles and regional ceramics.

There are two fixed-price menus, the cheaper one costing 64F ($14.61) and including some of the chef's specialties. You're likely to be offered rillettes (highly seasoned ground pork), grilled blood sausage, a round slice of veal with sautéed mushrooms, scalloped potatoes, the salad of the season, and the pastry of the day, perhaps made with fresh strawberries or cherries. The 112F ($25.57) menu gastronomique provides such specialties as quenelles made with crayfish and ris de veau (sweetbreads) seasoned with wine from Porto. The inn is closed from November 1 to March 20.

Au Gâteau Breton (N76) (tel. 29-90-14) is a refreshing place at which to dine or else have tea. In the heart of the village, within walking distance of the château, this little Breton-type inn opens toward its rear sun-terrace dining area. Gravel paths run between little beds of pink geraniums and lilacs, red tables rest under bright yellow canopies and umbrellas, and ivy grows over the walls.

Dining here is most satisfying. Madame Herembert, the wife of the patron, asks, "Have you had enough?" Everything her husband prepares in the kitchen is homemade, and he provides as well a cherry liqueur, a specialty of the region. Their front room is set aside for the selling of his tasty pastries; in cool months meals are served in the rustic rooms in the rear. There are several set menus, the lowest costing 25F ($5.71); more courses are yours if you order the 32F ($7.31) or 38F ($8.68) meal. Another menu, this for 45F ($10.27), might include a selection of hors d'oeuvres, then terrine du chef, smoked salmon on buttered toast, poultry, or grilled meat. Closed from December till February.

16. Orléans

Orléans suffered heavy damage in World War II, so those visiting who hope to see how it looked when the Maid of Orléans was there are likely to be disappointed. However, the reconstruction of Orléans has been judiciously planned, and there are many rewarding targets for visitors.

Orléans is the chief town of Loiret, on the Loire, about 80 miles from Paris. Joan of Arc relieved the city in 1429 from the attacks of the Burgundians and the English. That deliverance is celebrated every year on May 8, the anniversary of her victory. An equestrian statue of Joan of Arc stands in the **Place du Martroi**, which was created by Foyatier in 1855.

From that square you can drive down the rue Royale—rebuilt in the 18th-century style—across the **Pont George V**, erected in 1760. After crossing the bridge you'll have a good view of the town. A simple cross marks the site of the Fort des Tourelles which Joan of Arc and her men captured.

Back in the heart of town, you can go to the **Cathedral of St. Croix**, begun in 1287 in the High Gothic period, although burned by the Huguenots in 1567. The first stone on the present building was laid by Henry IV in 1601, and work continued on the cathedral until 1829. Inside, the church of the Holy Cross contains a gigantic organ from the 17th century, and some magnificent wood-work from the early 18th century in its chancel. You'll need a guide to tour the chancel and the crypt and to see the treasury with its Byzantine enamels and textiles, its goldwork from the 15th and 16th centuries, and its Limoges enamels. Admission is 2F (46¢).

The **Musée des Beaux-Arts** occupies the 15th-16th-century town hall, known as the Hôtel des Créneaux. This is mainly a picture gallery of French works from the 15th to the 19th centuries. Some of the works once hung in Richelieu's château. Other pieces of art include busts by Pigalle, *St. Sebastian with Lantern* by Georges de La Tour, and a fine array of portraits, including one of Mme. de Pompadour, of whom, when she crossed the Pont George V, the people of the town remarked: "Our bridge has just borne France's heaviest weight." See also works by Correge, Le Nain, Philippe de Champaigne, La Hire, Boucher, Watteau, and Gauguin, as well as a salon of pastels by Perron-neau. Several foreign works are also displayed, including a lovely Velásquez. The museum is open from 10 a.m. to noon and from 2 to 6 p.m. in summer (closes at 5 p.m. in winter), charging 2F (46¢) for admission. It is always closed on Tuesdays.

To the northwest of the cathedral, the **Hôtel de Ville** or town hall, a Renaissance mansion, was built under François I and Henri II, though restored in the 19th century. It has been occupied by the royalty of France from François II to Henri IV. The husband of Mary Queen of Scots, François II, died there in 1560. On a lighter note, Charles IX met his lovely Marie Touchet there. The statue of Joan of Arc praying (in the center of the porch) was by the daughter of Louis-Philippe, Princess Marie of Orléans. In the garden you can see the remains of the 15th-century chapel of St. Jacques.

Another church of much interest, lying near the Loire, is the **Church of St. Aignan**, which was consecrated in 1509. The choir and transept remain, but the nave was burnt by the Protestants. In a gilded, carved wooden shrine lie the remains of the church's patron saint. The crypt, completed in 1029, is intriguing, containing as it does some decorated capitals. This surely must be one of the earliest vaulted hall-crypts in all of France.

WHERE TO STAY (IN TOWN): Sofitel Orléans, 44-46 Quai Barentin (tel. 62-17-39), offers the finest accommodation right in the heart of town, within walking distance of the Place du Martroi with its statue of Joan of Arc. Bordering the river, the hotel stands at the Pont Joffre. A modern, bandbox structure, it offers 110 well-furnished rooms with all the conveniences. One person pays anywhere from 230F ($52.52) to 280F ($63.92), and two persons are charged from 265F ($60.50) to 320F ($73.06). The Sofitel even has two suites, one reserved for a bride and her groom, another for presidents. The restaurant and bar, Le Vénerie, serves regional specialties, a full table d'hote menu costing 75F ($17.12), including table wine. The hotel also has a big swimming pool.

Terminus, 40 rue de la République (tel. 870-24-64), facing the railway station, is a suitable place to stay in spite of its unromantic-sounding name. The decor of the rooms is ordinary but agreeably comfortable. The service is attentive, and the price is reasonable enough—85F ($19.41) in a single, rising to 130F ($29.68) in a double. Incidentally, the hotel is immaculately kept. There is no restaurant, although you can order breakfast for 9F ($2.05).

Less expensive, **St.-Martin,** 52 Boulevard A.-Martin (tel. 62-47-47), is a 22-room hotel on a broad boulevard near the cathedral, yet its rooms aren't too noisy. The hotel is conveniently situated for touring the sights of Orléans or else shopping for souvenirs of Joan of Arc. There is no restaurant, yet you will be close to some excellent ones (see below). The rooms are simply furnished but clean. A single rents for 50F (11.42), that tariff rising to 90F ($20.55) in a double. A few of the accommodations contain private baths.

On the Outskirts

Actually, one of the more comfortable hotels is not in Orléans at all but south of the town (head down the N20). There you'll find **Novotel Orléans Sud,** rue Honoré-de-Balzac (tel. 63-04-28). In a beautiful park with a swimming pool, this modern hotel offers such diversions as *pétanque* (French bowls) and Ping-Pong. The decor is tasteful and restrained, providing much comfort, such as air conditioning and color television. A single rents for 180F ($41.09), that rate going up to 200F ($45.66) in a double. On the premises is a grill, offering a set meal for 65F ($14.84) until 11 p.m.

Another possibility if you're a motorist is **Le Beauvoir,** rue du Beauvoir at Olivet, three miles south by D15 (tel. 66-02-16). Here 24 rooms are offered in a large modern building with a garden overlooking the river. The chambers are well furnished and impeccably maintained, renting for 60F ($13.70) in a single, that rate going up to 180F ($41.09) in a double. You can also stay here on half-pension terms, going from 155F ($35.39) to 180F ($41.09) per person. The food, under the direction of Madame Boitier, is quite good, including such specialties as rillettes, chitterling sausages, eel, crayfish, and delicious terrines, including a superb one made with larks. A wide selection of desserts and cheese is also featured. If you're not staying over, you can order a complete meal for 60F ($13.70), although you are likely to spend 120F ($27.40) on the à la carte menu.

THE BEST RESTAURANTS: La Crémaillère, 34 rue N.-D.-de-Recouvrance (tel. 53-49-17). Paul Huyart is perhaps the finest chef in Orléans. He serves food that is memorable, and although many authorities give him ratings, we haven't seen any yet that are high enough! Go here and plan to make an evening of it, savoring every course. His fresh duckling foie gras has a lively flavor. All of his main dishes we've sampled tasted original and imaginative—his ragoût of scallops with oysters (October to April only), his sautéed crayfish with asparagus tips, and his exquisite soup of strawberries with passion fruit. The chef is definitely talented. He calls his pièce de résistance "gigot de mer aux gousses d'ail." We'd suggest a Quincy wine if it fits in with your food order. This spicy, dry white wine is from a village on the Cher River, not far from Bourges, in central France, although it is considered a wine of the Loire Valley. The restaurant shuts down in August and on Sunday nights and Mondays. Expect to pay 130F ($29.68) for a meal.

Le Porte Barentin, 42 Quai Barentin (tel. 53-37-60), in the center of town, is a comfortably appointed restaurant—one of the best in the area—that attracts loyal habitués drawn to the cuisine of Monsieur Martel. Beautifully run, his restaurant is inviting and the cooking much in demand by the people of the city themselves, who come here for that special celebration. For a delightful meal, we'd suggest his salad, made with garden vegetables and crayfish, or else his terrine of rascasse, a Mediterranean fish generally used in bouillabaisse. In this pâté it is flavored with three different herbs. Other specialties include a sole soufflé, a pan-fried filet of beef with truffles, and excellently selected wines from the cellar, including a Quincy and a Chinon (the birthplace of the immortal Rabelais who made several references to Orléans in *Pantagruel*). The restaurant is closed in August and on Saturday nights and Sundays. A set menu is offered for 110F ($25.11), although you are likely to spend 220F ($50.23) ordering à la carte.

Auberge Saint-Jacques, 2 rue au Lin (tel. 53-63-48), on a small street near the river, is one of the top three restaurants of Orléans, the domain of Henri Fournier. The cooking is studied if not always delicate. In an old maison, the chef proudly presents his repertoire, which is likely to include the inevitable grilled Loire salmon (from the end of February until the end of May), a boneless rib of lamb, filets of zander (a freshwater fish with very white flesh), coq au vin de Champigny, and game dishes which are offered in the late autumn until Christmas. The turbot here is heavenly, served with a thick lobster sauce. Try also the sweetbreads with vegetables of the season and the pan-fried tournedos. The desserts are mouth-watering. Expect to pay 100F ($22.83) for a complete meal. The air-conditioned restaurant is closed in July and on Sunday.

Auberge de la Montespan, route de Blois, out N152 (tel. 88-12-07), lies about a mile from Orléans, its garden and terrace on the Loire. The house is from the era of Louis XV. The owner is Monsieur Fournier, who carefully selects a staff that shows consideration and most attentive service to each guest. The cuisine is the standard French repertoire, such as coq au vin, and it is done quite well. Of course, try the Loire salmon, although there are other fish dishes as well. The chef specializes in game pâté. If you want something unusual, he even does a veal head with a delicious-tasting sauce. A set meal costs 90F ($20.55), but is not available on Sunday. If you order à la carte, expect to pay from 140F ($31.96).

The restaurant is closed from Christmas until February 6. In addition, the host offers 10 well-furnished rooms with superb views of the Loire. A single rents for 145F ($33.10), that tariff rising to 220F ($50.23) in a double. Three of the rooms are bathless.

At Saint-Jean-de-Braye, **La Grange,** 205 Faubourg Bourgogne, route de Nevers (tel. 86-43-36), is an old mill restored in a neorustic style, offering choice grills and special platters. Monsieur Dupuy is in complete control, welcoming guests to his fine establishment which has much charm. It lies about two miles east of Orléans on the N152. You can come here for the drinking of fine wine and the contemplation of the menu, which is likely to include turbot mousse with watercress, boneless slices of duck with red pepper, sweetbreads with hurtleberries, and veal kidneys in a mustard sauce. The menus range in price from 52F ($11.87) to 100F ($22.83). Ordering à la carte is likely to cost you in the neighborhood of 200F ($45.66) to 340F ($77.62) per person. The restaurant is closed during most of August and January, as well as on Sunday nights and Saturdays.

17. Sully-sur-Loire

Southeast of Orléans stands the beautiful **Castle of Sully** where Joan of Arc persuaded Charles VII to go to Reims and proclaim himself king of France.

The château is named, however, for the Duc de Sully, the minister of Henri IV. The castle was mostly destroyed in World War II, but it has been restored. It was originally constructed in the 14th century, although enlarged after 1602 by Sully. Exiled from Paris, Voltaire spent much time with Sully. A theater was built for Voltaire in which his plays could be performed.

The castle is open from April 1 to October 1, from 9 a.m. to noon, and from 2 to 6 p.m., charging an admission of 5F ($1.14). Several apartments in the 14th-century wing of the castle are open to the public. Sully's remains were placed in the oratory. On the second floor, an apartment was covered with timberwork, which is considered the finest such work from medieval days. It is so well preserved it is hard to believe that it's actually 600 years old. In the Renaissance pavilion you can see the minister's study and his bedroom. Both rest under painted ceilings.

FOOD AND LODGINGS: **La Poste,** 11 rue Faubourg St.-Germain (tel. 35-26-22), is a typical French provincial hotel. Don't judge it by its façade, however. Inside it is cozy and comfortable. Its 30 bedrooms, five of which contain private baths, are simply furnished but well kept, costing 60F ($13.70) in a single, 130F ($29.68) in a double. The hotel has a lovely garden. In the pillared dining room the service is informal, the reception most hospitable, and the food good, with lots of local produce used when available. The chef does the usual range of Loire specialties exceedingly well, and the portions are ample, the menu having variety. The least expensive way to dine here is to order the 55F ($12.56) menu, although you could spend 180F ($41.09) if you're ravenously hungry. The hotel shuts down from January 15 to March 8.

Hostellerie Grand Sully, 10 Boulevard Champ-de-Foire (tel. 35-27-56), is also suitable if you're stopping over for the night, perhaps en route to Burgundy and the French Alps. It has only a dozen bedrooms, half of which contain private baths. The accommodations themselves are modestly furnished, costing from 55F ($12.56) in a single to a high of 130F ($29.68) in a double. The bar is pleasant, and there is also a garden. Food of good quality is served in the agreeable restaurant, where a set menu is offered for 50F ($11.42), an almost-more-than-you-can-eat one for 90F ($20.55).

18. Les Bézards

This village, at the edge of the Forest of Orléans, is the far eastern extremity of the Loire Valley. It lies on the main route between Paris and Nevers, and is a popular stopping-off point with Parisians, who stay at the following recommendation, exploring the lovely towns of Gien and Briare further along the Loire.

Auberge des Templiers, N7 at Boismorand (tel. 31-80-01), lies to the east of Orléans, a distance of 43 miles. The inn was once a stagecoach stop, and even that ancient *relais* was built on the site of an older hospice once belonging to the Knights Templars. The vine-covered auberge appears rustic, but that is a misleading first impression. Inside you'll find a haven of luxury, comfort, and recreation.

As you stroll to your room you'll wander through flower gardens, deciding on the annex, the thatched-roofed La Chaumière, or perhaps the handsomely appointed little manor house. The newest accommodations are in a pavilion by the pool. Ask for the tiny tower room if you prefer a snug nest. It's completely round, with old beams. The rooms are furnished with reproductions of antiques, and much use is made of velvet in the decor. Even the bathrooms are well decorated, with beautiful tiles and wallpaper. Naturally, the price for all this is high—a single costing from 220F ($50.23), that figure going up to 340F ($77.62) in a double, unless you select one of the even more expensive apartments. Breakfast is an extra 25F ($5.71).

On the grounds is a heated swimming pool, plus tennis courts. Out by the pool the hotel has been known to stage wild-boar barbecues, but not every day.

In the bar with its beamed ceiling you can enjoy an apéritif in front of a hearth with oak logs blazing and the glow soft from the brass chandeliers. Dining is by candlelight, of course. In autumn you are likely to be seated near a Parisian gourmet, drawn here to sample some of Monsieur Dépée's wild-game dishes. A profusion of wild game is to be found in the area, including woodcock and pheasant. Thus, in season you can order, perhaps, stuffed young rabbit for dinner. The chef's repertoire isn't confined to game, however. Try the white mousse of liver or veal liver cooked in cider vinegar, and especially the sole à l'orange or young guinea hen with lime. For dessert, perhaps you'll order the soufflé glacé with a whiskey-and-honey sauce. It's deliciously sinful. Meals are served in the garden in fair weather. Set menus are featured at 145F ($33.10) and 220F ($50.23). If you order à la carte, the tab is likely to be from 200F ($45.66) to 320F ($73.06). The finest of regional wines, such as Sancerre, are stocked here, along with more expensive choices. The auberge, if we can call it that, is closed from mid-January to mid-February.

19. Gien

A town of flowers, known for its porcelain, Gien was heavily bombed in the early months of World War II. But the reconstruction has been skillful, the town planners showing a healthy respect for traditional architectural styles. The town is in red brick which contrasts with the geometric designs and edgings in black brick.

Founded in 1820, the porcelain factory is in the western part of Gien, covering about 18 acres. Telephone 67-00-05 for permission to visit.

Stroll along the Loire river promenade with its shade trees, and cross the humpbacked bridge dating from the 15th century for a good view. If you're planning to stay over, avoid the weekends, especially in autumn. French hunters after wild game in the surrounding area (woodcock, pheasant, rabbit) seem to book up all the rooms.

The **Château of Gien**, rebuilt in 1484, once belonged to Anne de Beaujeu, the Comtesse of Gien, the eldest daughter of Louis XI. Installed in the castle is an **International Hunting Museum**, which is open to the public from Easter until the end of October—daily from 9 to 11:45 a.m. and from 2:15 to 6:30 p.m., charging an admission of 8F ($1.83). Off-season, it closes an hour earlier. Inside you'll find a collection of weapons, pictures, and prints, all devoted to *la chasse* down through the ages. The most interesting section of the restored castle is the Great Hall, with its paintings by Desportes. There is also a display of the famous Gien porcelain.

The **Church of Joan of Arc** stands nearby, but it is modern, the design pleasing and harmonious. Only the tower dates from the 15th century, the time of Anne de Beaujeu. After its destruction in 1940, the church was rebuilt in the postwar years in red brick with black geometric designs.

For a meal or a room, we'd suggest **Rivage**, 1 Quai Nice (tel. 67-20-43), an attractively situated hotel lying right by the river promenade with its shade trees. Sportsmen gravitate here on the weekends, getting a hearty welcome from the patron, Monsieur Gaillard. He offers a very good set meal (weekdays only) at 50F ($11.42). Otherwise, the menu is 90F ($20.55). Try to get a room overlooking the Loire. The accommodations are pleasantly decorated and most comfortable, costing 60F ($13.70) in a single, 115F ($26.25) in a double. The staff is attentive and friendly.

20. Langeais

The formidable gray *pile*, a true fortress of the Middle Ages, dominates the town. The façade is foreboding, but once you cross the drawbridge and go inside, the apartments are so richly decorated that the severe effect is softened or forgotten. The castle dates back to the ninth century, when the dreaded Black Falcon erected what was considered the first dungeon in Europe, the ruins of which remain to this day. The present structure was built in 1465 in the reign of Louis XI.

That the interior is so well preserved and furnished is due to Jacques Siegfried, who not only restored it over a period of 20 years but bequeathed it to the Institute of France in 1904.

"She arrived at Langeais carried in a litter decked with gold cloth, dressed in a gown of black trimmed with sable. Her wedding gown of gold cloth was ornamented with 160 sables." The date was December 6, 1491. The marriage of Anne of Brittany to Charles VIII was to be the golden hour of Langeais. Their symbols—scallops, fleurs-de-lis, and ermine—set the motif for the Guard Room. In the Wedding Chamber, where the marriage took place, the walls are decorated with a series of seven tapestries known as the *Valiant Knights*.

At the entrance to Langeais, a large tapestry illustrating the life of Nebu-chadnezzar shows him covered with hair and stricken with madness.

In a bedchamber known sardonically as "The Crucifixion," the 15th-century black-oak four-poster is reputed to be one of the earliest known. The room takes its odd name from a tapestry of the Virgin and St. John standing on a flower-bedecked ground. In the Monsieur's Room a rare Flemish tapestry depicts such motifs as Virginia snake-root leaves and pheasants on railings, surrounded by a border of fruit. The Chapel Hall was built by joining two stories under a ceiling of Gothic arches. In the Luini Room is a large fresco by that artist, dating from 1522, removed from a chapel on Lake Maggiore, Italy. It represents St. Francis of Assisi and St. Elizabeth of Hungary with Mary and Joseph.

The Byzantine Virgin in the drawing room is considered an early work of Cimabue, the Florentine artist. The best for last: the *Tapestry of the Thousand Flowers* in the Drawing Room is like an ageless celebration of spring, a joyous riot of growth, a symbol of life's renewal.

Langeais may be visited daily in summer except Monday mornings from 9 a.m. to noon and from 2 to 6:30 p.m., for 8F ($1.83) admission. The tab includes your entrance to the park, where you can see one of the earliest-known stone keeps to be built in France. In winter the château closes at 4:30 p.m. The town of Langeais lies between Saumur and Tours, the latter a 16-mile drive to the east.

FOOD AND LODGING: Hosten, 2 rue Gambetta (tel. 55-82-12), is a true country inn, with an informal atmosphere—no fancy airs, but excellent food and service. As a restaurant it qualifies as upper bracket, but as a hotel it is in the budget to medium-priced range.

The Hostens bought this 75-year-old hotel in 1948. Madame Hosten takes care of the guest accommodations, and her husband Jean-Jacques reigns in the kitchen (he was trained at the Savoy in London and the Ledoyen on the Champs-Élysées in Paris). The restaurant has accumulated honors for years.

In addition to those in the major dining room, tables are set up in the open courtyard under umbrellas and flowering trees. Three set meals are offered. The least expensive menu is 160F ($36.53), a more elaborate one 220F ($50.24). Monsieur Hosten even proposes a "menu de prestige" at 320F ($73.06), including foie gras d'oie frais des Landes, homard (lobster) cardinal, pintadeau farci aux pieds de cochons (guinea fowl stuffed with pigs feet), plus a selection of cheese, ending with a soufflé au Grand Marnier. The chef's specialties also include salmon with sorrel and filet à la moelle.

A double room with bath costs 160F ($36.53), but a double room with shower is only 80F ($18.26). Closed from December 1 to February 1 and on Tuesdays.

Family Hôtel-La Duchesse Anne, 9 rue de Tours (tel. 55-82-03), is a former coaching inn, family-operated as the name suggests. Monsieur Guerard is the chef, and Madame Guerard is in charge of the bedrooms and the dining room. The simple white-painted inn still possesses its covered central carriage passageway, leading to a courtyard. Garden tables are set out for dining, and cages of singing birds abound; there's even a tank of trout.

Regardless of your budget, chances are you'll find a meal here to suit your purse. The cheapest lunch or dinner costs 45F ($10.27) and includes three courses. A 70F ($15.98) dinner offers at least five of the chef's specialties, such as grilled Loire shad with the famous white butter and stuffed mushrooms.

Not all the rooms contain private baths, but they do offer hot and cold running water. The demi-pension tariff, for two persons, ranges from 185F ($42.24) to 220F ($50.23) daily in high season. The rooms are practical and keynoted by simplicity. The inn is closed from November 5 to mid-December, and Sunday night and Monday off-season.

21. Ussé

At the edge of the hauntingly dark forest of Chinon, the Castle of Ussé was the inspiration behind Perrault's legend of "The Sleeping Beauty" (called in French "Belle au Bois Dormant"). On a hill overlooking the Indre River, it is a virtual forest of steeples, turrets, towers, chimneys, and dormers. Originally conceived as a medieval fortress, it was erected at the dawn of the Renaissance.

Two powerful families—Bueil and d'Espinay—lived in the château in the 15th and 16th centuries.

Vauban, the military engineer who in the 17th century designed systems of fortifications for French cities, was a frequent visitor when Ussé was owned by his son-in-law, the Marquis de Valentinay. At one point in its history, Mlle. d'Ussé ordered royal apartments built for an anticipated visit of Louis XIV which never materialized. In time, the château was owned by the Duke of Duras and later by Mme. de la Rochejacquelin before coming into its present ownership by the Count of Blacas.

The terraces, laden with orange trees, were laid out in the 18th century. When the need for a "fortified" château had long since passed, the north wing was demolished, opening up a greater view, as the occupants wished to enjoy the sun and the landscape.

You used to have to settle for a look from the outside, but the count has opened some rooms to the public. The guided tour begins in the Renaissance chapel, with its sculptured portal and handsomely designed stalls. Then you are escorted through the royal apartments, furnished with tapestries and antiques, including a four-poster in red damask. One gallery displays an extensive collection of swords and rifles.

The château is open from March 15 to September 30 from 9 a.m. to noon and from 2 to 7 p.m., charging 8F ($1.83) for admission.

The hamlet of Ussé lies only nine miles from Chinon.

22. Chinon

Remember when Ingrid Bergman as Joan of Arc sought out the dauphin, even though he tried to conceal himself among his courtiers? The action in real life took place at Chinon, one of the oldest fortress-châteaux in France. Charles VII, mockingly known as the King of Bourges, centered his government at Chinon from 1429 to 1450. In 1429, with the English besieging Orléans, the maid of Orléans, that "messenger from God," prevailed upon the weak dauphin to give her an army. The rest is history.

The seat of French power stayed at Chinon until the Hundred Years' War ended. It was here that Louis XII in 1498 received Cesare Borgia, the son of the notorious Pope Alexander VI, when he brought permission from Rome to dissolve Louis's marriage to his "deformed" wife. Later he married Anne of Brittany.

On the banks of the Vienne, in the heart of Rabelais country, Chinon retains a medieval atmosphere with its grim feudal ruins. Nineteen miles from Langeais, it consists of winding streets and turreted houses, many built in the 15th and 16th centuries in the heyday of the court. For the best view, drive across the river, turning right onto the Quai Danton. From that vantage point, you'll have the best perspective of the town, seeing the castle in relation to the village and the river. The gables and towers make Chinon look like a toy village.

The most typical street is the **rue Voltaire,** lined with 15th- and 16th-century town houses. At No. 44, Richard the Lion-Hearted died on April 6, 1199, after suffering a mortal wound while besieging Chalus in Limousin. In the heart of town, the **Grand Carroi** was the crossroads of the Middle Ages.

The most famous son of Chinon, Rabelais, the great Renaissance writer, walked these streets. He was born at La Devinière, on D17 near N751, now the **Musée Rabelais,** open daily, closing for two hours beginning at noon, and charging 5F ($1.14) for admission. It is closed in December and January. He used his native scenery as background in many of his stories.

The château itself is actually three separate strongholds, badly ruined. Some of the grim walls remain, although many of the buildings—including the Great Hall where Joan of Arc sought out the dauphin—have been torn down. Some of the most destructive owners were the heirs of Cardinal Richelieu. Now gone, the **Château de St.-Georges** was built by Henry II of England, who died there in 1189. The **Château du Mileu** dates from the 11th to the 15th centuries, containing the keep and the clock tower, where a **Museum of Joan of Arc** has been installed. Separated from the latter by a moat, the **Château du Coudray** contains the Tour du Coudray, where Joan of Arc stayed during her time at Chinon. In the 14th century, the Knights Templar were imprisoned there (they are responsible for the graffiti on the walls) before meeting their violent deaths.

The château is open from 9 a.m. to noon and from 2 to 7 p.m. (till 5:30 p.m. in winter), charging 6F ($1.37) for admission. It is closed in December and January.

THE INNS AT CHINON: Hostellerie Gargantua, 73 rue Haute St. Maurice
(tel. 93-04-71), a brick-and-timbered building with a vine-covered courtyard,
stands in a row of ancient buildings, almost opposite the house where Richard
the Lion-Hearted died. Just a short walk from the river, it's in the old town
mansion of a bailiff. Chef-owner Francis Giacobetti runs it as an inviting
family-style inn. Named after Rabelais's amiable giant, the Gargantua features
a tiny glass-covered courtyard, complete with tall plants, which is used for
alfresco dining in good weather. A winding staircase leads to the simply furnished bedrooms.

Guests of the hotel are obligated to take meals, but that is no hardship
since the food is so good. The price of the rooms, doubles, ranges from a low
of 80F ($18.26) to a high of 170F ($38.81), the latter containing private baths
and decorated in either the Louis XIII style or else Directoire. Breakfast is an
additional 13F ($2.97).

But whether you stay here or not, do come for the excellent meals. A
not-to-be missed delicacy is the fluffy omelette Gargamelle. A creamy fondue
sauce is just one of its ingredients. A meal with wine costs about 130F ($29.68).
The hotel is closed from November 1 to March 1.

Grand Hôtel de la Boule d'Or (Golden Ball), 66 Quai Jeanne d'Arc (tel.
93-03-13), is a coaching inn, with the carriage yard now converted into an
almost lush dining area. The setting is one of glistening white walls and an
overhead arbor and trellis with trailing vines and red roses. White wicker chairs
and tables are set out for drinks and meals that range in price from 35F ($7.99)
to 55F ($12.56) to 85F ($19.41).

Owned by Béatrice Lebrun, the inn has long been a favorite with the
English. The front rooms open onto the river, but the quieter ones are at the
rear. Full-pension prices range from 150F ($34.26) per person. In rooms with
shower, one person pays 74F ($16.89), the cost going up to 94F ($21.46) for
two. In units with complete bath, the charge is 110F ($25.11) for one person,
130F ($29.68) for two, with breakfast costing extra. Madame Lebrun loves
cardinal red, using it whenever possible: front canopies, draperies, valances,
garden lounge cushions, bed covers, and draperies. The hotel is open every day
from April to October, closing Fridays off-season. Its annual closing is in
December and January.

THE LEADING RESTAURANT: Le Sainte-Maxime, 31 Place de l'Hôtel-
de-Ville (tel. 93-05-04), is a superior restaurant—really an unexpected discovery in such a provincial town. From its decor, you wouldn't expect such a fine
establishment. Set back from the main square, it is much like a tavern. Monsieur Bingler is the all-seeing proprietor.

His fixed-price meals cater to most budgets: 60F ($13.70) and 135F
($30.82), the latter a superb repast of exquisite quality, but the low-priced meals
are also satisfactory. On the à la carte menu, you can enjoy his pepper chateaubriand, a recommended specialty. The terrine du chef is a good beginning,
and other highly praised dishes include the stuffed escargots and the brochet
(pike) in a white-butter sauce. An à la carte dinner will cost about 80F ($18.26)
to 140F ($31.96) per person. The restaurant is closed from June 2 to 16, from
the end of September until mid-October, and on Sunday nights and Mondays.

23. Fontevraud-l'Abbaye

You're likely to trip over a British colonel muttering, "These tombs should
be in Westminster Abbey where they belong!" For in the Romanesque church

at Fontevraud-l'Abbaye the Plantagenet dynasty of the kings of England are buried. Why there? These monarchs, whose male line vanished in 1499, were also the Counts of Anjou, and they left instructions that they be buried on their native soil.

Contained within the 11th-century church—with its four Byzantine domes—are the remains of the eight English kings or princes, including Henry II of England, the first Plantagenet king, the one who fought with Thomas à Becket, and his wife, Eleanor of Aquitaine, perhaps the single most famous woman of the Middle Ages (at one time she was married to Louis VII of France). Her crusading son, Richard the Lion-Hearted, was also entombed here. The French State consistently refuses to surrender these tombs to Her Majesty's government, claiming them for the land of their origin in honor of those ancient requests. However, that refusal didn't prevent Prince Charles from driving down for an inspection. The tombs fared badly in the Revolution, as mobs invaded the church, desecrating the sarcophagi and scattering their contents on the floor.

More interesting than the tombs, however, is the octagonal Tour d'Evraud, the last remaining Romanesque kitchen in France. Surrounding the tower is a group of apses crowned by conically roofed turrets. A pyramid tops the conglomeration, capped by an open-air lantern tower pierced with lancets.

The abbey was founded in 1099 by Robert d'Arbrissel, who had spent much of his life as a recluse, although he enjoyed a reputation at one time as a sort of Billy Sunday of the Middle Ages. His abbey was like a public-welfare commune, very liberal in its admission policies. One part, for example, was filled with aristocratic ladies, many of them banished from court, including discarded mistresses of kings. The four youngest daughters of Louis XV were educated there as well.

Aside from the nuns and monks, there were lepers, and a hospital for the lame and sick who arrived almost daily at the abbey's doorstep. The foundation was controlled by powerful "abbesses" appointed by the king. Under Napoleon I the abbey was converted into a prison and remained so for 160 years. Now, the prisoners are gone, the abbey is being restored—actually rebuilt in parts—at great expense to the French government.

In the chapterhouse are some interesting 16th-century frescoes. A cloister dates from the same period, although one section goes back to the 12th century. The refectory is also from the 1500s.

Fontevraud-l'Abbaye lies about 10 miles southeast of Saumur, near the confluence of the Loire and Vienne Rivers. In winter, visiting hours are from 10 a.m. to noon and from 2 to 5 p.m.; in summer, from 9 a.m. to noon and from 2 to 6:30 p.m. daily except Tuesdays. You must take a guided tour, lasting 45 minutes and leaving every hour from 9 a.m. to noon and from 2 to 6:30 p.m. from Palm Sunday until September 30. The price of admission is 7F ($1.60) for adults, 3.50F (79¢) for students.

To reach the abbey, take Route N147 for about 2½ miles from the village of Montsoreau. If you have enough time, try to visit the 15th-century **Château of Montsoreau** itself, immortalized by Dumas's *La Dame de Montsoreau*, a highly fanciful tale bearing little resemblance to the actual historical events at this manor. The **Goumes Museum** is housed inside. It is open daily from 8 a.m. to noon and from 1 to 6 p.m. from May 1 to August 31 (off-season it closes at 4 p.m.), charging 5F ($1.14) for admission.

24. Saumur

At a point where the Loire separates to encircle an island, Saumur is set in a region of vineyards. (Do sample some of the local produce, like the Saumur Mousseux.) Founded in 1768, its Cavalry School, as well as its riding club, the Black Cadre, are world renowned. Its horsemen are considered among the finest in Europe (to see a rider carry out a *curvet* is to thrill at the training of both man and beast). The townspeople have even installed a **Musée du Cheval** —that is, a museum devoted to the history of the horse down through the ages, complete with stirrups, antique saddles, spurs, and whatever.

The museum is housed in the **Château of Saumur,** towering over the town from a promontory overlooking the Loire. The Poet Prince, René of Anjou, called it "the castle of love." In the famous *Hour Book* of the Duc de Berry at Chantilly, a 15th-century painting shows Saumur as a fairytale castle of bell turrets and gilded weathercocks. But these adornments are largely gone, leaving a rather stark and foreboding fortress.

Under Napoleon, the castle became a prison, eventually degenerating into a barracks and munitions depot. The town of Saumur acquired it in 1908 and began the herculean task of restoration. Now one of the most interesting regional museums (devoted to decorative arts) in the Loire has been installed. The galleries grew out of the collection begun by Count Charles Lair. The museum is noted mainly for its ceramics, dating from the 16th through the 18th centuries. A series of 13th-century enamel crucifixes from Limoges is remarkable, and also displayed are illustrated 15th-century manuscripts, polychrome sculpture (some from the 14th century), tapestries, and antique furnishings.

The château is open daily from July 1 to August 31, from 9 a.m. to 7 p.m. (evenings, 8:30 to 11), charging 7F ($1.60) for admission. From April 1 to June 30, and from September 1 to October 31, it is open from 9 a.m. to noon and from 2 to 6 p.m. Finally, from November 2 to March 31, it's open daily except Tuesdays from 10 a.m. to noon and from 2 to 5 p.m.

A MIDDLE-BRACKET HOTEL: Budan Hôtel, 3 Quai Carnot (tel. 51-28-76), is a practical, well-managed, and substantial establishment right at the hub of the town's activities. It's a four-story corner building, with an encircling balcony and tall windows providing views of the river from many of the bedrooms. Lovers of the belle époque period will admire the ceiling of the main reception lounge, with its art nouveau white-and-gold stained-glass dome filtering light upon the potted plants below.

The Budan is a good choice for an overnight stopover. Doubles with private baths rent for 160F ($36.53) to 220F ($50.23). Depending on the plumbing, singles range in price from 90F ($20.55) to 150F ($34.26).

Luncheon or dinner is available on the fixed-price menu for 80F ($18.26). Closed from November 1 to mid-March.

A BUDGET HOTEL: Roi René, 94 Avenue du Général de Gaulle (tel. 50-45-30), is a dignified hotel at the corner of a wide, tree-lined boulevard and the Loire River road. Well maintained, the hotel consists of four floors of rooms, with flowerboxes of geraniums at the windows.

For the best doubles with private baths, the charge is an out-of-the-bracket 220F ($50.23) nightly. But two persons who'll settle for a shower will pay 150F ($34.26). Meals are served in the wood-paneled dining room, its windows opening onto the riverside. Two set menus are offered: one for 55F ($12.56), a splurge for 85F ($19.41).

MEDIUM-PRICED DINING: Le Gambetta, 12 rue Gambetta (tel. 51-11-13), is on a side street in an old town house. Here Monsieur Bouhaud extends a gracious welcome to you to enjoy his food. A garden out back is used in fair weather. For openers, try the terrine de pâté maison at 18F ($4.11) or a dozen snails in garlic butter, 22F ($5.02). Main-dish specialties include tournedos Gambetta, filet steak with pepper flamed with brandy, 45F ($10.27), brochet au beurre blanc for 38F ($8.68), and a matelote d'anguilles (eels), also 38F. The dessert spectacular is soufflé maison at 42F ($9.59) for two. Everything tastes better with the wines of Saumur. Closed Sunday night and Monday and from December 20 to January 20.

A BUDGET BISTRO: L'Escargot, 30 rue du Maréchal-Leclerc (tel. 51-20-88). You'll know it's a French bistro by the row of tables and chairs on the sidewalk. Inside are two dining rooms suggesting a mellowed tavern atmosphere. In all, "The Snail" is an ingratiating setting for a tasty meal. One room has the coloration of the Barbizon school of painting, with sepias, gold, brass, and naturally aged wood. In the parlor dining room are a six-foot-high brass pedastal urn, a collection of pottery, plus lots of copper pans.

The quite talented *patron,* Monsieur Cupif, is also the chef de cuisine. He offers two set menus at 35F ($7.99) and 55F ($12.56), including hors d'oeuvres, a fish and a meat course, plus dessert. Service and drinks are extra. Some of the chef's specialties appear on the fixed-price menus. Special dishes include brochet (pike) in beurre blanc and grilled Loire salmon with a béarnaise sauce. Among meat dishes, M. Cupif does a delicious tournedos Saumurois. The restaurant is closed Monday nights and Tuesdays.

A CHÂTEAU-HOTEL ON THE OUTSKIRTS: Hostellerie du Prieuré, Chênehutte-les-Tuffeaux (tel. 50-15-31). The waiter serves you a heavenly rognons de veau sautés à moutarde (sautéed veal kidneys in a mustard sauce), while you look out at one of the finest views of the Loire—a span of 40 miles—in the château district. The "priory" is a château-hotel with a steep roof, dormer windows, and a large peaked tower, sitting on a plateau of a 60-acre park. Dating from the 12th century, it was restored in the 15th.

Designed for meditation, it is now turned over to organized recreation, with additional bungalows and a mini-golf course under the trees where monks of old used to stroll. There's even a heated swimming pool. While not rated as a luxury establishment, the hostellerie does offer completely comfortable and gracious living. The tone is set by the Grand Salon, with its ornately carved stone fireplace, clusters of crystal chandeliers, oak furniture, and the fleur-de-lis bar.

The bedrooms are traditional, each one treated differently, utilizing, for example, a few antiques and tufted head- and footboards. The three price levels set by the director, Mme. Bernard, make the accommodations possible for a number of budgets. Rooms vary considerably according to their size and placement. Two persons in a room with a complete bath pay from 180F ($41.09) to 285F ($65.07). In addition, 15% is added for service, and rates are lowered off-season.

The dining room has many windows, allowing everyone a chance to watch the sunset over the Loire. Two fixed-price menus are offered, at 100F ($22.83) and 140F ($31.96). On Sundays, those menus are increased to 120F ($27.40) and 190F ($43.38). Open from March 1 to January 5.

The hostellerie lies about four miles west of Saumur on N751.

Chapter VIII

NORMANDY

TEN CENTURIES HAVE gone by since the Vikings invaded the province of Normandy. The early Scandinavians might have come to ravish the land, but they stayed to cultivate it, bringing their cattle and their women. Of course, they didn't entirely revert from warriors to butter-and-egg men. Rather, they set out on conquests that were to give them England and even Sicily. The Normans produced great soldiers, none more famous than William the Conqueror, who defeated the forces of King Harold at Battle Abbey in 1066. The English and the French continued to do battle on and off for 700 years—a national rivalry that climaxed at the 1815 Battle of Waterloo.

Much of Normandy was later ravaged in the 1944 invasion that began on a June morning when parachutists and airborne troops dropped from the sky at Sainte-Mère-Église and Bénouville-sur-Orne. The largest armada ever assembled was about to begin one of the most momentous sagas in world history, the reconquest of continental Europe from the Nazis. Today, many come to Normandy just to see the D-Day beachheads.

Some of the province evokes a Millet landscape. Cattle graze sleepily in the fields turned a verdant green by the heavy Atlantic rainfall. Wood-framed houses exist side by side with postwar modern buildings that rose out of the ashes of World War II. Miraculously spared from the bombardments heaped on Normandy in the battle are stained-glass windows, sculptured woodwork, and Gothic architecture. Many great buildings, regrettably, were leveled to the ground.

The wide beaches attract those seeking a family holiday, though in August the sands at Deauville draw the most chic Europeans. Not far from the banks of the Seine, you come upon a tiny hamlet where Monet painted his world-famous water lilies. Transatlantic liners pull into Le Havre, the fishermen's nets are set off by a background of cliffs, and yachts clog the harbor. Normandy, like Brittany, seems to look toward the sea. Or so you think until you venture into its heartland and glimpse lush pastures and fragrant apple orchards.

The Normans are known not only as good soldiers but as hearty eaters. Their gastronomic table enjoys world renown. Many Parisians drive up for *le weekend* just to sample the rich Norman cuisine, which uses a lot of fresh butter and thick cream. Harvested along the seacoast are sole, brill, mackerel, and turbot. Shellfish is also common, especially those fat black mussels, the prawns of Cherbourg, the demoiselles of Dieppe. Try also Madame Poulard's feather-weight omelet, sole normande (stewed in rich cream), tripe à la mode de Caen, chicken from the Auge Valley, and duckling from Rouen. Normandy apples, especially those from the Auge Valley, produce a most potent cider. Matured in oaken casks, the apples also are turned into Calvados, a sort of applejack, a distillation of cider flavored with hazelnuts. A true Norman drinks this cider spirit at breakfast. Bénédictine, the liqueur made at Féchamp, also enjoys renown. The rich Norman Camembert is imitated but never equaled. Pont l'Évêque cheese has been known here since the 13th century. The Livarot is just fine for those who can get past the smell.

1. Rouen

"We've got one of the greatest cathedrals in Europe, many attractions," the woman at the Tourist Office laments, "but always, always they want to know where *she* was burned alive." *She* is Joan of Arc, and she died "on the Place du Vieux-Marché," answers the woman automatically.

The capital of Normandy, Rouen is the second most important tourist center in the north of France. It is also a hub of industry and commerce, the third largest port in France. Victor Hugo called it "the city of a hundred spires." Half of it was destroyed in World War II, mostly by Allied bombers, and many Rouennais were killed. In the reconstruction of the old quarters some of the almost forgotten crafts of the Middle Ages were revived.

On the Seine, 84 miles northwest of Paris, the city of Rouen is a good center for exploring much of Normandy. It is rich in historical associations: William the Conqueror died here in 1087, Joan of Arc in 1431.

THE SIGHTS OF ROUEN: This city has its share of formidable attractions, beginning with—

Rouen Cathedral

Most of the world knows the Rouen Cathedral, immortalized by Monet in an impressionistic series of plaintings depicting the three-portal main front with its galaxy of statues.

The present-day cathedral, a symphony of lacelike stonework, was reconstructed in part after the bombings of World War II. Consecrated in 1063, it was rebuilt after the "great fire" of 1200, the work lasting for centuries. Two soaring towers distinguish it; one, the **Tour de Beurre** ("Tower of Butter"), was financed by the faithful willing to pay good money in exchange for the privilege of eating butter at Lent. The tower is a masterpiece of the flamboyant Gothic style. Containing a carillon of 56 bells, a three-story lantern tower, built in 1877 and utilizing 740 tons of iron and bronze, rises to a height of almost 500 feet.

Especially interesting in the interior, the **Chapelle de la Vierge** is adorned with the Renaissance tombs of the Cardinals d'Amboise as well as Jean de Brézé. Also entombed inside was the "lion" heart of Richard the Lion-Hearted —a token of his affection for the people of Rouen.

The cathedral is closed from noon to 2 p.m. and on Sundays from 1 to 3 p.m. No admission is charged.

Behind the cathedral, the **Archbishop's Palace** was bombed out during the war. Now it stands naked against the sky. The broken arches and rosette windows witnessed the trial of Joan of Arc in 1431. At this same spot her rehabilitation was proclaimed in 1456.

To and Through the Place du Vieux-Marché

A lane running between the cathedral and Place du Vieux-Marché is called **rue du Gros-Horloge,** or "Street of the Great Clock." Now a traffic-free pedestrian mall, it is named for an ornate gilt Renaissance clock mounted on an arch, Rouen's most popular monument. The arch bridges the street and is connected to a Louis XV sculpted fountain with a bevy of cherubs and a belltower. At night the bells still toll a curfew. Visitors who purchase a ticket at the Beaux-Arts (see below) are entitled to visit the belfry to see the iron clockworks and the bells. Hours are from 10 a.m. to 12:15 p.m. and from 2:30 to 5:30 p.m. from Easter to mid-September.

Of course, you'll want to visit **Place du Vieux-Marché** ("Old Marketplace"), marking "the final abode" of Joan of Arc. Tied to a stake, she was burned alive on a pyre set by the English on May 30, 1431. Kissing a cross while she was being chained, she is reported to have called out "Jesus!" as the fire was set. Afterward, her ashes were gathered up and tossed into the Seine.

In the center of a monumental complex in the square is a modern church displaying stained-glass windows from St. Vincent. Beside it a bronze cross marks the position of St. Joan's stake.

Nearby, on **Place de la Pucelle** ("Square of the Maid"), stands **Hôtel de Bourgtheroulde,** which is Gothic-inspired, though it shows traces of the beginning of the Renaissance. It dates from the 16th century and was built by William the Red (Guillaume le Roux). The inside yard is exceptional. Once in the courtyard, look back at the Gothic building with its octagonal stair tower. The left gallery is entirely Renaissance. A bank uses the hôtel now, and access is free during working hours. On Saturday and Sunday, you can visit by ringing a bell and asking for the porter. On the square is a small outdoor market for fresh food.

More Churches

Besides the cathedral, two other Rouen churches seek attention. One is the **Church of St. Maclou,** behind the cathedral. It was built in the florid Gothic style, with a step-gabled porch and handsome cloisters. It is known for the remarkable panels on its doors, dating from the 16th century; our favorite (to the left) is the "Portal of the Fonts." The church was originally constructed in 1200, rebuilt in 1432, and finally consecrated in 1521, although its lantern tower is from the 19th century. It sits on a square of old Norman crooked-timbered buildings. Inside, pictures dating from June 4, 1944, document St.

Maclou's destruction (a fragment of a bomb was found in the choir of the chapel). All of its stained glass was shattered.

If you walk from rue de la République to Place du Général-de-Gaulle, you'll be at the **Church of St. Ouen,** the outgrowth of a seventh-century Benedictine abbey. Flanked by four turrets, its 375-foot octagonal lantern tower, in the Gothic style, is called "the ducal crown of Normandy." One of the best-known Gothic buildings in France, the present church represents the work of five centuries.

Its nave is of the 15th century, its choir from the 14th (but with 18th-century railings), and its remarkable stained glass from the 14th through the 16th centuries. Concerts on the huge 17th-century organ are presented on Sunday afternoons at 5 p.m. in August and September.

On May 23, 1431, Joan of Arc was taken to the cemetery of St. Ouen, where officials sentenced her to be burnt at the stake unless she recanted. An abjuration was signed by her, thus condemning her to life imprisonment; that sentence was later revoked.

Museums

The **Musée des Beaux-Arts,** entered on the Square Verdrel, is one of the most important provincial museums in France, with portraits by David, plus works by Delacroix and Ingres (don't miss his *La Belle Zélie*). One of the most important masterpieces in the museum is a retable by Gérard David called *La Vièrge et les Saints (The Virgin and the Saints).* A whole salon is devoted to Géricault, including a portrait he did of Delacroix. Other works are by Veronese, Velásquez, Renoir, Dufy, Guardi, and from the Schools of Fontaine-bleau and Barbizon. There is a large collection of paintings by Sisley and Monet, including a version of the latter's *Rouen Cathedral.* It is one of his most famous studies.

One of the greatest treasures of the Beaux-Arts is its Rouen faïence, which pioneered a special red in 1670. The exhibits provide a showcase for the talents of Masseot Abaquesne (1500-1564), considered the premier French craftsman in porcelain. In time, his position was usurped by Louis Poterat (1673-1696). As well, an exceptional showcase is devoted to chinoiseries dating from 1699 to 1745.

The museum is open from 10 a.m. to noon and from 2 to 6 p.m., charging 4F (91¢) for admission. It is closed all day Tuesday and on Wednesday mornings and holidays. The same ticket admits you to:

Le Secq des Tournelles (Wrought Ironworks Museum). Entered from the rue Jacques-Villon, this unique museum is housed in the 15-century Church of St. Laurent. Its collection ranges from what the press once called "forthright masculine forging to lacy feminine filigree, from Roman keys to the needlepoint balustrade that graced Mme. de Pompadour's country mansion." An aristocrat in Paris, Le Secq des Tournelles began the collection in 1870. So passionately was he devoted to it that his wife divorced him, charing alienation of affection. Donated to the city of Rouen, the collection now includes as many as 14,000 pieces.

Some of the pieces date from the days when English ships blocked French ports during the worst days of Napoleon's rule. Many French women—always concerned with fashion—went to their blacksmiths instead of their goldsmiths for sophisticated jewelry fashioned out of iron. These men could even turn out an orthopedic corset. Some of the collection is enlightening (including kitchen utensils dating from the 17th century), others merely amusing (a pair of scissors formed like a sea pelican, its beak making the blades). Removed from the d'Ourscamp Abbey, a 13th-century gate is remarkable for its filigree.

The Wrought Ironworks Museum keeps the same hours as Beaux-Arts.

Musée Flaubert et d'Histoire de la Médecine, 51 rue de Lecat, was the birthplace of Gustave Flaubert, the French novelist who wrote the masterpiece *Madame Bovary.* His father was the director of Rouen's public hospital. Flaubert was born in the director's quarters of the hospital and spent the first 25 years of his life in the city. The bedroom where Flaubert was born in 1821 is intact. In addition, family furniture and medical paraphernalia are displayed.

Only a glass door separated the Flaubert family from the ward filled with moaning patients. Contiguous to the family's billiard room was the dissection ward, where Flaubert would go to peek at the corpses.

Hours are from 10 a.m. to noon and from 2 to 6 p.m.; closed Sundays, Mondays, and holidays. Admission is 4F (91¢).

Flaubert fans may want to visit the author's family home at **Croisset,** an industrial suburb of Rouen. The Flaubert pavilion is open from 10 a.m. to noon and from 2 to 6 p.m.; closed Thursdays, Friday mornings, and most holidays. Admission is 3F (68¢), although it's free on Sundays and holidays. At the pavilion Flaubert wrote *Madame Bovary* and *Salammbô.*

HOTELS: Seven for the asking, beginning with—

Upper-Bracket Hotels
Frantel, rue Croix-de-Fer (tel. 98-06-98), is an excellent choice for those seeking the most up-to-date modern comforts in a city of antiquity. The location is unbeatable—right at the Cathedral of Rouen and the rue du Gros-Horloge. Air-conditioned bedrooms are well furnished and immaculately kept, costing from 220F ($50.23) in a single, that figure going up to 300F ($68.49) for the best doubles, all with private baths. The bedrooms are models of contemporary functional design. Its restaurant, Le Tournebroche, serves good food as well, a set meal costing 85F ($19.41), although you can spend far more, of course, by ordering à la carte.

Hôtel de Dieppe, Place Bernard Tissot (tel. 71-96-00), has been run by the Guéret family since 1880, and each new generation has modernized the premises somewhat. More recently, two new floors with 15 rooms have been added. Dieppe's essential character, however, remains that of a traditional French inn. In 1977, the fourth generation took over its responsibilities; Jean-Pierre Guéret, 10 years with Hilton International, is the general manager. Directly opposite the railway station, it is actually two buildings joined together. All its rooms have baths or showers, plus toilets. The newer rooms are preferable; many have been redecorated as well, and graced with art reproductions and period pieces. Singles range from 160F ($36.53) to 176F ($40.18); doubles, 187F ($42.69) to 215F ($49.08). In the adjoining newly redecorated rôtisserie, **Les Quatre Saisons,** you can select a menu for 80F ($18.26). À la carte specialties include beef filet "St.-Amand" with calvados cream sauce at 60F ($13.70) or sole poached in red wine at 55F ($10.27). Prices include tax and service. Expect to pay from 120F ($27.40) to 150F ($34.26) if you dine here.

Budget Lodgings
Le Viking, 21 Quai du Havre (tel. 70-34-95), right on the riverbank overlooking the Seine, provides charming views from its front rooms (the traffic can be thunderous at times, however). A completely modern establishment, Le

Viking has 37 bedrooms. Accommodations are clean-cut and utilitarian; twin-bedded rooms with private bath or shower start at 130F ($29.68). Bathless singles cost from 60F ($13.70) to 65F ($14.84), going up to 115F ($26.25) with bath. Breakfast at 10F ($2.28) is the only meal provided. In July and August, when the pilgrimage to Rouen reaches its zenith, you really should reserve at least two weeks in advance.

Hôtel de Québec, 18-24 rue de Québec (tel. 70-09-38), is a neat, modern, brick-built corner hotel, with 38 inexpensive bedrooms. A block from the Seine, within walking distance of the cathedral and some of the city's best restaurants, the hotel is well run and friendly. The bedrooms are small but serviceable, many opening onto a rear courtyard where parking is provided. The tariff for two persons in a room with private bath is 143F ($32.65), dropping to 68F ($15.52) in a double with hot and cold running water. A continental breakfast at 9.50F ($2.16) is the only meal served.

Hôtel de la Cathédrale, 12 rue St.-Romain (tel. 71-57-95), is a small, 25-room hostelry. Staying here is like being in a private home. The location is choice, behind the cathedral and opposite the Archbishop's Palace where Joan of Arc was tried. The street on which the hotel stands has been restored, the 19th- and 20th-century overlays giving way to the original black-and-white timbered-façades. Good, clean, but simply furnished double rooms peak at 150F ($34.26) with a private bath. Breakfast is an extra 11F ($2.51).

La Vieille-Tour, Place de la Haute-Vielle-Tour (tel. 70-03-27), is a small (23 rooms) modern hotel, on a square a block from the Seine, within walking distance of the cathedral. In fact, you'll often hear the chimes from your bedroom window. The lobby is tiny, the breakfast lounge small. But many of the bedrooms are spacious, some with two double beds. Furnishings are contemporary. The most desirable accommodations face the square. The cost for a double is 105F ($23.97). You'll pay an additional 10F ($2.28) for your croissants, coffee, and jam with Normandy butter for breakfast.

READERS' HOTEL SELECTIONS: "The **Hôtel des Arcades,** 52 rue des Carmes (tel. 70-10-30), charges 45F ($10.27) a night for a double without bath, 52F ($11.87) for a double with bath. A continental breakfast is 8F ($1.83) per person extra. We had a double room with a balcony from which the cathedral could be seen illuminated at night. The owner, Mrs. Kanji, is friendly, helpful, and speaks English. The hotel is in the middle of the city, and all sights can be reached by foot in five or ten minutes" (George J. Takacs, APO, New York). . . . "We can recommend **Le Richelieu,** 24 rue du Bac (tel. 70-10-57), right downtown but quiet after 7 p.m., when all commerce stops. It is on a small street, one block away from the cathedral. A room for two with shower (sink and bidet also) is 57F ($13.01). The owners are nice, professional, and kind. Petit déjeuner (breakfast) is 8.50F ($1.94). The coffee is delicious, the croissants fresh. The rooms are modern and clean. We prefer a hotel without restaurant, but the woman owner makes an excellent omelet. That, combined with a salad and good French bread, makes an excellent and inexpensive lunch or supper" (Alexander Brody, Toronto, Canada).

RESTAURANTS: Now it's time to sample the rich Norman cuisine we've been telling you about. We'll begin at—

The Leading Restaurant

La Couronne, 31 Place du Vieux-Marché (tel. 71-40-90), is not only the most ancient restaurant in Rouen, dating back to 1345; it lays claim as well to being the oldest *auberge* (inn) in France. Housed in a half-timbered building that looks like a setting for Hansel and Gretel, it stands directly on the square where Joan of Arc was burned at the stake. During World War II, a 500-pound bomb exploded in its rear courtyard, but, amazingly, wooden pegs held La

Couronne together. The dining rooms, on several floors, are reached by wooden stairs leading around fireplaces.

La Couronne has won fame for its caneton (duckling) à la Rouennaise, costing 150F ($34.26) for two persons. Many gourmets have compared it in quality to that of La Tour d'Argent in Paris. Certainly the prices are better in Rouen. The duck is roasted (after its neck has been wrung, so as not to lose any blood), then the breast slices are flamed in calvados before being covered in a blood sauce. The drumsticks are grilled until they are crisp. A superb dish. The seafood couldn't be fresher. Try especially the filet de sole Normande, 72F ($16.44), prepared with a smooth, creamy sauce and garnished with crayfish. Another excellent dish is barbue au cidre at 60F ($13.70)—that is, brill poached in a fish stock laced with cider. A hollandaise-type sauce is poured over the fish filets before they are placed in the oven. A good dessert is profiteroles glacées, covered with a chocolate sauce, 24F ($5.48).

The Middle Bracket

Dufour, 67 rue St.-Nicholas (tel. 71-90-62), is one of the best preserved of the 17th-century inns of Normandy. In the true Norman style, it's a five-story corner building, built of timber and plaster. Inside are several dining rooms, a veritable forest of aged and seasoned beams, and all the trappings necessary for a colorful atmosphere: copper pans and pots, spices, wood carvings, and engravings.

The dishes—prepared and served under the eagle eye of Monsieur Dufour—are so outstanding that it's difficult to single out specialties. An always reliable opener, those delicious black mussels in a creamy sauce, costs 20F ($4.57). The inevitable filet de sole Normande, 60F ($13.70), is the favorite fish entree. An excellent main dish is half a roast Rouen duckling with apples, costing 100F ($22.83) for two persons. The restaurant is closed Sunday nights and Mondays, and takes a vacation in August.

A Budget Brasserie

Vieux Marché, 2 Place du Vieux-Marché (tel. 71-59-09), specializes in fruits de mer, or fruits of the sea. The larder must be well stocked, as the chef offers the widest selection of food on his set menus of any kitchen in Rouen. For 35F ($7.99) you can enjoy the simplest meal, beginning with hors d'oeuvres and including a main dish, as well as a choice of cheese or dessert. A more elaborate menu at 65F ($14.84) includes some more expensive dishes, such as oysters and steak au poivre. If you dine à la carte, expect to pay from 100F ($22.83) to 130F ($29.68), plus 15% for service.

Up the Seine 17 miles from Rouen is the town of:

2. Jumièges

Called one of the most beautiful ruins in France, **Jumièges Abbey** was founded by St. Philbert in the seventh century, although it was rebuilt in the 10th century by Duke Guillaume ("Long Sword"). The abbey church was consecrated in 1067 by the archbishop of Rouen in the presence of William the Conqueror.

One of the architectural wonders of Normandy, Jumièges was seized by the state during the French Revolution. It was later sold to a wood merchant and subsequently vandalized. Salvaged finally in the mid-1800s, it has been turned over to the state. The 100-foot-high nave is complete, and the porch is surrounded by two towers, 150 feet high. In summer the hours are from 9 a.m.

to noon and from 2 to 6 p.m. (in winter from 10 a.m. to noon and from 1:30
to 4 p.m.). The cost is 4F (91¢), 2F on Sundays.

About six miles further on lies the village of—

3. Saint-Wandrille

The **Abbey of Saint Wandrille** was founded in 649 by Wandrille, an official
of the court of King Dagobert. Wandrille was called an "athlete of God"
because of his great spiritual training and influence. In the course of centuries
the buildings have suffered from fire, thunder and lightning, and the attacks of
men, among whom were the Vikings. That is why nothing survives of the
original seventh-century monastery. Ever since 649, monks have lived in the
abbey, except for a hundred years or so because of French political troubles.

A monumental blue gate from the 18th century frames the entrance to the
monastery. Inside the great courtyard you can see a building housing a factory
in which household products, such as wax and polish, are manufactured to help
the community make a living. Next to the factory stand the workshops, and
even a flour mill (perhaps the smallest one in France).

The cloisters are from the 14th to the 16th centuries. In the north gallery,
a lavabo (wash basin) is a beautiful and unique piece of work from about 1500.
The church is well worth even a short visit. A 14th-century barn originally
located 30 miles from the abbey was transplanted and reerected in 1967-69 as
the abbey church.

A guided tour is given weekdays at 3 and 4 p.m. (Sundays and holidays
at 11:30 a.m. as well), costing 4F (91¢) for adults and 2F (46¢) for children or
groups. Products by the monks are on sale.

In the village, the **Auberge Deux-Couronnes** (tel. 96-11-44) is an old
Norman inn that makes a good luncheon or dinner choice if you're in the
hamlet visiting the abbey and listening to Gregorian chants. The daily menus
at 60F ($13.70) and 75F ($17.12) are highly commendable. This gem of a
restaurant is beautifully run, and the chef, Jacques Grangier, does all the
Norman specialties well. That means a cuisine of butter, cream, cheese, and
cider. But there are other standard French dishes as well. In addition to the
good food, you get friendly service. The restaurant is closed from the end of
August until September 15, and it shuts down also February 1-20 and Sunday
nights. Monday is its weekly closing day all year.

4. Caudebec-en-Caux

Set in an amphitheater on the banks of the Seine, this charming little town
was nearly destroyed in World War II. At the end of the Ste.-Gertrude Valley,
it is the scene of the famous "Mascaret," which is a tidal wave occurring in the
estuary of the Seine at the time of the fall and spring equinoxes.

Its Gothic **Church of Notre Dame**, dating from the early 15th century, was
saved from the 1940 fires. Henri IV called the church "the handsomest chapel
in my kingdom." Restoration work in the 16th century was carried out by
Guillaume Le Tellier. On the west side is a trio of flamboyant doorways,
surmounted by a rose window.

Although damaged in the war, the **Maison des Templiers** has been restored, showing it to be an outstanding example of secular architecture from
the 13th century. It can be visited on Sundays in summer from 3 to 6 p.m. or
on Thursday and Saturday all year, 3 to 5 p.m.

On a hill, with a view of the Seine, stands the **Manoir de Rétival**, 2 rue
St.-Clair (tel. 96-11-22). Once a hunting lodge, it receives guests in its dozen

chambers, 10 of which contain private baths, from March 1 to December 15, charging 100F ($22.83) in a single, 240F ($54.79) in a double. The bedrooms are in the antique style, and some even have fireplaces. In warm weather guests like to sit out on the terrace overlooking the river and the heather-covered plains of Caux. The second-floor salon, where guests also retreat, is a lovely period piece with an interesting chimney.

Since the manor no longer serves meals other than breakfast, we'd suggest the **Normandie,** Quai Guilbaud (tel. 96-25-11), where Monsieur Guyot offers a simple, well-prepared cuisine in a setting overlooking the Seine. The chef prepares such dishes as grilled fresh sardines, eggplant fritters, fried sand eels, and a delicious-tasting Norman chicken. Menus are offered at 35F ($7.99), 55F ($12.56), and 75F ($17.12). In addition, the patron rents out about 10 simply furnished rooms, costing 55F ($12.56) in a double with toilet, 65F ($14.84) with shower, and a peak 110F ($25.11) with complete bath. The inn shuts down on Sunday night and for Monday lunch, and is also closed for the first two weeks in September.

5. Pont-Audemer

The father of William the Conqueror used to storm through this historic town of markets and tanners. A number of old houses still stand on the **rue de la Licorne** (the street of the unicorn). A few tourists pass through to see the **Church of St. Ouen,** dating from the 11th century, with a 1450 façade and Renaissance stained-glass windows. But the real reason foreigners head this way is because of a remarkable old Norman inn, detailed below.

Pont-Audemer is 23 miles northeast of Lisieux and makes a convenient stopover between Deauville and Rouen.

A 17TH-CENTURY NORMAN INN: Auberge du Vieux Puits ("The Inn of the Old Well"), 6 rue Notre-Dame-du-Pré (tel. 41-01-48), is a dreamy picture-postcard cliché of a mellowed 17th-century Norman inn. You'll recognize it quickly, with its half-timbered façade, small street-floor windows, and third-floor dormers. An L-shaped building, it partially encloses an old garden. Hopefully, you'll schedule at least a night's stopover.

Beamed ceilings, half-timbered walls, crude country chairs, and plain wooden tables mark the interior. Copper and brass pots and pans hang from the beams, and above the fireplace is a pewter collection.

The inn is owned and run by Monsieur and Madame Jacques Foltz, and the chef de cuisine is Monsieur Piquet. Those interested in the specialties should order à la carte, paying from 110F ($25.11) to around 160F ($36.53) per person for a complete meal. Especially recommended is the canard aux cerises (duck with cherries), the filets de sole "Vieux Puits," and the truite (trout) Bovary au champagne. Many diners prefer to finish their meal with the three classic cheeses of Normandy: Camembert, Livarot, and Pont-l'Évêque. For dessert, you can order a thick tart (hopefully strawberries will be in season) smothered in rich Norman cream, 17F ($3.88). The Norman cider is most appealing.

Madame Foltz offers eight bedrooms, all prettily furnished with antiques. A single is 58F ($13.24), a double 100F ($22.83), with breakfast costing another 16F ($3.65).

The Auberge is closed December 20 to mid-January and the first week in July, plus Monday nights and Tuesdays year round.

6. L'Aigle

A good center for touring the upper valley of the Risle, L'Aigle contains **St. Martin's Church** with its 15th-century square tower and another smaller tower dating from the 12th century. In addition, it also has an interesting waxworks—**Musée Juin 44: Bataille de Normandie**, with its recreation of some of the major personalities of that epic battle. Their voices, recorded at the time, can also be heard. The museum is open from 9 a.m. to noon and from 2 to 6 p.m., charging an admission of 6F ($1.37).

L'Aigle—its denizens are called "Aiglons," or little eagles—is a metal-working center, a tradition going back to ancient times. Frankly, the town itself isn't a major sightseeing attraction. Our main reason for recommending it for those touring in Normandy is because of—

The **Hôtel du Dauphin**, Place Hall (tel. 24-12-44), which has one of the most charmingly decorated interiors of any hôtel in Normandy. In grand provincial comfort, the Bernard family will welcome you to one of their color-coordinated rooms, some of which have the beams exposed. All 30 of their chambers are decorated in a different style, and most of them contain private baths. Depending on the room, singles begin at 100F ($22.83), the tariff rising to 170F ($38.81) in a double with private bath. In the handsomely decorated public lounges, you may find such style you won't want to leave the premises. Tea and pastry are a delight in the salon known as "Coin du Feu" with its fireplace. The food at du Dauphin is among the most outstanding in the area, specialties including sole Normande, langouste (lobster) au porto, saumon (salmon) braisé au Pouilly, caneton (duckling) à la bigarade, and homemade ice cream and delicious fruit tarts. An outstanding set meal is offered for just 58F ($13.24), although if you order à la carte you are likely to pay as much as 122F ($27.86).

7. Orbec

In a peaceful valley of the Pays d'Auge, near the source of the Orbiquet River, Orbec is a Norman town that has preserved its character. It lies 12½ miles from Lisieux, 22 miles from L'Aigle, and 43 miles from Caen. Although the town has an interesting **Church of Notre-Dame**, from the 15th and 16th centuries, the real reason people come here is to sample the food at—

Au Caneton, 28 rue Grande (tel. 32-73-32), a 17th-century Norman house in the rustic style, standing on this principal business artery. You dine in small dark rooms by lamplight reflecting on an illuminated chimney piece. Copper pots hang on the white walls. Monsieur Joseph Ruaux, a *Diplômé d'Honneur de Grand Palais,* is the chef and owner; he knows the value of classic simplicity and is an expert at seasoning and saucing. As cookery fads come and go, he has maintained his popularity over the years, drawing visitors who come all the way from Paris.

His feuilletté of lobster is outstanding. After sampling it, we thought our most recent meal could only go downhill. It didn't—far from it. The duckling St.-Antoine is his pièce de résistance. He also does a superb roast leg of duckling cooked in cider vinegar. Of course, this is calvados country, so one of those mellow mulled drinks with your meal would be in keeping with an age-old tradition. Menus are offered for 145F ($33.10) and 200F ($45.66), hardly expensive considering what you get. À la carte orders also run about 200F per person. It's important to call ahead to reserve a table. The restaurant is closed on Monday nights and Tuesdays.

8. Caen

On the banks of the Orne, the port city of Caen suffered great damage in the Allied invasion of Normandy in 1944. Nearly three-quarters of the city's buildings, some 10,000 in all, were destroyed, although the twin abbeys founded by William the Conqueror and his "good wife, Matilda" were spared. Eight miles from the English Channel, 150 miles northwest of Paris, the city today is essentially modern, with many broad avenues and new apartment buildings.

William the Conqueror made Caen his seat of government. The son of Robert the Devil and a tanner's daughter, young William had been known as "The Bastard" in the days before he conquered England. He proposed marriage to his cousin Matilda, the daughter of Baldwin V of Flanders. She is said to have told her ladies-in-waiting that she'd "rather take the veil than marry a bastard." However, William galloped on horseback to Flanders, grabbed Matilda by the hair—and she changed her mind. The Papal Council at Reims had prohibited the alliance because of their close kinship, but in 1059 Pope Nicholas II granted dispensation. To show their penance, William and Matilda founded the Abbaye aux Hommes and the Abbaye aux Dames at Caen.

The **Abbaye aux Hommes,** in the Norman Romanesque style of architecture, also includes the **Église St.-Étienne;** both are entered on the Place Monseigneur-des-Hameaux. During the height of the 1944 battle, denizens of Caen flocked to St.-Étienne for protection from the bombardments. Twin Romanesque towers, their spires dating from the 13th century, rise 300 feet into the air (Caen is known as "a city of spires"). Inside, a simple marble slab in front of the high altar commemorates the site of William's tomb. The Huguenots destroyed the tomb in the uprising of 1562, save for a hipbone that was recovered. However, in the French Revolution the last bit of William the Conqueror's dust was scattered to the wind.

For a tour of the abbey ensemble (entrance at No. 5) you must wait to be conducted by a guide. It is open daily except Tuesdays from 8 to 11 a.m. and from 2 to 6 p.m. for a 3F (68¢) admission fee. Inside, the handcarved wooden doors are exceptional, as is an elaborately sculpted wrought-iron staircase. From the cloisters, you get a good view of the two towers of St.-Étienne. Part of the former abbey houses municipal offices.

On the opposite side of town, the **Abbaye aux Dames** was founded by Matilda and it embraces the **Church of the Trinité.** Like St.-Étienne, its façade is flanked by two Romanesque square towers. Destroyed during the Hundred Years' War, its spires were never rebuilt. Inside, the ribbed vaulting is interesting architecturally. In the 12th-century choir rests the tomb of Queen Matilda. To see the choir, the transept, and the crypt, you must go on a guided tour between 9 a.m. and noon or between 2 and 7 p.m. (till 6 p.m. in winter).

If time remains, you may want to visit the **château,** close to the Relais des Gourmets. There you may enjoy a walk in the castle gardens, from which you can look out over Caen. The citadel is from the 14th and 15th centuries; it was badly damaged in the war. The approach ramp is from the front of the Church of St. Pierre.

AN UPPER-BRACKET HOTEL: Malherbe, Place Maréchal-Foch (tel. 84-40-06), occupies the prime position in the new part of Caen, on a wide, tree-shaded boulevard, opposite a large sports park. It's in the tradition of a businessperson's hotel, offering rooms at several price levels. The best twin-bedded rooms with private bath cost 220F ($50.23); double-bedded rooms with bath are 195F ($44.52). The rooms are comfortable and well furnished—the best in town, in fact. The bar draws many Americans who use Caen as a center for touring the 1944 beaches. The Malherbe was selected by Darryl F. Zanuck for his cast when he was shooting *The Longest Day*.

A MIDDLE-BRACKET HOTEL: Le Relais des Gourmets, 15 rue de Geôle (tel. 86-06-01), at the foot of the Château de Guillaume-le-Conquérant, is a charming little four-star hotel. Proprietor Jean Legras has been awarded many culinary honors, and you may dine (à la carte, if you wish) in the hotel's little terraced garden. Some caged songbirds are among the permanent residents of the hotel. Many pleasant antiques, including a 13th-century closet, and reproductions adorn the lounges and reception area. Bedrooms are of generous size, many with views of the garden or the château walls. The rate for two persons, in a double with shower bath, is 100F ($22.83), increasing to 150F ($34.26) with a complete bath. For single occupancy these rates are generally reduced by 15F ($3.42) per room.

A BUDGET STOPOVER: Bristol, 31 rue du 11-Novembre (tel. 84-59-76), is modesty itself, a simple hotel in a block of modern apartments and shops a short way from the park. Consider the Bristol more of a stopover hotel than an island of charm. If you want a private bath, expect to pay 120F ($27.40) to 145F ($33.10) for a double or twin-bedded room. But the double-bedded rooms with showers (no toilets) are the real money-savers at 85F ($19.41). An even better bet is one of the smaller rooms with a cabinet de toilette, costing just 55F ($12.56).

UPPER-BRACKET DINING: Le Rabelais, Place Maréchal-Foch (tel. 84-46-42), on the ground floor of the Malherbe Hôtel, is famous for its tripes à la mode de Caen. The restaurant takes its name from the French author, who wrote that Gargamelle gave birth to Gargantua after downing a large dish of godebillios (that is, the fat tripe of oxen). The house specialty is served in a terrine, the tripe flavored with aged calvados.

The restaurant is run by Madame Ville, who specializes in fish and seafood. Her most highly prized main courses include timbale Dieppoise at 65F ($14.84), coquilles St. Jacques at 50F ($34.26), and turbot cooked with sorrel, 65F ($14.84). She also has set menus for 50F ($34.26) and 90F ($20.55), the first including wine and coffee. Her place is closed on Sundays.

Le Dauphin, 29 rue Gémare (tel. 76-22-26), is not only one of the outstanding restaurants of Caen but also offers good accommodations. The decor of Monsieur Chabredier is provincial modern, and he offers meals for 50F ($11.42), 80F ($18.26), and 100F ($22.83). The cookery is quite imaginative, and there are many interesting sauced dishes and specialties, including a ragoût of small lobster with pâté, rabbit cooked in cider, sweetbreads Carême, and sea bream with chive butter. His dessert specialty is soufflé glacé with strawberries. Only the freshest of ingredients are used. The restaurant is closed on Saturday and from mid-July until August 9. Its 21 bedrooms are well furnished and maintained, renting for 76F ($17.35) in a single, 160F ($36.53) in a double.

THE "CUISINE SOIGNÉE" (BUDGET): Au Coq en Pâté, 35 rue Girard (tel. 82-08-16), is a modest little restaurant, offering the *cuisine soignée*—and that means first-rate cooking. It gives one of the best values in the city in its set meal for 28F ($6.39). The repast is likely to include stuffed clams, gigot d'agneau rôti (roast leg of lamb), artichokes vinaigrette, plus a choice of nearly a dozen desserts. A more elaborate menu costs 75F ($17.12). The decor is in the typical Norman bistro fashion. If you wish to stay overnight, the innkeeper offers 10 modestly furnished rooms for 45F ($10.27) to 50F ($11.42) per person, with breakfast costing an extra 10F ($2.28) per person. Closed Mondays and all of September.

LIVING AND DINING ON THE OUTSKIRTS (DELUXE): At Bénouville, 6½ miles northeast of Caen, **Le Manoir d'Hastings,** N814 (tel. 93-30-89), is a converted priory from the 17th century with an enclosed Norman garden. Its owner, Claude Scaviner, is an advocate of La Nouvelle Cuisine. If in your Norman tour you've tired of cream and calvados with everything, then head here for a refreshing lighter meal. The chef's creativity is inspired, and he has developed his own style and language with food. He might propose a ragoût of truffles or even a soup of truffles dedicated to Paul Bocuse, one of the leading exponents of the new cuisine in Lyon. Monsieur Scaviner makes a basil-flavored "pot-au-feu" with seafood, or else prepares a steamed bass so delicately flavored you'll want to kidnap him for your own kitchen. His cider-cooked ham and his Bresse squab herald him as a master of his art. For dessert, we'd suggest a sabayon with champagne and fruits of the season. You can order set menus for 85F ($19.41), 190F ($43.38), and 200F ($45.66). The manor is closed Sunday night and Monday off-season, and it is also closed for the first two weeks in February.

If you find living in Caen too bleak, you'll discover the most luxurious trappings at Audrieu, 11 miles from Caen (head out the D94). At Audrieu, the **Relais Château d'Audrieu** (tel. 80-21-52), is a beautiful 18th-century château set on its own park grounds. Here you can enjoy not only the setting and the swimming pool but the excellent specialties of the chef, Gilles Marcouiller, who offers a simplified menu for about 100F ($22.83) or an elaborate gourmet repast for around 200F ($45.66). Try his terrine of three fish, his steamed sole in butter with caviar, his stuffed pigs' feet, his soup of pears with caramel. His cuisine is extremely interesting, and his guests leave with an unfailing smile. Lovely rooms are rented to guests at rates of 200F ($45.66) in a single, from about 600F ($136.98) in a suite for two to three persons. In all, 22 chambers, including four suites, are available, each furnished with antiques and equipped with modern private bathrooms. The château is closed in December and January and on off-season Wednesdays.

9. Bayeux

The dukes of Normandy sent their sons to this Viking settlement to learn the Norse language. Bayeux has changed a lot since then, but miraculously it was spared from bombardment in the 1944 Allied invasion of Normandy. The first town liberated in France, Bayeux gave de Gaulle an enthusiastic welcome when he arrived there on June 14. Today, the sleepy town, 17 miles northwest of Caen, is filled with Norman timbered houses, stone mansions, and cobbled streets.

The **Cathedral of Bayeux** has been called "the Reims of Normandy." It was consecrated in 1077 by Odo, the brother of William the Conqueror. The ruler's son, Beauclerc, partially destroyed it in 1105. Left over from an earlier church, its Romanesque towers rise on the western side, although the central tower is from the 15th century, with an even later topping. Inside, the nave is a fine example of the Norman Romanesque style. Rich in sculptural decorations, the 13th-century choir contains handsome Renaissance stalls. To see the treasury, the crypt, and the chapter house (13th century), apply to the sexton. Incidentally, the crypt was built in the 11th century, then sealed. Its existence remained unknown until it was discovered in 1412.

Across from the cathedral, on the rue de l'Évêché, is the **Musée la Tapisserie de la Reine Mathilde,** containing Matilda's tapestry, the most famous in the world. Only problem is, the **Bayeaux Tapestry** isn't a tapestry but an embroidery, and it wasn't by Matilda, the wife of William the Conqueror. It was probably commissioned in Kent, the work of unknown Saxon embroiderers between 1066 and 1077. It's a band of linen stretching 231 feet, 20 inches wide, with worsteds of eight colors depicting some 58 scenes. The first recorded mention of the embroidery was in 1476, when it was explained that the tapestry was used to decorate the nave of the Cathedral of Bayeux.

Housed in a structure built for it, the embroidery is behind glass. It tells the story of the conquest of England by William the Conqueror, including scenes such as the coronation of Harold as the Saxon king of England, Harold returning from his journey to Normandy, "the mysterious personage of Aelfgyve," the surrender of Dinan, Harold being told of the apparition of a comet (a portent of misfortune), William the Conqueror in war dress, and the death of Harold. Decorative borders include scenes from *Aesop's Fables.* Men, horses, ships, and weapons—the panorama of history sweeps by.

The embroidery may be viewed from June 1 to September 15 without interruption from 9 a.m. to 7 p.m. At other times usually from 9 a.m. to noon and from 2 to 6 p.m. The admission is 5F ($1.14) for adults, 3F (68¢) for students. For 1F (23¢) you can rent an earphone which gives you a running lecture on the embroidery.

FOOD AND LODGING: Lion d'Or, 71 rue St.-Jean (tel. 92-06-90), is like an old French coaching inn, with a large open courtyard and mansard roof. Lush window boxes decorate the façade. You can sleep or dine well here. One meal is required. On the half-board plan, the rate in a simple room is 177F ($40.41) for one person, rising to 300F ($68.49) for two. In a room with shower and toilet, a single pays 235F ($55.93), two persons 340F ($77.62), both on the demi-pension plan. The most expensive units are the twin-bedded chambers with complete baths, costing two persons 370F ($84.47) for demi-pension. The hotel has been renovated especially to keep that inn atmosphere both pleasant and comfortable. The rooms are personalized with a lot of warmth; they are set well back from the street, which provides quiet.

The beamed dining room has elegant cloth-covered walls, decorated with painted reproductions of the famous Bayeux Tapestry. Hanging from the beams are ornate but beautifully fashioned curtains, providing a more intimate atmosphere. Windows look out onto a courtyard replete with palms and pots and baskets of bright-red geraniums. The cooking here is famous. Three set dinners are offered at 82F ($18.72) for the tourist meal, 92F ($21) for the regional meal, and 135F ($30.82) for the gastronomic menu. The regional meal might include a meatloaf (specialty of the house); a fresh poached trout with shallot butter; chicken à la Vallée d'Auge flambé, cooked in cider with cream and mushrooms; Normandy cheese and, to top it off, a sort of meringue cake called Saint-Eve, a specialty of Bayeux. Specialties of the house include rabbit pâté with hazelnuts, andouille chaude à la Bovary, lotte aux baies roses, and pavé des Ducs (a chocolate dessert). There are lots of excellent wines, plus an attractive bar with a fireplace decorated in the tartan style, which makes for a cozy atmosphere. Try the Battle of Hastings cocktail.

10. Port-en-Bessin

Those wanting to get away from the popular tourist centers may consider the Port, as it's called locally. In the Calvados section, 5½ miles from Bayeux, it opens onto a harbor enclosed by two half-moon jetties. Hopefully, you'll be there early in the morning, except Sundays, for a fish auction.

While there consider a stopover, either for a room or meal, at **Hôtel de la Marine,** right on the harbor (tel. 21-70-08). It's simplicity itself, but that may be what you're seeking. The air-conditioned dining room on the second floor faces the sea. The style is pleasant, with carpeting and rustic furniture. Everything is of good standard without any particular originality. For 30F ($6.85) a set meal is offered including, for example, an appetizer of small shellfish, followed by boeuf bourguignonne, cheese, and pastry. Specialties of the chef include a cassolette de homard (lobster) in a Newburg sauce, terrine de St. Jacques (scallops), paupiettes de sole with a scallop mousse, and a mousseline of turbot in a lobster sauce. Service is very good.

A clean and comfortable bedroom overlooking the sea, with either bath or shower and toilet, goes for 90F ($20.55) double nightly.

11. D-Day Beaches

From June 6 to the breakthrough on July 18, "the longest day" was very long indeed. The greatest armada the world had ever known—men, warships, landing craft, tugboats, jeeps, whatever—had assembled along the southern coast of England in the spring of 1944.

On June 5, at 9:15 p.m., the BBC announced to the French Resistance that the invasion was imminent, signaling the underground to start dynamiting the railways. Before midnight, Allied planes were bombing the Norman coast fortifications. By 1:30 on the morning of June 6, members of the 101st Airborne were parachuting to the ground on German-occupied French soil. At 6:30 a.m., the Americans were landing on the codename beaches of Utah and Omaha. One hour later, the British and Canadian forces were making beachheads at Juno, Gold, and Sword.

The Nazis had mocked Churchill's promise in 1943 to liberate France "before the fall of the autumn leaves." When the invasion did come, it was swift, sudden, and a surprise to the formidable "Atlantic wall." Today, veterans from Canada, America, and England walk with their families across the beaches where "Czech hedgehogs," "Belgian grills," pillboxes, and "Rommel asparagus" once stood.

The exploration begins at the modest little seaside resort of **Arromanches-les-Bains,** 6½ miles from Bayeux. In June of 1944 it was a little fishing port, until it was taken by the 50th British Division. Towed across the English Channel, a mammoth prefabricated port known as "Winston" was installed to supply the Allied forces. "Victory could not have been achieved without it," said Eisenhower. The wreckage of that artificial harbor—also known as "Mulberry"—lies right off the beach, *la plage du débarquement.* A **Museum of the Invasion** has been installed, featuring relief maps, working models, a cinema, and photographs showing such scenes as the opening "Pontoons." A diorama of the landing, with an English commentary, is featured. The museum is open daily from 9 a.m. to noon and from 2 to 6 p.m.

Moving along the coast, you arrive at **Omaha Beach,** where the wreckage of war can still be seen. "Hanging on by their toenails," the men of the 1st and 29th American Divisions occupied the beach that June day. The codename Omaha became famous throughout the world, although the French up to then had called the beaches St.-Laurent, Vierville-sur-Mer, and Colleville. A monument commemorates the heroism of the invaders. Covering some 173 acres, the **Normandy American Cemetery** is filled with crosses and stars of David in Carrara marble. More than 9300 remains of American military dead were buried there on territory now owned by the United States, a gift from the French nation. The cemetery is open from 8 a.m. to 6 p.m.

Further along the coast, the jagged lime cliffs of the **Pointe du Hoc** come into view. A cross honors a group of American Rangers led by Lt. Col. James Rudder who scaled the cliff using hooks to get at the pillboxes. The scars of war are more visible here than at any other point along the beach. Much further along on the Contentin Peninsula is **Utah Beach.**

Nearby you can visit **Sainte-Mère-Église,** which not too many people had heard of until the night of June 5-6 when parachutists were dropped over the town. They were from the 82nd U.S. Airborne Division, under the command of Matthew B. Ridgeway. Members of the 101st Airborne Division, commanded by Gen. M. B. Taylor, U.S. Army, were also involved. Thus, little Sainte-Mère-Église became the first French town to be liberated in the long war against Germany. In the town is a **Permanent Exhibit of the Airborne Troops,** at which you can see many relics. From April to November the museum is open daily from 9 a.m. to noon and from 2 to 7 p.m. From November to April it is open only on Sundays and holidays. The cost is 5F ($1.14) for adults, 3F (68¢) for students and military personnel. In the town is **Kilometer "O"** on the **Freedom Trail,** marking the first of the milestones the American armies reached on their way to Metz and Bastogne.

FOOD AND LODGINGS: At **Grandcamp-les-Bains,** near Omaha Beach, you'll find a little fishing village in danger of silting up. In summer, French families turn it into a modest but pleasant seaside resort. If you're passing through, we'd recommend a luncheon stopover at **Bar de la Marée** (tel. 22-60-55), right on the harbor and built in the typical Norman style. The fish soup there is excellent, and we'd also endorse the Norman sole. Everything tastes better with country bread and Norman butter. If you make selections among the fish specialties, your tab can easily rise to 120F ($27.40). The bar is closed on Mondays and in November.

Hôtel-Bar-Restaurant d'Arromanches (tel. 22-36-26) is simple but good. It faces the Musée du Débarquement in Arromanches-les-Bains. The small double rooms cost 40F ($9.13) with a toilet, 55F ($12.56) with a shower and toilet. A few rooms for three rent for 70F ($15.98) nightly, service included. A continental breakfast is an extra 9F ($2.05). The hotel is well maintained, and English is spoken. The restaurant specializes in "fruits of the sea," complete meals costing from 35F ($7.99) to 48F ($10.96), service included. The hotel remains open in winter, although it shuts down in October.

12. Cherbourg

At the tip of the Cotentin Peninsula, Cherbourg is a major point of arrival for transatlantic liners, and, historically, it was the chief supply port for the Allied landings in the invasion of Normandy in 1944. On the English Channel, at the mouth of the Divette River, Cherbourg is the third great naval base of France. Its naval port was begun on orders of Napoleon Bonaparte, and it contains extensive drydocks and shipbuilding yards. Because of its location, 60 miles south of England's Isle of Wight, it was connected by the famous "Pluto" pipeline under the ocean, supplying fuel from the Isle of Wight to Cherbourg. Today you can take a motorboat trip through the great artificial port.

The history of the battle at Cherbourg—in fact, the story of the Allied landings at Normandy—unfolds at the **Musée de la Guerre et de la Libération,** which is reached by a winding road. At the top you'll have a good view of the town and the port. The museum was installed in the Fort du Roule. Photographs show the Germans surrendering, and an armory room displays artillery and equipment, even uniforms of Luftwaffe pilots. That teleguided contraption, a "Goliath," is also shown. One of the most interesting sections is devoted to modern propaganda, including the underground press and a moving Paul Colin poster, *Wounded France Awakes to Liberty.* The French contribution to the Allied victory isn't neglected either. The museum is open April through September from 9:30 a.m. to noon and from 2 to 5:30 p.m., charging an admission of 3F (68¢). Off-season it is open daily except Tuesday from 9 to noon and from 2 to 6 p.m.

Back in town, the **Church of La Trinité,** on the south side of the Place Napoléon, was built from 1423 to 1504, and is a fine example of the flamboyant style. It is one of the few historic buildings still left in Cherbourg.

The **Hôtel de Ville,** or town hall, possesses the minor **Musée Henry,** which is open daily, except Tuesdays in summer, charging 2F (46¢) for admission. It has a collection of European paintings, including some Spanish and German ones. A statue of a local painter, Jean-François Millet, stands in the public garden, and inside the museum you can see examples of his work. Look for a panel by Botticelli.

FOOD AND LODGINGS: In bandbox modern, the **Sofitel Cherbourg,** Gare Maritime (tel. 44-01-11), is the best place to stay in the port. It faces the new Port de Plaisance, as well as the Gare Maritime where transatlantic liners arrive. Your room may open onto a fishing fleet, usually from Britain. The hotel offers 72 well-equipped bedrooms with either private baths or showers. The rates for one person range from 135F ($30.82) to 235F ($53.65), and two persons pay from 155F ($35.42) to a high of 210F ($47.99). On the premises, Le Chateaubriand faces the sea, featuring good food and specializing in fish dishes. The bar, La Timonerie, also faces the sea and is a scenic place to stop for a drink at sunset, watching the fleet in the harbor.

Le Louvre, 2 rue H.-Dunant (tel. 53-02-28), isn't a museum but one of the finest bargain accommodations at Cherbourg. It has no restaurant, and is admittedly modest in its appointments, yet it charges only 52F ($11.87) in a single, 150F ($34.26) in the most expensive doubles with private bath. The rooms are comfortable and well maintained, although only 18 of the 40 accommodations come equipped with private plumbing.

For dining, the **Café du Théatre,** Place Général-de-Gaulle (tel. 53-01-14), is your leading choice, as it offers excellently prepared grilled lobster in a prawn sauce and other tempting dishes made with "fruits de mer," although the chef also does meat dishes well. Try, in particular, his peppersteak or his mixed grill. A set menu is offered for just 36F ($8.22). If you order à la carte, you can easily spend 60F ($13.70). The cuisine is simple, but the ingredients are fresh, compelling enough reason to visit.

READER'S HOTEL SELECTION: "I had a single room with breakfast for 48F ($10.96) a night at the **Hôtel de la Gare,** 10 Place Jean-Jaurés. This is right across the street from the Cherbourg Gare—not the Cherbourg Maritime Gare, which lets you out by the ship. A few people sometimes like to arrive at a port a day before leaving, so this little hotel can be convenient" (Adrian Allen, Miami Beach, Fla.).

13. Mont St.-Michel

Considered one of the greatest sightseeing attractions in Europe, Mont St.-Michel is surrounded by massive walls measuring more than half a mile in circumference. Connected to the shore by a causeway, it crowns a rocky islet at the border between Normandy and Brittany. The rock itself is 260 feet high.

Mont St.-Michel is noted for its tides, considered the highest on the continent of Europe, measuring at certain times of the year a 50-foot difference between high and low tide. Unsuspecting tourists wandering across the sands—notorious for their quicksands—can be trapped as the sea rushes toward the Mont at a speed comparable to that of a galloping horse.

Every day there are two tides, varying from 20 to 50 minutes. The Tourist Office, in the old Guard Room of the Bourgeois at the left of the town gates, will provide you with free tables of the annual tides. About twice a month the granite hilltop is completely surrounded by water, but the causeway leading to it is never under.

Ample parking space is provided at the cost of 4F (91¢) per day. However, if you're going by train, you have to get off at Pontorson, the nearest station, six miles from "the Mont." Here you can make easy bus connections that will take you to the abbey, which lies 47 miles from Dinan, 30 miles from St.-Malo, and 80 miles from Caen. To reach the abbey, you have to climb the steep Grande Rue, lined with 15th- and 16th-century houses. Along the way, you may have to fight off souvenir peddlers and Normans hawking their omelet specialties.

Those who make it to the top can begin their exploration of the "Marvel of the West." The abbey is open year round from 9 to 11:30 a.m. and from 1:30 to 6 p.m., May 15 to September 15 (off-season, it is open from 9 to 11:30 a.m. and from 1:30 to 4 p.m.), charging 6F ($1.37) for admission, only 3F (68¢) on Sundays. You must go on a guided tour, leaving every 15 minutes and lasting 45 minutes. To enter the abbey gardens afterward, you pay an additional 2F (46¢) admission. No tours in English are conducted on Fridays.

In the eighth century an oratory was founded on the spot by St. Aubert, the bishop of Avranches. It was replaced by a Benedictine monastery, founded in 966 by Richard I, Duke of Normandy. That met with destruction by fire in 1203. Large parts of the abbey were financed by Philip Augustus in the 13th century.

Ramparts encircle the church and its ensemble of buildings, a part of which includes the "Merveille" (Marvel), one of the most important Gothic masterpieces in Europe. One of these, the Salle des Chevaliers, is most graceful. Begun in the 11th century, the abbey church consists of a Romanesque nave and transept, plus a choir in the flamboyant Gothic style. The rectangular refectory is from 1212, the cloisters with their columns of pink granite from 1225.

FOOD AND LODGING: Plan to spend at least a night here at one of the town's typically French inns. And be sure to sample—

Mother Poulard's Legendary Omelet

La Mère Poulard (tel. 60-14-01) is a gastronomic shrine. It's sacred to those who revere the omelet that the simple village woman Annette Poulard began making at the end of the last century. Her omelet "secret" has been passed on to the operators of the inn today, Monsieur and Madame Bernard Heyraud. Mother Poulard would hold her beaten egg mixture over a hearth fire in a long-handled copper pan. That same tradition exists today among village women wearing the traditional garb. Stacked on a counter are baskets holding hundreds of fresh eggs, which are broken into large bowls to be beaten with large metal whips, turning them into a foamy, frothy mixture.

In truth, it's more of an open-fire soufflé than an omelet. The secret lies partially in the use of the wood, traditional oak. Three set meals (including the omelet) are featured, costing 105F ($23.97), 170F ($38.81), and 210F ($47.94), taxes and service included, although your drink is extra. For the cheaper price you'll be served cold salmon with green sauce, the famous omelet, sauteed chicken with tarragon, plus a chocolate mousse for dessert.

In the true tradition of a French inn, upper-floor rooms are offered for sleeping. There are 27 in all, renovated and furnished in the typical Norman fashion. For demi-pension, including dinner (the cheaper menu), room, and a continental breakfast, the charge for two persons ranges from 350F ($79.91) to 430F ($98.17). In season the manager will ask you to take your meals on the premises (not a hardship). La Mère Poulard is open from April 1 to October 1.

The Budget Inns

Hôtel des Terrasses Poulard (tel. 60-14-09) is a reconstruction of several old village houses, perched prettily up the hill on the stone city wall. Its entrance is opposite a parish church founded in the 11th century. Two dining rooms provide a panoramic view of the sea, offering meals at two price levels. The 80F ($18.26) tourist menu gives a wider choice. A bargain feature is the 60F ($13.70) special, including mussels or an omelet, fish or chicken, plus a dessert. The inn opens at the end of March, closing in mid-October. It is also shut on Tuesdays in the off-season months.

Hôtel du Mouton Blanc (tel. 60-14-08) is a village house complex converted into a restaurant on its lower floors, with 20 bedrooms available for overnighters upstairs. Tables are set not only inside, which is decorated in the rustic Norman fashion, but outside on the terrace overlooking the sea.

True to the pattern of the restaurants of Mont Saint-Michel, the omelet is offered along with fruits de mer ("fruits of the sea"). Three fixed-priced meals are featured, at 42F ($9.59), 60F ($13.70), and 100F ($22.83). The 35F ($8) meal gives you an assortment of fruits of the sea, including oysters, coquillages (small shellfish), langoustines, and crevettes (prawns), roast chicken with pommes frites, plus dessert. A double room with private bath or shower costs anywhere from 90F ($20.55) to 145F ($33.10), dropping to just 50F ($11.42) in a bathless room. The inn is closed from mid-November to mid-December and from January 1 to mid-February.

Croix-Blanche & Belle-Vue ("White Cross & Beautiful View") (tel. 60-14-04) offers splendid dining rooms overlooking the water; you can almost smell the clean sea air. A Norman inn, it is pleasantly decorated in a provincial manner, with a beamed ceiling and tiny tables. The four set meals include many of the chef's specialties. A three-course lunch begins at 28F ($6.39), ranging upward to 45F ($10.27) and 50F ($11.42). You get the most value for the 50F ($11.42) meal, which offers, or did on one recent occasion, a choice of moules (mussels) marinières or an omelet Mont Saint-Michel, a selection of fruits of the sea, followed by roast lamb with white beans, then the Camembert cheese of Normandy, topped off by a tarte de maison. With your meal, we'd suggest a half bottle of Réserve. Doubles with bath range from 85F ($19.41) to 110F

($25.11), dropping to 70F ($15.98) with hot and cold running water. All the accommodations have been renovated, most of them furnished in a rustic style.

READER'S HOTEL SELECTION: "At **Avranches,** the nearest town to Mont St.-Michel, we found a delightful little inn on the town square where the memorial to General Patton is erected on U.S. territory. At the **Auberge Saint-Michel,** 7 Place Général-Patton (tel. 58-01-91), we had a double room for 120F ($27.40), which included a bath and W.C. Cheaper doubles, containing only a washbasin and a bidet, rent for 68F ($15.52). In the little dining room we ate a sumptuous meal, consisting of vegetable soup, pâté with bread, pickles, mussels, lamb chops, beans, tossed salad, a choice of 12 cheeses, apple cider, chocolate cake—for the cost of 40F ($9.13). It was one of the most complete meals we ate during our entire trip, and was delightfully served in the French fashion" (George L. McClintock Jr., Bethel Park, Pa.).

A Rustic Norman Farmhouse

If the casinos of Deauville or the tides of Mont Saint-Michel have begun to bore you, head for the rustic splendor of **La Verte Campagne,** Hameau Chevalier par Trelly (Manche) (tel. 47-65-33), about 30 miles north of Mont Saint-Michel. Take Route D7 north from Avranches to Lengronne and follow the signs north from town. A small road winds through groves and orchards bringing you to a white wooden barrier with an old farmhouse just beyond. You are welcomed by friendly dogs and a gentle donkey, but mainly by Madame Meredith, the gracious lady of the manor.

The farmhouse is timbered and entirely renovated, the decoration sumptuous, with antiques and lots of brass utensils. The bar is so comfortable that you may drink just a little too much of the lightly alcoholic apple cider without even noticing it (the cider, incidentally, is made next door on an old-fashioned cider press). The family cooking is excellent. The atmosphere is comfortably formal —a place where you feel you may be expected to dress for dinner, but don't mind doing so. On a 40F ($9.13) set menu, you can order, for example, consommé fermier (a true vegetable soup), lamb chops (from pré-salé lamb), plus apple pie. If you're spending the night, ask for the "splurge" bedroom at 190F ($43.38), offering red carpeting, curtains, bedcover, and vanity—everything in harmony with the pink "Vichy" pattern. Standard doubles cost 85F ($19.41). Based on double occupancy in one of these rooms, the pension rate is 150F ($34.26) per person; demi-pension, 120F ($27.40) per person. The farmhouse is closed from January 5 to February 5.

14. Pont-l'Évêque

Famous for its cheese since the 13th century, Pont l'Évêque, 11 miles from Lisieux, was severely damaged during the liberation of Normandy from the Nazis in 1944. Fortunately, the historic **Hostellerie de l'Aigle d'Or,** 68 rue des Vaucelles (tel. 64-06-21), was spared. An inn on this spot dates back to that epic year 1066. However, the present "Golden Eagle" is from the 16th century, when it was a stagecoach house. The Norman courtyard of the period has also been preserved. Go here for the outstanding, delicate cuisine of Madame Castelain. Her place is a friendly, inviting setting, with lots of pots and pans used for decor and (in summer) flowers placed everywhere. Offering a set menu for 90F ($20.55), she cooks chicken on a string swinging and spinning before the fire, prepares stuffed mussels, and does shrimp in the Norman style; she even features a specialty, lobster Castellain. The inn is closed from October 1 to May 1.

If you like the town you might want to stay over at **Le Lion d'Or,** 8 Place du Calvaire (tel. 64-00-38), which is attractive and charming, but often heavily booked for what the French call *le weekend.* It also serves good food, a set meal costing 45F ($10.27), although it's easy to spend at least 70F ($15.98). This Lion roars not too far from the railway station. The rooms are modestly furnished, well kept, and comfortable. Expect to pay 62F ($14.15) in a single, 180F ($41.09) in a double. Only four of the 16 rooms contain private baths. The hotel shuts down in December, January, and on off-season Wednesdays.

15. Deauville

This resort has always been associated with the famous. For example, Coco Chanel began her career here in the summer of 1913, opening a boutique selling tiny hats. The grand ladies of her day paraded by under the weight of fruits and flowers. "How can the mind breathe under those things?" she asked. That isn't the problem today. Bare heads, bare feet, bare virtually anything is de rigueur during the day. However, the briefest bikini-wearers often don evening dress for nocturnal activities, including concerts, ballets, or the casino nightclub where some of the major headliners in all of Europe appear in high season.

Parasols dot the beach, and beauties abound, especially in August. Many bathers just walk up and down the slat boards to see and be seen, dropping in occasionally for an apéritif at **Le Bar du Soleil.** One French countess confided that she diets for four months straight before making her summer appearance on the sands of Deauville. The **Plage Fleurie** is a beach aptly named, studded with bright flowers. The rich, the celebrated flock to Deauville in August, enjoying its golden sands.

The mayor of Deauville frankly conceded to the press, "We are looking for the élite, not the masses." Once the resort of Trouville, built in the days of Louis Philippe, was the most fashionable place to go—until 1866, when the Duc de Morny, a half-brother of Napoleon III, crossed the Touques River and founded Deauville, which quickly replaced the other resort with the fickle arbiters of taste. With its golf courses, its casino, its deluxe hotels, its racing season (two tracks: **La Touques** and **Clairefontaine**), its regattas, its yachting harbor, its polo grounds, its tennis courts, whatever, Deauville is a formidable contender for the business of the smart crowd. Though dress, customs, lifestyles, and morality have changed, Deauville has never completely left the Edwardian era in which it reached its zenith.

Launched in the 1920s, the **Casino d'Été,** open from mid-March to mid-September, is the heart of the nighttime complex, complete with the super-expensive, scarlet-flamed **Le New Brummell's** nightclub, as well as the superb but high-priced **Casino Grill Room** and the **Ambassadeurs** restaurant. You pay an 18F ($4.11) fee to enter the casino, but that merely gets you across the threshold.

Since 1959, the **Winter Casino** has been open from mid-September to mid-March. Its restaurant-cabaret, **La Malibran,** and **Ciro's,** for lunch only, are right on the beach.

Deauville casinos attract such celebrities as Elizabeth Taylor, Gregory Peck, Gunther Sachs, and Sydney Chaplin.

If you don't want to go swimming at the beach, you can visit the $2-million **La Piscine.** Opened to the public in 1966, the Olympic pool is 150 feet long. Entrance fee is 15F ($3.42), increasing to 20F ($4.57) on Sundays and holidays. In July and August, the price goes up to 20F ($4.57) daily and 25F ($5.71) on

Sundays and holidays. The tab includes a cabin and the use of a chair. Special prices are quoted for those under 18 years of age.

A DELUXE TRIO OF HOTELS: Normandy, rue Mermoz (tel. 88-09-21), is the largest of the deluxe hotel coterie that includes the Royal and the Hôtel du Golf, all of which are owned by the casino interests. To us, the Normandy is the most interesting—a block-long structure built to resemble a Norman village, with turrets, gables, and tiny windows peeking out of high-sloping roofs. Opposite the casino, this year-round hotel opens onto a park of trimmed shrubs, beds of red geraniums, tennis courts, and lawns.

The interior is as comfortable as a vast rambling country house. The many reception rooms are furnished in a warm manner. Activity centers around the main rotunda, which is encircled by a colonnade of marble pillars, and the dark-paneled drinking lounge, where in August you might even run into Gunther Sachs and his friends. Bedrooms are furnished with antiques or reasonably good reproductions.

The price of a room is determined by its view and its size, a double ranging in price from 340F ($77.62) to 600F ($136.98), including breakfast but not the 15% service charge. Full-pension terms of 150F ($34.26) per person in addition to the room tariff are granted for a minimum stay of five days. A complete luncheon or dinner costs about 30F ($6.85). Lunches are served in the dining room and in the open-air restaurant, where you dine under umbrellas.

Royal, Boulevard Eugène Cornuché (tel. 88-16-41), is also impressive. Adjoining the Casino, it occupies a key position, fronting a block-wide park between the hotel and the water. High-trimmed yew hedges are arranged to make various terrace levels for lawns and flower beds. The Royal is like a great regal palace, providing grandiose living for big spenders.

Each of its rooms—some mammoth-size—contains a private bath (some have showers, no tubs), the price of the accommodations varying widely according to room views and plumbing. The bedrooms are decorated with period furniture, with matching floral cretonne fabrics, loomed carpets, and (in some) spacious sitting-room areas fronting the ocean.

Open from Easter, and until the end of September, the *grand luxe résidence* charges from 350F ($79.91) for its simplest doubles with shower and toilet all the way to a peak 550F ($125.57) for doubles with complete bath and private balcony or terrace. A single begins at 275F ($62.78), going up to 420F ($95.89) with complete bath. Dinner, beginning in price at 120F ($27.40), is served in the elegant, highly stylized dining room with its period chairs, sparkling crystal, and wall of arched mirrored doors. In fair weather, lunch is provided on the terrace or lawn as well.

Hôtel du Golf, at New-Golf, 1½ miles from Deauville on D278 (tel. 88-19-01), is for sporting fans. Seemingly transplanted from some eastern U.S. resort area such as the Adirondacks, it is a focal point for golfers. A colossal mock-Norman structure with a beamed façade, this hotel adjoins the grassy golf course itself and is near the race track and stadium. Open at Easter, Whitsun, and from May through September, it charges 300F ($68.49) in a single, from 600F ($136.98) in a double. The furnishings are comfortable but set no design pace. Meals are served discreetly in the gracious dining room, where large-paned windows overlook the country setting. Guests gather in the tavern-style drinking lounge, relaxing in armchairs and exchanging golf scores.

BUDGET AND MEDIUM-PRICED HOTELS: Le Nid d'Été, 121 Avenue de la République (tel. 88-36-67). Success has done much to change this once-private villa opening onto Deauville's major boulevard. Originally a simple structure with a mansard roof covering a timbered and plaster façade, it has been expanded in front to make room for a rustic-style dining room which attracts many to its precincts. A woodshed at the rear has been converted to provide more dining and lounge space. With its fireplace, it, too, has a rural aura. A small rear garden has become an enclosed courtyard, and the former servants' quarters have been converted into studio bedrooms.

The hospitality of the Chanet family has made them many friends, who appreciate their uniqueness and informality. They work well together, sheltering their visitors in accommodations nicely equipped with reproductions of regional antiques. Based on double occupancy with private baths, the full-pension rate per person is 150F ($34.26); demi-pension, 130F ($29.68). In a bathless room, one person pays 135F ($30.82) for full pension, only 125F ($28.54) for half pension. For 60F ($13.70), a four-course meal is offered, including tax and service. There is another set meal, with fewer courses, for 29F ($6.62). The inn is open from April 1 to October 1.

"La Fresnaye," 81 Avenue de la République (tel. 88-09-71), is an upper-class private villa turned pension-hotel. Set back from the busy boulevard, about six blocks from the beach, the stone, brick, and timbered building is a crazy quilt of architecture, with towers, cupolas, and bays. At the rear of the house an area is set aside for parking in a tree-shaded garden.

Family-owned, "La Fresnaye" is managed by a gracious woman who speaks English; a bevy of town women are employed as chambermaids and waitresses. Since it was once a private villa, the bedrooms are of various sizes, the most expensive with private bath costing 260F ($59.36), including breakfast, tax, and service. A few bathless doubles go for a low of 130F ($29.68), with bathless singles costing 75F ($17.12). Breakfast is the only meal served, at 13F ($2.97) per person. On the main floor are a front parlor and a dining room opening onto the rear garden.

UPPER-BRACKET RESTAURANTS: Ciro's, Promenade des Planches (tel. 88-18-10). Should you arrive on your yacht, chances are you'll have lunch here. You couldn't get much closer to the water, or be more chic. Ciro's provides the best seafood in Deauville—it's expensive, but worth it. Tables are placed on two levels; both have walls of glass allowing a fine view of the sea. You can make your lobster selection from a tank as you enter. A specialty is an omelet with langouste (lobster), which many French people select to begin their repast. Favorite fish dishes are braised sole Ciro's or braised turbot with fresh vegetables. Among the meat selections, the piccata de veau Normande is excellent. Fish dishes are priced at 35F ($7.99) to 80F ($18.26), meat dishes are around 60F ($13.70), and desserts are 20F ($4.57).

Augusto, 27 rue Desire-le-Hoc (tel. 88-34-49), is an intimate, friendly bistro with a typical Norman cuisine. The restaurant is intimate with two attractively decorated dining rooms, the first with silk-covered walls, the second with a nautically inspired décor. The specialty is lobster, although other fresh seafood is available every day, including fresh shrimp, oysters, and baby crayfish. Mr. LeBreton took over from the former owner in 1974 and has maintained very high standards for cuisine and service. His culinary creations include a terrine de turbot in a green sauce, 48F ($10.96); mussels with sorrel and cream sauce, 32F ($7.31); stuffed oysters, 52F ($11.87); stuffed sole with lobster coulis, 58F ($13.24), and suprême of turbot with champagne sauce, 65F

($14.84). Lobster is prepared in a number of tempting ways—grilled with American sauce, à la Nage, in sauce Corail, in feuilleté, or with garlic sauce. It's priced according to weight and tends to be super-expensive. The restaurant is closed in January and February, and on Monday and Tuesday from September to June.

BUDGET BRASSERIES: Le Petit Vatel, 129 Avenue de la République (tel. 88-21-56), is a simple place offering good food at low prices. It's really a bistro with a bar on one side and dining tables on the other. The tables overflow onto the sidewalk, in the typical French fashion. The location is central but not chic, on the main boulevard of Deauville, overlooking a park. Open from Easter to October, it offers a set meal for 38F ($8.68), good value considering the quality. A typical menu might include a choice of pâtés, followed by coq au vin, plus a salad or a cheese selection, as well as dessert. A more elaborate meal is presented at 60F ($13.70). Service is an additional 15%.

Chez Miocque (Bar Cintra), 81 rue Eugène-Colas (tel. 88-21-52), is a bustling brasserie-café, doing a brisk business at sidewalk café tables. Right in the core of Deauville, Chez Miocque is within sight of the Casino, the luxurious Normandy, and the fashionable boutiques. Its owner is known simply as Jack. He's an American from New York City, and he'll welcome you for lunch or dinner, or for only a drink. His average price for a complete dinner (without wine) is about $15 (U.S.). We'd recommend his fish of the day at $9, his pepper steak at $10, his sole meunière at $9, and his tarte Tantin at $3.

DEAUVILLE BY NIGHT: Facing Chez Miocque, the disco **Gainsborough,** 92 rue Eugène Colas, is among the most popular at the resort, attracting an extremely handsome crowd. It is open on weekends, drawing a patronage of both young and older dancers. The entrance fee is 30F ($6.85) on weekends, and an alcoholic drink goes for around 45F ($10.27).

BRITTANY

THE OLD PEOPLE may be fading away, but while they live, so will the past. In the northwestern corner of France, in the ancient province and duchy of Brittany, the Bretons stubbornly hold onto their traditions. True, the young people head for Paris for "a better life," and the men who returned from World War II brought "alarming" new ideas. Nevertheless, deep in the heart of the interior, called l'Argoat, the old folks quietly live in stone farmhouses, with much the same ideas their grandparents had. The older women, at least on special occasions, still can be seen wearing their starched lace headdresses.

The Breton language is still spoken, better understood by Welshmen and the Cornish folk than by the French. Sadly, it may die out altogether, in spite of attempts by folklore groups to keep it alive. In that sense, Brittany is the Wales of France.

Conquered by Caesar in 56 B.C., the land was once called Armorica. However, the Celtic inhabitants of the British Isles, the Britons, crossed the Channel in 500 A.D., fleeing from the invading Angles and Saxons.

The true Bretons—except those whose parents married "foreigners" from Paris—are generally darker and shorter than their compatriots in France. These characteristics reflect their Celtic origin, which still lives on in superstition, folklore, and fairy tales. Breton *pardons* are famous. These are religious festivals, sometimes attracting thousands of pilgrims who turn up in traditional dress.

Nearly every hamlet has its own *pardon*. These observances are major attractions, drawing the French from as far away as Marseille and Scots from Glasgow. The best-known ones are on May 19 at **Treguier** (honoring St. Yves, who consoled the poor and righted wrongs); on the second Sunday in July at **Locronan** (in the footsteps of St. Ronan); on July 26 at **St.-Anne-d'Auray** (honoring the "mothers of Bretons"); and on September 8 at **Le Folgoet** (commemorating *ar foll coat*, or that "idiot of the forest").

Many Bretons consider themselves a nation within a nation. Movements for independence—particularly strong in the 19th century—come and go. Brittany was joined with the crown of France through Anne of Brittany's marriages to Charles VIII and later to Louis XII.

Traditionally, the province is divided into **Haute-Bretagne** and **Basse-Bretagne**. The rocky coastline, some 750 miles long, is studded with promontories, coves, and occasional beaches. Like the prow of a ship, Brittany projects into the sea. Hence, the province gives France its best sailors. The interior, however, is a land of sleepy hamlets, stone-built farms, and moors covered with yellow broom and purple heather. First-time visitors to the craggy peninsula would be better advised to stick to the coastline, where salt-meadow sheep can be seen grazing along pasture land whipped by sea breezes. Those leaving Mont Saint-Michel can center at the trio of tourist towns, St.-Malo, Dinan, or Dinard. Coming from the château country, visitors can explore the South Brittany coastline.

The province is rich in seafood, the mainstay of its diet, including Aulne salmon, pike (best with white butter), scallops, trout, winkles, cockles, spiny lobsters; and Lorient sardines. Of course, the pré-salé (salt-meadow lamb) is the best meat course, traditionally served with white beans. The finest artichokes come from Roscoff, the most succulent strawberries from Plougastel. Nearly every village has its own crêperie, specializing in those paper-thin pancakes with an infinite variety of fillings. Buckwheat griddlecakes are another popular item. The foodstuff is washed down with Breton cider (admittedly inferior to the Norman variety, but quite good nevertheless). Unlike much of France, the province lacks wine, except muscadet, a light white wine produced from the vineyards around the old Breton capital of Nantes in the lower Loire Valley.

Assuming you're beginning your exploration after leaving the Loire, your first major stopover will be uncharacteristic of Brittany:

1. Nantes

In western France, Nantes is the largest town of Brittany, though in spirit it seems to belong more to the château country along the Loire. The mouth of the Loire is about 30 miles away, and at Nantes the river divides into several branches. Nantes spreads itself over these Loire islands, though it lies mostly on the north bank. A commercial and industrial city, it is a busy port which suffered great damage in World War II. The city is famous for the Edict of Nantes, sponsored by Henri IV in 1598, guaranteeing religious freedom to Protestants (it was later revoked). Many famous people have lived here, from Molière to Madame de Sévigné to Stendhal to Michelet.

The **Cathedral of St. Pierre**, begun in 1434, wasn't finished until the closing years of the 19th century, yet it remained harmonious architecturally, a rare feat of which few European cathedrals can boast. The façade is characterized by two square towers, but it is the interior which is more impressive. It is 335 feet long. Its pièce de résistance is the Renaissance masterpiece of Michel

Colomb—the tomb of François II, Duke of Brittany, and his second wife, Marguerite de Foix. There is yet another impressive work of art, also a tomb, that of General Juchault de Lamoricière, a native of Nantes and a great African campaigner. The work is by the sculptor Paul Dubois, completed in 1879.

Between the cathedral and the Loire stands the second major sight of Nantes, the **Ducal Château,** once the seat of the dukes of Brittany. It was here that the previously mentioned Edict of Nantes was signed. The castle was founded in either the 9th or 10th century, although François II had it rebuilt in 1466 for Duchess Anne. It is flanked by large towers and a bastion. The Duchesse de Berry was imprisoned here, as was Gilles de Retz, known as "Bluebeard," who confessed to more than 100 murders.

Behind its walls the government has installed two museums—a **Museum of Decorative Arts** in the Grand Logis or southwest wing and a **Museum of Popular Regional Art** in the Grand Gouvernement building. Exhibits include a Breton house, costumes, arts and crafts, and wrought ironwork. The château and its museums are open daily except Tuesdays from 10 a.m. to noon and from 2 to 5 p.m., charging 4F (91¢) for admission (free on weekends).

If time remains, you might want to visit the **Musée des Beaux-Arts** on the rue Gambetta, east of the Place du Maréchal-Foch. It is one of the most interesting provincial galleries of art in western France, containing an unusually fine collection of sculptures and paintings, accenting the French modern schools. Sculpture and temporary exhibitions are displayed on the ground floor. See Ingres's portrait of Madame de Senonnes, a painting by Courbet, plus works by Delacroix and Georges de la Tour, and *Two Saints* by Bergognone. There are also examples from the Italian and Spanish schools, including works by Murillo, Ribera, Caravaggio, Andrea del Sarto, and even Botticelli. See also the collection of modern paintings, including works by Kandinsky, Hartung, Poliakoff, and Gorin. The museum is open daily except Tuesdays from 9:15 a.m. to 12:30 and from 1:30 to 6 p.m., charging 4F (91¢) for admission.

Of minor interest, the **Palais Dobrée** is a town mansion from the 19th century that was built by an important collector in Nantes, from whom the palace takes its name. It stands alongside the manor of Jean de la Touche from the 15th century, where the bishops of Nantes occasionally lived. Both buildings are museums, containing a varied collection gathered by Monsieur Dobrée, including prehistoric and medieval antiquities, along with Flemish paintings from the 15th century and many ecclesiastical relics. The museum is open daily except Tuesday from 10 a.m. to noon and from 2 to 5 p.m., charging 3F (68¢) for admission. The museum is in the vicinity of the Place Graslin, near the attractive Cours Cambronne.

Jules Verne, the French novelist (*Around the World in Eighty Days*), was born in Nantes in 1828, and literary fans like to seek out his house at 4 rue de Clisson in the Île Feydeau.

HOTELS: **Sofitel Nantes,** rue Alexandre, Île Beaulieu (tel. 47-61-03), stands on an island surrounded by the Loire. Five minutes from the heart of town and the railway station, it offers 100 well-furnished chambers that are a model of efficient hotel-planning. In fact, this chain hotel is the best place to stay in town for those seeking the most up-to-date amenities and modernity. Singles pay from 220F ($50.23) to 260F ($59.36); doubles, 260F ($59.36) to 300F ($68.49). All the rooms come with complete modern baths. The restaurant and bar, La Pecherie, offers a wide choice of seafood and fish dishes, with meals costing from 80F ($18.26) to 150F ($34.26). In addition, the hotel has a swimming pool with a lounging terrace, plus tennis courts.

Hôtel Central, 4 rue du Couëdic (tel. 20-09-35), is another excellent choice—*très confortable,* as the French say. The hotel has a discreet exterior and offers rooms that are pleasantly and agreeably decorated. In a single, expect to pay from 174F ($39.72), that tariff rising to 217F ($49.54) in a double. The Rôtisserie Crémaillère at the Central is a good dining choice. It does well-prepared grills, among other offerings. We recently enjoyed a crayfish bisque, a quiche Nantes-style, and a sorbet with muscadet. Such standard international fare is featured as minute steak, veal escalope Milanese, and steak tartare, a very popular choice. Menus run from 80F ($18.26) to 120F ($27.40).

France, 24 rue Crébillon (tel. 73-57-91), is right in the center, near the river. It's recommended for a suitable overnight stop, although you may find some of its rooms noisy. Furnishings are in the neat, clean, modern style, and the cost goes from 96F ($21.92) in a single to 210F ($47.94) in a double. The bar is pleasantly charming, and a tea salon is more formal. The restaurant is of good size and serves a top-notch set dinner for just 60F ($13.70).

Alternatively, you may prefer the comparable **Graslin,** 1 rue Piron (tel. 71-35-61), which doesn't have a restaurant, however. The hotel lies on a steep old street near the harbor. It is utterly unpretentious but, again, suitable for an overnight stop if you're economizing. Singles rent for 50F ($11.42), the cost going up to 95F ($21.69) in a double, a good bargain for Nantes. Only a few of the rooms contain private baths or showers, and these are grabbed up first.

RESTAURANTS: La Rôtisserie, Place Aristide-Briand (tel. 71-27-08), is filled with loyal, well-heeled Breton patrons who demand—and get!—gourmet food. Do not come to sample young Jean-Claude Thomzeau's cuisine expecting dainty, delicate fare served in petite portions. People dine in a long, lingering fashion, selecting their favorite seats and making an evening of it, or at least an afternoon. The restaurant deserves its good reputation.

From October to March, the dish to order is Breton scallops prepared with sherry, a splendid selection; or you may, alternatively, prefer the sole with vermouth. The menu changes with the season. For example, you might sample a leg of duckling with red currants or a galantine of turbot with pistachio nuts. For a smooth beginning, try foie gras de canard with apple, or a pâté of mussels with a brochette of scallops. À la carte diners can expect to pay from 120F ($27.40) to 150F ($34.26). The restaurant is closed on Sundays and for the annual August vacation.

Les Maraîchers, 21 rue Fouré (tel. 47-06-51), attracts those seeking lighter fare than the traditional cuisine served in most of the city's leading restaurants. The domain of Monsieur Pacreau, it offers food of exceptional quality, and locals debate endlessly and needlessly as to which restaurant offers the best cuisine, La Rôtisserie or Les Maraîchers. Both are good—they are just different. In a modern atmosphere, you can enjoy near-perfection or perfection in some dishes—steamed scallops, a salad of mussels, the foie gras of the house, grilled lobster, aiguillettes de caneton (duckling). Each dish, even a simple turbot, comes out of the kitchen as an original and imaginatively prepared concoction. Dining à la carte can easily run up your tab to 120F ($27.40) to 190F ($43.38). The restaurant is closed from September 1 to 23, for Saturday lunch and on Mondays.

Coq Hardi, 22 allée du Charcot, near the railway station (tel. 74-14-25), is the domain of Albert Athimon who is known for two accomplishments—his bass in the famous beurre blanc sauce and his canard du Muscadet. On a busy promenade near the river, this top-grade restaurant offers you a chance to dine in a refined, modern atmosphere, enjoying well-prepared dishes and formal, polite service. Menus go from 60F ($13.70) to 85F ($19.41), or at around 100F ($22.83) if you're ordering à la carte. The restaurant closes on Saturday and July 1-15.

In our search for the restaurant that serves the best meal in town at a low cost, we found **Petit Saint-Jean**, 9 rue Lapérouse (tel. 48-29-97), which offers one for 35F ($7.99). In unpretentious surroundings, you dine very well indeed here, enjoying regional specialties and a lot of dishes made with products of the sea, such as fish soup and shellfish. Lying right off the Place Royale, a beautiful square laid out in 1790, this bright restaurant concentrates on good, filling fare, and does so without a lot of fuss. If you elect to dine à la carte, your cost could go up to 80F ($18.26). The restaurant, regrettably, is closed on weekends and takes a long vacation from December 15 to January 15.

About five miles east of the city, on Route N751, near Basse-Goulaine, stands an exceptionally good little restaurant, **Mon Rève** (tel. 54-90-10). People of Nantes have been coming to this place for years, knowing they can dine well in a parklike setting with a rose garden. The chef, Ryngel Gerard, and his wife took over operation of Mon Rève in 1979 and have given free rein to the talent and inventiveness they showed previously in a four-star restaurant near Nantes. Monsieur Gerard produces such dishes as the fresh Loire salmon steak, wild duck with Bourjeuil sauce, and delicious pastries. He also makes the famous beurre blanc sauce, a specialty of Brittany. Menus are offered for 80F ($18.26), although you can spend at least 150F ($34.26) ordering à la carte. The restaurant is closed on Sunday nights and 15 days in February.

2. La Baule

Founded in the heyday of the Victorian seaside craze back in 1879, La Baule remains as fresh and inviting as the Gulf Stream that warms the waters of its wide, five-mile-long, crescent-shaped, white sandy beach—considered by many (and not just hoteliers) as the finest in Europe. It's in a bikini-for-bikini race with Biarritz for supremacy as the most fashionable resort on the Atlantic Coast, itself occupying a strip known as the Côte d'Amour ("Coast of Love").

That Prince of Gamblers François André founded the casino and the major resort hotels, claiming later that a hound tricked him by showing him the beach in fair weather and that La Baule, despite his considerable investment, was a losing proposition. However, his name is forever linked to the success of the resort. The weather is most unpredictable. Pines grow on the dunes. On the outskirts, Easter-egg villas, landscaped with honeysuckle, jasmine, pomegranates, figs, and palms, draw the wealthy chic in season, this lasting from the end of June till mid-September. Should you arrive at any other time, you might have La Baule to yourself. The movie stars go to Deauville or Cannes, La Baule drawing more of a middle-class clientele. But the wealthy with quiet money still come here, as the yachts in the harbor testify. Tennis, golf, and sailing are popular along the coast, which was used as the setting for the Jacques Tati film *M. Hulot's Holiday*.

Of course, there's the inevitable casino, which often books top talent.

This South Breton resort is still essentially French, drawing only a nominal string of sun-seeking foreigners. It lies 49 miles west of Nantes, the old capital of the dukes of Brittany.

HOTELS: Everything is here, from palatial digs to a simple villa. First—

Deluxe Living

Hermitage, Esplanade du Casino (tel. 60-37-00), is the regal palace of this beach kingdom. Impressively built seven stories high and studded with red balconies, it occupies a dominant position on the beach. The upper three floors, with green timbers, are a mélange of gables and dormers. Ornate and plush, the interior is in direct contrast to the casual beach.

The air-conditioned bedrooms, each with a marble or tiled private bath, are furnished with reproductions of English and French antiques. Several rooms have been transformed into the modern style. There is no shabby grandeur here; everything is kept up to a high standard. In July and August, a double room with bath costs 580F ($132.41) with a sea view, dropping to 350F ($79.91) if it opens onto the garden in the rear. Pension costs from 400F ($91.32) to 600F ($136.98) per person daily, and a 15% service charge is added to all tabs.

The Hermitage offers a choice of three dining places: a beach terrace, a grill, and a main dining room with arched windows, paneled ceilings, and glittering chandeliers. Behind the scenes is a corps of white-hatted chefs turning out top-drawer cuisine. The main drawing room is conservatively modern. A heated seawater pool is another facility. The Hermitage is open from May to October. Under the same management is an 18-hole golf course and 28 tennis courts.

Castel Marie Louise, Esplanade du Casino (tel. 60-20-60), is a Breton manor house (part of the Relais de Campagne chain) providing imaginative living in a pine-park estate along the oceanfront. Seemingly created as a private, overscale villa for some wealthy person, the stone-built, gabled castle now offers plush living for vacationers all year round except in January. The public rooms, including a salon for drinks, are furnished tastefully in the French provincial style, with mellow fruit woods set against autumnal colors. The wall tapestries depict stylized animals in brown and green.

Most of the 30 renovated accommodations on the upper floors come with private balconies; two rooms are in a tower. Furnishings reflect several styles, including Louis XV, Directoire, and rustic. In high season, from July 1 till the end of August, full pension ranges from 390F ($89.04) to 490F ($111.86) per person; off-season, 300F ($68.49) per person. These rates include taxes but not the 15% service charge. The excellent chef is reason enough to stay here; even if you aren't a guest, you may want to stop for a meal. Specialties include a terrine de caneton (duckling) aux pistaches at 30F ($6.85); nine oysters, 50F ($11.42); and grilled turbot in white butter at 60F ($13.70). A set meal is offered for 98F ($22.37).

The Middle Bracket

Alexandra, 3 Boulevard d'Armor (tel. 60-30-06), is one of the best of the modern hotels in the center of La Baule. Right on the oceanfront, the Alexandra boasts eight floors of ultramodern bedrooms with all-glass walls opening onto private balconies facing the beach. An open-air terrace with umbrellas and sidewalk tables, plus planters of flowers and greenery, set it off from the coastal road. The ninth-floor solarium is a popular spot for drinks or coffee, guests sitting under parasols.

Although the second-floor dining room is exposed through glass to the ocean, and the drinking lounge is *intime* with tufted velour chairs, the bedrooms are the best feature. In subdued white and oyster-gray, the sleek furnishings stand on forest-green carpets, with filmy curtains screening off the blue Atlantic. In July and August, the full-pension rate per person is 250F ($57.08) to 285F ($65.07), decreasing 10% in low season; these rates include service and taxes. The hotel is open from March 15 to October 15.

The Budget Range

Helios, 7 Boulevard d'Armor (tel. 60-22-38). The welcome is typically French, and the owner, who worked for several years at the Grand Hotel in Paris, speaks English. Facing the sea, this pleasant budget hotel has two glass doors opening into the lobby, whose walls are covered with a Toile de Jouy tapestry. A little sitting corner is furnished with rustic tables and chairs. From the lobby you ascend to the dining room, which is large with windows opening right onto the water in summer. The walls are covered with the same Toile de Jouy as the lobby. The furniture is Breton-rustic. The bedrooms are furnished without any particular originality but in a functional style, and they're kept clean and comfortable. Doubles with private showers or baths range from 145F ($33.10) to 170F ($38.81). All rooms are for two persons. Depending on the room, the full-pension rate ranges from 135F ($30.82) to 185F ($42.24) per person. The hotel is open from April 1 until the end of September.

Parc, Avenue des Albatros (tel. 60-24-52), is another "Hansel and Gretel" house, in a pine-studded residential setting, a short walk from the beach and the casino. It's a true French bourgeois villa, seemingly built around the turn of the century, of rugged fieldstone. The hotel is managed competently, the owner taking special care of guests. Open only during the season (closed in winter), the Parc charges 120F ($27.40) per person for a room with private bath, plus all three meals. In a bathless room the full-pension rate is 110F ($25.11) per person. Bedrooms are bright and cheerful and kept immaculately clean. Very good and somewhat bountiful meals are served on the veranda. Nonresidents pay 60F ($13.70) for a set meal.

THE BEST RESTAURANT: L'Espadon ("The Swordfish"), 2 Avenue de la Plage (tel. 60-05-63). Perched atop a tall apartment building complex, the most elegant of La Baule's restaurants overlooks the town and its beaches. The ambience is contemporary chic, the food excellent, the service traditional. Three set meals are offered: a club menu at 48F ($10.96), a tourist one at 80F ($18.26), and a gastronomic repast at 220F ($50.23). À la carte, you might begin with moules (mussels) à la crème at 35F ($7.99), then follow with suprême de St.-Pierre soufflé à l'oseille at 62F ($14.15), or perhaps grilled bass with fennel or fricassée de homard at about 170F ($38.81), or caneton au poivre vert at 62F ($14.15). For dessert, we'd most heartily recommend the fraises Romanoff at 30F ($6.85) or the succès glacé Espadon au coulis de fraises, 30F also.

3. Carnac

In May and June the fields are resplendent with golden broom. Sometimes the good weather at this seaside resort continues into October. But aside from "sea and sail," Carnac, 62 miles southeast of Quimper, is one of the most important centers in the world for seeing evidence of the human race's prehistoric past. For there you'll find the famous **Field of Megaliths,** the huge stones, numbering in the hundreds, considered the most important prehistoric find in northern France. Their arrangement and placement, however, remain a mystery. At **Carnac Ville,** the **Miln et Le Rouzie Museum** (named after its founders, one a Scotsman) contains a number of prehistoric relics. It opens daily in summer from 8 a.m. to noon and from 1 to 7 p.m., charging 2F (46¢) for admission.

Even if Carnac didn't possess dolmens, cromlechs, and menhirs, its pine-studded sand dunes would be worth the trip. Protected by the Quiberon Peninsula, **Carnac-Plage** is lately developing into a family resort.

BUDGET LODGINGS AND MEALS: **Lann Roz,** 37 Avenue de la Poste (tel. 52-10-48), is built in the Breton manner and surrounded by a private garden of flowers and lawns. Within walking distance of the water, it's a good, inexpensive oasis for budget-minded visitors in search of a sea holiday. Family-owned and operated, Lann Roz is under the wing of Madame Le Calvez, who is friendly and hearty, inviting guests to sunbathe on the wide stone terrace opening off the family-style living room. Also fronting the garden is a typical Breton dining room, where Madame has instructed the cook to keep the meals regional and the portions generous. In high season, half-pension terms range from 100F ($22.83) to 135F ($30.82) per person per day. The hotel is closed from November 20 to December 20 and on Wednesdays off-season.

Ker Ihuel, 59 Boulevard Plage (tel. 52-11-38), is a modest villa with a white plaster façade, set amid pine trees in a residential area, directly on the coast road. On a raised stone terrace, garden furniture is set out for drinks and sunbathing. Across the road is a strip of dunes and a sandy beach. Sun and the ocean breezes pour into the bedroom windows. The Ker Ihuel is a genial family-run place, attracting the French who like an informal holiday. The interior lounge and dining room are decorated in a provincial Breton style, that theme extending to the bedrooms as well. The rooms contain showers or tubs, plus hot and cold running water in the basins, but the toilets are in the corridors. In July and August, the full-pension rate ranges from 150F ($34.26) to 170F ($38.81) per person, these tariffs lowered in May, June, and September. The higher price is for an accommodation with private bath. In high season, from June 1 to September 15, a minimum stay of three days is required. The hotel is open from April 1 to 20 and from mid-May to September 25.

Les Alignements, 45 rue Cornély (tel. 52-06-30), is a 27-room establishment where the mother does the cooking, the father the managing, and the graceful and lovely daughter the welcoming. The front is sober and pleasant enough; the back looks out onto a garden. Inside, everything blends and is clean and efficient. On the second and third floors rooms have balconies or loggias. Those facing the street have double windows to keep down the noise. For decoration wall tapestries have been used effectively and fabrics have been color-coordinated. Incidentally, the keys to the rooms are made of brown leather in the shape of fish. Full pension, which is required in July and August, ranges from 135F ($30.82) to 150F ($34.26) per person. Nonresidents are welcome to dine here, in a modern room with a rustic touch created by tiles and wooden walls. The price of the set menus ranges from 50F ($11.42) to 65F ($14.84). For the second price, we recently enjoyed Breton oysters followed by grilled crab. Delicious. The inn is open from mid-May until October 1.

4. Quiberon

A sardine-fishing port, Quiberon is also a noted South Breton resort with a large white sandy beach attracting "family affair" tourists. It's on a peninsula which was once an island, connected to the mainland by what has been called "a narrow tongue of alluvial deposits." Aside from the beach, the best local sight is the rugged Breton fishermen hauling in their sardine catch.

The entire coast—the **Côte Sauvage** ("Wild Coast")—is rugged, the ocean breaking with fury onto the reefs, its waves lashing against the jagged rock at the cliff's edge, then surging with a roar into the grottos eating into the shore-line. Fierce northern winds, especially in winter, lash across the sand dunes, shaving the short pines that grow there. On the landward side, however, the beach is calm and relatively protected.

HOTELS IN THE UPPER AND MEDIUM BRACKETS: Sofitel-Quiberon, Pointe de Goulvars (tel. 50-20-00), is a blockbuster of a beachside hotel, part of an aggressive chain that doesn't look back, preferring to go all out in the contemporary mode. The bedrooms have private balconies opening directly onto the sea or the rear plaza. A wall of glass—screened nightly by soft pastel draperies—seemingly brings the outdoors in. In muted colors, the bedrooms are tasteful, and each contains a shiny tiled bath. The rates depend on the placement of the accommodation, two persons paying anywhere from 500F ($114.15) to 630F ($143.83) for demi-pension. The hotel is closed in January.

Behind its wall of glass, the lounge is sun-drenched, the marigold carpeting picking up the brightness. A chic bar-lounge in aqua and walnut provides a social center for predinner drinks. If you don't want to swim in the Atlantic, there is a covered Olympic-size pool with an all-glass front facing the sea. The **Restaurant Thalassa**, overlooking the water, combines a sophisticated modern decor with the best of the viands at the resort. For 90F ($20.55), you can order a complete dinner. On the à la carte menu, costing around 135F ($30.82), specialties include nine fines belons (oysters), palourdes farcies (stuffed clams), and barbue (brill) grillée. The restaurant is closed from the first week in January to February 2.

Ker Noyal, rue de St.-Clement (tel. 50-08-41). Monsieur and Madame Tanguy have a good thing going here. In a well-planned and tended garden a short walk from the beach, they have created a hotel with an intimate country-club atmosphere. Graveled walks are bordered by brilliantly colored flowers, the grounds are studded with pine trees, and white garden furniture is set under pagoda-style parasols.

The rooms, in the main building of the older annex, overlook either the sea or garden—or both. The newer building has sun balconies with wrought-iron furniture. Each comfortable accommodation is tastefully outfitted in con-temporary style, kept light and airy. For a room with private bath, in high season, the full-pension rate peaks at 230F ($52.51), dropping to 165F ($37.68) for a bathless; these tariffs include service and taxes. Meals—a *cuisine soignée* —are served in one of two dining rooms, with a view of a walled-off garden of summer flowers. A set menu is offered for 85F ($19.41). Open from March 1 till the end of October.

Ty-Briez, 23 Boulevard Chanard (tel. 50-09-90), is a stone-built hotel right on the water. Its owner, Madame Le Bideau, is friendly and gracious and speaks English. The bedrooms are furnished in a homey, comfortable style, and many open onto sea views. The rate in a single is 70F ($15.98), going up to 170F ($38.81) for the most expensive double with bath. The hotel offers snacks in its crêperie, and there is a bar as well, plus a lounge furnished in the typical Breton style. The hotel shuts down at the end of September.

5. Belle-Île-en-Mer

From Quiberon, you can take an inexpensive steamer (several run daily) to Belle-Île, the largest island off the coast of southern Brittany. The cost is

35F ($7.99) per person, 122F ($27.85) for a small car. Or else you can take a guided tour, "Les Cars Bleus," costing 54F ($12.33) per person. In season it is necessary to book a day in advance. About 10 miles off the coast, the island is dramatically eerie with its rocky cliffs, reef-fringed west coast, its **Grotte de l'Apothicairerie,** and its general sense of isolation and seclusion from the world. Valleys cut through the ravines, wending their way to such small ports as **La Palais,** the point at which you dock.

In the days before he made the Sun King jealous and was overthrown, Fouquet, the finance minister, erected a château on the island, and much later the great actress Sarah Bernhardt enjoyed spending her summers at Belle Île, occupying a fort.

If you're not over on the day tour and would like to stay on the island, exploring it in more depth, you'll find excellent accommodations at—

PORT DE GOULPHAR: One of the most charming spots on the island, attracting thousands of nature-lovers in summer, this port on a narrow inlet is framed by cliffs. It lies on the southern shores of the island, the boats docking at Le Palais on the north.

Castel Clara (tel. 52-84-21) is a hotel of warmth and color—bright oranges, reds, rose tones, and forest green. At an enchanting spot, this complex seems to extend itself to the ocean. There are few places along the coast where guests can enjoy such peace along with ideal service and a first-class cuisine.

From the first of April until October, the hotel rents out 41 bedrooms with private marble baths, TV sets, and phones. Under paneled ceilings, the rooms are well furnished, and, as you pull back the draperies, you can walk out onto your own wide balcony with a view of the sea. Rates begin at 250F ($57.08) in a single, rising to 320F ($73.06) in a double. Half pension costs 250F ($57.08) to 330F ($75.34) per person in summer, and it's obligatory, incidentally.

If you're just visiting the island for the day in your car, you'll find good food served here, with menus priced at 60F ($13.71) to 65F ($14.85). A set menu is featured for 90F ($20.55), although it will easily cost from 110F ($25.11) if you choose to dine à la carte. The hotel also offers a large terrace with a solarium around a heated seawater swimming pool. The cozy bar is *très intime,* and there's even a playroom for children and a billiard table.

Manoir de Goulphar (tel. 52-83-95) is a creamy white building under a blue roof with a round tower. The hotel is built in a traditional style, lying on the Goulphar Harbor, which many have compared to a fjord in Norway. The rocky landscape on the wild coast makes for a tranquil setting for "Le Manoir," which, although modern, looks from a distance like a country estate.

A first-class hotel built in the 1970s, it offers 55 stylish bedrooms with private baths, toilets, and sunny balconies opening onto the Atlantic and the harbor at Goulphar. A single costs 60F ($13.70), rising to 130F ($29.68) in a double. Most guests stay here on the pension plan, ranging from 140F ($31.96) to 170F ($38.81) per person. The restaurant offers excellent service in a pleasant atmosphere, set menus costing 55F ($12.56), although you can also order à la carte for anywhere from 85F ($19.41) to 110F ($25.11) per person. The dining room opens onto views of the coast, and the public sitting rooms, under paneled ceilings, are semiluxurious. The hotel receives guests from March to September.

6. Hennebont

. On the outskirts of this once-fortified town split by the Blavet River is one of the most delightful accommodations in all of South Brittany. It lies three miles south of the town, on a private road off N781, and is called the—
Château de Locguénolé (tel. 76-29-06). A hilltop estate of 900 acres over-looking the tree-covered Blavet River valley, it is a stately château owned by the same family for more than 500 years. It's filled with antiques, tapestries, and paintings accumulated over the centuries. Madame de la Sablière doesn't use her family title, wanting to live for today, not in another era. Not too long ago, she persuaded her husband that in order to preserve and restore the château they should take in paying guests.

The word has gotten around, and discriminating clients, such as writers, painters, and statesmen, beat a path to her door. The drawing rooms and the petit salons are furnished with old pieces. You ask her about a painting in the corner drawing room. "That is Lafayette, he married my great-grandmother" (or did she say "great-great"?). "Yes, those are two Vernet paintings, and those tapestries in the dining room are from the 17th century."

The bedchambers vary widely in size and furnishings, the price difference depending not only on that but on the view and position of the room as well. In high season, from July 1 to August 31, the full-board rate per person ranges between 380F ($86.75) and 420F ($95.89), including service and taxes. The demi-pension rate ranges between 280F ($63.92) and 330F ($75.34) per person. A bath has been installed in each of the 38 accommodations, with decorative floral sprays and harmonious colors. While the second floor has great old bedrooms, the upper-floor accommodations—the converted maids' rooms— are also charming. Some of the rooms are in a converted Breton cottage.

Even if you can't stay here, it would be wise to call ahead and request a meal in the dining hall, decorated with a room-wide Aubusson tapestry. While sitting on Louis XVI red-velvet and cane chairs, you can order such specialties as filet de boeuf poele au foie gras frais, suprême de barbue (brill) with cider and leeks, and saumon (salmon) grillé. A set meal is offered at 125F ($28.54), but you can order à la carte, selecting a fine wine from the cellar. Closed between December 1 and February 1.

7. Quimperlé

Built on a hillside, Quimperlé offers a refreshing sojourn into the charm of a former age. Because of its unique situation—where two rivers, l'Isole and l'Ellée, meet to form the Laïta—it is called a paradise for fishermen. The salmon and trout are fairly abundant.

In the lower town, the Basse-Ville, is **St.-Croix,** a unique Romanesque church with an 11th-century crypt. Its Greek-cross plan is based on that of the Holy Sepulchre in Jerusalem. The hill overhanging the town like a sugarloaf gives it the nickname "Mont St.-Michel of the land."

About a mile away, the **Carnoët State Forest** is a setting for romantic horseback riding, with its towering trees recreating the mood of the legends of the Breton Bluebeard and of St. Maurice, that charmer of birds. Six and a half miles away you can explore the beaches with their hidden coves, enjoying the adventure of the sea and practicing sailing at the school at **Le Pouldu.**

FOOD AND LODGING: Hôtel de l'Hermitage, Route du Pouldu (tel. 96-04-66), is known as the Manoir (Manor) de Kerroch, and it still clings to a garden of about five acres, enclosed by an old stone wall. At the edge of a forest which very likely belonged to the manor at one time, it is 1½ miles from Quimperlé, reached via D49. You drive along the Laïta River, passing under a Roman-esque-style bridge, till you reach a creaky iron gate and a most tranquil setting. The Hermitage is a complex of three buildings, surrounded by rose bushes and cherry trees and with a heated swimming pool. The owner, Monsieur Miniou, rents 20 bedrooms, one with a full tub bath, the others with private showers or simple hot-and-cold-running-water basins. The most expensive doubles cost 187F ($42.69); the others go for 160F ($36.53), plus 15F ($3.42) for a continen-tal breakfast. The rooms come in many shapes and sizes, and the furnishings are mixed; antiques, reproductions, and modern. The full-board rate ranges from 165F ($37.68) to 180F ($41.09) per person daily. Closed from mid-December to mid-March.

8. Pont-Aven

Paul Gauguin loved this village with its little white houses along the gently flowing Aven. In the late 19th century, a school of painters followed in his trail, led by Maurice Denis, Sérusier, and Émile Bernard. The colony of artists became known as the School of Pont-Aven.

Before departing for Tahiti, Gauguin painted *The Golden Christ* and *The Beautiful Angela* here. People can admire the crucifix which inspired *The Golden Christ* in the lovely Chapelle de Trémalo, not a mile away from the little town. Every year the Société de Peinture organizes an exhibition of paintings by other members of the School of Pont-Aven, including Sérusier, Bernard, and Delavallée.

Another famous resident of Pont-Aven was Théodore Botrel, who won his fame composing patriotic French songs during World War I.

Pont-Aven, 10 miles south of Concarneau, is quiet and peaceful today, a Breton market village with an exceptionally good and beautifully situated restaurant, described below.

WHERE TO DINE: Moulin de Rosmadec (tel. 06-00-22). When it comes to a charming setting, this 15th-century reconstructed stone mill has no peers in Brittany. Regional meals are served in a two-level dining room, where you're surrounded by antique furniture and decorative accessories. In addition (and this is preferred in good weather), you can enjoy your meal on an "island" terrace while listening to the water from the river churning past. Honeysuckle scents the air, red and pink roses climb the stone wall, and orchids and rhodo-dendrons edge up against the moulin.

The owners, Madame and Monsieur Sébilleau, serve some of the finest viands along the south coast of Brittany. The specialties include truit aux amandes (trout with almonds), homard grillé à l'estragon (tarragon), and pou-lardes farcies (stuffed pullets). Expect to pay from 130F ($29.68) to 170F ($38.81) per person for a good meal. Closed from October 15 to November 15 and from February 18 through 22, as well as on Wednesdays.

9. Riec-sur-Belon

The flat-shelled oysters found off the shores of this village are, without qualification, the finest in France. In other words, Riec-sur-Belon is not a sightseeing attraction but rather a haven for gastronomes. In this village is one of the finest restaurants in France, described below.

WHERE TO DINE: Chez Mélanie, 2 Place de l'Église (tel. 06-91-05). Throughout the war years, Curnonsky, the "Prince of Gastronomes," lived at this famous inn, eating, drinking, and talking with the legendary Mélanie. Both are gone now, but the tradition of great food is carried on by Mme. Trelly.

Each dining room is furnished with old Breton furniture and decorative accessories. The patina of age and much polishing have given luster to the armoires, the carved chests, the wooden shelves, and a grandfather clock. Contemporary paintings seem to cover every square inch of wall space in the dining rooms and corridors, and the skylit kitchen contains an elaborate collection of copper pots and pans.

From that bustling kitchen 12 specialties are produced, many of which are included on the set menus. Meals range in price from 70F ($15.98) to 200F ($45.66). Specialties include timbale de fruits de mer, palourdes farcies (stuffed clams), homard à la sauce crème, coquilles Saint-Jacques (scallops), pâté de volaille, huîtres (brown-flesh oysters) extra supérieures du Belon, and galette Bretonne.

If you want to stay overnight, reserve in advance. Each accommodation is furnished in a typical Breton style and is comfortable and decorative enough to tempt you to prolong your visit. A double with bath costs 120F ($27.40), from 82F ($18.72) to 100F ($22.83) without bath. One bathless single is available at 70F ($15.98). The inn is closed from mid-November to mid-December and on Tuesdays.

10. Concarneau

Painters love this port, never tiring of capturing on canvas the changes and subtleties of the colorful fishing fleet in the harbor. It's our favorite of the South Breton coastal communities—primarily because it doesn't depend on tourists for its livelihood. In fact, its canneries produce nearly three-quarters of all the "tunny" fish consumed in France.

Walk along the quays here, especially in the late evening, and watch the rustic Breton fishermen unloading their catch; enjoy the tang of the sea air, and later join the men for a pint of potent cider in their local taverns. Sometimes their words are unfathomable, but not their friendliness.

Of course, all tourists visit Concarneau to explore its **Ville-Close,** an ancient hamlet surrounded by ramparts, some of which date from the 14th century. From the quay, cross the bridge and descend into the isolated citadel world of the old town. Admittedly, the souvenir shops have taken over, but that shouldn't spoil it for you. You can easily spend an hour wandering the narrow, winding alleys, gazing up at the towers, peering at the stone houses, pausing for a moment on a secluded square snug behind monumental granite walls. For a splendid view of the port itself, walk the ramparts. The cost is 1F (23¢) for adults, .50F (11¢) for children.

Also in the old town is a fishing museum, **Musée de la Pêche,** which you can visit from 9:30 a.m. to 8:30 p.m., for an admission of 5F ($1.14), 2F (46¢) for children. In a 17th-century building, it displays ship models and exhibits tracing the development of the fishing industry.

HOTELS: After sightseeing, repair to one of the nearby beaches of **Les Sables Blancs.** Or check into one of the hotels of this port town and enjoy a relaxing seashore vacation, which might include boating, coastal fishing, tennis, golf, horseback riding, and canoeing.

Upper-Bracket Living

La Belle Étoile ("The Beautiful Star"), Plage du Cabellou (tel. 97-05-73), is a waterside retreat three miles from the center of the port. Madame Moreau has taken three villas, with their own sandy beach, wharf for mooring boats, and stone terraces with colorful parasols—all set amid old ivy-covered walls and several acres of pine trees. The main villa, with a steep, tall roof and square lighthouse tower, has large arched windows opening onto terraces and gardens. Individualized bedrooms on the upper floors overlook either the harbor or the trees. Across the road is a stone château-style annex, complete with a round tower and gables, and nearer the water is a pretty little bungalow for guests seeking privacy.

All of Madame's bedrooms are centrally heated—most of them containing private baths with tub or shower, plus toilets and telephones. The accommodations are decorated with good reproductions of English or French antiques. In high season, full pension ranges from 330F ($75.34) to 400F ($91.32), the latter rate for an apartment. All accommodations come equipped with private baths. Étoile opens on May 15, closing September 15.

There's a combination bar-lounge, plus a tea room for guests. An open and airy dining room looks out onto the harbor. Chef's specialties include grilled lobster seasoned with tarragon and brochette of Bréton scallops (only in winter). Nonresidents can enjoy a set meal for 120F ($27.40).

The Budget Range

Grand Hôtel, 1 Avenue Gueguen (tel. 97-00-28), is the best choice in the center of this colorful port. Directly on the quay, across from La Ville-Close, the Grand Hôtel overlooks the fishing fleet and the marketplace with its open stalls selling fresh vegetables, fruit, fish, even clothing. The bedrooms have different price levels, depending on the plumbing and the view. A double with twin beds and bath costs 146F ($33.33); a double with hot and cold running water goes for only 55F ($12.56).

The kitchen is reason enough for staying at the Grand. Even if you're just passing through, hopefully you'll consider it for lunch or dinner. A set meal is offered, including six courses, such as fish soup (a specialty of the chef), hake meunière, roast lamb flavored with herbs and served with new potatoes in country butter, a fresh salad of the season, your choice from the cheese tray, and, finally, dessert. The cost is 52F ($11.87). The Grand is open only from May 1 to October 1.

TWO BUDGET RESTAURANTS: If you love crêpes, be sure to visit **Noz Ha Deiz** ("Night and Day"), Place St.-Guénolé in La Ville-Close. Reached via a bridge and a cobblestoned street, the crêperie itself is in an old building with thick natural stone walls and a fireplace, plus a rough beamed ceiling. The husband-and-wife team, Michel and Josiane Chaze, combine elaborate and rich furnishings, such as a tapestry-covered armchair, with Louis XIII country-crude furniture and copper buckets and pots. Rare paintings by a well-known friend of Gauguin's are also displayed.

The proprietors bring crêpe-making to its highest level. For the set price of 38F ($8.68), you're given a meal that consists of one buckwheat crêpe with smoked salmon, Breton scallops, crab, and mussels, followed by a crêpe with ham, egg, cheese, tomato, and mushrooms, ending with a crêpe flambée with Grand Marnier. The most appropriate beverage is an 11F ($2.51) pewter jug of cool, locally made cider. The crêperie is open from March till the end of

September, generally from 11:30 a.m. to 11 p.m. It's quite wonderful to sit before a 17th-century fireplace savoring a crêpe topped with rich homemade ice cream.

Les Halles ("The Market"), 2 rue des Halles (tel. 97-11-41), is a Breton fisherman's restaurant opening onto the flower and vegetable markets. The cooking is not only regional and authentic but very well prepared. A 36F ($8.22) fixed-price meal includes (according to the catch of the day) araignée (spider crab) with mayonnaise, filet de merlan (whiting) bonne femme, noix de veau (filet of veal), plus vegetables and cheese or dessert. Two other set meals are offered as well—one at 55F ($12.56), another at 100F ($22.83). Closed in October.

11. La Forêt-Fouesnant

Set in an orchard district of South Brittany, La Forêt-Fouesnant turns out the best cider in the province. One of Brittany's finest manor houses—open to the public for both rooms and meals—lies in the environs of this sleepy village. It's reached by going along N783 and turning off at the clearly indicated sign, five miles from Concarneau, eight miles from Quimper.

FOOD AND LODGING: Manoir du Stang (tel. 56-97-37) is approached via a long, tree-lined avenue. Passing under a stone-built tower gate, you enter the graveled courtyard leading to the entrance of the ivy-covered, 16th-century manor house. On your right is a formal garden, with walks through beds of pink and red flowers. Raised stone terraces lead to 25 acres of rolling woodland. The Manoir du Stang is the domain of Monsieur and Madame Hubert, who provide gracious living in period drawing rooms, studies, lounges, and dining room liberally furnished with Breton antiques. Our favorite salon features Breton paneling, plus a fireplace, chunky crystal, and Louis XIII chairs.

Guests are lodged either in the main building or in the even older annex, the latter with a circular stone staircase. Your bedroom is likely to be furnished with silk fabrics and fine antiques. A maid in starched lacy Breton cap will bring a breakfast tray to your room each morning. Rates depend on the length of your stay, the time of the year, and the plumbing. In high season, from June 20 to September 20, one person pays 220F ($50.23) for half pension in a room with private bath, service and taxes included. The manor is open from Easter to September 30.

Equally beguiling are the meals, the chef's specialties being homard grillé à l'estragon, mousseline de turbot, côte de boeuf au poivre vert, fruits de mer, and huîtres de la baie de la Forêt-Fouesnant. If you are just stopping over, set meals range in price from 100F ($22.83) to 110F ($25.11).

12. Quimper

This is the town that pottery built. Its world-famous faïence decorates tables from Africa to Canada. Skilled artisans have been turning out the Quimper-ware since the 17th century, using bold provincial designs. You can visit one of the factories and learn their techniques. To discover the names and addresses of the factories receiving visitors during your stay at Quimper, inquire at the helpful Tourist Bureau.

At the confluence of the Odet and Steir rivers, Quimper was the medieval capital of Cornouailles. In some quarters it maintains its old-world atmosphere. Charming footbridges span the rivers. At the Place St.-Corentin, the **Cathedral of St. Corentin** is the town landmark, characterized by two towers that climb to a height of 250 feet. The cathedral was built between the 13th and 15th centuries, although the spires weren't added until the 19th. Inside, the 15th-century stained glass is exceptional—well worth a look.

Also on the square is the **Musée des Beaux-Arts.** Its collection of paintings includes works by such major artists as Rubens, Boucher, Fragonard, Oudry, Chasseriau, Corot, and Marquet. There's an exceptionally good exhibition from the northern schools and Pont-Aven school (Bernard, Sérusier, Lacombe, Maufra, Denis, Meyer de Haan). Charging 3F (68¢) for admission, the gallery is open daily except Tuesdays from 9:30 a.m. to noon and from 1:30 to 7 p.m. (10 a.m. to noon and 2 to 6 p.m. off-season).

FOOD AND LODGINGS: Tour d'Auvergne, 13 rue Réguaires (tel. 95-08-70), is the preferred hotel choice in busy Quimper, just a short block from the Odet. Even though centrally positioned, it is especially quiet. Recently renovated, it has a stylish modern look to it, with a little salon featuring a wall-size mural, a blow-up of an engraving of a battle scene. Most of the 45 well-furnished double rooms contain private baths and rent for 130F ($29.68) nightly. A bathless single costs 56F ($12.78). One of the principal reasons for staying here is the food, as the kitchen features Breton specialties. Set meals are offered for 45F ($10.27) and 70F ($15.98), the latter a menu gastronomique with expensive shellfish. However, the less expensive menu is invariably good, including on one recent occasion spider crabs with mayonnaise and a saddle of rabbit with mustard sauce. The restaurant is closed on Sundays from October to Easter.

In town, you'll find good food at the small restaurant **Les Tritons,** allées de Locmaria (tel. 90-61-78), run by Marcel Baïer. At his warmly decorated restaurant you get consistently good cooking. Some plates are simple although far from ordinary. Try, for example, his duck stew, his stewed anglerfish, or his Breton soup made in an earthenware pot with cabbage. The menu is varied, the service efficient. Menus are at 38F ($8.68) and 60F ($13.70), and à la carte orders average around 85F ($19.41) to 110F ($25.11). The restaurant is closed Mondays and in September.

Motorists may prefer the **Manoir de Moustoir** (tel. 94-80-80), which lies 6½ miles southeast by N783, on the route de Concarneau. The medieval stone mansion is more of a château, lovingly placed in a seven-acre woodsy park with a small decorative pond. The conversion from private home to its present use as a hotel has been intelligently and tastefully handled. Antiques of the period abound, and in one of the drawing rooms there is an exhibit of contemporary local painters. The bedrooms have been expertly and harmoniously provided with accessories, and a bathroom has been added for each chamber. The cost for a single is 120F ($27.40), rising to 240F ($54.79) in a double. Only breakfast at 15F ($3.42) is served. The manor receives guests only from July 1 until the first week of September.

13. Locronan

A gem among Breton villages, Locronan was once known as the City of Weavers, earning its fame in the 17th century when 300 workers labored seven days a week weaving sails for the Royal Navy. Today, two weaving concerns continue the tradition, but the village is mostly noted for its old bearded woodcarvers.

The Renaissance core of Locronan, the **Place,** is remarkably preserved, standing virtually intact from the 16th and 17th centuries, with granite houses, old beams, delicate cut stone, and open well. The church on the stone square is from the 15th century, containing an interesting Chapel of Pénity in which is the tomb of St. Ronan, the patron saint of Locronan. The hermit Ronan was driven from Ireland in the fifth century. In penitence he ran four miles every day of his life, 7½ miles on Sunday.

Every six years his memory is revived in a **Grand Troménie,** a pageant considered one of the most extraordinary in France. A colorful procession covers the 7½ miles, gathering numerous of the faithful along the way. The neighboring parishes display the relics of their patron saints.

On the Quimper-Crozon road, less than a mile outside Locronan, turn to the left at a wooden panel indicating—

FOOD AND LODGING: **Hôtel au Fer à Cheval,** Route du Bois-de-Nevet-Locronan (tel. 91-70-67). Alain Chipon built this hotel, "The Horseshoe," in the contemporary style, but has matched it well with the landscape. In the large lounge, bay windows open onto the countryside. The decoration, although modern, preserves some rustic elements, including tiled floors and a large fireplace of white stone. The dining room also avoids coldness, using ocher fishnet curtains, "glass balloon" lamps, and a tapestry. Some of the bedrooms have a mezzanine reached by a stairway. The accommodations are quiet and spacious, with large windows opening onto the scenery. Orange and yellow are employed effectively. The hotel is most pleasant, almost deluxe, but with reasonable prices: 70F ($15.98) to 85F ($19.41) in a single, 80F ($18.26) to 120F ($27.40) in a double, the higher tariff for the mezzanine rooms. Three persons are accommodated for 160F ($36.53); four persons, 180F ($41.09). A meal ranges in price from 35F ($7.99) all the way up to 160F ($36.53) or more.

14. Dinan

Once a stronghold of the dukes of Brittany, Dinan is still one of the best-preserved towns of Brittany. Characterized by houses built on stilts over the sidewalks, this walled town with a once-fortified château lies 19 miles south of St.-Malo. Contrasting with the medieval timbered houses are the granite dwellings erected in the 18th century.

For orientation and a panoramic view, head first for the **Jardin Anglais** ("English Garden"), a terraced garden huddling up to the ramparts. From that vantage point, you can look out over the valley. Spanning the Rance River is a Gothic-style bridge which was damaged in World War II but has been restored.

The most typical street of Dinan is the sloping **rue du Jerzual,** flanked with old buildings, some of which date from the 15th century. The street ends at **La Porte du Jerzual,** an ancient gate. The **rue du Petit-Fours** also contains a number of 15th-century **maisons.**

Dominating the town is the **château,** which has been turned into a museum. It is open from 8:30 a.m. to 12:30 p.m. and from 1:30 to 7 p.m. in summer, charging 3F (68¢) for admission. Otherwise, it is open from 9 a.m. to noon and from 2 to 5 p.m. You can visit the 14th-century Donjon de la Duchesse Anne and the Tour de Coëtquen, towers in which an historical and folklore exhibition, including a typical Breton room, has been installed.

The heart of Bertrand du Guesclin, who successfully defended the town when the Duke of Lancaster threatened it in 1359, was entombed in a position of honor in the **Basilica Saint-Sauveur.** Characterized by its outstanding Romanesque portals, the château is also noted for the rich ornamentation of its 16th-century chapels.

FOOD AND LODGING: In Dinan the accommodations are limited but quite good and moderately priced. The food, however, is superb. Many visitors prefer to use Dinan as a base for exploring St.-Malo, Dinard, and Mont Saint-Michel.

The Leading Inn

D'Avaugour, 1 Place du Champs-Clos (tel. 39-07-49), is the pet child of Madame Quinton, who has gutted an old building, turning it into the most up-to-date accommodation at Dinan. Small as it is, with just 25 rooms, it is the best hotel in town. All accommodations are with private baths and toilets, costing 200F ($45.66) for two persons, plus an additional 15F ($3.42) for a continental breakfast. The rooms are furnished with reproductions and occasional contemporary pieces. Half of them overlook the square; the others face the tiny rear garden with its birdcages, large stone fountain, and flower borders. The little front lounge has been treated stylishly, using a lot of natural stone and simple modern furnishings. A very good restaurant, with excellent service and well-prepared food, is in the garden overlooking the ramparts. Monsieur Quinton is the chef.

Where to Dine

La Caravelle, 14 Place Duclos (tel. 39-00-11). J. C. Marmion is a dazzling young talent who has awakened the sleepy taste buds of Dinan with his inventive cuisine. He is passionately devoted to the products of the season, fashioning his menu to keep it abreast of what is available, good, and fresh on the local markets.

In summer you can order his terrine of eel with a tomato mousse, his lobster fricassée, sweetbreads in a truffle sauce, oysters and lobster with peppermint, perhaps his delicious turbot with fresh green peas in an onion sauce, or a salad of scallops with fresh artichokes. In season he also does the finest game dishes in town, including jugged hare or rabbit. When the first of the spring turnips come in, he prepares a veal filet with these vegetables, served with an onion compote.

Surprisingly, he offers a little dinner for just 35F ($7.99), another at 70F ($15.98), though you'll pay from 150F ($34.26) if ordering à la carte. The reception, the welcome, and the service are flawless. It's one of our highest dining recommendations in all of Brittany.

Incidentally, Monsieur Marmion will also give you a room for the night, as the Caravelle rents out 11 simply furnished chambers at a cost of 60F ($13.70) in a single, 90F ($20.55) in a double. The establishment closes in October and on Wednesdays from November until the end of June.

Mère Pourcel, Place des Merciers (tel. 39-03-80), is in the very heart of Old Dinan, transporting you back to the 15th century. In an authentic *maison* of that era, it is filled with old beams and leaded-glass windows. It also enjoys an outstanding reputation for regional food. If you want to follow the set menus, you will pay either 45F ($10.27) or 78F ($17.81). Most diners, however, seem to prefer the à la carte menu, enjoying such house specialties as a pepper steak "Mother Pourcel" at 45F ($10.27). You might begin your meal with coquilles St.-Jacques (scallops) at 22F ($5.02) or a marinade of fresh sardines, 19F ($4.34). A coupe de glace, a specialty of the house, costs 12F ($2.74). It's closed in February and on Mondays.

"Le Connétable," 1 rue de l'Apport (tel. 39-06-74), is a colorful Breton crêperie ensconced on the lower level of a 14th-century building, with a beamed ceiling, rough stone walls, a fireplace, and an open wooden staircase leading to the private quarters of the Desbonnet family. You enjoy your crêpes while seated on provincial wooden chairs, eating off handmade ceramic plates, perhaps drinking locally made cider from a bowl, peasant fashion. You can have almost any kind of crêpe here, as well as the house specialties, crêpe le Connétable at 10F ($2.28) or crêpe Marrakech, also 10F. A banana chantilly crêpe makes a luscious dessert. Most crêpes range in price from 9F ($2.05) to 13F ($2.97), and most dessert crêpes go for 7F ($1.60). To begin your meal, you may prefer six oysters at 13F ($2.97) or onion soup gratinée at 12.50F ($2.85).

Breton Luxury on the Outskirts

Only 12½ miles from Dinan is one of the most charming houses in Brittany, **Manoir du Vaumadeuc,** on a country road near Pléven (route de Lamballe) (tel. 84-14-67). The Vicomtesse de Pontbriand welcomes guests to this manor dating from the 15th century, when it was presented as a dowry gift. Mme. de Pontbriand's husband was a colonel in the French army and she traveled widely with him, collecting antiques and objets d'art from all over the world. At the edge of a deep, cool vale, the manor is built of solid Breton granite, its severity softened by the "Vine of the Virgin" blooming across its stones. The entrance is through a Gothic doorway.

Under beamed ceilings, the interior is sumptuously decorated, with tapestries, Louis XV *chauffeuses,* Renaissance chests, wrought-iron chandeliers, and Brocatel marble. Carvings and doors represent the finest of craftsmanship, as practiced in Brittany in the 15th century. The manor contains seven carved chimneys, all of them different, each a work of regional art.

Only 10 bedrooms—each one decorated differently—are rented out, costing 200F ($45.66) in a single, 350F ($79.91) in the most elegant double. The hotel is closed from January until mid-March. In season, half pension is required, ranging from 420F ($95.89) to 600F ($136.98) for two persons.

Even the bedrooms have fireplaces. The most elegant chamber is No. 6, entered through a large oak door which opens onto a gallery with a wooden balustrade. Below is a huge room with a big "matrimonial" bed.

For such a small place, the cuisine of Mademoiselle Yvonne Le Terrien is so ambitious it would put to shame many a chef at a large restaurant. Meals are offered at 125F ($28.54) and 220F ($47.94). She does a tajine of pigeon in the Moroccan style, lobster gratiné with sherry, quenelle de brochet Nantua, roast quail (complete with quail eggs), sweetbreads with citrus, even a head of veal en Tortue. Brittany cider is available, along with a fine wine selection.

15. Dinard

One of the best-known seaside resorts in France, Dinard offers safe, well-sheltered bathing in **La Manche.** Its origins as a resort go back to the heyday of Queen Victoria, when it became popular with the Channel-crossing English, who wanted a continental holiday but one "not too foreign." Dinard offers a trio of beaches, the main one being the **Plage de l'Écluse** ("Beach of the Floodgate"), which tends to get crowded in July and August. Another, facing a backdrop of towering cliffs, is **Saint-Enogat.** Still a third, the **Prieuré,** honors a priory that stood nearby in the Middle Ages.

Dinard sits on a rocky promontory at the top of the Rance River, opposite St.-Malo. Ferryboats ply between the two resorts. Turn-of-the-century Victorian-Gothic villas, many now converted into hotels, overlook the sea. Gardens and parks abound. Even on rainy days English women, heavily protected from the elements, go for long walks along the promenades.

From June to September there is *musique et lumière* along the floodlit
seafront **Promenade du Clair-de-Lune.** The **New Municipal Casino** in the
Palais d'Emeraude is open year round, attracting devotees of roulette, baccarat,
and boule. And about five miles from Dinard is the 18-hole golf course at
Saint-Briac, one of the finest in Brittany.

UPPER BRACKET HOTELS: Le Grand, 46 Avenue George V (tel. 46-10-
28), is Dinard's leading hotel. Open from Easter until the end of September,
it commands an excellent view of the harbor. Most of the five floors of this
substantial brick-built structure have balconies and tall French windows. For
the most part, the bedrooms—some 100, all with bath—are decorated with
traditional pieces, including some in the Louis XVI style, with white-painted
wood and carnation-red upholstery. The baths are modernized, with tiled
showers in the tubs. In high season, from June 15 till September 15, the tariffs
for half pension range from 165F ($37.68) to 225F ($51.38) per person, taxes
and service included. The lobby has the look of a city hotel, although with a
resort overlay of rattan furnishings. Decorated invitingly in autumnal tones,
the bar is a popular spot before and after dinner. Good meals, with rather
generous portions, are offered in the dignified paneled dining room.

MEDIUM-PRICED HOTELS: Printania, 5 Avenue George V (tel. 46-13-
07), is an old-world Breton-style hotel. The antique-jammed sitting room, with
its dark carved oak, paneled furniture, old clocks, and provincial chairs, sets
the tone. A time-seasoned inn, the Printania draws many repeat guests, among
them writers and artists. *Everybody* has stayed here, from England's Edward
Heath to Americans such as Sinclair Lewis.

The main villa stands eight stories high, providing terraces for garden
sunbaths plus a "hothouse" glassed-in veranda with potted palms, Breton
cupboards, and ceramic pottery. Dinner at Printania, served by young women
in white bibbed aprons and starched headdresses, combines superb cookery
with a view of the coastline. On August 15, 1944, the hotel was bombed, but
the debris was removed in time for the Allied victory celebration.

The bedrooms are furnished with antiques and Breton decorations; some
offer private baths, others hot and cold running water. For a minimum stay of
five days in the peak of the season, from July 10 to August 31, one person is
charged anywhere from 140F ($31.96) to 200F ($45.66) for full pension per
day, including service and taxes. Tariffs are lowered at other times. The hotel
is open from March 30 to October.

Roche Corneille, 4 rue Georges-Clémenceau (tel. 46-14-47). This natural
stone villa, with a tall tower and a mansard roof, is right in the heart of Dinard,
and one side directly fronts the street. Nevertheless, Roche Corneille has a
French garden and a country-house atmosphere. Run like a private home and
furnished in the same style, it reflects excellent taste throughout, revealing the
interests and lifestyle of the proprietor, Madame Barreaud. Guests gather in
the drawing room, with its baronial fireplace, colonnaded arches, and wood-
paneled ceiling. Another favorite spot is the winter garden, with bowls of fresh
flowers, a colorful wall mural, and a heavy baroque oak refectory table.

The rooms are comfortably furnished and beautifully kept; all have private
baths. The cost for pension ranges from 200F ($45.66) to 275F ($62.78). The
hotel is closed from November 15 to December 15.

Frankly, the hotel's restaurant, **La Coquille,** offers the best food in Dinard. Guests dine in an upper-floor room with ladderback antique chairs and

picture windows, or in a ground-floor room more typically Breton, with reed-covered, high-backed chairs, pink-and-white-cloths, and an elaborate carved-oak cupboard, plus a wall of recessed windows with copper pots and fresh flowers from the gardens. If you're an "outsider" dropping in, you'll find a fixed-price dinner offered for 80F ($18.26). À la carte specialties include a cassolette de filets de sole à l'orange, 70F ($15.98), and rognons de veau (veal kidneys) à notre façon, 55F ($12.56).

BUDGET ACCOMMODATIONS: Des Bains, 38 Avenue George V (tel. 46-13-71), offers a wide variety of accommodations with meals. On the rise of a hill, it is within walking distance of the casino and the beach. The hotel has been considerably modernized, relying heavily on bright-red plastic-covered pieces. There are 40 bedrooms, also with plastic chairs plus chintz-covered beds and draperies. Twenty-five of them come with showers and toilets. In high season, from July 10 to August 31, you'll be charged anywhere from 120F ($27.40) to 145F ($33.10) per person for full pension, including taxes and service. In the dining room, the beamed ceiling, carved oak paneling, and red-and-white tablecloths add a provincial-inn touch. Jean Bor, the proprietor, has created "Papa's Bar," where guests gather for drinks. The hotel is closed in January.

Des Dunes, 5 rue Georges-Clémenceau (tel. 46-12-72), puts you in the center of Dinard life. Its façade is inviting, with cut fieldstone, elaborate white trim, tall French windows, and balustraded balconies. On the front terrace, garden furniture rests under parasols. High on a cliff away from the water, the hotel is open all year except between November 3 and December 20; highest rates are in July and August, when pension is required. You can stay here and take all meals for anywhere from 166F ($37.90) to 190F ($43.38). The bedrooms have a fresh seaside-holiday look, with white curtains and comfortable furnishings. The dining room and lounge overlook the front garden terrace.

16. St.-Malo

Built on a granite rock in the English Channel, St.-Malo is joined to the mainland by a causeway. Dinard is eight miles away. Popular with the English, especially those from the Channel Islands, it makes a modest claim as a bathing resort.

For the best view of the bay and the offshore islets at the mouth of the Rance, you can walk along the **ramparts** that date from the Middle Ages. These walls were built over a period of centuries, some parts of them going back to the 14th. However, they were mainly rebuilt in the 17th century, then vastly restored in the 19th. You can begin your tour at the 15th-century **Gate of St. Vincent.**

At the harbor you can book tours for the **Channel Islands.** Hydrofoils leave for the English island of Jersey at 8, 8:30, 10:15, and 11 a.m. and 4:30 and 8 p.m., returning at 7:45 and 8:30 a.m. and 2, 5, 5:30, and 6:30 p.m. The cost is 130F ($29.68) per person. A passport, of course, is necessary.

At low tide, you can actually walk to the Île du Grand Bé to the north-west, site of the lonely tomb of Chateaubriand, "deserted by others and completely surrounded by storms." Actually, the tomb—marked by a cross—is quite simple, unlike the man it honors, but the view of the Emerald Coast makes up for it. It's about a 25-minute stroll.

Called the "Bastille of the West," the **St.-Malo Castle** and its towers shelter a historic museum with souvenirs of Duguay-Trouin (1673-1736) and

Surcouf (1773-1827), the most famous of the St.-Malo privateers. The **Museum of St.-Malo** is in the donjon. You can visit year round except on Fridays, from 10 a.m. to noon and from 2 to 6 p.m., paying a 2F (46¢) admission. Guided tours are available.

The museum also contains memorabilia of the celebrated native sons of St.-Malo. The most famous, of course, was Chateaubriand, the romantic French writer and statesman who created the melancholy hero. However, as well known (even better by Canadians) was Jacques Cartier, the French explorer and navigator who discovered the St. Lawrence River in 1536, thus establishing a French claim. He named the country Canada. The third great son was the morbid Lamennais, the French priest and philosophical and political writer who was born in St.-Malo, the son of a ship owner. In 1834, he wrote *Paroles d'un Croyant (Words from a Believer),* which was widely circulated throughout Europe.

The **Galerie Qui Qu'en Groigne,** at Tour Qui Qu'en Groigne, is a wax museum installed in a tower. Historic scenes are recreated, along with effigies of the celebrities of St.-Malo. It is open April to September, charging 8F ($1.83) admission.

After the castle and ramparts tour, you'll hopefully have time to explore the cobbled plazas, the flagstone courtyards, the narrow streets, the fish market, the cathedral with a 12th-century nave, and the tall gabled houses. One of the most important of the Breton *pardons* is held at St.-Malo in February: the **Pardon of the Newfoundland Fishing Fleet.**

In the resort of St.-Servan, adjoining St.-Malo, you can visit the **Musée International du Long-Cours Cap-Hornier** in the Tour Solidor, a tower built in 1382, commanding the Rance estuary. Here a history of voyages around the world by way of Cape Horn is depicted in exhibits from the 16th century up to the 20th. Maps, manuscripts, ship models, and nautical instruments are on display. Guided visits are conducted annually from 10 a.m. to noon and from 2 to 6 p.m. for an admission of 2F (46¢).

FOOD AND LODGING: Recommended at St.-Malo are medium-priced and budget accommodations, plus one excellent seafood restaurant.

Central, 6 Grande Rue (tel. 40-87-70), is the leading hotel, and it has been entirely renovated. On a street near the harbor, it is provincial but in a sophisticated way. Most of the remodeled rooms contain private baths. The furnishings are contemporary, but originality shows in the color coordination. Doubles begin at 110F ($25.11), going up to 250F ($57.08). No singles are offered. Half pension ranges from 170F ($38.81) to 230F ($52.90) per person, depending on the plumbing. Before dinner you can have a drink in a bar with an *ambience sympathique.* One of the best reasons for staying here is the food. Two set meals are proposed—one at 60F ($13.70), the menu gastronomique at 100F ($22.83). A delicious fish soup and grilled red mullets with anchovy butter are often featured. On the à la carte, we're most enthusiastic about the plentiful seafood platter at 80F ($18.26). Especially delectable is the barbue pochée with white butter, at 60F ($13.70). The hotel is closed in January.

Hôtel de l'Univers, Place Chateaubriand (tel. 40-89-52), is the preferred choice for those seeking the more traditional French atmosphere. On a little tree-shaded square opposite the château, it lies behind a dignified façade. Set out on the sidewalk are tables overlooking the ramparts. A central courtyard is glass-covered and decorated with wicker chairs and potted palms, a throwback to another era. The entire hotel—the lounge, the dining room, and certainly the bedrooms—offers comfort and character.

Two persons can stay either in double-bedded or twin-bedded chambers at prices beginning at 65F ($14.84) and going up to 140F ($31.96), depending on the plumbing.

A favorite spot is the Bar Maritime, resting under a beamed ceiling, its walls covered with photographs of nautical objects such as ships' bells, models, and compasses, revealing the owner's enthusiasm for yachts.

Duchesse Anne, 5 Place Chateaubriand (tel. 40-85-33), is beguilingly built into the ramparts, right near the château. The atmosphere is mellow, with a white-and-gold-paneled ceiling and turkey-red walls. In the summer tables are placed under a large canopy and hydrangea abounds in wall vases. Try the fish specialties here. The fish soup made with hunks of freshly caught seafood, harmoniously spiced and cooked in an iron pot, is excellent at 35F ($7.99). Alternatively, you can sample six oysters from Cancale at 30F ($6.85). As a main dish, you may select grilled turbot with white butter at 50F ($11.42) or a pepper steak, also 50F. Desserts range from 15F ($3.42) to 25F ($5.71). The restaurant is closed in December, January, and on Wednesdays.

CHAMPAGNE COUNTRY

IN ABOUT THREE DAYS a visitor can travel from Paris on the N3—the Autoroute de l'Est—to a world of old cathedrals, battlefields, fantastic food, and some of France's most famous vineyards, topping the exploration with a heady glass of champagne.

On the "champagne trail," you can go first to the wine-producing center of Épernay, and then on to Reims, which lies some 90 miles to the northeast of Paris. After visiting Reims and its cathedral, you can leave on Route 31 east, heading in the direction of Verdun.

Old Roman roads criss-crossed Champagne, and the region has always stood in the pathway of invaders. The clashes here have gone on for two millennia. Even today, names such as Reims evoke ghastly memories of some of the worst fighting of World War I.

1. Épernay

On the left bank of the Marne, Épernay rivals Reims as a center for champagne. With only one-sixth of Reims's population, Épernay produces nearly as much champagne as does its larger sister.

Although the town itself is a rather pedestrian modern one, Épernay has nearly an estimated 200 miles or more of cellars and tunnels, a veritable rabbit warren, for storing champagne. These caves are really vast vaults cut in the chalk rock on which the town is built. Represented in Épernay are such champagne companies as Moët et Chandon (the largest), Pol Roger, Mercier, and de Castellane.

The **Moët Champagne Caves** offer guided tours in English, an expert member of the staff giving you a detailed description of the process of champagne-making. There you can see the *rémueurs* at work, twisting each bottle a quarter-turn. At the end of the tour each visitor is given a glass of bubbly. The cellars are open daily except Saturdays, Sundays, and French public holidays, from 10 a.m. to noon and from 2 to 6 p.m., from April 1 until the end of October.

Seventeen miles from Reims, Épernay has been either destroyed or burned nearly two dozen times as it lay in the path of invading armies, particularly the Germans. Therefore, few of its old buildings are left. However, try to visit the Avenue de Champagne, with its Musée du Champagne and its neoclassic villas and Victorian town houses, a curiosity at least.

By doubling back on the N51, you can visit the **Abbaye d'Hautvillers,** just north of Épernay, containing the tomb of Dom Pérignon. A blind monk, Pérignon was the cellar-master at the abbey from 1670 to 1715, when he died. He is credited with inventing the process for turning the still wines of the region into the sparkling temptation known as champagne. Of course, one of the most expensive bottles of that bubbly carries the monk's name to this day. Upon drinking champagne for the first time, Pérignon is reported to have said, "I am drinking stars!"

The gracious old abbey has been rebuilt several times since it was founded in the 12th century. When the monks were evicted during the French Revolution, the abbey was purchased by the Moët family. However, it is once more a working church and can be visited at any time of the day. A representative of the Moët company can arrange for you to see the beautiful interior gardens with their incomparable view of the champagne vineyards and the Marne Valley. The river was extolled in verse by La Fontaine and glorified by Corot in his landscapes.

If you're staying over, the best hotel—certainly the most scenically positioned—is called, appropriately, **Royal Champagne** (tel. 51-25-06). It lies some four miles from Épernay in the hamlet of Champillon, in the direction of Reims, on the N51. The château-inn offers 14 handsomely furnished bedrooms in its posting house which dates from the 18th century. Windows open onto views of the champagne vineyards. Singles begin at 170F ($38.81), going up to 200F ($45.66) in a double. The food is exceptional. Specialties include poached eggs "vigneronne," plus a soup made with freshwater crayfish which is subtly and delicately flavored and contains (as a surprise) cucumber. As a main dish, you might select little triangular-shaped slices of a white, flaky, delicate-tasting pike-perch, well flavored with herbs. A set meal will cost about 130F ($29.71). Expect to spend around 170F ($38.81) to 220F ($50.23) for a complete meal if you order à la carte.

In Épernay itself, the preferred choice for both food and lodgings is the little **Berceaux,** 13 rue Berceaux (tel. 51-28-84), where Monsieur Courgnaud is a fine host. In comfortable, pleasant surroundings, you'll be given one of two dozen bedrooms, costing 90F ($20.55) in a single, 150F ($34.26) in a double.

But where Monsieur Courgnaud really excels is in his Champenois cookery, among the best in the area. The portions, incidentally, are prodigious, so plan to make an evening meal here an event, and, if you can afford it, everything should be washed down with tremendous libations of champagne.

You might begin with a terrine of duckling with foie gras. Of course, the chef's sautéed chicken in champagne has been exciting visitors for years. There are, as well, small-size turbots (known as chicken turbot in English and *turbotins* in French) prepared with Bouzy, which is a white wine, one of the best wines of the champagne district.

A set meal runs 75F ($17.12), although you more likely will spend from 120F ($27.40) to 200F ($45.66) on the à la carte. The dining room is closed

August 10 to 24, on Sunday nights, and takes a long Christmas holiday in December.

For the budget, we'd recommend the more recently opened **Hôtel St.-Pierre**, 14 Avenue Paul-Chandon, a continuation of rue St.-Thibault (tel. 51-95-55). There you can rent pleasantly furnished rooms—only 14 in all—at a cost of 55F ($12.56) to 60F ($13.70) for two persons in a room with shower. Even cheaper are the bedrooms with hot and cold running water and a bidet, only 45F ($10.27) to 52F ($11.87) for two nightly. A single bedroom with only hot and cold running water goes for 40F ($9.13) nightly. The owners are most helpful and friendly and often extend themselves to make your stay a good one. They shut down from August 22 to September 12 for a well-deserved summer vacation. There is no restaurant, so it's recommended that you take your meals at the Berceaux, endorsed previously.

From Épernay, you can take the following most popular excursion.

2. Condé-en-Brie

The Marquis de Sade is alive and well in Condé-en-Brie, to the west of Épernay. Of course, it's not the same de Sade we all know, but his great-great-great-grandson, the Marquis Xavier de Sade (who prefers, by the way, to be called "count," as he considers it more modern). The present occupant of the château has devoted his life to clearing his family name of the reputation connected with his infamous ancestor. Unfortunately, the word "sadism," derived from the marquis's name, has become such an everyday term that it is a never-ending source of embarrassment to the de Sade family.

According to Count Xavier de Sade, the marquis was not a perverse, sadistic individual at all, but simply an ordinary, run-of-the-mill, dissolute man, irresponsible in his business affairs (he died a pauper in 1814), and intent on having every woman in France. His only real fault, the present count continues, is that he wrote down everything he did—or wished that he did. "Everyone else was doing it, too," the present de Sade maintains, "only they didn't record it." Today's count also claims that many of the attributes of his ancestor have been overlooked—that he was, in fact, a great believer in freedom and civil liberty and a fascinating innovator in literary style.

In his passion for restoring the family honor, the present Count de Sade has set about renovating the large château. After leaving Épernay, you'll come to the old village of Dormans, with its Louis XIII château. From there head southwest on the D41 until you reach D20. Get on the D20 and you'll see a sign pointing the way to the **Château de Condé-en-Brie**, which is the proper name—not the "De Sade château," as it is more popularly known.

The château is a large French Renaissance structure, with gabled roofs and domed turrets. The current count has passionately worked to restore the interior and exterior and has relandscaped the lovely grounds.

Although a portion of the château is not open to visitors, since it is the private domain of the count himself, the larger portion has been transformed into a museum honoring the de Sade family—especially their remarkable ancestor. Besides the several fine period pieces on view, many of which date from the 18th century, Count Xavier de Sade has collected some first editions of the works of his ancestor. These are kept under lock and key. One of the rooms was painted by Watteau and another, depicting scenes from the hunt, by Oudry. The Italian stage director Servandoni decorated one room completely in trompe-l'oeil. And, of course, there are letters and manuscripts from the marquis.

The de Sade château is open to visitors daily except Wednesdays from the first of June until the end of November. Visiting hours are from 10 a.m. to noon and from 2 to 6:30 p.m. From Easter until June 1, it can be visited only in the afternoon on weekends and French public holidays. The admission is 8F ($1.83).

3. Reims

Reims is an ancient city. French kings came there to be crowned. Joan of Arc escorted Charles VII there in 1429, kissing the feet of the silly man.

Aside from its historical monuments (of which there are many), Reims is visited chiefly because it is the center of a wine-growing district that gives the world a bubbly with which to make toasts. The champagne bottled in this district, of course, is said to be "the lightest and most subtle in flavor of the world's wines." Those planning more than a quick one-day trip can linger in the region, exploring the vineyards and wine cellars, the Gothic monuments, the World War battlefields. Trains leave from Gare de l'Est in Paris, the journey taking about an hour and a half, the distance some 102 miles northeast of the French capital.

On May 7, 1945, the Germans surrendered to General Eisenhower at the **Salle de Guerre**, 10 rue Franklin-Roosevelt, a brick building near the railroad tracks, once a little schoolhouse. The walls of the room are lined with maps of the rail routes, exactly as they were on the day of surrender. It may be visited daily except Tuesdays from 9 a.m. to noon and from 2 to 6 p.m. (it is closed, however, from mid-November to mid-March).

SEEING THE SIGHTS: Reims is dominated by the **Cathedral of Notre-Dame.** One of the most famous cathedrals in the world, the pointed Gothic edifice at Reims has suffered more bombardments than most fortresses. After World War I, it was restored largely with U.S. contributions. Mercifully, it rode out World War II relatively free. Built on the site of a church burned to the ground in 1211, it was intended as a sanctuary where French kings would be anointed. St. Rémi, the bishop of Reims, had baptized Clovis, the pagan king of the Franks, there in 496.

Laden with statuettes, its three portals on the western façade are spectacular. The central portal, dedicated to the Virgin, is surmounted by a rose window. The right portal portrays the Apocalypse and the Last Judgment; the left, Martyrs and Saints. At the northern door of the western façade is the guardian angel, often called the smiling angel.

Lit by lancet windows, the nave is immense, with many bays. In the palace beside the cathedral is the treasury, containing a 12th-century chalice used for the communion of French monarchs and a talisman said to have been worn around the neck of Charlemagne and to contain a relic of the True Cross.

In the sacristy are exhibited robes, ornaments, and chalices from the 13th to the 19th centuries, as well as pictures of the cathedral during World War I, and pictures and a clay model of the procession of the coronation. English is spoken. Open in June, July, August, and September from 9 a.m. to noon and 2 to 6 p.m.; admission, 7F ($1.60) for adults, 3.50F (79¢) for children.

In summer, the cathedral is decorated with a series of 17 tapestries, dating from the 16th century and illustrating scenes from the life of the Virgin. The choir is majestic. The cathedral is at Place du Cardinal-Luçon.

The **Church of St. Rémi**, at 53 rue Simon, is unfavorably compared to the cathedral; nevertheless, it is an outstanding achievement. Once a Benedictine abbey church, it contains a grand Romanesque nave leading to the choir. Not only the nave but the transepts, one of the towers, and the aisles also date from the 11th century. The portal of the south transept is in the flamboyant style of the early 16th century. Decorating the apse is stained glass, some from the 13th century.

Framed by a shell of stonework is the reconstructed tomb of St. Rémi, elaborately carved with figures and columns in the Renaissance style. The former abbey, rebuilt in the 18th century, has been turned into a historical and lapidary **museum,** open daily except Tuesdays from 10 a.m. to noon and 2 to 5 p.m. In the cloister is a Gallo-Roman sarcophagus said to be that of the consul Jovin, who died in 412. There is also a collection of medieval sculpture, mostly Romanesque.

Musée des Beaux-Arts: Housed in the 18th-century buildings belonging to the old abbey of St. Denis, this fine provincial art gallery is at 8 rue Chanzy. In the Salle Monthelon are more than a dozen portraits of German princes of the Reformation by both "the Elder" and "the Younger" Cranach. The museum has owned this remarkable collection since it first opened in 1795. In the same hall, the Toiles Peintes (light painting on rough linen) date from the 15th and 16th centuries, depicting such scenes as the vengeance of Christ.

In the Salle Diancourt hang the high-warp *Tapestries of St. Rémi,* made between 1505 and 1530 by the Flemish School. The *Minstrels' Statues* displayed there date back to the 13th century (the only example in Reims of the profane sculpture of that era).

Paintings include *The Descent from the Cross* by Pieter Van Moll and a Venus by the Le Nain brothers. In the first hall is an excellent series of Corot's tree-shaded walks. The museum also owns canvases by such artists as Millet, Pissarro, Monet, Sisley, Renoir, Gauguin, Bonnard, Matisse, Braque, Picasso, Dufy, Rouault, Vuillard, Daumier, and Courbet.

The hours are from 10 a.m. to noon and from 2 to 6 p.m. No admission is charged.

Open year round, the **Champagne Caves** are most interesting at the autumnal grape harvest. Many are immense, extending for 10 miles through chalky deposits. In some of these cellars the populace hid out during the German siege of 1914, many people living there for the length of the war. Even a daily paper was published, the harbinger of the underground press. Many have compared these caves to subterranean towns.

After the harvest, the wine is stored in vats. It takes four to five years before it appears in a bottle on your table. While in the chalk caves, a second fermentation of the wine takes place. The wine-growers wait until the sparkle has taken, as they say, before removing the bottles to racks or pulpits. For about three months a turner is paid just to move them a fraction every day, which is a process of bringing down impurities on the cork. After aging for a few years, the wines are mixed with a *dosage,* the amount determining the dryness.

All these methods take place in the caves, which, incidentally, may be 100 feet deep and are at a constant temperature of 50 degrees Fahrenheit. One of the most visited cellars is **Pommery & Greno,** at Place Général-Gouraud (tel. 05-05-01), open from 9 to 11:15 a.m. and from 2 to 5 p.m. Closed Saturdays, Sundays, and holidays.

HOTELS: If a day just isn't enough, you can stay overnight or dine at one of the following.

La Paix, 25-27 Place Drouet-d'Erlon (tel. 40-04-08), contends for a premier position. Inside and out, it is remodeled into a super-modern hotel. The sidewalk restaurant with its white chairs and tables is a social center. Decorated in a contemporary style, 100 bedrooms are spread across eight floors. Good strong colors are used throughout, and the beds are springy yet soft. The cost for two persons in a double or twin ranges from 156F ($35.61) to 180F ($41.09), including service and taxes. Singles range from 148F ($33.79) to 165F ($37.68). For a set meal, expect to pay about 120F ($27.40). Monsieur Renardias, the owner-manager, will aid you on a champagne cave tour.

Grand Hôtel du Nord, 75 Place Drouet-d'Erlon (tel. 47-39-03), provides an efficient, clean, and comfortable accommodation right in the heart of the city. An older building, entirely renovated, it contains small lounges on most bedroom floors where you can have breakfast. The bedrooms are adequate and modestly furnished. Doubles range from 75F ($17.12) with shower to 140F ($31.96) with bath. A continental breakfast is an extra 11F ($2.51). The rates include service and taxes.

Grand Hôtel Continental, 93 Place Drouet-D'Erlon (tel. 47-49-97), is on the formal park opposite the railway station. It's a long, low corner building with a mansard roof. In addition to old reception lounges with near-antiques, there are two attractive dining rooms, each with a traditional French look. The rate for two persons in a room with private bath is 160F ($36.53). Bathless singles cost 52F ($11.87).

READER'S HOTEL SELECTION: "**Hôtel d'Alsace,** at the corner of rue du Général-Sarraul and rue des Écrevées (tel. 47-44-08), is close to the railroad station. The façade looks expensive, but don't let that fool you. We paid only 60F ($13.70) for a double room with an enclosed bidet and hot and cold running water. The room was clean and large. Breakfast was an additional 10F ($2.28). To get to Hôtel d'Alsace from the railroad station, cross Boulevard Joffre, which runs in front of the station, and continue walking for a short block until you get to Boulevard Foch. Cross it and you will find rue Thiers. Walk about a block down rue Thiers until you reach rue du Petit-Four. Turn left and go a short block until you come to rue du Général-Sarrail, where the hotel is" (S. P. Hiam, Honolulu, Hawaii).

THE BEST RESTAURANTS: Boyer, 184 Avenue d'Épernay, N51 (tel. 06-08-60), on the outskirts of town, is a rustic restaurant with a fireplace. If you're willing to pay the price, you can get the finest viands in and around Reims. In fact, the restaurant is known for setting one of the best tables in all of France. It's run by Gaston Boyer and his son, Gérard, the latter trained at Lasserre in Paris. Once they operated a restaurant at Vincennes, but it wasn't until they moved to Reims that they won the fame they so richly deserve. They weren't long here when the champagne moguls—who pride themselves as gourmet diners—started beating a path to their door.

Of course, champagne is the great drink here, and the wine list is staggering—and super-expensive. The specialties are prepared by men who evidently care, putting time, money, effort, and imagination into their meals. Feuilleté d'escargots à la champenoise (snails in a light pastry shell, in a smooth cream-and-mushroom mixture) is an elegant beginning. Normally, you bypass an omelet in a top restaurant, but not here: the Boyers offer an omelette aux queues d'écrevisses for two persons, made with lobster and a creamy sauce that appears to be hollandaise but isn't. A favorite main-dish specialty is fresh salmon with sorrel. The most outstanding dessert is les délices de Marjorie. Expect to spend from 160F ($36.53) to 275F ($62.78) for a complete meal. The restaurant is closed Sunday nights, Mondays, and in August.

At Châlons-sur-Vesle, six miles west of the city on the N31, **Assiette Champenoise** (tel. 49-34-94) is a typical country auberge with untypical food. The chef, Monsieur Lallement, produces some award-winning specialties, and we'd highly recommend a lunchtime stopover if you're touring in the area. The food is cooked with great care and affection, and the prices are reasonable considering the service and attention given to the meal. You will spend about 120F ($27.40) to 170F ($38.81) for a complete meal. Specialties include a delicious dish of scallops or else a plate of three different types of poultry. We'd also recommend the poisson (fish) Bouzy Rouge. The wine list naturally offers champagne and some excellent bottles of Bouzy made from black grapes. The restaurant is closed for Sunday dinner and on Wednesdays and shuts down in February.

Back in Reims itself, **Le Florence**, 43 Boulevard Foch (tel. 47-35-36), is one of the leading restaurants. Despite its location across from the railway station, it is elegant inside. A gastronomique menu, four plates, is offered for 90F ($20.55), not including your wine. A tourist menu, however, goes for 42F ($9.59). On the à la carte menu, you might begin with pâté de canard truffé, then follow with one of the specialties, perhaps gratin de queues de langoustines au ratafia or poularde au champagne. Expect to spend from 85F ($19.41) to 130F ($29.68) if you order à la carte. Add 15% for service. The restaurant is closed Monday nights and from the end of July to mid-August.

Le Jardin du Crystal, 86 Place Drouet-de'Erlon (tel. 88-48-87), has been entirely renovated and completely upgraded. Monsieur Alemany is the chef de cuisine. His specialties include les rognons de veau (veal kidneys) flambés au marc de champagne, filet flambé au cognac in a sauce made with three mustards, le feuilleté of scallops, and turbot with a selection of vegetables prepared in the julienne fashion. A complete meal will cost from 120F ($27.40). The restaurant has a fine wine list, and the service is friendly and efficient. The "Crystal Garden" shuts down on Mondays.

4. Fère-en-Tardenois

For the most superb restaurant in the champagne area—in fact, one of France's greatest—head for Fère-en-Tardenois, 29 miles from Reims. You take the N31 northwest of the cathedral city, passing through Fismes, then turning southwest onto the N367. At a point a mile and a half north of this hamlet lie the ruins of the Château de Fère, a fortified castle dating from the 12th century. There is, as well, a Renaissance viaduct erected in 1560.

Near the colorful ruins stands the **Hostellerie du Château,** out the D967, route Forestière (tel. 82-21-13). If it's summer, begin your elegant repast in the sunny garden, sipping the apéritif of the house, a glass of champagne to which the juice of freshly crushed raspberries has been added. Then the serious business begins, and the cuisine here is very serious indeed.

The owners of the restored 16th-century château, the Blot family, oversee every detail, turning out imaginative and most original dishes. Of course, the turbot cooked in champagne may be familiar, but not perhaps the guinea hen with pink peppercorns or the breast of capon in truffle juice. The pièce de résistance is grenadin de veau (little slices of filet of veal cut in triangular shapes) Laguipière. The dish is named in honor of one of the great masters of French cookery who died in 1812. He'd followed Murat to Naples and later to Russia, only to freeze to death during the retreat from Moscow. The chef also specializes in some of the finest fish and shellfish dishes.

For all of this, however, expect to pay from 175F ($39.95) to 260F ($59.36). Although the desserts are mouth-watering, we always skip them and settle happily instead for a boulette d'Avesnes, which is a cone-shaped cheese flecked with herbs and crushed peppercorns, then coated with paprika.

If you'd like, you can reserve a room and spend the night. The family offers 20 guest rooms, all beautifully decorated in shades of burgundy and pink with touches of red, costing from 230F ($52.51) for one of the smaller doubles to a peak 330F ($75.34) for two housed in an apartment or suite. There are no singles. The château is closed in January and February.

EN ROUTE TO PARIS: If after your tour of the champagne country you have a full day, you can return to Paris leisurely, exploring battlefields and sampling the gastronomy along the way.

After leaving our last stopover at Fère-en-Tardenois, head southwest on the N367 to—

5. Château-Thierry

On the right bank of the Marne, 56 miles from Paris, Château-Thierry is where Jean de La Fontaine, the French poet and fabulist, was born in a 16th-century maison which is still open to the public on certain days (there is a small museum of his mementos). An industrial town, Château-Thierry contains the ruins of a castle crowning a hilltop which is believed to have been built for the Frankish king, Thierry IV.

Primarily, Château-Thierry is known in history because it was the farthest point reached by the German offensive in the summer of 1918. Under heavy bombardment, French forces were aided by the Second and Third Divisions of the American Expeditionary Force. At a point a mile west of the town are the battlefields of the Marne. Here thousands of Allied soldiers who died fighting in World War I were buried. Atop the hotly contested Hill 204 a monument stands honoring the American troops who lost their lives.

Those interested in this sad chapter in history may want to continue for a distance of two miles to—

BELLEAU WOOD: Known in French as Bois de Belleau, "The Battle of Belleau Wood" marked the second clash between American and German troops in World War I. The battlesite lies five miles northwest of Château-Thierry. After a struggle which lasted for two weeks of bitter fighting, the woods were finally taken by the Second Division of the U.S. Expeditionary Force under Major General Omar Bundy. Although the Germans suffered many losses, and some 1650 prisoners were taken, the U.S. casualties were appalling. Nearly 7585 men and 285 officers were wounded, killed, or missing in action. This battle demonstrated the bravery of the U.S. soldier in modern warfare.

In 1923 the battleground was dedicated as a permanent memorial to the men who gave their lives there. The American cemetery contains 2288 graves. You'll also see a chapel which was damaged in World War II fighting. Discarded weapons, now rusting, can still be seen along the scorched road. A gruesome sight. For far happier touring in the area, follow the N3 along the Marne to—

6. La Ferté-sous-Jouarre

At the hamlet of Jouarre itself, you can visit a Benedictine abbey dating from the 12th century and explore one of the oldest crypts in France, going back to the 7th century.

From the abbey, it is a drive of about a mile and a half back to La Ferté-sous-Jouarre, where Parisian gastronomes flock on the weekend to dine at the **Auberge de Condé,** 1 Avenue de Montmirail (tel. 022-00-07), one of the most exceptional of the restaurants in what is sometimes called "the ring around Paris."

The appointments aren't luxurious—in fact, the inn is decidedly old-fashioned, but also intimate, with lots of provincial character. It serves delicious dishes and regional specialties worthy of its two-star rating. The Tingaud family welcomes you, inviting you to partake of the cuisine of Emile Tingaud, beginning with feuilleté de truffes et foie gras. After that bit of elegance, you might order either sweetbreads "des gourmets" or filets de sole Vincent-Bourrel. The cookery is traditional, classical, and of grand quality, accompanied by the finest of champagne. For a complete meal, expect to pay from 150F ($34.26) if you order from one of the set meals. However, diners preferring the à la carte menu might easily spend 200F ($45.66) even more. The inn is closed on Monday nights, Tuesdays, from mid-August to September, and in February.

The Tingaud family also runs **Le Relais,** 4 Avenue Franklin-Roosevelt (tel. 022-02-03), which is more modest—and so are its prices. The meals here are well prepared, and the service is polite and friendly. Although the cuisine in no way matches that of the Auberge de Condé, it is, nevertheless, satisfying. Featured dishes include brill with sorrel, thin slices of sole in sauce, a cassoulet, and a mousseline of pike. Dinner is available only from an à la carte menu, costing from 80F ($18.26). The restaurant shuts down in July, in December, and on Wednesday nights and Thursdays as well as on public holidays.

After dining here, take the Autoroute de l'Est back to Paris, a distance of 42 miles.

7. Verdun

At this garrison town in eastern France Maréchal Pétain said, "They shall not pass!"—and they didn't. Verdun, where the Allies held out against a massive assault by the German army in World War I, evokes tin-helmeted soldiers in *All Quiet on the Western Front.* In the closing years of World War I an estimated 600,000 to 800,000 French and German soldiers died battling over a few miles of territory.

Today, stone houses clustered on narrow, cobblestoned streets give Verdun a medieval appearance. It lies on the muddy Meuse between Paris and the Rhine. Two monuments commemorate these tragic events: Rodin's *Defense* and Boucher's *To Victory and the Dead.*

A good tour of the battlefields is called **Circuit des Forts,** covering the main fortifications. On the right bank of the Meuse, this is a good 20-mile run, taking in **Fort Vaux,** where Raynal staged his heroic defense after sending his last message by carrier pigeon. After passing a vast French cemetery of 16,000 graves, an endless field of crosses, you arrive at the **Ossuaire de Douaumont.** Here, the bones of those killed in battle—literally blown to bits—were embedded. Nearby at the mostly underground **Fort de Douaumont** the "hell of Verdun" was unleashed. From the roof you can look out at a vast field of corroded tops of "pillboxes." Then on to the **Trench of Bayonets.** Bayonets of French soldiers instantly entombed by a shellburst form this unique memorial.

The other tour, the **Circuit Rive Gauche,** is about a 60-mile run and takes in the **Hill of Montfaucon,** where the Americans have erected a memorial tower, and the **American Cemetery at Romagne,** with some 15,000 graves.

FOOD AND LODGING: Hotel de la Poste et Restaurant Pergola, 8 Avenue Douaumont (tel. 86-03-90), is a member of the Fédération Nationale des Logis de France, a nonprofit national association of hotelkeepers. Members receive financial support from the government, providing they preserve the regional characteristics of an establishment. At de la Poste, accommodations contain spacious closets, writing tables, and in some cases a sofa in the bedrooms. A young woman, after our most recent check-in, arrived with a bottle of Vittel water and a bucket of ice. The room was pleasantly kept and well equipped. The least expensive single was priced at 50F ($11.42), the costlier doubles 90F ($20.55). Breakfast is served in the bedrooms, costing an extra 8.50F ($1.94). The Pergola restaurant offers fine dining, a multicourse meal costing 38F ($8.68), although a more "gastronomique" dinner goes for 75F ($17.12). Closed from January 20 to February 20.

8. A Detour to Amiens

Due north of Paris for about 75 miles, Amiens has one of the finest Gothic cathedrals in France. On the Somme River, a major textile center since medieval days, Amiens was the ancient capital of Picardy. Its old town—a jumble of narrow streets criss-crossed by canals—is worth exploring.

The **Cathedral of Notre-Dame** was begun in 1220 to the plans of Robert de Luzarches and completed about 1270, though two unequal towers were added later. It is 469 feet long, the largest church in France.

Surely the Amiens cathedral is the crowning example of French Gothic architecture. In John Ruskin's rhapsodical *Bible of Amiens,* which Proust translated into French, he extolled the door arches. The three portals of the west front are lavishly decorated, important examples of Gothic cathedral sculpture which must have influenced the builders of Notre-Dame in Paris. The portals are surmounted by two galleries. The upper one contains 22 statues of kings, and the large rose window is from the 16th century.

In the interior are beautifully carved stalls and a flamboyant choir screen. These stalls with some 3500 figures were made by local artisans in the early 16th century, and they are the loveliest in all of France. The interior is held up by 126 slender pillars, perhaps the zenith of the High Gothic in the north of France. The cathedral, like St. Paul's in London, somehow managed to escape destruction in World War II, and the architecture of Europe is richer for that.

WHERE TO STAY: Grand Hôtel de l'Univers, 2 rue Noyon (tel. 91-52-51), is the leading choice, lying 150 yards from the railway station in the business heart of town, within a short walk of the cathedral. The hotel is more than 100 years old, but it has been completely renovated. Its 40 rooms come in a completely modern Nordic styling, or else with reproductions of more traditional French pieces. Rooms with private baths and showers range in price from 105F ($23.97) in a single to a high of 170F ($38.81) for the best doubles. There is an elevator and an American bar, but no restaurant. Breakfast is an additional 15F ($3.42). English is spoken.

Chapter XI

ALSACE

1. Strasbourg
2. La Wantzenau
3. Illhaeusern
4. Colmar
5. The Wine Road of Alsace

OLD GERMANS still speak of it as one of the "lost provinces" of Alsace-Lorraine, whose ancient capitals are Strasbourg and Nancy. Alsace itself has been called "the least French of French provinces," perhaps more reminiscent of the Black Forest facing it across the **Rhine.**

This territory has been much disputed by Germany and France. In fact, it became German from 1870 until after World War I, and it was ruled by Hitler from 1940 until 1944. But now both of the old provinces are happily back under French control, although they are somewhat independent, remembering the days when they ruled themselves.

In its old cities and cathedrals and its castle-dotted landscape Alsace evokes memories of a great past, and its battle monuments or scars sometimes recall military glory or defeat.

1. Strasbourg

Capital of Alsace, Strasbourg is one of France's greatest cities. It is also the capital of pâté de foie gras. It was in Strasbourg that Rouget de Lisle first sang the "Marseillaise." In June of every year the artistic life of Strasbourg reaches its zenith at the **International Music Festival** held at the Château des Rohan and the cathedral.

Strasbourg is not only a great univeristy city, the seat of the Council of Europe, but one of France's most important ports, lying two miles west of the Rhine. Visits by motor launch and a number of Rhine excursions are offered from here. Go to the tourist office at 10 Place Gutenberg for the most up-to-date data on these excursions, whose schedules vary depending on the season and the number of passengers interested.

Despite war damage, much remains of old Strasbourg. It still has covered bridges and the old towers of its former fortifications, and many 15th- and 17th-century dwellings with painted wooden fronts and carved beams.

In 1871 Strasbourg became German and was made the capital of the imperial territory of Alsace-Lorraine, reverting back to France in 1918. Germans continue to invade it, but today's visitors are friendly ones, pouring over the border on the weekends to sample the fine food, wine, and beer of Alsace.

One street alone illustrates Strasbourg's identity crisis. A century ago it was called the Avenue Napoléon. In 1871 it became the Kaiser Wilhelmstrasse, turning into the Boulevard de la République in 1918. In 1940 it underwent another change, becoming Adolf Hitler Strasse, before ending up as the Avenue du Général-de-Gaulle in 1945.

The traffic hub of Strasbourg is the **Place Kléber**, which dates from the 15th century. Sit here with a tankard of Alsatian beer and slowly get to know Strasbourg. Eventually everybody seems to cross this square. The bronze statue in the center is of J. B. Kléber, born in Strasbourg in 1753. He became one of Napoleon's most noted generals, and was buried under this monument. Apparently, his presence offended the Nazis, who removed the statue in 1940. However, this Alsatian bronze was restored to its proper place in 1945 at the liberation.

From Kléber Square, you can take the rue des Grandes-Arcades to the **Place Gutenberg,** one of the oldest squares of Strasbourg. It was formerly a *marché aux herbes.* The statue in the center is by David d'Angers in 1840. It is of Gutenberg himself, who perfected his printing press in the Strasbourg winter of 1436-37. The former town hall, now the **Hôtel du Commerce,** was built in 1582, and is considered one of the most significant Renaissance buildings in all of Alsace.

With this small orientation, you can now make your way along the rue Mercière to the Place de la Cathédrale to see the crowning glory of Strasbourg.

The **Strasbourg Cathedral,** which inspired the poetry of Goethe, was built on the site of a Romanesque church of 1015. Today it stands proudly, one of the largest churches of Christianity, one of the most outstanding examples of German Gothic, representing a harmonious transition from the Romanesque. Construction on it began in 1176. The famous pyramidal tower in rose-colored stone was completed in 1439, and is the highest such one dating from medieval times, soaring a distance of 472 feet. You may want to ascend the tower, although "at your own risk," as the sign warns. The cost is 3F (68¢). You can do so from 8:30 a.m. to 7 p.m. in July and August. From April to June and in September, the hours are from 9 to 6:30; in March and October, 9 to 5:30; and from November through February, 9 to 4:30. You climb 329 steps to the platform, 556 steps to the bottom of the pyramid, and 635 steps to the top of the steeple. You cannot, of course, go up to the pyramid. From the highest viewing level, a panoramic vista unfolds of the Vosges and the Black Forest.

On the main façade, four large counterforts divide the front into three vertical parts and two horizontal galleries. Note the great rose window which looks like real stone lace. The façade is rich in sculptural decoration. On the portal of the south transept, the "Coronation and Death" of the Virgin in the tympanum is considered one of the finest such medieval works. In the north transept, see also the face of St. Lawrence Chapel, a stunning achievement of the late-Gothic German style.

A Romanesque crypt lies under the chancel. The chancel itself is covered with a square of stonework. The stained-glass window in the center is the work of Max Ingrand. The nave is vast and majestic, with windows depicting emperors and kings on the north aisle. Five chapels are grouped around the transept, including one built in 1500 in the flamboyant Gothic style. In the south transept stands the Angel Pillar, illustrating the Last Judgment, with angels lowering their trumpets.

The astronomical clock was built between 1547 and 1574. However, it stopped working during the Revolution, and from 1838 to 1842 the mechanism was replaced. The clock is wound once a week. People flock to see its 12 noon show of allegorical figures. The clock can also be inspected; tickets at 1.50F

(34¢) go on sale daily in the south portal at 11:30 a.m., and visits are allowed between 12:30 and 12:45. On Sunday Apollo appears driving his sun horses; on Thursday you see Jupiter and his eagle, and so on. The main body of the clock has a planetarium according to Copernicus.

From March 2 until the end of September you can view a son-et-lumiere show at the cathedral.

On the south side of the cathedral, at the Place du Château, the **Château des Rohan,** built from 1730 to 1742, is an architectural example of supreme elegance and perfect proportions. It is considered one of the crowning design achievements in eastern France in the 18th century, and is noted in particular for its façades. On the ground floor is an archaeological museum, and on the first floor a fine-arts museum, with works by Rubens, Rembrandt, Van Dyck, El Greco, Goya, Watteau *(The Copper Cleaners),* Renoir, and Monet. There is, as well, a museum devoted to decorative arts, including ceramics and the cock of the first astronomical clock of the cathedral. The museum, charging an admission of 4F (91¢), is open April 1 to September 30 from 10 a.m. to noon and from 2 to 6 p.m. Off-season, its hours are from 2 to 6 p.m. only.

On the southwest corner of the Place du Château, the **Musée de l'Oeuvre Notre-Dame** occupies a collection of ancient houses with wooden galleries. Its courtyards are known by their old names—the Stag, the Grooms, and the Bakery. Inside is a museum illustrating art of the Middle Ages and the Renaissance in Strasbourg and surrounding Alsace. The original building dates from 1347, although there have been many later additions. Some of the pieces of art were formerly displayed in the cathedral itself, where copies have been substituted. The most celebrated prize is a stained-glass head of Christ from a window originally at Wissembourg, dating from about 1070, one of the oldest known. There is also a stained-glass window depicting an emperor from about 1200. The medieval sculpture is of much interest, as are the works from the Strasbourg goldsmiths from the 16th through the 17th centuries. The museum's winding staircase and interior are in the pure Renaissance style. The 13th-century hall contains the loveliest sculptures from the cathedral, including the wise and foolish virgins from 1280. Hours and admission are the same as for the Château des Rohan.

The **Musée Alsacien,** 23 Quai St.-Nicholas, has been installed in a mansion dating from the 16th and 17th centuries. It is like a living textbook of the folklore and customs of Alsace, containing arts, crafts, and tools of the old province. It keeps the same hours as the museums described above, charging a 6F ($1.37) admission.

The **Church of St. Thomas,** built between 1230 and 1330, is peculiar in that it has five naves. A Protestant church, it is the most interesting one in Strasbourg after the cathedral. It contains the mausoleum of Maréchal de Saxe, a masterpiece of French art by Pigalle, dating from 1777. The church lies along rue St.-Thomas, near the Bridge of St. Thomas.

La Petite France, a long walk from the church down the colorful rue des Dentelles, is the most interesting quarter of Strasbourg. Its houses from the 16th century are mirrored in the waters of the Ill. In "Little France," old roofs with gray tiles have sheltered families for ages, and the crossbeamed façades with their roughly carved rafters are in the typical Alsatian style. Of exceptional interest is the rue du Bain-aux-Plantes. An island in the middle of the river is cut by four canals. For a view, walk along the rue des Moulins, branching off from the rue du Bain-aux-Plantes.

Finally, you may want to take a **Riverboat Tour of the Ill.** Off season, departures are at 4:15 p.m. and 6 p.m. only at a cost of 15F ($3.42) for adults,

8F ($1.83) for children. During summer there is an extra night trip at 9, costing 18F ($4.11) for adults, 10F ($2.28) for children.

HOTELS: Sofitel Strasbourg, Place St.-Pierre-le-Jeune (tel. 32-99-30), is the most attractive and glamorous of the contemporary blocks of hotels in the city center. It stands on a stately, tree-shaded square next to one of the city's oldest churches. From the garage basement there is direct elevator access to all floors, where you'll find such amenities as soundproofed windows, three-speed air conditioning, and wall-to-wall carpeting. The atmosphere, the architecture, the furnishings—French traditional combined with modern—are light and airy. Of course, you could be living in southern California instead of the old city of Strasbourg. Singles range in price from 250F ($57.08) to 380F ($86.75), and doubles go from 320F ($73.06) to 480F ($109.58). Once you get past the marble lobby, the lounges and the bar, Le Thomann, are warm and inviting. Its restaurant, Le Chateaubriand, opens onto the little plaza with its reflection pool and beds of seasonal flowers. The food is in the grand-hotel international style. Thus, you are likely to be offered Valencian paella for two, sauerkraut Alsacienne, roast lamb flavored with the herbs of Provence, and a zander suprême with Riesling. An à la carte meal will cost from 110F ($25.11) and up. The restaurant is closed on Sundays.

Terminus Gruber, 10 Place de la Gare (tel. 32-87-00). One of the leading modern hotels of Strasbourg, built at the railway station, the Terminus Gruber has a streamlined, contemporary façade that doesn't suggest the warmth and tradition of its interior. The bedrooms are comfortably furnished in a somewhat dated but still pleasing French fashion. Baths are tiled and immaculately maintained. In all, 80 rooms with bath or shower are offered at rates ranging from 110F ($25.11) in a single to a high of 230F ($52.51) in a double. The hotel offers two restaurants—Le Relais Gastronomique, which seems primarily a meeting place for Strasbourg business people at lunch, and the more inviting La Cour de Rosemont, which is a luxuriously appointed restaurant for dinner. The latter restaurant has very good food, including specialties of Alsace such as snails, and sauerkraut with pork products. In season the chef specializes in game dishes, such as roast pheasant. His fish dishes, such as a turbot soufflé, are sometimes artistic statements. Menus go for 58F ($13.24) and 108F ($24.66), plus 15% for service, and an à la carte dinner here averages around 170F ($38.81). Incidentally, the hotel also has a Brasserie Terminus-Gruber, serving a very good set meal for just 35F ($7.99).

France, 20 rue Jeu-des-Enfants (tel. 32-37-12), stands in the vicinity of the railway station. The designer employed know-how to produce rooms that are comfortable and attractive. Each chamber has its entry hall for luggage, as well as an all-tiled bath with a stall shower. The beds are soft, and the fruitwood and Formica furnishings slick and practical. Most accommodations also have velvet-covered armchairs and carpeting in rich colors. Singles cost 170F ($38.81), the double rate rising to 220F ($50.23). Breakfast is enjoyed in a room where a window wall opens onto a view of the plaza. The hotel is color-happy, relying a great deal on autumnal tones. The lounges are less skillfully decorated than the bedrooms, although pleasant.

Vendôme, 9 Place de la Gare (tel. 32-45-23), shelters Eurailpass holders and others, enjoying a central position opposite the railway station. The 39-room hotel occupies a fairly new building, offering rooms of comfort and style. Everything is modern, and there is a private bath or shower in each chamber. Furnishings are either provincial or else in sleek contemporary lines. Singles rent for 60F ($13.70), that tariff rising to 110F ($25.11) in a double. Breakfast at 11F ($2.51) is the only meal offered.

Gutenberg, 31 rue des Serruries (tel. 32-17-15), stands near the Place Gutenberg. Madame Lette welcomes you to her 1745 mansion, which offers a warm atmosphere with plenty of old furniture and pictures. There are no singles, but doubles start at 75F ($17.12) with hot and cold running water and private toilet, 100F ($22.83) with shower, and 135F ($30.82) with complete bath. A continental breakfast is another 10.50F ($2.39).

Victoria, 7-9 rue du Maire-Kuss (tel. 32-13-06), is conveniently perched on a main artery between the railway station (three minutes) and the center of town (10 minutes). Rooms are neatly and pleasantly furnished, costing 50F ($11.42) in a single, 70F ($15.98) in a double. A continental breakfast is included in these rates. The management is courteous and friendly.

READERS' HOTEL SELECTIONS: "This is a logical overnight stop for persons traveling by train from Luxembourg to the Black Forest, Bavaria, or Austria. We stayed at the **Hôtel du Rhin,** 7 Place de la Gare (tel. 32-35-00), immediately opposite the train station. There we had a spacious—downright enormous by European standards—room with a large, comfortable bed. A double room rents for 130F ($29.68) and a single for 75F ($17.12). Breakfast at 14F ($3.20) is served in a bright, cheerful dining room" (Richard and Eleanor Leary, Springfield, Ill.). . . . "**Hotel des Princes**, 33 rue Geiler, at the Conseil de l'Europe (tel. 61-55-19), is a two-star hotel—without doubt the best value we found in five months of European travel. Rooms are large, clean, and fresh, and the service is excellent, the location in a quiet neighborhood, a 15-minute walk from the cathedral and the center of town. A bathless room rents for 45F ($10.27) for one person, 65F ($14.84) for two. Or else two persons pay anywhere from 100F ($22.83) to 120F ($27.40) in rooms with private showers or baths, with a continental breakfast costing an extra 10.50F ($2.39)" (Carl and Jean Auer, Hillsborough, Calif.). . . . "For a room, try **Hôtel de la Gare**, 15 Petite rue de la Course (a half-block from the railway station) (tel. 32-18-45). The hotel is completely remodeled and has modern showers in most rooms. Two persons in a room with a double bed and shower pay 70F ($15.98), the tariff increasing to 100F ($22.83) in a twin-bedded chamber with shower. Breakfast is extra. The owner, Claude Faber, speaks English. You'll find him usually in the restaurant, which is excellent; a three-course, hearty dinner costs about 30F ($6.85)" (Sandy and David Ahl, Morristown, N.J.).

RESTAURANTS: Maison Kammerzell, 16 Place de la Cathédrale (tel. 32-42-14), is not only one of the best restaurants in Strasbourg but a sightseeing attraction in its own right. Dating from 1467, and facing the cathedral, it is an Alsatian gingerbread house reminiscent of Hansel and Gretel's. Its carved wooden framework is from the Renaissance period, and a cheese dealer known as Martin Braun built the three overhanging stories in 1589. It is richly decorated, and nowadays it is a shrine of gastronomy. Paul and Tony Schloesser are the owners, and their cuisine is exciting and varied. If you've never ordered it before, we'd suggest la choucroute formidable (two persons are required). This is the great specialty of Alsace, prepared with goosefat, Riesling wine, and juniperberries, and served with pork products, such as Strasbourg sausages, pork cutlets, and smoked breast of pork. Other specialties include duckling au Cassis, a filet of sole with a scallop mousse, even a zander fricassée. Venison, wild fowl, partridges, pheasant, hare, and wild boar are offered according to season. Fixed-price meals featuring many specialties, cost 95F ($21.69). There is a special *menu degustation* for 170F ($38.81), if you think you can eat a lot of food. The restaurant is closed Thursdays.

Crocodile, 10 rue Outre (tel. 32-13-02). This is a beautiful old restaurant where patrons go to taste the grande cuisine of Émile Jung. His food is generally more inventive, often more daring in concept, than the traditional restaurants of Strasbourg. On a summer day the golden light that pours down through yellow skylights might illuminate a boned quail which has been stuffed with foie gras, then braised slowly in goosefat and chilled in a meat gelatin. You might start your meal with a remarkable soup of frog legs or else the celebrated endive salad with hot goose liver. You might even order stuffed roast suckling pig here, or sausages that evoke memories of the smoked German wurst. Then there are turbot with thin strips of vegetables, timbale of sole and lobster, veal kidneys gratin with crayfish tails—always something interesting and probably some dishes you've never sampled before. Another grand specialty is a filet of beef en croûte. Naturally, you get the finest wines Alsace has to offer. Set meals cost 140F ($31.96), but expect to pay 200F ($45.66) to 260F ($59.36) if ordering à la carte. The restaurant is closed from July 13 to August 11 and on Sundays and Mondays.

Maison des Tanneurs, 42 impasse du Bain-aux-Plantes (tel. 32-79-70), is a timbered building established in 1572, standing on one of the most typical of the old streets of the quarter known as Petite France. Its dining terrace opens onto the canal. The decor is very warm, with many flowers and well-selected Alsatian antiques. In this characteristic sector, you dine very well on some of the outstanding specialties of the Alsatian kitchen. Sometimes the restaurant is called "La maison de la choucroute." Naturally, sauerkraut is the specialty, accompanied by a formidable array of pork products, although two persons must order the dish at a cost of 100F ($22.83). But the chef knows how to do other dishes equally well, including the classic opener, if you're feeling extravagant: a parfait of foie gras with fresh truffles. Main dishes we'd recommend include crayfish tails à la nage, or poulet—known as coq au Riesling—cooked in white wine, certainly braised squab served with green peas. Set meals are offered at 100F ($22.83). If ordering à la carte, expect to pay around 135F ($30.82). The restaurant is closed on Sundays and Mondays and takes a holiday July 2 to 12 and from December 22 to January 21.

Valentin-Sorg, 6 Place Homme-de-Fer (tel. 32-12-16), has long been a favorite dining room of ours, even when it stood on a street known as "the old winemarket street." But it long ago was transferred to the 14th (top) floor of a building called "the Tower," standing on the "Square of the Iron Man." Many would patronize it if only for the view. Fortunately, it not only offers a panoramic vista but is one of the finest restaurants in the city, often ranked as number two or three. Here you can order the classic dishes of the French menu—sauerkraut à l'Alsacienne, naturally, but also sole Pyramide, sweetbreads Demidoff, frog legs with Riesling, tournedos Rossini, duck in orange sauce, even beef Wellington (24-hour notice), which sounds strangely heretical in France. Menus are offered at 95F ($21.69) and 135F ($30.82). The restaurant is closed Sunday nights, Tuesdays, and from mid-August until September 1 and from mid-February until March 1.

Buerehiesel, 4 parc de l'Orangerie (tel. 61-62-24), is also known as "Chez Westermann." It is distinguished for two reasons—La Nouvelle Cuisine of Antoine Westermann and the setting in the Orangerie, which is a beautiful park, at the end of the allée de la Robertsau, near the Council of Europe. The park was planned by the famous landscape artist Le Nôtre and was offered to the Empress Josephine. In such a distinguished setting, you can enjoy the admirable specialties of the inventive chef—a terrine of sweetbreads with foie gras, sole and lobster à la nage (cooked in court-bouillon and flavored with herbs), salmis de pigeon au Bourgogne, zander with noodles, steamed spring chicken with cabbage. Set meals begin at 95F ($21.69), and à la carte orders average around 150F ($34.26). The restaurant is closed on Tuesday nights and Wednesdays, 15 days in August, and from February 20 until March 10.

À l'Ancienne Douane, 6 rue Douane (tel. 32-42-19), near the cathedral, enjoys one of the most romantic restaurant settings, its garden tables set out on the banks of the Ill. This old restaurant is rich in the antique Strasbourg atmosphere, with time-blackened beams, wood paneling, and tapestries. A lovely patina seems to coat everything. Inside are formal dining rooms, but of course if the weather's right, every diner makes for one of those tables overlooking the river banks, within sight of houses with highly pitched roofs peppered with chimneys. Specialties include meat pie with chicken liver, potted meat with hazelnuts, the famous Strasbourg foie gras, perch-pike in Riesling sauce, and a rib of beef (two diners required). A set meal costs as little as 32F ($7.31), one of the best bargain dinners of Strasbourg, considering quality of food and the large size of the portions. À la carte selections may bring the tab up to 70F ($15.98) to 110F ($25.11). The restaurant is closed on Wednesdays.

Pfifferbriader, 9 Place du Marché-aux-Cochon-de-Lait (tel. 32-15-43), behind the cathedral and close to Ill Quay, offers fast-food service in the popular tavern style. The plat du jour ranges from 16F ($3.65) to 28F ($6.39) at lunch, peaking at 22F ($5.02) to 30F ($6.85) at dinner. Desserts range from 4F (91¢) to 7F ($1.60). There is also a 28F ($6.39) set menu. À la carte orders will cost from 60F ($13.70) to 85F ($19.41) for the average repast. Many working Strasbourgers come here to enjoy their lunch break.

2. La Wantzenau

Instead of dining in Strasbourg, many motorists prefer to head north for 7½ miles to the village of La Wantzenau, which has very good restaurants and lots of regional specialties. Go northeast on the N68 if you'd like to follow their example.

There the Zimmer, rue des Héros (tel. 96-20-05), serves the famous chicken dish of the village—poussin à La Wantzenau. Gastronomes drive over from Germany just to sample it. Under the watchful eye of Mme. Zimmer, excellent regional specialties in large portions are served—matelote with Riesling, duckling with sauerkraut, turbot with sorrel, scallops with strips of sole. Menus are offered at 55F ($12.56) and 135F ($30.82). Featured wines include Pinot Noir and Edelzquicker. The restaurant is closed on Sunday nights and Mondays and takes a vacation in August.

À Moulin, 25 route de Strasbourg (tel. 96-20-01), is another favorite; it is set in a flower garden. A large house, it feeds diners well in a traditional setting. Not only is cookery exceptional, but the wine list is also rewarding, including Riesling, Pinot Noir, and Tokay. German diners from across the border come here with their list of dishes to order—such specialties as foie gras frais maison, matelote with white wine, poussin (pullet) Mère Clauss, omelet with fines herbes, and carré d'agneau (loin of lamb with ribs). Menus cost 95F ($21.69) and 135F ($30.82). The restaurant, run by Monsieur Clauss, is closed on Sunday nights and on Thursdays and in July.

Finally, À la Barrière, 3 route de Strasbourg (tel. 96-20-23), is on many a connoisseur's short list. It is urbanely run by Monsieur Aeby, who sees that wines and food are carefully served, although not in an ostentatious way. The chef likes nothing better than producing regional cooking for hungry diners. His foie gras with truffles adds an elegant touch, followed by his barbue (brill) suprême. In hunting season, he also offers roast pheasant and roebuck. Fish dishes are also recommended, especially the turbot served with a creamy hollandaise sauce and the salmon steaks with sorrel. Zander cooked in Riesling is also good. The least expensive meal goes for 75F ($17.12), and you will more likely spend 130F ($29.68) ordering à la carte. The restaurant is closed on

Wednesday nights and Thursdays and takes a vacation from August 20 to September.

3. Illhaeusern

Gourmets from all over the world flock to this sleepy village, eleven miles north from Colmar, for one important reason—**L'Auberge de l'Ill**, route de Collonges (tel. 71-83-23). The Haeberlin brothers have a total commitment to food. They combine the finest quality Alsatian specialties with La Nouvelle Cuisine and other classic offerings. They do this so well that their restaurant is one of the greatest in France.

In this small village east of Route N83, the brothers Haeberlin serve unforgettable meals in an elegant setting under the willows of the riverbank. The scene could have been painted by Watteau. It used to be the Haeberlins' family farmhouse, and it is furnished with antiques and highly polished silver holloware.

Jean-Pierre, a talented painter, is in charge in the dining room. He knows it well, considering he designed it for dining perfection. Paintings, some by Bernard Buffet, decorate the walls. Paul is in charge in the kitchen. Once the Haeberlin women did the cooking in the family, and Paul first learned cuisine from his mother and aunt. Soon he was taking dishes of Alsatian origin and making them into grande cuisine, as represented by matelote au Riesling, eel stewed in Riesling wine. He also came up with new and inventive ways to serve foie gras.

His dishes have perfect harmony. Jean-Pierre comes up with names for the new ones, such as turbot de l'Ill, for the river that flows through the hamlet. After frying, the turbot is surrounded by a cream sauce made with lobster, chopped tarragon, tomatoes, and almond-size pieces of cucumber. Another unusual dish is a mousse of pike surrounding a core of boned frog legs, all served in a velvety sauce atop a bed of spinach.

The partridge, pheasant, and duckling are hardly better anywhere in Europe, and the in-season-only main dishes are flavored deliciously. Sometimes braised slices of pheasant and partridge are served together with their dressing, the inevitable chestnuts, but also a rainbow of woodsy wild mushrooms. They are served with very light, almost airy Breton cornmeal pancakes, which come as a surprise. Of course, a winey game sauce is also used.

The salmon soufflé in a velvety smooth white sauce is surely unequaled in all of France and in fact is celebrated. A pale pink slice of salmon is peaked with a pike soufflé. This delicate concoction is glazed under a cream and Riesling sauce, spiced with just a dab of fresh tomato concassé.

For an appetizer, we'd suggest a salade de lapereau, if featured—filets of baby hare with slivered artichoke hearts. Morels are served with this dish.

"Cooking is an art, and all art is patience," you are reminded; and some dishes require a 24-hour notice.

The cheese selection is impressive. The local rye bread, sliced paper-thin, is studded with walnuts and served along with the array of cheese. The sorbets, particularly the pale grapefruit, literally melt in your mouth.

In the beautiful flower-filled garden of the inn you can take your apéritif or coffee and brandy at a table under the weeping willows, watching the quiet-flowing Ill go by.

Of course, reservations are imperative. Set meals cost from 160F ($36.53) weekdays, rising to 200F ($45.66) on Sundays and holidays. The restaurant is closed on Monday nights and Tuesdays and for one week in July and three weeks in February.

4. Colmar

One of the most attractive towns in Alsace, Colmar is filled with many wonderful old medieval and early Renaissance buildings, with half-timbered structures, sculptured gables, and gracious loggias. Little gardens and wash houses surround many of the old homes. Its old quarter looks more German than French, filled as it is with streets of unexpected twists and turns. As a gateway to the Rhine country, Colmar is a major stopover south from Strasbourg, 44 miles away. On the Ill River, Colmar is the third largest town in Alsace, lying near the vine-covered slopes of the southern Vosges.

Its major attraction is the **Musée d'Unterlinden** ("Under the Linden Trees"), one of the most visited and most famous of all French provincial museums, lying on the Place d'Unterlinden. The museum is housed in a former Dominican convent built in 1232. The convent was the chief seat of Rhenish mysticism in the 14th and 15th centuries. Converted to a museum around 1850, it has been a treasure house of art and history of Alsace ever since.

The jewel of its collection is a celebrated immense altar screen with folding, two-sided wing pieces. It was designed that way to show first the Crucifixion, then the Incarnation, framed by the Annunciation and the Resurrection. The carved altar screen shows St. Anthony visiting the hermit St. Paul. It also depicts the Temptation of St. Anthony, the most soothing and beguiling part of the work, which has some ghastly scenes of misshapen birds, weird monsters, and loathsome animals. The demon of the plague, for example, is depicted with a swollen belly and purple skin, his body blotched with boils, a diabolical grin spread across his horrible face. He stands on webbed feet, his hands rotting stumps reaching out to seize the hermit's breviary. One of the most exciting works in the history of German art, the *Issenheim Altarpiece* was created by the Würzburg-born Matthias Grünewald (1460-1528), called "the most furious of realists." His colors glow, his fantasy overwhelms you.

The museum has other attractions as well, including the magnificent altarpiece of Jean d'Orlier by Martin Schongauer from around 1470.

Also displayed are works of artists from the 14th to the 15th centuries who were painting in Colmar. In religious art, the former convent has a large collection of woodcarvings and stained glass from the 14th to the 18th centuries, plus some lapidary collections of the Gallo-Roman period, including funereal slabs. Its armory collection includes ancient arms from the Romanesque to the Renaissance periods, featuring halberds and crossbows. Charging 6F ($1.37) for admission, the museum is open daily from 9 a.m. to noon and from 2 to 5 p.m. between November 1 and March 31. From April 1 to October 31 it is open from 2 to 6 p.m.

St. Martin's Church, in the heart of old Colmar, is a collegiate church begun in 1230 on the site of a Romanesque church. It has a notable choir erected by William of Marburg in 1350. Its celebrated treasure, however, is Martin Schongauer's painting *Virgin of the Rosebush,* all gold, red, and white, with fluttering birds. It is to be found on the left side-altar. The church is crowned by a steeple rising to a height of 232 feet.

One of the most beautiful houses in Colmar is the **Maison Pfister,** a civic building erected in 1537 with wooden balconies. It stands at the corner of the rue Mercière and the rue des Marchands.

If you take St. Peter's Bridge over the Lauch River, you'll have an excellent view of Old Colmar and can explore the section known as **Petite Venice** because it is riddled with canals.

HOTELS: Le Champ-de-Mars, 2 Avenue de Marne (tel. 41-54-54), is an excellent hotel, the finest in Colmar, and it certainly has an agreeable setting in the park of le Champ-de-Mars, from which it takes its name. The building is in the typical Alsatian style, and the interior decoration is warm and inviting. Rooms are handsomely furnished and well maintained, costing 150F ($34.26) in a single, that tariff rising to 175F ($39.95) in a double. The hotel also has a restaurant, offering a set meal for 48F ($10.96), as well as an Alsatian "caveau."

The **Terminus-Bristol,** Place de la Gare (tel. 23-59-59), has been the traditional leader. It also contains within its precincts one of the finest restaurants and bars in Colmar, the Rendez-vous de Chasse, which is recommended separately as a dining choice. Right at the busy railway station, this hotel rents out 85 bedrooms, all done in a wide-ranging French styling using both sleek modern and provincial 18th-century-type pieces. Rooms come equipped with private baths and toilets. The single rate is 150F ($34.26), rising to 200F ($45.66) in a double. In the hotel's l'Auberge you can order a set meal for 35F ($7.99).

The **Park Hôtel,** 52 Avenue de la République (tel. 41-34-80), is less expensive and quite good, offering completely modern comfort at a rate of 75F ($17.12) in a single, 170F ($38.81) in a double. The hotel has sleek, contemporary styling, totally ignoring the Alsatian tradition. But it is well maintained, its rooms equipped with tiled baths and Danish-style showers. In addition, built-in headboards are used, and writing desks are provided, as are radios and televisions. So as not to ignore tradition completely, one end of the dining room is decked out in an Italian Regency period. The dining room serves good Alsatian food, set menus offered at 55F ($12.56) and 98F ($22.37). The hotel is closed from December 20 to January 10, and the restaurant shuts down from November 1 to March 31.

Hôtel Turenne, 10 route de Bâle (tel. 41-12-26), is a modern hotel with a nice reception. The furniture is in classic wood of good quality, and the rooms have a warm, inviting atmosphere. No singles are available, but doubles—no baths, only toilets—rent for 70F ($15.98), increasing to 90F ($20.55) with shower, 110F ($25.11) with complete bath. Breakfast is an extra 10F ($2.28) per person.

RESTAURANTS: Maison des Têtes, 19 rue des Têtes (tel. 41-21-10), is in a building that dates from 1608. Now a Colmar monument, this wine restaurant got its name from the sculptured heads in its stone façade. The entrance is through a covered cobblestone driveway and open courtyard with what must surely be the oldest grapevine in France. Two dining rooms contain time-aged wood paneling on the walls and the beamed ceiling. Art-nouveau lighting fixtures are clusters of glass grapes. Stained-glass and leaded windows, an elaborate hand-carved wooden clock, a free-standing stove with decorative tiles combine to give the "House of Heads" the atmosphere of a cozy Black Forest inn. The food is excellent, including the traditional foie gras with truffles and the special sauerkraut with pork products. If you're there in the right season you can enjoy roebuck served with morels. Fresh trout is braised in Riesling wine, as is the Rhine salmon. Young chicken is flavored with a tarragon sauce, and there is a delicious crayfish dish in the style of the chef. The meals here are monumental, and the Alsatian wines are superb. Menus are offered at 65F ($14.84), 85F ($19.41), and 140F ($31.96), plus 15% for service. À la carte diners pay in the neighborhood of 110F ($25.11) to 140F ($31.96). The restaurant is closed July 1 to 14, in February, and on Wednesdays.

Schillinger, 16 rue Stanislas (tel. 41-43-17), is what the French call a *belle maison,* with Louis XVI-style decor. Monsieur Schillinger is a chef of considerable talent. His cookery is now even better than it was, and dish after dish reflects his enthusiastic professionalism. Try, for example, his foie gras frais maison, his foie d'oie chaud au vinaigre, and his duckling in orange sauce (served only to two persons). Menus are offered at 90F ($20.55), 130F ($29.68), and 170F ($38.81), and the average à la carte order costs from 180F ($41.09), plus 12% service.

The restaurant is closed on Sunday nights and Mondays and from July 15 to August 15.

Fer Rouge, 52 Grande-Rue (tel. 41-37-24), is a black-and-white-timbered storybook building. A gable opens onto a small square. The windows are stained and bottle glass—shuttered, with outside boxes overflowing in summer with geraniums. There are two levels for dining, each with aged oak beams with carved trim. Many brass and copper kitchen implements hang from the beams. In such a traditional setting, Madame Fulgraff, the owner, has departed from the typical Alsatian fare of sauerkraut and foie gras. Her cuisine is more inventive, in the style of the legendary Paul Bocuse of Lyons or Monsieur Peyrot's Vivarious in Paris. Specialties include a timbale of sole, turbot suprême, a highly spiced duck, and a masterful rabbit pâté with foie gras. The mousseline of perch is smooth, and, if featured, we'd suggest the small roasted squab. The food selections are wisely balanced to give variety, and the staff has been well chosen to provide good service. Menus are at 66F ($15.08), 120F ($27.40), and 150F ($34.26). If you order à la carte, expect to pay from 160F ($36.53). The restaurant shuts down on Sunday nights and Mondays and takes a vacation from July 27 to August 8 and from January 4 to 25.

Rendez-vous de Chasse, 7 Place de la Gare (tel. 23-59-59), is in the previously recommended Hotel Terminus-Bristol at the railway station. Run by Richard and Ilonka Riehm, this hunter-style restaurant is popular with the local residents, especially on Sundays when entire families take up the big tables. The restaurant is the recreation of a lofty old tavern, with heavy ceiling beams. Its main architectural feature is a long stone wall with an open fireplace, where the white-hatted chef cooks some of his specialties over the open fire. Menus begin at 85F ($19.41), going up to around 180F ($41.09) if you order à la carte. A specialty of the chef is le foie gras au naturel à la cuillère. In season, game such as roebuck is featured, although all year you can order veal kidneys in a sauce of three mustards, similar to that celebrated dish of Raymond Oliver of Paris's Grand Véfour. The dessert concoction featured is a vacherin glacé à l'Alsacienne. The restaurant is closed December 24 to January 7.

On the Fringe

For those who'd like to stay or dine on the outskirts, we'd recommend the **Auberge Père Floranc,** with its annex, le Pavillon, 9 rue Herzog, at Wettolsheim, three miles out by way of roads N417 and D1 bis (tel. 41-39-14). At this idyllic spot you can eat and dine very well, enjoying Edelzwicker wine along with Riesling. Monsieur Floranc provides a first-class cuisine with many specialties, including a terrine of foie gras and a cassolette of snails with those flap mushrooms that is classic cookery at its finest. Quail is also featured in season. Another highly rated dish is stuffed pike en croûte, as well as a tender and delicious tournedos. One touch we like—his cake is named after Albert Schweitzer who was born nearby. Service is friendly and polite. Menus are offered at 60F ($13.70), 80F ($18.26), and 105F ($23.97), all the way up to 150F ($34.26). The decor of the 26 bedrooms is in a grand French style, making for an engaging and rewarding stopover. The cost is 50F ($11.42) in a single, rising to 150F ($34.26) for the best double rooms with private bath. The inn is closed on Sunday nights off-season, on Mondays, July 1 to 16, and from November 3 to December 4.

5. The Wine Road of Alsace

From Strasbourg, motorists heading south to the sights of Colmar, 42 miles away, can take the N83, a direct route. However, if you've got the time, the famous wine road of Alsace is one of the most rewarding sightseeing targets in eastern France. For some 60 miles the road goes through charming villages, many of which are illuminated on summer nights for your viewing pleasure. Along the way are country inns if you'd like to stop and sample some of the wine, perhaps take a leisurely lunch or dinner or a room for the night. The wine road runs along the foothills of the Vosges. Medieval towers and feudal ruins evoke the pageantry of a faded time.

Of course, the slopes are covered with vines, as there are an estimated 50,000 acres of vineyards along this road, sometimes reaching a height of 1450 feet. Some 30,000 families earn their living tending the grapes. The best time to go is for the vintage in September and October.

Riesling is the king of Alsatian wine, with its exquisitely perfumed bouquet. Other wines include Chasselas, Knipperle, Sylvaner, Pinot Blanc (one of the oldest of Alsatian wines), Muscat (a dry fruit wine), Pinot Auxerrois, Pinot Gris, Traminer, and Gewurztraminer.

The traditional route starts at—

MARLENHEIM: This agreeable wine town—noted for its Vorlauf red wine—lies 13 miles due west of Strasbourg on the N4. You might want to visit it even if you can't take the complete route, as it offers an excellent inn, **Hostellerie du Cerf**, 30 rue du Général-de-Gaulle (tel. 87-50-06), where Robert Husser, the patron, will feed you with such specialties as fresh foie gras, a cassolette of lobster, a ballotine of quail (in season only) with sweetbreads, scallops and oysters cooked in court-bouillon and flavored with herbs, roast turbot served with small strips of vegetables, or a trout with sorrel. The selection of pastries and sorbets is praiseworthy, and certainly the wine list of Alsatian vintages is commendable. Menus are priced at 110F ($25.11) and 175F ($39.95). The inn is closed from the end of June until July 12 and on Mondays and at Tuesday lunch. It also rents out 18 pleasantly furnished rooms, charging 60F ($13.70) in a single, 135F ($30.82) in a double, and 200F ($45.66) for a small apartment.

WANGEN: One of the many jewels along the route, Wangen contains narrow, twisting streets. A city gate is crowned by a tower. It's one of the most typical of the Alsatian wine towns. The road from Wangen winds down to—

MOLSHEIM: This is one of the 10 free cities of Alsace, called the "Decapolis." It retains its old ramparts and has a Gothic and Renaissance church built in 1614-19, plus a large fountain. Its Alte Metzig, or town hall, was erected by the Guild of Butchers and is a most interesting sight, with its turret, gargoyles, loggia, and a belfry housing a clock with allegorical figures striking the hour.

ROSHEIM: Nestled behind medieval fortifications, this old wine-growing town—another of the 10 free Alsatian cities of the empire—has a Romanesque house of the 12th century and the Church of Sts. Peter and Paul, also Romanesque, from two centuries later, which is dominated by an octagonal tower. Medieval walls and gate towers evoke its past.

OBERNAI: The patron saint of Alsace, Obernai, was born here. With its old timbered houses and colorful marketplace, the Place du Marché, it is one of the most interesting stopovers along the wine route. Its walls are partially preserved. The Place de l'Étoile is decked out in flowers, and the Hôtel de Ville of 1523 has a delightful loggia (inside you can view the council chamber). An old watchtower, the Tour de la Chapelle, is from the 13th and 16th centuries. The town's six-pail fountain is one of the most spectacular in Alsace.

BARR: The grapes for some of the finest Alsatian wines, Sylvaner and Gewurtztraminer, are harvested here. The castles of Landsberg and Andlau stand high above the town. Barr has many pleasant old timbered houses and a charming Place de l'Hôtel-de-Ville with a town hall from 1640.

MITTELBERGHEIM: Curiously perched like a stork on a housetop, this is a charming village. Its Place de l'Hôtel-de-Ville is bordered with houses in the Renaissance style.

The town has an excellent inn, **Winstub Gilg,** 1 route du Vin (tel. 08-91-37). Georges Gilg, its old-time chef, attracts a loyal following of habitués from Strasbourg who are drawn to his rustic Alsatian auberge. He specializes in the products of the region, including a delicious onion tart. Naturally, the formidable sauerkraut is among his hearty offerings, as is a more delicate foie gras en brioche. Main-dish specialties include a filet of sole with a julienne of vegetables and beef cooked in Pinot Noir. Menus are offered at 65F ($14.84) and 130F ($29.68). Monsieur Gilg also rents out 12 simply furnished rooms of modest comfort, charging from 70F ($15.98) in a single to 105F ($23.97) in a double. The inn is closed on Tuesday nights and Wednesdays and from June 26 to July 11.

ANDLAU: This gardenlike summer resort was once the site of a famous abbey dating from 887, founded by the disgraced wife of the emperor, Charles the Fat. It has now faded into history, but a church remains which dates from the 12th century. In the tympanum are noteworthy Romanesque carvings.

DAMBACH: In the midst of its well-known vineyards, Dambach is one of the delights of the wine route. Its timbered houses are gabled with galleries, and many contain oriels. Wrought-iron shop signs still tell you if a place is a bakery or a butcher. The town has ramparts and three fortified gates. A short drive from the town leads to the Saint Sebastian chapel, with a 15th-century ossuary.

Going through Chatenois, you reach—

SÉLESTAT: This was once a free city, a center of the Renaissance, and the seat of a great university. Its **Bibliothèque Humaniste** contains a rare collection of manuscripts, including Sainte-Foy's *Book of Miracles.* It is open to the public from 9 a.m. to noon and from 2 to 6 p.m., charging an admission of 2F (46¢). It is closed on Saturdays and at noon on Sundays. One of its most interesting Renaissance buildings is called **Maison de Stephan Ziegler.** The Gothic

Church of St. George contains some fine stained glass and a stone pulpit which was gilded and painted. Finally, see the **Church of Ste. Foy**, built of red sandstone from the Vosges in the Romanesque style in the 12th century. Towered battlements enclose the town.

From Sélestat, you can make an excursion to—

HAUT-KOENIGSBOURG CASTLE: Standing 2500 feet up on an isolated peak, this 15th-century castle—the largest in Alsace—treats you to an eagle's-nest view. From its platforms, a panoramic view of the Vosges unfolds. It once belonged to the Hohenstaufens. During the Thirty Years' War the Swedes dismantled the château, but it was rebuilt in 1901 after it was presented as a gift to Kaiser Wilhelm II. Guided visits are arranged from April 1 to September 30 from 9 a.m. to noon and from 1 to 6 p.m. In March and October, the hours are from 9 a.m. to noon and from 1 to 5 p.m.; November to March, 9 a.m. to noon and 1 to 4 p.m. Admission is 9F ($2.05), half price on Sundays and holidays.

Descending again, the trail picks up and leads to—

BERGHEIM: Renowned for its wines, this town has kept part of its 15th-century fortifications. There are many timbered Alsatian houses and a Gothic church.

RIBEAUVILLÉ: In September a fair is held here known as the "Day of the Strolling Fiddlers." At the foot of vine-clad hills, the town is charming, with old shop signs, pierced balconies, turrets, and flower-decorated houses. See its Renaissance fountain and its Hôtel-de-Ville which has a collection of Alsatian tankards known as "hanaps." Of interest also is the Tour des Bouchers, a "butchers' tower" of the 13th and 16th centuries. The town is also noted for its Riesling and Traminer wines.

In Ribeauvillé **Les Clos St.-Vincent**, route de Bergheim (tel. 73-67-65), is a Relais de Campagne, one of the most elegant dining and lodging choices along the Alsatian wine road. Bertrand Chapotin sells more here than his lovely view of the Haut-Rhin landscape in a vineyard setting. His food is exceptional—duck liver with green pepper, turbot with sorrel, roebuck (in season only) in a hot sauce, veal kidneys in Pinot noir. Of course, the wines are smooth, especially the Riesling and Gewurztraminer which everybody seems to order. A complete meal here costs from 170F ($38.81). The restaurant is closed Tuesday nights and Wednesdays and takes a vacation from mid-December to mid-February. Very comfortable and handsomely appointed rooms—only 10 in all—are rented out to lucky guests who can snare one: 220F ($50.23) in a single, rising to 320F ($73.06) in a double.

RIQUEWIHR: This town, surrounded by some of the finest vineyards in Alsace, appears much as it did in the 16th century. With its well-preserved walls and towers, its great wine presses and old wells, it is one of the most rewarding targets along the route. The town has many houses in the Gothic and Renaissance styles, with wooden balconies, voluted gables, and elaborately carved doors and windows. Its most interesting houses are the Maison Liebrich, built in 1535; the Maison Preiss-Zimmer, from 1686, and Maison Kiener, from 1574. If possible, try to peer into some of the galleried courtyards, where centuries virtually have stopped. The High Gate of Dolder, straddling an arch through which you can pass, is from 1291. Nearby, the pentagonal Tower of Thieves (sometimes called "the robbers' tower") contains a torture chamber. The château, from 1539, offers a minor museum devoted to the history of Alsace.

A good place to dine is the **Auberge du Schoenenbourg**, 2 rue de la Piscine (tel. 47-92-28), where meals are served in a garden setting. The cuisine of Monsieur Kiener contains many familiar regional and international dishes—onion soup, snails in the Alsatian manner, veal piccata, steak Dow Jones, trout with sorrel, duckling with green pepper, goose liver "housemade," and rack of lamb with green lemon. Meals begin at 80F ($11.42), and, if you're ordering à la carte, perhaps 100F ($22.83) to 120F ($27.40). The restaurant is closed on Wednesday afternoons, Thursdays, and all January.

READER'S HOTEL SELECTION: "We stayed in an old but clean and beautiful hotel, **Au Vieux Riquewihr**, 4 rue du Cerf (tel. 47-92-85), for just 70F ($15.98) for a double. The price quoted does not include breakfast which is 10F ($2.28) extra per person" (Myra Broadway, APO, N.Y.).

KIENTZHEIM: Famous for its wine, Kientzheim is one of the three colorful towns to explore in this valley of vineyards, ranking along with Kaysersberg and Ammerschwihr. Two castles, timber-framed houses, and walls that date from the Middle Ages make it an appealing choice for a visit. After you have passed through, it is just a short drive to—

KAYSERSBERG: Once a Free City of the empire, Kaysersberg lies at the mouth of the Weiss Valley, built between two vine-covered slopes and crowned by a feudal castle which was ruined in the Thirty Years' War. Kaysersberg rivals Riquewihr as one of the most colorful towns along the wine route. The church, from the 12th and 15th centuries, contains a splendid early 16th-century altarpiece. Many houses are from the Gothic and Renaissance eras, and there are remains of fortifications dating from the Middle Ages. Dr. Albert Schweitzer was born in this pleasant town in 1875. His house stands near the fortified bridge over the Weiss, and can be visited from 9 a.m. to noon and from 2 to 6 p.m. for a 2F (46¢) admission.

In Kaysersberg, **Chambard**, 9 rue du Général-de-Gaulle (tel. 47-10-17), is the domain of a chef of unusual versatility and imagination, Pierre Irrmann. Using the products of the region, he turns out such a fine cuisine that it is well worth planning your wine route tour to have a stopover at this exceptional place. Naturally, Riesling and Tokay should be the wines to order with the repast. Tokay, incidentally, was said to have been brought back by a captain of the imperial forces who fought in the Turkish wars in Hungary and introduced the grape to Alsace. Try Monsieur Irrmann's foie gras, a gratin of crayfish tails, his Bresse chicken sautéed with crayfish tails, his coq sauté au Riesling, or his heart of artichoke filled with goose liver. For dessert, we'd suggest the mousse Chambard. Meals are at 70F ($15.98) and 150F ($34.26). The restaurant is closed on Sunday nights, Mondays, and March 1 to 21.

Finally, to cap the wine road tour, as you move near the outskirts of Colmar—

AMMERSCHWIHR: Once an old Free City of the empire, it was almost completely destroyed in 1944 in World War II battles, but has been reconstructed in the traditional style. Motorists stop off here in increasing numbers to drink the wine, especially Käferkopf. A trio of gate towers, a 16th-century parish church, and remains of its early fortifications evoke yesterday.

The best news for last. The most superb restaurant we've ever found along the Alsatian wine route is here—**Aux Armes de France**, 1 Grande-Rue (tel. 47-10-12). In a lovely flower-filled setting, Monsieur Pierre Gaertner receives the finest gourmets of France and Germany who know of his superlative cuisine. If you go here for lunch, you may spend the afternoon, and you can even book one of the eight rooms with bath and toilet if you'd like to stay for dinner, too. The rate is 90F ($20.55) in a single, rising to 210F ($47.94) in a double, plus 12% service. The patron runs an immensely popular concern with enthusiasm and expertise. The cuisine, for such a small town, is definitely sophisticated, so much so it comes as a bit of a surprise. Of course, be prepared to spend fairly lavishly, but, then again, you won't need to dine until the third day after taking a meal here. If you can afford it, we'd suggest the fresh foie gras. Main dishes include a wide repertoire of the classic cuisine with imaginative variations: roebuck (in season) in a hot sauce, sole cooked with vermouth, lobster fricassée with cream and deliciously expensive truffles, sole with hazelnuts, beef cooked in Pinot rouge, a ragoût of kidneys with sweetbreads laced with Calvados, and soufflés and crêpes to stagger the imagination. Menus are at 110F ($25.11), 160F ($36.53), and 170F ($38.81), plus service. The restaurant is closed on Wednesday nights and Thursdays. It takes a vacation from January 7 to February 1 and from June 18 to July 4.

A charming little place to stay, if you don't want to press on to Colmar, is the **Arbre Vert**, 7 rue des Cigognes (tel. 47-12-23), which has a delightful interior decoration. Near an old fountain, it is warm and inviting, welcoming you to one of its dozen bedrooms at a low rate of 50F ($11.42) in a single, 100F ($22.83) in a double. The inn also serves very good Alsatian specialties. If you stay here in season, you must take the demi-pension tariff, ranging from 93F ($21.23) to 100F ($22.83) per person. The inn shuts down on Tuesdays and from November 25 to December 10 and from February 15 until March 20.

THE FRENCH ALPS

NO PART OF FRANCE is more dramatically scenic than the Alps. The western ramparts of the Alps and their foothills is a majestic section of grandeur. From the Mediterranean to the Rhine in the north, they stretch along the southeastern flank of France.

The skiing here has no equal in Europe, not even in Switzerland. Some of the resorts are legendary, including Chamonix-Mont Blanc, the historic capital of Alpine skiing, with its celebrated 12-mile Vallée Blanc run. Mont Blanc, of course, is the highest mountain in Europe, rising 15,780 snowy feet.

Most of our recommendations will fall in the area known as Savoy, taking in the French lake district, including the largest Alpine lake, which the French share with Switzerland. The French call it Léman, but most English-speaking people refer to it as Lake Geneva.

1. Évian-les-Bains

On the château-dotted southern shore of Lac Léman (Lake Geneva), 26 miles from the city of Geneva, Évian-les-Bains is a spa and tourist resort, one of the leading ones of eastern France. Its lakeside promenade lined with trees and sweeping lawns has been fashionable since the 19th century. In the 16th century Évian was ruled by Switzerland, but it passed to France in 1860.

In the 18th century the waters of Évian—still and tasteless—became famous, and the first spa buildings were erected there in 1839. Bottled Évian is one of the great French table waters, considered beneficial for everything from baby's formula to gout, arthritis, and salt-free diets.

In the center of town is the new Hôtel de Ville and the **Municipal Casino**, patronized heavily by the Swiss from across the lake. The casino, charging a 6F ($1.37) entrance fee to its gaming rooms, offers blackjack, baccarat, and roulette, among other games, and has a cinema and floor shows two or three nights a week from June to mid-September, the price depending on the attraction featured. The cost of entrance is usually lowered the rest of the week when music is played for dancing.

Here you'll also find the most elegantly appointed restaurant in Évian, **Lapierre** (also known as Le Cercle), au Cercle du Casino (tel. 75-03-78), where you'll dine well with formal service at a price ranging from 200F ($45.66). The chef, Roger Lapierre, specializes in a lobster soup flavored with basil, grilled duck liver in a sherry-flavored vinaigrette, and a brochette of grilled chicken in orange sauce. We'd also recommend trout en papillottes, and, for dessert, an iced soufflé of raspberries.

In addition to its spa buildings, Évian offers an imposing **Ville des Congrès,** or convention hall, earning for the resort the title of "city of conventions."

In summer, the **Nautical Center** is a popular attraction; it lies right on the lake; it has a 328-foot pool with a diving stage, a solarium, restaurant, bar, and children's paddling pool.

The major excursion in Évian is a boat trip on Lake Geneva. The boats of the **Compagnie Générale de Navigation** ply between landing stages on the lake. You can go the tourist office and pick up a schedule of tariffs and hours. You're given a choice of trips, including night cruises in summer. Those who want to see it all can tour both the Haut-Lac and the Grand-Lac. The quickest and most heavily booked of all trips is the crossing from Évian to Ouchy-Lausanne, Switzerland, on the north side.

Crescent-shaped Lake Geneva is the largest lake in Central Europe. In the 18th century, the name of Lac Léman was revived. Taking in an area of approximately 225 square miles, the lake is formed by the Rhône, and it is noted for its unusual blueness, almost a transparent look the farther one gets from the muddy Rhône.

A CHOICE OF HOTELS: Hôtel de la Verniaz et ses chalets, Avenue Verniaz (tel. 75-04-90), is the most glamorous and sophisticated place to stay at Évian, attracting a host of celebrated people that have included, in times gone by, the Aga Khan and Elizabeth Taylor. Up from the lake, the well-known country house stands on a hillside, allowing a panoramic view of woods, waters, and the Alps on the horizon. It is perhaps the most self-contained establishment in the area, and is beautifully run and managed by the Verdier family.

The central building is in the rustic style, with balconies, beams, and plaster or stone construction. The guest rooms are either here in the main house or in one of the separate chalets, such as "Le Cyclamen," which has its own garden and total privacy if you can afford it. The personable owners are delighted when honeymooners check into one of their chalets. The least expensive single in the main building goes for 280F ($63.92), although you'll spend as much at 500F ($114.15) for a large twin-bedded chamber with a complete private bath. The five chalets range in price from 600F ($136.98) to 1400F ($319.62).

On parklike grounds you'll find a trout and crayfish pool, a tennis court, some 20 horses for riding, a heated swimming pool, even a disco. The hotel, which remains open all year, also serves some of the best food at the spa (see our dining recommendations). Half pension in season is obligatory, costing from 330F ($75.34) to 450F ($102.74) per person.

Hôtel Royal, Plateau des Mateirons (tel. 75-14-00), was created for guests who want to live with a touch of splendor. There is dignity and serenity in this deluxe establishment with its top-grade hotel facilities. Set back from the resort and the center of town, it offers a panoramic view of the lake and the Swiss

Alps. The hotel is in a large park, with flowered terraces overlooking the lake. A heated private swimming pool is accessible by elevator from all the rooms. Almost every bedroom has an excellent vista from its balcony or loggia. The Royal offers 250 handsomely furnished rooms with private baths or showers, ranging from 250F ($57.08) to a peak 650F ($148.40), the latter price for a luxuriously appointed apartment best suited for Geneva bankers. It is open from April to October. You'll find very good food and excellent service in the Café Royal, where a set meal is offered for 120F ($27.40). The architectural and decorative style throughout the hotel is traditional. Many of the public rooms have arched and coved ceilings with beautiful Italian and French frescoes and murals. In fair weather there is dining on a wide lakeview terrace.

Cygnes, Grande-Rive (tel. 75-01-01), is one of the best bargains at the spa, although it's away from the center. It's a Norman-style villa opening onto a lake port, and it's characterized by dormer windows, a conically shaped tower, a decorative beam-and-plaster façade, a mansard roof, and an entrance court-yard surrounded by abundant flowers and shrubs. All this, plus a waterside terrace with a grape arbor and a boat pier extending into the lake, makes for a delightful holiday escape and evokes another era.

The hotel is family-run, and it's a homey place at which to stay, anchoring in for a few days and using it as a base from which to explore Lake Geneva. The bedrooms are pleasant but decidedly old-fashioned, as they should be. A single rents for 70F ($15.98), that tariff rising to 160F ($36.53) in a double. The good-size dining room, with its beamed ceiling and high-backed ladder chairs, always seems ready to serve a meal. On our latest rounds there, we enjoyed a delicious homemade soup, followed by oeuf (egg) poêle, then a veal escalope fried in butter with an accompaniment of fresh vegetables, ending with pears in syrup. Visitors not staying at the hotel are welcome to drop in for a meal, costing 52F ($11.87). Or, if you're staying at the hotel, you may want to take a full pension, ranging in price from 125F ($28.54) to 160F ($36.53) per person. The hotel is open only from May 25 to September 25.

One of the best and most scenic places to stay in the environs is at **Les Prés Fleuris,** on Route Thollon, 4½ miles from Évian (tel. 75-29-14). It's a casual, white-painted, attractive little villa with a lakeside location, and it's open from March 20 to October 20. There are only 12 bedrooms, but each is sumptuously furnished with antiques or reproductions. The rates range from 275F ($62.78) to 500F ($114.15). For guests there is a comfortable sitting room with big, soft armchairs, and many vases of fresh flowers are placed about in summer. Glass walls capitalize on the view. Checkered tablecloths and white wrought-iron chairs are set under the trees for meals in fair weather. The food served by Monsieur and Madame Demonceau-Frossard is exceptional. Full pension costs from 320F ($73.06) to 480F ($109.58) per person daily, but a minimum stay of three days is required for those terms. Set menus are featured at 105F ($23.97), 140F ($31.96), and 180F ($41.09), or you may select from the à la carte offerings.

WHERE TO DINE: Bourgogne, 73 rue Nationale (tel. 75-01-05), is a charming inn with many appealing decorative touches, located near the Congress Hall. Come here if you want a really delectable meal, irreproachable service, an attractive setting, and excellent wine. Main dishes include a filet of lake trout cooked with champagne and le ris de veau (sweetbreads) des gourmets. We'd also suggest le carré d'agneau (lamb) à la Provençale. The chef also does the delicious char (*omble chevalier* in French), a fish, somewhat like a trout that comes from the deep lakes of Savoy. Another specialty is crêpes flambées

Bourgogne, requiring at least two diners. Regional wines featured are Crépy and Roussette. Bourgogne offers the best set meal in Évian, costing 85F ($19.41), although the menu gastronomique runs as high as 180F ($41.09) and includes not only oysters or foie gras but a cassolette of crayfish, followed by a filet of beef with a béarnaise sauce. If you order à la carte, you will more likely pay 130F ($29.68). Incidentally, the inn—owned by Monsieur Riga—also offers 10 well-furnished and comfortable bedrooms, costing 170F ($38.81) for two persons. The restaurant is closed from November to mid-December and on Tuesday nights and Wednesdays in July and August.

Hôtel de la Verniaz et ses chalets, Avenue Verniaz (tel. 75-04-90), recommended previously as a hotel, serves an exceptional cuisine as well. The main dining room is a warm setting with provincial chairs and an open fireplace. Even more engaging is the rustic Rôtisserie, where tables are placed to catch the warmth of the wood-burning fire set in a raised brick fireplace. Olive wood is used in roasting, or else vine branches. When weather permits, white garden furniture is set on a graveled terrace under fringed umbrellas. Before a meal here, guests gravitate in the late afternoon to the luxuriously rustic **Le Bar,** with its wooden tower and ceiling decorated with an Alpine brass horn made into a chandelier. This is the center for whiskey tasters in the area, as at least 150 scotch whiskeys are available. Even the bagpipe clan meets here. Specialties of the restaurant include crayfish with dill, truite saumonée au champagne, a parfait de foie gras de canard, and the finest of spit-roasted game, poultry, and meat. Regional wines featured are Crépy and Roussette. A set meal is offered for 110F ($25.11), although you are more likely to spend 150F ($34.26) if you order à la carte.

Da Bouttau, Quai de Blonay (tel. 75-02-44), was originally founded in Nice in 1860, but it has been a good two-fork restaurant happily ensconced in Évian for many years. In fair weather, you can request a dining table outside. Even though in the Alps, Da Bouttau retains its Mediterranean provincial decor, with an elaborate use of copper pots. Not all those pots are used for decoration, however. The proprietor serves some of the best food at the spa. In honor of its past, Da Bouttau still specializes in dishes from Provence. Right near the casino, the restaurant fronts the lake. A set meal is offered for 50F ($11.42) and it is excellent, featuring on one recent occasion a salade Niçoise followed by poule à la Niçoise, then osso bucco, cheese, and dessert. Another more elaborate repast goes for 120F ($27.40). On the à la carte menu, you can order such specialties as a Mediterranean-style bouillabaisse at 100F ($22.83) or grilled loup, 90F ($20.55), even a most interesting chicken-and-crayfish dish, 65F ($14.84). The restaurant is closed January 15 to March 1 and on off-season Tuesdays.

2. Morzine–Avoriaz

The tourist capital of the Haut-Chablais district, Morzine stands in the middle of foothills and forest. The most northerly of the French Alp resorts, it offers such attractions as sleighrides and beautiful pine forests, as well as ice shows and more than a dozen cabarets. For years it was known as a summer resort, but now its acclaim as a winter ski center seems to have overshadowed that previous reputation.

Like Samoëns, Morzine was noted in the 19th century for its fraternities of artisans, particularly masons. When winter came, these artisans used to wander about the countryside, taking their skills with them.

Based in Morzine, you can visit **Lac de Montriond,** at an altitude of 3490 feet. A tour of this famous and beautiful lake takes about two hours for an 18-mile journey.

One of the most modern and sophisticated ski centers of Europe has been developed at **Avoriaz,** towering over Morzine. Even if you don't want to stay in one of its hotels, you may want to take a cable car up for a look and perhaps a meal. A round-trip ticket goes for 20F ($4.57).

By cable car or bubble car you can also go to **Le Pléney,** at 5367 feet, enjoying a view from its belvedere looking out on Mont Blanc. Through the Dranse Gap a vista of Lake Geneva unfolds. A round-trip ticket costs 20F ($4.57).

A WIDE RANGE OF HOTELS AT MORZINE: Parador de Saint-Alben (tel. 79-14-22) is for the grand and elegant life. With the same taste level as the best of the Iberian Paradors, this luxurious oasis is a twin-season holiday spot. Its central square tower blends architecturally with its chalet bedroom wing, and every room has an unmarred view of an Alpine vista. The reception facilities are dramatic in a salon with a large white fireplace, black and white marquetry-tiled floors, and Spanish-style furnishings.

The loggia dining room has windows high and wide to drink in the view, and for intimate get-togethers there is the bar, Le Puits de l'Ermite. Each bedroom offers an individual decor. Many of the beds are regal, with satin covers, matching headboards, and draped testers. Of course, they have balconies and wide windows for viewing the scenery. Four apartments are available, but the regular rooms cost from 230F ($52.51) in a single to 275F ($62.78) in a double. It's best to take the full-pension plan, costing from 185F ($42.24) to 290F ($66.21) per person. If you're not a guest and are touring in the area, you can call and reserve a table. A set meal, large and delicious, costs 75F ($17.12), although you can spend from 110F ($25.11) if you want to dine à la carte. Guests are welcomed between June 30 and the first of September and between December 20 and April.

Le Dahu (tel. 79-11-12) is a four-story modern structure, built on the side of a hill so as to offer panoramic views. Its white plaster façade is relieved by wooden balconies and picture windows opening onto the village and Alpine range. Although sleekly contemporary, the hotel has some old-fashioned warming touches, such as stone fireplaces around which guests gather to talk after a session on the slopes in winter. In summer the wide terraces become the social center, as guests gather for sunbathing and refreshments. There is also a shady lawn with flower gardens. Meals are served in a provincial-style dining room with reed-seated chairs and oxen-yoke chandeliers. The bedrooms are up to date, and many have been given homelike touches. All of them contain private baths. The charges range from 65F ($14.84) in a single to 190F ($43.38) in a double. The full-pension plan goes from 170F ($38.81) to 235F ($53.65) per person. The hotel is open from June 30 to August 31 and from mid-December to Easter.

Le Carlina (tel. 79-01-03) is an informal village chalet which, in spite of its modesty, has maintained a high respect among its skiing habitués. Its interior is rustic, with several lounges—from the library to the inglenook parlor—containing open fireplaces, plus an abundance of cozy conversation nooks. The decor accent is Alpine, with beamed ceilings and flagstone floors. While not fashion-setting, its bedrooms are pleasantly decorated and most comfortable, costing 170F ($38.81) in a single and from 210F ($47.94) in a double. All rooms come with private baths. In summer there is a refreshment terrace with umbrella tables on the street level. In evening life gravitates around the Carlina Club where you can either dance or join in the folk music. The cuisine is most agreeable, as is the polite, friendly service. The least expensive set meal, and it's a heartily recommendable one, costs 80F ($18.26). However, you can stay here on the full-pension plan, going from 115F ($26.25) to 240F ($54.79) per person. La Carlina is open from July until the end of August and from mid-December to mid-April.

Chamois d'Or (tel. 79-13-78) is a Logis de France, offering one of the best bargains at this increasingly popular resort. An overscale Alpine chalet, it has a façade of wooden trim and balconies—and two seasons, from July 1 to September 30 and from December 20 to April 10. In summer you can go on hikes or picnics, or else stay at the hotel and sunbathe. In winter skiers check in, sitting snugly in front of an open fire, meeting friends and drinking hot grog, when not on the slopes. All rooms have private baths and toilets and are furnished in a semirustic style. Tariffs are 70F ($15.98) in a single, increasing to 110F ($25.11) in a double. It's preferred that you take the full-pension plan, costing from 130F ($29.68) to 170F ($38.81) per person. The logis also serves one of the best set meals at the resort, many tempting courses for just 55F ($12.56).

AT AVORIAZ: Hôtel des Dromonts, Avoriaz 1800, par Morzine (tel. 74-08-11), stands on the crest of an Alp, an avant-garde complex that reigns unchallenged as the chicest Alpine retreat in France. A bizarre architectural wonder, it spreads out to include luxurious apartment villas, a cluster of boutiques, restaurants, a nightclub, and, of course, elaborate playtime facilities. The architectural theme evokes cliff-dwelling days with beehive balconies. Natural shingles cover the façade, and both the public and private rooms are oddly shaped. Long, winding ramps lead you through space over intimate fireplace nooks, past boutiques and drinking bars as well as restaurants. Every facility is here for the total *le weekend*—Le Solarium, Le Taverne, Le Drugstore, Le Roc-Club Disco. Your bedroom will probably be in an explosive modern design with a liberal use made of natural wood and bright colors, even "futuristic" furniture. The crowd attracted to these premises is usually youthful and brimming with energy. Ski runs and lifts are right at the door. Expect to pay from 220F ($50.23) to 320F ($73.06) per person for full pension. The highest prices are charged at Christmas, Easter, and in February. The hotel is closed from mid-April to mid-December.

Les Hauts Forts, Avoriaz 1800, par Morzine (tel. 74-09-11), does a sister act with Les Dromonts. With the same bizarre architecture, it offers almost as much for your money as Les Dromonts although its tariffs are lower. Bedrooms are furnished in an avant-garde style and often are irregularly shaped. Fifty bedrooms are rented out. In high season, two persons are charged from 300F ($68.49) to 350F (79.91) for a room, although in certain off-season periods the rate is lowered to 225F ($51.38) to 250F ($57.08). Singles occupying a double room are granted a 60F ($13.70) reduction. The hotel receives guests from July 1 to August 31 and from mid-December to April 15. Facilities include a cinema, heated swimming pool, many recreational facilities, a solarium, a gallery of boutiques, and, again, ski lifts virtually at your door. There's also a good restaurant, serving a set meal for 70F ($15.98) to 90F ($20.55) in case you're just visiting the Alp-high resort from Morzine. You can taste some of the specialties of the region—mountain trout, fondue, and snails.

3. Flaine

Flaine has made its debut as a ski center in recent times but is rapidly gaining in popularity. It enjoys a superb location, about 30 miles from both Morzine and Megève. Flaine boasts deep powder snow from November through April. The chalets of Flaine, at 5412 feet, are situated above the valley of the Arve and the Carroz-d' Araches.

From its cable-car station, inaugurated in 1969, you are whisked up to Les Grandes Platières. There you can admire the Désert de Platé and look out on a magnificent view of Mont Blanc. Skiers have a choice of downward trails—a thrilling descent in a four-minute run on the Diamant Noir ski trail or else a 60-minute run via the Serpentine trail.

Sofitel Le Flaine (tel. 90-80-30) is the leading hotel. Four famous designers—Arman, Saarinen, Agnoli, and Paulin—contributed to the decoration and furnishings of this luxurious holiday retreat. A spectacular building, it has a splendid view of winter landscape, snow-capped mountains, and the peaceful valley below. The hotel itself was built by Marcel Breuer. The open-air bar, cantilevered in space, is his masterpiece. Jutting out from a high wall of rocks, the hotel was designed so that each room would have individual balconies for sunbathing. The main lounge is uncluttered, with white leather molded chairs, rare wood, soft-colored fabrics, and a huge fireplace, the design of Breuer.

Guests can dine inside or else (for lunch only) on an open-air terrace, with its view of the slalom runs. Near the dining room, drinks are served in the Ziganthrope Night Club where you can also dance or else listen to jazz records. Bedrooms are stylish and comfortable, always with that awesome view from their windows. Open from December 15 until the end of April, the hotel charges from 190F ($43.38) in a single room and 340F ($77.62) in a double. Most guests stay here on the full-pension plan—from 300F ($68.49) to 360F ($82.19) per person. A large, quite superb set menu is offered for 75F ($17.12).

Gradins Gris (tel. 90-81-10) is another excellent choice, and it's less expensive. Fifty-one contemporary rooms come equipped with telephones, private baths, and all the modern conveniences. For these you pay 150F ($34.26) in a single and from 200F ($45.66) in a double. Full-pension plans range from 180F ($41.09) to 230F ($52.51) per person nightly. The hotel receives guests from mid-December until the end of April. The rooms open either onto the spruce forest or else the Forum, the center of life in Flaine, as in ancient times.

Marcel Breuer's passion for diamond-shaped panels is particularly noticeable on a moonlit night, as you stand looking at the façade of Les Gradins Gris. After a day on the slopes, skiers return to the warmth of Breuer's famous fireplace in the lounge. In the Salon-Cimaise you'll find a coffee table with a relief by Roy Adzak, canapes by Agnoli, armchairs by Aalto, and tapestries by Albers. From the Salon-Cimaise you can go out onto the sun terrace or else head for the main dining room, which offers an excellent cuisine. Motorists in the area might want to drop in to enjoy its 55F ($12.56) set meal, very good value.

Le Totem (tel. 90-80-64) is the daring challenger, and many frankly prefer Roger Giraud's establishment, primarily because of the cuisine of his young chef, Michel Guillaumou, another devotee of La Nouvelle Cuisine. A Relais de Campagne, Le Totem is very modern, with beautifully furnished and immaculately kept rooms costing from 220F ($50.23) to 300F ($68.49) per person in season if you stay there on the pension plan, as many guests seem to. If you're just visiting to sample the food, you'll find a meal offered at 150F ($34.26). Specialties include poulet with cucumbers, a feuille of pigeon with foie gras, and a grenadin of veal with morels. Service is friendly and efficient. The Totem is open only in July and August and from mid-December until the end of April.

4. Chamonix–Mont Blanc

At an altitude of 3422 feet, Chamonix, opening onto Mont Blanc, is the historic capital of Alpine skiing. Chamonix lies huddled in a valley almost at the junction of France, Italy, and Switzerland. Dedicated skiers all over the world know of its 10-mile **Vallée Blanche** run, considered one of the most rugged in Europe, certainly the longest. Daredevils also flock here for mountain climbing and hang-gliding.

A charming, old-fashioned mountain town, Chamonix has a most thrilling backdrop—**Mont Blanc,** Europe's highest mountain, rising to a peak of 15,780 feet.

When two Englishmen, Windham and Pococke, first visited Chamonix in 1740, they were thrilled at its location, and later wrote a travel book making the village known around the world. When their guide was published, it was believed that no human foot had yet trod on Mont Blanc. In the summer of 1786, Jacques Balmat became the first man to climb the mountain. In the old quarter of town a memorial to this brave pioneer stands in front of the village church.

With the opening of that seven-mile miracle **Mont Blanc Tunnel,** Chamonix became a major stage on one of the busiest highways in Europe. The tunnel provides the easiest way to go through the mountains to Italy by literally going *under* those mountains. Motorists now stop at Chamonix even if they aren't interested in winter skiing or summer mountain climbing.

Toll rates for vehicles going through the Mont Blanc tunnel are 7000 Italian lire ($8.40) for small cars and motorcycles (one way), 9000 lire ($10.80) for a round-trip ticket.

Because of its exceptional equipment, Chamonix is one of the major resorts of Europe, attracting a sophisticated international crowd.

The **Casino de Chamonix** is the hub of its nightlife activity. It's open daily from 3 p.m. to 2 a.m. (closes at 3 a.m. on weekends and holidays). A passport is required, and a 6F ($1.37) entry fee is assessed. You can also dine at the Casino's **Le Royal** restaurant, where meals begin at 140F ($31.96). Teas and dinner dances are offered in the grill room, and at the tables you can play such games as roulette, boule, and chemin de fer. In the casino club, live shows are presented.

CABLE-CAR RIDES: The belvederes which can be reached from Chamonix by cable cars or mountain railways are famous.

In the heart of town you can board a cable car heading for the Aiguille du Midi and on to Italy, a harrowing journey. The first stage of the trip, a nine-minute run to the **Plan des Aiguilles** at an altitude of 7544 feet, isn't so alarming. But the second stage, to an altitude of 12,602 feet, the **Aiguille du Midi** station, may make your heart sink, especially when the car rises 2000 feet between towers.

At the summit you are 1100 yards from the peak of Mont Blanc. From the belvedere you have a commanding view of the Aiguilles of Chamonix and the Vallée Blanche, the largest glacier in Europe (9.3 miles long and 3.7 miles wide). You also have a panoramic view for 125 miles of the Jura and the French, Swiss, and Italian Alps.

You leave the tram station along a chasm-spanning narrow bridge leading to the third cable car and the glacial fields which lie beyond. Or else you can end your journey at Aiguille du Midi, returning to Chamonix. Generally, the cable cars operate all year. Summer departures are from 6 a.m. to 6 p.m., leaving at least every half-hour. In winter the hours are from 8 a.m. to 5 p.m., leaving every hour. The round-trip fare to the Aiguille du Midi station is about 50F ($11.42).

For the final lap of the trip you go across high mountains and pass jagged needles of rock and ice bathed in a dazzling light. The final trip to **Pointe Helbronner** in Italy—at an altitude of 11,355 feet—requires a passport if you wish to leave the station and descend on two more cable cars to the village of Courmeyeur. From there you can go to nearby Entreves to dine at **La Maison de Filippo,** called a "chalet of gluttony," the Chamonix visitor's favorite restaurant across the border in Italy.

Reader Jeffrey Stanton of Marina del Rey, California, reports: "This third leg of the journey was acclaimed an engineering triumph when it was built in the early 1960s. Its three miles of cables are supported in only two intermediate places. Because support towers can't be placed on a glacier, one of the two intermediate supports is another cable attached to two adjacent peaks. The cars—traveling in threes to facilitate loading—at an altitude of 600 feet above the chasm-scarred glaciers, pass stupendous mountain vistas on the flank of Mont Blanc. On the Italian side, you can watch skiers on the snowfields even in summer."

The round trip from Chamonix to Pointe Helbronner is 100F ($22.83).

After all that, you may swear off cable cars for life. However, another aerial cableway takes you up to **Brévent** at an altitude of 8284 feet. From here you'll have a first-rate view (frontal) of Mont Blanc and the Aiguilles de Chamonix. The trip takes about 1½ hours round trip. Cable cars operate all year except from November 1 to December 15, beginning at 7 or 8 a.m., shutting down at 6 p.m. In summer, departures are at least every half-hour. The price of a round-trip ticket is 25F ($5.71).

A final aerial goal might be to **Le Montenvers,** at an altitude of 6276 feet. Here, from the belvedere at the end of the cable-car run, you'll have a view of the celebrated **Mer de Glace,** or sea of ice, which is four miles long. The **Aiguille du Dru** is a rock climb notorious for its difficulty. The trip takes 1½ hours, including a return by rail. Departures are from 7:30 a.m. until 6 p.m. in summer or 4:30 p.m. in winter. The round-trip fare is 25F ($5.71).

As a curiosity, you can visit a cave hollowed out of the Mer de Glace. A cable car connects it with the upper resort of Montenvers, the trip taking just three minutes. The fare is 6F ($1.37). To enter the cave costs an additional 6F ($1.37). There is, as well, a small zoo containing such animals as bison, nutria, beaver, and marten. The zoo may be visited from June 15 to October 5 from 9 a.m. to 7 p.m. for a 5F ($1.14) admission.

FOOD AND LODGING: Hôtel Mont Blanc et Restaurant Le Matafan, Place de l'Église (tel. 53-05-64), not only offers the best facilities of any first-class hotel in Chamonix, but enjoys a setting in tranquil gardens, with its own swimming pool and tennis courts. It also has one of the finest dining rooms at the resort. The seven-story, overscale villa has shuttered windows and balconies, plus a double-decker sun terrace, looking due south onto the Aiguille du Midi and the Mont-Blanc massif.

The Morand family owners close the hotel from November 1 through December·15, but are open otherwise, charging from 183F ($41.79) in a single to 143F ($32.65) per person based on double occupancy. The rooms have been completely renovated and furnished in a rustic style, with pine paneling. Each has its own private bath and telephone. The half-pension tariffs are 253F ($57.76) in a single, from 213F ($48.63) per person, based on double occupancy. Tariffs are reduced from May 19 to June 7 and from mid-September until the end of September.

Food is served in the dramatically impressive main dining room, featuring a circular raised fireplace with a wood-faced hood. Separated from the main dining room is the cozy restaurant-bar, Le Matafan, a favorite summer or winter rendezvous for ski teachers, mountain guides, and tourists. A specialty is fondue bourguignonne and fondue Savoyarde. The set meal on one recent occasion featured smoked salmon, followed by grilled tournedos with béarnaise sauce, plus a salad and a selection from the cheese board, climaxed by dessert.

Hôtel Albert ler et de Milan, 119 impasse Montenvert (tel. 53-05-09), is an expanded mountain chalet run by Monsieur and Madame Carrier. Set in the center of the resort, it is surrounded by its own informal flower gardens and a tennis court. From every window there is a view. Even the vision-clear dining windows provide spectacular panoramas of Mont Blanc. In winter clients meet for convivial gatherings around the open fireplace. The rooms are of decent size, many opening onto balconies, and they are traditionally furnished with reproductions in classic French styles. In all, 35 rooms are rented out at rates ranging from 110F ($25.11) in a single to a peak 280F ($63.92) in a double. The hotel is closed in May and again in October, reopening November 10. Full-pension terms range from 190F ($43.38) to 270F ($61.64) per person daily.

Even if you aren't a guest, you may want to call for a table at dinner, as the food is the best served in Chamonix, a meal costing from 70F ($15.98) to 100F ($22.83). Specialties include a terrine de saumon (salmon) sauce corail, ris de veau (sweetbreads) with crayfish, and an escalope with morels. Staying here on the pension plan, we recently enjoyed a dinner beginning with beef bouillon with toasted cheese croûtons, followed by chunks of white fish in a delicious creamy sauce on a heap of rice, then a platter of cold Alpine ham (all you want), accompanied by a cold vegetable salad, followed by the cheese board and fresh fruit of the season.

Hostellerie "Le Lion d'Or," rue du Dr.-Paccard (tel. 53-15-09), is a chalet-style inn with overhanging balconies and a façade graced with a pair of golden lions. Run by Paul Dervieux, it's one of the best independent restaurants in Chamonix, which usually have a hard time surviving because nearly all the hotels require pension in season. However, the Lion offers 10 serviceable bedrooms, and only pension guests are accepted at a rate of 160F ($36.53) a night, one of the best package deals in Chamonix.

Outside clients are invited to come here to sample the cookery of the maître rôtisseur, in a rustic atmosphere where the old tradition of French cuisine is maintained. Set meals run from 45F ($10.27) to 80F ($18.26), the latter for the menu gastronomique. As in most restaurants in the Alps, fondue is the specialty. Here the fondue bourguignonne is excellent, with hot melted Savoy cheese laced with kirsch. The chef also prepares a delicious mountain trout with almonds and veal medallions cooked in butter.

In the front dining room a fireplace burns on chilly winter nights, and in the rear a larger room has a more provincial atmosphere, with high-backed chairs and an ornate wooden chandelier. The inn closes in June and from October 20 to December 22 and on Mondays off-season.

Au Bon Coin, 80 Avenue de l'Aiguille du Midi (tel. 53-15-67), is the inexpensive little domain of René Moggino, who gives you a gracious welcome. The two-star hotel has much modern comfort and clean, well-kept rooms, often with views of the surrounding mountainside. Autumnal colors predominate. The chambers also contain private baths and terraces where you can soak up the sun, even in winter. Au Bon Coin is chalet-style, charging 85F ($19.41) in a single and from 115F ($26.25) in a double. The situation is tranquil, and the owner provides private parking as well as a garden.

5. Megève

Called a "cité verte," Megève is famous as a summer resort set in pine forests, foothills, and mountain streams. But it's even better known as a charming cosmopolitan town, referred to as a "capitale du ski." The old village with its turreted houses gathered around the church, dating from the 17th century, suggests what Megève looked like at the turn of the century.

However, after 1920 the new town came along, attracting people who like to go to the mountains just for fun and not just those fanatical about skiing, although they come in hordes, too. Megève was made popular by the Baroness de Rothschild.

Tennis, horseback riding, and cable railways add to the attractions. There are wide views of the Mont Blanc area from the top of each ski lift. The range of amusements includes a casino, nightclubs, discos, dancing, and shows. At the foot of Mont Blanc, Megève is actually one of the best equipped of the French winter sports resorts, a social center of international status.

In the environs you can take a chair hoist to **Mont d'Arbois,** at an altitude of 6000 feet. Here a magnificent panorama unfolds, including not only Mont Blanc but the Fis and Aravis massifs. Cable service is from July 1 to September 15 at every half hour, beginning at 9 a.m. and ending at 7 p.m. The round-trip fare is 15F ($3.42). To reach the station take the Route du Mont d'Arbois from the center of the resort, going past the golf course.

WHERE TO STAY: Megève has several accommodations, ranging from deluxe to budget:

Deluxe resort living

Le Mont d'Arbois, route du Mont-d'Arbois (tel. 21-25-03), is a grandiose, country-club-style hotel, built originally in 1921 for the mother of Baron de Rothschild. On the outskirts of Megève, at the foot of the towering Mont d'Arbois, it is set apart from the tourism of the resort. It not only has magnificent views from all its windows, but is surrounded by an 18-hole, Henry Cotton-designed golf course. The hotel also has its own tennis courts, ski lift, a ball-trap-shooting range, an equestrian ring, even a winter trail for colorful horse-drawn sleigh rides.

The main building has five floors with encircling balconies, and there is a more contemporary wing of rooms adjoining. The connecting passageway is an art gallery. The styling of the interior is done with originality and imagination. The more expensive suites and bedrooms are quite chic, all color coordinated. There is, as well, a 13-bedroom chalet with a private bar and a dining room that is open all year. Queen Juliana of the Netherlands once stayed here, not taking the best room but giving it to her offspring instead. In the regular rooms, singles begin at 420F ($95.89), rising to 750F ($171.23) in a double. In the chalet, a single room costs 550F ($125.57), a double, 750F ($171.23). There are several places at which to eat, including the chalet itself where a meal runs around 120F ($27.40), and can be enjoyed in the right weather on an outside terrace. The main restaurant is like an alpine tavern with whitewashed walls.

Here a meal runs from 110F ($25.11) to 140F ($31.96). By taking the ski lift you'll reach an atmospheric dining lodge, where on sunny days you can order your meal at a trestle table placed out on the terrace. Near the chalet is La Taverne Bavaroise, serving such Bavarian specialties as sauerkraut and sausages.

There is also a disco frequented by guests of all ages. During the day you can use a heated indoor swimming pool and an adjoining gymnasium with a sauna and massage tables. Except for the year-round chalet, the hotel is open from June 25 through September and from December 15 to April 15. When reserving a room, you must request a stay of three days. It's best to take the half-pension plan, ranging from 335F ($76.48) to 420F ($95.89) per person.

A First-Class Choice

Le Triolet, route du Bouchet (tel. 21-08-96), is a beguiling miniature chalet, built with a sun balcony and standing in a flower garden. It's almost like a private home, the owner being the chef de cuisine. He does much of his roasting and baking in a huge corner brick-oven fireplace. Each of the 10 bedrooms contains a private bath, and, happily, a glass wall with a sliding door leading to the terrace. A single rents for 250F ($57.08), the tariff rising to 450F ($102.74) in a double. It's best to request full pension, costing from 275F ($62.78) to 425F ($97.03) per person daily. The hotel lies just a few minutes' walk from the center of the village and the Palais de Sports, with its swimming pool, tennis courts, and ice curling rink. If you're dining at Le Triolet, you'll find a well-prepared set meal for 85F ($19.41). The hotel is closed from April 20 to May 31 and from September 29 to November 15.

The Medium-Priced Range

Coin du Feu, route de Rochebrune (tel. 21-04-94), is one of the best of the middle-bracket hotels, built in the modern grand-chalet style. It offers a lot of amenities, including an American bar and Ping-Pong. Connections are easily made to the Rochebrune cable car. Rooms are well furnished and beautifully maintained, and the hotel is most comfortable. Only 25 rooms are available, and the cost ranges from 230F ($52.51) in a single to a high of 320F ($73.06) in a double. At night you can order snacks. The hotel is open only from mid-December until the first of April.

A Budget Inn

Perce Neige, route de Rochebrune (tel. 21-22-13), blends in well with the local scene, complete with Alpine-green shutters and sun-seeking balconies. Inside, the owner has attempted a more cosmopolitan style with modern furnishings. There are a total of 20 pleasantly furnished bedrooms, costing from 80F ($18.26) in a single to 160F ($36.53) in a double. You can stay here on the full-pension plan at a rate going from 150F ($34.26) to 180F ($41.09) per person nightly. If you're dining only, a set meal costs 40F ($9.13). The hotel is open from June 20 through September and from December 20 to April 15.

WHERE TO DINE: Au Capucin Gourmand, route du Crêt-du-Midi (tel. 21-01-98), offers the best food in Megève outside of the hotel dining rooms. The chef of this Savoy inn, Monsieur Ripert, is a man of taste and skill, as reflected by his well-chosen menu and carefully selected staff whose professional service makes this a formal yet intimate place. The cookery certainly reflects talent, and the menu always contains much of interest, including grills. Monsieur Ripert's special opener is a pâté en croûte served hot. The appendage he attaches to its name is "Souvaroff." Or perhaps you'd prefer his mousseline of salmon or else his fresh artichokes with morels. In naming his trout mousse, he honors Richelieu. He also offers a delicious-tasting grilled chicken in orange sauce, and grilled lamb cutlets which are superb. In this part of the country you try to order a main dish that will go well with gratin Dauphinois—sliced potatoes baked with eggs, milk, and mountain cheese. The sorbets or petits fours make an excellent finish to your meal. Featured wines include Gamay and Apremont. You'll spend around 120F ($27.40) ordering à la carte. The restaurant is open from July 1 to November 5 and from December 15 to May 5. It is closed on Mondays.

6. Annecy

Right on Lac d'Annecy, the jewel of the Savoy Alps, the resort of Annecy makes the best excursion base for touring Haute-Savoie. The former capital of the counts of Geneva, Annecy opens onto one of the best views of lakes and mountains in the French Alps.

The resort is dominated by **Annecy Castle,** its Queen's Tower dating from the 12th century. It was in this castle that the counts of Geneva took refuge in the 13th century. You can go up to the castle, now being restored, and look out upon the town's roofs and belfries. The museum is open daily except Tuesday from 10 a.m. to noon and from 2-6 p.m., charging 4F (91¢) for admission. Students and children are admitted at half-price.

Canals cut through the old part of town, **Annecy-le-Vieux,** and because of this Annecy has been called "the Venice of the Alps." You can explore the arcaded streets of the old town where Jean-Jacques Rousseau arrived in 1728, sent there in the hope that the charismatic Mme. de Warens could save his soul from heresy. On the Place J.-J.-Rousseau, the house where the madame once lived has disappeared, but not her memory. There is a little monument with Rousseau's bust in the courtyard.

After exploring Annecy, we'd suggest a visit to the famous **Les Gorges du Fier,** six miles from Annecy, a 12-minute run by train from the Lovagny station (the Aix-les-Bains line). You can also go to the tourist office and get the latest schedule of daily motorcoach trips offered. This striking gorge is considered one of the most interesting sights in the French Alps. A gangway takes visitors through a winding gully, varying from 10 to 30 feet wide. The gully was cut by the torrent through the rock and over breathtaking depths. You'll hear the roar of the river at the bottom. Emerging from this labyrinth, you are greeted by a huge expanse of boulders—a "sea of rocks." The gorge is open from Easter to October, the tour taking less than an hour and costing 6F ($1.37). It remains open from 9 a.m. to 6 p.m. (till 7 p.m. in July and August).

In the area, you can also visit the 14th-century **Château de Montrottier.** From its tower a view of Mont Blanc unfolds. The château itself contains pottery, Oriental costumes, armor, tapestries, and antiques, as well as some bronze bas-reliefs by Peter and Hans Vischer of Nürnberg, their art dating from the 15th century. The castle is open daily from Easter to mid-October from 8 a.m. to noon and from 1:30 to 7 p.m., charging 6F ($1.37) for admission. You're shown through on a conducted tour.

Of course, one of the most interesting excursions is a tour of **Lac d'Annecy** itself. These tours leave from Easter until the end of September. In July and August, there are at least 12 steamers leaving from Annecy. It's best to take a combined ticket, costing 15F ($3.42), and allowing visitors to cruise the lake and take a cable car—called a téléphérique—to **Mont Veyrier.** In seven minutes you take a 2600-foot jump to the top of the mountain at 4280 feet. From the mountain's rocky slopes, a panoramic view unfolds—considered one of the most beautiful belvederes in the French Alps. If you're planning to tour the mountain, allow another hour in your schedule.

FOOD AND LODGINGS: Hôtel des Trésoms et de la Forêt, 3 Boulevard de la Corniche (tel. 51-43-84), is the best place to stay in Annecy, certainly the most tranquil and scenically positioned of all the hotels near the town itself. It's actually more of an attractive private villa than a hotel—set in its own three acres of a promontory overlooking Lac d'Annecy, the Alps, and Annecy itself. The hotel is a substantial villa, painted white with cherry-red shutters. Try to get a lakeview room if possible. However, all the accommodations are pleasant and attractively furnished, costing from 160F ($36.53) in a single to a peak 300F ($68.49) in a double with complete private bath. The rooms have a Swiss cleanliness, and you can stay here on a number of plans, including half pension, ranging in price from 270F ($61.64) to 380F ($86.75) per person daily. The wines of the region are gently handled and reasonably priced. The food is traditional and wholly reliable. If you're touring in the area, you can call up and reserve a table, ordering a complete meal from 100F ($22.83) to 200F ($45.66). The hotel shuts down from December 1 to February 15.

At Chavoires, three miles from Annecy, the **Pavillon de L'Ermitage** (tel. 44-81-09) is another charming candidate for lakeside tranquility seekers, although the villa is in the environs. A long, distinguished-looking, white-painted villa, it is set right on the water, in the midst of vineyards. It even has its own boat landing. Although the rooms are comfortable and well furnished, most guests come here to enjoy the food. Maurice Tuccinardi competes with the Auberge de Savoie (recommended below) in his cuisine. His dining room offers lakeside views, and in summer guests can eat out on the terrace under a cool, leafy arbor. A set meal will run 85F ($19.41). If you order à la carte, expect a bill ranging from 110F ($25.11) to 160F ($36.53). Specialties include omble chevalier ("char" in English), a fish somewhat like a trout found in the deep lakes of Savoy. It is prepared like salmon trout. Other main dishes are a soufflé de brochet (pike) and poularde de Bresse. Incidentally, we'd highly recommend the latter offering, because chicken from the ancient part of France known as Bresse has been eulogized by many gourmets, its praise sung in verse by many poets. The hotel contains only a dozen bedrooms, and these rent for 105F ($23.97) in a single, rising to a peak 170F ($38.81) in a double with private bath. The Pavillon is open from February until the first of November.

L'Abbaye, 15 chemin de l'Abbaye (tel. 23-61-08), is in Annecy-le-Vieux, the most interesting part of the town for history buffs, the Old Town itself. The hotel was converted from an 11th-century abbey. You approach it through a courtyard, allowing you to step back through the years. A family-run affair, the hotel has been subtly modernized without interfering with its quaintness and charm. There are only a dozen bedrooms. The price is the same for either single or double occupancy—from 110F ($25.11) with shower, from 135F ($30.82) to 220F ($50.23) with full bath. The accommodations themselves are furnished in a personable, helter-skelter manner.

Bargain seekers may also be drawn to the **Super Panorama** on the route du Semnoz, about 1½ miles from the heart of Annecy (tel. 45-34-86). With a name like that, this simple little inn had better have a view to sell, and it does. Admirably situated, the hotel opens onto a splendid vista of lake and mountain You can sit out on the terrace enjoying it, or else take a promenade in many directions. The hotel rents out only five bedrooms, which are modestly furnished. In season, demi-pension is obligatory, at a rate of 115F ($26.25) per person daily. This is one of the best values offered at this lakeside resort, considering that the Alpine food is good and hearty and the portions of generous size. The hotel is closed from January 5 to mid-February.

The best restaurant in Annecy—and this has been true since we first dined there back in 1959—is the **Auberge de Savoie**, 1 Place St.-François (tel. 45-03-05). Many of the townspeople prefer this restaurant as a luncheon rendezvous, although we gravitate to it in the evening when it is quieter. The setting is rustic, the cookery exceptional in a robust, regional sense. The atmosphere is informal, and such local wines as Crépy and Roussette are served at reasonable prices. To begin your meal, we'd recommend a terrine of pike served with a beurre neige, roughly translated as "snow butter." We find that Bernard Collon is at his most skillful when preparing a saddle of lamb served with a game sauce. His most noteworthy dessert is a soufflé glacé aux noisettes. If featured, his tarragon chicken and his crayfish à la Bordelaise are highly recommendable. Expect to pay from 85F ($19.41) to 160F ($36.53) for a complete meal. The restaurant shuts down from June 3 to July 4.

Le Belvédère, a mile out route du Semnoz (tel. 45-04-90). Born in La Rochelle, the patron, Jean-Louis Aubeneau, grew up with the sound of the ocean in his ear and fish on the table every night. Although he has long since moved to the Alps, he carries his heritage of the sea with him, offering the finest seafood cookery in all of Annecy, inventing dishes of his own instead of relying on classic methods of preparation. Call for a table at lunch or dinner, and you'll also get a good view of the lake. We'd recommend his pot-au-feu of the ocean, a marvelous meal, or perhaps his turbot sautéed with three different kinds of pepper. He also makes a soup of scallops with little strips of vegetables cut in the julienne fashion that is delicious, and his masterful touch is reflected in his stuffed brill with red mullet mousse and a caviar-laced sauce to add the proper zest. Menus are offered at 90F ($20.55) and 140F ($31.96). Monsieur Aubeneau also rents out a dozen simply furnished rooms which have beautiful views of the lake. Pension is obligatory in season, costing 145F ($33.10) per person. The hotel's restaurant doesn't serve on Sunday nights and Mondays, and the staff takes a vacation from mid-January to March 20.

7. Talloires

Eight miles from Annecy is our preferred spot on Lake Annecy, the charmingly situated village of Talloires. Chalk cliffs surround a pleasant bay. At the lower end a wooden promontory encloses a small port. An 18-hole golf course and water sports such as skiing, boating, swimming, and fishing make this a favorite spot with French holiday makers.

Talloires is a gourmet citadel, containing one of France's great three-star restaurants, the Auberge du Père Bise, and a Benedictine abbey founded here in the 11th century but now transformed into a deluxe hotel. First, the restaurant, in case you're just motoring through.

Auberge du Père Bise (tel. 44-72-01) is an elegant chalet restaurant in a private park at an enchanting spot on the lake. One food critic called its viands "gastronomic fantasies." It's a joyous recommendation for those who can afford the steep tariffs. Long before the automobile became popular, the Swiss came down from Geneva to dine with Père Bise, who opened his auberge at the turn of the century. Of course, he's gone now, but the heirs, Monsieur and Madame François Bise, carry on in his great tradition, having inherited his secret recipes.

You enter through a little tiled reception lounge directly onto the spectacular kitchen with its glistening copper pots and pans. The kitchen area is almost the same size as the generous dining room, with its sparkling silverware and bowls of fresh flowers. But in fair weather guests overlook even so tempting a setting and head instead for the vine-covered pergola with its view of the lake.

A chanteuse from Vienna confided in us that the food here tasted better in 1928. Frankly, we'll have to take her word for that. The chef specializes in omble chevalier, that most delicate of fish which tastes somewhat like a cross between a trout and a salmon. It appears at least four times on the menu—braised in port, with a Nantua sauce, a Vermeille sauce, and even as an entrée (meunière or with hollandaise) if you don't want to order it as a main course.

Main dishes that have enraptured such guests as the late Duke of Windsor include braised pullet in a tarragon sauce, carré de pré-salé au feu de bois (for two persons—that is, young lamb, most delicate, which has been fattened in meadows along the Alpine lakes and cooked over a wood fire). Seasonal dishes include braised pullet with fresh morels of the type Madame du Barry personally selected for Louis XV, roebuck Grand Veneur, roasted woodcock, and jugged hare. Another specialty—*sur commande*—is volaille Souvaroff, chicken filled with foie gras and truffles, sprinkled with a quality cognac, and baked in a casserole after being sealed with dough.

Whenever one of the Rothschilds—Edmond, Élie, or Guy—drops in, he naturally orders the soufflé Rothschild Grand Marnier, named in their honor, although Bardot preferred the strawberries with a heavenly selection of petits fours. The wine cellar is among the finest in France. For a regional choice, order either the Apremont or Seyssel.

The cost of all this—about 350F ($79.91) for what may be one of the most memorable meals of your life.

The auberge also rents out 18 rooms in either the main building or the annex. In season, you can stay in one of these comfortable chambers on the pension plan, which is obligatory, at a cost ranging from 650F ($148.40) to 850F ($194.06) per person daily.

Le Cottage (tel. 44-71-10). The brother of Père Bise, Georges Bise, founded this establishment around 1920. Nowadays his son, Fernand Bise, carries on, maintaining the high tradition. Monsieur Georges once entertained Sir Winston Churchill here. After World War I, the chef cooked a banquet for President Briand, converting a spinach-hater into a spinach devotee. If you want to know what tempted that president of long ago, you can still order épinards en branches Georges Bise here. At his terraced restaurant, the chef also specializes in the previously mentioned omble chevalier, that delicate salmonlike fish which is prepared in at least four different ways at Le Cottage.

For an appetizer, we'd suggest pâté chaud Lucullus. Highly praised main dishes include pintadeau (young guinea hen) truffé Lucullus, which is available in season only; selle de pré-salé truffé Cottage, and fonds d'artichauts Clamart. Other specialties include mousse de foies de volaille (cold pâté of chicken liver), homemade every day. The cuisine is in the grand style, and service is still carried on with flourish and charm. Set meals are offered at 95F ($21.69), 140F ($31.96), and 200F ($45.66), plus 15% for service. You can easily spend 180F ($41.13) on the à la carte menu.

The Cottage also offers 40 rooms, elegantly furnished and most comfortable, in traditional French styling, often using matching chintz draperies and bedspreads. In season, the half-pension rate is obligatory at a cost ranging from 180F ($41.09) to 240F ($54.79) per person. Otherwise, the rooms themselves rent for 100F ($22.83) in the most basic single to a high of 400F ($91.32) in one of the luxuriously appointed double rooms with complete private bath. The Cottage receives guests from mid-March to mid-October.

Nearby, the old Benedictine abbey is now **Hôtel de l'Abbaye** (tel. 44-70-81), a Relais de Campagne. The abbey has been turned into one of the most exceptional character hotels in France. The building itself was reconstructed in the 17th century. With its own landing stage, the hotel is completely secluded. Used as a rest camp for the army in World War II, it was turned into a hotel again in 1945 by Monsieur Tiffenat. In a former age, monks used to store wine in a cellar which is now a bar, an example of the changing times around here.

The entrance to the abbey is through an iron gateway. You stroll along shaded walks, bypassing formal French gardens. The great corridors lead to converted bedchambers—no two alike—where the atmosphere of the past has been carefully preserved, although the niceties of today (telephones, private baths) have been installed. Along this lofty hall are suspended wooden balconies leading to a second level of bedrooms. The furnishings are distinguished. Hopefully, you'll get a chamber with a frescoed ceiling. There are 42 rooms in all, renting for 200F ($45.66) to 240F ($54.79) in a single to a high of 350F ($79.91) in a double. In season, half-pension (obligatory) ranges from 280F ($63.92) to 310F ($70.77) per person daily, taxes and service included. The dining room with its large wooden chandeliers was the monks' dining hall. In summer guests can also dine outside under the shade trees, enjoying a view of the lake. Lovers eventually find a secluded spot by the old moss-covered stone well. The abbey receives from May 1 to mid-October.

Decidedly humble compared to its illustrious neighbors, **Hostellerie du Vivier**, route du Bout-du-Lac (tel. 44-70-54), is easier on the purse. This two-star hotel offers some 34 rooms extended motel-style along the lakefront. Bedrooms are shiny clean, although basic, with a French provincial decor. Doubles with bath peak at 115F ($26.25), and singles cost 72F ($16.44). The inn is owned by Monsieur (he's a superb cook) and Madame Berger. A complete meal at their place (and you don't have to be a guest of the hotel) costs in the range of 32F ($7.31), 40F ($9.13), and 56F ($12.78). The first set menu is one of the dining bargains of the resort. Specialties include pullet in a cream sauce with fresh morels, fondue bourguignonne, and gratin Dauphinois (sliced potatoes baked with eggs, milk, and cheese). The inn is open from mid-March to mid-October.

8. Aix-les-Bains

Forty-five miles north from Grenoble, Aix-les-Bains is the most fashionable spa of eastern France and one of the largest. Its hot springs, which offered comfort to the Romans, are said to be useful in the treatment of rheumatism. The spa is well equipped for visitors, containing flower gardens, a casino (the Palais de Savoie), a race course, a golf course, and a lake, Lac du Bourget, with a bathing beach.

It was at Aix-les-Bains that Lamartine, the French poet (author of *Poetic Meditations*), met the doctor's wife, Julie Desherettes, the "Elvire" of his early poems and the inspiration for his most famous piece, "Le Lac," composed in the autumn of 1817. His "Elvire" died in December of that year, and romantic French schoolgirls have been weeping ever since. Balzac also described the lake in his novel *Peau de Chagrin*.

The **Aux Thermes Nationaux d'Aix-les-Bains** is open all year. The New Baths opened in 1934, completing the structure that had been launched in 1857 by Victor Emmanuel II. To enter, go to the caretaker at the main entrance, across from the Hôtel de Ville, the former château of the marquises of Aix in the 16th century. Inside you can see the olympic swimming pool, the thermal caves, and the remains of the Roman baths. The baths are open from April until the end of October, daily except Sundays and holidays, from 3 to 6 p.m., charging an admission of 4F (91¢).

Also in the center of the spa are two other Roman remains—a **Temple of Diana,** a square building, and the **Arch of Campanus,** a triumphal arch 30 feet high.

The spa's most interesting museum is the **Musée du Docteur-Faure,** where you'll find a modern art collection, including watercolors by Rodin, plus works by Degas and Corot. It is open from 9 a.m. to noon and from 2 to 6 p.m., daily except Mondays from October 15 to June 15, and daily from June 15 to October, charging a 4F (91¢) admission.

In the environs you take a cable car up to **Le Revard,** at an altitude of 5080 feet. There you'll have a panoramic view of Mont Blanc. The round-trip fare is 15F ($3.42).

Regular steamer service also takes you on a four-hour boat ride on **Lac du Bourget,** a beautiful trip. The service is on Tuesdays, Thursdays, Fridays, and Sundays from July 10 to September, with departures at 2:30 p.m. The round-trip fare is 18F ($4.11). Boats depart from the landing stage at Grand Port.

The **Abbaye Royale de Hautecombe** can also be visited on a boat trip, with two to five steamers leaving every day from Easter until September 30. To board a boat, go also to the landing stage at Grand Port. The price is 20F ($4.57), the trip taking 2½ hours. The abbey, which has been called the Saint-Denis of Savoy, is the mausoleum of the princes of the House of Savoy. It stands on a promontory jutting out into the lake. It is open to the public from 10:30 a.m. to noon and from 2 to 6 p.m. The church was rebuilt in the 19th century in what is called the "Troubadour Gothic" style. If you'd like, you are permitted to attend mass in Gregorian chant on Sundays at 9:15 a.m. and on weekdays at 9:30 a.m. Vespers are at 6 in summer, at 5 p.m. in winter.

WHERE TO STAY: Hostellerie le Manoir, rue Georges-Ier (tel. 61-44-00), in the Parc du Splendide-Royal, is an old building with a rustic decoration that has the look of a country house in bygone times. Within walking distance of the thermal center, it is pervaded by an informal charm. Pathways weave in and about the old-world gardens at which outdoor furniture has been discreetly placed under shade trees. Most of the public rooms, as well as the bedrooms, open onto terraces and flowering shrubbery. The white-stucco hotel with its green shutters has an overhanging roof, and on the garden façade under the eaves is a large antique clock.

The interior furnishings are traditional, with a sprinkling of antiques. The dining hall has large wooden beams, a tall, open fireplace, and a center which opens onto a wooden mezzanine. Here a good cuisine is served, costing 65F ($14.84) to 90F ($20.55) for a set menu. We've enjoyed smoked salmon, trout cooked in vermouth, peppersteak, gnocchi, and a mouth-watering strawberry tart. When featured, the chef also does an excellent pâté de campagne.

The bedrooms are well furnished, with chintz draperies and provincial pieces. Each has its own private bath and telephone. The rate is 85F ($19.41) in a single, peaking at 200F ($45.66) in a double. You can ask for full pension rates, going for anywhere from 150F ($34.26) to 250F ($57.08) per person. The manor shuts down in January.

WHERE TO DINE: One of the best restaurants, **Lille,** le Grand Port (tel. 55-04-22), stands near the landing stages where you can get steamers for tours of Lac du Bourget. It is also possible to secure an accommodation here, as the inn rents out 14 simply furnished rooms at prices that begin at 80F ($18.26) in a single, going up to 210F ($47.94) in the best double. Guests of the hotel can also take the full-pension plan, at rates ranging from 170F ($38.81) to 190F ($43.38) per person daily. The hotel is closed January and February and on Tuesdays off-season.

But most guests go here for the truly superb cuisine. The food is rich and often quite subtle. The chef's preferred dish is char (*omble* in French), a fish somewhat like a trout found in the deep lakes of Savoy. Here it's made all the more elegant, as it's cooked in champagne. We'd also recommend the chicken "Mère Lille," and, in season only, a raspberry soufflé which is the best we've ever enjoyed anywhere. Featured wines are Gamay and Roussette. In season you can dine out on the large shaded terrace. A complete meal will cost from 80F ($18.26) to 140F ($31.96).

D'Albion, Avenue d'Albion (tel. 61-02-44), has a prime position. Its façade is an example of classic French architecture, with tall doors leading out onto tiny balconies. The restaurant opens onto the spa's major park, and lies within walking distance of the thermal establishment and the casino, farther away. D'Albion is surrounded on three sides by woods. Regional specialties and a standard international repertoire of dishes are featured, an à la carte meal costing from 110F ($25.11) to 170F ($38.81) per person. Opening off the lobby is **Le Bar,** styled in Nordic modern.

Davat, also at Grand Port (tel. 35-09-63), is not only another leading restaurant but also an excellent and modestly priced place at which to stay in beautiful surroundings. Its chief attraction is its lovely flower garden with potted plants and singing birds. Again, its bedrooms, only 10 in all, are simply furnished, costing from 120F ($27.40) in a single to 150F ($34.26) in a double. A continental breakfast is an additional 12F ($2.74). Guests at the Davat are allowed to take the full-pension terms, ranging from 160F ($36.53) to 180F ($41.09) per person. The cooking is robust, the drinking of regional wines most pleasurable, and the service is warm and gracious. If you're visiting only for a meal, you'll find one of the best set menus at the spa, costing only 70F ($15.98), although you could easily spend as much as 180F ($41.09). The hotel and restaurant are closed in November and December, reopening at Christmas. In addition they are closed on Wednesdays from September to May.

Finally, the **Restaurant de la Chambotte** (tel. 61-30-54) serves good food, but even if it didn't, people would come here for the view of the lake. The entrance to its panoramic terraces is free, and from that platform you can look out onto a sweeping aerial view of Lac du Bourget, and, on the horizon, at least three mountain chains. If we were ever compiling a guide to restaurants with a view in Europe, this would be one of our leading selections. If you're driving, head out the N201, cutting off onto the D991B. The food is irreproachable on a modest level. From Easter until the end of October, diners are received and are offered a set menu at 45F ($10.27) that is very good value. Depending on your appetite, you can order more expensively, of course, for around 130F ($29.68), but we've always found the less expensive menu more than adequate.

BURGUNDY AND MORVAN

VINEYARD CASTLES and ancient churches make La Province de Bourgogne in eastern France the land of the good life for those who savor food and drink. Once, Burgundy was as powerful as La Belle France herself, its dukes spreading their might across Europe. But they are gone now, leaving a legacy of vintage red and white wines to please and excite the palate.

The six major wine-growing regions of Burgundy are Chablis, Côte de Nuits, Côte de Beaune, Côte de Chalon, the Mâconnais, and the Nivernais.

1. Auxerre

This old town was founded by the Gauls and enlarged by the Romans. On a hill overlooking the Yonne River, it is the capital of Lower Burgundy and the center of vineyards, some of which produce Chablis.

Joan of Arc spent several days here in 1429. Napoleon met Marshal Ney here on March 17, 1815, on the former emperor's return from Elba. King Louis XVIII had sent Ney to stop Napoleon. Instead, Ney embraced him and turned his army against the king. For that gesture, Ney was later shot in Paris.

Pay a visit to the **Cathédrale St.-Étienne,** built during the 13th century though not completed until the 16th. It is a good example of the flamboyant

Gothic style. The front is remarkable, with its sculptured portals. Inside, the stained glass is famous, some of it being the original from the 13th century. In the crypt, all that remains of the Romanesque church that stood on this site, you can see frescoes from the 11th century.

Auxerre used to be a gastronomic relay on the road between Paris and Lyon, but the Autoroute du Soleil has mostly ended that. However, shops display interesting regional specialties, including chocolate snails filled with almond praliné, chocolate truffles with rum-soaked grapes, and garlic sausage baked in brioche, even sourdough bread from wood-fired ovens.

FOOD AND LODGING: Le Maxime, 2 and 4 Quai de la Marine (tel. 52-04-40), is run by Monsieur Fortune. At his attractive house at the edge of the Yonne, you can begin your meal with a terrine du chef at 28F ($6.39), then follow with darne de saumon sauce choron at 52F ($11.87). The pièce de résistance is tournedos périgourdine at 68F ($15.52). A half-bottle of wine goes for 14F ($3.20) to 17F ($3.88). Set meals are offered for 95F ($21.69). If you're staying overnight (tel. 52-14-19), you'll find pleasant rooms, costing 143F ($32.65) in a single, 160F ($36.53) in a double. All rooms are equipped with baths. Breakfast is an extra 15F ($3.42) per person.

You leave Auxerre by N6, following the valley of the Cure River to a town called **Sermizelles.** There you take the N151 to—

2. Vézelay

For many this is the high point of their trip through Burgundy and Morvan. Because it contained what was believed to be the tomb of St. Mary Magdalene, that "beloved and pardoned sinner," it was once one of the great pilgrimage sites of the Christian world.

On a hill 360 feet above the surrounding countryside, the town is characterized by its ramparts and its old houses with sculptured doorways, corbelled staircases, and mullioned windows.

The site of Vézelay was originally an abbey, founded by Girart de Roussillon, a count of Burgundy (troubadours were fond of singing of his exploits). It was consecrated in 878 by Pope John VIII.

On March 31, 1146, Saint Bernard preached the Second Crusade there; in 1190 the town was the rendezvous point for the Third Crusade, drawing such personages as Richard the Lion-Hearted and King Philippe-Auguste of France. Later, Saint Louis of France came here several times on pilgrimages.

Park outside the town hall and walk through the medieval streets past flower-filled gardens. After about a quarter of a mile of climbing streets, you reach the **Basilique Ste.-Madeleine.** The largest and most famous Romanesque church in France, this basilica is only ten yards shorter than Notre-Dame de Paris. The façade was rebuilt by Viollet-le-Duc, who restored Notre-Dame. You enter the narthex, a vestibule of large dimensions, about 4000 square feet. Look through the main door for a tremendous view of Burgundian-Romanesque glory. The high nave is built in white and beige chalk stones. It is full of light, and each capital shows a different sculpture. It's possible to visit the Carolingian crypt, where the tomb of Mary Magdalene formerly rested (today it contains some of her relics). From the narthex you can ascend the tower, 1F (23¢), for a view of the old town and the hilly landscapes.

Afterward, you can end your walk by going alongside the ancient walls and back to the Place du Champ-de-Foire at the lower end of town.

If you're dining or staying over, the preferred choice follows.

FOOD AND LODGING: Poste et Lion d'Or (tel. 33-21-23) is a local monument, the former *poste relay,* built at a time when owners had the materials and room to construct expansively and grandly. The present patron, Monsieur Danguy, has masterfully restored the inn to its former glory, and, as someone observed, "it smells of good times of another era." You feel you're being welcomed at a first-class place, although the tariffs are comparable to those at a modest Parisian hotel. Singles range between 95F ($21.69) and 130F ($29.68), depending on the plumbing. Doubles begin at a low 125F ($28.54) for a bathless version, and peak at 230F ($52.51) for a room with bath. Service and taxes are included, but breakfast is an additional 16F ($3.65). The food is exceptionally good. We especially like the escargots (snails) de Bourgogne in Chablis and the stuffed trout (truite farcie) with herbs. There are no set meals, and à la carte orders range in price from 120F ($27.40) to 200F ($45.66), the latter a Pantagruelian meal. Closed from November 3 to April 5.

On your way out of town, follow N485 to **St.-Père-sous-Vézelay** on the Cure River, 1¼ miles from Vézelay. You can stop and admire the **Église Notre-Dame,** a beautiful Gothic church dating from the 12th century.

From there, continue on to **Pierre-Perthuis,** some 10 miles southwest of Avallon. This little village is one of the most scenic spots in Morvan, with a view of the Cure River Valley. The ruins of its feudal castle date from the 12th century.

If you wish, you can detour to—

3. Avallon

The old fortified town is shielded behind its ancient ramparts, upon which you can stroll. A medieval atmosphere still permeates the town, and you'll find many 15th- and 16th-century houses. At the town gate on the Grande Rue is a **clock tower** from 1460. The Romanesque **Church of St. Lazarus** dates from the 12th century and has two interesting doorways. The church is said to have received the head of St. Lazarus in 1000. This turned Avallon into a pilgrimage site. Today, Avallon is used as a base for excursions to the north of the Massif du Morvan. But it is mainly visited because it is a gastronomic highlight of Burgundy, as reflected by the two following recommendations.

FOOD AND LODGING IN THE UPPER BRACKET: Hostellerie de la Poste, 13 Place Vauban (tel. 86-34-06-12), is beautifully furnished with rich tapestries and antiques. It serves, at deluxe prices, some of the most celebrated food in France, including amusettes (hors d'oeuvres) de l'Hostellerie, 90F ($20.55), followed by timbale de homard (lobster). At last report, this specialty cost 175F ($39.95), although we have no idea what the price will be when you arrive. Especially recommendable is pintadeau (guinea fowl) aux Baies roses de l'Île Bourbon, 105F ($23.97). By all means, round out your repast with one of the delicious pastries, dolce Borghèse, at 45F ($10.27). Chablis and Volnay are the featured wines. Everything comes under the eagle eye of Monsieur Hure. If the season's right, you can enjoy a walk in the beautiful flower garden later.

Those staying over will find 29 handsomely furnished rooms with modern amenities. A standard double with bath costs 260F ($59.36); a single, 180F ($41.09), plus 15% for service. The inn is open from February through November.

Equally enchanting—and also expensive—is the **Moulin des Ruats,** Vallée du Cousin (tel. 34-07-14), a Relais de Campagne two miles outside of town, reached by taking D247. On the banks of the Cousin, this country inn in the valley offers serene and elegant dining, and, under the direction of Monsieur Bertier, the restaurant serves some of the finest food in France.

Dining here is a delight because you can combine the pleasures of good food with attractive surroundings. In pleasant weather, the terrace overlooking the stream is a favorite spot for diners, but on foul days the inn's pleasant dining rooms are a wonderful alternative—and you can still listen to the comforting sound of the water cascading through the millrace.

As might be expected, freshwater fish is a specialty at the inn, with the honors going to truite au bleu beurre blanc crème du Major Thompson, a delicious stream trout tossed live into a broth of onions, vinegar, carrots, and cayenne, and then served with a white butter sauce made with shallots and cream. Named for a famous character in a novel by Pierre Daninos (who has been a favorite customer), the trout is only one of three fish—pike and salmon are the other two—cooked in this way.

Chicken is another popular dish at the Moulin des Ruats, and it is cooked in a variety of ways, including the traditional coq au vin. But the truly sensational dish here is the fondue de volaille à la crème des Ruats—a boned chicken breast sautéed in butter, flamed with cognac, and then simmered in the best Chablis. After the wines are reduced to their essence, cream and mushrooms are added to create a fantastic sauce. Another specialty is quail from the Dombes. Although the menu lists a variety of desserts, you should definitely try the homemade fruit tarts. These are custom-made after your order, requiring half an hour's wait. Your choice is assembled, popped into the oven, and delivered to your table sizzling.

In addition to the excellent menu, the hostellerie offers a fine wine list, plus a number of unusual after-dinner liqueurs. A complete meal usually costs from 115F ($26.25) to 170F ($38.81).

If you wish to spend the night, you can get a double room with bath for 200F ($45.66), a double without bath for a low of 110F ($25.11). Breakfast is an extra 15F ($3.42) per person. The Moulin is open from March through October.

Return to N485 and continue until you reach D42, at which you turn left to **Lormes,** a town on the border between Nivernais and Morvan. The cemetery provides the best panorama. In Lormes, take the D17 to—

4. Ouroux-en-Morvan

This is a pleasant little village with a dynamic mayor, Monsieur Coeurdacier. After seeing its little church and main square, you can take a road leading to a panoramic view over the hills to **Pannesière Lake.**

In Ouroux itself, if you like to ride horses it'll cost 25F ($5.71) an hour, even less if you take an all-day trek through the surrounding hills. In July and August, the village becomes an artisan center. If you plan to stay overnight, you'd better call the following recommendation for reservations.

FOOD AND LODGING: Hôtel de la Poste (tel. 91-11-47). When you push open the door, a cowbell sounds. Inside, the hôtel is a simple *salle de café* with a bar. Under a beamed ceiling, at a large table, you eat farm-style. Madame Julien is the reigning empress. Her meals are not only delicious but gargantuan. You'll need to be hoisted up from the table. Set meals cost 22F ($5.02), 35F ($7.99), and 50F ($11.42)—this last is spectacular. Some of the specialties include ris de veau (sweetbreads), beignets (batter-fried) frog legs, and canard (duckling) sauvage aux grisets (local mushrooms).

Madame Julien sets aside 14 bedrooms for overnighters, furnishing them in a country style with floral wallpaper and padded beds. A single costs 30F ($6.85), increasing to 48F ($10.96) in a double. Breakfast is an extra 8F ($1.83). From Ouroux, you can continue to—

5. Planchez .

Some people call this village the world capital of Christmas trees because of the forests surrounding it. The Nazis burned down nearly three-quarters of Planchez in reprisals against the French Resistance Movement. But that sad memory is blotted out today. From here you can take a road to **Lac des Settons,** a scenic spot of nearly 850 acres along the Cure River Valley. Its dam dates from 1861.

Back at Planchez, we have the following recommendation:

FOOD AND LODGING: Le Relais des Lacs (tel. 14) is another one of France's owner-run inns where you get a good night's sleep, excellent food, and low tariffs. The hotel stands on the only square in the hamlet, next to the pocket-size post office. The windows are small, and hanging baskets of flowers are placed outside to welcome travelers. Inside, the setting is in the typical bistro style. Adjoining the drinking area is a rustic dining room with small tables around a fireplace. Set menus go for 28F ($6.39), 45F ($10.27), 60F ($13.70), and 90F ($20.55). For 45F, we recently enjoyed an appetizer of the famous cold cuts of Morvan, then sole en papillottes, followed by beef-filet en croûte, fresh mushrooms, a salad, a selection of cheese, and a sherbet. An open bottle of wine costs 11F ($2.51). The wine list is impressive, and a lot of great bottles at inexpensive prices are available.

The owner, Monsieur François Dumarais, rents out 24 bedrooms. The chambers are more homey than impressive, but all is kept immaculate. Toilets and baths are in the corridors. Without bath, a single rents for 40F ($9.13), a double for 55F ($12.56). Ten doubles are equipped with private baths, these costing 90F ($20.55). Breakfast is a pleasant surprise, with lots of coffee, plenty of local butter, homemade toasted bread, and pots of homemade jam, costing an extra 8F ($1.83). Closed on Wednesdays off-season and for one week in February.

From Planchez, the D17 will bring you to the **Barrage de Pannessière Chaumard,** the great dam of the Yonne. Turn around and join the N444 to—

6. Château-Chinon

This scenic town was a natural fortress, looking out over the plains of Morvan and Nivernais. Once it was a feudal castle, and it's seen many battles. You can climb to the **Panorama du Calvaire** at 2000 feet, once the site of a Gallic settlement. The overall panorama is remarkable from this vantage point. You look over not only the town but the Morvan mountains in the distance. In clear weather you may even see westward to the Loire Valley and south to the summit of **Haut Folin** (3000 feet). Finally, if you have a car, take the **Promenade du Château** running along the side of the hill and making a circuit of the slate-roofed town.

FOOD AND LODGING: Le Vieux Morvan, Place de la Mairie (tel. 85-05-01), is a pleasant country-style inn where you can get good local cooking and a bed for the night. The location is central, and the dining room opens onto a panoramic view of the Valley of the Yonne. This inn is a favorite retreat of the socialist leader François Mitterand. On our last visit, we noticed that he skipped the 38F ($8.68) dinner in favor of the 90F ($20.55) repast. That included, incidentally, hors d'oeuvres, filet de lotte (anglerfish) à l'Américaine, pintade (guinea-fowl) rôtie, cheese or ice cream. There are 23 simply furnished bedrooms with varied plumbing. Singles begin at 48F ($10.96), and the most expensive doubles are 120F ($27.40). Breakfast is an extra 12F ($2.74). Closed November 10 to January.

You leave Château-Chinon by N78, heading toward Autun. At the town of **Arleuf,** take the D500 on your right, a narrow and rough road through a large, dark forest. At a fork, turn right to **Glux.** After Glux, follow the arrows to **Mont Beuvray** via D18. You reach the summit through D274, a narrow, winding, one-way road. After two miles of climbing, you're at **Oppidum of Bibracte,** capital of the Eduens, a famous Gallic tribe. At this altitude of 2800 feet, Chief Vercingétorix back in 52 A.D. organized the Gauls to fight Caesar's legions. From this summit the view is tremendous over Autun and Mont St.-Vincent. If the weather is clear, you can see the Jura and snowy Mont Blanc. All around are oaks and beeches, some of them more than 1000 years old. After leaving Mont Beuvray by the D274, you'll come to **St.-Léger-sous-Beuvray.** There you can head to Autun via D3.

7. Autun

Deep in Burgundy wine country, Autun is one of the oldest towns in France, lying some 30 miles west of **Beaune.**

In the days of the Roman Empire, it was often called "the other Rome." Some of the Roman relics still stand, including the remains of a theater, the **Théâtre Romain,** the largest in Gaul, holding some 15,000 spectators. It was nearly 500 feet in diameter. Outside the town you can see the curious quadrangular tower of the **Temple of Janus** rising incongruously 80 feet on the plain.

Once, Autun was an important link on the road from Lyon to Boulogne, as reflected by the **Porte d'Arroux,** with two large archways used now for cars, and two smaller ones for pedestrians. It's in the northwest section, rising 55 feet. Also exceptional is the **Porte St.-André,** or St. Andrew's Gate, about a quarter of a mile northwest of the Roman theater. Rising 65 feet high, it, too, has four doorways, and is surmounted by a gallery of ten arcades.

The crowning achievement of Autun, however, is the **Cathédrale de St.-Lazare,** standing on the highest point in Autun, built in 1120 to house the relics of St. Lazarus. On the façade, the tympanum in the central portal is famous, depicting the Last Judgment; it is one of the triumphs of Romanesque sculpture. Some of the stone carvings are by Gislebertus, one of the few artists at that time who signed their names to their works. Inside, a painting by Ingres depicts the martyrdom of St. Symphorien, who was killed in Autun. In summer you can climb the tower and from there enjoy a good view over the town.

The **Musée Rolin** is installed in a 15th-century *maison* built for Nicolas Rolin, who became a celebrated lawyer in his day (born in 1380). An easy walk from the cathedral, the museum displays a fine collection of Burgundian Romanesque sculptures. From the original Rolin collection are exhibited the *Nativity* by the Maître de Moulins, along with a statue that's a masterpiece of 15th-century work, *Our Lady of Autun.* From mid-March until the end of September, hours are from 9:30 a.m. to noon and from 2:30 to 7 p.m. Otherwise, you're admitted from 10 a.m. to noon and from 2 to 4 p.m. (Sundays 2:30 to 5 p.m.). Off-season the museum is closed on Tuesdays, holidays, and for most of February. Admission is 5F ($1.14), half-price for students.

WHERE TO STAY: Hôtel St.-Louis et de la Poste, 6 rue de l'Arbalète (tel. 52-21-03), is an old posting inn built in 1696 on the main Paris-Nice road. Napoleon slept there twice, once with his wife, Josephine, on January 10, 1802, and again on March 15, 1815, upon his return from the island of Elba on his victorious march to Paris. If you want to have the feeling of the period, ask for the Napoleonic chamber, relatively inexpensive at 170F ($38.81) per night. Inside are two canopied mahogany beds and an Empire fireplace. A more "republican" double with bath rents for 160F ($36.53), and you can get even more republican in a double with shower at 135F ($30.82). Most of the bedrooms have rustic furniture and floral wallpaper, and some contain brass beds. Owner Monsieur Barra provides an imperial reception to guests, either in the American bar or the rococo reception lounge. His dining-room walls and ceiling are covered with tapestries. Malmaison-style, and the furnishings are Empire, with large bay windows overlooking the courtyard (once the stables). Waiters in black and white serve good meals, set menus beginning at 65F ($14.84). The hotel is open from February 1 to mid-December.

Hostellerie du Vieux Moulin, Porte Arroux (tel. 52-10-90), is a good bargain both for meals and for lodging. There are 18 simple but clean rooms, ranging in price from 70F ($15.98) is a bathless single up to 170F ($38.81) for the most expensive doubles with private baths. Breakfast is an additional 15F ($3.42). In summer you can sit out at a table overlooking the garden and a tiny millstream nearby. Most guests are content to order the 58F ($13.24) meal, although a huge 90F ($20.55) "gastronomique" special is featured.

Leave Autun on the N73. After six miles, turn left onto D326 toward Sully. There you can admire the Château de Sully, although you can't go inside. This Renaissance residence was known as the Fontainebleau of Burgundy.

Leave Sully by taking the D26 until you cross the N73. Turn left toward Nolay and go through this small village. Three miles past Nolay, you'll reach La Rochepot with its magnificent castle. It is a medieval-style fortress with an aisle built during the Renaissance. Hours are from 10 a.m. to noon and from 2 to 6 p.m. (5 p.m. in winter). Entrance is 5F ($1.14).

After La Rochepot, head toward Beaune, first on the N6, then on the N74. When you're on the N74 you're on the wine road, passing through some of the most famous Burgundy vineyards, including Chassagne Montrachet, Puligny-Montrachet, Meursault, Auxey Duresses, Volnay, and Pommard.

8. Beaune

This is a small but famous city. It's the capital of the Burgundy wine country and is also one of the best-preserved medieval cities in the district, with a girdle of ramparts. Its history goes back more than 2000 years.

Twenty-four miles south of Dijon, Beaune was a Gallic sanctuary, later a Roman town. Until the 14th century it was the residence of the dukes of Burgundy. When the last duke, Charles the Bold, died in 1447, Beaune was annexed to the crown of France.

Its Hôtel-Dieu et Musée is a perfectly preserved 15th-century hospice which remains a working hospital—one of the world's richest hospitals, since it owns vineyards producing such renowned wines as Aloxe-Corton and Meursault. (On the third Sunday of November the wines are auctioned.) This Gothic masterpiece has a multicolored tile roof, and it shelters treasures of Flemish-Burgundian art. In the *chambre des pauvres* ("room of the poor") you can admire painted, broken-barrel-style, timbered vaulting. Most of the furnishings are authentic. In the museum the masterpiece is a 1443 polyptych of the **Last Judgment** by Roger van der Weyden.

In season, tours leave every 30 minutes from 9 a.m. to 11:30 a.m. and from 2 to 6 p.m. Off-season, tours leave every 45 minutes from 9 to 11:15 a.m. and from 2 to 5:45 p.m. The charge is 6F ($1.37) per person, 4F (91¢) for students. Children under 14 are admitted free.

North of Hôtel-Dieu, **Collégiale Notre-Dame** was begun in 1120, in the style of Burgundian Romanesque. In the sanctuary of this church are displayed some remarkable tapestries illustrating scenes from the life of Mary. They may be viewed from Easter to Christmas.

In the former mansion of the dukes of Burgundy the **Musée du Vin de Bourgogne** has been installed. The history of the Burgundy vineyards is presented. The hours are from 9 a.m. to noon and from 1 to 5:45 p.m. (on Thursday and Friday, from 2 to 5:45). A guided tour, costing 4F (91¢), leaves every hour.

WHERE TO STAY: Hôtel de la Poste, 3 Boulevard Clemenceau (tel. 22-08-11), has been in the Chevillot family for almost 70 years. Although its members have improved everything, they have kept the original rustic style. The reception hall is spacious, with many nooks for lounging. The style of the bedrooms is personalized; some beds are made of brass, others are padded. Half pension in a single is from 250F ($57.08) and up. Menu specialties include crayfish in cream and duckling au poivre vert. If you dine here à la carte, expect to spend from 125F ($28.54) to 190F ($43.38) per person. The hotel is open from March 27 to November 25.

Hotel de Bourgogne, Avenue du Général-de-Gaulle (tel. 22-22-00), offers 120 very comfortable bedrooms at 134F ($30.59) for a single, 156F ($35.62) for a double. Breakfast is an extra 13.50F ($3.08). The hotel belongs to the hotel owners' association of Beaune. It stands just outside the walls, about a quarter of a mile from the old city. The furnishings are up-to-date, and the style is very handsome. You can also dine in the hotel, either in the snackbar for a low 30F ($6.85) or in the more elaborate dining room where prices begin at 60F ($13.70) for a set meal. Reception is very courteous and helpful.

READERS' HOTEL SELECTION: "**Hostellerie de Bretonnière**, 43 Faubourg Bretonnière (tel. 22-15-77), offers rooms in a courtyard off a main entrance to the city. It is very comfortable with quiet modern rooms for 130F ($29.68), plus a continental breakfast at 11F ($2.51). There is off-street parking at no charge" (Warren and Dorothy Hemphill, Blythe, Calif.).

From Beaune you might consider the following detour, before picking up our Burgundian wine trail again.

9. Chagny

Eleven miles southwest of Beaune, Chagny is a busy, bustling commercial and industrial town. Its major antiquity is a church with a Romanesque tower dating from the 12th century. Although it wouldn't be included in an average sightseeing tour of Burgundy, gourmets flock here from all over the world to sample the viands in the following establishment:

Lameloise, 36 Place d'Armes (tel. 87-08-85), is a *relais gourmand,* a hotel and restaurant in an ancient Burgundian maison that sets about the best table in the entire province where the competition is really tough. The cuisine of Jean and Jacques Lameloise, father and son, is inspired. These men are passionately devoted to good food and wine. One pleased diner told us, and we concur, "with the Lameloise family, food is truly raised to an art."

The service and decor are impeccable. If we gave out stars, we'd award Lameloise three, making it one of the premier tables of France. Their salad of fresh green beans and crayfish might sound ordinary, but it is extraordinary. The kitchen also does a delicious feuilleté of sweetbreads that is delicately flavored. Sweetbreads are employed again in something else on the menu, a salad with crayfish. Other specialties include a blanquette of salmon with pearl onions and aiguillettes of duckling with fresh figs. From the ancient cellars emerge some of the finest in wines. Try, in particular, Rully and Santenay. Meals are in the 150F ($34.26) to 210F ($47.94) range.

The establishment also rents out beautifully furnished and comfortable rooms, costing from 112F ($25.57) in the simplest single to a high of 270F ($61.64) for the best doubles with private baths. The restaurant is closed Thursday for lunch and on Wednesday and from mid-November to mid-January.

Leaving Beaune on the D2, the most colorful route is to—

10. Bouilland

The drive to this village takes you through one of the most famous white-wine roads of Burgundy, along the narrow valley of the Rhoin. Soon Bouilland, circled by wooded hills, comes into view. Its church is 900 years old and in remarkably good shape. Here in this secluded oasis you may wish to follow your gastronomic nose to the following recommendation.

FOOD AND LODGING: **Hostellerie du Vieux Moulin** (tel. 21-51-16) has won respect for its owner, Monsieur Heriot, who has turned this small inn at the edge of the village into an excellent place for dining. He sets one of the best tables in Burgundy. The dining room, overlooking a mill and the Rhoin, is comfortable, with stone floors, tapestry-covered seats, and Burgundy-style furniture. Three set meals are offered, at 85F ($19.41), 112F ($25.57), and 185F ($42.24). À la carte specialties include terrine de brochet, lotte en gigot, and pigeon fermier en cocotte. In season there is a large choice of game. We recently enjoyed a pâté chaud, mousse de truite, veau au Marsala with carrots and spinach, plus cheese and a warm tart. We'd suggest that you order half a bottle of Savigny Vergelesse from the vineyard of Monsieur Bize (the vineyard is five miles away).

Only eight rooms are offered, all of them nicely decorated in the Louis XV style, with padded beds. A double with basin costs only 65F ($14.84), increasing to 160F ($36.53) with bath. Breakfast is an extra 14F ($3.20). The "old mill" is closed on Wednesdays, for Thursday lunch, and from June 4 to 12 and from December 24 to January 1.

THE WINE ROUTE TO DIJON: Back on the N74, the road takes you through the wine district en route to Dijon.

Along the way you'll pass through **Aloxe-Corton,** where the Emperor Charlemagne once owned vineyards. The Corton-Charlemagne is still a famous white Burgundy. **Comblanchien** is known for a white stone quarried from neighboring cliffs. At **Nuits-St.-Georges,** a wine is produced that enjoyed great renown during the reign of Louis XIV.

The next village is **Vougeot,** whose vineyards produce an excellent red wine. Here you can visit the **Château du Clos de Vougeot,** a Renaissance building associated with the Brotherhood of the Knights of Tastevin, known for its lavish banquets. Surrounding the château is one of the most celebrated vineyards of France. You can explore the great 12th-century cellar. Hours are from 9 to 11:30 a.m. and from 2 to 5:30 p.m.; an entrance fee of 2F (46¢) is charged. Open all year.

Leave the N74 for D122. This will take you through **Chambolle Musigny,** a spot of great scenic beauty, then to **Morey St.-Denis** and **Gevrey-Chambertin,** marking the beginning of the Côte de Nuits wine district.

11. Gevrey-Chambertin

This world-famous wine-producing town eight miles south of Dijon was immortalized by the writer Gaston Roupnel. Typical of the villages of the Côte d'Or, Gevrey added Chambertin to its name, which is, of course, the name of its most famous vineyard. In the village itself lie the ruins of a fortified castle which was once owned by the abbots of Cluny. The village church with its Romanesque doorway dates from the 14th century.

In Gevrey-Chambertin, the gourmet trail in Burgundy leads to—

La Rôtisserie du Chambertin (tel. 34-33-20). You would think that the owner of this unusual restaurant intentionally hid it to keep people from going there, so inconspicuous is it. The only indication is an unmarked door in the open courtyard with a menu posted next to it. You enter through a museum devoted to the history of barrel-making (the owner's great-grandfather was the town cooper on this very spot), then pass beneath the vaults dating from the 11th century, and finally arrive in a modern, almost psychedelically lit room. The electronic decor is offset by several traditional pieces, creating a warm, friendly atmosphere in which to sample the cuisine.

As the name suggests, the restaurant specializes in grilled and spit-roasted meats, but grilled sole and turbot are also on the menu. For an appetizer, we'd suggest tourte de pigeon (pigeon pie) or terrine de foie de volaille truffé (chicken liver pâté with truffles), both excellently prepared by Mme. Menneveau.

In spite of the variety on the menu, we'd recommend passing everything by to order the spit-roasted ham. This whole, fresh ham has been marinated for several days in white wine, then basted for hours with its own marinade as it slowly turns on the rôtisserie. Accompanying this—and most main dishes—are fresh spinach and potatoes au gratin. For a salad, try the salade vigneronne, a chicory salad wilted with hot bacon and sausage. After such a heavy meal, you may prefer to nibble on some of the delicious cheeses, but if you crave a sweet finale, you'll be overwhelmed by the mouth-watering chocolate cake.

Above all, don't neglect the inn's wines. Chambertin has been called "the wine for moments of great decision." Perhaps that is why Napoleon always took it on his campaigns—even to Moscow. Although the wine list is not extensive, it includes the best of recent vintages. A complete meal, including wine and service, is likely to cost from 130F ($29.68) to 150F ($34.26). The restaurant is closed on Sunday nights and Mondays, in August, and from February 8 to 16.

If you're staying over, we'd recommend the **Hôtel les-Grands-Crus** (tel. 34-34-15), a 24-room charmer, a tiny château that traces its origins back to the 12th century. Opened in 1977, the hotel is run by Pierre Mortet, a helpful host who speaks English. Your bedroom window opens onto views of the vineyards of Burgundy and of two churches, one going back to the 11th century. Prices begin at 130F ($29.68) in a single, going up to 160F ($36.53) in a double with bath. Most rooms contain telephones and TV sets, and some of the furniture is in the Louis XV style. The hotel does not have a restaurant, but serves a continental breakfast for 11F ($2.51). In addition, guests can enjoy the fine wines of Burgundy in a "Cellier d'Exposition et Degustation." Grands-Crus shuts down in January and on Sundays from October 1 to May 1.

READER'S HOTEL SELECTION: "Hôtel les Terroirs, route Dijon (tel. 34-30-76), is small (only 18 rooms) and looks fairly ordinary on the outside. It is right on the main road, not a particularly attractive location, although a convenient one for anyone exploring the wine country. But it is one of the most tastefully and imaginatively decorated places I've seen on my entire trip. A double costs 160F ($36.53)" (Frances Jennings, Evanston, Ill.).

At **Brochon,** you're at the boundary between the Côte de Nuits district and the Côte de Dijon. Further on, at **Fixin** you can stop to visit **Parc Noisot** for a view of the environs of Dijon. **Marsannay-la-Côte,** next, produces a rosé wine from black grapes. At **Chenove,** the vineyards were once owned by Autun monks and the dukes of Burgundy. Finally, you reach—

12. Dijon

Dijon is known overseas mainly for its mustard. In the center of the Côte d'Or, it is the ancient capital of Burgundy. Here good food is accompanied by great wine. Between meals you can enjoy Dijon's art and architecture.

The remains of the former palace of the dukes of Burgundy (**Ancien Palais des Ducs de Bourgogne**) has been turned into the **Musée des Beaux-Arts** (Fine Arts Museum), which is open from 9 a.m. to noon and from 2 to 6 p.m. Entrance is 4F (91¢). One of the oldest and richest museums in France, it contains exceptional sculpture, ducal kitchens from the mid-1400s (six great chimneypieces), a representative collection of European paintings from the 14th through the 19th centuries, and modern French paintings. Take special note of the Salle des Gardes, built by Philip the Good. It was the banqueting hall of the old palace. The grave of Philip the Bold was built between 1385 and 1411 and is one of the best in France. A reclining figure rests on a slab of black marble, surrounded by 41 mourners.

A mile from the center of town, on N5, stands **Chartreuse de Champmol,** the Carthusian monastery built by Philip the Bold as a burial place; it is now a mental hospital. Much was destroyed during the Revolution, but you can see the Moses Fountain in the gardens designed by Sluter at the end of the 14th century. The Gothic entrance is superb.

Major churches to visit in Dijon include the **Cathédrale St.-Benigne,** a 13th-century abbey church in the Burgundian-Gothic style; the **Église St.-Michel,** in the Renaissance style; and the **Église Notre-Dame,** built in the 13th century in the Burgundian-Gothic style with a façade decorated partly with gargoyles. On the Jaquemart clock, the hour is struck by a mechanical family.

FOOD AND LODGING IN THE MIDDLE BRACKET: Hôtel Central, 10 rue du Château (tel. 30-44-00), is one of the biggest hotels in the center of Dijon. The reception areas are traditional and attractive, the bedrooms comfortable with excellent furnishings. Depending on the plumbing, singles range from 85F

($19.41) to 130F ($29.68); doubles, 90F ($20.55) to 160F ($36.53), although some of the special and more luxurious twins are tabbed at 260F ($59.36).

Meals are served daily in the grill room. On the à la carte menu you can find such items as soup au pistou and an entrecôte with a béarnaise sauce. We especially recommend ice cream with black currant liqueur for dessert. Expect to pay around 100F ($22.83) for an average meal.

READER'S HOTEL AND RESTAURANT SELECTIONS: "I stayed at the **Hostellerie du Sauvage,** 64 rue Monge (tel. 41-31-21). In a courtyard set back from the street in the old part of town, it is built like a medieval inn rather than a hotel, is covered with greenery, and is very well kept, comfortable and reasonable. Depending on the plumbing, singles range in price from 50F ($11.42) to a high of 80F ($18.26), and doubles are priced from 60F ($13.70) all the way to 92F ($21), these prices including a continental breakfast.
. . .The **Brasserie du Théâtre** on the Place du Théâtre, right across the street from the opera house, serves a very good meal at moderate prices. I even enjoyed half a dozen snails as my first course on (if I remember correctly) the 35F ($7.99) menu" (Frances Jennings, Evanston, Ill.).

TOURING NOTES: You can leave Dijon on the N5, heading toward **Paris.**

For a few miles you run on a new road in the **Vallée de l'Ouche,** alongside the Burgundy Canal. The scenery is severe, with large fields spreading over the hills. At **Pont de Pany** keep going on N5 toward **Sombernon.** After Aubigny, on your left lies the artificial lake of **Grosbois.** The scenery is typical of agricultural France, with isolated farms, woods, and pastures.

You pass through **Vitteaux** and just before the next village, **Posanges,** stands a magnificent feudal château. You can't visit it, but it's worth a picture. Continue on N5 for a few miles after Posanges until you come to a railroad crossing. There on your left is another old castle, now part of a farm.

The next village you reach is **Pouillenay.** Turn right there onto D9, heading toward **Flavigny-sur-Ozerain.** Park your car outside the walls and walk through the old streets. This once-fortified town is filled with decaying grandeur.

You leave Flavigny on the D29, crossing the D6 and turning left on the small D103 toward **Alise-Ste.-Reine.** This was the site of the famous camp of Alésia. In 52 B.C., Caesar overcame Gallic forces here. Millet sculpted a statue of the leader of the Gauls, Vercingétorix. Visitors can explore the excavated ruins of a Roman-Gallic town from 9 a.m. to 7 p.m. in summer for a 2F (46¢) admission fee. The **Monastery of Ste.-Reine** honors a Christian girl who was decapitated for refusing to marry a Roman governor, Olibrius. As late as the 17th century, a fountain at the site of the beheading was said to have curative powers.

After Alise-Ste.-Reine you can head back toward the village of **Les Laumes,** a railroad center. Before entering the village, make a U-turn to the right, taking the N454 to **Baigneux-les-Juifs.** After the village of **Grésigny** there is a curious farm-fortress surrounded by water on your left.

One mile further on, turn right toward the **Château de Bussy Rabutin.** Roger de Rabútin was the cousin of letter-writing Madame de Sévigné. He also wrote, ridiculing the foibles of the court of Louis XIV. For this he had to spend six years in the Bastille. The façade of his former château is characterized by two round towers. The château, miraculously, has survived mostly intact, including the interior decoration ordered by the count himself. The gardens and park are attributed to Le Nôtre. Guided tours leave every hour from 9 to 11 a.m. and from 2 to 6 p.m. in summer (10, 11, and 4 in winter). Closed Tuesdays. Admission is 4F (91¢).

Going back to Grésigny, turn right before the farm-fortress, then left. Outside the village, turn right again toward **Menetreux Le Pitois.** You're now off the main road and into some real country.

Once back on N5, head on to **Montbard.** After six miles you reach the village of **Marmagne.** There you can turn right on D32 toward the **Abbey of Fontenay.** Isolated in a small valley, Fontenay is one of most unspoiled examples of a 12th-century Cistercian abbey. The abbey was once a paper mill but it's now been restored. The church, from 1139, is one of the oldest Cistercian churches in the country. The cloisters are especially elegant. Open from 9 a.m. to 6:30 p.m., the abbey charges an admission fee of 9F ($2.05).

13. Montbard

On the Burgundy Canal, this busy port was the birthplace of Comte Georges Louis Leclerc de Buffon, born there in 1707. The French naturalist was the author of the monumental *Histoire Naturelle,* published in 1749-1804 in 44 volumes.

In spite of his international fame, he remained simple in his tastes, preferring to live in Montbard rather than Paris. Most of his books were written in Montbard.

Though Buffon died in Paris in 1788, he was buried in Montbard in a small chapel next to the **Church of St. Urse.** The **Parc Buffon** was laid out by the great master himself. You can visit **Tour St.-Louis,** where mementos of Buffon are displayed; it is open from 10 a.m. to noon and from 3 to 6 p.m. except Wednesdays. Buffon's study, **Cabinet de Travail de Buffon,** where he wrote his many volumes, is also open to the public.

ON THE ROAD: Leaving Montbard, cross the Burgundy Canal and take the N80 toward **Semur-en-Auxois.** A few miles away from the city on the right stand the impressive ruins of the feudal **Château de Montfort.** In Semur you can visit **Église Notre-Dame,** rebuilt in the 13th and 14th centuries. You can also spend an hour or so touring the ramparts of the old château there.

The N80 carries you toward **Saulieu.** At the crossroads at N70, turn left towards the ruins of **Thil,** a collegiate church founded in the 14th century. The ruins of the 12th-century château nearby can't be visited without a guide. It was built on the site of a Roman oppidum, and some of the walls date back to the ninth century. The panorama over the countryside is pleasant.

At the village of **Precy-sous-Thil,** join the N80. The road passes through a forest. After 10 miles, you reach—

14. Saulieu

Although the town is fairly interesting, its gastronomy has given this small place international fame. On the boundaries of Morvan and Auxois, the town has enjoyed a reputation for cooking since the 17th century. Even Madame de Sévigné praised it in her letters. So did Rabelais.

The main sight is **Basilique St.-Andoche** on the Place de la Fontaine, which has some interesting decorated capitals. In the art museum you can see many works by François Pompon, the well-known sculptor of animals. His bull, considered his masterpiece, stands on a plaza off the N6 at the entrance to Saulieu.

FOOD AND LODGING: Hôtel de la Côte d'Or, 2 rue d'Argentine (tel. 64-07-66). Chef Albert Dumaine long ago made this hotel world-famous. After him, his pupil and equal, François Minot, took over. He eventually retired, passing the hotel on to another great, Claude Verger, and now Verger has turned the operation over to a younger chef, Bernard Loiseau. Regardless of who was chef, the cooking has always been fabulous here. The former stage-coach stopover serves one of the finest cuisines in France, even in Europe, for that matter. The cooking is less traditional than in times past, but fans of the "new cuisine" will prefer it, as the emphasis is less on sauce and more on herbs. Among the specialties, you may select cassolette d'écrevisse (crayfish) à la nage, the sole filets on a spinach bed, or the poularde de Bresse with tarragon. Service is an extra 15%. Expect to pay around 120F ($27.40) to 200F ($45.66) per person with wine. All the great burgundies are on the wine list. The food is strictly from farm and garden—no tricks, nothing frozen.

If you want to stay overnight, if you've had a little too much burgundy, you'll find recently renovated singles renting for 80F ($18.26), doubles for 120F ($27.40) to 165F ($37.68). Breakfast is an additional 25F ($5.71). Your bed will be comfortable, although it's likely to be 200 years old. The style of the rooms ranges from Empire to Louis XV, an accumulation of several generations of innkeepers.

Another possibility, if you can't afford these prices, is **La Tour d'Auxois,** Place de l'Abreuvoir (tel. 64-13-30). The food is good and the welcome from Monsieur Perié friendly. The rooms are simple but comfortable, costing 35F ($7.99) in a single, from 40F ($9.13) to 55F ($12.56) in a double, the latter with shower. Meals are served on the terrace overlooking the square. Set meals are offered for 50F ($11.42) and 80F ($18.26). Wine is available for as little as 18F ($4.11) a bottle. The inn is closed on Sunday night and Monday and from December 1 to January 10.

From Saulieu you can head north until you reach the Autoroute. From there, it takes two hours of steady driving to reach Paris. However, you may want to continue south en route to the Riviera.

Chapter XIV

THE VALLEY OF THE RHÔNE

1. The Beaujolais Country
2. Lyon
3. Pérouges
4. Roanne
5. Vienne
6. Valence

LE RHÔNE, just as mighty as the Saône is peaceful, is famous for the excellence of its table. These two great rivers form a part of the French countryside that is often glimpsed only briefly by motorists rushing south to the Riviera on the thundering Mediterranean Express. But this land of mountains and rivers, linked by a good road network, invites more exloration than that; it is the home of the Beaujolais country; France's gastronomic center, Lyon; Roman ruins, charming villages, and castles.

It was from the Valley of the Rhône that Greek art and Roman architecture made their way to the Loire Valley, the château country, and finally to Paris itself. The district abounds in pleasant old inns and good restaurants, offering a regional cuisine that is among the finest in the world.

1. The Beaujolais Country

The vineyards of Beaujolais start about 25 miles north of Lyon. This wine-producing region is small—only 40 miles long and less than 10 miles wide—yet it is one of the most famous areas in the nation, and has become increasingly known throughout the world because of the "Beaujolais craze" that began in Paris some 25 years ago. The United States is now one of the three big world markets for Beaujolais. In an average year this tiny region produces some 25 million gallons of the wine.

Léon Daudet once wrote, "Lyon has three rivers, the Rhône, the Saône, and the Beaujolais." Unlike the wine road of Alsace, the Beaujolais country does not have a clearly defined route. Motorists seem to branch off in many directions, stopping at whatever point or wine cellar intrigues or amuses them. We can't think of a way to improve on that system.

However, in the capital of Beaujolais, **Villefranche,** it would be wise to go to the Syndicat d'Initiative (the tourist office) at 7 rue de la Paix in front of the Hôtel de Ville. There you can pick up a booklet on the Beaujolais country, containing a map of the region and giving many itineraries. The booklet lists some 30 villages that maintain wine cellars open to the public.

In Le Beaujolais—the countryside, not the wine—you'll find a colorful part of France: not only vineyards on sunlit hillsides but pleasant golden cottages where the vine growers live, as well as historic houses and castles. It has been called the "Land of the Golden Stones."

If you really want specific sites to visit, we'd suggest the monastery at **Salles,** a Romanesque cloister built in the 12th century out of mellow golden stones. The tour through the complex takes about half an hour. Salles lies northwest of Villefranche. Before you reach it, you might want to stop first at—

Saint-Julien-sous-Montmelas, six-and-a-half miles northwest of Villefranche. This charming village was the home of Claude Bernard, the father of physiology, who was born there in 1813. The small stone house in which he was born—now the *Musée Claude-Bernard*—contains mementos of the great scholar, including medieval instruments and books that belonged to him. The museum is open on Thursdays, Saturdays, and Sundays from 9 a.m. to noon and from 2 to 6 p.m., charging an admission of 3F (68¢).

Most people don't come to the Beaujolais country to visit specific sites but rather to drink the wine. There are some 180 châteaux scattered throughout this part of France. At many of these a wine devotee can stop and sample the Beaujolais or else buy bottles of it.

One of the friendliest and most inviting of these châteaux is the **Domaine de Bois-France,** just beyond Jarnioux. There you are invited to enter a large, deep room. One side of this cellar is lined with huge barrels of Beaujolais; their spigots are decorated in summer with wildflowers, a nice touch. Tables and chairs are placed in front of the barrels, and you can select a seat for enjoying your Beaujolais-tasting adventure. You can also enter another long, narrow room down a flight of steps. This cellar has a vaulted stone ceiling supported by pillars. The air is pungent with the aroma of Beaujolais. In the deep cellar, you'll find a vine grower in an indigo-blue apron ready to hand you samples. You can drink as many vintages as you like, or as much as you can hold. But the man in the apron is keeping count. At the end of your spree he'll present you with a bill. You can also buy bottles of Beaujolais here.

Juliénas is a village that produces a full-bodied, robust wine. In this village people go to the **Cellier dans l'Ancien Église,** the old church cellar, to sip the wine. A statue of Bacchus with some scantily clad and tipsy girl friends looks on from what used to be the altar.

At **Chenas,** three miles south of Juliénas, you might want to schedule a luncheon stopover. A popular eating place, one of the best dining rooms in the Beaujolais country, is **Robin,** aux Deschamps (tel. 36-72-67). Daniel Robin is an excellent cuisinier, having worked with the great Alain Chapel. He does superb regional dishes, including a Bresse chicken cooked in Beaujolais and some of the finest andouillette (chitterling sausage) we've ever sampled. His gratin of crayfish and his Charollais à la bourguignonne have drawn the praise of gastronomes. At his lovely old house you can enjoy a meal for 85F ($19.41) or 150F ($34.26). Naturally, you can order the best of Beaujolais. The restaurant is closed on Wednesdays and for the entire month of February.

Heading south, you reach **Villié-Morgon,** which produces one of the greatest of Beaujolais wines. In the basement of the Hôtel de Ville, in a village-owned park, the **Morgon Cellar** is open daily from 9 a.m. to noon and from 2:30 to 5 p.m., charging no admission.

If you'd like to stay in the Beaujolais country instead of heading back to Lyon, we'd suggest driving south from Villié-Morgon to the junction of D37. Head due east to—

Belleville-sur-Saône. There **Le Beaujolais,** 40 rue Maréchal-Foch (tel. 66-05-31), run by the Dalmaz family, is one of the leading restaurants in the whole district, some say the very best. Diners enjoy a rustic medieval ambience and the cuisine of the Beaujolais country, which is likely to feature andouillette (chitterling sausage) with Beaujolais, crayfish in a cream sauce, coq au vin which is rich and tasty, and rosette Lyonnaise, a large, dry sausage. In this provincial setting the service is polite and considerate. In all, a friendly stopover. Menus are offered at 48F ($10.96), 70F ($15.98), and 100F ($22.83). The restaurant is closed Tuesday night, Wednesday, and from November 27 to December 18. In addition, if you'd like to stay over, ten simply furnished rooms are rented out at a cost of 45F ($10.27) in a single, 62F ($14.15) in a double.

Or, as an alternative, you can continue for an 11-mile run to **Chatillon-sur-Chalaronne,** where you'll find a charming inn, **Chevalier Norbert,** Avenue C. Desormes (tel. 55-02-22). The rooms are well furnished and comfortable, costing 80F ($18.26) in a single, 160F ($36.53) in a double. You'll also be able to order a good dinner (except Mondays when the restaurant is closed) for just 50F ($11.42).

2. Lyon

At the junction of the turbulent Rhône and the tranquil Saône, a crossroads of western Europe, Lyon is the third largest city in France. It is a leader in book-publishing and banking and is the world's silk capital. It is also the gastronomic capital of France.

Some of the most highly rated restaurants in the country, such as Paul Bocuse (about which more below), are found in and around Lyon. Such dishes as Lyon sausage, quenelles (fish balls), and tripe à la lyonnaise enjoy international renown. The region's succulent Bresse poultry is the best in France.

Forty-five minutes by plane and less than four hours by train from Paris, 319 miles away, Lyon makes a good stopover en route to the Alps or the Riviera.

Founded in 43 B.C., the city became known as Lugdunum, capital of Gaul, a cornerstone of the Roman empire. Although its fortunes declined with those of Rome, it revived during the French Renaissance.

A seat of learning, Lyon has a university that is second only to the Sorbonne of Paris. Incidentally, the university has a veterinary school founded in 1762, the oldest in the world.

SEEING THE CITY: A good beginning for your tour of Lyon is **Place Bellecour,** one of the largest and most charming squares in France. A handsome equestrian statue of Louis XIV looks out upon the encircling 18th-century buildings. Going down rue Victor-Hugo, south of the square, you reach the *Basilique Romane de St.-Martin-d'Ainay,* the oldest church in Lyon, dating from 1107.

Nearby are two of the city's most important museums. The first, at 30 rue de la Charité, is the *Musée des Arts-Decoratifs,* in the Lacroix-Laval mansion built by Souffiot in 1739 (he was the architect of the Panthéon in Paris). It contains furniture and objets d'art, mostly from the 17th and 18th centuries, although the medieval and Renaissance periods are also represented—a little bit of everything, from ivory-decorated rifles to four-posters in red velvet. It is open from 10 a.m. to noon and from 2 to 5:30 p.m. except Mondays, charging 6F ($1.37) for admission. Your ticket entitles you to visit not only the Museum of Decorative Arts but the even more interesting **Musée Historique des Tissus,** next door at 34 rue de la Charité. In the 1730 Palace of Villeroy, the museum, one of the most unusual attractions of Lyon, contains a priceless collection of fabrics from all over the world and spanning 2000 years—a woven record of civilization. Some of the finest fabric made in Lyon from the 17th century to the present day is displayed. The textiles embroidered with religious motifs in the 15th and 16th centuries are noteworthy, as are the 17th-century Persian carpets. The museum keeps the same hours as its next-door neighbor.

Back at the Place Bellecour, head north along rue de l'Hôtel-de-Ville, which leads to the **Place des Terreaux.** Dominating this square of buildings is the **Hôtel de Ville,** one of the most beautiful town halls in Europe, dating from 1746. The outside is dark and rather severe, but the inside is brilliant and friendly to visitors, just like the people of Lyon. On the south side of the square stands the **Palais des Arts** (also called the Palace of St. Pierre), a former Benedictine abbey, with an outstanding collection of paintings and sculpture displayed in its **Musée des Beaux-Arts.** Built between 1659 and 1685 in the Italian baroque style, the palace is open from 10 a.m. to noon and from 2 to 6 p.m. daily, charging no admission. First, you step into the most charming courtyard in Lyon, graced with statuary, chirping birds, and shady trees. On the ground floor is a large sculpture collection. Some of the oriental porcelain displays humorous motifs. The parade of art history passes by: Etruscan, Egyptian, Phoenician, Sumerian. See in particular Perugino's altarpiece. The top floor is devoted to more contemporary art, with works by Dufy, Léger, Picasso, Matisse, Braque, Bonnard, Sisley, Manet, Monet, Degas, Van Gogh, Rodin, and especially Gauguin.

Nearby at 13 rue de la Poulaillerie, the **Musée de l'Imprimerie et de la Banque** is housed in a 15th-century mansion that was the Hôtel de Ville of Lyon in the 17th century. It is devoted to mementos of Lyon's position in the world of printing and banking. Printing exhibits include a Gutenberg Bible, 17th- to 20th-century presses, manuscripts, 16th- and 18th-century woodcuts, and more than 2000 engravings. The museum is open daily from 9:30 a.m. to noon and from 2 to 6 p.m. except on Mondays and Tuesdays. Admission is free.

Vieux Lyon

From the Place Bellecour cross the Pont Bonaparte to the right bank of the Saône. You'll be in Vieux Lyon, one of France's leading tourist attractions, the result of massive urban renewal. Covering about a square mile, Old Lyon contains one of the finest collections of medieval and Renaissance buildings in Europe. Many of these houses were built five stories high by thriving merchants to show off their newly acquired wealth. After years as a slum, the area is now fashionable, attracting antique dealers, artisans, weavers, sculptors, and painters, who never seem to tire of scenes along the characteristic **rue du Boeuf,** one of the best streets for walking and exploring.

Greeting you first, however, is the **Primatiale St.-Jean,** a cathedral built between the 12th and 15th centuries. Its apse is a masterpiece of Lyonnais Romanesque. Exceptional stained-glass windows are from the 12th to the 15th centuries. Seek out in particular the flamboyant Gothic chapel of the Bourbons. On the front portals are medallions depicting the signs of the zodiac, the story of creation, and the life of St. John which number among the finest examples of French medieval sculpture. The cathedral's 16th-century Swiss astronomic clock is intricate and beautiful; it announces the hour at noon, 2 p.m., and 3 p.m. grandly, with roosters crowing and angels heralding the event. Incidentally, the axis of the cathedral curves slightly to suggest the curve of Christ's body on the cross.

South of the cathedral is **Manécenterie,** noted for its Romanesque façade from the 12th century. The boys who sang in the medieval choir at the church were housed there, making it the oldest residence in Lyon.

North of the cathedral is the major sector of Old Lyon, where restoration is proceeding financed in part by the French government. It is a true *musée vivant,* or living museum, with narrow streets, courtyards, spiral stairs, hanging gardens, and soaring towers. The most outstanding of these courtyards is the overhanging gallery of the **Hôtel Buillioud,** built in 1536 for a bureaucrat by Philibert Delorme, who designed the Tuileries Palace in Paris.

On the rue de Gadagne (No. 10) stands the **Hôtel de Gadagne,** an early 16th-century residence. Rabelais described its rich décor. It now houses the **Musée Historique de Lyon,** with interesting Romanesque sculptures on the ground floor. Other exhibits include 18th-century Lyon furniture and pottery, Nevers ceramics, a pewter collection, and numerous paintings and engravings of Lyon vistas. It is open from 10 a.m. to noon and from 2 to 6 p.m. except Tuesdays. No admission is charged. In the same building is the **Musée de la Marionnette,** which has three puppets by Laurent Mourguet, creator of Guignol, the best known of all French marionette characters. It keeps the same hours as the history museum.

While still in Vieux Lyon, try to visit the 16th-century **Maison Thomassin,** Place du Change, a mansion with exceptional Gothic arcades; the 16th-century **Hôtel du Chamarier,** 37 rue Saint-Jean, where the Marquise de Sévigné lived; and, finally, the **Church of St. Paul,** with its octagonal lantern tower dating from the 12th century. The church has been rebuilt, although it traces its history back to the sixth century.

Rising to the west of Vieux Lyon on a hill on the west bank of the Saône is—

The Fourvière

Covered with greenness surrounding colleges, convents, hospitals, a big Roman theater, and a complete Gallo-Roman museum, this hill affords a panoramic vista of Lyon, with many bridges on its two rivers and rooftops of pinkish tiles, and, in clear weather, of the countryside up to 44 miles. Looming over it is the 19th-century **Basilique de Notre-Dame de Fourvière,** fortresslike with its four octagonal towers and crenelated walls. Its interior is covered with mosaics. Adjoining is the ancient chapel, dating from the 12th to the 18th centuries. On top of its belfry is a monumental gilded statue of the Virgin. Two funiculars service this hill, a ride costing only 1F (23¢).

In a park south of the basilica are the excavated **Théâtres Romains,** a Roman Theater and odeum at 6 rue de l'Antiquaille. The theater is the most ancient in France, built by order of Augustus Caesar in 15 B.C., and greatly expanded during the reign of Hadrian. It had a curtain which was raised and lowered during performances. The odeum, which was reserved for musical performances, apparently was once sumptuously decorated. Its orchestra floor, for example, contains mosaics of such materials as brightly colored marble and porphyry. From March to October the site is open from 9 a.m. to noon and from 2 to 6 p.m. daily except Sunday mornings. You can visit with a guide on Sundays and holidays between 3 and 6 p.m. Admission is 4F (91¢). The rest of the year it is open only on weekdays. Performances are given at both theaters in summer.

Croix-Rousse

North of Lyons's downtown district lies **Colline de la Croix-Rousse,** crowned by the baroque church of **St.-Bruno-des-Chartreux.** This sector has been the center of the French silk industry since the 15th century. Until fairly recently the old houses along the hill were still inhabited by weavers who both lived and worked there. You can visit a workshop at **Musée des Canutes,** 10-12 rue d'Ivry, where weavers work at their age-old craft. Lyon is famed for its renewed silk industry.

The area is distinguished by its *traboules*—rather long and dimly lit passageways running under the Gothic vaulting of the houses. Often they extend from one building to another and even from one street to another.

On the Outskirts

Built on the slope of Croix-Rousse, near **Condate,** a Gallic village at the confluence of the Rhône and Saône Rivers, stands the **Arena of the Three Gauls,** a partly excavated amphitheater. It's known to have existed several centuries before the Romans arrived. Delegates from 60 tribes from all over Gaul met here in the earliest known example of a French parliamentary system—in fact, it is sometimes referred to as the world's first parliament. For this reason the 2000th anniversary of France, its bimillennium, will be celebrated in Lyon in 1989.

Across the Rhone, the 290-acre **Parc de la Tête** is the setting for a son-et-lumière from June to October. Surrounded by a wealthy residential quarter, the park has a lake, illuminated fountains, a fine little zoo, and a botanical garden with greenhouses. Its rose garden, with some 100,000 plants, is unique.

In the tiny village of **Hautevilles** near Lyon stands one of the strangest pieces of architecture in the world, representing the lifelong avocation of a French postman, Ferdinand Cheval. It is a palace of fantasy in a high-walled garden. One is reminded of Simon Rodia, who built the unique Watts Tower in Los Angeles. During his lifetime Monsieur Cheval was ridiculed by his neighbors as a "crackpot," but his palace has been declared a national monument. The work was finished in 1912, when Cheval was 76 years old; he died in 1925. The north end of the façade is in a massive rococo style. The turreted tower rises 35 feet, and the entire building is 85 feet long. The elaborate sculptural decorations include animals, such as leopards, and artifacts, such as Roman vases.

At **Rochetaillée-Saone,** seven miles north of Lyon on La Route Nationale 433, Henry Malartre's **Musée Français de l'Automobile** is installed in the historic **Château de Rochetaillée.** One of the earliest cars exhibited is an 1898 Peugeot; a 1908 Berliet, a 1900 Renault, and such later models as a 1938 Lancia-Astura delight as well. The château itself is surrounded by a large park. From March 15 to the end of October the museum is open from 9 a.m. to noon and from 2 to 7 p.m., the rest of the year from 10 a.m. till noon and from 2 to 6 p.m. The admission is 6F ($1.37).

HOTELS: Lyon has never been as renowned for its hotels as for its restaurants; however, there are many worthy candidates.

The Upper Bracket

Sofitel Lyon, 20 Quai Gailleton (tel. 842-72-50), is like a resort hotel, with a patio containing tropical plants, a heated indoor swimming pool, and a panoramic restaurant, Le Melhor, where set meals start at 85F ($19.41). Another restaurant, Les Trois Dômes, is located upstairs on the eighth floor; a repast there starts at 120F ($27.40). Opening onto the Rhône, it also tempts with its views of Vieux Lyon. The bar, Le Frégoli, is a favorite predinner rendezvous. The 200 combination bed-sitting rooms have warm decorative themes in autumnal colors, along with picture windows, televisions, radios, direct-dial phones, and individually controlled air conditioning and heating. Singles rent for 300F ($29.68); doubles peak at 500F ($114.15).

P.L.M. Terminus, 12 cours de Verdun (tel. 837-58-11), is a modern hotel of much comfort which stands next to the train station. If you've flown to Lyon from Paris, the bus from the airport will take you to the terminal here. Although the front rooms of P.L.M. may be noisy, they are large, clean, and beautifully maintained, among the best in Lyon. Singles begin at 130F ($29.68), rising to 280F ($63.92) in a double. The lobby is decorated in an amusing fin-de-siècle style. Nice big drinks are served in the hotel's bar, Tahonga; and the restaurant, Le Relais Perrache, serves passable food if you don't want to go bistro shopping. It is closed on Sundays, but otherwise offers meals beginning at 60F ($13.70) and 80F ($18.26).

The Middle Bracket

Le Roosevelt, 48 rue de Sèze (tel. 852-35-67), is attractive, offering four different styles of furnishings: Louis XV, Louis XVI, Directoire, and Scandinavian modern. Built in 1966, the hotel is air-conditioned, and the bedrooms contain showers or tub baths. Singles go for 135F ($30.82), and you can pay as much as 190F ($43.38) for a double.

Hôtel des Artistes, 18 Place Céléestins (tel. 842-04-88), is a little gem. Right in the city center, it's home base for many singers, actors, and revue artists who appear in the theater across the square. Autographed photographs are kept under glass at the reception desk. The rooms have varied plumbing and are priced accordingly, singles averaging around 85F ($19.41), doubles peaking at 200F ($45.66). The furnishings are modern, and all is clean and comfortable.

The Budget Range

Bayard, 23 Place Bellecour (tel. 837-39-64), opposite the Lyon Tourist Office, is a remake of an old town house, opening directly onto the landmark Place Bellecour midway between the two rivers. Don't be put off by the rather shabby entrance, which is down a narrow hallway on the second floor. Inside, you'll find special accommodations, each with a different name, price, and décor, ranging from rustic to Louis XIV to Directoire to "grandmère." Singles rent for 75F ($17.12), doubles for 125F ($28.54). Parking is available.

Grand Hotel des Terreaix, 16 rue Lanterne (tel. 827-04-10), is recommended for its location and its price. While the façade is old-fashioned, the interior has been updated. Style the hotel doesn't have, but it's a good, clean, comfortable base for your gastronomic foray into the Lyon environs. Although the lounge has a "Louis touch," the bedrooms are basic modern, a single renting for 85F ($19.41), a double for 135F ($30.82).

READERS' HOTEL SELECTION: "The centrally located *Hôtel des Étrangers,* 5 rue Stella (tel. 842-01-55), is very comfortable at 200F ($45.66) for a double with bath. The staff speaks English and was very helpful. Parking is a problem, however" (Warren and Dorothy Hemphill, Blythe, Calif.).

RESTAURANTS: The food in Lyon, as we've noted, is among the finest in the world, as exemplified particularly by the following recommendation.

The Upper Bracket

Paul Bocuse, Pont de Collonges (tel. 22-01-40). The man is the most famous contemporary chef in the world. His restaurant—one of the greatest in France—is on the banks of the Saône at Collonges-au-Mont-d'Or, more than 5½ miles north of Lyon on Route N433. Monsieur Bocuse is also one of the great Gallic ambassadors. Once called an enfant terrible, he's been known to dance on the tables at the end of the evening and even toss champagne glasses in the air. He specializes in regional produce and cookery and is one of the leading exponents of La Nouvelle Cuisine.

Most repasts at his establishment begin with a Burgundian apéritif, Kir (champagne and a crème de cassis or black currant liqueur, or even a touch of raspberry liqueur). Our favorite main course, which we invariably have when we pass through the area, is an impeccably constructed loup en croûte. This is a sea bass on a bed of tarragon and other herbs and stuffed with lobster mousse. It's then baked in a pastry shell symbolically decorated to represent the fish inside. It is served with a light tomato-and-cream sauce Choron ladled over it. But Monsieur Bocuse does many other dishes well, too. For openers, try his warm pâté of game birds becassines served with truffles, or his terrines of foie gras and squab. The fruit sorbets are among the best we've ever had, particularly the strawberry. For a complete meal, expect to pay at least 250F ($57.08) to 350F ($79.91), which may turn out to be one of the best investments you've ever made. Set meals are offered for 210F ($47.94) and 275F ($62.78), plus 15% for service.

Although Paul Bocuse is our admitted favorite, Lyon has many great restaurants, which is why we always spend several days there on our journeys through France.

Whenever we're in Lyon, we always strike out for at least one meal at **Alain Chapel** (tel. 91-82-02) in the hamlet of Mionnay, 12½ miles north from Lyon. This Relais Gourmand is one of the great restaurants of France. A stylish place with a flower-garden setting, it at first evokes an Iberian parador. But once you enter you'll be treated to some of the finest food the Lyon district has to offer, in a three-star restaurant. Monsieur Chapel is one of the premier cuisiniers of the world. He even knows how to take a calf's ear and make it interesting (by breading it and stuffing it with sweetbreads). But you can find far more temptations on the menu than that.

We'd recommend, as an opener, the gâteau de foies blondes, for which the chef is celebrated. This is a hot mousse of chicken livers and marrow, pale-gold in color, which has been covered with a pink Nantua sauce. Perhaps you'd prefer instead a velvety-smooth eel pâté in a puff pastry with two butter sauces. (Be warned: Monsieur Chapel's specialties change, depending on the shopping or the season, and some of the items recommended may not be available during your visit.) Yet another seasonal offering is a pan-fried skillet of fresh mushrooms that grow in the woods. His poulette de Bresse en vessie is incomparable. This is a truffled chicken poached and sewn into a pig's bladder (to retain its juices) baked and served with a cream sauce with a bit of foie gras. Accompanying it are discreetly chosen vegetables of the season, often turnips or parsnips or carrots cooked *al dente*.

We could go on and on—a lobster salad with truffles and breast of squab, a trinity of salads (including mushrooms of the woods and violet artichokes flavored with fresh chervil from the garden), fois gras with crayfish tails, a hot pâté of young rabbit. To dine here will cost around 250F ($57.08) to 350F ($79.91), but it may be one of the most memorable meals of your life. The restaurant is closed on Mondays and from January 9 to 31. Gastronomes are fond of booking one of the beautifully furnished bedrooms, only 10 in all, costing 300F ($68.49) for a single, 420F ($95.89) for a double.

Roger Roucou, Quai J.-J.-Rousseau, Lyon La Mulatière (tel. 851-65-37), is an elegant domain. On the right bank of the Saône, this restaurant offers cookery you rarely find. Dining in La Salle Louis XV, you're presented with an array of dishes likely to include steak with foie gras de canard (duckling) au poivre vert, truffles Périgourdine, or chicken flavored with saffron and served with rice Creole. Set menus cost 140F ($31.96) and 180F ($41.09); à la carte orders can add up to 200F ($45.66) per person, plus an extra 15% for service. The restaurant is closed on Sunday nights, Mondays, and in August.

Nandron, 26 Quai Jean-Moulin (tel. 842-10-26), is a salon and restaurant (air-conditioned on the second floor) that opens onto the river, near Pont Lafayette. Gérard Nandron is a chef of considerable talent who knows how to do both simple and complex dishes that are virtually flawless. His sauces are light and well balanced, and he uses fresh local ingredients whenever possible. Specialties include the Bresse chicken cooked in tarragon vinegar, a sole soufflé Nandron, salmon steak with tomato, braised sweetbreads with mussels, veal liver in mustard sauce—all excellently prepared regional specialties. But some of his newer and more challenging fare could go into that rapidly expanding repertoire of La Nouvelle Cuisine: a vegetable pâté with tomato mousse, sole or turbot simmered in court-bouillon with herbs, fresh mushrooms "of the woods," raw salmon with citron. Set menus are offered at 110F ($25.11), 140F ($31.96), and 210F ($47.94), plus 15% for service. On the à la carte menu, expect to pay from 200F ($45.66) to 270F ($61.64). The service, by the way, is friendly, the waiters most helpful, and English is spoken. Nandron is closed on Saturdays and from July 25 to August 25.

Vettard, 7 Place Bellecour (tel. 842-07-59), stands on a large open square bordered by plane trees. It adjoins the Café Neuf-Glacier. Jean Vettard is a man of grand talent who knows how to turn out a superb regional cuisine in a gastronomic capital where standards are high. No dish is more typical here than pike quenelles with a Nantua sauce made with bits of crayfish. But also try his chicken sautéed in champagne, his filet of herb-flavored sole Vettard, and, as a side dish, his delicious morels in a velvety-smooth cream sauce. A superb dish, done with a masterful touch, is veal kidneys sautéed with cucumbers. Try, if featured, his caneton (duckling) Louhans Fourré with foie gras, or his pan-fried tournedos. For dessert, you might order the crêpes souflées for two persons. A set meal goes for 140F ($31.96), and à-la-carte meals average around 170F ($38.81). The restaurant is closed on Sundays.

Chez La Mère Brazier, 12 rue Royale (tel. 828-15-49), in the vicinity of Pont Morand, has grown from a lunchtime rendezvous for silk workers in Lyon to a citadel of good food, attracting gastronomes from all over the world. The restaurant is presided over by Mme. Brazier herself. Unmistakably Gallic with simple décor and wood paneling, it is an attractive setting for a long, leisurely lunch or an outstanding supper. Here you can order some excellently prepared regional dishes, accompanied by such local wines as Mâcon, Juliénas, Morgon, and Chiroubles. Perhaps you'll begin with artichoke hearts stuffed with foie gras, or maybe the smoked Nordic salmon. Her main-dish specialties are volaille (poultry) demi-deuil, stuffed veal en vessie (sealed with a pig's bladder to retain its juices), cervelas (Saveloy sausage) with pistachio nuts, and superbly smooth quenelles de brochet (pike). More extravagant fare includes lobster Belle Aurore. Not only is the food admirable; the service is solicitous. Fixed-price meals are offered at 100F ($22.83) and 115F ($26.25) plus 15% for service. On the à la carte menu, expect to pay from 120F ($27.40). The restaurant is closed at noon on Saturdays, on Sundays, and from July 26 to August 26.

Léon de Lyon, 1 rue Pléney (tel. 828-11-33), has a typically Lyonnaise atmosphere. It lies on a somewhat hidden but colorful street, well worth the effort to locate. Downstairs is a restaurant and bar in the style of Old Lyon, but you can also dine upstairs. Hydrangeas are planted above the entrance in summer. The atmosphere may be traditional and typical, but the food certainly isn't. When we first visited this place 20 years ago, it was a family dining room where guests tucked their napkins under their chins. Now its owner, Paul Lacombe, has been called a daring challenger to the top chefs of Lyon. His cuisine is most inventive. Some of his Lyonnaise customers claim he serves the finest food within the city proper and ranks right after Paul Bocuse and Alain Chapel in the environs. Monsieur Lacombe does a regional cuisine, based upon the products of the season. Therefore, you might be eating oysters accompanied by a Pouilly-Fuissé, the dry white Burgundy, or enjoying his pike quenelles or his entrecôte Marchand de vin, or, in season, his snails bubbling in butter. As part of his standard repertoire he offers coq au vin Beaujolais, la poularde Mère Léon aux morilles (à la crème), and filets de sole aux nouilles (noodles). Newer and more challenging fare includes a terrine of sweetbreads with spinach, a feuilleté of scallops, and even a quenelle of hare with a purée of turnips, a culinary first for us. In season he also offers those flap mushrooms known as cèpes. His sorbets made with fresh fruits are rewarding desserts. In the center of Lyon, the restaurant offers menus at 92F ($21) and 175F ($39.95). It is closed on Sundays, for lunch on Mondays, and from June 21 to July 15 and from December 24 to January 5.

The Middle Bracket

Chez Juliette, 25 rue l'Arbre-Sec (tel. 828-64-06), is an enduring favorite. A bistro on a narrow street, it offers first-rate food at fair prices. What makes the restaurant recommendable is its set meal for 110F ($25.11). On our latest rounds, it included hors d'oeuvres, followed by a quenelle de brochet au gratin, next a pepper steak, then ice cream for dessert. Recommendable main-dish specialties include filets de sole Vignard and fabulous Bresse chicken. The restaurant is closed Sundays and from June 15 to July 15.

La Tour Rose, 16 rue Boeuf (tel. 837-25-90), stands in Veiux Lyon, near the Palais de Justice. Its chef, Philippe Chavent, has been called a culinary genius, a rising star on Lyon's cookery horizon, where so many great chefs get their training. Still a young man, he has opened this elegant restaurant in a historic building with a pink tower and hanging gardens for al fresco dining. Monsieur Chavent is a disciple of La Nouvelle Cuisine, and he is so passionately devoted to cooking that he is an artist at his work. We'd suggest his spinach salad; but since his main dishes are likely to depend on the season, we hesitate to recommend particular ones. However, he can make beautiful dishes out of turbot or red mullet, and his chicken fricassée is sublime. Many of his desserts are not complicated, but great care goes into the selection of ingredients. Set meals begin at 105F ($23.97), rising to 170F ($38.81), the latter a remarkable meal. Always call far ahead for a reservation. The restaurant is closed on Sundays and in August.

The Budget Range

Tante Alice, 22 rue Remparts-d-Ainay (tel. 837-49-83), has the flavor of a country inn. Up front is an old-fashioned bar and in back is a bistro. The cuisine is rich, and many of the specialties are featured on the set menus at 42F ($9.59) and 70F ($15.98). The traditional beginning is quenelle de brochet maison. For a main course, we're especially fond of filet de sole Aunt Alice. (Our Aunt Alice could never make a sole that good.) The restaurant is closed Friday nights, Saturdays, and from July 25 to September 1.

La Tassée, 20 rue Charité (tel. 837-02-35). Go here if you're seeking a real Lyonnaise atmosphere, the kind of bistro of legend that made Lyon celebrated for its cuisine. The chef here isn't interested in a lot of fancy show or frills. Instead, he believes in serving good food and plenty of it, at prices most people can afford. The Lyonnaise believe in eating, and workers often take a break at 10 a.m. for a mâchon. Perhaps its equivalent would be a coffee break in American offices or an "elevenses" in London. La Tassée serves a mâchon that is quite large. From the kitchen emerge hot sausages, salads, and herb-flavored cheese, among other offerings. On our most recent visit we arrived at the bar just as the Beaujolais nouveau had come in. It is a thin, sharp wine, bearing little resemblance to the real Beaujolais with its uncomplicated taste and flowery bouquet. The wine is served in a shallow metal cup known as a *tastevin*. As its name indicates, it is used by wine tasters. So intrigued were we with the place we returned for dinner, which we found most soul-satisfying. Huge portions are served, and you might be offered anything from strips of tripe with onions to game or perhaps sole. A set meal begins at 60F ($13.70), very good value. A more elegant repast costs 100F ($22.83). You can also select from the à la carte menu, which will cost from 110F ($25.11) to 170F ($38.81). The restaurant is closed on Sundays and from August 2 to 25 and from December 23 to January 2.

Chez Raymond, 21 rue de Rancy (tel. 860-58-67). Lyon's reputation for food, it is generally conceded, is based not so much on haute cuisine as on good home-cooking done by the revered *mères lyonnaises*. Trouble is, the men seem to have taken over in the kitchen at most of the city's major restaurants. However, at Chez Raymond Jeannine Caillot clears out the card-playing customere so she can serve lunch. Her husband, Raymond, will greet you; he used to be the maître d' at Paul Bocuse's. Go here to sample an avalanche of dazzling salads, known as a saladier lyonnais. On our latest rounds Madame Caillot displayed at least 20 or more imaginative salads, artistically presented, including on one spring day fat asparagus cooked perfectly (in other words, not mushy). You can eat as much as you like. What follows is a limited choice of four or five main dishes, which included roast turbot when we were there. Cheese comes after the main course, then a cascade of desserts—more than two dozen are presented for your inspection. Meals are offered at 60F ($13.70) and 75F ($17.12), plus service. The restaurant is closed Sunday nights and in August.

Auberge Rebelais, 39 rue Saint-Jean (tel. 837-07-43), is good and inexpensive, a winning choice in Le Vieux Lyon. It's new but with an old look. You can enjoy meals at 42F ($9.59), 60F ($13.70), and 80F ($18.26). Specialties include quenelles de brochet, scallops with saffron, chicken cooked with fruits, and a thick steak known as pavé Rabelais. The chef also serves a hearty salade Niçoise, which you might want to order if you're there for lunch. The restaurant is closed on Sundays.

Chevallier, 40 rue Sergent-Blandan, off rue Terme (tel. 828-19-83), is on a cobblestoned street where horse chestnuts bloom in spring. It's a short walk from Place Sathonay, one of the oldest and most characteristic of Lyon's squares. The setting is simple, although many refined touches such as stemmed glassware are used. An exceptionally good meal is offered here for 28F ($6.39), one of the finest bargains in the city. It is served.from noon to 1:30 p.m. and from 7 to 9 p.m. The restaurant is closed Tuesdays, Wednesdays till 6 p.m., and all of September.

Marc, 12 rue Mazenod (tel. 860-05-57), offers one of the finest meals at a low cost we found in Lyon. For 40F ($9.13) you can enjoy a superb dinner with a carafe of Rhône wine. Near the river, the restaurant is done in bentwood modern. The place is closed Tuesday nights, Wednesdays, and all of August.

3. Pérouges

The Middle Ages live on. Saved from demolition by a courageous mayor in 1909 and preserved by the government, this village of crafts people often attracts movie crews; *The Three Musketeers* and *Monsieur Vincent* were filmed here. The town sits on what has been called an "isolated throne," atop a hill some 22 miles northeast of Lyon off Route 84, near Meximieux.

Follow **rue du Prince**, once the main business street, to **Place du Tilleul** and the Ostellerie du Vieux Pérouges, a fine regional restaurant (described below) in a 13th-century house. In the center of the square is a **Tree of Liberty** planted in 1792 to honor the Revolution. Nearby on the **Place de la Halle** stands the **Musée de Vieux Pérouges**, displaying such artifacts as handlooms. In the village's heyday in the 13th century weaving was the principal industry, and linen merchants sold their wares in the Gothic gallery.

The whole village is a living museum, so wander at leisure. The finest house is on the rue des Princes: it's the **House of the Princes of Savoy.** You can visit its watchtower. Also ask to be shown the garden planted with "flowers of love." In the eastern sector of the **rue des Rondes** are many stone houses of former hand weavers. The stone hooks on the façades were for newly woven pieces of linen.

FOOD AND LODGING: Ostellerie du Vieux Pérouges, rue du Prince (tel. 61-00-88), is one of the treasures of France, a handsome and lavishly restored group of 13th-century timbered buildings. The proprietor, Monsieur Thibaut, runs a museum-caliber inn furnished with polished antiques, Norman cupboards with pewter plates, iron lanterns hanging from medieval beams, glistening refectory dining tables, stone fireplaces, and wide plank floors. The restaurant is run in association with **Le Manoir**, where overnight guests are accommodated at rates ranging from 220F ($50.23) to 300F ($68.49) in a double. The annex is cheaper: 160F ($36.53) for a room.

The food is exceptional, especially when it's served with the local wine, Montagnieu, a sparkling drink that's been compared to Asti-Spumante. Set meals range in price from 75F ($17.12) to 165F ($37.68). Specialties include terrine truffée Brillat-Savarin, écrevisses (crayfish) Pérougiennes, and a dessert called galette Pérougienne à la crème (a type of crêpe). After dinner, ask for a liqueur made from a recipe from the Middle Ages and called Ypocras, "the liqueur of the gods." It's unique in the world.

4. Roanne

On the left bank of the Loire, this is an industrial town which is often visited from Lyon, 54 miles away, or Vichy, 44 miles away, because it contains one of France's greatest three-star restaurants, previewed below.

Roanne was an ancient station on the Roman road from Lyon to the sea. Its principal sightseeing attraction is its **Musée Joseph-Déchelette,** which has some excellent medieval sculpture and even some prehistoric and Celto-Roman artifacts. The museum is open from 10 a.m. to noon and from 2 to 6 p.m. It is closed on Tuesdays.

The major church, *St.-Étienne,* dates from the 13th and 14th centuries with overhauls in the 19th century.

The **Hôtel des Frères-Troisgros,** Place de la Gare (tel. 71-66-97), is the magnet referred to earlier. Frankly, when you see this nondescript railway-station hotel, operated by Jean and Pierre Troisgros, you may think you've come to the wrong address. But just as you shouldn't judge a book by its cover, so you shouldn't judge this hotel/restaurant by its appearance or placement. It is one of the great dining rooms of France.

For an appetizer alone, you might be presented with a mousse of grives (a juniper-scented pâté of larks), or perhaps oysters in butter "in the style of Julia," or else thin escalopes of salmon in a sorrel sauce. The celebrated opener, however, is the mosaic pâté of mixed vegetables with truffles, a delectable dining experience. We also like the mussel soup flavored with saffron.

Among the main dishes, recommendable are legs of duck served au vinaigre, a panache of fish, thyme-scented chops of a ewe, Charolais beef with marrow in a red-wine sauce, and a superb-tasting squab.

You might follow with an interesting assortment of cheese, or request a praline soufflé. The petits fours with candied citrus peel may make you linger longer than you intended. Set menus are in the 180F ($41.09) to 220F ($50.23) range—quite steep; but then, you're paying for an acclaimed cuisine, beautiful service, and quality dishes excellently and creatively prepared. À la carte tabs range from 240F ($54.79) to 280F ($63.92). The restaurant is closed in January and on Tuesdays.

The hotel also rents out 18 rooms, which do not match the style of the restaurant; they cost from 180F ($41.09) in a single to a high of 280F ($63.92) in a double.

5. Vienne

Of course, every gourmet knows of Vienne because it contains one of the world's greatest restaurants (see below). But even if you can't afford to partake of the haute cuisine at that deluxe citadel, you may want to visit Vienne for its sights. About 17 miles south from Lyon, on the left bank of the Rhône, it is a wine center, the most southern of the Burgundian towns.

A Roman colony founded by Caesar in about 47 B.C., Vienne contains many embellishments from its past, making it a true *ville romaine et medievale.* Near the center of town on Place du Palais stands the **Temple d'Auguste et de Livie,** inviting comparisons with the Maison Carrée at Nimes. It was ordered built by Claudius, and was turned into a temple of reason at the time of the Revolution. Another outstanding monument is **La Pyramide du Cirque,** a small pyramid that was part of the Roman circus. Rising 52 feet high, it rests on a portico with four arches and is sometimes known as the tomb of Pilate.

Take rue Clémentine to the **Cathédrale Saint-Maurice,** dating from the 12th century, although it wasn't completed until the 15th. It has three aisles but no transepts. Its west front is built in the flamboyant Gothic style, and inside are many fine Romanesque sculptures.

In the southern part of town near the river stands the **Church of St. Pierre,** a landmark that traces its origins to the fifth century, making it one of the oldest medieval churches in France. It contains a **Musée Lapidaire** displaying architectural fragments and sculptures found in local excavations.

A large **Théâtre Romain** has been excavated at the foot of **Mont Pipet**, east of town. Theatrical spectacles were staged here for an audience of thousands. Ruins of ancient aqueducts are also to be seen.

WHERE TO DINE: **Pyramide,** Boulevard Fernand-Point (tel. 53-01-96), is run by Madame Point, widow of Fernand, one of the undisputed geniuses of French cookery. Madame Point has continued in his tradition. In fact, she became the first woman in history to be chosen one of the Meilleurs Ouvriers de France, a single honor. Specialties include stuffed trout, turbot au champagne, and poularde (chicken) de Bresse. Expect to pay at least 220F ($50.23) for one of the spectacular meals of your life. The restaurant is closed Monday nights, Tuesdays, and from November 1 to December 15.

6. Valence

Valence stands on the left bank of the Rhône, between Lyon and Avignon. A former Roman colony, it later became the capital of the Duchy of Valentinois, which was set up by Louis XII in 1493 for Cesare Borgia.

The most interesting sight in Valence is the **Cathédrale St.-Apollinaire,** consecrated by Urban II in 1095, although it certainly has been much restored since that long-ago time. Built in the Auvergnat-Romanesque style, the cathedral stands on the Place des Clercs in the center of town. The choir contains the tomb of Pope Pius VI, who died here a prisoner at the end of the 18th century.

Adjoining the cathedral is a **Musée** noted for its nearly 100 red-chalk drawings by Hubert Robert, done in the 18th century. The museum is open from 9 a.m. to noon and from 2 to 5:30 p.m., charging 3F (68¢) for admission.

On the north side of the square, on the Grand' Rue, you'll pass the curiosity known as the **Maison des Têtes,** built in 1532 with sculptured heads of Homer, Hippocrates, Aristotle, and other famous Greeks.

RESTAURANTS: **Restaurant Pic,** 285 Avenue Victor-Hugo (tel. 44-15-32), is worth the drive down from Paris. It is perhaps the least known of the great three-star restaurants of France but one of the best. Not only is the cookery exceptional, the wine list is most rewarding, featuring such regional selections as Hermitage and St. Péray as well as Côtes du Rhône. The restaurant was begun a generation ago by Jacques Pic's father. It was known only to the snugly bourgeois merchants and prosperous farmers from nearby, until word of its great cuisine spread to Paris. Then it was placed on every gourmet's list of stopovers between Lyon and Avignon.

The villa itself, with a flower-garden courtyard, is charming. In the dining room big tables and ample chairs invite you to spend a long time dining.

First, you have to face a dazzling choice of appetizers—a ballotine of squab, pâté de froie gras en croûte, an emincé of duck flecked with truffles and a slice of fresh duck liver, or a corn salad with truffles (which is one dish you are not likely to encounter often in France). Notable also are the delicate breasts of small game birds.

For a main course we always gravitate to the filet of sea bass served in a velvety velouté and crowned by caviar. Do not overlook, however, the chicken cooked in a pig's bladder, the filet of sole in champagne, or the lamb stew seasoned with basil (it also includes nuggets of sweetbreads and kidneys for added flavor). In season, we'd suggest one of the chef's masterpieces—noisettes of venison that are tender and served in a wine-dark sauce light as chiffon. His sweetbreads flavored with saffron and his mint-flavored veal kidneys are sublime—as are the warm welcome and impeccable service.

The cheese selection is exceptional, everything accompanied by rye bread studded with walnuts. The desserts are a rapturous experience, from the grapefruit sorbet to the cold orange soufflé. Set meals are 220F ($50.23) and 280F ($63.92), plus 15% for service. Ordering à la carte usually costs from 200F ($45.66) to 280F ($63.92). The restaurant is closed on Sunday nights, Wednesdays, January 21 to 30, and in August, much to the disappointment of the mass migration from Paris that descends on Pic on its way down to the Riviera.

The Pic also rents out ten charmingly furnished rooms overlooking the garden. Rates go from 135F ($30.82) in a single to 200F ($45.66) in a double. Always reserve as far in advance as possible.

If the rarified prices at Pic are not for you, we'd suggest dining at the utterly simple but good **Chaumont**, 79 Avenue Sadri-Carnot (tel. 43-10-12), where André Margier will give you a fine meal for just 25F ($5.71). The food is prepared in ways that are familiar—tender country ham, sole cooked in butter, a deliciously rich coq au vin, artichokes with potatoes, a fine selection of cheese, and some very filling desserts. More expensive menus are offered, at 32F ($7.31), 48F ($10.96), and 65F ($14.84). If you like the place, you might ask to book one of his modestly furnished rooms, 11 in all, renting for 40F ($9.13) in a single to 50F ($11.42) in a double, which is the best bargain accommodation we were able to find in Valence.

Chapter XV

BORDEAUX AND THE ATLANTIC COAST

1. Bordeaux
2. The Wine Country
3. Angoulême
4. Cognac
5. La Rochelle
6. Poitiers

FROM THE HISTORIC port of La Rochelle to the Bordeaux wine district, the southwest of France is too briefly glimpsed by the motorist rushing from Paris to Spain. But, hopefully, the area is becoming better known for its Atlantic beaches, its medieval and Renaissance ruins, its Romanesque and Gothic churches, its vineyards and charming old inns that still practice a splendid regional cuisine.

In our journey through this most intriguing part of France we will not stay entirely on the coastline, visiting such cities as Bordeaux and La Rochelle as the title of the chapter suggests, but will dip inland for a glass of cognac and trips to such nearby art cities as Poitiers and Angoulême.

Allow at least three days for this journey—just enough time to sample the wine, savor the gastronomic specialties, and see at least some of the major sights of this ancient region over which the French and English fought so bitterly for so many years.

1. Bordeaux

The great port city of Bordeaux, on the Garonne River, struck Victor Hugo as "Versailles, with Antwerp added." As the center of the most important wine-producing area in the world, Bordeaux attracts many visitors to the offices of wine exporters here, most of whom welcome guests. (For an actual trip through the Bordeaux wine country refer to our next section.)

Bordeaux is a city of warehouses, factories, mansions, and exploding suburbs, as well as wide quays five miles long. Now the fifth-largest city of France, Bordeaux was for 300 years a British possession, and even today it is called the most un-French of French cities, although the same has been said of Strasbourg.

Your tour can begin at the **Place de la Comédie**, which lies at the very heart of this venerated old city, a busy traffic hub that was a Roman temple in olden days. On this square one of the great theaters of France, the **Grand Théâtre,** was built between 1773 and 1780. A colonnade of 12 columns graces its façade. Surmounted on these are statues of goddesses and the Muses. Apply to the porter if you'd like to visit the richly decorated interior, a harmonious setting of elegance and refinement.

From here you can walk to the **Esplanade des Quinconces** to the north, which was laid out between 1818 and 1828, the largest square of its kind in Europe, covering nearly 30 acres.

A smaller but lovelier square is the **Place de la Bourse,** bounded by quays, opening onto the Garonne. It was laid out between 1728 and 1755, with a fountain of the Three Graces at its center. Flanking the square are the Custom House and the Stock Exchange.

The finest church in Bordeaux is the **Cathédrale St.-André,** standing in the south of the old town. It lacks only twenty feet of being as long as Notre-Dame in Paris. At the 13th-century Porte Royale or "royal door" the sculptures are admirable. See also the sculptures on the North Door, dating from the 14th century. Separate from the rest of the church is the Tour Pey Berland, a belfry begun in the 15th century and rising 155 feet high.

Bordeaux also has another church with a separate belfry. It's the **Tour St.-Michel,** the tallest tower in the south of France. Rising 374 feet high, it was erected from 1472. Those willing to climb 228 steps will be rewarded with a panoramic view of the port. For a 2F (46¢) admission, the tower can be climbed from April to September—10 a.m. to noon and from 3 to 7 p.m.

In the crypt of St. Michael's tower is the ghoulish **Caveau des Momies.** In this mummy vault, corpses stand against the walls. Originally these bodies were buried in the cemetery of the basilica. When the graves were dug up, it was found that a property in the soil had preserved the bodies, which were transferred to this crypt. The figures are like parchment, and such a gallery of the dead can't be seen this side of Palermo. The guide is extremely graphic in exposing the intimate details of these mummies. To visit this bizarre and gruesome sight costs an additional 2F (46¢).

Bordeaux has yet another interesting church, the **Église St.-Seurin,** whose most ancient sections, such as its crypt, date from the 11th century. See the porch, which was left over from an earlier church. It has some capitals from the Romanesque era.

The **Musée des Beaux-Arts,** Cours d'Albret, in the Hôtel de Lalande, built in 1779, contains a fine collection of medieval and Renaissance art, including works by Botticelli, Veronese, Tiepolo, Rubens, Cranach, Perugino, Titian, and Delacroix. It can be visited from 10 a.m. to noon and from 2 to 6 p.m. (till 5 p.m. off-season) for an admission of 2F (46¢). It is closed on Tuesdays.

The **Pont de Pierre,** with 17 arches, stretches 1594 feet across the Garonne and is considered one of the most beautiful bridges in France. Ordered built by Napoleon I in 1813, the bridge can be crossed on foot for a fine view of the quays and the port itself.

And, for an even better view, we'd suggest a **Tour of the Port,** embarking from the Esplanade des Quinconces. There you can take a boat trip which goes all around the port, the tour lasting 1¼ hours and costing from 10F ($2.28) per person. The boat leaves only on Mondays and Thursdays from June 1 to September 30. In April, May, and October, departures are only on Thursdays. The tours leave at 2:30 p.m.

HOTELS: Frantel, 5 rue Robert-Lateulade (tel. 90-92-37), is a luxurious hotel of distilled sophistication and personalized decoration, standing near the Place

Gambetta in the heart of town, which was the old Place Dauphine in the era of Louis XV. In a setting of such antiquity, the most up-to-date contemporary comfort provides a contrast. The staff is friendly and helpful, and the maid service is efficient. In a single the tariff is 235F ($53.65), rising to 300F ($68.49) in a double. On the premises is a grill, Le Sarment, serving a respectable meal for 75F ($17.12), but if you'd like to make an evening of it, we'd suggest dining at the hotel's **Le Mériadeck,** its main restaurant, one of the finest in Bordeaux. The chef, Christian Clément, has been compared favorably to the innovative and now celebrated Senderens of l'Archestrate in Paris. The Bordeaux wine merchants who visit this hotel are often first-rate gastronomes who have come to expect the best in cuisine and service, and Monsieur Clément delivers. He can take consommé, a fairly ordinary soup, and make his own statement with it, adding crayfish, oysters, and spinach to turn it into an exceptional dish. His sweetbreads with prunes are marvelous, as are his medallions of veal with ginger, his veal kidneys in salmis sauce, or his sautéed John Dory (a flat, oval-shaped fish) with cabbage. His desserts are special concoctions as well, especially his peach sabayon with Bordeaux. Expect to spend from 135F ($30.82) to 180F ($41.09). The restaurant is closed on Sundays and in August.

Sofitel Bordeaux-le-Lac, Zone Hôtelière du Lac (tel. 50-90-14), lies north of town near the Pont d'Aquitaine, in the vicinity of its chain-fellow and rival, the **P.L.M.**-Aquitania. It is close to the lake and the Palais des Expositions, and it attracts a large clientele of international business people. Its 100 bedrooms with private baths are warmly decorated, color coordinated, containing no distracting frills, although all the required facilities are provided. In a single the rate ranges from 210F ($47.94) to 230F ($52.51); in a double or twin, from 240F ($54.79) to 295F ($67.35). To relax tired muscles, there is a heated swimming pool with a terrace and a refreshment bar. For dining, you'll find regional specialties and other dishes offered at La Pinasse, where a meal will cost in the neighborhood of 120F ($27.40), and lighter food and quicker service at Le Café de Bordeaux, where a lunch or dinner begins at 55F ($12.56).

Le Majestic, 2 rue Condé (tel. 52-60-44), is very recommendable if you're more traditional-minded and want an oasis of comfort right in the heart of the city, near the Grand Théâtre. Modernization for creature comforts has not disturbed its antique qualities. Now 37 of its 43 bedrooms contain private baths. Rates are 80F ($18.26) in a single, rising to 170F ($38.81) in a double. The hotel does not have a restaurant, but serves breakfast at 13F ($2.97).

Français, 12 rue du Temple (tel. 48-10-35), is liked by travelers who want to be in an old part of Bordeaux, away from noise and traffic. Here you'll find, surprisingly enough, peace and a good night's sleep. There's a renovation program going on. It's a good choice and economically priced—from 65F ($14.84) in a single to 170F ($38.81) in a double.

Etche Ona, 11 rue Mautrec (tel. 44-36-49), is small but tranquil and central, and one of the best bargain accommodations we've been able to find in Bordeaux. It lies within walking distance of many of the city's major attractions, including the Grand Théâtre, the Cathedral St.-André, the Place de Bourse, and the quays. The rooms, 30 in all, are nicely furnished, costing from 70F ($15.98) to 90F ($20.55) in a single, 145F ($33.10) in a double. Breakfast at 11F ($2.51) is the only meal served.

READER'S HOTEL SELECTIONS: "Try the **Hôtel des Pyrénées,** 12 rue St.-Rémi (tel. 48-66-58), which is a five-minute ride on bus 1 from the Bordeaux rail station. The hotel is spotless, with large rooms, and run by the most courteous French couple I've met. The cost of the double is 100F ($22.83), and singles pay 60F ($13.70). This hotel is recommended by a number of touring associations, and is well worth the money" (Harvey G. Lockhart, Brooklyn, N. Y.).

RESTAURANTS: Dubern, 42 allées de Tourny (tel. 48-03-44), is the favorite for traditional cuisine in a Louis XV setting. We know of no better place for your introduction to classic French food Bordeaux-style. The place bulges with the richest treasures of produce from the countryside. Downstairs is a little bar-restaurant graced with ferns, and upstairs is a room where splendid food is cooked splendidly and served splendidly, along with such regional wines as Médoc and Graves. You might also like Château Castera and Château Bouteil-ley. Prepare for an array of tempting dishes—crayfish bordelaise, a ragoût of kidneys in sherry, the classic woodcock with foie gras (as good as that offered by Lucas-Carton in Paris), chicken suprême, even stuffed eggplant. A superb dish is lamb cooked with Pauillac, the wine that comes from the celebrated little town in Hart-Médoc. The soufflé Grand-Marnier will make every other seem like pudding grandmère! Set meals begin at 73F ($16.67). À la carte dinners are in the 150F ($34.26) range on the average. The restaurant is closed July 14 to 31, January 1 to 12, on Sundays, and on Saturdays for lunch.

   Saint-James, 2 cours de l'Intendance (tel. 52-59-79). Monsieur Amat is the exciting, innovative, and creative chef of Bordeaux today, waking up the palates of the wine merchants with his daring Nouvelle Cuisine. From his second-floor restaurant he operates a Relais Gourmand near the Grand Théâtre, right in the heart of Bordeaux. The world comes to his door, even chefs on vacation who decide to drop in to see why this fellow-professional generates such admiration and enthusiasm among his loyal habitués. When he serves his sautéed lobster with a tarragon-flavored mousseline, you begin to understand. Perhaps you'll sample his chicory salad with capon, or else his beautifully conceived salad of artichoke hearts with foie gras. From May to October he offers small baked lobsters that are delicious. One of his finest dishes is a pullet with a broth of truffles. Monsieur Amat is perhaps best known for his duck. Around that noble bird he builds an entire dinner, complete with bouillon made from the duck. He takes its skin and makes it crisp, which also makes for delicious eating. He grills the legs, and the tender breast is sliced and served with a sauce that has been thickened with blood. Other recommendable specialties include sea perch or bass with a thyme-flavored cream sauce, glazed and grilled duckling, squab with a caramel glaze, and a blanquette de veau with fresh kidney beans. An elegant meal here will run from 130F ($29.68) and up, plus 15% for service. The restaurant is closed April 15 to 30 and for most of August. It is also closed on Sundays and Mondays.

   Tupina, 6 rue Porte de la Monnaie (tel. 91-56-37), is small and cozy, the very special statement of one of Bordeaux's most talented young chefs, Jean-Pierre Xiradakis. His cookery is inspired, and duck is his specialty. For example, your meal might begin with croûtons that have been spread with duck rillettes, a most delicious concoction. Shredded duck preserved in its own fat is another dish that allows Monsieur Xiradakis's talents to show themselves at advantage. His salads often use giblets, skin, and livers from his prized ducks. Of course, he doesn't ignore the classic regional specialties such as truffles and foie gras; a recent potato salad sampled here contained slices of the famous black truffles of the Périgord region. His foie gras often comes steamed en papillote. Try, if featured, his veal ragoût, which is made with leeks and carrots, or his tripe of veal in a well-seasoned stock. He also keeps a good wine cellar. Expect to pay from 100F ($22.83) to 120F ($27.40) for a meal here. The restaurant closes for part of July, part of February, and on Saturdays and Sundays.

Chez Le Chef, 57 rue Huguerie (tel. 48-67-07), is an excellent little restaurant where you can dine in a garden setting right in the heart of Bordeaux. Mrs. Vidal, the owner, and her chef, Henri Laplace, hire only the finest cooks and waiters, and their standards are high. They offer one of the best set meals in the city, charging 36F ($8.22), a remarkable bargain, as they insist on using the freshest of produce and quality meats, along with fine regional wines of the Bordeaux district. The cookery is traditional, including such specialties as mutton in a tarragon-flavored cream sauce, chicken fricassée with those flap mushrooms, duckling with green pepper. Try also the sole with flap mushrooms. You can order more intricate set menus for 54F ($12.33) and 100F ($22.83), and à la carte orders are likely to make your bill climb to 110F ($25.11) per person. The restaurant is closed on Sunday nights and in October.

Au Chipiron, 56 cours de l'Yser (tel. 92-98-59), is the best Basque restaurant in the city. Its owner, Mme. Urtizvéréa, sees to that, using fresh ingredients, and quality produce, all cooked with care and imagination. The fish soup served here is most noteworthy, as is the ham pipérade. The decor is agreeable, the service friendly. Meals are in the 80F ($18.26) to 120F ($27.40) range. The restaurant is closed on Sunday nights, Monday lunch, and in August.

Les Allées, 9 allées de Tourny (tel. 44-71-36), is on the same street as Bordeaux's leading restaurant, Dubern. But its prices and style of cookery are quite different. Monsieur Maillard offers a superb set meal (he's closed on Sundays) for just 45F ($10.27). It's not just bargain dining here. Care and concern go into the preparation of the food. You get a friendly welcome and solicitous and personal service, although everything is unpretentious. The food is traditional, including a marvelous turbot in hollandaise sauce. The chef also serves codfish in the Basque style, a worthy specialty. Ordering à la carte costs in the neighborhood of 70F ($15.98) to 100F ($22.83). The restaurant is closed on Sundays.

At l'Alouette

For a lovely tranquil setting for both rooms and meals, we'd suggest you leave Bordeaux altogether, driving five miles up the D109 until you come to **La Réserve,** Avenue de Bourgailh (tel. 45-13-28). Set in a park, this hotel rents out 18 beautifully furnished rooms to discerning clients who pay from 110F ($25.11) in a single to 270F ($61.64) in a double.

But La Réserve is mainly a restaurant that attracts guests from all over the wine district who are eager to try the cuisine of the remarkable Francis Aguirre. This young chef of merit has great style and flair, his innovative dishes drawing those diners who take the Relais de Campagne trail through France. The house itself is managed and owned by Claudine and Roland Flourens.

Try, for example, the chef's sweetbreads with flap mushrooms, his sea bass with pickles, his fresh duckling foie gras. In season he offers the highly prized lamprey, an eel found particularly in the Atlantic. These eels cluster at the mouth of the Gironde and are prized by gastronomes. His pièce de rèsistance is his entrecôte with three different sauces. We'd also suggest his garlic-flavored kidneys and his frog legs in a saffron creme sauce. Set meals are offered at 75F ($17.12), and average à la carte orders come to 150F ($34.26), plus 15% for service. The place shuts down over the Christmas holidays, reopening on January 5.

2. The Wine Country

Bordeaux is one of the capitals of French gastronomy. Many consider the district the equal of Lyon. Dugléré, born here, became one of the great men of classical French cookery.

The major wine districts of Bordeaux are **Graves, Médoc, Sauternes, Entre-deux-Mers, Libourne, Blaye,** and **Bourg.**

North of the city of Bordeaux, the Garonne River joins the Dordogne. This forms the Gironde, a broad estuary comprising the heart of the Bordeaux wine country. More than 100,000 vineyards produce some 70 million gallons of wine a year. Some of these are among the greatest red wines in the world. The white wines are lesser known.

ALONG THE GIRONDE: Northwest of Bordeaux, along the south bank of the wide Gironde River, are the vast vineyards of the great Médoc and Haut-Médoc wines. South of Bordeaux lie other fine grape-bearing districts. On the east bank is the Côtes de Bordeaux, on the west bank the Graves and Sauternes area. Two villages, Esconac-Cambes and Langoiran, offer inns with attractive possibilities for wining and dining. Esconac-Cambes is 12 miles from the city of Bordeaux; Langoiran, 15 miles.

At Esconac-Cambes

Hostellerie à la Varenne, Route D10 (tel. 21-31-15), was built as a dignified and stately mansion in 1930. But over the years it's become an inn, housing guests not only in its main building but in a row of joined bungalows. The accommodations open onto a garden and the impressive river. In summer, red chairs and tables are set out on a wide terrace where wine is sampled.

The owner, Madame Naronian, handles her guests well, supervising the cleaning of the attractive, tidy rooms, pouring Bordeaux wine in the tavern, or serving in the more formal dining room.

The cottage bedrooms have tiled baths. A room with bath costs 95F ($21.69), although other units with hot and cold running water only go for 60F ($13.70). Set meals range between 45F ($10.27) and 70F ($15.98), including a simple wine from the area. The super-gastronomic repast costs 80F ($18.26). À la carte suggestions include hors d'oeuvres, terrine du chef, trout with almonds, and duck à l'orange.

At Langoiran

Miremont, 13 rue Verdun (tel. 23-01-37), is for the simple life. Near the slow-moving river, the hotel specializes in the regional cuisine. A complete meal is offered for 40F ($9.13), served in one of the two tavern-style dining rooms. The good-natured wife of the owner knows how to keep the rooms tidy, and her husband rules in the kitchen. Their house fronts the river and has a large covered patio for breakfast, lunch, and wine drinking. The four bedrooms contain hot and cold running water, renting for 44F ($10.05) nightly. Preferred is the demi-pension rate of 85F ($38.81) per person, based on double occupancy. Closed Mondays and in October.

Hôtel-Restaurant St. Martin, Place Aimé Goozy (tel. 67-02-67), is a typical little country inn at the edge of the village, directly on the river. Lower and upper vine-covered terraces have tables set out for fine country-style meals and wine drinking. Set meals go for 38F ($8.68) and 78F ($17.81), including plenty of wine and service. It's more recommendable to rent one of the 13 simple but clean bedrooms, taking all your meals here. The rate for full pension ranges from 90F ($20.55) to 110F ($25.11) per person. Most of the accommodations have hot and cold running water, although two contain private showers. The owner, Monsieur Allegre, has won local fame for his specialty, eels. Other specialties include foie gras, confits de canard (duckling), terrines, fish soup, and entrecôte à la Bordelaise. The hotel is easy to find. Travel along the river road through the village until you see a sign at the edge. Closed in October.

LIBOURNE: This is a sizable market town with a railway connection. At the junction of the Dordogne and Isle Rivers, Libourne is considered roughly the center of the St.-Émilion, Pomerol, and Fronsac wine districts.

In the town itself, a large colonnaded square still contains some houses from the 16th century, including the **Hôtel de Ville.** In addition, you can explore the remains of 13th-century **ramparts.**

In the center of town the **Syndicat d'Initiative** on rue Thiers will give you complete information on how to visit the Bordeaux vineyards.

Where To Stay

Hôtel Loubat, 32 rue Chanzy (tel. 51-17-58), stands across from the railroad station plaza and has an exterior that warms the heart at once. Although it suggests a small country inn, some provincial decorator has given its interior a "new look" by using reproductions of French country pieces intermixed with semimodern. Nevertheless, it's the leading hotel in town, offering 55 rooms at rates that are quite reasonable. A double costs 180F ($41.09) and a single goes for 100F ($22.83). Best of all is the 70F ($15.98) set meal, including the wine of the region (but not the 15% service charge). There is as well an impressive à la carte menu, which could mean a check of 160F ($36.53). The chef's specialties include turbot cooked in champagne, duckling with mushrooms, and sweetbreads with crayfish. Off the dining room is a summer garden used primarily for wine tasting, a favorite gathering place for foreign buyers. Monique and Jacques Douté are your friendly, helpful proprietors, and they have a fine reputation in the town for their outstanding food specialties and cellar of Bordeaux wine. The place is closed Saturdays off-season.

Gare Hotel, 43 rue Chanzy (tel. 51-06-86), is exactly that—a hotel at the railway station. That may not sound attractive, but the station is small, and there is a pleasant parking plaza separating the hotel from the terminus. The hotel is neat, with 12 bedrooms, plus an inviting combination dining-and-drinking lounge on the street floor. In a double the price for two is 60F ($13.70), rising to 85F ($19.41) in a twin, each with shower and water basin. The food is abundant, and two set meals are featured, one at 28F ($6.39), another at 42F ($9.59). In the evenings and late afternoons, it's pleasant to order wine at one of the sidewalk tables. The restaurant is closed Sundays and holidays.

A Budget Restaurant

Castaing, 34 rue Lyrot (tel. 51-23-25), is a recommendable independent restaurant. The cuisine features specialties of the area and, of course, some of the finest wines in France. Even the house wine is a delight. The cheapest meal, including wine, costs 35F ($7.99). However, an appetite and enough curiosity might run the tab to as much as 80F ($18.26). Closed Sundays and in July. Castaing is about two blocks from the railway station, toward the center of town and the Dordogne River.

St.-Émilion: This wine-growing district is world renowned. It is also an archaeological gem of the Middle Ages. The town is named after a saint who founded a hermitage here in the eighth century. The wine of St.-Émilion was called "Wine of Honor," and British sovereigns nicknamed it "King of Wines." Saint-Émilion is about 24 miles east of Bordeaux.

Food and Lodging

Hostellerie de Plaisance, Place du Clocher (tel. 24-72-32), is the choice hotel of this little medieval town, and it blends in easily with the antiquity all about. Many of its bedrooms open onto stone monuments and towers. The rooms have been tastefully styled, with full knowledge that some of the most sophisticated wine tasters and buyers in the world will be sleeping in them. The smaller singles with private baths rent for 130F ($29.68) although the most luxurious doubles cost 220F ($50.23). These have sun terraces where you can enjoy breakfast, viewing the old village buildings and nearby vineyards. Three excellent set meals are offered, featuring wines of the region. The costs are 75F ($17.12), 95F ($21.69), and 130F ($29.68), service included. Free parking is available in the courtyard.

Logis de la Cadène, Place Marché-au-Bois (tel. 51-71-40), is a modest inn near the Syndicat d'Initiative. The Logis offers a typical inn experience, including moderately priced regional fare. The two popularly priced set meals include the local wine. The least expensive dinner is 30F ($6.85). If you want a wider selection, you can order the 40F ($9.13) set dinner. A gastronomic repast, including the best wines of the house, will cost about 80F ($18.26). The logis is closed Mondays all year, from mid-June until the end of that month, and September 1 to 15.

WINE TOURS: At **Le Doyenné,** Place des Créneaux, St.-Émilion (tel. 51-72-03), the Syndicat d'Initiative provides excellent tours of the Bordeaux wine area. The staff there will even rent you a cassette in English to guide you on the 1½-hour tour of the medieval village, at a cost of 25F ($5.71) for two, 14F ($3.20) for one. In addition, you can pick up a list of all the nearby vineyard châteaux. In this region even a small vineyard with a tiny cottage is called a château. But there are many great ones, including some of architectural interest.

Visits to vineyards can be arranged free at the Syndicat d'Initiative, where English is spoken. You can visit at least 13 vineyards which produce wine in the Premiers Grands Crus Classes, and nearly 70 in the Grands Crus Classes. You can, of course, purchase sample bottles and order cases to be shipped.

3. Angoulême

On a hill between the Charente and Aguienne rivers, Angoulême lies 72 miles north of Bordeaux. It can easily be visited on the same day as Cognac. A "Balzac town," Angoulême first saw the novelist in 1831 when he came here and much admired his host's wife, Zulma Carraud.

The hub of the town is the Place de l'Hôtel-de-Ville, with its **Town Hall** erected in 1858-66 on the site of the old palace of the dukes of Angoulême, where Marguérite de Navarre, sister of François I, was born. All that remains of the ducal palace are the Tower of Valois from the 15th century and the Tower of Lusignan from the 13th century.

The **Cathédrale St.-Pierre** was begun in 1128, though it suffered much restoration in the 19th century. Flanked by two towers, its façade has a total of 75 statues—each in a separate niche—representing the Last Judgment. This church is one of the most startling examples of the Romanesque-Byzantine style in the country. Some of its restoration was questionable, however. The architect, Abadie (the designer of Sacré-Coeur in Paris), tore down the north tower, then rebuilt it with the original materials in the same style! In the interior you can wander under a four-domed ceiling.

Adjoining the cathedral is the former Bishop's Palace, which has been turned into the **Musée Municipal,** with an interesting collection of European paintings, mainly from the 17th through the 19th centuries. It is open daily except Tuesdays from 10 a.m. to noon and from 2 to 5 p.m.

Finally, you can take the **Promenade des Remparts,** boulevards laid down on the site of the town walls. Going along, you'll have a superb view of the valley almost 250 feet below.

FOOD AND LODGINGS: France, 1 Place Halles (tel. 95-47-95), is an old hotel with a well-tended flower garden, lying close to the encircling Promenade des Remparts. The bedrooms here, 61 in all, are nicely furnished in a traditional manner, and 44 of them contain private baths. Singles pay 70F ($15.98), and two persons are charged 200F ($45.66) in a room with private bath. Demi-pension rates are offered at 120F ($27.40) to 160F ($36.53) per person. The hotel has a small but honest menu of traditional French dishes. If you'd like to drop in to dine, you'll find meals priced at 55F ($12.56) and 80F ($18.26).

For the most luxurious accommodations you'll have to drive to Asnières-sur-Nouère, 5½ miles out the N139 to **Le Moulin du Maine-Brun** (tel. 96-92-62). This is an old mill, set in the Charente countryside, which has been converted into a distinguished and comfortable inn on the road from Paris to Spain. The Ménager family, who made this their private home until 1964 when they started receiving paying guests, are antique collectors. With flawless taste and an eye for authenticity, they set about furnishing this hotel, where no two bedrooms are alike. Under the beams of the old mill, they have added Napoleonic beds, a Louis XIV bar, Charles X pieces, whatever. At night guests gather around a cozy fireplace or enjoy candlelit dinners.

The old water mill is now the main house, and guest rooms have been added in a pavilion overlooking the millstream and the gardens. The hotel is surrounded by 12 acres of beautiful grounds. The single rate is 220F ($50.23), rising to 260F ($59.36) in a double. All that cardinal-purple velvet costs money, as does lounging around a swimming pool in this part of the country.

The cuisine is exceptional at this Relais de Campagne. In season, it is obligatory to take the demi-pension rate, costing 275F ($62.78) per person daily. If you're visiting just for a meal, you'll find menus at 85F ($19.41) and 160F ($36.53).

Specialties include a pike mousse with an asparagus sabayon, an omelet with small snails, fresh duckling foie gras with old cognac, a feuilleté of mussels with Pineau des Charentes, lobster suprême with tarragon, a côte de boeuf Charentaise, and some of the finest trout we've ever tasted.

Monsieur Ménager is justly proud of his wine cellars, which contain some of the finest Bordeaux and rare cognacs. The vegetables for your meals are grown on the family's own farmland. They even have their own special cognac du Maine-Brun and their own cheese, which is mild and white. The moulin is closed from mid-November to mid-December.

4. Cognac

Cognac, 23 miles west of Angoulême and about 70 miles southeast of La Rochelle, is a celebrated center for making brandy that has ennobled the tables of history. It's worth a detour to stop off here to visit one of the château warehouses of the great cognac bottlers. Martell, Hennessey, and Otard welcome visits from the public, and will even give you a free drink at the end of the tour. If you'd like to visit a distillery, go to its main office during regular business hours and make your request. The staffs are generally receptive.

François I was born in the town's ancient but dilapidated château in the center. It dates from the 15th and 16th centuries and was a former residence of the House of Valois. It is now a cognac warehouse.

Cognac has two beautiful parks which should be visited: the **Parc François Ier** and the **Park de l'Hôtel-de-Ville**. The Romanesque-Gothic **Church of St. Léger** is from the 12th century, its bell tower from the 15th century.

FOOD AND LODGINGS: **Moderne**, 24 rue Mousnier, opening onto the Place Sous-Préfecture (tel. 82-19-53), is a modest little 26-room inn in the center of town. Rooms are comfortably although simply furnished, and the welcome is polite and friendly. A single rents for 85F ($19.41), a double going for 98F ($22.37). Rooms contain private baths and toilets. The hotel doesn't have a restaurant, but serves a continental breakfast at 11F ($2.51). There is a garage if you're driving.

Logis de Beaulieu, N141 (tel. 82-30-50), has an excellent location in the hamlet of St.-Laurent-de-Cognac, four miles from the center of Cognac itself. The logis stands in a six-acre park and has enjoyable views. It offers bowling, boating, and a volleyball court. There are 21 pleasantly furnished bedrooms, 12 with private baths. The cheapest singles rent for 54F ($12.33); doubles are 180F ($41.09). The hotel also serves good meals at 48F ($10.96) and 100F ($22.83).

5. La Rochelle

Once known as the French Geneva, La Rochelle is a historic port, formerly the stronghold of the Huguenots. From the port sailed the founders of Montreal and many others who helped to colonize Canada. On the Atlantic coast, the city lies 90 miles southeast of Nantes on the railway line to Bordeaux. From the 14th to the 16th centuries it enjoyed its heyday as one of France's great maritime cities.

As a hotbed of Protestant factions, it armed privateers to prey on Catholic vessels. But it was eventually besieged by Catholic troops. Two strongmen led the fight—Cardinal Richelieu himself (with, of course, his famous Musketeers) and Jean Guiton, formerly an admiral and then mayor of the city. Richelieu proceeded to blockade the port. Although La Rochelle bravely resisted, on October 30, 1628, Richelieu entered the city. From the almost 30,000 citizens of the proud city, he found only 5000 survivors.

La Rochelle became the principal port between France and the colony of Canada, but the loss of Canada by France ruined its Atlantic trade.

SEEING THE CITY: There are now two different aspects of La Rochelle, the old and untouched town inside the Vauban defenses and the modern and industrial suburbs. Its fortifications have a circuit of 3½ miles with a total of seven gates.

The oldest tower is the **Tower of St. Nicholas,** dating from 1384. From the top you can enjoy a view over the town and the islands in the bay, **Ré** and **Oléron.** The tower is open from 9 to noon and from 2 to 6 p.m. in season (2 to 5 off-season), charging 2F (46¢) for admission.

Opposite St.-Nicholas is the **Tour de la Chaîne,** a sister tower from which was anchored a large chain that closed the harbor at night. It, too, dates from the 14th century.

The **Tour de la Lanterne,** once a lighthouse, keeps the same hours as St.-Nicholas. It was built in the 15th century and was used mainly as a jail. The famous La Rochelle sergeants were imprisoned there in the 19th century.

The town itself with its arch-covered streets will please the walker. The port is still a bustling fishing harbor and one of the greatest sailing centers in Western Europe. Try to schedule a visit in time to attend a fish auction at the harbor.

The best streets for strolling are **rue du Palais, rue Chaudrier,** and **rue des Merciers** with its ancient wooden houses. On the latter street, seek out in particular the houses at Nos. 17, 8, 5, and 3.

You may also want to visit the **Maison Henri II,** rue Augustin, which was built in the mid-16th century. The **Hôtel de Ville** is also interesting architecturally. From April to September it's open from 9 to 11:30 a.m. and from 2:30 to 5:30 p.m. (from 2:30 to 4 p.m. off-season), charging an entrance fee of 2F (46¢).

The town has at least three museums that merit a short visit. They are **Lafaille, d'Orbigny,** and **Beaux-Arts.** Hours of opening for all of them are 10 a.m. to noon and 2 to 6 p.m. in season (2 to 5 p.m. off-season).

Outside La Rochelle you may want to visit the commercial port at **La Pallice,** three miles to the east. The Germans erected large submarine bases there in World War II, some of which can still be seen, although the port was heavily bombarded by the Allies. Buses to La Pallice are available at the railway station in La Rochelle. The price is 2F (46¢) to La Pallice, although you may prefer an 8F ($1.83) round trip by ferry.

A toll bridge leads to the resort island of **Oléron,** 4 miles wide and 20 miles long. It is covered with beaches, dunes, and pines.

FOOD AND LODGINGS: Yachtsman, 23 Quai Valin (tel. 41-20-68), is a hotel of high-level modernity set in the midst of well-restored old houses, overlooking the harbor. There's a swimming pool, and yachts practically arrive at your doorstep. The hotel is just the right size for intimacy, with 36 compact and attractively decorated bedrooms, each having the desirable little amenities tired travelers appreciate. But the prices aren't cheap, as this hotel is semiluxurious, charging 220F ($50.23) in a single, 300F ($68.49) in a double. Many guests stay here on the demi-pension plan, at rates ranging from 270F ($61.64) to 290F ($66.21) per person. At the hotel, Jacques Le Divellec has created one of La Rochelle's most outstanding restaurants, **Le Pacha.** In the restaurant, with its beautiful modern decor, you can enjoy such specialties as lobster pâté, red mullet cooked in cider vinegar, young rabbit with citrus mustard, a pot-au-feu of snails, John Dory with a compote of algae (definitely La Nouvelle Cuisine). Of course, fish features prominently on the menu, and the fresh oysters from Brittany are superb. For an intriguing beginning to your repast, we'd suggest the smoked bass. A menu is offered for 180F ($41.09), although à la carte orders average 200F ($45.66), plus 15% for service. The restaurant is closed on Sunday nights and Mondays.

Les Brises, Chemin de la Digue-Richelieu (tel. 34-89-37), is the most tranquil and scenically positioned hotel at La Rochelle, occupying a prime perch facing the sea. It's just past the old port—actually, the "new port," where the situation is peaceful. Naturally, there are those fresh sea breezes. Each of the 46 bedrooms is neatly arranged, immaculately kept, and contains a private bath. The single rate is 160F ($36.53), rising to 300F ($68.49) in a double. A continental breakfast is the only meal served. There is a garage for your car.

France-Angleterre, 24 rue Gargoulleau (tel. 41-34-66), is run by Monsieur Coutanceau, who provides 76 attractively decorated bedrooms for guests and also operates one of the port's most acclaimed restaurants, **Le Richelieu.** His establishment is in the center, a stroll from the old port or Parc Charruyer. The hotel provides private baths and very satisfactory furnishings, and there is an emphasis on cleanliness and order. Singles are rented at 85F ($19.41), doubles going for 175F ($39.95). Many of the rooms overlook a beautiful courtyard garden, and a garage is also available. At Le Richelieu the menu offers highly commendable seafood dishes, including a terrine of pike with scallops, pike steamed with algae and served with a velvety smooth beurre blanc, a feuilleté of lobster with a watercress mousse, a pot-au-feu of the sea, and turbot with small vegetables. For dessert, we'd recommend the raspberry charlotte. Service is friendly—not rushed, and even the side dishes are cooked to perfection. Meals are offered at 90F ($20.55) and 120F ($27.40), and à la carte orders average 100F ($22.85). Le Richelieu is closed on Sundays from October to Easter and takes a vacation December 15 to 30.

Hôtel François I, 13 rue Bazoges (tel. 41-28-46), is a nice, private hotel run with a lot of taste and kindness. You have the feeling of living two centuries ago. Nevertheless, the rooms are pleasantly furnished and the plumbing is quite modern. Service is efficient as well. The price range of the 35 rooms goes from 95F ($21.69) to 120F ($27.40), the higher tarriff for those accommodations with private baths. Breakfast is the only meal served, costing 11.50F ($2.62).

There are plenty of restaurants at La Rochelle, especially at the harbor. We'd suggest **Les Flots,** 1 rue de la Chaîne (tel. 41-32-51), which offers two meals, one at 38F ($8.68) and a gargantuan repast at 80F ($18.26). Naturally, shellfish and other fruits of the sea are featured. From the restaurant you have a good view of port traffic. Closed on Mondays and in February.

For smaller budgets, we'd recommend **Aux Fruits de Mer,** 5 bis rue du Port, in a pedestrian alley reaching the harbor. The food is extremely good, the style more "port bistro" than at Les Flots. Two set menus are offered, one at 32F ($7.31), another at 48F ($10.96). For the latter price you get five courses, with a lot of fish, of course.

For younger people seeking a nautical atmosphere, the **Midship,** 23 Quai Valin, will entertain with its good cooking and candlelight. Prices are fair, with main dishes running from 18F ($4.11) to 50F ($11.42).

And those who want to rest under the sunshine and enjoy the life of the harbor may settle for a snack at the **Cafeteria,** Quai Valin, right in the middle of the port. There's an interesting set menu for 30F ($6.85).

6. Poitiers

This city, the ancient capital of Poitou, the northern part of Aquitaine, is filled with history and memories. Everybody has passed through here, from England's Black Prince to Joan of Arc to Richard the Lion-Hearted.

Some 200 miles southwest of Paris on the rail line to Bordeaux, Poitiers stands on a hill overlooking the Clain and Boivre rivers. It was this very strategic location that tempted so many conquerors. Charles Martel proved the savior of Christendom by chasing out the Moslems in 732 and perhaps altering the course of European civilization. Poitiers was the chief city of Eleanor of Aquitaine, who discarded her pious French husband, Louis VII, in favor of England's Henry II.

For those interested in antiquity, this is one of the most fascinating towns in France. That battle we learned about in the history books was fought on September 19, 1356, between the armies of Edward the Black Prince and those of King John of France. It was one of the three great English victories of the Hundred Years' War, distinguished by the use of the longbow in the skilled hands of English archers.

In the eastern sector of Poitiers the twin-towered **Cathedral of St. Pierre** was begun in 1162 by Henry II of England and Eleanor of Aquitaine on the ruins of a Roman basilica. It was completed much later, but it has always been undistinguished architecturally. However, the interior, which is 295 feet long, contains some admirable stained glass from the early 13th century.

From the cathedral you can walk to the **Baptistère St.-Jean,** which is considered the most ancient Christian monument in France. It was built as a baptistery in the first half of the fourth century on Roman foundations, then extended in the seventh century. Opening onto the rue Jean-Jaurès, this monument contains frescoes from the 11th to the 14th centuries and a collection of funereal sculpture. Visits are from 10 a.m. to 12:30 p.m. and from 2:30 to 6 p.m. The fee is 1.50F (34¢), and the building is closed on off-season Wednesdays.

A favorite place of pilgrimage in times gone by, the 11th-century Église **Ste.-Radegonde,** in the eastern section of Poitiers, commemorates the patroness of Poitiers. In its crypt is her black marble sarcophagus. Radegonde, who died in 587, was the consort of Clotaire, king of the Franks.

Notre-Dame-la-Grande is from the late 11th century, built in the Romanesque-Byzantine style and considered one of the most richly decorated churches in the country. See especially its west front, dating from the mid-12th century. Surrounded by an open-air market, the façade is characterized by pine-cone-shaped towers. Carvings on the doorway represent biblical scenes.

In the center of town, the Place du Maréchal-Leclerc is dominated by the Hôtel de Ville, constructed in 1869. The town hall now houses the **Musée des Beaux-Arts,** which is open from 10 a.m. to noon and from 2 to 6 p.m. (till 5 p.m. off-season), charging an entrance fee of 2F (46¢). It is closed on Tuesdays. The collection is eclectic, including some remarkable portraits, one of Ferdinand of Aragon.

From the square you can take the rue Carnot to the Romanesque church of **St.-Hilaire-le-Grand,** dating from the 11th and 12th centuries. The church, after much destruction, was restored in the 19th century.

The **Église-de-Montierneuf** was begun in 1077 by William VI, Duke of Aquitaine, who is now buried within its precincts. Once attached to a Benedictine monastery, the church was much restored during the Gothic and baroque eras. After he proclaimed the First Crusade, Urban II in 1096 consecrated the choir.

The **Palais de Justice** incorporates the 14th-century keep and some other parts of a ducal palace that stood here. It was here that Joan of Arc was questioned by the doctors of the university who composed the French Court of Parliament, and also here that Richard the Lion-Hearted was proclaimed Count of Poitou and Duke of Anjou in 1170. It is open to the public daily except Sunday from 9 a.m. to 12:30 p.m. and from 3 to 7 p.m.

FOOD AND LODGINGS: France, 28 rue Carnot (tel. 41-32-01), is almost semiluxurious, a place where the food equals the excellence of the setting. In the attractive garden is a covered terrace where you can take your morning coffee and croissants before plunging into the historic sights of Poitiers. The hotel has been superbly transformed, and is now the choice place to stay in this venerated old city. Especially restful are the attractively furnished rooms overlooking the gardens. All the bedrooms, however, have fine furnishings and accessories. Seventy-five of the 86 bedrooms come with private baths. Singles cost 160F ($36.53), and two persons pay 260F ($59.36). The hotel also has a good restaurant, offering meals at 50F ($11.42) and 70F ($15.98). The chef specializes in regional cookery, and does so exceedingly well—grills "from the woods," tender beef, saffron-flavored scallops, and blood sausage. The hotel and restaurant are open all year.

Le Chalet de Venise, 6 rue de Square (tel. 88-45-07), is a little discovery, a 10-room inn near a small church in a pleasant location for those who don't want to be right in the heart of town. Each chamber has a distinct personality, and the hotel and the restaurant with its glowing fireplace are warmly furnished, relying heavily on autumnal colors. Guests can also enjoy a shaded, graveled terrace, taking drinks at the tables which have been invitingly set out. Take the D88 south for 2½ miles from Poitiers. The chalet is surrounded by trees and shrubbery and opens onto the water. Prices are reasonable, and the bedrooms, although simply furnished, are comfortable and immaculately kept, costing 85F ($19.41) in a single, 115F ($26.25) in a double. Seven rooms contain private showers, and the rest come with complete baths. Personally, though you may disagree, we found the food among the best served in the Poitiers area. The town doesn't have an acclaimed restaurant, but it offers exceedingly good meals, although dieters may find the portions overly large. Set menus are offered for 65F ($14.84) and 90F ($20.55), and for many of the specialties of Poitou you'll have to order à la carte. The inn is closed on Sunday nights, Mondays, and during the entire month of January, reopening in mid-February.

THE BASQUE COUNTRY AND THE PYRÉNÉES

THE CHIEF TOURIST interest in the Basque country, a land rich in folklore and old customs, is confined to a small corner of southwestern France, near the Spanish frontier. There you can visit the Basque capital at Bayonne and explore the coastal resorts, chic Biarritz and St.-Jean-de-Luz. In the Roman arena at Bayonne in July and August you can see a real Spanish bullfight. The typical costume of the Basque—beret and cummerbund—isn't as plentiful as it once was, but still evident.

Stretching the length of the Spanish frontier, the vast Pyreneean region of France is a land of glaciers, wild summits, thermal baths, subterranean grottoes and caverns, winter sports centers, and trout-filled mountain streams. Pau is a good base for excursions in the western Pyrénées; and Lourdes, of course, is the major religious pilgrimage center in all of France.

We'll begin in the west, working our way east across the mountain range to Perpignan.

1. Bayonne

The leading port and pleasure-yacht basin of the Côte Basque, Bayonne is a cathedral city and capital of the Pays Basque. It is characterized by narrow streets, quays, and ramparts. Enlivening the local scene are bullfights, pelota games (jai alai), and street dancing at annual fiestas. The town is divided by the Nive and Adour rivers. While here you may want to buy some of Bayonne's famous chocolate at one of the arcaded shops along **rue du Port-Neuf,** later enjoying a coffee at one of the cafés along **Place de la Liberté,** the hub of town.

Grand Bayonne, the old town, is within the ramparts of Vauban's fortifications, lying on the left bank of the Nive. This part of town is dominated by the **Cathédrale Ste.-Marie,** one of the most outstanding in the southwestern part of the country, dating from the early 13th century. A Gothic building, it is characterized by two towers, one built as late as the 19th century. Incredibly beautiful, it is distinguished by its stained-glass windows in the nave. Many niches along the walls contain elaborate sarcophagi. From the 13th-century cloister you have a view of the remarkable architecture of the cathedral itself.

Nearby stands the **Château-Vieux,** built on the original Roman walls. Such prisoners as du Guesclin were held here in one of the towers waiting for their ransom money to be raised.

Across the river is **Petit Bayonne,** the museum district. Here the **Musée Basque,** 1 rue Marengo, at the foot of a Nive-spanning bridge, is one of the finest regional museums in France. Certainly it's the best museum for understanding the original and highly imaginative Basque people. Regional costumes, many reserved for dancing, and scale models of Basque architecture, both French and Spanish, fill the precincts, along with prints, paintings, and sketches (the latter depicting such customs as bull-baiting). In one room is a replica of a large country kitchen. Downstairs on a stone floor are displayed implements used in boating, trapping, tilling the soil, and other activities. Many exhibits are related to Basque maritime exploits. Ancient tombstones prepare the way for your visit to a chapel and sacristy. The top floor is most unusual, a tiny **Musée de la Pelote,** with illustrations from this popular Basque game, including examples of the *chistera,* the wicker bat used. Models of costumes are exhibited, along with photographs of famous players. The museum is open from 10 a.m. till noon and from 3 to 6 p.m. in season (2:30 to 5:30 p.m. off-season), costing 4F (91¢) for admission. Closed Sundays and holidays.

The other important museum is the **Musée Bonnat,** 5 rue Jacques-Laffitte, containing a collection of artwork the painter Léon Bonnat donated to the city, including his own. Bonnat was especially fond of portraits, often of ladies in elegant 1890s dresses. In his own *Jacob Wrestling with the Angel,* the angel is so delicate and effete it's really no contest. Far greater painters whose works are represented include Degas, David, Goya, Ingres, Daubigny, Rubens, Piero della Francesca, Van Dyck, Rembrandt, Tiepolo, El Greco, Turner, Ribera, Murillo, Constable, even Leonardo da Vinci. The museum is open from 10 a.m. till noon and from 2 to 8 p.m. in season, charging 3F (68¢) for admission. Closed Tuesdays. From mid-September to mid-June the museum is open on Monday, Wednesday, and Thursday from 1-5 p.m., on Friday from 4 to 8 p.m., and on Saturday and Sunday from 10 a.m. to noon and from 3 to 7 p.m.

A Château-Hotel

Château de Larraldia, Villefranque (tel. 25-41-05), is the most outstanding château-hotel in the Basque country, and a very expensive place. A 17th-century building, it stands on a 120-acre domain, overlooking the village of Villefranque between two rivers, the Nive and Adour. Just a 12-minute drive from Biarritz, it is 2½ miles from Bayonne. Surrounding the château are lawns, formal gardens, vineyards, clumps of magnolia trees, and vegetable gardens.

Inside the château are beautiful salons for relaxing, dining, and entertainment. Each is furnished with rare antiques, valuable paintings, and fine porcelain. Many of the handsomely furnished bedrooms on the second floor contain private sitting areas, and all have an accompanying bath. On the third floor rooms are smaller but more appealing to some, as they're installed under a sloping mansard roof. Scattered about the property are stone terraces, an outdoor barbecue, and a blue-tiled swimming pool. No singles are available. Doubles cost from 320F ($73.06) up.

The restaurant of the château is in a vine-covered auberge, a converted stable. The dining room, which serves nonresidents as well, has been decorated in a rustic 17th-century style, with time-darkened beams, whitewashed walls, and antique Spanish rugs placed on the tiled floors. The china was designed by Limoges to match the traditional Basque ceremonial linen. The bar is intimate with a stone fireplace and a ceramic collection. The chef prepares delicious regional specialties and international dishes. Menus begin at 130F ($29.68), although you'll spend far more ordering à la carte. The vineyard provides Larraldia with an excellent white wine which is prized among French gastronomes. The château is open only from the end of May until October.

FOOD AND LODGINGS: On the outskirts of Bayonne you'll find a whole different world and price structure at the **Mendi Alde** (tel. 25-17-79), 1½ miles outside of town on the D932, route de Cambo-les-Bains. This little 11-room hotel is for budgeters, charging only 50F ($11.42) in a single, 130F ($29.68) in a double. There is no restaurant, but breakfast at 10F ($2.28) is served. The bedchambers are simply furnished, and the hotel is well kept, doing a thriving family business in summer. Boule and Ping-Pong are also offered. The inn is closed in September and on Sundays off-season.

For dining in Bayonne itself, try **La Tanière**, Quai Mousserolles (tel. 25-53-42), which has some of the best seafood in the port. Monsieur Dubet has decorated his restaurant in a Louis XIII style, and in such a setting you'll be offered filets of sole with flap mushrooms, sea bass cooked in Riesling with thinly cut strips of vegetables, grilled duckling, and an array of seafood dishes that are always fresh, always tempting. Service is friendly and polite. Expect to spend from 85F ($19.41) to 120F ($27.40) for a fine meal. The restaurant shuts down on Wednesdays and takes a vacation from June 20 to July 10.

Beluga, 15 rue des Tonneliers (tel. 25-52-13). Jean-Claude Géudon is probably the most creative chef in Bayonne. In a charming quarter of the old city, Petit-Bayonne, between the Adour and the Nive, he has opened this restaurant, serving an array of specialties to tempt the most fastidious of diners. His filet of brill is served with small vegetables cut julienne style, and he does superb fresh frog legs in Charentes. We even like what he calls his "blood sausage of the country." His medallion of veal is served with a compote of onions, and his sea bass comes with seaweed in the style of La Nouvelle Cuisine, an inspiration of Michel Guérard. There is a fine wine list as well. Meals are offered at 75F ($17.12) although you'll average 110F ($25.11) to 130F ($29.68) if you order à la carte. The restaurant is closed on Sunday nights from July 13 to September 7 and in February.

For really authentic Basque cookery, head for **Euzkalduna,** 61 rue Pannecau (tel. 59-28-02). Although we've never learned to pronounce her name completely to her satisfaction, we have only the highest commendation for the regional cuisine of Madame Muruamendiaraz. Her fish soup is excellently prepared. We've enjoyed it on at least three different occasions, and it always tasted different but good, its ingredients depending on the catch of the day. She also prepares superb mussels in vinaigrette, plus an array of other Basque dishes. Meals begin at 65F ($14.84) and go up, depending on what you order. The restaurant is closed Sunday nights, Mondays, and from June 1 to 8 and October 28 to November 5.

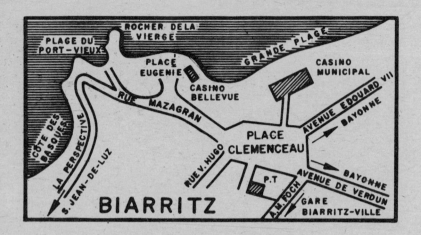

2. Biarritz

One of the most famous seaside resorts in the world, Biarritz in southwest France was once a simple fishing village near the Spanish border. Favored by the Empress Eugénie, the Atlantic village soon attracted her husband, Napoleon III, who launched it on the road to fashion. Later Queen Victoria showed up, and her son Edward VII visited more than once. Toady, it is busy from July to September, quietly settling down for the rest of the year. Frankly, we prefer it in June, when the prices are lowered, the blowers are in bloom—especially the spectacular hydrangea—and there's space on the beach. Surfboarding, rarely practiced in France, is most popular here, drawing many Stateside youths.

On the fringe of the Basque country, Biarritz has good wide sandy bathing beaches (the surf can be dangerous at times on the Grand Plage). Cliff walks, forming a grand promenade planted with tamarisks, are one of the most enduring attractions of Biarritz. The most dramatic point is **Rocher de la Vierge** ("Rock of the Virgin"), connected to the shore by a footbridge. Enclosed by jetties, **Port des Pêcheurs** ("Port of the Fishermen") is yet another scenic spot.

ACCOMMODATIONS: Biarritz offers a wide choice of places to stay in all price ranges.

A Deluxe Choice

Hôtel du Palais, Avenue de l'Impératrice (tel. 24-09-40), is and has been the playground for the international elite of this century. Originally, it was built in 1854 by Napoleon III as an imposing residence for his Empress Eugénie so that she wouldn't get homesick for nearby Spain. He picked the most commanding position on the beach, in view of the rocks and rugged shoreline. It's a true palace, with grand halls and staircases, marble columns, and art nouveau trappings. Edward VII of England stayed here in 1906 and 1910; Alfonso XIII (the last king of Spain) in 1909; the Duke of Windsor in the 1940s; and Haile Selassie in 1956. Guests are especially attracted to the free-form swimming pool on the lower terrace, with its encircling umbrellas and pads for sunbathing. At night, excellently prepared meals are served dramatically in the classic columned dining room, softly lit by glittering crystal chandeliers.

Of course, there are elaborately furnished suites, but even the average bedrooms are decorated with style, employing period furnishings, silk draperies, marquetry, and bronze hardware. Open from Easter till mid-October, the hotel charges its highest prices from mid-July till September 15: from 350F ($79.91) in a single, from 550F ($125.57) in a double. To be given pension rates, you must stay a minimum of three days. Room tariffs are based primarily on the view and the size of the room.

A Château-Hotel

Château de Brindos, Lac de Brindos (tel. 23-17-68), is the most romantic stopover on the Côte Basque for those heading for Spain. Once you've arrived here, you may change your mind and never make it to San Sebastián. In the vicinity of the airport, the Château de Brindos lies about 1½ miles from Biarritz. Set on its own park grounds, it even has a private lake. Inside, the decoration of both the public rooms and the 17 bedrooms is in period styles, imaginatively conceived and beautifully executed. Guests gather in comfortable armchairs around the large stone fireplace, and take regional specialties in the hotel's dining hall. For the pinnacle of Basque charm and comfort, you pay dearly—from 275F ($62.78) in a single to 500F ($114.15) for the best double rooms. The cuisine is superb, including Bayonne ham, a mousseline of turbot in caviar sauce, duckling with small vegetables, and sea bass grilled with fennel. If you'd like to drive out there to dine, always call for a reservation. You'll average around 135F ($30.82) to 220F ($50.23) on the à la carte menu. The hotel shuts down only between January 1 and 15.

The Upper Bracket

Eurotel, Avenue la Perspective (tel. 24-32-33), is an upper-bracket hotel for the true dollarwise traveler who wants all the modern luxuries and amenities without the belle-époque trappings that usually fatten the tab. Although not on the beach, its position is even more striking—perched on top of the cliff, away from the center of town, with panoramic views from every window.

The design concept of the 12-story structure is enlightened, with the rooms extending out beyond sliding glass doors onto a private open-air loggia. The soft sofas are turned into beds at night, converting back to sofas during the day. You can ask for a streamlined, completely equipped kitchenette with a stove and refrigerator, for which you'll pay 45F ($10.27) extra per day. The baths have showers, decorative tiles, and all sorts of gadgets to make life more convenient. In addition, the rooms are air-conditioned and soundproofed. Open all year, even in winter when the deluxe palaces are closed, the hotel charges its highest rates between June 1 and September 30. The rooms are priced according to facilities, the least expensive with a large bed, the costliest with a loggia and twin beds. Two people can pay a low of 225F ($51.38) or a high of 281F ($64.15), including taxes and service. Singles range in price from 154F ($35.16) to 281F ($64.15). There are two bars and one snackbar, as well as a bar on the 10th floor of the building affording the most spectacular view in all Biarritz. Set meals cost 75F ($17.12), not including wine. A continental breakfast is an extra 20F ($4.57).

The Middle Bracket

El Mirador, 10 Place Ste.-Eugénie (tel. 24-13-81), enjoys a dreamy position right on the most favored square of Biarritz, set near the edge of a cliff overlooking the sea. Most of its 40 rooms have not only a sea view but private baths. The accommodations are quite nice, with a homey mixture of modern furniture and traditional pieces. Since the hotel owns what is considered the second-best restaurant in the resort, the Rôtisserie du Coq Hardi (see below), it's wise to take the complete pension at El Mirador. Including service and taxes, the full-board tariff is 200F ($45.66) to 280F ($63.92) per person, lower off-season. In summer, half pension is required. The place is closed from mid-January to March.

The Budget Range

Marbella, 11 rue du Port-Vieux (tel. 24-04-06), opens onto two narrow streets. It has been renewed in the style of Louis XV. In the rear courtyard you can enjoy the flowers of the garden while dining. Many of the upper bedrooms have a view of the sea. In high season, the cost for a double is 130F ($29.68), lowered to 95F ($21.69) in a single, plus 12F ($2.74) for breakfast. Half board averages around 135F ($30.82) per person daily. The Marbella is a beehive of activity, with a friendly, helpful staff.

Hôtel du Port-Vieux, 43 rue Mazagran (tel. 24-02-84), is warmly recommended, especially for those who desire *chambres sans pension.* You're free to travel for your lunch and dinner, perhaps to sample the fish restaurants of St.-Jean-de-Luz or the Basque cuisine in Spain's San Sebastián. In high season (July 10 to September 15), you pay 100F ($22.83) for the best double rooms, with twin beds and a shower and water basin, that tab including a continental breakfast, service, and taxes. Bathless doubles drop in price to only 78F ($17.81). The "Old Port" was recently built and decorated and is neat as can be. Closed from December 15 to January 15.

Océan, 9 Place Ste.-Eugénie (tel. 24-03-27), right in the heart of restaurant row, is an older, six-story, white-painted corner building next to a church, on the ocean end of the park. It's rated highly for convenience, cleanliness, and good food. The bedrooms vary considerably in size, but each is comfortable and well tended by a bevy of scrubbing and polishing maids. The view from some of the rooms is memorable, overlooking the plaza and the sea beyond. Full pension is 135F ($30.82) to 160F ($36.53) per person. For just a room, it's 135F ($30.82) for two. The hotel is closed from November 30 till March 29. You can dine at the sidewalk tables under a canopy.

Lauretta, Plateau de l'Atalaye (tel. 24-16-77), sits on a special little plaza, with rows of hotels on one side, a belvedere with a sea view on the other. The creamy façade with green shutters opens onto a trellis of roses in front. It's owned and managed by a chic woman who runs everything with the smile of assurance. Her best rooms, with private baths, face the garden and rent for 125F ($28.54), including breakfast. Her other doubles are priced according to the plumbing, a double with basin costing 85F ($19.40). Breakfast is included. All her rooms are practical and clean. The hotel is open from May 1 to October 31.

Izarra, 5 Place de l'Atalaye (tel. 24-08-91), is a tiny, 18-room hotel facing two streets; on one side it fronts an open plaza with a sea-view belvedere. It's most attractive, made of gray stone and adorned with white shutters and ornate iron balconies. Away and up from the crowds, it enjoys its own private world. A single with basin goes for 60F ($13.70), increasing to 90F ($20.55) with a shower. Doubles, depending on the plumbing, range from 100F ($22.83) to 120F ($27.40). The Izarra is open from mid-May until the end of September.

READERS' HOTEL SELECTION: "At the Washington Hôtel, 34 rue Mazagran (tel. 24-10-80), a twin-bedded room with bath is 130F ($29.68); with shower, 90F ($20.55); with basin, 65F ($14.84). A continental breakfast is an extra 11F ($2.51), although all taxes and service are included. The hotel has an indoor and an outdoor breakfast room and is managed efficiently by its *propriétaire*, Madame Marcé. She is American-born and has been living in France since the age of 12. Her English is flawless and her manner gracious" (Mr. and Mrs. Joseph Cohen, Forest Hills, N.Y.).

DELUXE DINING: Café de Paris, 5 Place Bellevue (tel. 24-19-53), is one of the greatest restaurants along the Basque Coast. Across from the casino, it sits on a charming belvedere overlooking the sea. The Messieurs Laporte, father and son, bring elegance not only to the setting but to the cuisine. Here you get not only haute cuisine, but on occasions haute couture. While sitting under the potted palms, you can—just for openers—get started with truffes (truffles) au vin de champagne. After years of serving traditional French cookery, the chef now specializes in the new cuisine. Specialties include a soup of mussels which is most savory, followed perhaps by a vegetable pâté with a mousse made of flap mushrooms. Wild duckling with cucumbers is one of the featured main dishes, as is squab with hurtleberries. If featured, order the delicious tart made with fresh asparagus. Smoked fresh salmon is very good here, as is the brochette of lobster. For a fine finish, try the different types of sorbet with sauterne. Expect to pay from 200F ($45.66) to 275F ($62.78) for a complete meal. The restaurant is closed in February and on Mondays off-season.

OTHER DINING SELECTIONS: Rôtisserie du Coq Hardi ("Bold Rooster"), 8 Place Ste.-Eugénie (tel. 24-13-81), occupies the ground floor of El Mirador Hotel. Its tables are arranged to let guests enjoy the view at the edge of the ocean walk. The chef features excellently prepared specialties, many of them appearing on the set menus, these going for 80F ($18.26) and 120F ($27.40). Three out of four dishes served here are true creations. Try moules (mussels) poulettes or the delicious Bayonne ham. The coquilles St.-Jacques is yet another seafood favorite. Main dishes include the specialty, côte de boeuf à la broche, served only for two. Cèpes (flap mushrooms) are another good offering, served à la Bordelaise. Easily recommendable are the poulet de grain à la broche and escalope de veau Mirador. Closed January 15 to March 1.

"Chez Ramuntcho," Plage du Port-Vieux (tel. 24-19-94), is a unique establishment in a colorful setting, right above the old port and opening onto a terrace. You can dine inside or on the terrace, watching the lights from the bobbing boats in the harbor. Like a summer house, the setting is sophisticated, with rattan chairs and potted palms. Two set meals are available, for 32F ($7.31) and 72F ($16.44), the latter offering an extra course, pipérade with Bayonne ham. Pipérade is an omelet made with tomatoes and pimientos, a leading Basque specialty. However, order the more expensive meal only if you're ravenously hungry. It's truly enormous. A first course consists of a delicious Basque bouillabaisse, then follows with the omelet and a Basque-style paella with chicken and fresh mussels, and finishes with cheese and a regional cake. The restaurant is open Easter through September.

Français, rue Lavernie (tel. 24-14-85), near the Municipal Casino, is set back from the beach, with an enclosed front terrace. The chef, the son of the owner, Monsieur Guidon, ranges around France for his repertoire, freely borrowing from both the Provençal and Basque kitchens. Le Français can hardly be claimed as a discovery by us. It has long ago passed the test among hard-to-please diners at Biarritz. But it deserves even more attention than it has received, for taking basic elements and turning out memorable meals. For example, try its escargots (snails) as an opener, or a plate of les cochonnailles, compliments of your "friendly pork butcher." The crab salad is excellent, as is the freshly caught turbot. Two especially good dishes are raie au beurre noir (skate in black butter) and steak poêle à ma façon (pan-fried steak). Expect to spend from 70F ($15.98) to 110F ($25.11) here for a complete dinner. Full pension is also available in the simple but comfortable rooms, a dozen in all. For full board, expect to pay from 160F ($36.53) to 195F ($44.52) per person, depending on the plumbing. These prices are most reasonable for Biarritz.

AFTER DARK: Nightlife in Biarritz revolves around the **Casino Bellevue,** which opens July 1, closing September 15. You pay only 5F ($1.14) to enter, and you must bring your passport.

Otherwise, you can patronize the **Municipal Casino,** which is open all year (4 p.m. till 2 a.m.). Charging 6F ($1.37) for entrance, it lets you in providing you have a passport and are more than 21 years of age. Within the building, the **Taboga** is a cavelike club offering music for dancing. The minimum charge is taken care of by ordering a whiskey for 30F ($6.85).

The **Royalty,** 11 Place Clemenceau, is most sophisticated. It is managed by one of the best barmen in France, Monsieur Pennes. The scene outside is the Biarritz version of Rome's Via Veneto.

The à la mode club is **Chez Albert,** Port des Pêcheurs (tel. 24-43-84), where *tout Biarritz* comes and spends most of the night in a cabaret-style ambience.

3. St.-Jean-de-Luz

This Basque country tuna-fishing port and beach resort is the goal of many a person's pipedream. About 10 miles south of Biarritz moving toward the Spanish frontier, St.-Jean-de-Luz lies at the mouth of the Nivelle.

In its principal church, the 13th-century **Église St.-Jean-Baptiste,** Louis XIV and the Spanish infanta, Marie Theresa, were married in 1660. The interior is among the most handsomely decorated of all Basque churches, with painted wooden panels. Surmounting the altar is a statue-studded gilded retable.

At the harbor, the brick and stone **Maison de l'Infante,** a mansion in the Louis XIII style, sheltered the Spanish princess. The Sun King, meanwhile, dreamed of another woman at the **Château Lohobiague,** on the Place Louis XIV, the center of the old port.

Many narrow streets flanked by old houses provide interesting strolls in this port town. If possible, try to attend a fish auction.

Livening up the resort are pelota, fandangos, and a celebration beginning on June 24 called **Toro del Fuego.** Highlight of the festivities is when a snorting papier-mâché bull is carried through town. The townspeople literally dance in the streets.

HOTELS: L'Hôtel de Chantaco, Golf de Chantaco, a mile from the center of St.-Jean-de-Luz out the D918 (tel. 26-14-76). This Basque mansion is surrounded by an 18-hole golf course and parklands and lies just a mile from the ocean. There are 30 bedrooms, each with complete bath, each luxuriously furnished and equipped. It seems more like a country palace, with Moorish arches, a side patio garden, and an interior that has been skillfully decorated with taste and restraint. The reception hall has two stone fireplaces, a wrought-iron gallery, and high-backed tapestry-covered chairs. The drawing room contains two superior grand pianos, in addition to a formal white fireplace, large book-filled cases, and luxurious velvet sofas, along with a collection of prints, pictures, and ship models. There is a refectory table where you can write your letters by the light of two silver candelabra. Breakfast is served in a patio with wisteria-covered arches. As you bite into your croissant, you listen to the sound of water splashing in a fountain. Rates are 180F ($41.09) in a single, rising to 300F ($68.49) in a double. The hotel's restaurant, El Patio, serves a high-quality regional cuisine. Try the filets of sole Chantaco and the gâteau Basque. It's better to stay here on the demi-pension plan, ranging from 250F ($57.08) to 350F ($79.91) per person in high season, plus 15% for service. The hotel is open from Easter to October.

A good choice in the middle-bracket range is **Stella Maris,** 21 rue de la République (tel. 26-04-57). At the top of the beach, it's a complex of two white buildings with red wooden shutters. The reception is on the second floor of the main building, giving you access to the breakfast lounge from which you can enjoy a view of the sands. Deep carpeting covers the floors, the walls are white, and the furnishings are in the Basque style. Minimum for a single with shower is 90F ($20.55), the best doubles with bath peaking at 140F ($31.96). No pension is offered. The hotel is open from May 20 until October 10.

In the budget range, **Hôtel de la Plage,** 33 rue Garat (tel. 26-06-46), is well located right by the beach. It is warmly furnished in the Basque style. Everything is kept immaculate, and the welcome is friendly; the owners are Monsieur and Madame Garraialde. There are only 30 rooms. A single with toilet and bidet goes from 62F ($14.15), rising to 90F ($20.55) with complete bath. Two persons pay from 120F ($27.40) to 170F ($38.81) in units containing showers or complete baths. The cost of full board is another 155F ($35.39) to 185F ($42.24) per person daily. For a four-course dinner, you pay 45F ($10.27). The inn is open from March to mid-October.

Finally, **Hôtel Le Mazarin,** 39 rue Tourasse (tel. 26-04-74), is worth considering. A small, traditional hotel, it has yellow-painted walls and red wooden shutters. Depending on the plumbing, its prices range from 95F ($21.69) to 135F ($30.82) in a double. It is open from April 1 to October 30.

RESTAURANTS: La Vieille Auberge, 22 rue Tourasse (tel. 126-19-61), is a Basque-style tavern specializing in fish, the platters going from 45F ($10.27) to 55F ($12.56). Monsieur and Madame Grand offer two set menus: 52F ($11.87) and 62F ($14.15), the latter a gargantuan repast. The tavern is closed Wednesdays and from September 30 to May 1.

Le Petit Grill Basque, 4 rue St.-Jacques (tel. 26-03-53), is a small auberge with a low ceiling and many small round tables covered with fresh napkins. Three set meals, each featuring Basque specialties, are offered: 26F ($5.94), 32F ($7.31), and 48F ($10.96), the latter one, with four courses, most highly recommendable. The grill is closed Wednesdays and from January 15 till February 15.

Ramuntcho, 24 rue Garat (tel. 26-03-89), is a typical Spanish Basque-style restaurant with lots of beams and wooden tables. In this tavern setting, you can order a three-course meal, a simple one at 32F ($7.31), or a more elaborate one at 60F ($13.70), with fish specialties. The restaurant is open from Easter until the end of September.

4. Pau

High above the banks of the Gave de Pau River, the all-year resort of Pau is a good halting point in your trek through the Pyrénées. The town was once the residence of the kings of Navarre. The British discovered it back in the early 19th century, launching such innovative practices as fox hunting, a custom which has lingered.

Even if you're just passing through, go along the **Boulevard des Pyrénées,** an esplanade erected on orders of Napoleon I. You'll have what is perhaps the most famous panoramic view in the Pyrénées. After seeing the white-capped peaks of the Anie and Midi-de-Bigorre, Lamartine, the poet, said, "The land-view at Pau is, like the sea-view at Naples, the finest in the world."

At the western end stands the **Château de Pau,** dating from the 14th century and still steeped in the Renaissance spirit of the bold Margaret of Navarre, who wrote the bawdy *Heptaméron* at 60. This collection of tales amused her brother, François I. The castle, however, has seen many builders and many tenants. Louis XV ordered the bridge that connects the castle to the town, while the great staircase hall inside was commissioned by Margaret herself. Inside are many souvenirs, including a crib made of a single tortoise shell for Henry of Navarre, who was born here. There is a splendid array of Flemish and Gobelin tapestries, many collected by Margaret. The great rectangular tower, Tour de Montauzet, is from the 14th century. The castle is open daily from 10 a.m. to noon and from 2 to 5:30 p.m. in summer (off-season from 10 a.m. to noon and from 2 to 4:30 p.m.), charging an admission of 4F (91¢).

On the château's third floor a **Musée Régional** has been installed, containing ethnographical collections of Béarn, the old name of the county of which Pau was the capital. It is open mornings from 9:30 a.m. to 12:30 p.m. year-round, afternoons from 2:30 to 6:30 p.m. from April through October and 2:30 to 5:30 the rest of the year. Admission is 3F (68¢).

The **Musée des Beaux-Arts,** on the rue Mathieu-Lalanne, displays a collection of European paintings, including some Spanish masters, El Greco, Murillo, Zurbaran, as well as works by Corot, Degas, and Boudin. Hours are daily except Tuesday from 10 a.m. to noon and from 2 to 6 p.m. No admission is charged.

Finally, you may want to walk through the beautiful **Parc National,** the famous gardens (or what is left of them) which used to surround the château in the 16th century.

FOOD AND LODGINGS: **Hôtel Continental,** 2 rue du Maréchal-Foch (tel. 27-69-31), is from all points the leading hotel of Pau. In the center of town, convenient for local sights and shopping, it has undergone an extensive modernization program, including soundproofing of its windows. Nearly all of its 110 bedrooms have been equipped with private baths and stylishly decorated. A single rents for 140F ($31.96), rising to 220F ($50.23) in a double. The demi-pension rate is 200F ($45.66) in a single, from 155F ($35.39) per person based on double occupancy. The hotel also employs a brilliant chef, Paul Nantas, who attracts not just guests but lots of nonresidents, too, to the Continental's restaurant, **Le Conti.** Both the staff and the food they serve are outstanding, the cuisine going beyond professional showmanship, including such specialties as scallop pâté, fresh foie gras with prunes, a smooth, tender, tasty chicken suprême, and a pipérade that is as superb as any you'll be served in the Basque country. A set menu is featured for 60F ($13.70); you are likely to spend 130F ($29.68) ordering à la carte. The restaurant remains open all year.

Europe, 9 Place Clemenceau (tel. 27-73-40), is a comparatively small hotel—only 33 rooms—right in the center of Pau. Fortunately, it's peaceful, escaping most of the noise of the town. Almost all of the bedrooms are pleasant and nicely decorated, although varying in size, price, and plumbing arrangements. Half of the chambers have accompanying private baths. The best doubles cost 135F ($30.82), and singles begin at 70F ($15.98). There is no restaurant at the hotel, but a classic French breakfast is brought to your room for 11F ($2.51). However, the hotel is not without its public facilities, which include a dignified British-style bar.

Pierre, 16 rue Louis-Barthou (tel. 27-76-86). Roland and Raymond Casau are among the finest cuisiniers in Béarn, where, according to *Larousse Gastronomique,* "the art of cookery has never ceased to be honored and practiced." Their specialties include sole with morels, foie gras, and fresh salmon braised with Jurançon, a rather sweet, golden Pyrenean wine, celebrated in history and legend and much loved by Henri IV. The cassoulet with beans at Pierre is a dish worthy of an award. The cuisiniers take natural products of the region and use them creatively. For example, the lamb comes from the Ossau valley and has been called "as tender as a strawberry." In air-conditioned comfort, you can enjoy splendid service and a rewarding cuisine, with most dinners ranging in price from 110F ($25.11) to 160F ($36.53).

Résidence de l'Étrier, 70 Avenue Général-Leclerc (tel. 02-58-68), is an unusual and pleasant little inn where the chef-owner, Monsieur Orth, cooks in a classic French way. He is pleased when his dinner guests stay overnight so they can dine leisurely. He rents out 10 bedrooms, charging 75F ($17.12) in a single, 110F ($25.11) in a double. Meals are offered at 55F ($12.56) and 85F ($19.41), although you can also order à la carte. The restaurant is closed on Saturdays.

Hostellerie de Canastel, Avenue Rausky, route d'Oloron (tel. 32-37-14), lies in the hamlet of Jurançon, after which the famous wine is named. It is reached by going south on the N134 for about a mile. This is an inn-style hotel where the atmosphere is delightful, the food superior. The owner, Madame Bensoussan, has installed a swimming pool for the enjoyment of her guests. The hostelry is an overhanging roadside place, yet it is private enough. The owner has provided many comforts and conveniences in her attractively furnished rooms, for which she charges 120F ($27.40) in a single, 170F ($38.81) in a double. Most guests stay here on the demi-pension plan, costing from 185F ($42.24) to 195F ($44.52) per person daily. You'll be served breakfast on the terrace if you wish. If you dine here, you'll find menus at 55F ($12.56) and 70F ($15.98).

5. Eugénie-les Bains

A century ago the Empress Eugénie came here to "take the cure." Now some of the most discerning people in the world are following in her footsteps, but for a slightly different attraction. In the Landes section of France, in the foothills of the Pyrénées, about 33 miles from Pau, this spa village is better known today than it ever was because of—

Les Prés et les Sources d'Eugénie (tel. 58-19-01), the creation of Michel Guérard, the now-famous master chef whose *cuisine minceur* started a revolution in French cooking in the early 1970s. In this gracefully fashionable country hotel and restaurant, M. Guérard practices his art assisted by a staff of 16 chefs. Dieters may choose from a tasty variety on the minceur menu, but gourmets are not ignored here, either. The "grand menu gourmand" draws devoted fans from all over the world.

When you first enter the cheerfully decorated restaurant operated by Michel and his wife, Christine, you may want to select your dessert before you decide on the rest of the meal because all pastries are cooked to order. Then you may settle into a light appetizer such as eggs scrambled with chives and caviar or a delicate cream-of-crayfish soup. Seafood is plentiful, as indicated by an array of entrees that include whiting in white-wine sauce and mullet steamed with seaweed and oysters. Grilled breast of duck in cream sauce and braised rabbit are choice game dishes. One of the house favorites is the pot-au-feu, as delicious here as it was in Monsieur Guérard's former restaurant in Paris. If you wish to stick to the *minceur* cuisine, you may select tender lamb steamed with fennel or a number of fresh fish dishes. The vegetables are always fresh and in season, often chosen personally by Monsieur Guérard from the local farms. Desserts—most of these are non-*minceur*—include a tasty coffee cream or a delicious puff-pastry apple tart. Prices for meals range from 240F ($54.79) to 320F ($73.06), really a "big splurge," but a worthy investment to true lovers of good food.

The establishment also offers 35 guest rooms, each individually decorated and all contributing to the fairytale-like atmosphere. Room rates range from 180F ($41.09) for a single to 390F ($89.64) for a double per night. Both the hotel and restaurant are open from April 1 through November 3.

6. Lourdes

Muslims turn to Mecca, Hindus to the waters of the Ganges; but for Catholics Lourdes is the world's most beloved shrine. Nestled in a valley in the southwestern part of the Hautes-Pyrénées, it is the scene of pilgrims gathering from all over the world. Nail down your hotel reservation in overcrowded August.

On February 11, 1858, the Virgin is believed by the Roman Catholic world to have revealed herself to a poor shepherd girl, Bernadette Soubirous. Eighteen such apparitions were reported. Bernadette, subject of the film *Song of Bernadette,* died in a convent in 1879. She was beatified in 1925, then canonized in 1933.

Her apparitions literally put Lourdes on the map. The town has subsequently attracted millions of visitors from all over the world, the illustrious and the poverty-stricken. Many of the truly devout are often disheartened at the tawdry commercialism that hangs over Lourdes today. And some holiday-seekers are acutely disturbed by the human desperation of victims of various afflictions spending their hard-earned savings of a lifetime seeking a "miracle," then having to return home without a cure. However, the church has recognized many "cures" which took place after patients bathed in the springs, labeling them "true miracles."

THE SIGHTS OF LOURDES: From July 1 to September 20, tourists and pilgrims on a short visit can join the **Day Pilgrims,** a pilgrimage conducted in English that gathers at 9 a.m. at the statue of the Crowned Virgin for a prayer meeting in the meadow facing the Grotto. Part of these services include a 9:30 a.m. Stations of the Cross and a mass at 11:15 a.m. In the afternoon, assembling at the same spot at 2:30 p.m., pilgrims are taken on an explanatory visit to the Sanctuaries or places associated with Bernadette. At 4:30 there is a Procession of the Blessed Eucharist, starting from the Grotto. The 9 p.m. Marian celebration, rosary, torchlight procession, all start from the Grotto as well. For more information about this dramatic tour, apply to the information center under the right-hand ramp when you're going toward the Grotto.

In the Sanctuaries there are hostesses to welcome you all year at the **Office of Touristes et Isolés,** under the ramp on the right when you face the Basilica. Hours are from 9 a.m. to noon and from 2 to 7 p.m. The hostesses present the *Story of Lourdes and of Bernadette,* told with slides. The free film (in English) runs about 15 minutes.

At the **Grotto of Massabielle** the Virgin is said to have appeared 18 times to Bernadette between February 11 and July 16, 1858. This venerated site is accessible to pilgrims both day and night, and a Holy Mass is celebrated there every day.

The Statue of Our Lady depicts the Virgin in the posture she is said to have taken and in the place she reputedly appeared when she made herself known to Bernadette, saying to her in Pyrenean dialect, "I am the Immaculate Conception."

At the back of the Grotto, on the left of the altar, is the **Miraculous Spring** that reportedly welled up on February 25, 1858, during the ninth apparition, when Bernadette scraped the earth as instructed. The Virgin is said to have commanded her, "Go and drink at the spring and wash there." The water from this spring is collected in several big reservoirs, from which one can drink it.

Other Sanctuaries associated with St. Bernadette include the crypt, the first chapel built on top of the Grotto, the Basilica of the Immaculate Conception, the Rosary Basilica, and the underground Basilica of St. Pius X. In town, there are the house where Bernadette lived, the Cachot, the baptismal font in the parish church, and the hospital chapel where she made her first communion.

The **Upper Basilica,** at Place du Rosaire, was built in the 13th-century ogival style, though it was consecrated in 1876. It contains one nave split into five equal bays. Lining its interior are votive tablets. On the west side of the square is the **Rosary Basilica,** with two small towers. It was built in 1889 in the Roman-Byzantine style and holds up to 4000 persons. Inside, 15 chapels are dedicated to the "mysteries of the rosary."

The oval-shaped **Basilica of Pius X** was consecrated in 1958. An enormous underground chamber covered by a concrete roof, it is 660 feet long and 270 feet wide, holding as many as 20,000 pilgrims. After St. Peter's in Rome, it is the world's largest church.

Nearby, the **Musée Bernadette** contains scenes representing the life of the saint. It is open from 9 a.m. till noon and from 2 to 6 p.m. The true Bernadette devotee will also seek out the **Moulin de Boly,** rue Bernadette-Soubirous, where the saint was born January 7, 1844, the daughter of a miller. Her former home is open Easter through October, from 8 a.m. till 7:30 p.m. This was actually her mother's house. Bernadette's father, François Soubirous, had his family home in another mill, **Moulin Lacadé,** also on rue Bernadette-Soubirous. Visiting hours are from 9 a.m. till noon and from 2 to 7 p.m. None of these attractions charges admission.

Crowning the resort is the **château,** scene in summer of a son-et-lumière program. From the terrace, a handsome vista spreads before you (take the elevator from below). An excellent example of medieval military architecture, the castle contains the **Musée Pyrénéen,** with its collection of handicrafts and costumes from this mountain region. There's a curious collection of dolls in nuns' habits. In the courtyard are scale models of different styles of regional architecture, including Spanish. Both the château and museum may be visited from 9 to 11 a.m. and from 2 to 7 p.m.

EXPLORING THE PYRÉNÉES: Lourdes is one of the finest bases for exploring the Pyrénées. You can take tours into the snow-capped mountains across the border into Spain or go horseback-riding near **Lac de Lourdes,** two miles northwest of the town.

The Tourist Office at 2 Place Église-Paroissiale (tel. 94-15-64) will pinpoint particular highlights on a map. Outstanding ones include **Bagnères-de-Bigorre,** a renowned thermal spa; **Pic du Jer,** for a magnificent vista; **Béout,** for a panoramic view and an underground cave where prehistoric implements have been found (reached by cableway); **Pibeste,** for another sweeping vista of the Pyrénées; the **Caves of Medous,** an underground river with stalactites; and the **Heights of Gavarnie,** at 4500 feet, one of France's great natural wonders, requiring a full day.

HOTELS: **Grand Hôtel de la Grotte,** 66-68 rue de la Grotte (tel. 94-58-87), is a traditional favorite, decorated in typical upper-bourgeois French taste. The hotel, built in 1872, lies only five minutes from the sanctuaries. Open from April 1 to November 1, it offers 90 well-furnished rooms, charging from 130F ($29.68) in a single to 210F ($47.94) for the best twin. Depending on the room, the compulsory full-board tariff ranges from 230F ($52.51) to 250F ($57.08) per person per day.

Galilée et Windsor, 10 Avenue Peyramale (tel. 94-21-55), has a traditional façade, although it's modernized inside, often with plastic furnishings. Air-conditioned, the hotel offers pleasant rooms in flowery chintz. All have private baths and toilets. The rate is from 180F ($41.09) to 220F ($50.23) for a double, service included. Meals cost 70F ($15.98) per person. The hotel is open from April to October.

Panorama, 13 rue Sainte-Marie (tel. 94-33-04), is also a good hotel, lying close to the Grotto. The carpeted bedrooms contain typically modern and functional furniture, and there is a pleasant dining room, plus a spacious and comfortable lounge. Guests are preferred to take the full-board arrangement which costs from about $45 (U.S.) per person, including service. English is spoken. The hotel is open from the end of March to October 31.

Notre-Dame de France, 8 Avenue Peyramale (tel. 94-20-77), next to the Windsor, is another good budget hotel, clean and simple, offering a total of 61 units, each with a minimum of furnishings although they contain either private baths or showers as well as toilets. The cost for two persons is 110F ($25.11). In high season, the full-board rate runs from 130F ($29.68) to 150F ($34.26) per person. You can drop in just for a meal, from 50F ($11.42), service included.

READERS' HOTEL SELECTION: "We stayed at **Hôtel d'Annecy,** 13 Avenue de la Gare, only two minutes from the station at Lourdes. It is quite nice and clean, charging 85F ($19.41) for two persons, including a continental breakfast with only coffee and croissants" (Graham and Rhonda Kelly, Peakhurst, Sydney, Australia).

RESTAURANTS: The best food is at the **Taverne de Bigorre et Albert,** 21 Place du Champ-Commun (tel. 94-11-79). There you'll pay 110F ($25.11) for the gastronomic menu, 35F ($7.99) and 85F ($19.41) for the tourist menus. The place also rents out 25 rooms, costing from 65F ($14.84) in a single, from 145F ($33.10) for the best doubles. The tavern is closed from January 1 to February 6. No meals are served on Wednesdays from November 1 to May 1.

A very good budget restaurant in the center of town is **Le Bourguignon,**

10 rue des 4-Frères-Soulas (tel. 94-20-55). For only 32F ($7.31), we recently enjoyed a wide selection of crudités, followed by a grilled steak with pommes frites, plus a salad, cheese, and dessert. A bottle of the local wine was only 10F ($2.28). The dining room is pleasant, without any particular style—functional, but with large windows opening onto the square.

7. Cauterets

The souvenir peddling and the aggressive commercial atmosphere of Lourdes offends many visitors. If you are among them, we'd suggest that you strike out for the mountains. One sylvan retreat, 18½ miles south from Lourdes, is Cauterets. The site of a dozen curative thermal springs, this little hamlet composed mainly of hotels has been famous since Margaret of Navarre, arriving with her court, put it on the map. Even George Sand and Victor Hugo came this way, seeking cures for various ailments. The local folk will tell you, "You can be cured of whatever ails you at Cauterets, and that means everything."

Cauterets is also a center for touring some of the most majestic sights of the Pyrénées. The most popular tour is to the **Pont d'Espagne** and the **Lac de Gaube,** south of Cauterets. The road goes along for about 10 miles to the Pont d'Espagne. After that, only the hearty continue on foot. The **Cascade du Pont-d'Espagne** is considered the most dazzling of the waterfalls in and around Cauterets. If you're willing to walk for about an hour, you can take the path that leads to the Lac de Gaube. This lake occupies a magnificent setting, extolled by such visitors as Chateaubriand and Vigny. It has been used to illustrate almost every guide written about the Pyrénées since the Romantic period.

FOOD AND LODGINGS: Le Lys, rue Féria (tel. 97-54-30), is almost new yet has already earned a good reputation for providing satisfactory accommodations, good service, and a fine regional cuisine. In this part of France you're fortunate in being able to knock on the door of almost any hotel, where you'll find a plentiful cuisine prepared with concern and skill and a friendly, welcoming atmosphere. Although there are several modest inns at Cauterets, we prefer this bigger one, because it is newer and more up to date than some of the other creaky choices. With 113 rooms offered, you stand a better chance of securing an accommodation even in the peak summer months. A single rents for 135F ($30.82); a double, for 155F ($35.39). Menus are offered at 45F ($10.27) and 60F ($13.70). The hotel is closed from the first of October, reopening right before Christmas.

If you'd like to be truly remote, we'd suggest you journey to La Fruitière, four miles from Cauterets along the N21C. There you'll find a petite inn, **Hostellerie La Fruitière** (tel. 97-52-04). The "Fruit Shop" is only a simple inn, renting out eight bedrooms for 50F ($11.42) in a single and 60F ($13.70) in a double. In high season demi-pension is required, at a rate of 85F ($19.41) to 105F ($23.97) per person. Set apart from all the commercialization, the inn is most tranquil, decorated in an amusingly rustic style with antlers, open stone-built fireplaces, pitchforks, and blacked-beamed ceilings. It lies on a paved road, although in the midst of a national forest. From the inn there are many walks through woodlands, along lanes, and up hills. It is open only from May 20 until October 1.

8. Ax-les-Thermes

READERS' TOURING, HOTEL, AND RESTAURANT SELECTIONS: "Ax-les-Thermes, a small, pretty town in the French Pyrénées, is a good starting point for a one-day return trip to **Andorra.** There is a daily bus service in the summer from Toulouse to Barcelona, via Ax-les-Thermes and Andorra. In the summer months there are daily return excursions from Ax-les-Thermes to Andorra la Vella, capital of Andorra. This involves a spectacular bus ride through the French Pyrénées into the valleys of Andorra, where the local farmers still cut and harvest their hay by hand. At Ax-les-Thermes, we stayed at the **Hôtel Carrière,** on the main street, for 55F ($12.56) per night for a double room, plus 8.50F ($1.94) per person for breakfast. We also had an excellent dinner at **Hôtel de la Lauzeraie** (tel. 64-24-52) for 30F ($6.85) per person. Rooms range in price from 46F ($10.50) for a single to 95F ($21.69) for the best doubles with shower and toilet" (Jim and Adrienne Jago, Adelaide, Australia).

9. Perpignan

At Perpignan you may think you've already crossed the border into Spain. Actually, Perpignan was once the second city of Catalonia, ranking after Barcelona. Even earlier, it was the capital of that curiosity the kingdom of Majorca. But when the Roussillon—the French part of Catalonia—was finally partitioned off, Perpignan became French forever, authenticated by the Treaty of the Pyrénées in 1659. However, Catalan is still spoken, especially among the country people. There is much traffic between Perpignan and Barcelona.

Perpignan derives its name from the legend of Père Pinya, a plowman who is said to have followed the Tet River down the mountain to the site of the town today, where he started cultivating the fertile soil, with the river carrying out its promise to water the fields.

Among the chief things to see, the **Castillet** is a machicolated and crenellated building of red brick. It's a combination of a gateway and fortress, dating from the 14th century. If you ask the keeper, you can climb the tower for a good view of the town.

The second-best-known building is the **Loge de Mer,** a sort of maritime stock exchange erected in 1397, though enlarged in the 16th century. With its arcaded court, it is rather Venetian in style.

The **Cathédrale St.-Jean** dates from the 14th and 15th centuries. The cathedral has an admirable nave and some interesting 17th-century retables. Leaving by way of the south side of the door, you'll find a chapel on the left containing the curious Dévot Christ, a magnificent woodcarving depicting a Jesus contorted with pain and suffering, his head, crowned with thorns, drooping on his chest.

At the top of the town, the Spanish citadel encloses the **Palais des Rois de Majorque,** or the palace of the kings of Majorca. This structure from the 13th and 14th centuries has been restored by the government. It is built around a court which is encircled by arcades. You can see the old throne room with its large fireplaces, and a square tower with a double gallery. From the tower there is a fine view of the Pyrénées. The former palace can be visited daily from 9:30 a.m. to noon and from 2:30 to 6:30 p.m. for a 3F (68¢) admission.

If you'd like to take an excursion, you can visit **Thuir,** where Byrrh, the famous apéritif with a red-wine base, is made. The cellars, among the largest in Europe, can be viewed from 8:30 a.m. to 11 a.m. and from 2:30 to 5 p.m. weekdays. Thuir itself lies 10 miles southwest of Perpignan.

FOOD AND LODGINGS: Park Hôtel, 18 Boulevard Jean-Bourrat (tel. 61-33-17), is favored by most travelers heading for Spain's Costa Brava. Certainly its position is desirable, facing the Jardins de la Ville with their bird sanctuary. Rooms are well furnished and handsomely maintained, and there is an air of professionalism about the place. Singles begin at 100F ($22.83), rising to 170F ($38.81) in a double. The rooms have a nice ambience, are fully equipped, and most of them overlook the gardens. The hotel also runs a good restaurant, Chapon Fin, offering set menus at 85F ($19.41) and 120F ($27.40). The restaurant is closed on Sundays and from mid-December to mid-January.

La Loge, Place de la Loge (tel. 34-54-84), is a beguiling little hotel of only 29 bedrooms. Although modern, it has a charmingly tasteful interior. The location is right in the heart of town, near not only the Loge de Mer, from which it takes its name, but the Castillet as well. It is also near a canal outlet of the Tet. More than half the attractively furnished bedrooms contain private baths, and others water basins with access to immaculate hallway baths and toilets. Singles begin at 82F ($18.72), rising to 150F ($34.26) in a double. Breakfast at 14F ($3.20) is the only meal served.

Athéna, 1 rue Queya (tel. 34-37-63), lies in the old part of town, handy for all sights, just a short stroll from the cathedral. Even though it is centrally located, the hotel itself is in a tranquil zone. The building dates from the 18th century and has been considerably modernized and updated. Now, 19 of its 29 bedrooms come with private baths. Singles rent for 60F ($13.71); doubles, 90F ($20.57). There is no restaurant, but breakfast is provided at 8.50F ($1.94).

François Villon, 1 rue du Four St.-Jean (tel. 51-18-43), is installed in an authentic Catalonian house dating from the 14th century, with vaults, a special bread oven, and rustic decorations. You're offered the best cuisine in town, and it's heavily influenced by France's gastronomic center, Lyon. The menu is subject to change, depending on the availability of products and the season. So, even though you don't know what you're going to be offered when you go there, the chances are it will be fresh and skillfully prepared by the young chef, Pierre Charreton. His specialties made with local products and regional wines include foie gras mi-cuit au Banyuls, ris d'agneau (sweetbreads) au Mas Amiel, and truffes du Roussillon. Many of your fellow diners are likely to be from Barcelona, as François Villon is known by discerning visitors from that Catalonian port city. Monsieur Charreton offers a unique meal at 110F ($25.11), including a large choice of regional produce. The restaurant is closed on Saturdays, Sundays, and from mid-July to mid-August.

Chapter XVII

LANGUEDOC AND THE CAMARGUE

1. Auch
2. Toulouse
3. Albi
4. Castres
5. Carcassonne
6. Nîmes
7. Aigues-Mortes

LANGUEDOC, one of the great old provinces of southern France, is a loosely defined area encompassing such famous cities as Nîmes, Toulouse, and Carcassonne. It's one of the leading wine-producing areas of France, and is fabled for its art treasures.

The Camargue is a marshy delta lying between two arms of the Rhône. South of Arles, this is cattle country. The strong wild black bulls are bred here for the arenas of Arles and Nîmes. The small white horses, most graceful animals, were said to have been brought to the Camargue by the Saracens. They are ridden by *gardians,* French cowboys, who can usually be seen in black wide-brimmed hats. The whitewashed houses, the plaited-straw roofs, the pink flamingos who inhabit the muddy marshes, the vast plains, the endless stretches of sandbars—all this qualifies as Exotic France.

1. Auch

On the west bank of the Gers, in the heart of Gascony, the town of Auch in southwestern France is divided by an upper and lower quarter, each connected by several flights of steps. In the old part of town the narrow streets are called *pousterles.*

These streets center on the **Place Salinis,** from which there is a good view of the Pyrénées. Branching off from here, the **Escalier Monumental** leads down to the river, a truly monumental descent of 232 steps.

On the north of the square stands the **Cathédrale Ste.-Marie,** built from the 15th to the 17th centuries, one of the handsomest Gothic churches in the south of France. It has 113 Renaissance choir stalls made of carved oak. The stained-glass windows, also from the Renaissance era, are impressive. Its 17th-century organ was considered one of the finest in the world at the time of Louis XIV.

Next to the cathedral stands an 18th-century archbishop's palace with a 14th-century bell tower, the **Tour d'Armagnac.**

FOOD AND LODGINGS: Hôtel de France, Place de la Libération (tel. 05-00-44). If you could spend only one night in a sleepy provincial town, sampling the regional cuisine, we'd suggest you make it André Daguin's Hôtel de France. In the center of town, close to the cathedral, the hotel has been newly renovated, with a modern restaurant, a cozy bar, and two lounges. There are only 32 bedrooms, but each has been given a semiluxurious treatment, and you'll revel in the comforts. Singles begin at 80F ($18.26), although regular doubles rent for 190F ($43.38). If you want to spread your family out in a suite, the charge is 340F ($77.62).

The restaurant is exceptional—Monsieur Daguin constantly astonishes with his culinary feats, many of which are La Nouvelle Cuisine selections. Hopefully, your meal might start with a thinly sliced Gascon ham, or perhaps sweetbreads in a delicate béarnaise sauce. Among his main-dish specialties, you might select small cuts of lamb (taken from the choicest part) with crayfish tails, lou magret (a grilled breast of duck with a delicate flavor), fresh liver with vegetables, a brochette of salmon with foie gras, and a heavenly concoction of chicken breast with mussels. For dessert, you might be offered several flavors of homemade ice cream, divinely light pastries, or small side dishes of sweets belle époque. Meals are offered at 95F ($21.69) and 155F ($35.39), with à la carte orders averaging 140F ($31.96) to 160F ($36.53). The inn is closed in January.

Bargain hunters will seek out **Le Moulin de la Ribère,** a mile or so out the N21, route de Tarbes, at La Ribère (tel. 05-21-84). At this rustic inn everything is diminutive. There are only four bedrooms—modestly decorated, but also modestly priced, going for 55F ($12.56) nightly. Breakfast is an additional 11F ($2.51). The Moulin also serves good meals, offering demi-pension rates (obligatory in season) at 100F ($22.83) per person. The mill is closed on Saturdays off-season and from October 15 until November 5.

2. Toulouse

The old capital of Languedoc, France's fourth-largest city, is cosmopolitan in flavor. One of the major cities of the southwest, it is the gateway to the Pyrénées. A distinctive city of gardens and squares, it is especially noted for its red brick buildings.

Built on both sides of the Garonne River at a wide bend, Toulouse is an artistic and cultural center. It's had a stormy history, playing many roles—once it was the capital of the Visigoths and later the center of the counts of Toulouse.

It lies 60 miles west of Carcassonne, but a long 443 miles southwest of Paris, though easily reachable by air.

SEEING THE SIGHTS: The city's major monument is the **Basilica of St. Sernin,** Place St.-Sernin. Consecrated in 1096, it is the largest and finest Romanesque church extant. One of its most outstanding features is the Porte Miègeville, opening onto the south aisle and decorated with 12th-century sculptures. The door opening into the south transept is called Porte des Comtes, and its capitals depict the story of Lazarus. Nearby are the tombs of the counts of Toulouse. Entering by the main west door, you can see the double side aisles, giving the church five naves, an unusual feature in Romanesque architecture. An upper cloister forms a passageway around the interior. Look for the Romanesque capitals surmounting the columns. In the axis of the basilica, 11th-century bas-reliefs depict "Christ in his Majesty." The ambulatory leads to the crypt (ask the custodian for permission to enter), containing the relics of 128 saints, plus a thorn said to be from the Crown of Thorns.

Opposite St.-Sernin is the **Musée St.-Raymond** (tel. 23-11-44), housed in a college dating from 1523. It contains one of the finest collections of Imperial busts outside Rome itself. Open from 10 a.m. to noon and from 2 to 6 p.m. (until 5 p.m. off-season), it charges 1F (23¢) for admission. Closed Tuesdays.

Another important museum is the **Musée des Augustins,** corner of rue de Metz and rue d'Alsace-Lorraine (tel. 25-02-19). In its 14th-century cloisters is the most important collection of Romanesque capitals in the world. The sculptures or carvings are magnificent, and there are some fine examples of early Christian sarcophagi. On the upper floors is a large painting collection, with works by Murillo, Toulouse-Lautrec, Guardi, Gérard, Delacroix, Rubens, and Ingres. The museum also contains several portraits by Antoine Rivalz (1667-1735), a home-grown artist of surprising talent. Open from 10 a.m. to noon and from 2 to 6 p.m. (closes at 5 p.m. off-season), it charges 1F (23¢) for admission. Closed Tuesdays.

The other major ecclesiastical building is the **Cathédrale St.-Étienne,** at the east end of the rue de Metz. It has a bastardized look (probably because it was built between the 11th and 17th centuries). The rectangular bell tower is from the 16th century. It has a unique ogival nave to which a Gothic-style choir has been added.

One final church worthy of attention is **Jacobins,** in Old Toulouse, west of the Place du Capitole. A Gothic brick church, it dates from the 13th century. The convent, daring in its architecture, has been restored and forms the largest block of buildings in France in use as a monastery.

In civic architecture, the **Capitole,** Place du Capitole, is outstanding. Built in 1753, it houses the Hôtel de Ville, or city hall, plus a theater in its right wing. It is open from 9 a.m. till noon and from 2 to 6 p.m. except Tuesdays (closes at 5 p.m. off-season). Admission: 2F (46¢).

Toulouse has a number of fine old mansions. More than 50 survive, most of them dating from the Renaissance when Toulouse was one of the richest cities of Europe. The finest is **Hôtel d'Assézat,** on the rue de Metz. It contains a 16th-century courtyard where a son-et-lumière program is given between mid-June and the end of September. The mansion houses the Académie des Jeux-Floraux, which since 1323 has presented flowers made of wrought metal to poets.

After all that sightseeing activity, head for the oval-shaped **Place Wilson,** a 19th-century square sheltering the most fashionable cafés of Toulouse.

HOTELS: Frantel Wilson, 7 rue Labéda (tel. 21-21-75), is the city's leading hotel, even though it doesn't have a restaurant. It places its emphasis instead on attractive, air-conditioned, and soundproofed accommodations. The interior design of the bedrooms is contemporary, and you'll have many conveniences, including a minibar for your beverages (you report what you drank to the desk clerk when you go to pay the bill). Other amenities include TVs, radios, and a device to awaken yourself automatically. Rates charged are 182F ($41.55) in a single, 325F ($74.20) in a double. Breakfast is an additional 21F ($4.79). The Frantel Wilson is in the center of Toulouse, and there is a garage for your car.

Le Concorde, 16 Boulevard Bonrepos (tel. 62-48-60), has a touch of the deluxe, but just a touch. Opposite the Canal du Midi, it stands at the Gare Matabiau, the railway station. Rooms are functional and practical, and there are 100 of them, containing private baths, televisions, and radios. They're also air-conditioned. Rates are 170F ($38.81) in a single, rising to 250F ($57.08) in a double. There is also a garage for your car. On the premises, the Rôtisserie de l'Écluse provides good food with fast, efficient service, offering a menu at 50F ($11.42). The restaurant is closed on Sundays and in August.

Sofitel, Toulouse Aéroport de Blagnac (tel. 71-11-25), is one of the simpler versions of this chain hotel, not unlike a motel. It lies about 200 yards from the entrance to the airport, about a 10-minute drive into the center of Toulouse. Half of its bedrooms are twins, and all the accommodations are "climate controlled" and soundproofed. There is a liberal use of solid color combinations in the bedroom decor, and the theme is cheerful, with many amenities. Singles pay from 230F ($52.51) to 260F ($59.36); doubles, from 260F ($59.36) to 290F ($66.21). There is a restaurant, Croix du Sud, the "southern cross," serving both grills and regional specialties, a set menu costing from 95F ($21.69). Especially nice are the indoor heated swimming pool, the sauna, and the tennis courts.

Those wanting to escape Toulouse moderne can head for **La Flânerie,** route de Lacroix-Falgarde (tel. 73-39-12), at Vieille-Toulouse, 5½ miles south by way of D4. It's so peaceful a place it's worth the drive. The ancient residence stands in its own six-acre garden. The room furnishings have been well selected, setting a high style level. Some of the bedchambers are outfitted with rich, tasteful antiques, including canopy-tester beds, fine marquetry desks, and bronze lighting fixtures, most elegant. However, there are only 15 chambers, so reservations are important. Singles cost from 130F ($29.68), the rate rising to 170F ($38.81) in a double. No meals are served, other than breakfast at 16F ($3.65).

d'Occitaine, 5 rue Labéda (tel. 21-15-90), is a hotel school. Maybe because the staff is young, everybody seems to try harder. We've received the best service here of any place in the city. The rooms are well furnished and handsomely maintained, costing from 85F ($19.41) in a single to 250F ($57.08) in the best double. However, the hotel shuts down for school vacations, usually from the end of June until the first of October. Even if you don't stay here, we'd recommend its delicious fixed-price menu for 60F ($13.70). The restaurant is closed Saturdays and Sundays.

Nearby is the **Royal,** 6 rue Labéda (tel. 23-38-70), which is done in a sophisticated style using wrought iron and tiles. Rooms here are attractively comfortable, costing 85 F ($19.41) in a single, 150F ($34.26) in a double. There is no restaurant, although breakfast at 14F ($3.20) is served.

The **Hôtel de France,** 5 rue Austerlitz (tel. 21-88-24), is one of the best bargains in Toulouse. It has recently been renovated, and its modernized rooms are comfortable and handsomely maintained. The price is reasonable, too—55F ($12.56) in a single, rising to 60F ($13.70) in a double. These accommodations have been fitted with shower baths. Some of the doubles are quite large. The hotel also has an elevator, a facility lacking in many of the less expensive choices.

READER'S HOTEL SELECTION: "We chanced upon the superb little **Hotel Raymond IV,** 16 rue Raymond IV (tel. 62-89-41), which turned out to be super-clean, very pleasant, bright, and modern. Our room with shower, a double, cost only 109F ($24.88), which is very good as prices go in France. The personnel were friendly. We had a room off the street, so there wasn't a sound, but we think that even on that street, there would have been very little noise" (James L. Busey, Manitoba Springs, Colo.).

RESTAURANTS: **Vanel,** 22 rue M.-Fonvielle (tel. 21-51-82). Lucien Vanel stirs the magic of his craft, turning out scrumptious fare. The patronage is heavily Gallic, and the restaurant is nearly always full—so you'll need a reservation. He gives new meaning and discovers new taste sensations in regional dishes, adding constantly to his own rapidly growing repertoire. His braised sea bass with lettuce is every bit as good (or better) than the seaweed style made famous by Michel Guérard. An endless variety of quality meats and produce, skillfully and creatively prepared, are presented for your selection—marinated veal liver (from the school of La Nouvelle Cuisine), a cassolette of snails with nuts, a fricassée of pigs' feet (it may sound unappetizing, but it's delicious), a pâté of pike with eel, a duckling ragoût with sweetbreads. The wine list is imaginative with many interesting selections, including Cahors and St.-Saturnin, and the service is impeccable. Expect to pay from 120F ($27.40) to 150F ($34.26) for a meal. The restaurant is closed on Sundays and in August.

The other leading restaurant is **Le Belvédère,** 11 Boulevard Recollets (tel. 52-63-73), which offers a panoramic view of the Garonne and Old Toulouse from its eighth-floor precincts. Under the careful eye of its patron, this exceptional restaurant serves an array of local specialties, including the typical cassoulet au confit and a confit en ratatouille. Set meals are offered for 60F ($13.70). The restaurant is closed on Sundays and holidays.

Le Cassoulet, 40 rue Peyrolières (tel. 22-18-99), takes its name from a shellbean stew originating in Languedoc. The dish is prepared with goose, pork, or mutton. Each is delicious. At this restaurant you can order à la carte at a cost of 60F ($13.70) to 85F ($19.41) per person. The restaurant is closed from July 1 to 22 and from December 21 to January 3, and on Mondays.

The best bargain meal we've come across in Toulouse is served at a simple little bistro called **Euzkadi,** 39 rue Gambetta (tel. 22-45-45), where we enjoyed a three-course meal for only 25F ($5.71). The service is polite. More elaborate meals are offered for 30F ($6.85), 35F ($7.99), and 45F ($10.27). The food is better than you might expect for the price. The restaurant is closed on Saturdays and from mid-July to mid-August.

3. Albi

The "red city" (for the color of the building stone) of Albi, 47 miles northeast of Toulouse, straddles both banks of the Tarn River, and is dominated by its brooding, fortified **Cathédrale Ste.-Cecile,** dating from 1282 and lying near the Place du Vigan, the medieval center of town. After viewing the cathedral, one writer claimed that if it were in Italy, "the French would spend a day in the train to go and see it and that stupendous view." Fortified with ramparts and parapets outside, and containing transepts or aisles inside, it was built by local bishops during a struggle for power with the counts of Toulouse. Inside, look at the 16th-century rood screen. It's exceptional.

Opposite the northern side of the cathedral is the Archbishop's Palace, or **Palais de la Berbie,** another fortified structure dating from the late 13th century. Inside, the **Musée Toulouse-Lautrec** contains the world's most important collection of that artist's paintings, more than 600 specimens of his work. His family bequeathed the works remaining in his studio. Toulouse-Lautrec was born at Albi on November 24, 1864. Crippled in childhood, his legs permanently deformed, he lived in Paris most of his life and produced posters and sketches of characters in music halls and circuses. His satiric portraits of the demimonde at the turn of the century were both amusing and affectionate. The museum also owns paintings by Degas, Bonnard, Vuillard, Matisse, Dufy, Utrillo, and Rouault. From May 1 to October 1 it is open daily from 10 a.m. to noon and from 2 to 6 p.m. (closes at 5 p.m. and on Tuesdays off-season). Admission is 6F ($1.37).

FOOD AND LODGING: Hostellerie St.-Antoine, 17 rue Saint-Antoine (tel. 54-04-04). Madame Rieux, a talented and inventive interior decorator, dipped heavily into the Toulouse-Lautrec palette when designing this hotel. Her grandfather was a close friend of the painter and was given a few of his paintings, sketches, and prints. Some of these are placed in various spots in the lounge, which opens onto a rear garden with fig trees and flagstone paths. The atmosphere evokes a private country estate. The bedrooms have been delightfully decorated, with a sophisticated use of color, good reproductions, and occasional antiques. A single with shower rents for 100F ($22.83), increasing to 160F ($36.53) with bath. Doubles are 130F ($29.68) with shower, rising to 250F ($57.08) with bath. Three set menus are offered: 50F ($11.42), 70F ($15.98), and 120F ($27.40).

La Réserve, route de Cordes à Fonviane (tel. 60-79-79), is a country-club villa on the outskirts of Albi, managed by the aforementioned Madame Rieux. It is built in the Mediterranean style, with a swimming pool and fine garden where you can dine. Step-terraces lead to the banks of the Tarn River. The upper-story bedrooms have sun terraces and French doors. Half of the accommodations are decorated in a light and cheery modern way, the other in Empire with top-grade reproductions. The colors are coordinated, and the decorative accessories are imaginative. Madame Rieux has even made the baths a delight. The price runs from 160F ($36.53) to 220F ($50.23) in a single to 200F ($45.66) to 320F ($73.06) for the best double. Three set menus are offered: 55F ($12.56), 75F ($17.12), and 130F ($29.68). On the à la carte menu, specialties include pâté de grives (thrush), carré d'agneau (lamb) aux cèpes, and tournedos Périgeux. A meal ordered à la carte is likely to run about 170F ($38.81).

Le Relais Gascon, 1 rue Balzac (tel. 54-26-51), is a low-cost establishment, offering only 15 rooms, which are clean and pleasant but without any particular refinement. Prices run from 60F ($13.70) in a single to 130F ($29.68) in a double. The restaurant offers a decent set meal for 45F ($10.27).

4. Castres

READER'S SIGHTSEEING AND RESTAURANT SELECTION: "I stopped overnight in Castres, 27 miles from Albi, where I had read that there was a museum with a collection of Goya paintings, Musée Goya. The museum is in the Hôtel de Ville, with a lovely garden in the rear. The Goya paintings are few, but another exhibit proved especially exciting to a history buff like me. Jean Jaurès, the Socialist leader, was a native of Castres (1859-1914), and his father had been mayor of the town and the family had lived in the Hôtel de Ville. There was family furniture, memorabilia, and Jaurès's personal possessions, including an issue of L'Aurore containing Zola's famous 'J'accuse' article from the Dreyfuss affair. What a wonderful way to make history come alive. Incidentally, from June 20 to September 15, a very nice and reasonable restaurant is open near the river, La Caravelle, 150 Avenue Roquecourbe (tel. 59-27-72), where a set meal can be ordered for around 50F ($11.42). It's closed Sundays" (Isabel Marovich, Kalamazoo, Mich).

If you'd like to spend the night, you'll find good comfort at Grand Hotel, 11 rue Libération (tel. 59-00-30), which is the best of the moderately-priced rooming establishments in town. It is run by J.P. Fabre, who also manages La

Caravelle, the best restaurant in town. The Grand offers 40 well-furnished rooms costing from 60F ($13.70) for its least expensive unit, rising to 140F ($31.96) for the best double with private bath. The hotel shuts down from December 15 to January 15.

5. Carcassonne

Evoking bold knights, fair damsels, and troubadours, the greatest fortress city of Europe rises against a background of snow-capped Pyrénées. Floodlit at night, it captures fairytale magic, but back in its heyday in the Middle Ages, all wasn't so romantic. Shattering the peace and quiet were battering rams, grapnels, a mobile tower (inspired by the Trojan horse), quicklime, catapults, flaming arrows, and the mangonel.

Carcassonne, 57 miles southeast of Toulouse, consists of two towns, the **Ville Basse** ("Lower City") and the medieval **Cité.** The former has little interest, but the latter is among the major attractions in France, the goal of many a pilgrim. The fortifications consist of the inner and outer walls, a double line of ramparts.

The inner rampart was built by the Visigoths in the fifth century. Clovis, the king of the Franks, attacked in 506, but he failed. The Saracens overcame the city in 728, until Pepin the Short (father of Charlemagne) drove them out in 752. During a long siege by Charlemagne, the populace of the walled city was starving and near surrender until a woman named Dame Carcas came up with an idea. According to legend, she gathered up the last remaining bit of grain, fed it to a sow, then tossed the pig over the ramparts. It is said to have burst, scattering the grain. The Franks concluded that Carcassonne must have unlimited food supplies and ended their siege.

The walls were further fortified by the viscounts of Trencavel in the 12th century and by Louis IX and Philip the Bold in the following century. However, by the mid-17th century Carcassonne's position as a strategic frontier fort was over. The ramparts decayed. In the 19th century, the builders of the lower town began to remove the stone for use as material in new construction. But interest in the Middle Ages revived, and the French government ordered Viollet-le-Duc (who restored Notre-Dame in Paris) to repair and where necessary rebuild the walls. Reconstruction continued until recently.

Enclosed within the walls is a small populace, numbering no more than 1000 persons. The **Cathedral of St. Nazaire** dates from the 11th and 12th centuries, containing some beautiful stained-glass windows and a pair of rose medallions. The nave is in the Romanesque style, but the choir and transept are Gothic. The organ, one of the oldest in southwest France, is from the 16th century. The tomb of Bishop Radulph is well preserved, dating from 1266 A.D.

WHERE TO STAY: Hôtel de la Cité, Place de l'Église (tel. 25-03-34), is the prestigious ivy-covered inn of Carcassonne, built within the city walls, adjoining the cathedral. Many of the accommodations open onto the ramparts and a garden. An adaptation of a church palace, the inn maintains the same medieval architectural heritage of thick stone walls and leaded Gothic windows. You enter into a long Gothic corridor-gallery leading to the lounge and dining room, the latter in strong colors with gilt fleur-de-lis on the walls. Logs burn in the ceiling-high fireplace on nippy nights. A small Louis XV-style salon is an inviting spot, with antiques and red-and-cream tapestry panels. The bedrooms feature either antiques or reproductions. The price range varies along with the plumbing and the view. For the best doubles with private baths, you pay 350F ($79.91), although there are many fine doubles with bath renting for 175F ($39.95) to 275F ($62.78). A continental breakfast is served in the hotel, other meals in **Restaurant Le Senechal.** The hotel is closed from mid-October to mid-April.

Hôtel du Donjon, 2 rue Comte-Roger (tel. 25-11-13), is well positioned, a modest little hotel big on charm—the best choice for an inexpensive stopover. It even has a garden. Built in the style of the old Cité, it lies behind a honey-colored stone exterior studded with windows with iron bars. The interior is a jewel, reflecting the taste and sophistication of its owner, Madame Christine Pujol, who loves to collect antiques. Rather elaborate Louis XIV-style furniture graces one of the reception lounges, decorated with gilt-encrusted and tapestry-covered chairs. The 20 bedrooms are small but nicely styled. A double room with a complete bath costs 150F ($34.26), although two persons will pay only 100F ($22.83) in a room with a shower. A continental breakfast at 11F ($2.51) or a full one with orange juice at 15F ($3.42) is the only meal served.

Montségur, 1 Avenue Bunau-Varilla (route de Pamiers) (tel. 25-31-41), is a stately old town house in the Lower City, resting under a mansard roof with dormers. The front garden is screened from the street by trees and a high wrought-iron fence. Monsieur and Madame Lucien Faugeras have furnished the hotel with antiques or reasonably good reproductions, avoiding that institutional look. Modern amenities include air conditioning and an elevator. The bedrooms are cheaper than you'd imagine from the looks of the place. A few doubles with shower go for as little as 115F ($26.25), although they range upward to 160F ($36.80) in a twin-bedded room with bath. A continental breakfast is available for another 11F ($2.51), and you can take your other meals at the highly recommended (see below) Le Languedoc restaurant nearby. Closed December 15 to January 15.

Hotel St.-Joseph, 81 rue de la Liberté (tel. 25-10-94), gave us our biggest welcome of any place in the city. A busy little place, it lies only 200 meters from where the trains pull in. An elevator will take you to one of its well-furnished rooms. In a unit with a double bed, two persons are charged 42F ($9.59). However, some of the rooms are large enough for three guests, who pay 46F ($10.50). Four guests in a room with shower are charged 65F ($14.84). The location is in the Ville-Basse, about a mile and a half from La Cité. Parking is free, and there's also a quiet garden.

WHERE TO DINE: Logis de Trencavel, 286 Avenue Général-Leclerc (tel. 25-19-53), is where the famed restaurateur Monsieur Ayméric is the star of his own show. Featured in *Joies de la Gastronomie,* he has done what many chefs dream about—discovered an attractive inn where he can produce his specialties and have enough room to serve his guests properly. Just outside Carcassonne he has created this auberge, designed in the Languedoc style. An old stucco villa with a tiled roof, the establishment is set back from the roadway and surrounded by its own garden, blossoming with petunias and geraniums. A raftered reception lounge, with dark beams and an open wood fireplace, leads to 12 bedrooms. Demi-pension, required in high season, ranges in price from 180F ($41.09) to 220F ($50.23).

Hopefully, you'll meet the rotund lover of good food himself: his enthusiasm is unbounded, and he enjoys being appreciated. For 70F ($15.98), he offers a fixed-price luncheon or dinner. On the à la carte menu, you might begin your meal with foie gras de canard (duckling) with apples or a hot pâté of scallops. Fish specials include stuffed trout Trencavel. His most popular dishes are cassoulet de Carcassonne and confit d'oie (goose meat delicately cooked in

its own fat and kept in earthenware pots). Ordering à la carte will bring your
tab into the 100F ($22.83) range. The restaurant is closed on Wednesdays and
the Logis is closed completely from January 4 until February 10.

Le **Languedoc,** 37 allée d'Iéna (tel. 25-22-17), is the pride of Monsieur
Lucien Faugeras, who also owns the previously recommended 19th-century
hotel, Montségur. He's an excellent chef, and has created a warm Languedoc
atmosphere as a proper setting for his culinary repertoire. The inviting ambience is achieved by rough plaster walls, a beamed ceiling, an open brick fireplace, and provincial cloths draped over peasant tables. It's a real country
tavern. You can order two set meals—a fine one for 45F ($10.27) and an even
more elaborate one for 60F ($13.70), including service. His house specialty is
le cassoulet au confit de canard (the world-famed stew made with duck cooked
in its own fat), 45F ($10.27). His paella Valenciana is superb, but his pièce de
résistance is tournedos Rossini, served with foie gras truffé (truffles, the Marquis de Cussy's "subterranean empress") and Madeira sauce, 75F ($17.12). A
delicious dessert is his crêpes flambées Languedoc, 23F ($5.25).

Le **Restaurant du Comte-Robert,** just next to the Hôtel du Donjon, offers
a fixed-price menu for 35F ($7.99), and what a dinner! The hors d'oeuvres are
practically a meal in themselves—they're what the French call *pantagruelic.* A
home-cooked cassoulet is the main-dish feature. If you eat it all, you won't need
another meal for the rest of the day. The restaurant itself is a nice, clean French
café-type place. In summer you can enjoy a little courtyard just behind the
hotel.

L'Ostal, 5 rue Violet-le-Duc, right in the heart of the old city (tel. 47-88-
80), is known for both its music and food. Old-fashioned in styling but newly
equipped, it presents a live folk show of troubadors. The food is typical of the
region, and the grill stays open until late at night. Many consider L'Ostal the
funniest and cheapest place for dining in the city. Set menus are featured at 18F
($4.11), 27F ($6.16), and 43F ($9.82). If you want to drop in just for drinks
and to hear the music, that too is possible. Drinks cost from 15F ($3.42) if
you're not eating.

Another inexpensive dining choice in La Cité is **Le Vieux Faus,** 9 rue
St.-Louis, which is a little pizzeria with live music and wood-oven cookery. It
presents set menus from 27F ($6.16) to 39F ($8.90), and you can visit late to
enjoy a good-tasting pizza costing 20F ($4.57).

READERS' RESTAURANT SUGGESTION: "There are two or three cheap restaurants
in rue de la Liberté, about two blocks from Hôtel St.-Joseph. The best of these is the
Tivoli, in which a four-course meal costs 28F ($6.39), service included, per person, plus
5F ($1.14) for a half-carafe of wine. The Tivoli is well patronized by the locals, a good
recommendation" (Jim and Adrienne Jago, Adelaide, Australia).

6. Nîmes

Nîmes, the ancient Nemausus, is one of the finest places in the world for
wandering among Roman relics. A busy industrial city today, about 27 miles
southwest of Avignon, it is the gateway to the Rhône Valley and to Provence.

THE SIGHTS: Pride of Nîmes is the **Maison Carrée,** Place de la Comédie,
built during the reign of Augustus. On a raised platform with tall Corinthian
columns and built in the Greek style, it is one of the most beautiful and
certainly one of the best-preserved Roman temples of Europe. Louis XIV
wanted to move it to Versailles, and it inspired the builders of the Madeleine
in Paris. The temple houses the **Musée des Antiques,** displaying antique works

of art found at Nîmes, including Roman statues, bronzes, and mosaics. Featured is the *Venus of Nîmes,* with one arm missing. Also exceptional are a bronze head and a statue of Apollo, plus a sumptuous exhibition, the "Frieze of Eagles."

The elliptically shaped **Amphitheater,** Place des Arènes, a twin to the one at Arles, is far more complete than the Colosseum of Rome. It is two stories high, consists of 60 arcades each, and was built of huge stones fitted together without mortar. One of the best preserved of the arenas existing from ancient times, it held more than 20,000 spectators who came to see gladiatorial combats and wolf or boar hunts. It's in good enough condition today to be used for bullfights.

The **Jardin de la Fontaine,** at the end of the Quai de la Fontaine, was laid out in the 18th century, using the ruins of a Roman shrine. It was planted with rows of chestnuts and elms, adorned with statuary and urns, and intersected by grottos and canals—one of the most beautiful gardens of France. Adjoining the garden is the ruined **Temple of Diana** and remains of some Roman baths. Over the park towers **Mont Cavalier,** surmounted by the **Tour Magne,** the city's oldest Roman monument, which you can climb for a panoramic view.

Nîmes also has a number of museums, notably the **Musée Archéologique** and the **Musée du Vieux Nîmes.** Our favorite is the **Musée des Beaux-Arts,** rue Cité-Foulc, containing paintings by Van Loo, Vernet, Watteau, Rubens, Canaletto, and some Rodin busts. Seek out in particular G. B. Moroni's fascinating *La Calomnie d'Apelle.* There's an interesting Gallo-Roman mosaic as well.

Finally, the Boulevard Amiral-Courbet leads to the **Porte d'Arles,** the remains of a Roman city gate erected during the reign of Augustus.

To visit the Roman monuments, you can buy one comprehensive ticket costing 10F ($2.28). The monuments are open from 9 a.m. to noon and from 2 to 7 p.m. (till 5 p.m. off-season). The Amphitheater stays open in June, July, and August from 8:30 a.m. till 7:30 p.m. The museums are open from 9 a.m. till noon and from 3 to 6 p.m. (2 to 5 p.m. off-season).

Outside the City

The **Pont du Gard** is a Roman bridge spanning the Gard River. Its huge stones were fitted together without mortar, and it has stood the test of time. Consisting of three tiers of arches, it dates from about 19 B.C. Take Route N86.

About 10 miles further on lies **Uzes,** a historic city, the "Premier Duchy of France." Standing on a hill, it is full of narrow streets and the former mansions of aristocrats which encircle the **Duché,** a château with a Renaissance façade. The Duché itself dates from the 11th century, and can be visited from 9 a.m. to noon and from 2 to 7 p.m. for an admission of 5F ($1.14). The **Cathedral of St. Théodorit,** built mainly in the 17th century, is distinguished by its 12th-century **Fenestrelle,** a circular six-story bell tower with many windows. This campanile is unique in Mediterranean France.

HOTELS: Nîmes offers good accommodations in all price ranges.

The Upper Bracket

Imperator, Place Aristide Briand (tel. 21-90-30), leads all others. It's near the city center and the Roman monuments, opposite Jardins de la Fontaine. The hotel's rear gardens are enticing. You can order lunch here, enjoying the private park, later walking along the graveled paths under shade trees. Bedrooms vary somewhat in character. The best have skillfully reproduced Proven-çal pieces. Most of them are old-fashioned in a pleasant way. Half of them have been renewed in a traditional way to preserve their character. Singles cost 200F ($45.66), the tariff rising to 320F ($73.06) in a double. All rooms come with private baths or showers, plus toilets. Prices include taxes and service.

Sofitel Nîmes, Chemin de l'Hostellerie, Nîmes-Ouest (tel. 84-40-44), lies outside of the city proper, yet is only about a five-minute drive from the arena and the Maison Carrée. In pure Sofitel-chain style, it has a contemporary design, allowing for air conditioning and soundproofing as well as private baths and attractively built-in furnishings. In all, 100 bedrooms are offered, costing from 180F ($41.09) to 210F ($47.94) in a single, from 220F·($50.23) to 290F ($66.21) in a double. Taxes and service are included, but not breakfast. Adjoining the hotel is a swimming-pool area and a sun terrace. In the Café de Nîmes you get simple meals and rapid service, a meal costing around 80F ($18.26). However, La Grazille serves grills and regional specialties, in the 85F ($19.41) to 120F ($27.40) range.

The Middle Bracket

Le Cheval Blanc, Place des Arènes (tel. 67-20-03), lies behind a stark façade directly opposite the arena. You enter a classical and large reception hall furnished with Provençal pieces. The dining room is impressive, with fine furniture plus plenty of silver and crystal. Most of the bedrooms are sound-proofed, and a few have air conditioning and television. The furniture is mainly Directoire, with assorted murals and tapestries. The baths are tiled, the walls covered with special matching paper. A single with shower rents for 110F ($25.11), increasing to 180F ($41.09) with bath. A double with shower is 115F ($26.25); you'll pay 180F ($41.09) with a complete bath. The restaurant is a grill.

Carrière, 6 rue Grizot (tel. 67-24-89), has been modernized. The furnishings are functional, not stylish. A single with shower costs 75F ($17.12). Doubles, all with bath, range from 120F ($27.40) to 165F ($37.68). The restaurant, with light wood tables and chairs, provides three menus—the cheapest one at 30F ($6.85), the most expensive one at 60F ($13.70).

The Budget Range

Hôtel l'Amphithéâtre, 4 rue des Arènes (tel. 67-28-51), stands on a narrow, quiet street just behind the Arènes. It offers 21 rooms which are furnished either with antiques or modern pieces. Every room has its own color scheme, with matching carpeting, bedcovers, and curtains. Two-thirds of the rooms contain private baths. A single with hot-and-cold running water is priced at 44F ($10.05), rising to 70F ($15.98) with private bath or shower. A double with shower goes for 70F ($15.98), increasing to 90F ($20.55) with a complete bath. The best bargain is a room for four, at a rate of 110F ($25.11) with bath.

Menant, 22 Boulevard Amiral-Courbet (tel. 67-22-85), is on one of the main boulevards, about 300 yards from the Maison Carrée. It's a little corner hotel, offering moderately priced, comfortably furnished rooms. The decor is modern, and the plumbing has been much improved in recent years. The simplest singles rent for 45F ($10.27). Doubles with hot-and-cold running water cost 65F ($14.84), rising to 120F ($27.40) with private bath. You can order breakfast at 11F ($2.51), although no other meals are served.

RESTAURANTS: Au Chapon Fin, 3 rue Château-Fadaise (tel. 67-34-73), is a tavern-style restaurant about two blocks from the arena, opening onto a little square behind a church. It's nicely decorated, with beamed ceilings, pictures on the walls, small lamps, and a white-and-black stone floor. The owner's wife comes from Alsace, which explains the many Alsatian specialties on the menu. On the à la carte menu you can order such specialties as a salmon terrine, 35F ($7.99); foie gras d'oie, entrecôte Périgourdine, and duckling with orange sauce, each costing 55F ($12.56); and a special garnished sauerkraut, 50F ($11.42). Monsieur Bartoletti, the proprietor, makes his own confit d'oie from geese direct from Alsace, 95F ($21.69). Two set menus are offered—one at 38F ($8.68), another at 75F ($17.12) and each offers a wide choice. Closed in August and on Tuesdays.

La Pergola, 11 rue Enclos-Rey (tel. 67-08-13), is the domain of Daniel Thème, who has a special flair for cooking and definite integrity in the kitchen. On our most recent visit we sampled his favored specialty, a filet of beef en croûte with a sauce made of flap mushrooms, and it was a delicious success, the crust flaky. He also does seafood dishes well, particularly scallops with sorrel and a gratin of mussels. He offers two menus, one at 55F ($12.56), another at 85F ($19.41), or else you can order à la carte for about 120F ($27.40). As the name of the restaurant suggests, you can take your meals in the garden. The dining room itself is charming and intimate. He closes his restaurant on Sunday nights and for Monday lunches.

Le Niçois, 10 rue Grizot (tel. 67-50-86), next to the Hotel Carrière, is a good-looking restaurant in the typical Provençal style, with wooden tables and paper napkins. It's a good place for a small purse, as you can have a choice here of four set menus: 25F ($5.71), 35F ($7.99), 45F ($10.27), and 65F ($14.84). Specialties include soupe de poissons (fish soup), bouillabaisse, caille (quail) provençale, peppersteak, and a special dessert of the day.

READERS' RESTAURANT SUGGESTION: "In Nîmes we discovered the **Restaurant Terminus,** just steps from the Hôtel de Milan. When we ordered just one of the most expensive dinners, at 55F ($12.56), the multicourse meal was so huge is sufficed to fill the two of us. The lowest fixed-price menu was 32F ($7.31) each, which we enjoyed another evening" (Pearl and Leslie Kay).

7. Aigues-Mortes

South of Nîmes you can explore a lot of the Camargue country by car. The most rewarding target in this curious landscape is Aigues-Mortes, the city of the "dead waters." In the middle of dismal swamps and melancholy lagoons, Aigues-Mortes is the most perfectly preserved walled town in France. Four miles from the sea, it stands on four navigable canals. Once Louis IX and his crusaders set forth from Aigues-Mortes, then a thriving port, the first in France to be built on the Mediterranean. The **walls** which still enclose the town were constructed between 1272 and 1300. The **Tour de Constance** is a model castle of the Middle Ages, its stones looking out on the marshes today, perhaps recalling the former greatness of the port. The tower is open from 9 a.m. to noon and from 2 to 6:30 p.m. (from 10 a.m. to noon and from 2 to 5 p.m. off-season), charging an entrance fee of 5F ($1.14), half price on Sundays. Sixty feet in diameter, the tower rises some 90 feet. Although built for defensive purposes, it saw little military action, becoming in time a prison for the Huguenots. Inside is an Oratory of St. Louis. From the tower you can go through a door leading out onto the ramparts, a walk around the town that takes about 40 minutes. These ramparts are studded with 15 towers.

A 21-mile drive east from Aigues-Mortes takes you to **Les Saintes-Mar-ies-de-la-Mer,** on the most southerly Mediterranean tip of the Camargue. There, according to legend, the three Marys landed in 45 A.D. and converted Provence to Christianity. They were Mary, sister of the Virgin Mary; Mary Magdalene, and Mary, mother of the Apostles John and James. The bodies of Mary, sister of the Virgin, and Mary, mother of the Apostles, were believed to have been buried in the fortresslike Church of Les Saintes-Maries-de-la-Mer, which dates from the 10th to the 15th centuries. A crypt in the basement believed to be that of their black servant, Sarah, is the object of special venera-tion by the gypsies who make pilgrimages there, as Sarah is their patron saint.

If you drive north on the road to Nîmes, you'll pass through **St.-Gilles,** with its church which was founded in the 12th century, then rebuilt in the 17th century. St. Aegidius (or Giles) died there in 721 after having founded an abbey. The hamlet turned into one of the most famous places for pilgrimages in the Middle Ages, an important stopping-off point on the road to Santiago de Compostela in northwestern Spain. The church has an elaborate west front, considered a Romanesque masterpiece. The three doorways are linked by a colonnade and richly adorned.

FOOD AND LODGINGS AT AIGUES-MORTES: Hóstellerie Remparts, 6 place d'Armes (tel. 88-33-67), is an ancient inn where the cookery is note-worthy for its regional dishes, the atmosphere in the lounge colorful, and the bedrooms warm, inviting, and most comfortable. Each of the nicely furnished bedchambers comes with its accompanying private bath, and you'll pay 180F ($41.09) in a single, that tariff going up to 320F ($73.06) in a double. As there are only 19 rooms, you must reserve well in advance. The food is excellent, set menus going for 65F ($14.84), although à la carte dining bills come to an average of 125F ($28.54). Specialties include aiguillettes de canard (duckling), quenelles de loup (sea bass) in a Nantua sauce, fresh foie gras, and coquilles St. Jacques (scallops) à la Provençale. The inn, which stands at the foot of the Tower of Constance, doesn't serve meals on Wednesdays off-season and is closed entirely in November.

St.-Louis, rue Amiral-Courbet (tel. 88-30-14), is a small inn near Place St.-Louis. There are 20 bedrooms, attractively furnished and containing private baths. Singles rent for 135F ($30.82), although you'll have to pay 150F ($34.26) in a double. Even though it is modest, the amenities and facilities are more than adequate, and you can not only sleep well here but dine well, too. Menus cost from 55F ($12.56) and 100F ($22.83). The cooking is regional. The restaurant is closed on Wednesdays, and the inn itself is closed from November through February.

Camargue, 19 rue de la République (tel. 88-31-57), is the scene of whatever nighttime activities there are in "the city of dead waters." Downstairs is a charming and elegant restaurant with a patio in an old house. There the owner offers some excellent grills and local dishes, including game dishes in season. A set meal costs 85F ($19.41), and is a good one, hearty, satisfying, and filling. The restaurant is closed Mondays and in January.

PROVENCE

PROVENCE, IN SOUTHEAST France, has been called a bridge between the past and present. Yesterday blends with today in a quiet, often melancholy way.

The Greeks and Romans founded cities here, complete with Hellenic theaters, Roman baths, amphitheaters, and triumphal arches. Medieval man erected Romanesque fortresses and Gothic cathedrals. By the 19th century the light and landscapes of Provence were attracting illustrious painters such as Cézanne and Van Gogh.

Despite changes over the years, withered black cypresses and dark-haired, hazel-eyed Provençal people remain. And the howling laugher of the mistral will forever be heard through broad-leaved plane trees.

Provence has its own language and its own customs. Naturally it has its own wines, ranging from elegant Châteauneuf-du-Pape to vins de pays, and its own dishes, such as ratatouille and bouillabaisse.

A part of Provence, the glittering Côte d'Azur will be dealt with in the chapter on the French Riviera. Provence is bounded on the north by the Dauphiné, on the west by the Rhône, on the east by the Alps, and on the south by the Mediterranean.

1. Toulon

This fortress and modern town is the principal naval base of France, the headquarters of the Mediterranean fleet, lying 42 miles east of Marseille. A beautiful harbor, it is surrounded by hills and crowned by forts. The place is protected on the east by a large breakwater and on the west by the great peninsula of **Cap Sicié**. Projecting from Sicié is **Cap Cépet**. Separated by the breakwater, the outer roads are known as the **Grande Rade** and the inner roads are called **Petite Rade.** On the outskirts is a winter resort colony.

In Vieux Toulon, lying between the harbor and the Boulevard de Strasbourg (the main axis of town), there are many remains of the port's former days before it developed along more modern lines. Visit the **Poissonerie,** the typical Provençal-style covered market, which is busy and bustling in the mornings with fishmongers and buyers. Another colorful market is called simply **Marché,** and it spills over onto the narrow streets around the Cours Lafayette. Go in the morning, when it is at its peak.

Also in old Toulon, the **Cathédrale Ste.-Marie-Majeure (St. Mary Major)** was built in the Romanesque style in the 11th and 12th centuries, though much expanded in the 17th century. Its badly lit nave is Gothic, though the belfry and façade are from a much later period, the 18th century.

In contrast to the cathedral, tall, modern buildings now line the **Quai Stalingrad,** which opens onto the Vieille d'Arse. On the Place Puget, look for the *atlantes* or caryatids, figures of men used as columns. These interesting figures support a balcony at the Hôtel de Ville and are also included in the façade of the naval museum.

The **Musée Naval** contains many figureheads and ships' models, and is open from 10 a.m. to noon and from 1:30 p.m. to 6 p.m. daily except Tuesdays and holidays, charging adults 6F ($1.37) for admission, children 3F (68¢).

An annex of the museum has been installed in the **Tour Royale,** built by Louis XII in the early 16th century. Over the years it has been a prison. The nautical collection is of passing interest. From June 1 to September 15, hours are from 2 to 6 p.m.; the rest of the year it is open from 3 to 6 p.m., charging adults 4F (91¢) for admission and children 2F (46¢).

You can also tour the **Arsenal Maritime,** where guided excursions of the graving-docks and quays are conducted, leaving between 9 and 11 a.m. and between 2 and 4:30 p.m. Naturally, you tip the guide.

The **Musée d'Art et d'Archéologie** contains both old and contemporary works, its earliest paintings dating from the 13th century. Exhibited are the works of such artists as Fragonard, David, Vuillard, Pieter Breughel, and Van Loo, as well as Egyptian, Greek, and Roman antiquities and relics from prehistoric times. The museum is open from 10 a.m. to noon and from 3 to 6 p.m. daily except Mondays and Wednesdays.

An hour or two before sunset, we'd suggest a drive along **La Corniche du Mont Faron,** a splendid boulevard along the lower slopes of Mont Faron. From this highway you'll have views of the busy port, the town itself, the cliffs, and in the distance the blue Mediterranean.

At Quai Stalingrad you can make arrangements with boatmen (always agree on the price beforehand) to take you on several excursions. The best known is to the **Island of Porquerolles,** a 1¼-hour trip. This is the largest and most westerly of the Hyères Islands. You arrive at the tiny village of Porquerolles, from which the privately owned island takes its name. The island is sparsely inhabited, containing vineyards and much Mediterranean vegetation. If you feel like exploring, you can take a two-hour hike to the **Phare** (lighthouse) and **Calanque de l'Oustau de Diou.** This will take you to the sourthern tip of the island. From there you'll have a panoramic vista over the entire island. On the winding return path, you'll have great views over the cliffs.

FOOD AND LODGING: Frantel, Tour Blanche, Boulevard Amiral-Vence (tel. 24-41-57), is the best hotel at the naval port, even though it's located away from the center, standing as it does at the foot of the cable car that carries passengers up Mont Faron. Here you get excellent accommodations, with all the modern comforts you'd want. The rooms are nicely furnished, both the bedrooms and the public salons, and there are attractive gardens with terraces and a swimming pool. One hundred streamlined accommodations are rented, costing 180F ($41.09) in a single, 235F ($53.65) in a double. The hotel also offers a restaurant with a panoramic view, serving a set meal for 85F ($19.41). The restaurant is closed on Sundays from the first of October until the end of June.

The **Maritima,** 9 rue Gimelli (tel. 92-39-33), lies only a short walk from the railway station and a few minutes from Jardin Alexandre Ier. Its 47 rooms are modestly furnished but well kept and comfortable, costing 70F ($15.98) in a single, 120F ($27.40) in a double. There's no restaurant, but you can order breakfast at 12F ($2.74).

Le Dauphin, 21 bis rue Jean-Jaurès (tel. 93-12-07), serves the best food in Toulon. Henry Vergeloni is an advocate of La Nouvelle Cuisine. He takes many of the regional specialties of Provence, giving them skillful and creative preparations—a gratin of eggplant and zucchini, lamb roasted with olives, a gâteau of chicken livers, a filet of veal in a cream sauce, or sole in a crayfish sauce. Menus are offered at 65F ($14.84), although you are likely to spend 110F ($25.11) ordering à la carte. The restaurant is closed at noon, on Sundays and from June 25 to July 15.

2. Marseille

Bustling Marseille is the second city of France in size but the premier port of the country. A crossroads of world traffic, the city is ancient, founded by Greeks from the city of Phocaea, near present-day Izmir, Turkey, in the sixth century B.C.

The city is a place of unique sounds, smells, and sights. It has seen wars and much destruction, but trade has always been its raison d'être.

Perhaps its most common association is with the national anthem of France, "La Marseillaise." During the Revolution, 500 volunteers marched to Paris, singing this rousing song along the way. The rest is history.

Many visitors never bother to visit the museums, preferring to absorb the unique spirit of the city as reflected on its busy streets and at its sidewalk cafés, particularly those along the main street, **Canebière.** The street, filled with hotels, shops, and restaurants, is filled with sailors of every nation and a wide range of foreigners, especially Algerians. It winds down to **Vieux Port,** dominated by the massive neoclassic forts of **St.-Jean** and **St.-Nicholas.** The port is filled with fishing craft and yachts, and is ringed with seafood restaurants offering that specialty of Marseille, bouillabaisse. The Nazis blew up the old quarter in 1943, destroying the narrow streets and subterranean passages (and the houses of prostitution).

Motorists can continue along to the **Corniche Président-J.-F.-Kennedy,** a promenade running for about three miles along the sea. You pass villas and gardens along the way, and have a good view of the Mediterranean as well.

To the north, the **Port Moderne,** the "gateway to the East," is man-made. Its construction began in 1844, and a century later the Germans destroyed it. Motorboat trips are conducted along the docks.

From **Quai des Belges** at Vieux Port, you can take one of the motorboats on a 20-minute ride to **Château d'If,** the round-trip fare costing 18F ($4.11). Boats leave about every 15 minutes. On the sparsely vegetated island, François I built a fortress to defend Marseille; the place later housing a state prison that sheltered such illustrious guests as Mirabeau. Carvings by Huguenot prisoners can still be seen inside some of the cells. Alexandre Dumas used the Château as a setting for *The Count of Monte Cristo,* although the adventure he invented never took place here. Its most famous association—that with the legendary *Man in the Iron Mask*—is also apocryphal.

A futuristic touch for Marseille is the 17-story **Cité Radieuse,** Boulevard Michelet, an avant-garde housing development and a landmark in modern architecture designed by the late Le Corbusier, the Swiss architect who introduced influential concepts in functional architecture. Built between 1947 and 1952, and also known as Unité d'Habitation, it is considered the first structure of its kind. Its flawed units have been much criticized, but they are credited with ushering in city planning in France.

MUSEUMS, CHURCHES, AND VIEWS: The **Palais Longchamp,** Place Bernex, was built in the era of the Second Empire. With its spectacular fountain and colonnade, it is one of the most scenic oases in Marseille. In back is a **Jardin Zoologique** with an exceptional collection of birds. Housed in a northern wing of the palace is the **Musée des Beaux-Arts,** displaying a vast array of paintings, both foreign and domestic, from the 14th through the 20th centuries. The ground floor exhibits paintings by Monticelli (a 19th-century artist), including his *Les Flamants,* plus works of other lesser-known Provençal artists. The museum also displays works by Corot, Millet, Vuillard, Ingres, David, Courbet, Perugino, Philippe de Champaigne (*The Ascension*), Puget (*The Baptism of Clovis*), and Rubens (*Wild Boar Hunt*). Interesting Dufy cubist landscapes plus a collection of other charming works by that artist are also on display, as is a gallery of sculpture by Pierre Puget (1620-1694). One salon on the second floor is devoted entirely to the works of Honoré Daumier, the French caricaturist and painter who was born in Marseille in 1808. Displayed are satiric lithographs and 36 bronzes of the series known as *The Parliamentarians.* The museum is open from 10 a.m. to noon and from 2 to 6 p.m. (closed Tuesdays and Wednesday mornings). Admission is 4F ($91¢), free on Sunday mornings. Students are admitted free at all times.

Nearby is the **Musée Grobet-Ladabié,** 140 Boulevard Longchamp, housed in a mansion and containing what was once a private collection, bequeathed to the city in 1923. It possesses exquisite Louis XV and Louis XVI furniture, as well as an outstanding collection of medieval Burgundian and Provençal sculpture, including capitals from Notre-Dames-des-Doms at Avignon. A music salon displays antique violins, bagpipes, and guitars, plus a letter from Beethoven. Paintings on view are by Monticelli, Corot, and Daubigny. Other exhibits include 17th-century Gobelins tapestries, 15th-century German and Flemish paintings, and 17th-century faïence. The museum is open from 10 a.m. to noon and from 2 to 6:30 p.m. (closes on Tuesdays and Wednesday mornings). Admission: 3F (68¢). Students are admitted free.

At the **Musée Cantini,** 19 rue Grignan, the temporary exhibitions and works of contemporary art often exceed the permanent collection. Housed in what was once a private mansion of the 17th century, this museum is devoted mainly to the most outstanding examples of Provençal ceramics, including a superb fountain by Leroy and works by Veuve Perrin, who often used fish in his motifs. Opening onto a beautiful courtyard, the museum may be visited from 10 a.m. to noon and from 2 to 6:30 p.m., for an entrance fee of 3F (68¢). Closed Tuesdays and Wednesday mornings.

Musée du Vieux-Marseille, in the Maison Diamantée, rue de la Prison, near the Town Hall, is a historical and folklore museum known for its collection of *santons,* little statuettes made of colored clay representing characters associated with the Nativity. They are traditionally made by a few families living in the outskirts, the models and moulds passed down from generation to generation. The *santons* appear at a traditional fair in December in Marseille. Other exhibits include furniture, pottery, old maps and engravings, 19th-century paintings by Provençal artists, antique costumes, a scale model of Marseille in 1848, and a costume room. The museum is open from 10 a.m. to noon and from 2 to 6:30 p.m., for an admission fee of 3F (68¢). Closed Tuesdays and Wednesday mornings.

Musée des Docks Romains du Lacydon, Place Vivaux, is devoted to the remains of the Roman docks unearthed in the old quarter of town. Some discoveries came to light as a result of the German bombings of the port in World War II. There is an outstanding collection of urns (photos show how undersea divers rescued them), plus fragments of Roman statuary and pottery. Open from 10 a.m. to noon and from 2 to 6 p.m. (closes an hour earlier off-season), it charges an admission of 3F (68¢). Closed Tuesdays and Wednesday mornings.

For a city as ancient as Marseille, antique ecclesiastical monuments are few. However, the seemingly fortified **Basilique St.-Victor** has a crypt that dates from the fifth century, when the church and abbey were founded by St. Cassianus. The crypt, which also reflects work done in the 10th and 11th centuries, may be visited from 10 a.m. to noon and from 3 to 6 p.m. (Sundays, 3 to 6 p.m. only). Admission: 2F (46¢). With its battlemented towers, the present church is from the 11th century. It's reached by going out the Quai de Rive-Neuve (near the Gare du Vieux-Port).

There are two cathedrals on Place de la Major, near Old Marseille. Their domes and cupolas may remind you of Istanbul. The **Ancienne Cathédrale de la Major** dates chiefly from the 12th century, having been built on the ruins of a Temple of Diana. In its left aisle is the Chapel of St. Lazare, in the early Renaissance style. Nearby is a Lucca della Robbia bas-relief. The newer edifice, **Cathédrale de la Major,** was one of the largest churches built in Europe in the 19th century, some 450 feet long. Its interior is adorned with mosaic floors and red-and-white marble banners, and the exterior is in a bastardized Romanesque/Byzantine style.

The landmark **Basilique de Notre-Dame de la Garde,** Place du Colonel-Edon, crowns a limestone rock overlooking the southern side of Vieux-Port. It was built in the Romanesque/Byzantine style popular in the 19th century, and was topped by a 30-foot-high gilded statue of the Virgin. The pilgrimage to this sanctuary dates from 1214. Visitors come here not so much for the church as for the panoramic vista—best seen at sunset—from its terrace. Spread out before you are the city, the islands, and the sea. On the square is a World War II tank, the "Jeanne d'Arc." Motorists can drive to the site, and pedestrians can take bus 60, which runs every half-hour from Vieux-Port. A restaurant serves food from 7 a.m. to 8 p.m. in summer.

Another vantage point for those seeking a panoramic view is **Parc du Pharo,** a promontory facing the entrance to Vieux-Port. You stand on a terrace overlooking **Château du Pharo,** built by Napoleon III for his empress, Eugénie. Fort Saint-Jean and the old and new cathedrals can be seen clearly.

HOTELS: In general expect a poor lot. We'll deal with the exceptions, beginning in—

The Upper Bracket

Sofitel Marseille Vieux-Port, Boulevard Charles-Livon (tel. 52-90-19), lies in a strategic position at the old port, all of its 222 bedrooms overlooking this active and colorful harbor. The hotel, at the Palais du Pharo, is the most outstanding choice for overnighting in Marseille. It is recently built, wisely taking advantage of its memorable location. All of its well-furnished bedrooms are individually air-conditioned and soundproofed, providing streamlined comfort and such amenities as TV, radio, direct-dial telephone, and, of course, a well-equipped private bath. Many of the modern chambers have private balconies where you can order breakfast at a garden table under a sun umbrella, with a view of the sea. Singles range in price from 265F ($60.50) to 420F ($95.89); doubles, from 310F ($70.77) to 500F ($114.15). The hotel has two restaurants: Les Trois Forts which has an ambitious menu and a panoramic situation, charging from 120F ($27.40) to 230F ($50.23) for a meal, and Le Jardin, with an open terrace overlooking the sea and near the pool, where a good menu is presented for 66F ($15.08). There's a wood-paneled, rather spacious bar, La Dérade, though you might prefer the other "bar panoramique," l'Astrolabe, which serves delicious cocktails.

Le Grand Hôtel Noailles, 66 La Canebière (tel. 54-08-48), has for years been one of the port's leading hotels. In its renovated bedchambers you have a choice of modern or traditional styles. The main lounge is stylish, with ornate bas-relief walls, a draped Campagne ceiling, and Louis XV-style furniture, although the wood-paneled bar, Le Samoa, with its Windsor chairs, old prints, and guns, seems more English. The single rate begins at 140F ($31.96) with bath; a double with one large bed costs from 170F ($38.81) with bath; twins are 190F ($43.38) to 370F ($84.47) with bath in the new section. The hotel's restaurant, Via Veneto, serves both a continental cuisine and Mediterranean specialties.

Le Concorde Prado, 11 Avenue de Mazargues (tel. 76-51-11), is the pacesetter in hotel design in Marseille. Created in the '70s, it is located away from the harbor in the newer section. Zippy bronze elevators take you to six floors of gadget-mad accommodations. Beside your bed is a master electronic-control panel. Bedrooms are often done in vivid plaids. You have a choice of rooms opening onto the busy street or else the garden with its reflection ponds. Singles go for 220F ($50.23); doubles are 240F ($54.79).

The Middle Bracket

Beauvau, 4 rue Beauvau (tel. 33-62-00), is right at the old port, a most convenient hotel for tourists. The lobby pays allegiance to Provence, but emphasis is on the good-size rooms, renting for 190F ($43.38) to 250F ($57.08) in a single, increasing to anywhere from 220F ($50.23) to 300F ($68.49) in a double.

Résidence du Vieux-Port, 18 Quai du Port (tel. 90-79-11), is a hotel where you should request a portside bedroom with balcony. This modern nine-story hotel is highly recommended to those who want to be in the swim of Marseille waterfront life. It's entered through a sidewalk café and bar, leading to a miniature lobby and reception area. Every room has a bath or shower. A single rents for 130F ($29.68), a double for 150F ($34.26). Families may want to consider one of the apartments, housing as many as five persons, for a peak rate of 265F ($60.50).

Grand Hôtel Genève, 3 bis rue de la Reine-Élisabeth (tel. 90-51-42), provides a great deal of style and comfort for the francs charged. It's not far from the old port, and even though it doesn't have a restaurant, all of its bedchambers have accompanying private baths. Singles rent for 110F ($25.11), and doubles go for 210F ($47.94). There are radios and individual refreshment bars in each bedroom. The attendant downstairs will direct you to a nearby public garage if you're driving.

The Budget Range
   La Résidence Bompard, 2 rue des Flots-Bleus (tel. 52-10-93), sits on a cliff at the outskirts of Marseille, a 10-minute drive along the coastal road, Corniche Président-J.-F.-Kennedy. A group of buildings surround a large courtyard and garden. The Antoun family welcomes guests, charging them 135F ($30.82) in a single, 155F ($35.39) in a double. All rooms have TVs. The Bompard is best for motorists seeking a tranquil retreat.
   Le Corbusier, 280 Boulevard Michelet (tel. 77-18-15), occupies space in the apartment complex designed by the world-famed architect and described previously. On the fourth floor, the hotel opens onto a club-style living room with a bar and dining room. The 25 rooms, based on designs by Le Corbusier, were originally intended for students. Hence they are small and simply furnished with functional pieces. Singles with showers rent for 80F ($18.26); doubles with showers, 110F ($25.11); and doubles with bath (private toilet), 125F ($28.54).

READERS' HOTEL SELECTIONS: "We decided to splurge a bit and stayed at an absolutely delightful place overlooking the port, Hôtel Belle-Vue, 34 Quai du Port (tel. 91-11-64). The balcony of our room had a fantastic view of the harbor and the Basilique de Notre-Dame de la Garde. Quai du Port is the street of the final chase in *The French Connection II.* Double rooms at the hotel range in price from 85F ($19.41) to 100F ($22.83). It's generally full, so it's wise to reserve ahead. If you really want to relive *The French Connection II,* walk from the railway station to the port, through the Arab quarter as depicted in the film" (Sandy and David Ahl, Morristown, N.J.).... "We ran into a nice hotel strategically located about midway between Toulon and Marseille, with frequent bus connections to Marseille. It's the Hôtel Le-Petit-Nice (tel. 26-22-91), Piage des Lecques, St.-Cyr-sur-Mer, about a quarter of a mile from the through highway. It's a quiet, clean place, and stands across the street from the beach. The hotel is modern, with excellent food. The owner speaks English. A double without bath is about 60F ($13.70); with bath and private toilet (as well as a balcony), 135F ($30.82). With shower only, the charge is 75F ($17.12) in a double, these tariffs excluding breakfast which is 11F ($2.51) extra. Dinner, including wine and tip, is about 75F ($17.12)" (Karel F. Zaluda, Skokie, Ill.).

RESTAURANTS: At restaurants in Marseille you'll eat some of the best seafood in Europe.

The Upper Bracket
   New-York, 7 Quai Belges (tel. 33-60-98), is where you can dine elegantly by picture windows overlooking the port. Table settings, service, and the general atmosphere match the distinguished cuisine, prepared to the exacting demands of Monsieur Venturini. Of course, both specialties here are brimming with fish—bouillabaisse marseillaise at 120F ($27.40) and bourride Provençale at 110F ($25.11). Exceptional is suprême de sole au champagne at 85F ($19.41), plus 15% service. An appropriate ending would be cherries jubilee at 30F ($6.85). Expect to pay at least 185F ($42.24) for a complete meal. Closed Sundays.
   Jambon de Parme, 67 rue La-Palud (tel. 54-37-98), is the leading Italian restaurant in Marseille. The cuisine of Monsieur Givravalli is both classic and

original. The wine list is extensive, the atmosphere exquisite, the decor a Louis XVI style, although complemented by framed engravings of Italian towns. The fried scampi and the homemade ravioli are as good as any you'd find in the homeland. The veal kidneys in a Marsala sauce are exceptional. Or perhaps you'll try tortellini in a smooth cream sauce or filets of capon cooked with champagne. The soup with truffles is a masterpiece, and the sweetbreads with cream is yet another skillfully prepared dish. Naturally, there is ham from Parma. Expect to pay from 130F ($29.68) to 170F ($38.81) for a memorable meal. The restaurant is closed on Sunday nights and Mondays and from mid-July to mid-August.

Calypso, 3 rue des Catalans (tel. 52-64-00), is a fish restaurant right on the water where the old port meets the sea. Guests go here not only for the cuisine of Mme. Paguet but to watch ships and sunsets. As at the New-York, the two featured main dishes are bouillabaisse and bourride Provençale—both served here with lobster, which increases the price tremendously. You might, as an alternative, order fish soup first, then follow with loup (Mediterranean sea bass) with fennel. The homemade pastries are excellent. Expect to pay at least 150F ($34.26) for a complete meal. Closed Sundays, Mondays, and in August.

The Middle Bracket

Au Pescadou, 19 Place Castellane (tel. 78-36-01), is one of the finest restaurants in Marseille, specializing in *fruits de mer et de poissons,* although it's nowhere near the harbor. Rather, it's on a circular traffic hub in the downtown section close to the freeway to Nice. Overlooking a fountain and an obelisk, it can be identified by its open oyster stands on the sidewalk. Nearly all forms of crustaceans, including many indigenous only to Mediterranean waters, are here. A savory opener might be mussels stuffed with almonds. But for the greatest variety of tidbits, order the "hors d'oeuvres of the fisherman." Main dish specialties include bouillabaisse de Marseille and gigot de lotte (a monkfish stewed slowly in a cream sauce with fresh vegetables). Try also the coquilles Saint Jacques aux morilles (scallops cooked in a mushroom sauce). You'll have to pay from 100F ($22.83) to 150F ($34.26), depending on the choice of fish. Closed in July and August.

Michel-Brasserie des Catalans, 6 rue Catalans (tel. 52-64-22), serves absolutely the finest bouillabaisse in Marseille. The Visciano family who run this place will also tempt you with their bourride, another type of fish stew with an ailloli sauce. This is one of the best old-time restaurants in the port city, serving about everything that creeps and crawls through the Mediterranean. There are few mysterious sauces and fancy dishes. Rather, the culinary emphasis is on the flavor of the seafood. Spices are added discreetly. A meal averages around 200F ($45.66). The location is agreeable, too, at one side of the old port, just beyond the Parc du Pharo. The restaurant is closed on Tuesdays, Wednesdays, and in July.

The Budget Range

Le Petit Caveau, 4 rue Mazagran (tel. 48-72-79), consistently serves one of the finest low-cost meals in Marseille. On a cobblestoned street about a 10-minute walk from the harbor, it will give you a complete meal for only 28F ($6.39). Italian dishes are featured. We recently enjoyed cannelloni, followed by beef pizzaiola with risotto, then fresh fruit for dessert. Closed July 14 to August 16 and Sundays.

Le Tonkin, 54 rue Vacon (tel. 33-71-20), is recommendable as a change of pace. It serves some of the finest Vietnamese dishes in the city, and, if you like your food hot and spicy, you can dine here for about 32F ($7.31), which makes it one of the most reasonably priced meals you are likely to find in the port. The restaurant, run by a polite, helpful staff, lies about three minutes from the old port, just off the rue Paris. It is closed on Mondays and in July.

Living on the outskirts

At Gémenos, 14½ miles from Marseille, the **Relais de la Magdeleine** (tel. 82-20-05) is a fine country mansion at the foot of the Sainte-Baume mountain range. Surrounded by park and woodland, the hotel lies near the spot where Mary Magdalene is believed to have ended her days. (Her grotto has long been the site of veneration.) The *relais* offers only 17 rooms, costing from 140F ($31.96) in a single, from 220F ($50.23) in a double. The inn has fine architectural details and appropriate furnishings. Over the fireplace in the entry hall is an old carving of the Virgin and Child, and throughout the mansion are portraits and scenic paintings. The drawing room has fine antiques intermixed with traditional reproductions. The rooms, which contain private baths, are appealingly furnished in a personal way. The *relais* also serves good meals in the 110F ($25.11) to 160F ($36.53) range, including such regional dishes as lamb cooked with the herbs of Provence and filet of sole Beau Manoir. There are a good-size swimming pool and several tennis courts at your disposal. The inn is open from mid-March until the end of October.

3. Aix-en-Provence

The celebrated son of this old capital city of Provence, Paul Cézanne, immortalized the countryside nearby. Just as he saw it, Montagne Sainte-Victoire still looms over the town, although a string of highrises have now cropped up on the landscape. The most charming center in all of Provence, the faded university town was once a seat of aristocracy, its streets walked by counts and kings. Aix still contains much of the atmosphere acquired in the 17th and 18th centuries before losing its prestige to Marseille, 20 miles to the south. The highlight of the season is its annual **music festival,** one of the best on the continent.

Its **Cours Mirabeau,** the main street, is one of the most beautiful in Europe. Plane trees stretch their leafy branches across the top to shade it from the hot Provençal sun like an umbrella, filtering the light into shadows that play on the rococo fountains below. On one side are shops and sidewalk cafés, on the other richly embellished sandstone hôtels (mansions) from the 17th and 18th centuries. Honoring Mirabeau, the French revolutionist and statesman, the street begins at the 1860 landmark fountain on **Place de la Libération.**

The **cathedral,** on Place de l'Université, is dedicated to Christ under the title Saint Sauveur, i.e., Holy Savior or Redeemer. Its Baptistery dates from the fourth and fifth centuries, but the architectural complex as a whole has seen many additions. Decorating its Gothic nave is a series of Flemish tapestries depicting scenes from the life of Christ and the Virgin. They were commissioned in 1511, originally for Canterbury Cathedral. The cathedral contains a brilliant triptych, *The Burning Bush,* a work of Nicolas Froment in the 15th century. One side depicts the Virgin and Child, the other Good King René and his second wife, Jeanne de Laval.

Nearby in a former archbishop's palace is the **Museum of Tapestries,** on the Place des Martyrs de la Résistance. Lining its white and gilded walls are tapestries made at the old factory at Beauvais de Natoire-le-Prince. Berain designed a fanciful and charming series of six, rich in amusing details, depicting such scenes as musicians and Bacchanalian revelry. Charging 5F ($1.14) admission, the museum is open from 10 a.m. to noon and 2 to 5 p.m. It is closed Tuesdays and in January.

Up the rue Cardinale is the **Museum of Beaux-Arts,** also called Musée Granet-Palais-de-Matte. The salon devoted to "Cézanne and His Friends." The museum owns mainly sketches, a not very typical collection of the great artist's work, Matisse contributed a nude in 1941. Housed in the former center of the Knights of Malta, the fine-arts gallery contains work by Van Dyck, Van Loo, portraits by Pierre and François Puget, Rigaud, Monticelli, and (the most interesting of all) a *Jupiter and Thetis* by Ingres. Ingres also did an 1807 portrait of the museum's namesake, François Marius Granet (1775-1849), showing him to be remarkably handsome. Granet's own works abound. Yet another salon contains Celto-Ligurian statuary discovered at the Roman town of Entrement. Hours are from 10 a.m. till noon and from 2 to 8 p.m. The museum shuts down at 5 p.m. from November to March 1; on Saturdays and Sundays it closes at 6 p.m. in summer, 5 p.m. in winter. Admission costs 8F ($1.83). Closed Tuesdays.

Outside town, at 9 Avenue Paul-Cézanne, is the **Atelier de Cézanne,** the studio of the painter who is considered the major forerunner of cubism. Surrounded by a wall, the house was restored by American admirers. Repaired again in 1970, it remains much as Cézanne left it in 1906, "his coat hanging on the wall, his easel with an unfinished picture waiting for a touch of the master's brush," as Thomas R. Parker wrote. The atelier may be visited from 10 a.m. to noon and from 2 to 5 p.m. daily except Tuesdays, holidays, and the month of November; from June to September, it remains open till 6 p.m. Admission: 4F (91¢).

Even more recommended than a visit to Cézanne's studio, and much more than the Musée Granet's Cézanne mementos, is a walk along the **Route de Cézanne,** D17, which winds eastward through the Provençal countryside toward the Sainte-Victoire. From the east end of the Cours Mirabeau, take rue du Maréchal-Joffre across Boulevard Carnot to Boulevard des Poilus, which becomes Avenue des Écoles-Militaires and finally D17. The stretch between Aix and the hamlet of Le Tholonet is full of twists and turns where Cézanne often set up his easel to paint. Although it is a longish walk (3½ miles), it is possible to do it at a leisurely pace by starting early in the morning. Le Tholonet has a café or two where you can rest and refresh yourself while waiting for one of the frequent buses back to Aix.

READER'S FOOTNOTE TO HISTORY: "The 17th and 18th centuries have indeed left a permanent stamp on the architecture and atmosphere of Aix, somewhat obscuring its earlier Roman and medieval history. Founded in 122 B.C. by a Roman general, Caius Sextius Calvinus, who named it Aquae Sextiae in his own honor, Aix was successively a Roman military outpost and then civilian colony, administrative capital of a province of the later Roman Empire, seat of an archdiocese, official residence of the medieval counts of Provence and thus its political capital. Even after Provence's union with France, Aix remained, until the French Revolution, a judicial and administrative headquarters. Aix's composite history is best reflected in its cathedral and in the City Hall bell tower just down the street: both incorporate architectural elements spanning the centuries from the Roman era to the 17th century. The cathedral's small and charming Romanesque cloister provides a tranquil oasis to visit" (Patricia Hagan, New Haven, Conn.).

LODGINGS: You have a good choice of hotels in Aix.

Upper-Bracket Living

Hôtel P.L.M. Le Pigonnet, Avenue du Pigonnet par route de Marseille (tel. 59-02-90), at the edge of town, is a Provençal villa surrounded by verdant gardens. Behind the salmon-pink façade is an interior with provincial furnishings, either antiques or reproductions. There are 50 rooms, all with private baths or showers. Singles cost 220F ($50.23), with doubles going for 300F ($68.49). In the garden, you can have your breakfast set on a table under the colonnaded veranda overlooking the courtyard reflection pool. There is also a swimming pool. You can dine in summer under the deep shade trees or else at the hotel's restaurant, Le Patio, which offers both a table d'hôte and an à la carte menu.

Paul Cézanne, 40 Avenue Victor Hugo (tel. 26-34-73). The modest façade on a street of sycamores hardly prepares you for such a distinguished interior. Created by its director-proprietor, Georges Delorme, it is a special and tasteful world. Using antiques from his own house, he made every room distinguished. Your accommodation might have mahogany Victorian furniture, Louis XVI-style chairs, marble-topped fruitwood chests, gilt mirrors, and oil paintings. Handmade and hand-painted tiles make the baths consistently attractive. Singles range from 175F ($39.95) to 220F ($50.23); doubles, 200F ($45.66) to 300F ($68.49). A recently built new floor is reserved for the most attractive deluxe rooms and suites of the hotel, costing from 320F ($73.06) to 400F ($91.32). A small breakfast room with opera-red chairs opens onto a rear courtyard. The lounge seems more like a private sitting room than the lobby of a hotel. Closed in January.

The Middle Bracket

Résidence Rotonde, 15 Avenue Belges (tel. 26-29-88), is a contemporary hotel right in the heart of town. It has gone to considerable trouble to create a streamlined accommodation in which all is bright and cheerful. Occupying part of a residential building, it has an open spiral cantilevered staircase, with lots of molded plastic and chrome furniture. Doubles with twin beds and a complete bath are 180F ($41.09). Singles rent for 110F ($25.11). Tax and service are included in these prices, but breakfast is extra. The rooms are jazzy, with ornate patterned wallpaper, balloon lamps, Nordic-style beds, and, novelty of novelties, a wardrobe set on a revolving pole. There is no restaurant—just the red-and-gold breakfast room.

READERS' HOTEL SELECTIONS: "Hôtel Cardinal, 24 rue Cardinal (tel. 26-14-49), is immaculate, decorated with antiques and French provincial furniture, and the service is excellent. A room with twin beds and an attached private bath with shower and tub is 99F ($22.60) a night. Breakfast is 10.50F ($2.39) extra. The hotel is centrally located, within walking distance of all places of interest in Aix" (Esther Kirschner, Huntington Woods, Mich.). . . . "We stayed at the Hôtel de France, 63 rue Espariat, in a double with two beds and full bath for 110F ($25.11). Optional breakfast costs about 9.50F ($2.16) extra. Furniture and decor is tasteful modern, and the owner is friendly. Be warned—ask for a room off the street if possible, as rue Espariat appears to be the nighttime rendezvous point for the motorcycle and scooter set of Aix" (Patricia Hagan, New Haven, Conn.).

WHERE TO DINE: La Rotonde, Place Jeanne-d'Arc (tel. 26-01-95), enjoys the most central position in the heart of Aix-en-Provence. It is a white-shuttered villa with a canopy over its garden terrace. Its tables, covered with colored cloths, are placed to give the diners a view of the fountain in the middle of the roundabout. The chef offers a number of excellently prepared appetizers, including such regional specialties as soupe au pistou (a garlic-flavored vegetable soup popular along the Riviera), 85F ($19.41). You might prefer half a dozen escargots à la Provençale at 20F ($4.57). The main-dish fish specialty is a bourride des pêcheurs Provençaux, 45F ($10.27). In grilled meats the chef excels, particularly his chateaubriand grillé with a béarnaise sauce, costing 120F ($27.40) for two persons. He also does a superb beef Wellington, 150F ($34.26) for two persons. Homemade ice creams are the dessert feature at 15F ($3.43) per serving.

If you're seeking something less expensive, try the **Brasserie Royale,** 17 Cours Mirabeau (tel. 26-01-63), renovated in the modern style. Right on this plane-tree-lined boulevard, it is brassy and animated, invariably crowded at mealtimes. With not the least bit of pretense, it dispenses excellent regional cooking at low prices. There are two interior dining rooms, but most habitués gravitate to the glass-enclosed section on the sidewalk under the canopy. Informality reigns, the bustling waiters offering you set dinners for 30F ($6.85) and 50F ($11.42), plus 15% for service. On our most recent rounds we sampled a more expensive meal, five whole courses, at 82F ($18.72), including asparagus vinaigrette, then escargots (snails) in garlic butter, veal with mushrooms, a selection of country cheese, and dessert (juicy little strawberries with freshly whipped cream). You pay extra for your beverage.

There are two very good inexpensive restaurants in Aix. At **Le Carillon,** 10 rue Portalis, for 30F ($6.85), you can order four complete courses, featuring a selection of hors d'oeuvres, an omelett, gratin dauphinois, a small steak, cheese or fruit. This restaurant is popular with workmen.

And at **Hacienda,** 7 rue Mérindol, a restaurant in the typical Spanish style, for only 29F ($6.62) you can order a complete meal, including a small carafe of wine. The cooking is simple, as would be expected, but the price is right.

READERS' RESTAURANT SELECTIONS: "An excellent restaurant is **La Vieille Auberge,** 63 rue Espariat (tel. 27-90-15). We had a fairly deluxe meal for the price of 30F ($6.85). Wine was extra, of course. La Vieille Auberge is truly old and the dining room is dominated by a magnificent fireplace. Our waiter was attentive, and conversed with us in English" (Esther Kirschner, Huntington Woods, Mich.). . . . "**Chez Nénette,** at the beginning of rue Aude near rue Espariat and Place d'Albertas, has a 28F ($6.39) menu, wine extra, and an extensive and inexpensive à la carte menu costing from 18F ($4.11) to 30F ($6.85) for the plat du jour. It is a small, unpretentious family operation with long tables, paper tablecloths, and paper napkins. You're served large portions of very good French cooking at more than reasonable prices. Try the boeuf en daube, a savory Provençal-style beef stew. This restaurant is popular with Aix's student population and fills up quickly. If you're not fond of crowds in close quarters, go early" (Patricia Hagan, New Haven, Conn.).

FOOD AND LODGING IN THE ENVIRONS: At Beaurecueil, 15 minutes south of Aix-en-Provence, toward Nice, **Le Logis du Maistre** (tel. 28-90-09) is ideal for those who want a charming three-star hotel set against the backdrop of a Cézanne landscape. This rendezvous spot is at the foot of the Montagne Sainte-Victoire. Here under a tiled roof a sophisticated crowd of Riviera people gather for receptions, marriages, cocktails, and seminars. You'll find a dozen beautifully furnished rooms in the provincial style, with immaculately tiled baths. In the evening you and your dog (if you brought him along) can sit in front of the fireplace in the lounge with its soft lighting and stucco walls. The next morning you can go for a swim in the large pool set on the inn's beautiful grounds. A single pays 160F ($36.53) and a double goes for 190F ($43.38).

For dinner, you can walk next door to the *Relais Ste. Victoire* (tel. 28-91-34), where a set menu is offered for 60F ($13.70). The restaurant doesn't serve on Sunday nights or for Tuesday lunch. From November to March it is also closed on Mondays. The inn rents 15 modestly furnished rooms costing 48F ($10.96) in a single, from 75F ($17.12) in a double. No guests are accepted in October.

At Meyrargues, 10 miles from Aix-en-Provence, the **Château de Meyrargues** (tel. 57-50-32) provides historical and architectural fascination, as well as a semiluxurious accommodation in a 12th-century château which was converted into a hostelry in 1952. It is considered one of France's oldest fortified sites, having been a Celtic outpost in 600 B.C. The entrance is imposing, with a reflection pool and twin high stone towers flanking a sweeping, curved, balustraded set of steps. From its terraces and rooms you can enjoy a panoramic view of the Valley of the Durance. Once the lords of Les Baux lived here, but now it is the domain of Monsieur Drouillet, who has turned it into an award-winning holiday retreat. So far, he has restored only 14 bedchambers, which vary in size, view, and decoration, although all of them are handsomely furnished, in keeping with the tradition of the château. You'll pay from 145F ($33.10) in a single, from 230F ($52.51) in a double. In high season demipension is obligatory, costing from 200F ($45.66) to 235F ($53.65) per person daily. Meals are served in the grand and lofty lounge which was the receiving hall of the nobility who once occupied the château. In fair weather meals are served on a covered terrace. The château is closed from December to February, and the restaurant is closed on Sunday nights and for Monday lunch off-season. Otherwise, nonresidents can order meals in the 85F ($19.41) to 160F ($36.53) range.

4. Vauvenargues

In forbidding hill country 10 miles east of Aix-en-Provence the body of Pablo Picasso is buried. Here in this village of mainly retired persons, the artist, who died at 91, painted his *Luncheon on the Grass* and did a portrait in red and black of his wife, the former Jacqueline Roque.

The ocher stone walls of the turreted **château** date from the 14th century, though the buildings in the square style are from the 16th and 17th centuries. On top of the Louis XIII porch is the coat of arms of the Vauvenargues family, who were the owners from 1790 until 1947. The castle was purchased by antique dealers, who sold all the furnishings. Picasso acquired it in 1958 and lived here between 1959 and 1961. Visitors aren't allowed inside, although they can see some of his sculptures in the castle park.

FOOD AND LODGING: **Chez Jo** (tel. 24-92-02) is a typical French bistro, the only one on the short main street. There you can have a tourist menu for 40F ($9.13).

About the only place to stay is **Au Moulin de Provence** (tel. 24-93-11), which offers only a dozen rooms, renting for 45F ($10.27) for the lone single, 110F ($25.11) in a double. It also serves a good meal for 40F ($9.13), although you can order more elaborate repasts for 70F ($15.98) to 100F ($22.83). The English-speaking host, Magdeleine Yemenidjian, is always pleased to take care of Americans. Closed January 4 to February 28.

5. Arles

It's been called "the soul of Provence." Art lovers, archaeologists, and historians are attracted to this town on the Rhône. Many of its scenes, painted so luminously by Van Gogh in his declining years, remain to delight. The great Dutch painter left Paris for Arles in 1888. It was in that same year that he cut off part of his left ear. But he was to paint some of his most celebrated works in the Provençal town, including *Starry Night, The Bridge at Arles, Sunflowers,* and *L'Arlésienne.*

The Greeks are said to have founded Arles in the sixth century B.C. Julius Caesar established a Roman colony here in 46 B.C. Under Roman rule Arles prospered. Constantine the Great named it the second capital in his empire in 306 A.D., when it was known as "the little Rome of the Gauls." It wasn't until 1481 that Arles, 55 miles northwest of Marseille by road, was incorporated into France.

SEEING THE SIGHTS: The town is full of monuments from Roman times. It's best to go to the local Tourist Office and purchase a comprehensive ticket for 15F ($3.42), allowing you to visit all the major sights.

All the museums (except Museon Arlaten) are open from 8:30 a.m. to noon and from 2 to 7 p.m., May 1 to September 30. In spring and autumn they close at 5:30 p.m., at 4:30 p.m. in winter.

The general vicinity of the old Roman forum is now occupied by the **Place du Forum,** shaded by plane trees. Once Van Gogh's "Café du Nuit" stood on this square. Two columns in the Corinthian style and pediment fragments from a temple can be viewed at the corner of the Hôtel Nord-Pinus.

South of this square lies the **Place de la République,** the principal plaza of Arles. A blue porphyry obelisk some 50 feet high dominates this square. On the north is the impressive **Hôtel de Ville,** the town hall from 1673, built to Mansart's plans. It is surmounted by a Renaissance belfry.

On the east side of the square is the **Church of St. Trophime,** noted for its 12th-century portal, one of the finest achievements of the sourthern Romanesque style. In the pediment the figure of Christ is surrounded by the symbols of the evangelists. Frederick Barbarossa was crowned king of Arles on this site in 1178. The cloisters are built in both the Gothic and Romanesque styles and are noted for their medieval carvings. For special expositions the price of admission is 4F (91¢), dropping to 3F (68¢) at other times.

Opposite the main portal is the **Museum of Pagan Art,** housed in the **Church of St. Anne,** dating from 1602. It contains a museum of Roman sarcophagi, a collection of Roman relics, including four large mosaics and a colossal statue of Augustus, plus Etruscan pottery, altars, and prehistoric finds.

The **Museum of Christian Art,** entered on the rue Balze, is considered one of the finest lapidary museums in Europe. Displayed in the chapel of a Jesuit college dating from 1654 is a collection of marble sarcophagi from the fourth and fifth centuries. Many are intricately designed, although headless. Some of them depict scenes from the life of Christ. A charming, but badly mutilated tombstone depicts children gathering olives. Some fragments of medieval sculpture from the Abbey of Montmajour are also on view. Notable is a complete set of coins struck at Arles and dating from the days of Constantine the Great (313-314).

Adjoining but entered on the rue de la République is the **Museon Arlaten,** the name written in the old Provençal style. It was founded by Frédéric Mistral, the Provençal poet and leader of a movement to establish modern Provençal as a literary language. The museum was founded with the money he received with his Nobel Prize for literature in 1904. As a setting he selected the former Hôtel Laval-Castellane of the 16th century. Collections illustrate the everyday life of Provence. In reality, it's a folklore museum, with regional costumes, portraits, fans, furniture (much of it black walnut), dolls, a salon of music, and one room devoted entirely to mementos of Mistral himself: Among its curiosities is a letter (in French, no less) from Theodore Roosevelt to Mistral, bearing a letterhead from the "Maison Blanche" in Washington, D.C. The museum is open daily except Monday from 9 a.m. till noon and from 2 to 6 p.m., charging 4F (91¢) for admission. From October to February its morning hours are the same, but its afternoon hours are 2 to 4 (2 to 5 in March).

The two great classical monuments of Arles are the **Roman Theater** and the **Amphitheater.** Little remains of the original theater, as it was later used as a quarry. It dates from the first century A.D. and was begun by Augustus. Only two marble Corinthian columns remain. Now rebuilt, the theater is the setting for an annual drama festival in July. Incidentally, the famous *Venus of Arles* was discovered here in 1651. The theater is open daily from 8:30 a.m. till noon and from 2 to 7 p.m. (closes earlier off-season). Take the rue de la Calade from the town hall. Nearby, the Amphitheater, or arena, was built in the first century A.D., seating almost 25,000 spectators screaming for blood. When aficionados gather for to-the-death bullfights here in summer, history seems to repeat itself. The arena is a huge, colonnaded, oval-shaped structure. The government warns you to visit the old monument at your own risk. Three towers remain (scale one for the view) from medieval times, when the amphitheater was turned into a fortress. Hours are from 9 a.m. till noon and from 2 to 6 p.m. daily.

Perhaps the most memorable sight in Arles is **Alyscamps,** once a necropolis established by the Romans, converted into a Christian burial ground in the fourth century. As the latter it became a setting for legends in epic poetry in medieval times. Today it's long and leafy, lined with poplars as well as what remains of the sarcophagi. Arlésiens escape here to enjoy a respite from the heat.

One final ancient monument is the **Baths of Constantine,** near the banks of the Rhône. The thermae are all that remain of a once-grand imperial palace. It's been stripped till just the walls remain. Entrance is on Rue Dominique Maisto. Visiting hours are the same as at the Amphitheater.

Nearby, with an entrance on rue du Grand-Prieuré, is the **Musée Réattu,** containing the collection of Jacques Réattu (1760-1833), a local painter. His private collection was donated to form the museum, but it's been updated by more recent works, including etchings and drawings by Picasso, some depicting bullfighting scenes. Other works are by Gauguin, Dufy, Utrillo, and Léger. The Arras tapestries from the 16th century are distinguished. One entire salon is devoted to Henri Rousseau. The museum is in the former Commandery of the Order of Malta from the 15th century.

UPPER-BRACKET LIVING AND DINING: Jules César, Boulevard des Lices (tel. 96-49-76), in the center of Arles, was a Carmelite convent in the 17th century. But it's been skillfully adapted, emerging as a stately, gracious country-town hotel. In spite of the noisy neighborhood, most of the rooms are quiet, as they face the unspoiled cloister. The decoration is luxurious, as most of the rooms are furnished with antique Provençal pieces. The owner attends auctions throughout the countryside, always adding new pieces to complete the harmony. Prices range from 160F ($36.53) in a single to as high as 375F ($85.61) in a double. You wake up in the morning to enjoy the scent of roses, the songs of the birds.

The hotel's restaurant, **Lou Marques,** is the best in Arles. Tables for alfresco dining are on the front terrace. The food, served by waitresses in costume, is extremely fresh. The set menus begin at 75F ($17.12). On the à la carte menu, we'd recommend foie gras frais de canard at 75F ($17.12); turbotin à la Provençale at 100F ($22.83); baudroie (an extremely ugly angelfish or frogfish that's simply delicious) à l'aïgo, 75F ($17.12); and poulet à l'ailet au thym at 58F ($13.24). The restaurant is open all year.

BUDGET LIVING AND DINING: Hôtel d'Arlatan, 26 rue du Sauvage (tel. 96-36-75), was created from the former residence of the counts d'Arlatan de Beaumont. It's been managed by the same family since 1920. The hotel was built in the 15th century on the ruins of an old palace ordered by Constantine. You can still admire a wall dating from the fourth century. The rooms are furnished with authentic Provençal antiques, the walls covered with tapestries in the Louis XV and Louis XVI styles. Hopefully, your bedroom will overlook the garden with its palms, pond, and climbing vines. Rooms are available with hot-and-cold running water or complete private baths. Singles go for 90F ($20.55) to 155F ($35.39); doubles, 160F ($36.53) to 220F ($50.23).

Calendal, Place Pomme (tel. 96-11-89), stands on a quiet square not far from the arena. Behind the building is a shadowy garden with laurels. The Calendal is a family affair, where you're welcomed with a smile by Madame and Monsieur Fieloux. The rooms are furnished in the Provençal style, some of the pieces authentic antiques. Flowery wallpaper is popular here. Most of the accommodations have a view of the garden with its ivy-covered trees. All rooms are equipped with showers and toilets, the singles costing 80F ($18.26), the doubles 140F ($31.96). In the lobby are a few curious showcases containing stuffed birds.

Hôtel du Cloître, 18 rue de Cloître (tel. 96-29-50), is right in the St. Trophime cloister—hence its name. It's a modest rural hotel, with rustic rooms facing the yard. A bathless single goes for 55F ($12.56), a double with either private shower or bath runs from a low of 85F ($19.41) to a peak of 150F ($34.26). The dining room overflows into a private garden, where tables are set against the old convent wall. The food is simple, honest, family-style cooking. Food is served only to residents; for half pension the charge ranges from 120F ($27.40) to 150F ($34.26) per person daily.

Brasserie Provençale, 38 rue Amédée-Pichot (tel. 96-37-59), a half-block from the Rhône, is warmly Provençal and doesn't strain too hard to be regionally interesting. Red-and-white cloths and country-style reed-seated chairs are placed in front of a 10-foot-wide fireplace with a raised hearth. The woman owner grills steaks and fish over burning root chunks. A set menu is offered for 32F ($7.31). The cooking is simple and standard but good. The brasserie shuts down from June 2 to July 1 and on Sundays.

READERS' HOTEL SELECTIONS: "The Hôtel Terminus and Van Gogh, Place Lamartine (tel. 96-12-32), is exceedingly nice—very clean and hospitable, and a bargain for two adults and a 12-year-old in a warm room with bath and toilet (breakfast delicious and service compris). Rates range from 45F ($10.27) to 70F ($15.98). Breakfast is 9F ($2.05) per person" (Dr. K. R. Niswander, Lausanne, Switzerland). . . . "I would like to recommend Hôtel Réattu, 3 rue Réattu (tel. 96-46-57). It is economical, costing from 65F ($14.84) to 88F ($20.09) per night for two twin beds in a room that was spotlessly clean, sweet smelling or 'no smelling,' colorful, and attractive. The shared toilet was as clean as the bedrooms. The hotel is on a narrow, quiet street, near some of the most interesting sights in Arles. Not least, the woman who manages the hotel is courteous, helpful, and gracious" (Rebecca Williams, Greenbelt, Md.).

6. Fontvieille

Just 6½ miles from Arles, this sleepy little town in the foothills of the Alpilles enjoys associations with the 19th-century novelist Alphonse Daudet. Writing his first novel at the age of 14, this handsome young man in time became a member of the inner circle of the fashionable, bohemian literary figures of his day. In 1884 he published the novel *Sappho.* He later became a patron of the young Marcel Proust. Daudet died in 1897, his health having been undermined by venereal disease.

On top of a small hill stands the mill which provided the title for Daudet's *Lettres de Mon Moulin.* The mill has been restored and turned into a little museum with memorabilia of the novelist.

In the town also is one of the most tranquil oases in Provence, which we shall now visit.

FOOD AND LODGING: La Régalido (tel. 97-70-17) is a member of the Relais de Campagne. A charming auberge, it is like a Provençal manor, tastefully decorated by the Michel family. It was converted from a 17th-century olive mill. Only 11 rooms are offered, at prices ranging from 200F ($45.66) in a single to 375F ($85.61) in the most expensive double. Staying here is somewhat like being the guest in a private home of a very fine and friendly family. Bedrooms are named after spices and herbs that grow in the region.

The Michel son is a maître-cuisinier, following in the footsteps of his father, who was one of the leading chefs of France. In the dining room you're impressed by the flower arrangements from Madame Michel's garden. The young chef specializes in the following dishes: gratin de moules aux épinards (tender Mediterranean mussels with spinach), pièce d'agneau en casserole et à l'ail (lamb delicately flavored with garlic and herbs), and canard farci au poivre vert (stuffed duckling with green peppercorns). A meal will cost anywhere from 120F ($27.40) to 170F ($38.81).

The inn shuts down from November 30 to January 15, and the restaurant doesn't serve on Mondays.

7. Les Baux

Cardinal de Richelieu called this village a nesting place for eagles. In its lonely position high on a windswept plateau overlooking the southern flank of the Alpilles, Les Baux is a mere ghost of its former self. Once it was the citadel of the powerful seigneurs of Les Baux, who ruled with an iron fist and sent their conquering armies as far as Albania. The town lies just 50 miles north of Marseille and the Mediterranean, nestling in a valley surrounded by mysterious, shadowy rock formations.

Hewn out of rock, Les Baux became a mighty fortress. In medieval times troubadours from all over Europe came this way. Here they recited western Europe's earliest known venacular poetry.

Eventually, the notorious "Scourge of Provence" ruled Les Baux, sending his men throughout the land to kidnap people. If no one would pay ransom for one of his victims, the poor wretch was forced to walk a gangplank to death over the cliff's edge.

Fed up with the rebellions against Louis XIII in 1632, Richelieu commanded his armies to destroy Les Baux. Today the castle and ramparts are a mere shell, though remains of great Renaissance mansions are to be seen. The population of Les Baux, which once numbered in the thousands, is reduced to only a few hardy souls who endure the fierce sun of summer and the harsh winds of winter.

FOOD AND LODGING: In this unlikely setting you come upon one of the greatest restaurants in all of France, which is, of course, in—

The Upper Bracket

L'Oustau de Beaumanière (tel. 97-33-07). Raymond Thuilier, now in his 80s, describes his restaurant as a "memory of the past," where excellent cuisine and unparalleled attention go hand-in-hand. With a twinkle in his bright eyes, he adds, "That isn't very modern, is it?" L'Oustau de Beaumanière certainly isn't modern, but it is the finest country restaurant in France. Its noble vaulted rooms are a delight to visit, whether you are simply stopping for a meal or staying overnight in the guest rooms, furnished in the elegance of the same era.

The dining rooms are decorated with a rare mixture of paintings, tapestries, and antique furniture. In winter, you can dine in front of a fireplace, into which are thrown gnarled trunks of olive trees. The cuisine is in the same rich tradition as the environment in which it is served. Only the finest meat and produce go into Monsieur Thuilier's dishes. He is as concerned with what goes into the creations of his culinary art as he is with the art itself. Because he doesn't trust many sources of supply, he has standing orders with special farmers near Lyon for eggs and poultry; he has a yearly contract with one producer for lamb. Lamb is the specialty at La Beaumanière, and it's best served as the gigot d'agneau au poivre vert (saddle of lamb cooked with green pepper kernels). Monsieur Thuilier raises his own artichokes for his popular mousseline d'artichauts. Pork for excellent pâtés and ham dishes come from the pigs raised on his own estate.

The menu is not large, but its listings include some very elegant dishes. For an appetizer, try the mousse de grives (made from the breast of thrush). An excellent seafood dish is loup (bass) en croûte. Desserts include no less than three kinds of soufflé, of which the orange is favored. A repast here will cost at least 175F ($39.95) per person. There is almost no ceiling on what you can pay; it depends on your selection of wine.

When Monsieur Thuilier opened his restaurant after the war, it grew into a cult center for a true gourmet adventure. From a small, cozy restaurant it developed a country-club atmosphere, complete with a swimming pool, without losing any of its original courtesy.

The cost of staying here depends on where you are housed. Beaumanière itself has rooms in a 16th-century stone battlement, furnished in the style of that era. The Résidence, on the other hand, is an old Provençal manor house, and the Manoir evokes the 17th century in its grandiose setting and tranquil climate. For two persons, for a minimum of three nights, the demi-pension rate is from 700F ($159.81) per day.

The Medium-Priced Range

Bautezar (tel. 97-32-09). You reach this hotel by going down some steps, arriving in a large vaulted dining room with a medieval touch. The furniture is in the rustic Provençal style. The walls of white stone are decorated with cloth tapestries. At the end of the dining room is a terrace with a view of Val d'Enfer. The rooms, containing private baths, are carefully decorated in the Louis XVI style. A double, depending on its view, ranges from 145F ($33.10) to 220F ($50.23). The food is also good, a set meal costing 65F ($14.84) to 100F ($22.83). It is closed from January 10 to February 28 and on Wednesdays.

The Budget Range

Hostellerie de la Reine-Jeanne (tel. 97-32-06) is the best bargain at Les Baux. The view is even better than at l'Oustau de Baumanière. You enter a typical provincial French bistro where you're welcomed by Monsieur Guilbard, standing behind a bar of waxed wood. The inn is immaculate, the atmosphere warm. In the bedrooms, everything has been carefully considered with the guest's comfort in mind. Three of the rooms have their own terraces with a view of the valley. The most expensive room—the blue room at 120F ($27.40)—is beamed, its walls covered with a flower paper in shades of blue. Less expensive doubles go for 75F ($17.12). Two set menus cost 50F ($11.42) and 60F ($13.70).

8. St.-Rémy-de-Provence

Nostradamus, the French physician and astrologer whose reputation is enjoying great vogue today, was born here in 1503. In 1922 Gertrude Stein and Alice B. Toklas found St.-Rémy after "wandering around everywhere a bit," Ms. Stein wrote to Cocteau.

But mainly St.-Rémy, eight miles north of Les Baux, is associated with Van Gogh. He commited himself to an asylum here in 1889 after cutting off his ear. Between moods of despair, he painted such works as *Olive Trees* and *Cypresses.*

The cloisters he made famous in his paintings can be visited today at the ancient Monastery of St.-Paul-de-Mausolé, dating from the 12th century and still run as an asylum. The cloisters are open from 9 a.m. till noon and from 2 to 6 p.m. Finding the cell to which this genius was confined requires some genius on your part. The monastery/asylum is about 1½ kilometers from the town center.

Further out, south of the town, is Glanum, a Gallo-Roman city (follow the road signs to "Les Antiques"). Its historical monuments include an Arc Municipal, a triumphal arch dating from the time of Julius Caesar, and a cenotaph called the Mausolée des Jules. Garlanded with sculptured fruits and flowers, the arch dates from 20 B.C. and is the oldest in Provence. It is also decorated with bas-reliefs representing chained prisoners. The mausoleum was raised to honor the grandsons of Augustus and is the only monument of its type to have survived. In the area are entire streets and the foundations of private residences from this first-century A.D. town. Some remains are from an even earlier Gallo-Greek town dating from the second century B.C. Glanum is open from 10 a.m. to noon and from 2 to 6 p.m., charging 4F (91¢) admission.

FOOD AND LODGING: Les Antiques, Avenue Pasteur (tel. 92-03-02) is a great old villa which has been in the same Provençal family for 150 years. This medium-priced hotel is in a beautiful seven-acre park with a swimming pool. A magnificent reception lounge, with marble floors and tapestries on the walls, opens onto several salons. Everything is rich and stylish; the furnishings are pure Napoleon III. The winter dining room is in the former library, although in summer guests dine in what used to be the Orangerie. The rooms are handsomely furnished, usually in pastels or a delicate rose. Some of the accommodations are in a private pavilion in the modern style, with direct access to the garden. Rooms range from 160F ($36.53) to 220F ($50.23). Full pension runs from 275F ($62.78) to 325F ($74.20) per person daily. Guests are lodged at the villa from April 1 until the end of October.

Les Arts, 30 Boulevard Victor-Hugo (tel. 92-08-50), is in the heart of town, on the main boulevard. The restaurant is attractive, with a colorful, shady terrace. You get plenty of Provençal atmosphere here and a lot of charm. From the terrace you enter a *salle de bistrot* with a beamed ceiling and a wooden bar. Sylvio, the boss, has filled the walls with paintings by regional artists. From the bar you enter a long and narrow dining room with beams and pictures, many signed by famous names. The rooms upstairs are pleasantly decorated, many in the Provençal style, with beams and flowery fabrics. A single with bath costs 55F ($12.56); doubles with bath or shower are 120F ($27.40) to 140F ($31.96). The restaurant offers a set menu for 65F ($14.84). The Sunday dinner at 95F ($21.69) is gargantuan. Specialties include frog legs Provençale, duck with orange sauce, bouillabaisse upon request, and trout meunière. An à la carte meal is likely to hit the 100F ($22.83) mark. The establishment is closed on Wednesday from mid-October to mid-March and also from November 1 to 8 and from February 1 to 20.

Auberge de la Graïo, 12 Boulevard Mirabeau (tel. 92-15-33). We discovered this one rainy night by accident and have been among its admirers ever since. The owners are among the nicest people in town. Dr. Alex Norman, of the Hospital for Joint Diseases and Medical Center in New York, characterized them well: "Madame Roulin (charming) and Monsieur Herrenschmidt (looks like a salty seaman)." These fine people combine their individual skills to shelter guests comfortably in one of their clean, pleasant, and beautifully furnished rooms, only 10 in all, each with private bath. Their vine-covered old Provençal auberge is warmly decorated, and guests often sit out in the flower-filled garden under umbrella tables, or retreat into the cozy dining room where on nippy nights a fire glows. The least expensive singles cost 90F ($20.55), the tariff peaking at 140F ($31.96) in the best doubles. The food is first-rate, the cost of a meal ranging from 50F ($11.42) to 90F ($20.55). The restaurant is closed on Mondays.

9. Avignon

In the 14th century Avignon was the capital of Christendom; the popes lived here during what the Romans called "the Babylonian Captivity." The legacy left by that "court of splendor and magnificence" makes Avignon even today one of the most interesting and beautiful of Europe's cities of the Middle Ages. It lies 66 miles northwest of Marseille.

SEEING THE SIGHTS: Even more famous than the papal residency is the ditty *"Sur le pont d'Avignon, l'on y danse, l'on y danse,"* echoing through every French nursery and around the world. Ironically, Pont St.-Bénézet was too narrow for the *danse* of the rhyme. It was all you could do to pass, much less dance. Spanning the Rhône and connecting Avignon with Villeneuve-lès-Avignon, the bridge is now only a fragmented ruin. It may be visited from 8 a.m. to noon and from 2 to 7 p.m., till 6 p.m. off-season, for an admission of 2F (46¢). According to legend, the bridge was inspired by a vision a shepherd boy had while tending his flock in the field. His name was Bénézet. Actually, the bridge was built between 1117 and 1185, and it suffered various disasters from that time on. Finally, in 1669, half of the bridge toppled into the river. Leading citizens have—as yet unsuccessfully—tried to get the government to repair it.

Dominating the city is the **Palais des Papes.** In 1309 a sick man, nearing the end of his life, arrived in Avignon. His name was Clement V, and he was the leader of the Christian world. Lodged as a guest of the Dominicans, he died in the spring of 1314 and was succeeded by John XXII. The new pope, unlike the popes of Rome, lived modestly in the Episcopal Palace. When Benedict XII took over, he greatly enlarged and rebuilt the palace. Clement VI, who followed, built an even more elaborate extension called the New Palace. After Innocent VI and Urban V, Pope Gregory XI did no building. Inspired by Catherine of Siena, he was intent upon returning the papacy to Rome, and he succeeded. In all, seven popes had reigned at Avignon. Under them art and culture flourished, as did vice. Prostitutes blatantly went about peddling their wares in front of fat cardinals, rich merchants were robbed, and innocent pilgrims from the hinterlands were brutally tricked and swindled.

From 1378, during the Great Schism, one pope ruled in Avignon, another in Rome. The reign of the pope and the "anti-pope" continued, one following the other, until both rulers were dismissed by the election of Martin V in 1417. Rome continued to rule Avignon until it was joined to France at the time of the French Revolution.

The ramparts (still standing) around Avignon were built in the 14th century, and are characterized by their machicolated battlements, turrets, and old gates. Olga Carlisle called them "squat and very thick, like huge children's blocks placed there according to a playful up-and-down design." The fortifications were rebuilt in the 19th century by Viollet-le-Duc, the busiest man in France, who restored Notre-Dame in Paris and the fortified walls at Carcassonne.

The fortress Palais de Papes stands on a hill. Guided tours lasting 50 minutes leave on the half-hour from 8 a.m. until 6 p.m., costing 10F ($2.28) for adults, 5F ($1.14) for students. In the off-season the hours are from 9 to 4. No tours are conducted between noon and 2 p.m.

The **Musée du Petit Palais,** Place du Palais des Papes, is housed in a palace dating from the 14th and 15th centuries. It contains an important collection of paintings from the Italian schools from the 13th through the 16th centuries, including works from Florence, Venice, Sienna, and Lombardy. In addition, salons display paintings done in Avignon in the 15th century. Several salons are devoted to Roman and Gothic sculptures from Avignon. The museum is open from 10 a.m. to noon and from 2 to 6 p.m., charging 5F ($1.14) for admission. It is closed on Tuesdays.

The long tour of the papal palace is somewhat dull and monotonous, as the rooms, for the most part, have long been stripped of their finery. The exception is **St. John's Chapel,** with a series of frescoes depicting scenes from the life of John the Baptist and St. John the Evangelist, painted by Matteo Giovanetti in 1346 and 1348. In a secular vein, the **Stag Room**—the study of Clement VI—was frescoed in 1343 with hunting scenes. Added under the same Clement VI, who had a taste for grandeur, the **Great Audience Hall** contains frescoes of the prophets, also attributed to Giovanetti and painted in 1352.

Nearby is the **Cathedral of Notre-Dame** dating from the 12th century and containing the flamboyant Gothic tomb of John XXII, who died at the age of 90. Benedict XII is also buried there. Crowning the top is a gilded statue of the Virgin from the 19th century. From the cathedral, you can enter the **Promenade du Rocher des Doms,** strolling through its garden and enjoying the view across the Rhône to Villeneuve-lès-Avignon.

The **Calvet Museum,** 67 rue Joseph-Vernet, is housed in an 18th-century mansion with a courtyard praised by Stendhal. It shelters a collection of prehistoric stoneware, Greek marbles, and many paintings. Our favorite oil is by Brueghel (the Elder), *Le Cortège Nuptial (The Bridal Procession).* Look for Bosch's *Adoration of the Magi* as well. Other works of art are by Vasari, Mignard, Joseph Vernet, David, Manet, Delacroix, Daumier, Vuillard, Rouault, Renoir, Sisley, Cézanne, Dufy, Utrillo (his *Lapin Agile*), Toulouse-Lautrec, and Seurat. A good collection of contemporary painting, including works by Modigliani and Vasarely, is also displayed. The museum is open from 9 a.m. to noon and from 2 to 6 p.m., charging 5F ($1.14) for admission. Closed Tuesdays.

An annex of the Musée Calvet, the **Musée Lapidaire,** is entered at 18 rue de la République. In a Jesuit church dating from the 17th century it displays a fine and important collection of sculptures from the Gallo-Roman time through the Gothic era. It is open from 9 a.m. to noon and from 2 to 6 p.m. There is no charge for admission. The museum is closed on Tuesdays.

The modern world is impinging on Avignon, but across the Rhône at **Villeneuve-lès-Avignon** the Middle Ages slumber on. When the popes lived in exile at Avignon, wealthy cardinals built palaces or *livrées* across the river. Many tourists prefer to live or dine there rather than in Avignon (see our recommendations set forth below). However, even if you're staying at Avignon or just passing through, you'll want to visit Villeneuve, especially to see its **Hospice,** or Carthusian monastery of the Val de Bénédiction, in the heart of town. It is open daily except Tuesdays from 9 a.m. to 11:30 a.m. and from 2 to 6 p.m. (off-season, it is open from 10 to 11:30 a.m. and from 2 to 5 p.m.), charging 6F ($1.37) if you wish to visit its museum. Inside, a remarkable *Coronation of the Virgin* by Enguerrand Charonton is enshrined. Painted in 1453, the masterpiece contains a fringed bottom that is Bosch-like in its horror, representing the denizens of hell.

Crowning the town is **Fort St.-André,** found in 1360 by Jean-le-Bon to serve as a symbol of might to the pontifical powers across the river. The Abbey of St. André, now owned privately, was installed in the 18th century. You can visit the formal garden encircling the mansion. The mood here is tranquil, with an aviary of fantail pigeons, a rose-trellis colonnade, fountains, and flowers. Charging 3F (68¢) for admission, the grounds are open April 1 to September 20, 10 a.m. to 12:30 p.m. and 3 to 7:30 p.m.; October 1 to March 31, 10 a.m. to noon and 2 to 5 p.m.

Try to visit the **Church of Notre-Dame,** founded in 1333 by Cardinal Arnaud de Via, in the center of the hamlet. Its proudest possession is a 14th-century "Virgin of Ivory," considered one of the great French art treasures.

UPPER-BRACKET LIVING IN AVIGNON: Europe, 12 Place Grillon (tel. 82-66-92), was built originally in 1580 as a palace for the Marquis of Gravezon, but it has been a hotel since 1799. You enter through a courtyard, where tables are set in warmer months. The interior has a remarkable collection of antiques acquired by the hotel's distinguished owner, M. J. Valat. Whether you go into the grand hall or any of the salons, you'll find tastefully arranged antiques and decorative accessories, such as Aubusson tapestries, Empire consoles, gilt-framed paintings, and an especially fine assortment of Directoire pieces. Equally impressive is the dining room, with its fine fireplace, although the courtyard is more festive. The bedrooms are also tasteful, with handsome decorations and period furnishings. Most of the doubles, with a large bed and a full bath, rent for 320F ($73.06), although a few "Directoire doubles" with shower go for

220F ($50.23). A set meal is offered for 80F ($18.26), plus 15% service. You can also order à la carte.

Sofitel Avignon, Avignon Nord (autoroute 7) (tel. 31-16-43), lies on the N542, about an eight-minute drive to the Palais des Papes on the *voie expresse.* The position allows for more expansive living. Surrounding the hotel is a swimming pool with a little refreshment bar, plus tennis courts. The 100 bedrooms, half of which are twins, are attractively conceived, with basic built-in units, private baths, air conditioning, and soundprooofing. Singles range in price from 225F ($51.38) to 310F ($70.77); doubles, 300F ($68.49) to 350F ($79.91).

For meals, Le Majoral serves either regional specialties or fast food, at prices ranging from 90F ($20.55) to 160F ($36.53). Adjoining is an attractive bar, Le Fustier.

Cité des Papes, 1 rue Jean-Vilar (tel. 86-22-45), is a pleasantly modern hotel in the center of Avignon, hugging close to its namesake, the Palais des Papes. Its rooms are newly furnished in a streamlined, contemporary vein, and each of the 62 chambers has an accompanying private bath. Singles go for 165F ($37.68), and doubles cost 220F ($50.23). Breakfast at 16F ($3.65) is the only meal served.

THE BUDGET HOTELS: Le Midi, 55 rue de la République (tel. 81-08-76), boasts a slick modern front and glassed-in lobby. The remodeling has been gradual, but successful. Half of the accommodations have been furnished in a contemporary mode, the others with reproductions of provincial pieces. All are neat and clean, appropriate for an overnight stay. The most expensive doubles, with private bath, rent for 150F ($34.26), although bathless singles cost only 60F ($13.70), these prices including service and tax. A continental breakfast is the only meal served, at 11F ($2.51) per person.

Hôtel d'Angleterre, 29 Boulevard Raspail (tel. 86-34-31). The entry opens onto a large lobby with a tiled floor. From the lobby, you go into a little sitting room where the walls are covered with rose-and-gray tapestry. The hotel has no particular originality, although all is clean and pleasant. The walls of the bedrooms are covered with florid paper, the furniture is in the functional style. The baths are tiled, the colors harmonized with those of the bedrooms. A single with basin rents for 55F ($12.56), increasing to 65F ($14.84) with complete bath. Doubles cost from 72F ($16.44) to 120F ($27.40).

Hôtel Le Jaquemart, 3 rue Félicien-David (tel. 86-34-71), is similar to the d'Angleterre, but even more modest. Bedrooms are modern, clean, and comfortable. The walls are covered with flowery tapestries. Singles with basin cost 62F ($14.15); doubles begin at 75F ($17.12), rising to 125F ($28.54), depending on the plumbing. Service, taxes, and a continental breakfast are included.

Hôtel de la Bourse, 6 rue des Vieilles-Études (tel. 81-18-65), is also modest but good. Only eight rooms are offered, ranging in price from 55F ($12.56) to 80F ($18.26). Each floor has a shower. In the family-style restaurant the cookery is simple, but tasty. Three set menus are offered—28F ($6.39), 32F ($7.31), and 50F ($11.42).

READER'S HOTEL SELECTION: "At less than 6½ miles from Avignon, just off the Remoulins highway (Route 100), about two miles from the Remoulins Interchange of the Lyon-Nîmes Expressway, stands Hôtel La Fenouillière, 30 Estezargues (tel. 01-01-47). No English is spoken. The bill for a double room with a modern clean bath, plus breakfast, came to 88F ($20.09). La Fenouillière is a motel-type establishment in a rural setting with ample parking" (Karel F. Zaluda, Skokie, Ill.).

THE BEST RESTAURANTS: Hiely-Lucullus, 5 rue République (tel. 81-15-05), is one of the finest restaurants in Provence. It has a long and devoted following of gourmets. A few years ago, *Holiday* magazine honored it as one of the best restaurants in Europe. For our tastebuds, it has remained so, consistently adhering to an excellent cuisine.

The menu is most impressive, and offers a 120F ($27.40) fixed-price menu. To begin your repast, you can try one of four specialties, including la petite marmite du pêcheur, a savory fish soup ringed with black mussels, carrying a 10F ($2.28) supplement. Main-dish specialties include la brochette de ris de veau et rognons (veal sweetbreads and kidneys) carrying a 10F supplement also. The pièce de résistance is l'agneau des Alpilles grillé (Alpine lamb) sur feu de bois, also a 10F supplement. Wines in a carafe include Tavel rosé or Châteauneuf-du-Pape, costing from 25F ($5.71). Closed Mondays off-season, Tuesdays year round, and from June 18 to July 11.

Auberge de France, 28 Place Horloge (tel. 82-58-86), is not only a respected hotel, but is better known for its cuisine, which is among the finest served in Avignon. The location is adjacent to the Palais des Papes, and there is a parking area nearby for your car. Monsieur Tassan serves a honey of a cuisine —stuffed mussels, a gratin of scallops, and his pièce de résistance, which he calls Poragneu Coumtadino (stuffed pork and truffles and a roast leg of lamb). His dessert spectacular is a charlotte with nuts and honey. Regional wines featured include Châteauneuf-du-Pape and Beaumes de Venise. Menus are offered for 65F ($14.84), although you will more likely spend 110F ($25.11) ordering à la carte. The restaurant is closed on Wednesday nights and Fridays, from mid-June to the first week in July, and for most of January. The accommodations at the auberge are reasonably priced, and half the rooms contain private baths. Singles go for 55F ($12.56), and doubles are charged 100F ($22.83). The chambers are pleasant, nicely furnished—no frills.

La Fourchette, 7 rue Racine (tel. 81-47-76), is an enlightened bistro where you can get creative cookery at a low price. There are two dining rooms, one like a summer house, with walls of glass, the other more of a tavern, with oak beams, burlap-covered walls, and hanging converted oil lamps. Creating the ambience are ladderback chairs, checked tablecloths, baskets of fresh cherries (in season), wooden kegs, ceramic jugs, copper urns of trailing plants, cages of birds, even a doll's buggy. For just 50F ($11.42), you can have this sample menu: (1) le flan d'épinard et aubergine aux tomatoes; (2) le foie d'agneau grillé (grilled lamb's liver) with raisin sauce; (3) crêpe de pommes de terre; and (4) a superb dessert, orange pelée à vig purée de frambois (raspberries). The restaurant is closed during parts of the year—best to call ahead.

FOOD AND LODGING IN VILLENEUVE: Le Prieuré, Place du Chapitre (tel. 25-18-20), dates back to 1322 when it was built by a wealthy cardinal—a nephew of the pope—as a palace, or *livrée*. During its checkered career, it was everything from a private school to a boarding house for artists, until it was taken over in 1943 by Monsieur Roger J. Mille, who turned it into an inn, installing modern amenities. The rooms are graced with a remarkable, eclectic group of antiques and accessories, covering a wide range of French decor and history, with harmoniously coordinated fabrics. All of the 30 rooms contain some form of private bath. The least expensive room is 240F ($54.79), although a suite will run as high as 650F ($148.40). Regular double rooms with private baths range in price from 275F ($62.78) to 475F ($108.44).

Country-estate living rooms open one into the other, with lavishly rich furnishings. The rooms are off a maze of gardens overgrown with trees and

seasonal flowers. You dine in front of a huge stone fireplace in the Great Hall
or on the flagstone terrace. Meals are good, but expensive, costing between
130F ($29.68) to 190F ($43.38). The specialty is sole au plat Pétrarque, named
after the Italian poet who spent so much time lambasting the papacy. Le
Prieuré is closed from November 1 to March 1.

La Magnaneraie Hostellerie, 37 rue Camp Bataille (tel. 25-11-11), offers
a hard-to-find combination—a superb cuisine and attractive rooms. Monsieur
and Madame Prayal have brought their homemaking and culinary skills to a
full flowering. This 15th-century villa (which once served as a wine-tasting
center for owners of the surrounding vineyards) has been totally renovated and
furnished with antiques and reproductions. In the high season, March 1 till the
end of October, half pension is required (and desired, as the chef-owner has
been awarded at least eight medals for his cookery). Based on double occupancy, the charge for half board ranges from 180F ($41.09) to 250F ($57.08) per
person daily. The big news is that Monsieur Prayal includes many of the
specialties from his repertoire on his set menus. For nonresidents, he offers set
meals from 85F ($19.41) to 120F ($27.40). If you dine à la carte, expect to pay
from 160F ($36.53) per person. Each bedroom has its own personality, al-
though we prefer 10 with its terrace balcony and bed on a dais, or else 19, on
the top floor, with its view of the old walls of the town. The oldest rooms in
the house, with heavy beamed ceilings, are on the ground floor. Many American guests have arrived for a stay of only one night and have remained for days,
enjoying the good food, the friendly atmosphere, and the restful retreat enhanced by the rear garden and swimming pool. La Magnaneraie is highly
recommendable.

Villeneuve's budget offering is the Hôtel de l'Atelier, 5 rue de la Foire (tel.
25-01-84), a 16th-century village house which has preserved much of its original style. A tiny, two-story, all-purpose central lounge is dominated by a
walk-in stone fireplace. In the sun-pocket rear garden, potted orange and fig
trees grow, the cook picking the first figs to serve with the morning meal. The
inn offers only 17 bedrooms, costing from 100F ($22.83) to 150F ($34.26) in
a double with either a shower or private bath. The accommodations are furnished informally, and are certainly comfortable, tidy, and immaculate. In the
old bourgeois dining room, breakfast is the only meal served.

AFTER DARK: In the evening, you can go to a little nightclub, La Chouette,
8 rue Devaria, where you can hear good jazz on and off between 6 p.m. and
midnight. Drinks are priced at 6F ($1.37).

LIVING ON THE OUTSKIRTS: At Noves, 8½ miles from Avignon, the
Auberge de Noves, out the D28 (tel. 94-19-21), is an elegant hostelry run by
the Lalleman family, who offer 18 modern and attractively decorated rooms.
On its own hilltop park, it seems a cross between a Riviera villa and a Beverly
Hills movie-star mansion of the '20s. When Monsieur and Madame Lalleman
purchased it in 1950, it was a religious retreat. Very painstakingly they set
about to transform it into one of the finest luxury country estates in Provence.
Their bedchambers are furnished with period pieces, and each room has been
individually conceived. Views are exceptional, and a few rooms have their own
sun terrace. A single costs 220F ($50.23); a double, 360F ($82.19) to 420F
($95.89). In high season, two persons can stay here on the demi-pension plan
(obligatory) at a cost going from 700F ($159.81) to 880F ($200.90). It is
imperative to make reservations as far in advance as possible. The food is

among the best served in the province, including such gastronomic specialties as herb-flavored filet d'agneau (lamb), a chicken-liver mousse, superb sole, veal kidneys Printanier, rabbit in a mustard sauce. From the first-class wine cellar come such selections as Châtaeuneuf-du-Pape and Lirac. The auberge is closed from January 10 to February 10.

At Pontet, three miles north on the N7, the **Hostellerie de Cassagne**, route de Vedène (D62) (tel. 31-04-18), might be your best bet for food and lodgings in the Avignon area. It's an enchanting little rustic-style Provence inn with only 14 bedrooms. These are rented for 125F ($28.54) in a single, 260F ($59.34) in a double. The bedchambers have a country look and are provided with all the necessities. The rooms overlook a park with a swimming pool and adjacent tennis courts. Half pension is required in season, at rates ranging from 150F ($34.26) to 190F ($43.38) per person. The cuisine here is exceptionally good. You take your meals in a rustic dining room, or else at a table in the garden. The owner, Monsieur Thomas-Bourgneuf, features such dishes as coquille St. Jacques and petits legumes, loup or turbot, and deviled lamb. Meals go for 70F ($15.98) and up if you'd like to visit just to dine. However, call first for a reservation. The restaurant takes a vacation in January.

10. Gordes

Past typical Provençal vegetation, the winding road leads to Gordes. All around are curious stone huts called *bori*. Some of these *bori* are a thousand years old. Gordes itself is 25 miles from Avignon and 40 miles from the airport at Marseille.

The **castle** dominating the town was built in the 11th century, then later rebuilt during the first half of the 16th. To visit, check with the guard on the right inside the yard. Entrance is 6F ($1.37).

The **Musée Vasarely** is in this imposing Renaissance château. The painter Victor Vasarely is one of the founding fathers of kinetic art. He has a house nearby, and has leased the château from the village for 35 years for a rental of 1F a year. On the first floor are tapestries in brilliant colors. Betraying a surrealist influence, older works are on the second and third floors. In all, the château houses 1500 paintings (not all Vasarely's), of which 800 are permanently displayed. The museum is open daily except Tuesday from 10 a.m. to noon and from 2 to 6 p.m. Admission is 10F ($2.28).

In the neighborhood of Gordes is **Vénasque**, seven miles southeast of Carpentras on the way to Orange. In this village a baptistery dates from the sixth century. Even closer to Gordes is **Sénanque**, on the D15 and D177. The **Abbey of Sénanque** is one of the three Cistercian abbeys of Provence. It was founded in 1148 and remains almost untouched. Summer hours are from 10 a.m. to 12:30 and from 2 to 7 p.m. in July and August; other months, 10 a.m. to noon and 2 to 6 p.m. The entrance fee is about 5F ($1.14), subject to change.

FOOD AND LODGING: La Mayanelle, rue Combe (tel. 72-00-28), is a stone-built patrician mansion, tracing its origins back to the 12th century. It is owned by Monsieur Julien Mayard, who welcomes guests to one of his 10 beautifully furnished and accessorized bedchambers, for which he charges 120F ($27.40) for single occupancy, 160F ($36.53) in a double. It's preferable that you take the demi-pension rate, ranging from 160F ($36.53) to 190F ($43.38) per person. In the vaulted dining room, with its high ceilings, you'll be served such regional specialties as roast guinea fowl, duck with olives, lamb flavored with the herbs of Provence, grilled salmon, and homemade fruit tarts.

If you're visiting only for a meal, you'll find menus at 110F ($25.11) and 140F ($31.96). The entry with its informal terrace, weeping willow, open stone staircase, arched windows, and flower planters makes for an inviting welcome. The small mansion, which overlooks the rolling hills of Vaucluse, is closed for dining on Tuesdays and takes a vacation in January and February, reopening on March 20.

Les Bories (tel. 72-00-51) is about 1½ miles outside Gordes (take D177). It takes its name from those dried stone constructions called *bori*. In this countryside of antiquity, Les Bories blends in with its background, providing a kind of rustic luxury. Near the inn stands the Abbey of Sénanque which dates from the 12th century. Monsieur Rousselet is the chef-owner, and he relies on his spontaneous inspiration in the planning of meals. Although he's a classic cook, he likes innovative dishes as well. He always uses fresh products which he personally selects. His specialties include a croustade of guinea-fowl, an omelet with truffles, an orange soufflé, and nougat ice cream. Meals cost from 90F ($20.55) to 150F ($34.26). There are only two bedrooms with private bath, which are rented for 140F ($31.96) to 170F ($38.81). In fair weather you can dine on a covered terrace with a view. The inn is closed on Wednesdays and in December.

11. Orange

Overlooking the Valley of the Rhône, Orange tempts visitors with: (1) the third-largest triumphal arch extant in Europe, and (2) the best preserved Roman theater in Europe. Of the latter, Louis XIV, who toyed with the idea of moving it to Versailles, said: "It is the finest wall in my kingdom."

In the southern part of town, the theater—le **Théâtre Antique**—dates from the days of Hadrian. Built against a hill, it once seated 8000 spectators in tiered seats divided into three different sections (classes weren't allowed to mix). It is nearly 350 feet long, 125 feet high. Carefully restored, the theater is noted for its fine acoustics, and is used today for outdoor entertainment. In season it is open from 8 a.m. to 7 p.m., charging an admission of 2F (46¢). At the end of July, a drama, dance, and music festival takes place here, called **Les Chorégies d'Orange.** To reach its bureau of information or to inquire about ticket sales, telephone 34-15-52 or 34-24-24.

To the west of the theater once stood one of the biggest temples in Gaul which, combined with a gymnasium and the theater, formed one of the greatest buildings in the empire. Across the street at Place des Frères-Mounet, the **Musée de la Ville** displays fragments excavated in the arena. Your ticket to the ancient theater will also admit you here.

Even older than the theater is the **Arch of Triumph,** which shows some decay but is still fairly well preserved. Built to honor the conquering legions of Caesar, it rises 72 feet and is nearly 70 feet wide. It's composed of a trio of arches held up by Corinthian columns. The sculptural decorations are well preserved. In the Middle Ages it was used as a dungeon for prisoners.

Orange gets its name from the days when it was a dependency of the Dutch House of Orange-Nassau. It lies about 75 miles northwest of Marseille (Avignon is about 16 miles to the south).

Before leaving Orange, head for the hilltop park, the **Colline Saint-Eutrope,** for a view of the surrounding valley with its mulberry plantations.

FOOD AND LODGING: Arène, Place Langes (tel. 34-10-95), overlooks a quiet square with plane trees. The rooms are warm, comfortable, and well furnished, with rich tapestries and attractive bedcovers. The top price of 150F ($34.26) is for a double with bath; for a double with shower and toilet, the tab is 110F ($25.11). The restaurant is the best in town. Monsieur Arène catered to Queen Juliana when she visited. But even if you're not from the House of Orange, you're still treated royally. The food is excellent as well, and you have a choice of two menus. The first one, at 60F ($13.70), offered us at last visit a choice of two homemade pâtés with pickles, followed by a pork chop cooked with tomatoes in the Provençal style, then a homemade sorbet flavored with fresh black currants. The more expensive one goes for 90F ($20.55). With it, we'd suggest you order a bottle of Monsieur Arène's own rosé. The Arène is highly recommended.

On the Outskirts

At Rochegude, 6½ miles from Orange, the **Château de Rochegude** (tel. 04-81-88) is a magnificent turreted castle standing in its own 37 acres of parkland. It goes back to the 11th century, and throughout its centuries it has been added to by its distinguished owners, which have ranged from the pope to the dauphin. Stone-built, at the edge of a hill, it is surrounded by its own vineyards. Because of its location in Provence, it is spread out, not drawn in protectively as it might be if it were in Normandy. There are several sunny terraces for refreshments.

The present owner, Monsieur Galibert, has brought in many 20th-century innovations, although touches of antiquity survive, including a Roman dungeon. The furnishings and decor throughout the hotel are outstanding. Each of the 25 bedrooms is done in a period, such as Napoleon III and Louis XVI. Some rooms have tapestries, some are mirrored, and others are richly adorned with gilt, crystal, and fine carpeting. The bathrooms are deluxe as well. Singles begin at 150F ($34.26), and doubles cost 550F ($125.57). Special features include a marble swimming pool that would have pleased Nero and a tennis court.

Reservations are necessary. The château is open from mid-March until the end of October. Perhaps you'd like to stop for a meal. Prices range from 120F ($27.40) to 170F ($38.81).

We've left the best for last—the food, which is exceptional, as is the service. You can enjoy meals in the stately dining room, surrounded by pots of flowering plants. Specialties include a basil-flavored bass suprême, stuffed quail, tournedos with truffles, and spectacular desserts.

Chapter XIX

THE FRENCH RIVIERA

1. Menton
2. Roquebrune and Cap Martin
3. Monaco
4. Eze and La Turbie
5. Beaulieu
6. St.-Jean and Cap Ferrat
7. Villefranche
8. Nice
9. St.-Paul-de-Vence
10. Vence
11. Cagnes-sur-Mer
12. Biot
13. Antibes and Cap d'Antibes
14. Juan-les-Pins
15. Golfe-Juan and Vallauris
16. Mougins
17. Grasse
18. Cannes
19. La Napoule-Plage
20. St.-Tropez
21. The Riviera After Dark

IT'S BEEN CALLED the world's most exciting stretch of beach. The towns, ports, and hamlets of the Riviera are best approached as if on a safari, going from chic St.-Tropez in the west to sleepy Menton at the Italian frontier, climbing into the hill towns such as St.-Paul-de-Vence when you tire of the sands.

Every habitué has a favorite oasis and will try to convince you of its merits. Some say, "Nice is passé." Others maintain that "Cannes is queen." Still others shun both resorts in favor of Juan-les-Pins, and yet another discriminating crowd would winter only at St.-Jean/Cap Ferrat. If you have a large bankroll, you may prefer Cap d'Antibes, but if money is short, you may find companions at the old port of Villefranche. Truth is, there is no best resort. Each place along the Riviera—Beaulieu by the sea or eagle's-nest Eze—offers its unique flavor and special merits. It's a question of taste, and the French Riviera—Stephen

Liégeard's "Côte d'Azur" ("Azure Coast")—is famous or infamous for catering to every taste.

The coast is steep and rocky in the main, but it's studded with harbors, ports, gambling casinos, and beach resorts. It's a sun-drenched land, with olive groves and vineyards, where everybody from Harold Robbins to Curt Jurgens has a villa. Cactus, eucalyptus, bougainvillea, lemons, almonds, mimosa, wild anemones, oranges, roses, and laurel grow in abundance, at the foot of the last spurs of the Alpine chain.

A trail of modern artists attracted to the brilliant light and the setting of the Côte d'Azur have left a rich heritage: Matisse in his chapel at Vence, Cocteau at Menton and Villefranche, Picasso at Antibes (and seemingly everywhere else!), Léger at Biot, Renoir at Cagnes, and Bonnard at Le Cannet. The best collection of all is at the Maeght Foundation at St.-Paul-de-Vence.

The Riviera's high season used to be winter and spring. Fashion dictated that no one went in the summer. However, with changing tastes, July and August have become the most crowded months, and reservations are imperative. In summer the average temperature is 75 degrees Fahrenheit. In winter the temperature averages around 49 degrees Fahrenheit, particularly in January, when Nice experiences its coldest weather.

In hotels the choice is perhaps the most varied in the world, ranging from a belle époque palace to a stone-built grape-grower's vineyard in the hills. Gourmets go to the Riviera, too. The food, especially fish, tends to be exceptionally good. It also tends to be expensive, though we'll offer many suggestions where you can dine well at reasonable prices. Bouillabaisse, said to have been invented by Venus, is the area's best-known dish. Usually spiny lobster and whiting are the main ingredients, but each chef has his own ideas on the subject. Racasse, a fish found only in the Mediterranean, is invariably put in. One of the best seafood selections, rouget (red mullet) sometimes appears on fancy menus as bécasse de mer (sea woodcock). Yet another is loup (bass) de mer, cooked with fennel, an expensive dish. Aïoli, mayonnaise with a garlic and olive-oil base, is usually served with hors d'oeuvres or boiled fish.

Other specialties include soupe au pistou (vegetable soup with basil), salade Niçoise (likely to include everything, though traditionally it's made with tomatoes, beans, olives, tuna, anchovies, and radishes), pan pagnat (bread cooked in olive oil and served with olives, anchovies, and tomatoes), and ravioli, which needs no introduction.

The **Corniches of the Riviera,** as depicted in countless films, stretch from Nice to Menton. The Alps drop into the Mediterranean, and roads were carved along the way. The lower road, about 20 miles long, is called the **Corniche Inférieure.** Along this road you'll reach the port of Villefranche, the Cap Ferrat peninsula, Beaulieu, and Cap Martin.

Built between World War I and the beginning of World War II, the Middle Road, or **Moyenne Corniche,** 19 miles long, also runs from Nice to Menton. Winding in and out of tunnels and through mountains, it is spectacular. The highlight of the trip is at mountaintop Eze.

Finally, the **Grande Corniche**—the most spectacular of the roads from Nice to Menton—was ordered built on the ancient Aurelian Way by Napoleon in 1806. La Turbie and Le Vistaëro are the principal targets along the 20-mile stretch which reaches an altitude of more than 1600 feet at Col d'Eze.

In this chapter, we'll explore the Riviera beginning in Menton and ending in St. Tropez. But first—

GETTING THERE: The Nice Airport, serving the Côte d'Azur, is the second largest in France. Air France will fly you there from Paris in just one hour and 20 minutes. It's also possible to go by train, the trip from Paris taking 10½ hours on the super-express "Le Mistral." Both first-class Pullman cars and first-class standard carriages are available on this run. The "Train Bleu" (setting of an old Agatha Christie thriller) leaves Paris's Gare de Lyon.

1. Menton

It's Italianate more than French. Right at the border of Italy, Menton marks the eastern frontier of the Côte d'Azur. Its climate, incidentally, is considered the warmest on the Mediterranean coast, a reputation that attracts a large, rather elderly British colony throughout the winter. Menton experiences a foggy day every 10 years, or so they say. And it doesn't have one puddle of posh the way Cannes or Juan-les-Pins does. For that reason, it is sought out and widely praised by its habitués, many of whom are complaining that more and visitors are discovering Menton's charms every year.

According to a local legend, Eve was the first to experience Menton's glorious climate. Expelled from the Garden of Eden along with Adam, she tucked a lemon in her bosom, planting it at Menton because it reminded her of her former stamping ground. The lemons still grow in profusion here, and the fruit of that tree is given a position of honor at the Lemon Festival in February. Actually, the oldest Menton visitor may have arrived 30,000 years ago. He's still around—or at least his skull is—in the Municipal Museum (see below).

Don't be misled by all those "palace-hotels" studding the hills. No longer open to the public, they have been divided and sold as private flats. Many of these turn-of-the-century structures were erected to accommodate elderly Europeans, mainly English and German, who arrived carrying a book written by one Dr. Bennett in which he extolled the joys of living at Menton.

The town used to belong to Monaco, five miles to the west. The Corniches de la Riviera will take you from Nice to Menton, a distance of 21 miles. On the Golfe de la Paix ("Gulf of Peace"), Menton sits on a rocky promontory, dividing the bay into two parts. The fishermen's town, the older part with narrow streets, is in the east; the tourist zone and residential belt is in the west.

Jean Cocteau liked this resort, and today there is a **Musée Jean Cocteau** in a 17th-century fort near the harbor. The museum contains the death portrait of Cocteau sketched by MacAvoy, as well as MacAvoy's portrait of Cocteau in a better day. Some of the artist's memorabilia are here—stunning charcoals and watercolors, ceramics, signed letters, and 21 brightly colored pastels. Two Aubusson tapestries based on cartoons by Cocteau are also on display. The museum is open from 9 a.m. to noon and from 2 to 6 p.m. except Monday and Tuesday.

Cocteau decorated the **Salle des Mariages** at the **Hôtel de Ville**, which is open daily except Sunday from 9 a.m. to noon and 2 to 6 p.m. For 3F (68¢) you'll be admitted to it and to the museum. The frescoes are allegorical, and depict, among other things, the legend of Orpheus and Eurydice.

The **Municipal Museum**, rue Lorédan-Larchey, contains the head of the Grimaldi man, found in 1884 in the Baoussé-Roussé caves. In addition, it has an interesting archaeological and folkloric collection. The museum is closed on Tuesdays.

The **Palais Carnolès**, 3 Avenue de la Madone, contains a collection of 14th-, 16th-, and 17th-century paintings from Italy, Flanders, Holland, and the French schools, as well as an exhibition of modern paintings, including works by Dufy, Valadon, Derain, and Leprin—all of which were acquired by a British subject, Mr. Wakefield-Mori. Acquisitions of modern art are also displayed biannually. The museum is open daily except Mondays and Tuesdays from 10 a.m. to noon and from 3 to 6 p.m. (2 to 5:30 p.m. in winter), charging 3F (68¢) for admission.

HOTELS: Menton, you will notice, contains a number of seedy hotels. The following recommendations, however, are quite acceptable.

The Middle Bracket

Napoléon, 29 Porte de France (tel. 35-89-50), is built on a palm-tree-shaded avenue, and it has its own free-form swimming pool, set in a small garden and stone terrace. Guests unpack, slip into their bikinis, and jump into the pool. Afterward, they meet on the rooftop terrace, enjoying meals in an air-conditioned restaurant, entirely refurbished and redecorated. Furnished with 18th-century English and Italian pieces, the main lounge, with a bar at one side, is really like a large living room.

The bedrooms—40 in all, each with bath, and balcony—are decorated in vivid colors contrasting with mahogany pieces. All the sea-view rooms are air-conditioned, with a clear view over the sea and the old town. The demi-pension rate for two persons ranges from 185F ($42.24) to 215F ($49.09), the latter price for the sea-view units. If you are just stopping by, a luncheon or dinner in the panoramic restaurant on the sixth floor costs 90F ($20.55). The hotel is closed from November 4 to December 16.

Viking, 2 Avenue du Général-de-Gaulle (tel. 35-80-44), brings contemporary Scandinavian comfort and style to the Côte d'Azur. Under Swedish management, the hotel is set back one street from the beach and contains its own small swimming pool. The rooms are designed to take maximum advantage of the sun and air, most of the accommodations having tall, wide glass doors opening onto private balconies.

In season, from mid-June to mid-September, the hotel charges from 150F ($34.26) to 220F ($50.23) in a double, from 130F ($29.68) to 150F ($34.26) in a single, breakfast included. We've rarely encountered such a complicated rate system, the rooms falling into four different categories, based on everything from the position of the afternoon sun to the size of the balconies. In addition, studios with kitchens and refrigerators are available, housing from one to four persons (seven days minimum). On the sixth floor is a sun terrace, and there's a massage unit with a sauna as well, reflecting the Viking's Scandinavian ties.

The Budget Range

Le Dauphin, 28 Avenue du Général-de-Gaulle (tel. 35-76-37), was totally rebuilt in 1967. Just off the beach, its balconies open toward the sea. Of the 30 soundproofed hotel rooms, 25 contain private baths. The decor is uncluttered, with stark-white walls, floral draperies, picture windows, and Louis XVI-style chairs and beds.

A sea-view double with full bath rents for 170F ($38.81), the tariff dropping to 127F ($28.99) for a room with shower and a mountain view. But in a bathless double, the price is only 95F ($21.69). In glistening marble, with gray carpeting, the entry hall is inviting. More popular than the drinking lounge is the raised front terrace overlooking the sea, which comes complete with garden furniture, a fringed canopy, and stone planters of marigolds, geraniums, and

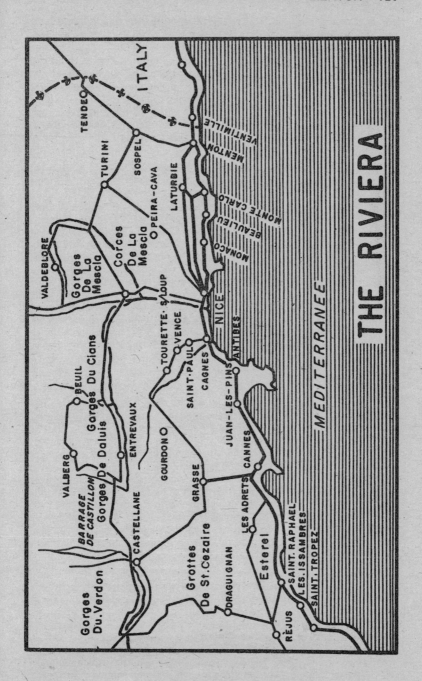

THE RIVIERA

birds of paradise. The chef is of Greek origin—hence the menu offers such specialties as moussaka, at 20F ($4.57).

Rives d'Azur, 30 Avenue du Général-de-Gaulle (tel. 35-72-09), is a large family-type mansion, with rooms furnished in a rather modern idiom. The hotel is on the seafront, facing the promenade near the casino. It's possible to go directly from your room to the sea. In summer, if you stay a minimum of three days you'll be granted a full-pension tariff ranging from 140F ($31.96) to 170F ($38.81) per person, the latter price for a room with bath. Mr. and Mrs. Costa, the owners, offer a choice of two dining rooms, one outside on a terrace. Nonresidents can drop in for a 45F ($10.27) set dinner.

RESTAURANTS: French and Italian cuisine, with emphasis on fish, are on the bill of fare in Menton.

A Medium-Priced Restaurant

Roc Amadour, 1 Square Victoria (tel. 35-75-04), is an especially fine fish restaurant overlooking the port. You dine at tables set under a canopy, where colored lights are turned on at night, adding a bit of gaiety. The chef, Monsieur Martal, offers meals at 58F ($13.24) to 120F ($27.40). You can also order à la carte, sampling such tasty dishes as omelet with herbs, grilled scampi, or trout meunière. Special favorites are confit de canard (duckling) for two. The patron is fiercely proud of how fresh his fish is, and of the delicate spices of the region that add "that magic touch." Depending on your choice of a main dish, expect to spend from 85F ($19.41) to 100F ($22.83) per person here for a complete meal. Closed Thursdays off-season and during most of November.

Budget Dining

La Calanque ("The Creek"), 13 Square Victoria (tel. 35-83-15), is the best for the budget along the port. Tables are set out under shade trees in the fair weather—within full view of the yachts moored in the harbor. Here, in pleasant and colorful surroundings, you can order a complete meal for 40F ($9.13). For just a little more, 55F ($12.56), you'll be fed very well indeed. Service is included. On the à la carte selections, you can allow your tastebuds to wander back and forth across the French and Italian borders. Recommended are the spaghetti Napolitaine, tripe à la Niçoise, soupe de poissons, and fresh sardines (very savory—grilled on charcoal). A specialty of the house is the bouillabaisse at 60F ($13.70). For an à la carte dinner, expect to spend from 70F ($15.98) to 100F ($22.83) per person. If the weather forbids alfresco dining, find a table inside, where it's pleasantly decorated in the style of a provincial inn, with pine paneling, beamed ceilings, and gourds hanging from the rafters. Closed from mid-November to mid-December.

2. Roquebrune and Cap Martin

Roquebrune, along the Grande Corniche, is a charming little mountain-perched village, with vaulted streets. The only one of its kind, the **Château de Roquebrune** was originally a 10th-century Carolingian castle, although the present structure dates in part from the 13th century. Characterized by two square towers, it contains a historical museum. From the towers, you'll have a spectacular view along the coast to Monaco. The castle gates are open every day from 9 a.m. to noon and from 2 to 7 p.m. during July and August. In June and September, hours are 9 a.m. to noon and 2 to 7 p.m.; in winter, 10 a.m.

to noon and 2 to 5 p.m. The château is closed on Fridays. Admission is 3F (68¢) for adults, 2F (46¢) for children under 14.

Three miles west of Menton, Cap Martin is really a satellite of the larger resort. It has long been associated with the wealthy and the famous, ever since the Empress Eugénie wintered here in the 19th century. In time, the resort was honored by the presence of Sir Winston Churchill. Don't go there thinking you'll find a wide, sandy beach. You'll encounter plenty of rocks, against a backdrop of pine and olive trees.

FOOD AND LODGING: Some excellent selections are to be found.

Deluxe Living in the Clouds

Vistaëro, Grande Corniche, Route Nationale 7 (tel. 35-01-50). For years, stopping here at least for a drink has been one of the major thrills in driving along the Grande Corniche. This spectacular hotel and "restaurant panoramique" stands like the figurehead of a ship on the outer ridge of the mountains, running parallel to the coast. Featured in many a Riviera espionage or jewel-theft flick, the "airplane view" of Monaco is spectacular. Equally imposing is the design of the Vistaëro itself. Interlocked by steel girders into the rocks, three levels are cantilevered out into space, so that every room seems to float on cloud nine.

Descending to the lower lounges and rooms, you reach a large reflection pool, edged with rows of colorful subtropical plants and flowers. Ocean-view dining rooms open off that. Even if you don't sleep here, consider a deluxe luncheon or dinner. With that view, the food could be mediocre and people would still come. Actually, it's on a high level—expensive, but worth it. Set menus are offered for 200F ($45.66). On the à la carte, you may prefer to begin your meal with a lobster mousse or perhaps smoked salmon. Fish and meat specialties include sole Vistaëro and carré d'agneau aux herbes (loin of lamb, flavored with herbs, roasted on a spit). An orange tart makes a good dessert. Even if you can't take a meal, stop at the clublike drinking lounge and terrace, selecting a bamboo chair.

To balance the avant-garde architecture, the director decided to furnish the hotel with tastefully traditional pieces. For example, the dining room has classical 18th-century-style chairs. The lounge areas—several of them on different levels—contain Oriental rugs, antique bronze torchiers, and strong colors. The bedrooms are individually conceived, each with a vibrant personality, be it in bamboo, plaid, or floral. Every room has a bath, and, of course, a view. For demi-pension, in season, one person pays anywhere from 350F ($79.91) to 430F ($98.17). The crowning glory of the hotel is its swimming pool, seemingly jutting into space. A supreme holiday retreat!

The Budget Range

Plaza, Avenue de la Gare, Cap Martin (tel. 35-00-06), is a pleasant hotel overlooking the lower part of the cape. The beach at Buze is 1500 feet away. The hotel is well kept, the furniture made of olive and wicker. In a double room with private bath or shower, you can stay here and enjoy full pension for 120F ($27.40) to 140F ($31.96) per person. If you're just passing through, a four-course meal costs only 35F ($7.99); a five-course repast, 50F ($11.42).

Moderate Dining at the Seafront

Hippocampe, 44 Avenue Winston-Churchill (tel. 35-81-91), is the best restaurant along the seafront. Lodged almost below the coastal road, occupying a garden shelf on the sea, it offers a full view of the bay and even the Italian coastline. Made safe by a thick stone wall, a terrace is shaded by five crooked pine trees. The "Sea Horse" is a garden house of stone and glass, persuasively attractive with its tiled roof and scarlet and pink potted geraniums. The host, Jack Teyssier, offers two set meals costing 90F ($20.55) and 170F ($38.81). A la carte specialties include filets de sole en brioche, 60F ($13.70), and coq au vin, 50F ($11.42). Especially favored are the loup (bass) flambé with fennel, 80F ($18.26). The restaurant is closed from January 1 to 20, May 1 to 20, October 1 to 20, and on Monday nights in season. Off-season it shuts down on Monday, Thursday, and Sunday nights.

A Meal in a 16th-Century Setting

Au Grand Inquisiteur, 18 rue du Château (tel. 35-05-37), is a culinary find. It's a miniature restaurant in a two-room cellar (actually an old converted sheep pen) near the top of the medieval mountaintop village of Roquebrune. On the steep, winding road to the château, it is made of rough-cut stone, with large oak beams. Every nook is crammed with bric-a-brac, pewter plates, copper utensils, an old painting of a knight, and a wrought-iron torchère. Taped music contributes to the 16th-century atmosphere. At lunch a cold buffet is offered for 45F ($10.27) plus 15% for service, and for a dinner costing 65F ($14.84) you're given a choice from among five different appetizers, ten different main dishes, and five different desserts. During the season (March to September) a well-known artist will entertain in the evening. The English-speaking owner, who is German, is a gracious host.

3. Monaco

The outspoken Katharine Hepburn called it "a pimple on the chin of the south of France." She wasn't referring to the principality's lack of beauty but rather to the preposterous idea of having a little country, a feudal anomaly, taking up some of the choicest coastline along the Riviera. Hemmed in by France on three sides and facing the Mediterranean, Monaco staunchly maintains its independence. Even Charles de Gaulle couldn't force Prince Rainier to do away with his tax-free policy. As almost everybody in an overburdened world knows by now, the Monégasques do not pay taxes. Part of their country's revenue comes from tourism and gambling.

Monaco, or rather its capital of Monte Carlo, has for a century been a symbol of glamor. Its legend was further enhanced by the marriage in 1956 of the world's most eligible bachelor, Prince Rainier, to an American film star, Grace Kelly. She met the prince when she attended the Cannes Film Festival to promote the Hitchcock movie she made with Cary Grant, *To Catch a Thief*. A daughter, Caroline, was born to the royal couple in 1957; a son, Albert, in 1958; and finally a second daughter, Stephanie, in 1965. The Monégasques welcomed the birth of Caroline, but went wild at the birth of Albert, a male heir. According to a treaty drawn up in 1918, Monaco would become an autonomous state under French protection should the ruling dynasty become extinct.

Monaco became a property of the Grimaldi clan, a Genoese family, as early as 1297. With shifting loyalties, it has maintained something resembling independence ever since. In a fit of impatience, the French annexed it in 1793, but the ruling family recovered it in 1814, although the prince at the time couldn't bear to tear himself away from the pleasures of Paris for "dreary old Monaco."

The second-smallest state in Europe (Vatican City is the tiniest), Monaco consists of the old town, **Monaco-Ville,** sitting on a promontory, the Rock, 200 feet high—the seat of the royal palace and the government building, as well as the famous Oceanographic Museum (see below). On the west of the bay, **La Condamine,** the home of the Monégasques, is at the foot of the old town, forming its harbor and port sector.

Up from the port (walking is steep in Monaco) is **Monte Carlo,** once the playground of European royalty and still the center for the wintering wealthy, the setting for the casino and its gardens and the deluxe hotels, such as the Hôtel de Paris. The fourth part of Monaco, **Fontvieille,** is an industrial suburb, surprisingly neat; but this entire principality is kept tidy.

Ironically, **Monte Carlo Beach** (about which more below), at the far frontier, is on French soil. It attracts a chic, well-heeled crowd, including movie stars in bikinis so perishable they would disappear should they get wet. The resort consists of a freshwater swimming pool, an artificial beach, and a sea-bathing establishment.

No one—just no one—used to go to Monaco in the summer. That has totally changed now—in fact, July and August tend to be so crowded that it's hard to get a room. Further, with the decline of royalty and multimillionaires, Monaco is developing a broader base of tourism (you can live there inexpensively, as you'll see from some of our restaurant and hotel recommendations). You can also lose your shirt. "Suicide Terrace" at the casino though not used as frequently as in the old days, is still a real temptation to many who have foolishly gambled away family fortunes.

Life still focuses around the **casino** (see "Riviera After Dark"), which has been the subject of countless legends and the setting for many films. High drama is played to the fullest here. Depending on the era, you might have seen Mata Hari shooting a tsarist colonel with a jewel-encrusted revolver when he tried to slip his hand inside her brassiere to discover her secrets—military, not mammillary. Before his death, King Farouk, known as "The Swine," used to devour as many as eight roast guinea hens and 50 oysters before losing thousands of dollars at the table. *Chacun à son goût.*

Nine miles east of Nice, Monaco reaches its zenith of excitement at its annual **Rallye** and its **Grand Prix** in May.

SEEING THE SIGHTS: In summer, most visitors—many of whom come over from Nice just for the day—want to see the Italian-style **Palace Grand Apartments** of Prince Rainier and his American-born Princess Grace. You can visit from 9 a.m. to 5 p.m. daily, including Sundays and holidays, from July to September, for an entrance fee of 10F ($2.28) for adults, 5F ($1.14) for children 6 to 14. The ideal time to arrive is 11:50 a.m. to watch the changing of the guard. The palace was originally built in the 13th century, and part of it dates from the Renaissance era.

A major attraction of Monaco is the **Oceanographic Museum and Aquarium,** founded by Prince Albert, the great-grandfather of the present prince. In the main rotunda is a statue of Albert in his favorite costume—that of a sea captain. Displayed are specimens he collected during 30 years of expeditions aboard his oceanographic boats. The Aquarium—one of the finest in Europe—contains more than 75 tanks.

In the oceanography room is exhibited Prince Albert's collection. Some of the exotic life he brought up were unknown species before he captured them. You'll see models of the oceanographic ships aboard which the prince directed his scientific cruises from 1885 to 1914. Prince Albert's last cruises were on board the *Hirondelle II*. The most important part of its laboratory has been preserved and its activities reconstituted as closely as possible. The cupboards contain all the equipment and documentation necessary for a scientific expedition.

On the main floor are skeletons of such specimens as a giant whale that drifted ashore at Pietra Ligure in September 1896, and which is believed to have been the same that was harpooned by the prince in May of that year. The skeleton is remarkable for its healed fractures sustained when a vessel struck the animal drifting asleep on the surface. In addition, underwater movies are continuously shown in the lecture room. The museum is open daily June 1 to September 30 from 9 a.m. to 7 p.m. (at 9:30 a.m. from October 1 to May 31). Entrance fee: 16F ($3.65), 8F ($1.83) for children 6 to 16.

The **Monaco Zoo** (du Centre d'Acclimation Zoologique de Monaco) contains a large and varied collection of animals (mostly monkeys), and, once there, you can look out over Cap d'Ail and the water from the vantage point of a belvedere. From July 1 to September 30, it is open daily from 10 a.m. to noon and from 1:30 to 5 p.m., charging 10F ($2.28) for adults and 5F ($1.14) for children. Off-season it is open 2 to 6 except Tuesdays and Fridays. On Sundays and holidays, its hours are from 10 a.m. to noon and from 2 to 6 p.m.

There's also an interesting **Musée du Souvenir Napoléonien** which can be visited from July 1 to September 30 from 9:30 a.m. to noon and from 2 to 6:30 p.m. for an admission of 8F ($1.83) for adults and 4F (91¢) for children. Off-season its hours are daily except Mondays from 9 to 11 a.m. and from 2 to 5:30 p.m.

Finally, you may want to visit the **Jardin Exotique** ("Exotic Garden"), built on the side of a rock and known for its collection of cacti. You can also explore the **Grottos** in this garden, as well as a **Museum of Prehistoric Anthropology.** They are open daily, including Sundays, from June to September from 9 a.m. to 7 p.m.; admission is 10F ($2.28) for adults, 4F (91¢) for children 6 to 14. From October to May, the hours are from 9 a.m. to noon and from 2 to 6 p.m. From here, the view of the principality is splendid.

HOTELS: In accommodations, the attention focuses on—

The Monte Carlo Deluxe Trio

Hôtel de Paris, Place de Casino (tel. 50-80-80), is a Rolls-Royce-and-caviar experience in a prime position, right on the main plaza of Monte Carlo, opposite the casino. The ornate façade of the Paris sets the mood, with its marble pillars and nude mermaids rising from the top of the arched entrance doors. In the impressive reception lounge, an art-nouveau rose window at the peak of the dome is said to make any woman appear attractive. It casts a glow over the handloomed carpeting, potted plants, classic pillars, and patent leather banquettes. At least two dozen movie companies have used this lobby as a background.

Constantly being overhauled, the high-style bedrooms are kept fresh by frequent painting, and their furnishings are well tended to by a smoothly trained maintenance staff. High-season tariffs are charged at Christmas, New Year's, Easter, and in May, July, and August. A double with bath ranges in

MONACO **423**

price from 500F ($114.15) to 730F ($166.66) for two persons. Singles begin at 400F ($91.32).

The ornateness is dazzling, with marble pillars, statues lining the wall, crystal chandeliers, sumptuous carpets, Louis XVI chairs, and a wall-size fin-de-siècle mural. To support this ambience, an orchestra softly plays Chopin. The food is superb—appropriate to the memory of Escoffier, who helped organize the kitchens and planned the menus.

The evening usually begins in the bar, which combines a rustic paneled ceiling with a baroque gilt bas-relief carving against a backdrop of carnation-red walls. On top of the Hôtel de Paris, the Grill Room with a sliding roof is vaguely styled in the Louis XIV period, with wrought-iron lanterns and carved woods. While you receive the best service possible, you can watch the arrival and departure of the world's greatest yachts. In back of the distinguished cuisine served at the hotel is a collection of 130,000 bottles of rare and fine wines kept in a dungeon chiseled out of the rocks, a honeycomb of passageways with racked bottles. In the Grill Room a complete meal can be enjoyed at a price ranging from 135F ($30.82) to 180F ($41.09).

Other facilities available include the St. Louis Club Discothèque and the Black Jack Club, as well as boutiques, a beauty parlor, and an underground passageway leading to an indoor swimming pool, "Dès Terrasses," perhaps the most spectacular on the coast. Winter winds don't matter, as it's protected, the curving heated pool carved out of a cliffside. A protective glass wall overlooks the yacht-filled harbor. In fair weather, the wall can be opened onto an open-air terrace, with umbrella tables and sundeck chairs, set in the midst of palms. There is an authentic Finnish sauna, constructed with natural pine from the north and shaped slatted shelves on which to lie. Massages are available as well.

Métropole, Avenue de Grand Bretagne (tel. 50-57-41), is built palace-style, just off the Casino Park, with surrounding gardens, terraces of palms, and an open-air swimming pool. The position of the hotel commands a view of the sea or gardens from most of the rooms. The aura is one of graciousness, decidedly old-world. On the ground floor, the architect has relied on the classic style, with Greek revival columns offset by walls of Wedgwood-blue trimmed in white. Softening this severity are Louis XVI fruitwood chairs, much satin and velvet, marble and brass, stone sculpture on pedestals, and baroque bronze chandeliers.

Guests are received all year, paying anywhere from 260F ($59.36) to 650F ($148.40) per person for demi-pension. The least expensive rate is for a single room with shower, the most expensive based on double occupancy with a private bath. Add 15% for service to all tariffs. Each bedroom has its own color-coordinated theme; Louis XVI painted beds, Bombay chests, and reasonably fine antiques or reproductions make the accommodations inviting.

In typical Riviera fashion, the daytime life revolves around the pool, where an international mélange of guests relax in wicker chairs under date palms, swimming or dining alfresco. At the outdoor "Summer Restaurant," a nightly dinner-dance is held during the height of the winter season and from July 10 to September 10. The **Restaurant des Ambassadeurs** is recommended for its first-rate cuisine.

Hermitage, Square Beaumarchais (tel. 50-67-31). Picture yourself sitting in a wicker armchair, being served drinks in a belle époque rotunda under an ornate stained-glass dome with an encircling wrought-iron balcony of trailing ivy. Such is the setting of the Hermitage. There is no better example of turn-of-the-century architecture in all of Monaco. The "palace" was the creation of Jean Marquet (the same man who gave the world marquetry, work inlaid with different pieces of variously colored fine wood).

Just a few minutes from the casino, clinging to the edge of a cliff top, this hotel provides remarkable views of the harbor of yachts and the royal palace. The trappings are appropriate for the period, including large brass beds and decoratively framed doors opening onto balconies. Bathrooms feature baroque floral-patterned porcelain sinks with bronze fixtures. The rates are adjusted according to the season, and the policies are set by the general manager, who also directs the adjoining Hôtel de Paris, connected by a block-long arcade lined with tapestries, paintings, and antiques. High season is Christmas, New Year's, Easter, May, July, August, and September. A double with bath ranges from 360F ($82.19) to 520F ($118.72). Singles begin at 250F ($57.08). Full pension is an additional 200F ($45.66) per person.

The hotel's splendidly styled dining room is called **La Belle Époque,** with marbled Corinthian columns, potted palms, paneled walls, and glittering crystal chandeliers. A set meal is offered at 110F ($25.11), and most à la carte orders average 170F ($38.81) to 200F ($45.66).

The Middle Bracket

Bristol, 25 Boulevard Albert Ier (tel. 50-18-61), deserves hymns of praise for its situation directly on the water, its totally contemporary design, plus its good style and taste. There are 50 bedrooms, each with its own bath and private balcony, and half of which open directly onto the harborside. The air-conditioned bedrooms combine modern pieces with traditional, enhanced by soft carpeting and tiled and well-maintained baths. What drama, having your morning coffee and croissants on one of the balconies, inspecting the yachts! The high-season tariffs apply from July 1 to September 20, from December 20 to April 30, and during the week of the Grand Prix. At that time, two persons pay anywhere from 235F ($53.65) to 320F ($73.06) for demi-pension. All rates include taxes and service. These tariffs apply after a minimum stay of three days. Just for the room, two persons pay anywhere from 195F ($44.52) to 270F ($61.64).

On the ground floor is a nautical-style bar, with exposed laminated wood running up the walls and across the ceiling like the exposed ribs of an old boat. The combined reception area and lounge is small but pleasant, with a decorative nautical star and globe across one wall. On the second floor is the **Restaurant Panoramique,** facing the sea. Sitting on red leather and wood chairs, guests enjoy regional cooking in one of the most glamorous modern settings in Monaco. A set luncheon or dinner is offered at 105F ($23.97), although you can order à la carte as well.

Balmoral, 12 Avenue de la Costa (tel. 50-62-37), was built in 1898 by the grandfather of the present owner, Jacques Ferreyrolles, when Monte Carlo was rising to its heights. The niceties of that era are still respected at the Balmoral. Its position is cliff-hugging, halfway between the casino and the Royal Palace, directly overlooking the yachting harbor. The street entrance makes the building seem low, but from the waterfront you can count eight floors of bedrooms and lounges with sea views. In the little lounge, many family antiques remain, although subtle additions have been made over the years.

The bedrooms remain consistent in theme with the public rooms—homelike, immaculate, and quiet. So inviting is the Balmoral that guests are likely to extend their stays (perhaps taking advantage of lower tariffs). A double room with bath or shower ranges in price from 200F ($45.66) to 250F ($57.08); a bathless single room, 100F ($22.83), increasing to 150F ($34.26) to 175F ($39.95) with bath or shower. A continental breakfast costs 20F ($4.57); a lunch or dinner, from 65F ($14.84).

Hôtel du Louvre, 16 Boulevard des Moulins (tel. 50-63-25), is built in the style of a traditional grand mansion. The furniture, in the main, is antique. Rooms are comfortable and carpeted, the colors in harmony. Each accommodation is different, incidentally. Higher tariffs are charged for rooms facing the sea. Singles begin at 185F ($42.24), going up to 215F ($49.09); and doubles cost from 235F ($53.65) to 260F ($59.36), the higher tariffs for units with air conditioning.

The Budget Range

Hôtel de Russie, 25 Avenue de la Costa (tel. 30-62-66), is a pleasantly old-fashioned hotel right in the center of the business section, about a five-minute walk from the casino. Outside, the main coast road whizzes past, and traffic tends to be noisy, but the Russie is on the top three floors. Forty-five bedrooms are offered, 13 of which contain private baths, the rest having hot-and-cold running water. In high season, doubles with bath peak at 200F ($45.66), while bathless doubles cost only 120F ($27.40). Singles with bath go for 135F ($30.82), but only 100F ($22.83) without bath.

The accommodations are decidedly in the old French style, with large combination wardrobes, brass beds, and chunky leather-and-wood armchairs. The living rooms are family style, with plastic armchairs, a console set out in the center for flowers, and a glass cupboard for Madame Collomb's treasured oddments.

Hôtel des Palmiers ("Palm Trees"), 20 Boulevard de Suisse (tel. 30-55-12), is a hillside villa converted into a hotel, right in the business area, about a five-minute walk from the casino. While undistinguished and without style, it provides good value and great deal of comfort. A double room with bath—sort of casually furnished—costs 145F ($33.10). There are some bathless doubles going for 130F ($29.68). Singles with bath are 125F ($28.54), but only 90F ($20.55) is charged for one of the bathless "Cinderella rooms." Guests can congregate in the lounge, with its writing desks and sofas, or else frequent *le bar* for inexpensive drinks. Meals are served on the flower terrace, where a fixed-price luncheon or dinner costs 45F ($10.27).

Résidence des Moulins, 27 Boulevard des Moulins (tel. 30-26-23). The owner, Mrs. Maxime Randall, is American, and she personally manages this bourgeois mansion. The rooms have pleasant personalities, and each is different. Bedcovers and curtains are in flowery harmony. Depending on the plumbing, singles range from 52F ($11.87) to 68F ($15.52); doubles, 90F ($20.55) to 110F ($25.11). Breakfast costs an extra 12F ($2.74).

Diana, 17 Boulevard du Général-Leclerc, at Beausoleil (tel. 78-47-58), is a fence straddler. One side of the street is Beausoleil, the other Monte Carlo. This is a clean, functional hotel without any particular style. Its prices are its main lure. Rooms are available with or without private baths. Singles cost from 45F ($10.27) to 75F ($17.12); doubles, 60F ($13.70) to 105F ($23.97). Breakfast is an additional 11F ($2.51).

Olympia, 17 bis Boulevard du Général-Leclerc, Beausoleil (tel. 06-12-95), is next to the Diana, and is preferable. The lounge is inviting, as is a small but warm bar. Each of the bedrooms has a different flowery wallpaper and comfortable wood furniture. The third-floor rooms provide a view of the sea. Singles with hot and cold running water cost 50F ($11.42); with shower, 85F ($19.41). Depending on the plumbing, doubles are 80F ($18.26), 115F ($26.25), or 140F ($31.96). A continental breakfast, service, and taxes are included.

RESTAURANTS: Monaco boasts many fine restaurants. We'll start with—

The Leading Restaurants

Rampoldi, 3 Avenue des Spélugues (tel. 30-70-65), has risen to a high acclaim through sheer effort. Rampoldi is one of the leading independent restaurants, serving some of the finest cuisine in Monte Carlo. The classic French viands are dispensed in a compatible setting, under a balcony terrace at the edge of the Casino Gardens. Celebrities dine here frequently: Umberto (the deposed king of Italy), Princess Grace and Prince Rainier, and (in days of yore) Maria Callas, Aly Kahn, and W. Somerset Maugham.

Owned by Monsieur Rampoldi, ex-chef of the Hôtel de Paris, Monte Carlo, the restaurant is the eating club of "the great," but its tabs are not dazzlingly high. For example, a set meal is offered at 100F ($22.83), although most guests prefer to order à la carte, paying from 150F ($34.26). To begin your repast, try the soupe de poissons, the chef's specialty. The fish dishes are universally good, including a rarity, mostèle (a Mediterranean fish which that "apostle of gastronomy" Jean Montafian translates as "smooth hound"). The peppersteak is a delight. A soufflé au Grand-Marnier for two might be the proper finish for a meal. The restaurant is closed on Fridays from mid-July to mid-September and from mid-November to mid-December.

Le Petit Bec, 11 Avenue Grande-Bretagne (tel. 50-97-48), is fast rising to stellar position, and it has attracted a devoted following of habitués. The chef brings a refinement to the classic French cuisine and includes some innovative La Nouvelle Cuisine dishes as well. There is a great emphasis on fish. In fair weather guests can dine on a sheltered open-air terrace, or else retreat, on a hot summer day, to the air-conditioned room inside. Specialties include fresh foie gras, a turbot suprême, a soup of mussels, a pot-au-feu of fish, a terrine of sea bass, and duckling. Dining à la carte will run your tab around 160F ($13.70). Le Petit Bec is closed on Sundays and in August.

The Middle Bracket

Quick Silver, 1 Quai President-Kennedy (at La Condamine) (tel. 50-69-39), is a portside restaurant built under the highway. It is especially noted for its well-prepared dishes served at its sidewalk tables under an arbor. Monsieur Henri offers a varied set menu at 70F ($15.98), including soup, pasta, or a terrine, plus a fish or meat course. A savory Mediterranean cuisine is presented, with emphasis on fish dishes. A much more elaborate menu at 110F ($25.11) is also presented, including on one recent occasion a soupe de poissons (fish) with roche, followed by a gratin of crayfish in Nantua sauce, plus lamb cutlets grilled with herbs, topped by a tart made with fresh fruit of the season, the tariff including service and taxes.

Brazil, 2 Boulevard des Moulins (tel. 30-75-53), is divided in two. The wrap-around glass portion sits under a bright canopy, with picture windows opening directly onto the Casino Gardens. It ranks along with Quick Silver as the best choice in Monaco for good cooking at moderate prices. There's a 48F ($10.96) set meal—although you may have to ask the waiter to show you the menu. Among the à la carte selections are onion soup and stuffed mussels. Those will get you going, preparing the way for the grilled lamb cutlets or the sole meunière. The pastry tray contains fresh fruit tarts that are light, moist, and creamy. À la carte tabs generally range from 70F ($15.98) to 100F ($22.83). Brazil is closed from mid-November to December 20.

Le Bistroquet, 11 Galerie Charles-II (tel. 50-65-03), has a charming fin-de-siècle atmosphere, attracting those who want rather simple but enjoyable food. There's a bar for nighttime drinks before dinner, and, weather permitting, you can dine on the terrace. Le Bistroquet is most attractive to an international young set, who prefer this kind of cookery to more elaborate Escoffier techniques. Here they can order such dishes as an omelet with pork lardoons, côte of beef, and a leg of lamb roasted with herbs and garlic. Expect to pay from 130F ($29.68) for a full meal. The restaurant is open until 2 a.m., closed on Tuesdays.

Sam's Palace, Palais de la Scala (tel. 50-89-33). There had to be such a place in Monte Carlo, a friendly restaurant/bar attracting those who prefer such dishes as Texas-style chili con carne, a super-hamburger, and French fries. Sam's is a gratifying stopover during lunch, but in the evening it almost turns into a social club, it's so informal. The average tab comes to 90F ($20.55). You can also order good, big drinks at the American-style bar.

An Economy Trio

If the prices of the citadels of luxury have frightened you, and if you consider the St. Louis Club, the Summer Sporting Club, and the Hôtel de Paris better suited for the purse of Gunther Sachs, then you may need to know about an unprepossessing street in Monaco known as the **rue de la Turbie**. Not all the Monégasques are rich, as a stroll along this narrow, crescent-shaped street of budget restaurants will convince you. The government labels these restaurants "no class" (that is, unclassified, falling into no particular category).

De La Roya, 21 rue de la Turbie (tel. 30-99-96), will give you a filling and tasty meal for only 36F ($8.22). This fixed-price dinner might include a rich and juicy beef bourguignonne. If you want to splurge a bit, you can order a more elaborate repast for just 45F ($10.27). The specialty of the house is Spanish paella at 36F ($8.22), but it must be ordered in advance.

De Tende, 19 rue de la Turbie (tel. 30-37-72), a family-run pension, is also good, but basic. Also called Chez Cinto, it offers fixed-price meals ranging from 28F ($6.39) to 40F ($9.13). The chef does a good escalope Milanese. In the afternoon, men gather over card games.

Finally, **Bacchus,** 13 rue de la Turbie (tel. 30-19-35), may tempt you if the others don't. For sheer economy, it is the best target on the street, offering the widest choice of set menus. Although you can dine here more expensively, you can select a complete dinner for just 32F ($7.31). One recent meal included asparagus vinaigrette, followed by cervelle d'agneau meunière (lamb's brains in butter) accompanied by braised fennel with butter, and topped by rice cake. English is spoken.

The Major Refueling Stop

Café de Paris, Place du Casino. If you frequent the Café de la Paix or Deux Magots in Paris, you'll gravitate to their counterpart in Monte Carlo. Everyone seems to end up here at least once a day. Directly opposite the casino and the Hôtel de Paris, the Café de Paris provides a front-row seat to the never-ending spectacle in the "living room" of Monte Carlo. Inside the café you can gamble on the slot machine. There's even a bowling alley and a glorified *le drug store.*

The café attracts a well-dressed and affluent-looking crowd which switches from one language to another with apparent ease. Sandwiches (a wide choice) cost from 18F ($4.11); an omelet, 17F ($3.88); a salad, 15F ($3.42). You can even order a hamburger at 21F ($4.79).

At Monte Carlo Beach (Expensive)

Old Beach Hotel, route du Beach (tel. 78-21-40), is another property of the Société des Bains de Mer, which controls the Paris and Hermitage in Monte Carlo. On the headland of La Vigie, the hotel provides 46 air-conditioned rooms, furnished in the main with painted furniture and metal beds. What it really offers is beach-club-style living, its crescent-shaped three floors opening onto loggias and curving around the rocks.

The May-to-September hotel charges "in-season" rates except in June, which for some reason is a traditionally slow period at Monte Carlo. For a double in the peak period, you'll pay 400F ($91.32) to 440F ($100.45), as much as 350F ($79.91) in a single. A complete meal here costs from 220F ($50.23) to 270F ($61.64). In addition, the "Old Beach" offers seven bungalows on a higher terrace, affording more privacy. Life centers around an adjoining Olympic-size swimming pool and beach restaurant, set apart from the main building. In summer, many guests from the Paris and Hermitage come here for their noonday luncheons, modeling the latest bathing attire.

DAYTIME SWIMMING: On French soil, Monte Carlo Beach adjoins the Old Beach Hotel. Opening the first week in May for the summer season, the beach club becomes an integral part of the social life of Monaco. The entrance fee in May and June is 12F ($2.74), increasing to 20F ($4.57) between July 1 and September 15. Besides the artificial beach, there are two pools, one for children.

Leaving Monte Carlo Beach to the international set, the Monégasques themselves frequent the Stade Nautique Rainier III, at La Condamine. Dramatically built to overlook the yacht-clogged harbor, it is a stupendous pool, a gift from the prince to his loyal subjects. But you don't have to have a passport to swim here. Rather, you pay an entrance fee of 10F ($2.28), which is lowered to 8F ($1.83) in summer. The pool is open in spring and fall from 9 a.m. to 6 p.m.; in July and August, from 9 a.m. until midnight.

4. Eze and La Turbie

Reached via the Moyenne (Middle) Corniche, Eze occupies an eagle's-nest perch where once medieval villagers were safe from Corsairs raiding the coast and capturing the young girls for harem duty or the strong men for slaves. You park your car in the little square below, then scale the narrow medieval maze to the top, the streets becoming steps. Ancient stone houses, often occupied by artisans who have restored them to their natural beauty, line the way.

At the top is an old château, set in a garden of cacti (admission, 1F). Many prefer to visit Eze at night, savoring the twinkling lights 1300 feet below.

After Eze, a road leads to La Turbie, on the Upper Corniche. At the highest point along the Grand Corniche, 1500 feet above sea level, stands Emperor Augustus' Trophy of the Alps. At the base of the Tête de Chien ("Head of a Dog"), it was erected in 6 B.C. The monument—restored with funds donated by Edward Tuck—was erected by the Roman Senate to celebrate the subjugation of the people of the French Alps. You can visit the Musée du Trophée des Alps in summer from 9 a.m. to noon and 2 to 7 p.m. (till 6 p.m. off-season), for an admission of 5F ($1.14), 2.50F (57¢) on Sunday. At night, from June to September, the Trophy is floodlit, a striking sight along the Upper Corniche. From the terraces, there's a panoramic view of Monaco.

TWO DELUXE HOTELS: Hostellerie du Château de la Chèvre d'Or (tel. 41-12-12), rue du Barri, in Eze-Village, is a miniature retreat not unlike a luxuriously converted monastery. On the side of the stone-built medieval village, off the Moyenne Corniche, the Hostellerie is a well-preserved complex of village houses on many levels, all with views of the coastline. The owner, Bruno Ingold, has had the interior of the "Golden Goat" flawlessly decorated to maintain its old character, yet has seen to it that it is most comfortable in today's terms. Heavy beams and French and Italian antiques are used throughout. Even if you don't arrive for a meal or a room, try to stop in for a drink in the bar-lounge, with its picture-window views. French doors open onto a terraced swimming pool.

The food is most worthy, living up to the traditions of "Old France." You can begin with a generous selection of hors d'oeuvres, follow with carré d'agneau (loin of lamb) aux arômes de Provence, or perhaps sole farcie (stuffed sole) Pompadour. For a bit of festivity, try the crêpes de Monsieur Seguin.

Only nine bedrooms are offered, each with private bath. Some open onto terraces. Singles range in price from 220F ($50.23), with doubles going for 430F ($98.17), plus 15% service added to all tariffs. In season, demi-pension is obligatory, ranging from 330F ($75.34) to 380F ($86.75) per person.

Take time out to enjoy the old ivy-covered wall, the Norman arches of the towers and the colonnades. Closed Wednesdays in off-season and from mid-November to mid-February.

At one of the most dramatic points along the Côte d'Azur, between Nice and Monte Carlo, Le Cap Estel is a rocky promontory jutting out into the azure sea. Just two miles from Beaulieu, the following hotel is reached along the Lower Corniche.

Le Cap Estel, Eze-Bord-de-Mer (tel. 01-50-44), is a successful reincarnation of a turn-of-the-century seacoast villa built for a princess. Now it is transformed into a luxurious hotel, where you can live and dine in style. Below the coastal road, Le Cap Estel is on five acres of terraced, landscaped gardens reached by a sweeping staircase. At the point where the waves dash against the rocks, a covered, heated swimming pool projects out like the bow of a ship. Exotic birds are kept in cages; mauve petunias add color, and the reflection pool is graced with a spraying fountain, lit with colored lights at night when cocktail parties are in progress under a banyan tree.

Because of its situation, all of the rooms overlook the sea, each near a terrace and each with a private bath. From June 1 to October 1, high-season prices are in effect, costing from 500F ($114.15) to 645F ($147.25) per person daily for demi-pension, based on a minimum stay of three days. At other times of the year, the hotel charges anywhere from 420F ($95.89) to 600F ($136.98) per person for demi-pension, including service and taxes.

In the public rooms, modern furnishings rather than antiques have been used. Guests can either dine inside, on an open-air terrace, or else under the trees where umbrella tables have been placed. Occasional barbecues and chicken-on-the-spit dinners are featured. The hotel is closed from November 1 to February 1.

THE BUDGET RANGE: Hôtel Motel du Cap Roux, Eze-Plage (tel. 01-51-23), is an older traditional hotel, offering a terrace with a view of the sea, a garden, and parking space for cars. It's a colorful place, with standard but convenient furnishings. Two persons in a room with bath will pay 135F ($30.82) off-season, increasing to 180F ($41.09) in season, a continental breakfast included. Many combinations of rooms are offered, including some with a kitchenette. In the same building, but under separate management, is a simple restaurant featuring a three-course meal at 35F ($7.99), a four-course one at 45F ($10.27).

Le Mas Provençal, rue de Verdun (tel. 01-51-93), is a very clean, white country house with wooden shutters. Mr. Gazzano is the owner, welcoming you to a nicely furnished room, for which he charges 105F ($23.97) per person for demi-pension, increasing the tab to 140F ($31.96) per person for full pension. Nonresidents are invited to stop in for one of the set dinners costing 38F ($8.68).

5. Beaulieu

Protected from the cold north winds that blow down from the Alps, Beaulieu-sur-Mer is often referred to as La Petite Afrique. Like Menton, it enjoys the mildest climate along the Côte d'Azur, and is especially popular with the wintering wealthy, including in days gone by James Gordon Bennett, the founder and editor of the New York *Herald* (he sent Stanley to find Livingstone). Originally, the English visitors staked it out, after an industrialist from that country founded a hotel here between the rock-studded slopes and the sea. The **Beaulieu Casino** fronts **La Baie des Fourmis,** the beautiful gardens attracting the evening promenade crowd.

The **Villa "Kerylos"** is a replica of an ancient Greek residence. It was painstakingly designed and built by an archaeologist, Theodore Reinach (1860-1928). Inside, the cabinets are filled with a collection of Greek figurines and ceramics. But most interesting is the reconstructed Greek furniture, much of which would be extremely modish and fashionable today. One curious mosaic depicts the slaying of the minotaur and provides its own labyrinth (if you trace the path, expect to stay for weeks). The villa is open daily, except Mondays and during the month of November, from 3 to 7 p.m. in July and August, from 2 to 6 p.m. September through June. Admission is 8F ($1.83).

Graced with lush vegetation, including oranges, lemons, and bananas, as well as palms, Beaulieu lies between Nice (six miles away) and Monte Carlo (seven miles away). The golf course of Mont Agel is 10 miles from the resort.

FOOD AND LODGINGS: Beaulieu offers choices in all price ranges, beginning with—

Super-Deluxe Living by the Sea

La Réserve, 5 Boulevard Général-Leclerc (tel. 01-00-01), has risen to stellar heights along the Côte d'Azur, richly deserving its reputation as one of the Riviera's most famous oases. Right on the Mediterranean, it is a pink-and-white palace, offering drama in its scope and refined atmosphere. A number of the public lounges open onto a courtyard, with urns of cascading flowers, bordered grass, and bamboo chairs. The social life centers around the main drawing room, with its harmonious oyster-white sofas and patterned floors—much like the grand living room of a country estate. In Louis XIV-style chairs, guests sit under a Pompeian ceiling in the drinking lounge, discussing their latest adventures (or lack of them!).

The hotel has been rebuilt in stages, hence its bedrooms range widely in size and character. All 50 are deluxe, distinctly different in style, including one with richly embossed white-and-gilt furniture, elaborately carved headboards and chests, chalk-white fabrics, and bronze and crystal lighting fixtures. The baths are equally stylish, with double sinks. Of course, all the bedrooms are air-conditioned, and each has a beautiful view, either of the mountains or the sea.

In high season, from July 1 to September 30, you pay anywhere from 600F ($136.98) in a twin-bedded room, plus 15% for service. Singles during that peak period go for anywhere from 500F ($114.15), plus service. In July and August, demi-pension is compulsory, costing an extra 175F ($39.95) per person.

The cuisine is world renowned (La Réserve won its fame as a "rendezvous of queens and kings" when it was founded as a restaurant by the Lottier family in 1894). The dining room is consistent in design and general aura with the rest of the hotel, providing a quiet, restful ambience, with its coved frescoed ceiling, parquet floors, provincial armchairs, crystal chandeliers, and arched picture windows opening onto the Mediterranean. Specialties include lobster "Roy George," bass Réserve, a pancake of the "fruits of the sea," and a dreamy soufflé of fresh raspberries.

Built into a huge stone terrace overlooking the water is a swimming pool, heated from October until May. Other facilities include a private harbor for yachts, submarine fishing gear, sauna, and thalassotherapy.

The Upper Bracket
Bedford, Avenue Blundell-Maple (tel. 06-57-00), is a great old waterfront hotel, totally renovated, and boasting its own formal garden of several acres, with a beautiful swimming pool amid rows of clipped hedges, flower beds, and palms. The rooms are well furnished, clean, and comfortable. Each contains its private shower bath. Most rooms overlook the garden and sea. Two persons off-season pay 650F ($148.40) for full pension, this tariff rising to 800F ($182.64) in high season. Half board for two guests is 550F ($125.57) in low season, going up to 650F ($148.40) in high season. The main lounge is classically styled. Many guests check in to spend "the season." The hotel is open December 15 to October 31.

Bedford Residence SA is also a resort condominium, where you can become a shareholder. The purchase of shares entitles the buyer to a lifelong stay on a time-sharing basis.

The Budget Range
Primerose, 2 Montée des Orangers (tel. 01-04-30), is a great old mansion with somewhat standard furnishings and a beautiful garden in which you can linger under a parasol. The hotel is quiet, and the obligatory full-pension prices most reasonable: 135F ($30.82) per person in a room with hot and cold running water, 150F ($34.26) with shower. A family atmosphere prevails.

6. St.-Jean and Cap Ferrat
It has been labeled Paradise Found. Of all the oases along the Cote d'Azur, no place has the snob appeal of Cap Ferrat. It is a nine-mile promontory sprinkled with luxurious villas, outlined by sheltered bays, beaches, and coves. Vegetation is lush. In the port of St.-Jean, the harbor democratically accommodates both yachts and fishing boats.

Somerset Maugham once lived at Cap Ferrat, quite grandly, receiving friends and confiding to them such tidbits as that he hadn't read *Of Human Bondage* since it was published or (in later years) that he longed for death. Leopold II of Belgium once had a villa here (now taken over by the owner of Grand Marnier). Today, Brazilian millionaires as well as movie stars (David Niven, Gregory Peck) own villas along the pine-studded peninsula.

The **Musée Île-de-France,** Avenue Denis-Séméria, affords you a chance to visit one of the most legendary villas along the Côte d'Azur. It was built in the Italianate style by the Baroness Ephrussi, a Rothschild. She died in 1934, leaving the building and its magnificent gardens to the Institut de France and the Académie des Beaux-Arts. According to her reputation, "she pinched everything from all Europe." The wealth of her collection is preserved: 18th-century furniture, Tiepolo ceilings, Savonnerie carpets, screens and panels from the Far East, tapestries from the factories of Gobelins, Aubusson, and Beauvais, original drawings by Fragonard, canvases by Renoir, Sisley, and Boucher, and rare Sèvres porcelain. Covering 12 acres, the gardens contain fragments of statuary from churches, monasteries, and torn-down palaces. One entire section is planted with cacti. The museum and its gardens are open every day, except Mondays and in November, from 2 to 6 p.m. from September 1 to June 30, from 3 to 7 p.m. July 1 to August 31. The gardens are also open in the morning from 9 to noon. Admission is 12F ($2.74) for museum and gardens, 6F ($1.37) for the gardens only.

FOOD AND LODGING: There's no lack of fine—and expensive—accommodations at Cap Ferrat, but some inexpensive suggestions are included in our list as well.

"Golden Sails" in the Sunset (Deluxe)

La Voile d'Or ("Golden Sail"), Avenue Mermoz (tel. 01-13-13), is a brilliant tour de force. It's compressed luxury, run on a personal and intimate scale. An antique collector turned hotelier, Jean Lorenzi had the good sense to turn over not only the design of the building but its interior to his architect. The location is at the edge of the little fishing port and yacht harbor, on a plateau with a panoramic view of the coast. Living at La Voile d'Or is like being a guest at a house party. The bedrooms, the lounges, and the restaurant open onto terraces, with lawns, flagstones, and gnarled olive and orange trees. On the edge of the upper terrace is a swimming pool, where you feel you're almost in the Mediterranean itself.

Partial tribute goes to English-speaking Mme. Lorenzi, a lovely woman from the Netherlands. She's equally comfortable inviting Danny Kaye to "make yourself at home" in the kitchen as welcoming Sam Spiegel ashore when he arrives on his luxurious yacht.

The bedrooms—50 air-conditioned ones in all—are unique. Each has its own decorative theme, utilizing hand-painted reproductions of antiques, gilt carved headboards, baroque paneled doors, parquet floors, antique clocks, paintings, and baths that are a hallmark of luxury. Open February 1 to October 30, the hotel experiences three seasons, the accommodations priced according to whether the rooms open onto the yacht harbor (more expensive) or the sea and garden. From July to September, demi-pension (required) is 350F ($79.91) to 550F ($125.57) per person.

Guests gather on the canopied outer terrace for luncheons. In the evenings, they dine in the more formal and stately room with Spanish armchairs and white wrought-iron chandeliers. Dining is quite festive, the menu sophisticated, offering regional specialties, plus a few international dishes as well as the classic French cuisine. Richly decorated, the drawing room is most attractive, using handloomed fabric-covered sofas and armchairs, Iberian tables, Italian chests, and oil paintings. Most intimate is a little drinking bar, with Wedgwood-blue paneling and antique mirroring. Guests make it their club room: introductions seem hardly necessary.

The Middle Bracket

Résidence Della Robbia, Boulevard du Général de Gaulle (tel. 01-33-07), serves memorable food, perhaps the finest along Cap Ferrat. Lodged on a hillside, it offers a panoramic view of the coast, the bay, and the yachts. In honor of its namesake, della Robbia-style terra-cotta sculptures adorn the façade. In 1960, Monsieur and Madame Davignon transformed the villa into a restaurant and hotel. (Originally, the country house was owned by Mrs. Benson, the wealthy English cigarette manufacturer.) Monsieur Davignon quickly became celebrated for his cuisine. At one time, he was the chef to George VI of England ("His Highness liked his food too plain!"). The interior of the villa is most livable, the furnishings (a generous use of antiques) and the style most tasteful. Fourteen handsome double rooms are rented to guests for 180F ($41.09) daily, plus another 15F ($3.42) per person for a continental breakfast.

The dining terrace is under an arbor, and below are a citrus grove, palms, and eucalyptuses. A set meal, including four courses, is offered for 80F ($18.26). On the à la carte, good openers include soupe de pêcheurs (fisherman's soup) and the seafood cocktail. Specialties are carré d'agneau (loin of lamb) with herbs of Provence for two persons, and loup de la Méditerranée farci (stuffed bass), also for two persons. À la carte, a meal will cost from 120F ($27.40) to 160F ($36.53).

The hotel is open from January 1 to mid-October.

Les Tourterelles, 27 Avenue Denis-Séméria (tel. 01-33-31), is a small hillside apartment house where you can live economically, independent of a hotel staff. It is a three-floor building, surrounded by a small garden, reached via a narrow lane with roses and geraniums. Guests gather to sunbathe in the garden and swim in the pool. The big news is the living space you get: a private sun terrace, a living room, a dining area, a twin-bedded room, a private tiled bath with shower, and a complete kitchen with all the necessary equipment to prepare a meal. Each apartment is named after a famous painter and contains reproductions of the artist's work—Rousseau, Utrillo, Gauguin, Degas. Most apartments accommodate from one to three persons, the rates remaining the same, varying only according to the time of year. In June and September, you pay from 220F ($50.23) daily, although it's cheaper to book by the week. In July and August, the daily rate increases to 280F ($63.92) and a month's stay is required.

Brise Marine, Avenue Mermoz (tel. 01-30-73), is a bargain paradise for so chic a situation. On a hillside terrace, it is a three-story villa with a front and rear terrace. It's up from the road, behind a stone balustrade, with statues and urns of pink geraniums. A long rose arbor, beds of subtropical flowers, palms, and pines provide an attractive setting. The atmosphere is casual and informal. Guests either have breakfast in the beamed lounge or under the rose trellis. No other meals are served, although there is a little corner bar for afternoon drinks. In comfortably furnished and immaculately kept bedrooms, two persons are housed and given demi-pension for 275F ($62.78) a day. The hotel is open from February 1 until the end of October.

La Belle Aurore, Avenue Denis-Séméria (tel. 01-31-03), is a hillside villa which has been converted into an informal little hotel offering 19 rooms, all with private baths or showers. The majority of the accommodations also have private balconies. Between the coastal road and the bay, it offers an attractive garden, with palm trees, large figs, and pink and red oleander surrounding a swimming pool. Chaise longues are set around the pool, where guests gather for relaxing hours. In addition the proprietor has installed a sauna bath with a jet-stream massage. In summer you can dine outside, enjoying barbecued meals. The cost per person for a room with bath and all three meals (quite good ones at that) ranges from 180F ($41.09) to 230F ($52.51). Nonresidents can drop in for a meal, ordering a six-courser for 65F ($14.84).

The Budget Choice

Le Dauphin, Place Clemenceau (tel. 01-30-37). Walking along the main street of the port with its high-priced seafood restaurants, you'd never suspect that such a plain little pension could have such an attractive rear patio and garden, on which are served excellently prepared but inexpensive meals. You pass along a narrow hallway to the intimate courtyard, covered by a split bamboo pergola. A few tables are set out, with a view of a garden on a higher level, where roses come in every color and red geraniums grow five feet high. A typical 45F ($10.27) dinner might include a bowl of fish soup (very rich, with toasted grated cheese), a crêpe stuffed with ham, followed by sole meunière with potatoes, plus cheese, fruit, or ice cream for dessert. The 15 rooms are very plain, but adequate, clean, and comfortable. Full pension for one person costs 150F ($34.26) per day, dropping to 110F ($25.11) for demi-pension.

7. Villefranche

According to legend, Hercules opened his arms and Villefranche was born. It sits on a big blue bay that looks like a gigantic bowl, large enough to attract U.S. Sixth Fleet cruisers and destroyers. Quietly slumbering otherwise, Ville-franche takes on the appearance of an exciting Mediterranean port when the fleet's in. Four miles from Nice, it is the first town reached along the Lower Corniche.

Once popular with such writers as Katherine Mansfield and Aldous Huxley, it is still a haven for artists, many of whom take over the little houses—reached by narrow alleyways—that climb the hillside. The **rue Obscure** is vaulted, one of the strangest streets in France (to get to it, take the rue l'Église). In spirit, it belongs more to a North African casbah. People live in tiny houses on this street, totally protected from the elements. Occasionally, however, there's an open space, allowing for a tiny courtyard.

One artist who came to Villefranche left a memorial. His name was Jean Cocteau, and he decorated the 14th-century Romanesque **Chapel of St. Pierre,** presenting it to "the fishermen of Villefranche in homage to the Prince of Apostles, the patron of fishermen." One panel pays homage to the gypsies of the Saintes-Maries-de-la-Mer. In the apse is a depiction of the Miracle of St. Peter walking on the water, not knowing that he's supported by an angel. On the left side of the narthex, Cocteau honored the young women of Villefranche in their regional costumes. The chapel is open from 9 a.m. to noon and from 2 to 6 p.m. Admission is 3F (68¢).

HOTELS: Versailles, Avenue du Maréchal-Foch (tel. 80-89-56), is a hill-clinging, sunpocket hotel, where you can swim in a pool surrounded by a mosaic-tiled terrace, palms, and bright flowers. Set back several blocks from the harbor, and outside the main part of town, it gives you a perspective of the entire coastal area. Constructed in the 1960s, it offers bedrooms with picture windows, so every room has a view. The tariffs vary according to the season. In high season you'll pay from 240F ($54.79) to 300F ($68.49) per person for full pension, including service and taxes. A minimum stay of three days is required. The high season is Christmas and April 1 to September 30. Otherwise, tariffs are reduced. Guests congregate on the roof terrace. You can have breakfast here, or even lunch under a white-fringed blue umbrella. In the panoramic dining room, decorated in Mediterranean blue, set luncheons or dinners are offered for 80F ($18.26). The hotel is closed from November 1 until February 1.

Welcome, Quai Courbet (tel. 55-27-27), involves you instantly in Mediterranean port life. Within hailing distance of the fishing and motor boats, it is a six-floor, villa-style hotel, painted an old Roman gold with deep-green shutters and balconies. The sidewalk café—set under a canopy—is the focal point of town life, serving coffee at any time of the day or night. The lounge and restaurant have an open fireplace, thick arches, handhewn beams, and fruitwood furniture. The bedrooms are good looking, 40 in all, 36 with private baths. The steepest tariffs are charged in high season (Easter, as well as July through September). For full pension, the rate ranges from 200F ($45.66) to 250F ($57.08) per person. A set menu is featured at 75F ($17.12). Once Pope Paul III embarked from this site with Charles V, but nowadays the departures are much more casual, usually on a fishing expedition.

RESTAURANTS: La Mère Germaine, Quai Courbet (tel. 80-71-39), is the best of a string of restaurants directly on the port. It's popular with U.S. Navy men, who have discovered the bouillabaisse made here from tasty morsels of freshly caught fish, and mixed in a caldron with savory spice. On the à la carte menu, you'll discover grilled loup (bass) with three herbs, 110F ($25.11), and a salade Niçoise, 50F ($11.42). A delicious apple tart costs 18F ($4.11). Plan to relax over a long lunch while watching the fishermen repair their nets. Closed Wednesdays and from July 15 to September 1.

La Méditerranée, Avenue Sadi-Carnot (tel. 80-78-56), is a modern restaurant, in the lower level of the Zig-Zag apartment house, with an all-glass façade, permitting guests to enjoy a stunning view. Every local as well as many visiting residents from Nice know about the delicious 60F ($13.70) fixed-price meal offered here. For that low price, you're likely to get mussels marinières or trout with almonds, finishing with a rich meringue chantilly for dessert. More expensive menus are offered at 100F ($22.83). Add 12% for service. The restaurant is closed Wednesdays, from July 1 to 20, and for most of January.

Le Dauphin, Quai Courbet (tel. 80-75-13), is a portside restaurant that often fills its tiny tables when other local eateries are empty. Its blue-and-white-clothed tables are set out for the fresh air and the view—a true bistro. You can order a very filling—and very good—meal here for just 50F ($11.42), service included. One recent repast included gratin de fruits de mer, filet de daurade (a fish), vegetables, and dessert. An even more elaborate meal is presented for 75F ($17.12). For this more expensive price, we recently enjoyed sautéed lobster in the Provençal style.

8. Nice

The Victorian upper class and tsarist aristocrats loved Nice in the 19th century, but it is solidly middle class today. In fact, of all the major resorts of France, from Deauville to Biarritz to Cannes, Nice is the least expensive. It is also the best excursion center on the Riviera, especially if you're dependent on public transportation. For example, you can go to San Remo, the queen of the Italian Riviera, returning to Nice by nightfall. From the Nice Airport, the second largest in France, you can travel by bus along the entire coast to such other resorts as Juan-les-Pins and Cannes.

Nice is the capital of the Riviera, the largest city between Genoa and Marseille (also one of the most ancient, having been founded by the Greeks, who called it "Nike," or victory). Because of its brilliant sunshine and relaxed living, artists and writers have been attracted to Nice for years. Among them were Matisse, Dumas, Nietzsche, Apollinaire, Flaubert, Victor Hugo, Guy de Maupassant, George Sand, Stendhal, Chateaubriand, and Mistral.

In 1822 the orange crop at Nice was bad, and the workers were facing a lean time. The English residents put them to work building the **Promenade des Anglais,** which today remains a wide boulevard fronting the bay and split by "islands" of palms and flowers, stretching for a distance of about four miles. Fronting the beach are rows of grand cafés, the **Musée Masséna,** the **Palais de la Méditerranée** gambling casino, villas, and hotels—some good, others decaying.

Crossing this boulevard in the briefest of bikinis are some of the most attractive people in the world, who come all the way from Israel or Minnesota. They're heading for the beach—"on the rocks," as it is called here. Tough on tender feet, the beach at Nice is shingled, one of the least attractive (and least publicized!) aspects of the cosmopolitan resort city. Many bathhouses provide mattresses for a charge.

In the east, the promenade becomes the **Quai des États-Unis,** the original boulevard, lined today with some of the best restaurants in Nice, each of which specializes in bouillabaisse. Rising sharply on a rock is the **château,** the spot where the dukes of Savoy built their castle, which was torn down in 1706. The steep hill has been turned into a garden of pines and exotic flowers. To reach the château, you can take an elevator, a round-trip ticket costing 2F (46¢). The park is open until 8 p.m. from May 1 to August 31, closing at 7 p.m. off-season. Actually, many prefer to take the elevator up, then walk down.

In the **Tour Bellanda** is the **Naval Museum**—sitting on "The Rock"— receiving guests from 10 a.m. to 12:30 p.m. and from 2:30 to 7 p.m. daily except Tuesdays for a 3F (68¢) admission (free on Saturdays). Off-season hours are from 10 a.m. to noon and 2 to 7 p.m.; closed entirely from November 15 to December 15. The tower sits on a precariously perched belvedere overlooking the beach, the bay, the old town, and even the terraces of some of the nearby villas. Of the museum's old battle prints, one depicts the exploits of Caterina Segurana, the Joan of Arc of the Niçois. During the 1543 siege by Barbarossa, she ran along the ramparts, raising her skirts and showing her shapely bottom to the Turks as a sign of contempt, although the soldiers were reported to have been more excited than insulted.

Continuing east from the Rock one reaches the **Harbor,** where the restaurants are even cheaper and the bouillabaisse just as good. While sitting here over an apéritif at a sidewalk café, you can watch the boats depart for Corsica (perhaps take one yourself). The port was excavated between 1750 and 1830. Since that time, an outer harbor—protected by two jetties—has also been created.

The "authentic" Niçois live in **Vieille Ville**, the old town, beginning at the foot of the Rock. Under sienna-tiled roofs, many of the Italianate façades suggest 17th-century Genoese palaces. The old town is a maze of narrow streets, teeming with local life and studded with the least expensive restaurants in Nice. Buy an onion pizza *(la pissaladiera)* from one of the local vendors. It's delicious. Many of the old buildings are painted a faded Roman gold, and their banners are multicolored laundry flapping in the sea breezes.

While there, try to visit **Marché aux Fleurs**, the flower market at Cours Saleya. The vendors start setting up their stalls at noon. The market opens between 2 and 4 p.m. Wheeled in on carts is a flamboyant array of carnations, violets, jonquils, roses, and birds of paradise.

The center of Nice is **Place Masséna**, with its pink buildings in the 17th-century Genoese style and a **Fontaine du Soleil** ("Fountain of the Sun") by Janoit, dating from 1956. The **Municipal Casino**, now closed, was built in 1883. Stretching from the main square to the promenade is the **Jardin Albert Ier**, with an open-air terrace and a **Triton Fountain.** With its palms and exotic flowers, it is the most relaxing oasis at the resort.

At certain times of the year, Nice is caught up in frenzied carnival activities. The **Nice Carnival** is famous, of course, drawing visitors from all over Europe and North America to this ancient spectacle. The **Mardi Gras of the Riviera** begins 12 days before Shrove Tuesday, celebrating the return of spring with parades, floats *(corsi),* masked balls *(veglioni),* confetti, and battles in which pretty girls toss flowers, and only the most wicked throw rotten eggs instead of carnations. Climaxing the event is a fireworks display on Shrove Tuesday, lighting up the Bay of Angels. King Carnival goes up in flames on his pyre, but rises from the ashes again next spring.

TRANSPORTATION TIP: If you're going to be in Nice for a week, we'd suggest that you purchase a 35F ($7.99) ticket at the bus station, allowing you to ride on all the city buses for that period.

Those with the time and inclination can explore—

THE MUSEUMS OF NICE: If the pebbles of the beach are too sharp for your tender toes, you can escape into some of the finest museums along the entire Riviera. Fronting the promenade itself is:

The Masséna Museum

This fabulous villa was built in 1900 in the style of the First Empire as a private residence for Victor Masséna, the Prince of Essling and grandson of Napoleon's marshal. The city of Nice has converted it into a museum of local history and regional art. Next door to the deluxe Negresco Hotel, it is entered on 65 rue de France, and is open daily, except Mondays and holidays, from 10 a.m. to noon and from 2 to 5 p.m. If you buy a comprehensive ticket at the door for 12F ($2.74), you'll be admitted to five other museums, including one devoted to Matisse. However, the ordinary entrance fee is 6F ($1.37), 3F (68¢) for students and children.

On the ground floor is a remarkable First Empire drawing room, completely furnished in the opulent taste of that era, with mahogany-veneer pieces and ormolu mounts. Of course, there's the representation of Napoleon as a Roman Caesar and a bust by Canova of Marshal Masséna.

The collection of Niçois primitives is notable, including works attributed to the painters of the 15th century, Bréa and Durandi. In addition to the Niçois primitives there are also examples of the Italian, Spanish, and Flemish schools. There are art galleries devoted to the history of Nice and the memories of Masséna and Garibaldi. Yet another gallery is reserved for a display of views of Nice during the 19th century. Folklore and the ethnographia of the County of Nice are presented in three other galleries, together with examples of the history of "the Carnival" in Nice. It should also be noted that the museum contains an excellent collection of arms and armor, as well as ceramics and jewelry.

The Musée Chéret

More distantly located, on the western fringe of the city, this fine-arts museum is open from 2 to 7 p.m. June 1 to September 30, 10 a.m. to noon and 2 to 5 p.m. October 1 to May 31. Admission is free. The museum was named in honor of Jules Chéret, a contemporary of Toulouse-Lautrec's; he died in Nice, leaving a series of posters and drawings as well as paintings. In a way, he was the inventor, before Toulouse-Lautrec, of modern poster art.

The museum is visited mainly for its outstanding gallery devoted to a dynasty of painters, the Van Loo family of Flemish descent. One of its best-known members, Carle Van Loo, was born in Nice in 1705. He was Louis XV's *Premier Peintre.*

European schools of the 17th, 18th, and 19th centuries are also represented, as are masterpieces by Fragonard, Hubert Robert, and Natoire. A wide panorama of the French masters of the 19th century includes Guérin, Besnard, Blanche, Cabanel, B. Constant, Flameng, and Marie Bashkirtseff and her friends. The gallery of sculptures includes works by J.-B. Carpeaux and Rodin.

A fine collection of pre-Impressionists is displayed, along with Impressionists Boudin, Renoir, Monet, Guillaumin, and Sisley. Paintings by Vuillard, Marquet, Laurencin, Lebasque, and Camoin round out the collection. Important works of Raoul Dufy (28 paintings, 15 aquarelles, 87 drawings, 46 engravings, along with ceramics and tapestry) and Kees Van Dongen (*Chimera* and *The Tango*) may be seen. Four huge canvases by Léopold Sauvage (1928), ceramics by Picasso, and glassworks by Marinot are also displayed.

Villa des Arènes

In the once-aristocratic hilltop quarter of **Cimiez,** Queen Victoria would spend her winters at the Hôtel Regina, bringing half the court of England with her. Founded by the Romans, who called it Cemenelum, Cimiez was the capital of their province of the Maritime Alps. To reach the suburb, take bus 17 at the right of the Municipal Casino, the ride costing 3F (68¢). On the way back down to Nice, you can board either bus 15 or 17.

Recent excavations uncovered the ruins of a Roman town. For a 2F (46¢) admission, you can wander among the diggings between 10 a.m. and noon and from 2 to 7 p.m., June through August. The site shuts down at 6 p.m. in September and October and at 5 p.m. from November through May. The arena was big enough to hold at least 5000 spectators, who watched contests between gladiators and wild beasts shipped in from Africa.

The **Cimiez Convent** embraces a church that owns three of the most important works from the primitive painting school of Nice by the Bréa brothers. See the carved and gilded wooden main altarpiece. In the sacristy, frescoes are of a most peculiar style, suggesting an esoteric imagination. Most of these works are in the private rooms of the monastery and can only be seen on the guided tours, which take place daily at 10 a.m., 11 a.m., 3, 4, and 5 p.m. (plus

6 p.m. from May to September), and cost 4F (91¢) for adults, 2F (46¢) for students.

In the little Italianate gardens you can get a magnificent view of Nice and the Bay of Angels. Matisse and Dufy are buried in the cemetery.

An 18th-century mansion, surrounded by gardens, houses the **Museum of Archaeology,** displaying in a new and attractive presentation artifacts removed from the diggings. The fragments of Roman sarcophagi are intriguing. Upstairs is the **Matisse Museum,** honoring the great artist who elected to spend the last years of his life at Nice, dying there in 1954. Even in his final years, he continued to develop his technique of bright color and flattened perspective. Seeing his nude sketches today, you wonder how early critics could denounce them as "the female animal in all her shame and horror." The famous *Flowers and Fruits* models he did for the Matisse Chapel at Vence are displayed here, as well as an example of his stained glass. Don't miss the collection of the artist's furniture, which he frequently painted. The museum is open in summer from 10 a.m. to noon and 2 to 6 p.m. (in winter, open daily except Mondays from 2 to 5 p.m.). No admission is charged. Closed in November.

Chagall Museum (Musee National Message Biblique Marc Chagall)

For the first time in France, the state has built a museum to house the works of a single living artist. In the hills of Cimiez above Nice, the single-story museum is devoted to Marc Chagall's treatment of biblical themes. The handsome museum is surrounded by shallow pools and a garden planted with thyme, lavender, and olive trees. Born in Russia in 1887, Chagall became a French citizen in 1937. The artist and his wife donated the works—considered the most important collection of Chagall ever assembled—to the French state in 1966 and 1972. Displayed are 450 of his oil paintings, gouaches, drawings, pastels, lithographs, sculptures, ceramics, a mosaic, three stained-glass windows, and a tapestry. This museum offers some first-rate concerts of classical music at least once a month in a splendid concert room specially decorated by Chagall with outstanding stained-glass windows. Temporary exhibitions are organized each summer about great periods and artists of all times. Special lectures in the rooms are available both in French and English (for appointments, call 81-75-75). The advantages to its members include such things as half-price for the concerts, signed posters by Chagall, and the like.

The museum is at the corner of Boulevard de Cimiez and Avenue du Dr.-Ménard. It is open daily except Tuesdays from 10 a.m. to 7 p.m. July 1 to September 30, from 10 a.m. to 12:30 p.m. and 2 to 5:30 p.m. October 1 to June 30. The entrance fee is 5F ($1.14), half price on Sundays.

READER'S SIGHTSEEING TIP: "For a nice trip and the most beautiful spot I found in France, go to a little town called **Carros.** Take a bus from the Gare Routière (main terminal). The bus goes out past the airport, turns, and heads up the river past the industrial section. On the opposite side of the river and up a 4000-foot mountain is this 11th-century castle/village, with a French château. There is a small restaurant and store. Some families have lived in the same houses for up to 10 generations. The view one way is about 20 miles out into the Mediterranean and the other way is of the Italian Alps" (G. Wayne Lawhorn, Hanover, Virginia). *Authors' Note:* For lunch, visit **Hostellerie Lou Castelet** (tel. 08-12-49), where a set meal is offered for 48F ($10.96). The food is of excellent quality, and about 20 rooms are rented out if you desire to spend the night. Closed from October to December and on Tuesdays.

HOTELS: Nice has something to please every pocketbook, beginning with—

The Leading Deluxe Hotel

Negresco, 37 Promenade des Anglais (tel. 88-39-51), is one of the super-glamor belle époque hotels strung along the French Riviera. When Madam Augier-Mesnage took over the hotel, wiseacres predicted she'd assumed a "white elephant," or what the French call a "pink elephant." However, she has triumphed, showing what taste and imagination—not to mention money—can do. The Negresco, named after its pre-World War I founder, who died without a franc in Paris in 1920, draws two reactions: (1) some say the original glamor has been restored; (2) others maintain that even in its heyday the Negresco wasn't as good as it is today! The deluxe hotel was built right on the seafront, in the "French château" style, with a Mansard roof and a domed tower.

Under a dome of stained glass, the rotunda is encircled by columns and decorated with an elaborate handwoven carpet on which Louis XVI-style chairs are arranged in color groups of royal-purple, carnation-red, and Versailles gold. Opening onto this grand salon is "Le Bar," with a mezzanine of tables—richly decorated in plush opera-red and blue, evoking a clublike atmosphere.

Inspired by the châteaux and museums of France, the decorators of the bedrooms scoured Europe, gathering antiques, tapestries and paintings, and objects of art to lend prestige and drama. Some of the bedrooms have personality themes, such as the Louis XIV chamber, with its green-velvet bed set under a brocaded rose tester. The "Chambre Impératrice Josephine 1810" regally recreates the Empire bedroom, with a huge rosewood "swan bed" set in a fleur-de-lis draped recess. At the foot and bottom stand two bronze torchiers. Ultra-feminine is the Napoleon III bedroom, with swagged walls and a half-crowned canopy in pink, resting on a leopard-skin carpet. Not only are the rooms extravagantly furnished, but the staff completes the scene by wearing 18th-century costumes. You're greeted at the door by a porter in black boots, a royal-blue and scarlet cape, gold braid, and a red-plumed hat.

Two seasons spin around this hotel, the costliest time to visit being from March 20 to October 1. During this peak period demi-pension is required, coming to 110F ($25.11) above the room tariff. Rooms themselves range from a minimum of 250F ($57.08) in a single to a high of 220F ($50.23) in the best, most sumptuously decorated doubles. The most expensive rooms, of course, open onto the Mediterranean.

Meals are served in La Rotonde grill room (open from 7 till midnight), with an art nouveau counter in the shape of a horseshoe. You're served by waitresses in hoop skirts. The featured restaurant, however, is the Chantecler, where an excellent chef dazzles foreign visitors with his lobster pâté, his crayfish salad, his fricassée of fish, and his pear soufflé, among other delightful offerings. Expect to pay from 220F ($50.23) if you dine here.

The Upper and Middle Bracket

Splendid-Sofitel, 50 Boulevard Victor-Hugo (tel. 88-69-54), is the most modern of the upper-bracket hotels of Nice, built on the corner of a wide boulevard lined with large shade trees. The beach with its promenade is just four blocks away. On the eighth and ninth floors is an open-air swimming pool, surrounded by a deck with parasol tables, a loggia bar for poolside drinks, a sauna, a sunbathing deck, even a bath for children. It's a celestial experience to swim there, with a panoramic view of the city, the sea, and the surrounding hills.

The four-star chain hotel is well conceived, with a clean-cut yet not cold decor. Balancing the contemporary architecture are autumnal colors and warmly grained wood paneling. Likewise, the bedrooms are soothingly balanced in style, with walls of daffodil yellow, white candlewick counterpane, and classic headboards set against paneling of rare imported wood. Every room contains a sparkling tiled bath with shower, a radio with five programs of piped-in-music, a television outlet, direct-dial telephone, and air conditioning. In addition, most of them open onto balconies or good-size terraces. There's a slight variation in price, due to room placement and size. Doubles range between 320F ($73.06) and 380F ($86.75), and singles go for anywhere from 260F ($59.36) to 290F ($66.21). Pension is not obligatory, and à la carte meals are available in the Grill Room and Coffeeshop. However, for demi-pension, one person pays anywhere from 230F ($52.51) to 320F ($73.06).

The entire hotel was newly built and furnished in 1964, created on the site of the 1883 Splendid, which had been the residence of the king of Wurtemberg. Since 1910, it has been under the control of the same family, who have wisely seen fit to keep their attentive staff, many of whom have been with the hotel for years. Added for guests are a hairdresser, money exchange office, a garage, and boutiques.

Westminster, 27 Promenade des Anglais (tel. 88-29-44), stands proudly in the center of the beach promenade, with most of its bedrooms facing the warm Mediterranean sun and sea. It maintains a belle époque atmosphere. Decor-wise, the interior is impressive. The grandeur of the Westminster bravely holds its own.

The bedrooms, too, are of another era, with brass or older wooden beds, gilt mirrors, cretonne-covered armchairs, and formal draperies with tasseled tiebacks. The view determines the price. Doubles range from 250F ($57.08) to 300F ($68.49), the latter with tiny balconies opening onto the seafront. Singles with bath go for anywhere from 180F ($41.09) to 220F ($50.23). A "free" continental breakfast is served either at your balcony window or else on the street-front loggia where guests congregate at all times of the day and evening, reclining in bamboo chairs under a canopy, surrounded by ferns, palm trees, and subtropical flowers.

A rather surprising restaurant, **Il Pozzo**, 1 rue Meyerbeer (tel. 87-02-87), is on the premises—a recreation of a "quaint" Italian tavern, with thick white-washed rough-plaster arches, a beamed ceiling, a stone well with a bucket, and a raised open fire where meat is grilled. Pizzas range from 20F ($4.57) to 45F ($10.27).

The **Westminster** is a wine and cocktail bar decorated in the English colonial style. **Le Farniente** offers good service on a flowered terrace; it features an international haute cuisine. A set meal costs 90F ($20.55), although you can order à la carte as well.

The **Gounod Splendid**, 3 rue Gounod (tel. 88-26-20), a few minutes from the sea, has been taken over by the Sofitel Splendid next door. It has been entirely modernized, and although it retains its old Niçois exterior, with ornate balconies and domed roof, the inside is new. The attractive lobby and adjoining lounge are festive, with Boussac cloth on the walls, old prints, and copper pots with flowers.

All the bedrooms are entirely renovated, with modern tiled bathrooms or showers, toilets, piped-in-music, TV, and air conditioning. Most rooms are quiet, overlooking the gardens of private homes on both sides. There is a garden where breakfast is served in summer. The rates, including a continental breakfast, service, and taxes, are 220F ($50.23) to 240F ($54.79) for a twin-bedded room, and 160F ($36.53) to 190F ($43.38) for a single. All rooms now also have direct-dial telephones, and guests can dial a United States number direct from their rooms if they wish.

Guests at the Gounod can enjoy the amenities of the Sofitel next door: swimming pool, sauna, panoramic bar, and beauty parlor. The staff of the Gounod was trained at the Sofitel.

West-End, 31 Promenade des Anglais (tel. 88-79-91). Time has been kind to this old-fashioned, stately hotel, strongly holding onto its glamorous position on the waterfront. Most of the rooms look out onto the front garden, with its tall date palms, flowers, shrubbery, and a splashing fountain. The entrance is formal but small, with a fine 19th-century tapestry behind the desk, and (to your left) a petit reception salon in yellow. With its baronial fireplace and paneled walls, the bar seems to belong in a château.

The special advantage of the West-End is its wide range of rates for accommodations, the most expensive with tall French windows opening onto tiny balconies fronting the sea, the cheapest facing the rear garden. The prices quoted include a continental breakfast, taxes, and a 15% service charge. Double rooms with bath range downward in price from 220F ($50.23) to 175F ($39.95), and singles go from 185F ($42.24) to 130F ($29.68). Most of the room furnishings are of the Provençal style. No meals are served at the West-End, but you'll be near some of the better restaurants of Nice.

Busby, 36-38 rue du Maréchal-Joffre (tel. 88-19-41), should please those desiring a centrally positioned hotel with a touch of quiet elegance, plus all the modern amenities. Totally renovated, the hotel kept its old Niçois façade, with balconies and shutters at its tall windows. It's on a corner, allowing for more outside bedrooms. The bar is a cozy spot, with walls paneled in Wedgwood blue and white. The long dining room is divided by butterscotch marble columns and decorated with gilded pier-glass mirrors and ladderback fruitwood chairs with rush seats.

The bedrooms, dignified yet colorful, might contain a pair of mahogany twin beds set in a red recess and flanked by two white-and-gold wardrobes. In a room with private bath, the rate for two persons is 200F ($45.66); for one, 150F ($34.26). All tariffs include a continental breakfast, service, and taxes. The restaurant is open only from December 15 until the end of May. Meals (lunch or dinner) cost from 55F ($12.56).

Windsor, 11 rue Dalpozzo (tel. 88-59-35), right in the heart of Nice, a short walk from the Promenade des Anglais, seems more like a stone villa than a hotel. In the moderately priced bracket, it's a charmer, with about 60 rooms, all excellently kept and containing color TVs, radios, and minibars. Many of its tall French windows open onto a verdant rear garden, where guests congregate on the graveled terrace, pleasantly surrounded by coconut date palms and pots of red geraniums. After a while, they can be seen jumping into the swimming pool. The drawing room, with a blue-and-white coffered ceiling, chestnut-paneled walls, a raised fireplace, and armchairs, is small enough to be intimate. The bedrooms contain private baths or showers. The owner, Mr. Redolfi-Strizzot, charges 160F ($36.53) in a double with shower and toilet, 200F ($45.66) with complete bath, these tariffs including service, taxes, and a continental breakfast. Singles with showers or baths go from 150F ($34.26) to 160F ($36.53). Garage facilities are available, as is a sauna.

La Résidence, 18 Avenue Durante (tel. 88-89-45), was built in 1963 and is owned by Monsieur Matlowski. The exterior is pristine, with apple-green shutters. Accommodations (34 rooms in all, most with private bath) are very comfortable, although the decor goes a little haywire with colored floral wallpaper, kelly-green bedspreads, and red carpets and slipcovers. From July to September, the highest rates apply: 190F ($43.38) for a double room with private bath, 115F ($26.25) for a bathless double. Suites are available at 260F ($59.36) for three and 270F ($61.64) for four persons. All rates include a continental breakfast, served either in your room or in one of the lower-floor salons. These little sitting lounges have their own styles—one is Regency, another modern.

La Pérouse, 11 Quai Rauba-Capeu (tel. 88-89-45), was once a prison on a rock, but it's been reconstructed and is now a unique Riviera hotel. This little cliff-hanging establishment overlooking the sea is entered through a lower-level entrance lobby, where an elevator takes you up to a handsome setting with gardens and a pool. La Pérouse is built right into the gardens of an ancient château-fort. The hotel itself is like an old Provençal home, with low ceilings, white walls, and antiques. All is silent, and the atmosphere is near-luxurious. Most of the rooms have a loggia overlooking the bay. Depending on the situation of the room, singles range from 115F ($26.25) to 180F ($41.09); doubles, 145F ($33.10) to 220F ($50.23), breakfast included. Accommodations have either private showers or baths.

The Budget Range

Georges, 3 rue Henri-Cordier (tel. 86-23-41), is a real discovery. Nestled on a ledge, in a tuck-away corner of Nice, it is only an 18-room hotel, furnished in a personal way, employing an instinctive high taste level. Although they had never run a hotel before, Monsieur and Madame Raymond Vidal are doing wonders with this one, adding little touches where many a hotelier would have compromised or cheated. The building itself, of course, is streamlined and contemporary, but the furnishings employ provincial or perhaps Louis XVI reproductions. An attractive reading room has been added, and there is sunbathing on the third floor.

Double wardrobes, twin beds, rich brass hardware, lush towels, and fine bedspreads are used throughout. Picture windows with filmy drapes let in the brilliant Mediterranean sun. The accommodations come with private baths, the cheaper doubles costing 120F ($27.40), the upper-floor units going for 165F ($37.68). Service and taxes are included in the rates. A continental breakfast, served on a flower terrace or in the rooms, is 10F ($2.28) extra. Down the street is the major hotel school of Provence. The students could learn from the Vidals.

St.-Georges, 7 Avenue Georges Clemenceau (tel. 88-79-21), stands on a quiet street near the railway station. Its façade is like a wedding cake, with ornate architectural details painted oyster-white, the shutters a muted aqua, the awning a faded red. Tradition has been maintained inside as well. Antiques have been used generously in the sitting room and the reception lobby. Even the bedrooms contain interesting old pieces, such as high brass beds, bronze chandeliers, and cretonne floral fabrics. The baths are brightly colored with tiled walls and floors. A double with bath and either twin or "matrimonial" beds costs 135F ($30.82), although bathless accommodations go for 94F ($21.46). Singles range from 58F ($13.24) to 92F ($21), depending on the plumbing. Included are a continental breakfast, service, and tax.

Locarno, 4 Avenue des Baumettes (tel. 96-28-00), is better suited for motorists who don't mind its somewhat out-of-the-way location in Les Baumettes, about an eight-minute ride from the center. Entirely renovated and redecorated, the Locarno offers 16 air-conditioned bedrooms. It is about 50 yards from the sea. The style is French modern, and each of the 50 well-furnished bedrooms contains a bath or shower plus a toilet, as well as a radio and automatic "wake-up" service. Half the rooms are air-conditioned and have television sets. Doubles with complete bath rent for 185F ($42.24) to 205F ($46.80). One person pays on the average of 120F ($27.40), all tariffs including a continental breakfast. The exterior is inviting as well, with aqua shutters and arched windows opening onto small balconies. To use the garage of the hotel, an additional charge of 20F ($4.57) is imposed.

Flots d'Azur, 101 Promenade des Anglais (tel. 86-51-25), is an inexpensive place directly on the sea, not too long a walk from the more elaborate and costlier promenade hotels of Nice. It's a prim, three-story, square villa, set back from the street, with two coconut trees on either side of the entry. Seemingly, every bedroom of this villa-turned-hotel has a good view, as well as sea breezes. There's a small sitting room and sun terrace in front. The accommodations vary widely in size and decor, a double room with private bath costing 130F ($29.68), but only 110F ($25.11) with a shower. Singles go from 70F ($15.98) to 80F ($18.26), depending on the plumbing. The quotations include service and tax. A continental breakfast, costing 10F ($2.28), is served on the front terrace.

Villa Eden, 99 bis Promenade des Anglais (tel. 86-53-70), is a 19th-century villa right on the seafront, previously owned by a Russian countess. Tall palms lead to the entrance to the rear garden, with its 18-foot-high hedges of ivy and red roses. Among parasol tables and bright geraniums, guests gather here in garden chairs. Owned by the Prone family, the Eden offers individualized accommodations. The father and mother have turned over the major responsibilities to the younger generation, the principal task falling on Michèle.

The living room—much like that in a private home—contains a charming collection of antiques, including Empire armchairs covered in harmonious gold. Opening onto the rear garden, the dining room is treated more in a provincial manner. As is to be expected in this converted villa, the bedrooms vary greatly in size, although all have a liberal sprinkling of old furniture, attractive and comfortable. Half pension, required in July and August, costs 180F ($41.09) for two persons in a room with private shower bath, but only 155F ($35.39) in a bathless double, these rates including taxes and service. Reductions are granted in low season.

Magnan, Square Général-Ferrié (tel. 86-76-00), is a simple, modern hotel, about a 10-minute bus ride into the heart of town, but only a minute or so from the Promenade des Anglais and the bay. A guest can put on his or her bathing suit in the room, then walk to the sea in a beach robe. A six-story building, the Magnan is reached through an entry of marble and glass, with a pair of potted shrubs at the front door. If possible, try to book an upper-floor accommodation, as the traffic noise will disturb you less, and the view of the Mediterranean will be better from your balcony. A double-bedded room with shower goes for 115F ($26.25) for two, rising to 145F ($33.10) if occupied by three. A twin-bedded room with private bath and toilet is 162F ($36.99) for two, 220F ($50.23) for three, and 235F ($53.65) for four guests, these tariffs including taxes, service, and continental breakfasts.

Suisse, 15 Quai Rauba-Capeu (tel. 85-62-20), is unusually positioned, in the old town near the sea, just below the château. Up a flight of steps, it is seemingly interlocked with an old tower. The rooms, furnished in a modified modern style, are priced according to the view you get as well as the plumbing. Strong colors are used throughout. In July and August and during the festival, you'll be asked to have one main meal at the Suisse plus breakfast. A seafront double with bath costs 131F ($29.91), 187F ($42.69) with bath and toilet. Bathless doubles (some with sea views) cost only 89F ($20.32). On weekdays, a set meal is offered for 45F ($10.27). Owned by Mme. Gazia and Mme. Giordan, the Suisse is open all year.

Little Palace, 9 Avenue Baquis (tel. 88-70-49), is for those who yearn for a personalized, old-fashioned atmosphere. This private little world is the domain of Mme. Commette, who is totally Gallic, maintaining the best traditions of another era. Her sitting rooms look as if they were her very own. You expect to see her family in the parlor. The furnishings are a collection of Spanish chairs, Flemish tapestry-framed needlepoint, library tables with pots of ferns and Chinese lamps with fringed shades. Even the reception desk reminds you of an old inn, with spindles of receipts and an elaborate book for allotting rooms. Doubles with bath or shower range in price from 128F ($29.22) to 145F ($33.10), although bathless accommodations cost only 76F ($17.35) to 93F ($21.23). Singles with bath or shower go from 115F ($26.25) to 128F ($29.22), all these tariffs including service and taxes. The Little Palace is open year round; it is, in fact, Mme. Commette's home.

Helvétique, 47 rue Hôtel-des-Postes (tel. 85-47-38), is one of a cluster of hotels in Nice in the heart of the city, near the Place Masséna. It's sheltered in a neat building with a marble-faced entry. Half of the accommodations still have the old Niçois look, with brass beds and floral cretonne fabrics as draperies and spreads. Others have been modernized, with new tiled baths. For bed and breakfast in a twin-bedded room with bath or shower, you'll pay 125F ($28.54), that rate dropping to 110F ($25.11) for two persons in a bathless room. Singles without bath cost 62F ($14.15), rising to 100F ($22.83) with private bath. You can stay here with or without pension, although the well-cooked meals may tempt you. Closed in November.

Victoria, 33 Boulevard Victor-Hugo (tel. 88-39-60), is a new hotel, part of the Mapotel chain, about five blocks from the seafront, facing one of the major boulevards of Nice. The façade is classic, with balconies and shutters on the wide French windows. Best of all in the quiet, rather casually kept rear garden and lawn studded with peach, fig, and palm trees. The interior furnishings are of good standard. A living room opens onto the garden. The whole hotel is decorated with style. The immaculately kept bedrooms are of good size, with bath or shower, direct-dial telephones, television, and minibars. Doubles with shower or bath cost 210F ($47.44) to 230F ($52.51).

Les Cigales ("The Cicadas"), 16 rue Dalpozzo (tel. 88-33-75), is an unheralded, tiny economy gem. It's a pretty, two-story villa, about three blocks from the promenade. The façade is classic and formal, with wrought-iron balconies and French doors. It stands next to a private garden. Inside, it's as homey as can be. There are only 12 rooms, half of which contain private showers. For a double with shower, you pay 65F ($14.84), but with hot and cold running water, the tariff drops to just 55F ($12.56). These prices include service and taxes. A continental breakfast costs another 9F ($2.05).

Le Panorama, 38 rue Segurane (tel. 55-89-36), is operated by Madame Sournas on the second floor of a building overlooking the port, close to the beach. Although the furnishings are clean and modern, the little hotel still has a personal touch. Two persons pay only 60F ($13.70) for a room with hot and cold running water and a kitchenette furnished with pots and pans. Four persons get a great bargain for 90F ($20.55) in a large room with shower, toilet, and kitchenette, although some cheaper doubles with less facilities go for 52F ($11.87). Those in accommodations without showers pay an extra 7F ($1.60) for use of the public ones. The German philosopher Nietzsche once lived here.

Prior, 5 rue d'Alsace-Lorraine (tel. 88-20-24), is an immaculately kept small hotel run by a pleasant and charming woman, Mme. Lodi. Near the train station, the Prior has a lounge and doors decorated in plaids; the stairs and floors are of marble. Most of the rooms have antique furnishings, with chintz bedcoverings and curtains. Depending on the plumbing, two persons are charged from 60F ($13.70) to 120F ($27.40). Three to four persons can also be accommodated, at tariffs going from a low of 85F ($19.41) to a high of 115F ($26.25), the latter with shower only. A continental breakfast, included in the rates, is most often taken on the terrace.

Central Hotel, 10 rue de Suisse (tel. 88-85-08), is the domain of Madame Cornacchini, a gracious hostess who receives customers as if they were guests in her own home. Her rooms are spacious, light, and airy, and are attractively furnished. One person pays 52F ($11.87) nightly, the tariff rising to 60F ($13.70) for two persons. In a room suitable for three guests, the rate goes up to 85F ($19.41). All these tariffs include a petit déjeuner. The location is on an attractive square, within walking distance of the railway station.

READERS' HOTEL SELECTIONS: "Hôtel Durante, 16 Avenue Durante (tel. 88-84-40), is a 'must,' particularly for film buffs who want to keep posted on the current film fare in Nice (and Cannes). The patronne, the beautiful Madame Dufaure, is the most knowledgeable and charming manager in France. The tastefully decorated rooms (all facing a court) go for a peak 120F ($27.40) in a double. Sixteen have kitchenettes. If you love films, this is the only place to stay. The woman is fabulous" (Norman F. Lareau, New York, N.Y.). . . . "My husband and I recommend the Hôtel Monclar, 29 Boulevard de Magnan (tel. 86-70-66). Madame Heckendum, the owner, and her mother make you very welcome, and nothing is a trouble. Double rooms cost 75F ($17.12) to 85F ($19.41) with breakfast or use of the kitchen; singles are 52F ($11.87). Our room had a sundeck, which was useful for drying clothes, a definite advantage these days when so many places forbid washing in your room. Car parking space is also available" (Evelyn Seicombe, New Plymouth, New Zealand). . . . "I came upon the Hôtel de la Mer, 4 Place Masséna (tel. 85-61-54), a small hotel with 12 good-size rooms, all with either a bath or a shower. It is in a perfect location: right in the heart of Nice and only 50 meters from the seafront. It is also quite close to Old Nice. The hotel is run by an extremely congenial and accommodating couple, who strive hard to please their clients. A room for two, with an exceptional view of the grand *place* of Nice, costs 115F ($26.25)" (Susan Brawley, Arundel, Sussex, England). . . . "We stayed at the Hotel-Pension Gilbert, 14 rue Pertinax (tel. 85-16-60), five minutes from the railway station, eight minutes from the sea. The charge is 45F ($10.27) in a single, rising to 55F ($12.56) in a bathless double. The proprietor, Jeanne Bernon, is a charming woman who speaks some English. Pertinax intersects the Avenue Jean-Médicin" (Bill and Jeannie Kaye Beanshaw, Franklin, La.).

RESTAURANTS: This city will feed you Italian food, Niçois dishes, even specialties from Lyon and Périgord, and, of course, bouillabaisse. Some of its local restaurants charge the lowest tariffs on the Riviera.

The Leading Restaurants

Le Madrigal, 7 Avenue Georges-Clemenceau (tel. 88-79-23), is one of the newer restaurants of Nice, and it has quickly distinguished itself by its stellar cuisine, served in a tasteful tavern setting. Jean Pierre Robert is the chef, and he's an outstanding one; Paul Cappa is the gracious host. They serve many fine dishes of the nouvelle cuisine school, using only fresh produce from the market, and offering two set meals at 100F ($22.83) and 150F ($34.26).

A good many blocks from the waterfront, the restaurant is next to the St.-Georges Hotel, and has honeysuckle growing at its door. Fresh flowers are placed throughout, and you'll notice that the service is friendly and attentive without being ostentatious. The garden is a cool and inviting oasis on a summer day.

The food is most imaginative, including such openers as a puff pastry of vegetables or strips of guinea fowl in a shallot cream sauce. Main-dish specialties include veal kidneys Cézanne and stuffed young rabbit. We've also found the desserts well cooked and appetizing. The restaurant is closed on Sundays and from mid-August until the first week of September.

La Poularde ("Chez Lucullus"), 9 rue Deloye (tel. 85-22-90), is the domain of Monsieur Normand, who rules with a velvet fist over this Provençal inn, dedicated to serving his guests the finest viands in the city. The patron insists on using only the best vegetables, meats, and fish from the local markets, and he doesn't believe in compromise. Even on our most hurried visits to Nice we try to have at least two meals at La Poularde. What to order? Everything is good, although you might consider the tasty Niçois hors d'oeuvres as a starter, costing 40F ($9.13). Some of the best main dishes are rouget (red mullet) à la sauvage, 55F ($12.56); capilotade de poularde (pullet) paysanne, 55F also; loupe grillé (grilled bass) with fennel, 90F ($20.55); châteaubriand for two, 150F ($34.26). The pastry of the house is usually moist and creamy, costing 23F ($5.25). The doors shut every Wednesday and all of July.

Petit Brouant ("Chez Puget"), 4 bis rue Deloye (tel. 85-25-84), offers the pride of its patron: perhaps the finest bouillabaisse des pêcheurs along the Riviera. It's crammed full of freshly caught seafood, soothingly spiced—everything from "hogfish" to conger eel to spiny lobsters. The right amount of garlic, the right amount of saffron—the kettle would please epicures. One food expert wrote, "If the bouillabaisse is well made, you should be able to distinguish the flavor of each variety of fish." Chef de cuisine-propriétaire Monsieur Gaston Puget (Meilleur Ouvrier de France) succeeds.

For more conventional meal planning, you might start with soupe de poissons (fish soup) or smoked salmon. A highly praised dish is poulet de Bresse à la crème. The pastries, made fresh daily, incorporate fresh peaches or strawberries, whatever is in season. Most tabs range in price from 85F ($19.41) to 175F ($39.95) for a complete meal, although if you order anything with lobster in it, your bill will easily climb beyond the 220F ($50.23) mark. The garden, with its subtropical flowers and terrace of tables, is most enjoyable. Closed Mondays and in June.

St.-Moritz, 5 rue Congrès (tel. 88-54-90), is only a short walk from the Promenade des Anglais, down the street from the American Express and behind the Palais de la Méditerranée. One American journalist wrote: "If I were 22, possessed of plenty of money, and had a movie starlet to beau around (three preposterous postulates), I would dine at the St. Moritz every night." In this mock-chalet setting, celebrities from Cannes often drop in, enjoying the setting with lighting that makes everybody (well, nearly) look glamorous.

But it's the food that wins in the long run. The patron, Monsieur Marti, grows his own herbs in his garden, using them for his sauces as well as his broiled or grilled dishes. For example, he makes a superb sauce verte with freshly cut chives, tarragon, chervil, basil, mint, and marjoram. The bouillabaisse—one of the most savory we've ever sampled in Nice—is superb. Other interesting side dishes include lobster in puff pastry, cheese soufflé, and the chef's special tart. Expect to spend from 110F ($25.11) to 140F ($31.96) per person. The restaurant is closed on Thursdays and from January 4 to February 4.

L'Esquinade, 5 Quai des Deux-Emmanuel (tel. 89-59-36), on the far side of the harbor near the car ferry, is rustic. The view of the harbor, the wooden water wheel, the bright-tablecloths, the rough plaster walls, and the chandeliers with sheaves of oats and corn make it somewhat of a stage setting, a romanticized *moulin.* The waiters in regional costumes bring dishes to the canopied front—past goldfish tanks—from the large grill at the rear of the restaurant. The chef's specialities include tournedos poêle au Roquefort and loup (sea bass) en chemise with a Mondesir sauce. Sorbets round out most repasts. A complete meal will cost from 170F ($38.81) to 200F ($45.66). Monsieur Béraud closes his restaurant on Sundays and in July.

Bouillabaisse on Fishermen's Row

Girelle Royale, 41 Quai États-Unis (tel. 85-63-97), enjoys the most acclaim of all the restaurants on this promenade bordering the sea. Torchères at night draw attention to its second-floor panoramic deluxe dining room. The 60F ($13.70) dinner includes a fish or a meat course, such as scampi in tarter sauce or grilled Alpine lamb with delicately scented herbs. The gastronomic menu at 90F ($20.55) is dazzling, offering a choice of the chef's specialties, including "la véritable bouillabaisse," turbotin de mer farci, or rognon de veau (veal kidneys) au safran (saffron). After 10:30 p.m. you can select only from the à la carte menu. A meal here on a moonlit Mediterranean night is an experience not easily forgotten. The restaurant is open every day from April 1 to September 30, closed on Wednesdays during the winter months.

Prince's, 57 Quai des États-Unis (tel. 85-71-56), is an economy seaside restaurant, also on "Fish Restaurant Row." The bouillabaisse is the specialty here, made with rougets (red mullet), 100F ($22.83). If you can't abide fish and everybody else in your party loves it, you can order an entrecôte, priced at 62F ($14.15). The menu gastronomique costs 130F ($29.68). Prince's is a colorful little place, Mediterranean in ambience, with sidewalk tables and provincial cloths. Closed Thursdays.

Seafood at the Harbor

La Cassine, 26 Quai Lunel (tel. 55-23-34), offers one of the best bargains at the harbor, an entire meal for 80F ($18.26). On our most recent expedition, this rather large fixed-price repast featured a seafood salad, followed by friture de la Baie des Anges (a fish fry from the Bay of Angels), a generous serving of ratatouille (a Niçois dish of eggplant, tomato, onions, garlic, peppers, and olive oil), ending with a selection of cheese and dessert. À la carte, you can order a delicious bouillabaisse at 80F ($18.26), chock-full of tasty hunks of the day's catch, spiced traditionally, and served with hunks of crusty bread. One fascinating column of the à la carte menu presents the special dishes for which Niçoise cuisine is famous. These include ravioli Nice-style at 35F ($7.99), ratatouille both hot and cold, costing 25F ($5.71), and salade Niçoise, also 25F. The set dinner is served between noon and 2 p.m. and from 7 to 9 p.m. Dress simply, unless you want to impress the crabs and lobsters. The restaurant is closed on Sundays and in August.

Barale, 39 rue Beaumont (tel. 89-17-94), is presided over by Catherine-Helene Barale, who believes in preserving a "Nissarda" cuisine—a unique Riviera blend of Italian and French. Her charmingly rustic restaurant, a museumlike assemblage of antiques including kitchen utensils, is bustling and usually overstuffed with hungry diners who know they can obtain some of their most memorable Côte d'Azur meals here. Madame Barale was born here, and she's learned the family secrets well. Her wares are listed on a blackboard menu hung with garlic pigtails. Her menu depends on her whim—or shopping—on any particular day. However, she nearly always sells squares of the Nice pizza called pissaladière and, of course, the classic salade Niçoise. For a second course, you might be served gnocchi or green lasagna. For a main dish you are likely to be offered pieche—poached veal stuffed with fresh Swiss chard, cheese, ham, eggs, and rice. It's superbly delicious. A fresh fruit tart rounds out most meals. Expect to pay around $20, which will include a bottle of the house's red wine.

Moderately Priced Dining

Don Camillo, 5 rue Ponchettes (tel. 85-67-95), set back from the coastal road near the foot of the château and the Naval Museum, is run like a country inn. The dining room is long and narrow, with a decorative clutter of paintings and colorful plates set in niches. A still-life table displays wines, elaborately prepared foodstuff, and desserts. The restaurant is simple but pleasant, serving what is generally considered the tastiest Italian food in Nice. The fettuccini is excellent, costing 28F ($6.39). Main-course selections include osso bucco, the Milanese specialty, 40F ($9.13), and saltimbocca à la Romaine, also 40F. Some prefer the ravioli maison at 26F ($5.94), others the tripe maison at 38F ($8.68). For dessert, a smooth choice is zabaglione with sherry, 40F ($9.13), for two persons. Closed Sundays and in July.

Taverne Alsacienne, 49 rue Hôtel-des-Postes (tel. 85-44-38), is one of the best brasseries in Nice. Next door to the Helvétique Hôtel, it is furnished in a typically Alsatian manner, with dark oak paneling, scrubbed wooden tables, and bowls of fresh flowers. And, of course, there's plenty of wonderful-tasting beer. The chef's larder is well stocked. The set meal at 40F ($9.13) plus 15% service merely gives you a preview. The choucroûte speciale (sauerkraut) at 45F ($10.27) is magnificent. River trout has always been a favorite on Alsatian menus, and it's served here meunière at 23F ($5.25). Try also the boeuf bourguignonne at 36F ($8.22). Food is served until 1 a.m., in case your pension didn't feed you well at 7.

Best for the Budget

Le Relais ("The Posting House"), 8 rue de la Suisse (tel. 88-11-48), in the style of a Provençal inn, specializes in dishes from Lyon, the gastronomic center of France. Inside, the decor of stained-glass windows, rustic lamps, bits of copper, beamed ceilings, wine bottles lining one wall, and terra-cotta floors provides a rustic atmosphere. Some of the English visitors who frequent the establishment look like characters from early Somerset Maugham stories.

The food is exceptionally good and the prices are low. Two menus of the day are provided: at 35F ($7.99) and 50F ($11.42), the latter including both a fish and a meat course. In season, fresh and tender asparagus is served with aïoli, the garlic-based mayonnaise praised by Dumas and Mistral. One superb dish—the pièce de résistance of the chef, Etienne Sipos—is lapereaux (rabbits) aux herbes de Provence. The sole meunière is also good. Closed on off-season Saturdays and in November, Le Relais is opposite the Church of Notre-Dame.

La Nissarda, 17 rue Gubernatis (tel. 85-26-29), is utterly unpretentious, specializing in a cuisine Niçoise and drawing a steady stream of locals who appreciate the cookery of Monsieur Devos Daniel. It lies on a tree-shaded square in the heart of the city and is entered through a front bar, where friendships are easily made if you speak French. Strangers are regarded with a certain curiosity around here but are warmly welcomed. One bearded artist, who seemed influenced heavily by Van Gogh, took us there with the stipulation that "you must taste tripe in the Niçoise style before you leave: And if you eat tripe, you must try it at La Nissarda." He was right, it turned out, although the chef does all the local dishes well. For example, on his 35F ($7.99) fixed-price menu he offers two courses, usually stuffed sardines or ravioli and a main course such as roast chicken, followed by dessert. For 50F ($11.42) you get another course, usually a savory fish soup or Niçoise salad. On Sunday noon his most elaborate menu is offered, costing 55F ($12.56); on Sunday night the price drops back to 35F ($7.99) for a more simple meal. Hours are daily except Wednesday from noon to 2 p.m. and from 7 to 9 p.m.

Le Saëtone, 8 rue d'Alsace-Lorraine (no phone), offers one of the best bargains in town. For just 30F ($6.85) you can enjoy a well-prepared four-course meal, beginning with hors d'oeuvres, then half a roast chicken, a salad, and crème caramel. This low price includes service. For 40F ($9.13), you can order five plates, but you must pay an additional 12% service charge. This miniature restaurant contains only two sidewalk tables, and is decorated in a rustic style, using wrought iron and natural woods. It is closed on Tuesdays and from mid-November to mid-December.

L'Étoile, 3 rue de Belgique, also offers one of the best bargains in town, rivaling Le Saëtone. Here you can order a three-course menu (and that includes wine) for only 25F ($5.71). We most recently enjoyed fisherman's soup, followed by roast beef with pommes frites, then an apple tart. At night the dinner costs 28F ($6.39).

Maire, 10 rue de Suisse, is another great bargain. The menu at 26F ($5.94) includes both wine and service. The specialty is quiche Lorraine, that hot cheese pie which is served as an appetizer. The atmosphere here, too, is Provençal, with beams and brass utensils. The cotton curtains are decorated with Provençal sketches. It's a short walk from Boulevard Jean-Médecin.

La Trappa, rue de la Préfecture (tel. 85-64-90), is deep in Vieille Ville (the old town). It was founded 100 years ago to feed the fishermen and flower growers in the area. It still has an aura of yesterday. It's crowded every night with habitués who know they can get good, simple food at inexpensive prices. The service is friendly and informal, the atmosphere enhanced by salami sausages and Italian cheeses hanging from the ceiling. The fish is fresh. For a beginning, try the soup au pistou, followed by a main course or the green noodles. For dessert, try the fresh strawberries or the apple tart. You can trust the vegetables; they come directly from the owner's gardens overlooking Nice. Expect to spend 40F ($9.13) to 80F ($18.26) per person here for a complete meal. At night, and even at noon, you'll enjoy the amateur singer who entertains you with "bel canto."

Snacks and Light Meals

Le Koudou, 28 Promenade des Anglais (tel. 87-33-74), is a tearoom-coffeehouse-snackbar right on the promenade, with luxurious sidewalk tables and chairs, under an ultramodern apartment house next to the Negresco Hôtel. You can relax on a canopy-shaded terrace, comfortably sipping your beverage, watching the passing parade. The crêpes are particularly good, including one made with a banana flamed in liqueur. The ice creams—everything from "African Queen" to peach Melba—are a specialty, averaging 12F ($2.74), and are often elaborate concoctions. A wide assortment of drinks is offered, from a Pimm's No. 1 at 13F ($2.97) to sangría at 11F ($2.51).

Mayfair Brasserie, Avenue des Phocéens, is opposite the Fountain of the Sun on the Place Masséna. It makes brasserie dining quite a treat. The decor and the setting are well styled. While primarily for drinks and snacks, it also serves regular meals. An all-glass terrace fronts the sidewalk, with lattice-covered boxes of flowers, bamboo chairs, and scrubbed natural-wood tables. At the bar, there is a simulated turn-of-the-century atmosphere with gaslight globes and chandeliers. In the food department, the terrine du chef is good at 14F ($3.20); likewise the chicken salad, 16F ($3.65), and the onion soup gratinée, 18F ($4.11). A hamburger costs 24F ($5.48), and there are sandwiches at 9F ($2.05). The chef's tart is 13F ($2.97). Closed Mondays.

READERS' RESTAURANT SELECTION: "Very close to the railway station is an inexpensive, real home-type French restaurant, **Le Bayeux,** 20 rue Miron. The complete meal was only 28F ($6.39). The restaurant is run solely by an elderly man and his wife. We were the only non-French in the place and really enjoyed being with the French in Nice" (Nels and Dotty Consalves, Hayward, Calif.).

AN EXCURSION TO LEVENS: Levens is an attractive residential town guarding the **Valée de la Vésubie.** At a point 15 miles from Nice on the D19, it is at an altitude of 1800 feet. Excursionists come this way to see some of the most beautiful spots in the mountains.

A trip to the **Saut des Français** ("Frenchmen's Leap") is recommended. It's at the exit from the village of Duranus. French Republican soldiers in 1793 were tossed over this belvedere by Barbets, guerrilla bands from Nice. The fall—without a parachute!—was some 1200 feet down to the Vésubie.

At another 15 miles you'll come upon **La Madone d'Utelle,** at an altitude of 3900 feet. Here a panoramic view of the Maritime Alps unfolds.

Malausséna, Place de l'Hôtel de Ville (tel. 91-70-06), stands right in the center of the village. A three-story hotel, it offers clean, comfortable rooms, a dozen in all. For full pension the charge ranges from 110F ($25.11) to 140F ($31.96) per person. The plumbing in most of the bedrooms is quite luxurious. Although the inn is fairly simple, the welcome is definitely first class. The food is excellent, although this is not the place to patronize if you're on a diet. Two set meals are offered: a substantial dinner costing from 35F ($7.99) and a huge repast for 80F ($18.26). The inn shuts down in November.

9. St.-Paul-de-Vence

Of all the perched villages of the Riviera, St.-Paul-de-Vence is the best known. It was popularized in the 1920s when many noted artists lived there, occupying the little 16th-century houses that flank the narrow cobblestoned streets. The hill town was originally built to protect its inhabitants from Saracens raiding the coast. The feudal hamlet grew up on a bastion of rock, almost blending into it. Its ramparts (allow about 30 minutes to encircle them) overlook a peaceful setting of flowers and olive and orange trees. As you make your way through the warren of streets you'll pass endless souvenir shops, a charming old fountain carved in the form of an urn, and a Gothic church from the 13th century. St.-Paul lies 17 miles from Cannes, 19 miles from Nice, and 3 miles from Vence.

THE MAEGHT FOUNDATION: The most important attraction of St.-Paul lies outside the walls at **Fondation Maeght.** It's the most modern art museum in all of Europe. On the slope of a hill in pine-studded woods, the Maeght Foundation is like a Shangri-la. Not only is the architecture daringly avant-garde, but the building itself houses one of the finest collections of contemporary art on the Riviera. Nature and the creations of men and women blend harmoniously in this unique achievement of the architect, José Luis Sert. Its white concrete arcs give the impression of a giant pagoda.

A stark Calder rises like some futuristic monster on the grassy lawns. In a courtyard, the elongated bronze works of Giacometti (one of the finest collections of his works in the world) form a surrealistic garden, creating a hallucinatory mood. Sculpture is also displayed inside, but it's at its best in a naturalistic setting of surrounding terraces and gardens. The museum is built on several levels, its many glass walls providing an indoor-outdoor vista.

The foundation, a gift "to the people" from Aimé and Marguerite Maeght, also provides a showcase for new talent. Exhibitions are always changing.

Everywhere you look, you see 20th-century art: mosaics by Chagall and Braque, Miró ceramics in the "labyrinth," and Ubac and Braque stained glass in the chapel. Bonnard, Kandinsky, Léger, Matisse, Barbara Hepworth, and many other artists are well represented.

There are a library, a cinema, a cafeteria, and lounges. In one showroom you can buy original lithographs by such artists as Chagall and Giacometti and limited-edition prints. Admission costs 12F ($2.74), with students paying 7F ($1.60). The museum is open daily including Sundays and holidays from 10 a.m. to 12:30 p.m. and from 3 till 7 p.m. (in the afternoons from October 1 through April 30 the hours are from 2:30 till 6 p.m.).

FOOD AND LODGING: The best choices in St.-Paul-de-Vence are the following:

The Upper Bracket

La Colombe d'Or ("The Golden Dove") (tel. 32-80-02), is a nugget of graceful antiquity. At the edge of this attractive old hamlet, this Renaissance-style villa lies behind tall stone walls, encircling a voluptuous Roman garden and terrace as well as a swimming pool. The proprietors bring an eclectic awareness of fine contemporary paintings to this old inn. It's almost like visiting a museum of contemporary art. You see—just hanging, unguarded—works by Chagall, Rouault, Dufy, Braque, Picasso, and Miró. According to what is now a Riviera legend, many of the paintings were left by artists in the '20s who "painted for their supper." Once featured in a Jean Seberg movie, the flock of snow-white doves hovering about turn "golden" at sunset.

Staying here is like being a member of a private club. The bedrooms, 16 in all, are consistently well planned, with very fine antiques and brightly colored tiled baths. Demi-pension is obligatory in season, costing 400F ($91.32) per person, plus 15% for service. Rooms rent from 320F ($73.06) in a single to a high of 400F ($91.32) in a double. Even if you can't stay here (reservations are imperative), you may want to have a meal. Most informal is the junglelike dining patio, with its tables set under umbrellas in the midst of ferns, geraniums, and pink flowering vines growing over trelliswork. Inside, there's a stately pair of dining rooms, with an elaborately carved Renaissance fireplace and provincial chairs. A set menu costs 100F ($22.83), and the average à la carte tab ranges between 160F ($36.53) and 220F ($50.23). A delicious meal we recently ordered included a wide selection of hors d'oeuvres, trout meunière, tender loin of lamb, a salad, and a soufflé Grand-Marnier. Enjoy an after-dinner drink before the fireplace in the lower "pit lounge." The hotel is closed from November 10 to December 20.

Other Selections

Orangers (tel. 32-80-95) is the hotel and Les Oliviers (tel. 32-80-13) is the restaurant in a pair of villas near the road on a hillside terrace less than a mile from the heart of the village. They are drenched with the scent of roses, oranges, and lemons. The main lounge is impeccably decorated with original oil paintings and lithographs by Picasso, Rousseau, Bernard Buffet, and Rouault. You are treated like a house guest, accommodated in a bedroom lavishly decorated

with antiques and opening onto a superior view. On the adjoining sun terraces
are banana trees, flower beds, and climbing geraniums. Madame Biancheri,
who began with just a restaurant in 1960, has created a lovely living oasis. In
high season she asks 350F ($79.91) per person for full board, from 230F
($52.51) to 270F ($61.64) for half pension.

Meals are a delight, served in a tavern-style room or, better yet, on the
wide, shaded terrace. Two set meals are offered for 72F ($16.44) and 95F
($21.69), the latter repast including a buffet hors d'oeuvre selection. Specialties
include grilled sea bass (loup) as well as a gigot of lamb cooked on a spit. The
inn shuts down from November 15 to December 20, and the restaurant is closed
from January 7 to February 7.

Le Café de la Place (tel. 32-80-03) is owned by French actor Yves Montand and Monsieur Roux, the proprietor of the world-famed La Colombe d'Or
("The Golden Dove") across the way. On the ground floor is a café where
guests sit sipping drinks and looking at the *pétanque* players. You can eat
brasserie-style cooking here, including plats du jour at 32F ($7.31) and half a
bottle of wine at 14F ($3.20). Large stairs with brass bars bring you to the
second floor, where you can overnight in one of 14 rooms, each of which looks
out over the walls of St.-Paul to the valley beyond. Accommodations are large
and furnished in the Provençal style. A double with hot and cold running water
is 110F ($25.11), increasing to 180F ($41.09) with bath. These prices include
breakfast and the use of a large swimming pool. From the terrace you can enjoy
a panoramic view of the valley. At night, with a little bit of luck, you can chat
with Monsieur Montand himself, or with some other star who might happen
to drop in.

In the budget range, **Les Remparts** (tel. 32-80-64) is a narrow stone
hostelry built right into the ramparts, offering a magnificent panoramic view.
A skinny rustic staircase connects five floors of this homey auberge, which is
furnished with many antiques—an individualized collection, reflecting the taste
of Madame Prébin, who has operated Les Remparts since 1949. Paintings and
sketches are placed throughout the rooms, some of which have a Morocco-
inspired decor.

The accommodations are oddly shaped, individually named, and totally
ingratiating. All have private baths or showers. The Rose Room costs 150F
($34.26) for two persons and contains a large bed on a raised platform. Con-
tinuing in a flowery mood are the Lilac Room and the Tulip Room. Some of
the less expensive doubles go for just 130F ($29.68). Half pension costs from
140F ($31.96) to 170F ($38.81), depending on the room. Meals—a tasty example of regional fare—are served in the provincial, cozy, old-world dining room.
If you drop in just for lunch or dinner (and there is no better bargain in
St.-Paul-de-Vence, considering the quality and the price), the cost is 40F
($9.13). There's a shaded terrace for meals. The dining room is closed Tues-
days, and the whole place shuts down from October 25 to December 20.

Auberge Le Hameau, 528 Route de la Calle (tel. 32-80-24), stands on the
outskirts of St.-Paul-de-Vence, on the road to Colle at Hauts-de-St.-Paul. It is
a holiday retreat, a hilltop villa with views of the surrounding hills and valleys.
It was conceived by a tasteful architect and designer who provided comfort in
a romantic Mediterranean setting. Most of the bedrooms, only 13 in all, overlook the vine-trellised courtyard, and others open onto the expansive sun
terrace with stone planters of fruit trees and flowering shrubs. With whitewashed walls and beamed ceilings, the bedrooms come in various shapes and
sizes, a single renting for 185F ($42.24) to 235F ($53.65), a double for 200F
($45.66) to 250F ($57.08). The provincial furnishings are just right for the

setting, although baths are completely modern and tiled. The hotel staff takes a holiday from mid-November to mid-December.

10. Vence

Travel up into the hills 15 miles northwest of Nice—across country studded with cypresses, olive trees, and pines, where bright flowers, especially carnations, roses, and oleanders, grow in profusion—and Vence comes into view. Outside the town, along Boulevard Paul-André, two old olive presses carry on with their age-old duties. But the charm lies in the **Vieille Ville** ("Old Town"). Visitors invariably have themselves photographed on **Place du Peyra** in front of the urn-shaped **Vieille Fontaine** ("Old Fountain"), a background shot in several motion pictures. The 15th-century **square tower** is also a curiosity.

If you're wearing the right kind of shoes, the narrow, steep streets of the old town are worth exploring. Dating from the 10th century, the **cathedral** on Place Godeau is unremarkable except for some 15th-century Gothic choir stalls. But if it's the right day of the week, most visitors quickly pass through the narrow gates of this once-fortified walled town to where the sun shines more brightly, at the—

MATISSE CHAPEL: It was a beautiful golden autumn along the Côte d'Azur. The great Henri Matisse was 77 years old, and, after a turbulent personal search, he set out to create his masterpiece, or, to quote the artist, "the culmination of a whole life dedicated to the search for truth." Just outside Vence, Matisse created a Chapel of the Rosary for the Dominican nuns of Monteils. From the front you might find it unremarkable and pass it by—until you spot a 40-foot crescent-adorned cross rising from a blue-tiled roof.

Matisse wrote: "What I have done in the chapel is to create a religious space. . .in an enclosed area of very reduced proportions and to give it, solely by the play of colors and lines, the dimensions of infinity." The light picks up the subtle coloring in the simply rendered leaf forms and abstract patterns: sapphire-blue, aquamarine, and lemon-yellow. In black-and-white ceramics, St. Dominic is depicted in only a few lines. The most remarkable design is the black-and-white-tiled Stations of the Cross with Matisse's self-styled "tormented and passionate" figures. The bishop of Nice came to bless the chapel in the late spring of 1951. The artist's work was completed. He died three years later.

The chapel is open only on Tuesdays and Thursdays, from 10 to 11:30 a.m. and from 2:30 to 5:30 p.m. (tel. 58-03-26). Admission is free but offerings are welcome.

DELUXE CHÂTEAU LIVING: Le Château du Domaine St.-Martin, route de Coursegoules (tel. 58-02-02), two miles outside of Vence, is romantically positioned in a 35-acre park on the crest of a high hill. Built in 1936 on the grounds where the "Golden Goat treasury" was reputedly buried, the country house is a rambling hacienda with spacious courtyards and terraces—an idyllic retreat. When the present owners, the Geneve family, purchased the estate, they had to sign a bill of sale agreeing to share the treasure, if found, with the assignees. Since there were only 18 guest rooms in the main building, a complex of tile-roofed villas was built in the surrounding terraced gardens, set in the midst of age-old olive trees. On one terrace where the sun beats down strongest, a kidney-shaped swimming pool was installed, surrounded by a flagstone terrace. You can walk through the gardens on winding walks lined with tall cypresses, past the crumbling chapel ruins and flowering orange trees. Tall arched windows let in the coastal sunlight in the handtiled loggia, a gracious gallery with such successfully coordinated antiques as eight-foot-high torchères, Louis XVI armchairs, and gilt mirrors. Equally well furnished, the main drawing room opens onto the sea, making for a private-seeming retreat that has attracted such guests as Truman, Isaac Stern, and Adenauer. One statesman called the château "the anteroom of paradise." The bedrooms have been equipped with fine furnishings and private baths. A single rents for 600F ($136.98), a twin-bedded room for 800F ($182.64). The hotel is closed in December and January. Not to be ignored is the cuisine, served in a glassed-in-restaurant opening onto a fantastic view of the coastline. Even if you aren't staying here, you can enjoy the food, a set meal costing from 185F ($42.24) plus 15% for service, although you can spend as much as 250F ($57.08) ordering à la carte. If a dinner or lunch is impossible, you may want to drive up for afternoon tea on the wide terrace, feeling the sense of peace, enjoying the colors and sky as Matisse did.

BUDGET LIVING AND DINING: Auberge des Seigneurs ("Inn of the Noblemen"), Place du Frêne (tel. 58-04-24), is an authentic village inn where you'll experience the France of another century. A stone hostelry in the old part of town, the inn is shaded by one of the largest trees on the Côte d'Azur, giving the plaza its name of "Ash Square." Fascinating decorative objects and antiques are placed everywhere. Inside is a long wooden dining table, in view of an open fireplace with a row of hanging copper pots and pans. Corner cupboards, ladderback chairs, wooden casks of flowers, dark beams, an open spit for roasting and grilling—all this is but a background to the truly superb food, "the cuisine of François I." Set meals are offered at 60F ($13.70) and 95F ($21.69). If you stay the night, you'll pay 140F ($31.96) for a double room with a private shower, 105F ($23.97) in a single. The inn is closed on Mondays and from mid-October to December 1.

La Farigoule, 15 rue Henri-Isnard (tel. 58-01-27), serves regional cooking in a setting of well-preserved, crooked old beams and antique furnishings, including a Welsh cupboard, a collection of dolls, and a grandfather clock. In summer, it's best to dine in the rear garden under a rose arbor. Meals are grilled on an open fire. The patronne, Madame Gastaud, keeps things humming and doesn't even get flustered when a long line forms on Sunday afternoons. There are three set meals offered; the cheapest, 35F ($7.99), includes soupe aux poissons (fish soup), truite (trout) meunière, a vegetable, and cheese or dessert. You pay extra for service and your beverage. The 42F ($9.59) menu, however, is far more enticing. On our latest rounds, we ordered asparagus vinaigrette, langoustines with Niçoise mayonnaise, a tender rabbit with seasonal vegetables, plus cheese and dessert, with drinks and service extra. An even more elaborate menu is featured at 60F ($13.70). The restaurant is closed Fridays off-season and from mid-November to mid-December.

La Vieille Douve ("The Old Barrel-Stave"), 10 rue Henri-Isnard (tel. 58-10-08), has a narrow and unobtrusive entrance leading to a corridor which ends in a protected terrace in front of the Matisse Chapel. The restaurant and its little bar are much frequented by the people of the town—a sure sign of good cooking, good wine, and value for money spent. There is a change of menu every day. Hors d'oeuvres, the main course, salad, and cheese or dessert go for 32F ($7.31). The plat du jour (a single main dish) is good value at 25F ($5.71). The house wine is selected by the proprietor from the vineyards of Cobassi, a half-bottle costing 6F ($1.37). There is also a cellar of fine vintage wines, naturally more expensive, but choice.

On the Outskirts: La Gaude

Hostellerie Hermitage (tel. 59-40-05) is the kind of crow's-nest villa that artists have been occupying along this hilly coast for more than half a century. In the heart of the artists' belt, the inn is lodged on the brow of a hilly ridge, surrounded by terraces of tall cypresses. A graveled area with a reflection pool is edged by flower beds, and climbing over the walls of the villa are magenta and orange bougainvillea. Opening onto a solarium, the dining room is splashed with color. However, many diners prefer tables set under umbrellas on a small terrace. As for the food, it's worth the expedition up here, even if you aren't staying over. Specialties include páillardines (veal scallops) à la sauge, fricassée de poulet (chicken) à l'estragon, and chaussons de morilles.

Lyon-born Monsieur Polette offers 10 bedrooms, a few with private bath. He charges from 90F ($20.55) to 110F ($25.11) in a double. There are two set menus, one at 50F ($11.42) and a much larger and better one at 100F ($22.83). If you order à la carte, expect to spend from 110F ($25.11) per person.

How to get there? First of all, a car is imperative. From the coastal road between Antibes and Cagnes, take D18 leading to St.-Jeannet. The inn is about a 15-minute drive from Vence.

The dining room is closed on Fridays, and the whole place shuts down from mid-October to mid-December.

11. Cagnes-sur-Mer

Between Nice and Antibes, Cagnes-sur-Mer, like the Roman god Janus, shows two faces. Its hilltop town, **Le Haut-de-Cagnes,** is one of the most charming spots on the Riviera. Its seafront **Cros-de-Cagnes** is an old fishing port and an unimaginative but rapidly developing beach resort. Its racecourse is considered one of the finest in France. In the "hinterlands" of Nice, Le Haut-de-Cagnes "crowns the top of a blue-cypressed hill like a village in an Italian Renaissance painting," to quote Naomi Barry. For years, the town has attracted the French literati (Simone de Beauvoir wrote *Les Mandarins* here) and a colony of painters (Renoir made it famous, selecting it as "the place where I want to paint until the last day of my life").

In a setting of orange groves and fields of carnations, the upper village consists of narrow cobblestoned streets with houses dating from the 17th and 18th centuries. You can drive your car to the top, the **Place du Château,** where you can enjoy the view, have lunch, drink an apéritif in a sidewalk café, and pay a visit to:

THE CASTLE MUSEUM: Once a stronghold of the Middle Ages, the fortress was built by Rainier Grimaldi in 1301. He was a lord of Monaco and a French admiral (a portrait inside shows what he looked like, and charts reveal how the defenses were organized). In the early 17th century, the dank castle was converted into a more gracious Louis XIII château. The historical monument, owned by the town of Cagnes-sur-Mer, consists of both a **Musée de l'Olivier** ("Museum of the Olive Tree") and a **Musée d'Art Moderne Méditerranéen.** The ethnographical museum shows the steps involved in the cultivation and processing of the olive. The modern-art gallery displays work by Kisling, Carzou, Dufy, Cocteau, and Seyssaud, among other painters, along with temporary exhibitions. In one salon is an interesting fresco depicting *La Chute de*

Phaeton in *trompe l'oeil* by Carlone, an Italian. From the tower, you get a spectacular view of the Côte d'Azur.

The museum is open daily except Tuesdays from 10 a.m. to noon and from 2 to 6 from June 15 to September 30, from 10 a.m. to noon and from 2 to 5 p.m. from October 1 to June 14, and is closed entirely from October 15 to November 15. Admission is 3F (68¢). Each year from July to September the International Festival of Painting takes place, with the official participation of 40 nations.

FOOD AND LODGING: Le Grimaldi, 6 Place du Château (tel. 20-60-24), enjoys the prime position on the main square. Guests dine on the front terrace under bright umbrellas, enjoying the cookery of the chef de cuisine, Monsieur Perrouly. Two set meals are offered, the least expensive one going for 50F ($11.42), which might begin with a salade Niçoise, followed with lapin (rabbit) chasseur, potatoes, and salad, then a selection of cheese or fruit. For 70F ($15.98), you can order a more elaborate menu featuring more expensive dishes, such as escargots (snails) Bourgogne. These fixed-price meals include service and beverage. Six rooms with hot and cold running water are rented out at prices ranging from 60F ($13.70) to 70F ($15.98). You can stay here and take half pension at 90F ($20.55) per person. The restaurant is closed Tuesdays off-season, and the whole place shuts down from October 28 to November 6 and during the month of February.

OUTSIDE THE TOWN: On the outskirts are two museums honoring famous Frenchmen.

Les Collettes has been restored to what it was when the great Renoir lived there, from 1908 until his death in 1919. Here at his *maison* he turned to sculpture, even though he was crippled by arthritis and had to be helped in and out of a wheelchair. Assistants aided in his work, and he also continued to paint with a brush tied to his paralyzed hand. One of his last paintings, *Rest After Bathing*, completed the year he died, is owned by the Louvre.

The house itself was built in 1907 in a setting of olive trees and an orange grove. In the entrance hall is a bust of Madame Renoir. On your own, you can explore the drawing and dining rooms before going upstairs to the artist's bedroom. In his atelier are his wheelchair, and his easel and brushes. From the terrace of Madame Renoir's bedroom is a stunning view of Cap d'Antibes and Le Haut-de-Cagnes. The museum owns only two paintings, but it has nine sculptures. On a wall hangs a photograph of one of Renoir's sons, Pierre, as he appeared in the 1932 film *Madame Bovary*. Inaugurated in the summer of 1960, the museum is open daily except Tuesdays from 2 to 6 p.m. (till 5 p.m. in winter), charging 3F (68¢) for admission. Closed from October 15 to November 15.

In the charming little hamlet of Villeneuve-Loubet in the Alps-Maritimes, Auguste Escoffier was born in 1846. Later he was to earn the appellation "the king of chefs and the chef of kings." His career began in 1859 at the age of 12. He was to work until his retirement from London's Carlton in 1921, although he lived until the age of 89, dying in 1935 at Monte Carlo. In the 1890s in London, as chef of the Savoy, he became world famous. In 1959 a museum was created in Escoffier's honor at Villeneuve-Loubet. A culinary center dedicated to the art of cookery, the museum is international, preserving mementos from the 14th to the 20th centuries from great chefs and gastronomes including many sugar creations by famous French pastry cooks. Known as **Le Musée de** l'Art Culinaire, it contains memorabilia of Escoffier's life. Charging adults 5F ($1.14), children 2F (46¢) for admission, the museum is open from 10 a.m. to noon and from 2 to 5 p.m. except Mondays and bank holidays. It is closed in November.

Food and Lodging

In the general neighborhood of the two museums just described, a short drive from Vence, lies—

Le Cagnard, rue du Pontis-Long, au Haut-de-Cagnes (tel. 20-73-22). To Madame Barel's 18th-century inn come some of the most outstanding members of the French literati, such as Simone de Beauvoir. At the cusp of the ramparts of this medieval feudal hamlet, two village houses have been joined. A vaulted candlelit dining room, a vine-draped terrace, and 14 bedrooms were created from the once-private dwellings. Artists who have dined or lodged here include Renoir, Soutine, Chagall, and Modigliani. The bedrooms as well as the salons are furnished intuitively and with authority by Mme. Barel, using many family antiques and decorative accessories: fruitwood provincial chests, armoires, Louis XV-style chairs, copper lavabos, plus a few "other era" paintings mixed with some modern works from the Côte d'Azur school.

A fixed-price meal for 165F ($37.68) is offered, including many of the chef's specialties. On the à la carte menu, don't miss some of the hot hors d'oeuvres, including such delicious little tidbits as a prune stuffed with foie gras (goose liver) and wrapped in bacon. The meat specialty is Sisteron lamb (carré d'agneau), spit-roasted with Provençal herbs, served only for two persons. A côte de boeuf is delicious and tender. The extravagantly prepared dessert pièce de résistance is mousseline de glace aux charmeuses de bois. A 15% service charge is added. If you order à la carte, your tab is likely to range from 90F ($20.55) to 170F ($38.81). After dinner, join the other guests for coffee in the little salon if it's a cool night, or on the ramparts terrace if it's balmy.

Staying overnight is a treat worth the trouble of a reservation. Behind painted doors, opening off the well-preserved stone steps and corridors, each bedchamber has its own style. For half pension, one person pays anywhere from 220F ($50.23) to 310F ($70.77) in a room with bath. Le Cagnard is closed from November 1 to December 15.

12. Biot

Cranes, acrobats, scaffolding, railroad signals, buxom nudes, casings, and crankshafts—all these subjects occupied the mind of Fernand Léger (1881-1955). At the place where he chose to work till the day he died, his widow, Madame Nadia Léger, has assembled the greatest collection of his art in a museum in this little town four miles from Antibes. From his first Cubist paintings, he was ironically called a "Tubist" rather than a Cubist.

The stone-and-marble façade of the museum is enhanced by Léger's mosaic and ceramic mural. On the grounds is a polychrome ceramic sculpture, Le Jardin d'Enfant. Inside, on two floors, you can wander through gallery after gallery of geometrical forms in pure, flat colors. The collection embraces gouaches, paintings, ceramics, tapestries, and sculptures, showing the development of the artist from 1905 until his death. Perhaps the most unusual work depicts a Léger Mona Lisa contemplating a set of monumental keys, a wide-mouth fish dangling at an angle over her head.

One critic wrote that "Léger has been attacked by several varieties of 'humanists' for 'dehumanizing' art by mechanizing his figures; but has he not at the same time helped to humanize the machine by integrating it in the painting?" Living in the United States, mainly in New York, during World War II, Léger gloried in "the bad taste, one of the valuable raw materials of the country."

The museum, inaugurated in 1960, is open daily from 10 a.m. to noon and from 3 to 6:30 p.m., closing at 5 p.m. off-season; it charges 8F ($1.83) for admission, 4F (91¢) for students.

13. Antibes and Cap d'Antibes

On the other side of the Bay of Angels, across from Nice, sits the ancient, once-fortified port of Antibes. Thirteen miles from Nice by road, it is an old Mediterranean town whose quiet charm is perhaps unequaled along the Côte d'Azur. Jutting out into the sea, it contains a little harbor filled with pleasure yachts and fishing boats. Its potential as a flower-growing center—mainly roses and carnations—is best reflected in the marketplace. If you're staying over in the evening, you can watch fishermen playing the popular Riviera game of *boule.* The Bonaparte family was there in 1794, and it is said that the future princesses stole artichokes and figs from the nearby farms.

On the ramparts stands the **Château d'Antibes,** now turned into the **Picasso Museum,** housing one of the greatest single Picasso collections. Once it was the home of the princes of Antibes of the de Grasse family, who ruled the city from 1385 to 1608. But Picasso, lodged in a small hotel room at Golfe-Juan after his bitter war years in Paris, needed more space to work. The museum director at Antibes—in one of the smartest moves he ever made—invited the great Spaniard to work and live at the museum. Picasso did, and when he left for better pastures, he permanently lent the museum all the work he'd done at Antibes that year. And what a prolific 1946 it was, a year of goats and centaurs. Displayed are two dozen paintings, nearly 80 pieces of ceramics, some 35 drawings, as well as 27 lithographs, 11 oils on paper, two pieces of sculpture, and one tapestry. In addition, a gallery of contemporary art exhibits works by Léger and Calder, among other modern artists. In contrast, antiquity is reflected in the display of Ligurian, Greek, and Roman artifacts. Charging 6F ($1.37) for admission, the museum is open from 10 a.m. to noon and from 3 to 7 p.m. (till 5 or 6 p.m. off-season).

Spiritually, Antibes is totally divorced from the celebrated **Cap d'Antibes,** a peninsula studded with the villas and swimming pools of the wealthy. Long a playground of the rich, particularly in the 1920s, it was depicted in *Tender Is the Night,* with F. Scott Fitzgerald's hero, Dick Diver, seen in an atmosphere of "old villas rotted like water lilies among the massed pines." Photographs of film stars lounging at the Eden Roc have enlivened many a Sunday supplement.

Although one doesn't usually think of visiting a museum at Cap d'Antibes, there is, in fact, the **Musée Naval et Napoléonien.** An ancient military tower, it houses an interesting collection of Napoleonic memorabilia, naval models, paintings, and army mementos. A toy-soldier collection depicts various uniforms worn by the men, including one used by Napoleon in the Marengo campaign. A wall painting in wood shows Napoleon's entrance into Grenoble; another tableau depicts his disembarkation at Golfe-Juan on March 1, 1815. In contrast to Canova's Greek-god image of Napoleon, a miniature pendant by Barrault reveals the Corsican general as he really looked, with pudgy cheeks and a receding hairline. In the rotunda in the rear is one of the many hats worn by the emperor. You can climb to the top of the tower for a view of the coast that is worth the price of admission, including a wide sweep of Juan-les-Pins and the harbor studded with sailboats. The museum is open daily, except

Tuesdays and the month of November, from 10 a.m. to noon and from 3 to
7 p.m. (off-season, September 2 to October 31 and December 16 to May 31,
it's open from 10 a.m. to noon and from 2 to 5); admission is 6F ($1.37).

FOOD AND LODGING: The best choices in all price ranges for meals and
accommodations follow:

Deluxe Living and Dining

Hôtel du Cap d'Antibes, Boulevard Kennedy (tel. 61-39-01). Around its
swimming pool built in the rugged rocks next to the lapping waves of the
Mediterranean lie what Fitzgerald called "the notable and fashionable people."
The celebrities change with the season, but have included Lloyd George, Anatole France, Bernard Shaw, Somerset Maugham, Chaplin, Fairbanks, Gable,
Bogart, Boyer, Orson Welles, Marlene Dietrich, Rita Hayworth, Mary Pick-
ford, Sophia Loren, Picasso, Chagall, Gary Cooper, and the Ford, Kennedy,
and Du Pont families. Set in the midst of splendid acres of gardens is the
palatial hotel itself, a monument to a bygone era, inaugurated in 1870. The
interior is like a great country estate, with spacious, well-decorated public
rooms, marble fireplaces, scenic paneling, crystal chandeliers, and clusters of
velvet-tufted armchairs.

All bedrooms are air-conditioned, with private baths and deluxe accessories, the period furnishings ranging from regal to merely sumptuous. Double
rooms peak at 750F ($171.23), singles going for 550F ($125.57), plus 15% for
service. The hotel is open between Easter and mid-October. In the peak of the
season, guests can dine in the seafront pavilion, the world-famous **Eden Roc,**
its all-glass windows fronting on the Mediterranean. Venetian chandeliers,
iris-blue Louis XV-style chairs, and toile draperies form a dramatic setting.
Luncheons are served on the outer terrace, under umbrellas and an arbor. At
noon there is a selection of ten hors d'oeuvres to get you started. At dinner,
the price of three specialties—bouillabaisse, lobster thermidor, and sea bass
with fennel—depends on the weight. Also good are le feuilleté bonne bouche,
l'escalope de veau aux fruits de mer, and le coquelet polonaise. A peach Melba
makes a beautiful dessert. Expect to pay from 220F ($50.23) to 270F ($61.64)
if you dine here.

The Upper Bracket

La Résidence du Cap, 161 Boulevard Kennedy (tel. 61-09-44), requires
special classification, it's that unique. Surrounded by a six-acre garden in the
heart of the cape, it is a stone-built, spread-out, once-private villa which has
been converted into a seasonal April-through-October hotel. The owner has
done a remarkable conversion and extension, entertaining guests in a stylish,
personalized manner. Installed was a "sun-trap" social area around a swimming pool at which barbecues (with steaks and spit-roasted lamb) are staged
twice weekly, complete with music for dancing under the stars.

Open from March 15 to October 20, the hotel charges 350F ($79.91) in
a single, that tariff rising to 500F ($114.15) in a double. A few apartments are
suited for occupancy by three to five persons. Exceptionally personalized, the
bedrooms fall into two categories: traditional ones furnished with such provincial pieces as carved beds, and newly built compact accommodations in "enlightened modern."

Across the back of the villa is a pergola-covered dining terrace, where you
can enjoy a lunch or dinner at set prices going from 120F ($27.40) to 200F

($45.66), almost within touching distance of the flowering vines and plants. Two inner courtyards are graced with colonnaded arches, pink geraniums trailing over the balcony, and a reflection pool with a stone fountain. The newer rooms opening off a central gallery are a veritable museum of contemporary art.

Medium Bracket and Budget

Auberge de la Gardiole, Chemin de la Garoupe (tel. 61-35-03), is run like a glorified country inn by Anne Marie Arama in a delightful, personal way. She knows all about food, supervising its buying at the markets and its preparation. She also directs the service in the dining room and takes care of the 20 bedrooms. The auberge is a large villa, spilling out into the surrounding gardens and pergola.

Set in a district of largely private estates, it welcomes guests into an all-purpose, high-beamed room where tables are set up for meals when the weather is nippy. It's cheerful, with colored cloths and (on cooler nights) a fire burning on a raised brick hearth, and hanging pots and pans. In fair weather, you can dine under a trellis covered with a wisteria vine.

Bedrooms, on the upper floors of the inn and in the little buildings placed in the garden, offer simplicity and charm, with provincial furnishings and good strong colors. In high season, demi-pension rates range from 165F ($37.68) to 200F ($45.66) per person, depending on the plumbing. Guests are accepted between Easter and October 1. The cuisine is skillfully prepared. Two fixed-price meals await nonresidents: 65F ($14.84) and 80F ($18.26). You pay extra for your drink, but service is included. On a recent visit, our salad contained delicious greens, including chard and dandelions, with a smoothly blended dressing.

Castel Garoupe, Boulevard Garoupe (tel. 61-36-51), is a villa-hotel-apartment house built in the Mediterranean style, with a tiled roof, private balconies, arches, and shuttered windows. Set back on a private lane in the center of the cape, it is surrounded by its own grounds and a freshwater swimming pool, along with a tennis court amid gnarled olive trees and a rock garden. It is highly recommended because it gives you an apartment for the same price you'd pay for a bedroom elsewhere. The rates are uncomplicated, 280F ($63.92) per person per day, based on either single or double occupancy, including a continental breakfast. In all, the hotel offers 28 rooms, each handsomely equipped and appointed. There is, as well, a shady garden, and under a pine tree you can find tranquility on the Riviera. The hotel is open all year.

Beau Site, 141 Boulevard Kennedy (tel. 61-53-43), is a three-story villa surrounded by eucalyptus trees, pines, and palms. Off the main road, with a low wall of flower urns and wrought-iron gates, it is a tile-roofed, white-stucco structure with heavy shutters. Although not on the beach, it has its own rustic charm; the interior is like a country auberge with oak beams and antiques. In high season, July and August, the demi-pension rate for one person ranges in price from 160F ($36.53) to 170F ($38.81). A minimum stay of three days is required, and the rates quoted include service and taxes. The villa receives guests from April 4 to September 25.

Hôtel de la Garoupe & Réserve du Cap, Boulevard F. Meilland (tel. 61-54-97), is a pleasant old villa in the center of the cape, set in a small grove of pine trees. The bedrooms are clean, fresh, and comfortable, although lacking in particular style. In high season, from June 15 to September 15, one person is charged from 180F ($41.09) to 220F ($50.23) for full pension, taxes and service included. Although you can dine inside, the open-air loggia is preferred, exposed as it is to the pines and flowers. Closed from November 1 to January 31.

Deluxe Dining

La Bonne Auberge, Quartier la Brague, route N7, 2½ miles from Antibes (tel. 33-36-65), is a special event. One of the most famous restaurants along the Côte d'Azur, it is a salmon-pink villa along the coastal highway with an impressive crescent-shaped driveway entrance. Covered with ivy, it is fronted by a long row of arbors and arches. The interior is like what "back-lot" MGM used to be, with pink walls, deep arches, black oak beams, carved provincial sideboards, and wrought-iron lanterns casting flickering lights. But most important of all is the proud chef, who provides a cuisine that has won acclaim from visitors from every continent.

Under the direction of Monsieur Rostang, the restaurant turns out a Nouvelle Cuisine that is ranked among the best along the Riviera. The specialties here are so beautifully prepared and so delicious that it is hard to recommend specific dishes. Nevertheless, you are likely to be tempted by such pleasurable dishes as fricassée of St.-Pierre made with leeks and truffles, mousseline of red mullet with red caviar, crayfish salad, duckling with a compote of pears, foie gras with celeriac, and a peach soufflé that is one of life's enchantments. The service and reception are grand. Menus go from 180F ($41.09) to 225F ($51.38) to 250F ($57.08), and ordering à la carte will run in the neighborhood of 270F ($61.64) to 370F ($84.47). Add 15% for service. Featured wines are Château-Simone and Bellet. The restaurant closes from November 1 to December 15 and on Mondays.

Budget Dining

Les Vieux Murs ("Taverne Provence"), Avenue Amiral-de-Grasse (tel. 34-06-73), is a provincial tavern, charmingly located on the ramparts of Antibes with a few outside tables. It produces fine food and isn't overly expensive, unless you succumb to the delectable house specialty, lobster thermidor. The interior is rustic, a colorful setting for such good seafood. Three highly recommendable dishes include fish soup, rognons de veau à la crème (veal kidneys in a cream sauce), and filet de sole in a champagne sauce, served only for two. A complete meal ranges in price from 110F ($25.11) to 165F ($37.68). The patron makes certain that only the best of fish—and the freshest— is bought at the early-morning market. Closed Wednesdays and from November 13 to December 18.

La Marine ("Chez Lou Lou"), 28 rue Aubernon (tel. 34-11-66), is an informal, rustic-style tavern a short walk from the Grimaldi Museum. You can dine outdoors under an arbor; the emphasis is on good food, not elegant manners or elaborate service. There's an economy meal for 32F ($7.31), although you'll pay 20F ($4.57) extra for a pitcher of the regional wine. À la carte, a large portion of the soupe de poissons (fish soup) is savory. Grilled scampi is done to perfection, and loup (sea bass) flambé is yet another superb dish. À la carte orders will bring the tab to around the 70F ($15.98) to 85F ($19.41) mark. Closed Wednesdays and from mid-November to mid-December.

14. Juan-les-Pins

This suburb of Antibes is a controversial resort, drawing highly mixed reactions. Frank Jay Gould developed it in the 1920s and lived there in his own villa. In those days, people flocked to "John of the Pines" to escape the "crassness" of nearby Cannes. In the 1930s Juan-les-Pins was drawing a chic crowd of the wintering wealthy of Europe. Today the resort is popular with the better-heeled young Europeans. Maybe their parents aren't rich any more, but—to judge from the money spent—these attractive young people are high-salaried at least. Activities reach frenzied heights at the July **jazz festival.**

Juan-les-Pins is often called a honky-tonk town or the Coney Island of the Riviera. Anyone who calls it that hasn't seen Coney Island in a long time. One writer referred to it as "a pop-art Monte Carlo, with eye-popping strip shows, burlesque, and bikini exhibitionists on its nudist-strewn beaches." Perhaps that description is too enticing or provocative for what is such an obviously middle-class resort.

As a nightlife center it is a major contender along the Riviera, attracting many of the resort-hoppers after dark. Many revelers stay up all night in the smoky jazz joints, then sleep it off the next day on the beach. The **casino** in the center of town offers cabaret entertainment, sometimes till daylight breaks. Then skin-diving and water-skiing predominate. The pines sweep right down to the coast and the sandy beach, which, incidentally, is excellent. Trouble is, you'll need a bulldozer to remove some bronze bodies in July and August if you'd like a spot just for yourself.

ACCOMMODATIONS: From the out-of-reach to the affordable, Juan-les-Pins has them all. We'll begin with—

Belles-Rives, Boulevard du Littoral (tel. 61-02-79), at the edge of the resort, is in an enviable position, with its formal entrance on the coastal road, its seaside façade fronting the bay. The lower terraces are devoted to garden-style dining rooms and a waterside aquatic club with a snack-lounge and a jetty extending out into the water. You'll find facilities for boating, water-skiing, sailing, fishing, plus plenty of room to swim. There's also a private sandy beach. Dinners are served on the terrace with a panoramic view of the bay, especially romantic when the lights begin to twinkle at night. The interior is rather subdued, as are the bedrooms; prices depend on the season and the view. Demi-pension is required from May 15 to September 15. At that time, the daily half-board rate with bath or shower and air conditioning ranges from 520F ($118.72) to 640F ($146.11) per person, with balcony, sea view, breakfast, and dinner. The hotel is open from Easter to October.

The Upper Bracket

Juana, Avenue Gallice (tel. 61-08-70), is separated from the sea by park-like grounds studded with cypresses and flower beds. The flowers are changed in the front garden three times a year (hopefully, you'll arrive when the pink and purple petunias are in bloom). The Juana has been owned and managed by the Barache family for three generations. The bedrooms are individually designed and decorated, varying greatly in price, size, and view. Because of the high culinary standards, the demi-pension rate, required in high season, is no problem here. One person pays 380F ($86.75) to 550F ($125.57). The bedrooms are pleasantly furnished, with good light colors. Some have private terraces, and all open onto good views of the garden.

On the grounds, in a setting of shady palms, are brown-and-white umbrella tables. Right across the park is the private swimming club, where you can rent your own "parasol and pad" on the sandy beach at reduced rates for hotel guests. The Juana receives guests from March 15 to October 20. The chef has developed a reputation for providing an outstanding offering of buffet hors d'oeuvres, with a repertoire of some 150 dishes ranging from stuffed grape leaves to "demoiselles" de Cherbourg to peppers filled with Spanish rice. This array is offered at lunch, costing 175F ($39.95). Meals are served in an open-air dining room.

The Middle Bracket

Pré Catelan,. Avenue Lauriers (tel. 61-05-11), is a substantial villa in a residential area just a few minutes' stroll from the town park and the sea. It has the kind of garden a northern European dreams about: rock terraces, towering palm, lemon, and orange trees, large pots of pink geraniums, and trimmed hedges with nooks and crannies for outdoor furniture where you can sneak away for a discreet rendezvous. The atmosphere is casual. The half-pension rate ranges from 165F ($37.68) to 200F ($45.66) per person daily, the more expensive rooms including private terraces. The hotel closes from November 1 to January 31.

Le Passy Parc Hôtel, 15 Avenue Louis-Gallet (tel. 61-11-09), is a recently enlarged and renovated, centrally positioned 60-room hotel. One side opens onto a small garden with palm trees and a wide flagstone terrace, the other fronts the sea and coastal boulevard. Generally, furnishings are Nordic modern; all the rooms have private baths (the newer ones have their own little balconies). There are three seasons, the highest tariffs charged between June 15 and September 15, when singles cost from 140F ($31.96) to 180F ($41.09); doubles, 175F ($39.95) to 280F ($63.92).

The Budget Range

Cecil, rue Jonnart (tel. 61-05-12), is only 50 yards from the beach. The owner-chef, Monsieur Romain, provides a very friendly welcome. The house is well kept, with beige corridors and many antiques in the rooms. The tapestries are in the Provençal style. In summer guests eat on a patio. You stay here on the full-pension plan, paying 135F ($30.82) per person in high season. On each floor is a free shower. Open from March 20 to October 15.

DINING: Bijou-Plage, Promenade du Soleil (tel. 61-39-07), at the edge of Juan-les-Pins on the coastal road to Cannes, is where you can order that famous bouillabaisse du pêcheur, costing 100F ($22.83) per person. It'll be made with freshly caught seafood, spiced just right and filling enough to make an entire meal. Decorated in a nautical style, the restaurant is right on the beach—a proper setting for its cuisine. A 60F ($13.70) set meal is offered, including the service charge. À la carte, such delectable dishes are featured as local grilled fish. A tarte maison rounds out most meals. If you order à la carte, expect to spend from 95F ($21.69) to 110F ($25.11) per person. Closed from mid-October to Christmas.

Le Perroquet ("The Parrot"), Avenue Gallice (tel. 61-02-20), is a tavern-like restaurant overlooking the central park. Not unlike a brasserie, it offers one of the most economical and best-prepared meals in the resort town. For 38F ($8.68) you can get a complete five-course luncheon or dinner, with service included. This fixed-price meal often features a choice of such dishes as rabbit in a white wine sauce or osso buco, the Lombard specialty. Closed from mid-October to March 1.

Beach shacks line the road west of Juan-les-Pins. Here you can order some of the best and freshest fish in the area. You can have more elaborate seafood meals at the already recommended Bijou-Plage, but these shacks are more adventurous. One favorite, **Chez Claude,** route de Golfe-Juan (tel. 61-58-68), offers a set meal for 35F ($15.98), including a big bowl of savory fish soup as a first course, then grilled fish (whatever was caught that day), a green salad, plus a choice of cheese and dessert. Claude will also make a bouillabaisse for you especially, 120F ($27.40) for two persons. The couscous is also delicious. Another specialty is a seafood paella served only for two. A la carte meals range in price from 55F ($12.56) to 110F ($25.11). You can rent a beach mattress or cabin and make a day of it.

15. Golfe-Juan and Vallauris

From his exile in Elba, Napoleon and 800 men landed at Golfe-Juan in 1815 to begin his Hundred Days. In time Golfe-Juan was to be favored by the American Navy, but primarily it is a family beach resort, well sheltered by protective hills planted with orange trees. Just three miles from Cannes, it contains one notable restaurant, **Tétou** (see below). A short road leads to Vallauris, once merely a stopover along the Riviera, until Picasso made it and its potters famous.

Its ceramics and souvenirs—many the color of rich burgundy—line the street. Frankly, most of the shops display tasteless ware. One notable exception is **Madoura** (tel. 63-74-93), where Suzanne and George Ramié are the only people licensed to sell reproductions of Picasso's works. The master knew and admired their work for a long time, ever since he ventured into this small Provençal town after World War II and occupied an unattractive little villa known as "The Woman from Wales." Madoura is open from 9 a.m. to noon and from 2 to 6 p.m. Some Picasso reproductions are limited to 150 copies, others to as many as 500.

Half the members of the world press clustered one day around the central square where Picasso's statue **Homme et Mouton** *(Man and Sheep)* stands. But they weren't admiring it. Everybody was there to take pictures of a couple getting married: Aly Khan and Rita Hayworth. The council of Vallauris had intended to ensconce this statue in a museum, but Picasso insisted that it remain on the square "where the children could climb over it and the dogs water it unhindered."

At the **Place de la Libération** stands a chapel of rough stone shaped like a Quonset hut, a horizontal half-cylinder. Picasso decorated the chapel with two paintings: *La Paix (Peace)* and *La Guerre (War).* The paintings tug the viewer in two directions—toward love and peace on the one hand, toward violence and conflict on the other. In 1970 a house painter gained illegal entrance to the museum one night and substituted one of his own designs, after whitewashing a portion of the Picasso original. When the aging master ventured out to inspect the damage, he said, "Not bad at all." The Museum of Vallauris is open from 10 a.m. to noon and from 2 to 6 p.m. (off-season, until 5 p.m.), charging 4F (91¢) for admission, 2F (46¢) for students.

DINING: Tétou, Boulevard de la Mer (tel. 63-71-16), fulfills one's fantasy of finding a white beach cottage right on the water where one can get a most delicious bouillabaisse. The bouillabaisse, usually served for two, is not only savory and delicately spiced, but each succulent chunk of fish can be tasted individually. On the à la carte menu, one of the best buys is poissons (fish) de pays, accompanied by tomatoes à la Provençale. The soupe de poissons (fish soup) makes a good opener, followed by an excellently prepared sole meunière. After all that seafood, fresh fruit from the hills is a good finish. Expect to spend from 180F ($41.09) to 220F ($50.23) for a complete meal. The restaurant is closed from the first of October until around Christmas and on off-season Wednesdays.

16. Mougins

Crowning a hill, this once-fortified town provides a viable choice for those who want to be near the excitement of Cannes but not in the midst of it. The international resort is just five miles away, but spiritually it is a continent away from the quiet life as lived at Mougins. The wealthy set from Cannes, however, has discovered its golfing potential. Picasso knew its possibilities for living. No wonder artists love the rugged, sun-drenched hills covered with gnarled olive trees. In the little valleys, gentle streams go by. Mougins is the answer to those who feel the Riviera is overrun, overspoiled, and overbuilt.

THE DELUXE LIFE: Le Moulin de Mougins, Notre-Dame de Vie (tel. 75-78-24), was a 16th-century olive-oil mill. Now it coddles guests in comfort and serves one of the finest and most imaginative cuisines in France. On entering, you pass the 10-foot-wide stone oil vat, complete with a wooden turn screw and a grinding wheel. Roger Vergé (described as having "the handsome face of a playboy") took over the mill in 1969, making it his own culinary kingdom. The "maître cuisinier de France" provides an idyllic setting for a fine meal: thick stone arches, rough old beams, ladderback chairs, Spanish paintings, and open cupboards with copper and painted china.

One day we asked him to list what he considered his best dishes. Our pencils wore down after he cited 30. Our favored viands include le suprême de loup maître Escoffier, le filet de Charolais (an excellent Bourgogne beef) au foie gras de canard et aux truffes, and le poulet d'allier au vinaigre, this last dish served for two only. His particular forte is fish from the Mediterranean. Each morning he buys directly from the local fishermen. If you dine here, expect to pay anywhere from 280F ($63.92) per person. Of course, the price depends a great deal on the wine you select. Monsieur Vergé has a lot of fantastic, even historic bottles. But there is also a good local wine selection at humane prices.

The old mill offers six beautifully decorated apartments, each a honeymoon lair, with provincial beds, Louis XVI chairs and chests, bay windows with white ruffled curtains, and matching flowered toile coverings for furniture and beds. Doubles range from 280F ($63.92) to 450F ($102.74), the latter for a suite with terrace. The inn is closed from November to mid-December, and the restaurant shuts down every Monday.

If you can't obtain a reservation, you might try Monsieur Vergé's other place, l'Amandier de Mougins (tel. 90-00-91), in the village in a 14-century olive-oil mill, where a set meal costs 160F ($36.53).

THE MIDDLE BRACKET: Le Clos des Boyères, 89 Chemin de la Chappelle, Notre-Dame de Vie (tel. 90-01-58), is a family villa in a tranquil setting where you can hear the birds chirping and smell the pines. On the side of a tree-covered hill, it is surrounded by a lawn, with a swimming pool on a lower terrace. The rambling entry driveway is edged by lawns and trees. The inn, a member of the Société of Mapotel, is especially recommended for families with children, as there is room to romp and play. The furnishings are pleasant, informal, and "countrified." Each of the 25 bedrooms has its own bath and telephone. Three sets of rates are charged, the most expensive applying in July and August, when two persons pay 350F ($79.91) for demi-pension; one per-

son, 250F ($57.08), including service and taxes. The hotel is open from March
1 to October 31.

17. Grasse

Grasse boasts the most beautiful fragrance of any town on the Riviera. Go
there to visit the perfume factories. One of the best known, the **Fragonard
Parfumerie,** is named after the French painter of the 18th century. It is open
daily, including Sundays and holidays, from 8:30 a.m. to 6:30 p.m. There is a
guided tour by an English-speaking young woman; you'll see "the soul of
flowers" extracted. After the tour, you can explore the **Museum of Perfumery,**
displaying bottles and vases that trace the industry back to ancient times. The
Parfumerie is at 20 Boulevard Fragonard.

Since the 19th century, Grasse—10½ miles from Cannes—has been the
world's perfume capital, set in the midst of jasmine and roses, violets and
lavender, orange blossoms and jonquils. Once it was famed as a resort, attracting such widely diverse personages as Queen Victoria and Pauline Borghese.

Of particular interest is the **Musée d'Art et d'Histoire de Provence,** 2 rue
Mirabeau, housed in the **Hôtel de Clapiers-Cabris,** constructed in 1771 by
Louise de Mirabeau, the Marquise de Cabris and sister of Mirabeau. The
museum is rich in paintings, four-poster beds, marquetry, ceramics, brasses,
costumes, kitchenware, jewelry, bonnets, pottery, urns, even archaeological
finds from the area. Visitors are welcomed from 10 a.m. to noon and from 2
to 6 p.m. in summer for an admission of 5F ($1.14), which also entitles you
to visit the Musée Fragonard (see below). In winter, the afternoon hours are
from 2 to 5 p.m.; it is closed on Sundays and in November.

Nearby is the **Villa Fragonard,** where the **Musée Fragonard** is now
housed. Here are displayed the paintings of Jean-Honoré Fragonard, born at
Grasse in 1732, and those of Marguerite Gérard and Alexandre and Théophile
Fragonard, sister-in-law, son, and grandson of Jean-Honoré Fragonard. The
grand staircase was decorated by Alexandre. The museum is open from 10 a.m.
to noon and from 2 to 6 p.m. in summer; in winter, afternoon hours are from
2 to 5 p.m. Closed Sundays and in November.

18. Cannes

When Coco Chanel went there and got a suntan, returning to Paris
bronzed, she startled ladies of society. Nonetheless, they quickly began copying
her, abandoning their heretofore fashionable peach complexions. Today, the
bronzed bodies—in the briefest of bikinis—which line the sandy beaches of this
chic resort continue the late fashion designer's long-ago example.

Popular with celebrities, Cannes is at its most frenzied during the **International Film Festival** at the **Palais des Festivals** on the Promenade de la
Croisette. Held either in April or May, it attracts not only film stars but those
with similar aspirations. On the seafront boulevards flashbulbs pop as the
starlets emerge—usually wearing what women will be wearing in 1990. International regattas, galas, *concours d'élégance,* even a Mimosa Festival in February
—something is always happening at Cannes, except in November, which is
traditionally a dead month.

Sixteen miles southwest of Nice, Cannes is sheltered by hills. For many
it consists of only one street, the **Promenade de la Croisette,** curving along the
coast and split by islands of palms and flowers. It is said that the Prince of
Wales (before he became Edward VII) contributed to its original cost. But he
was a Johnny-come-lately to Cannes. Setting out for Nice in 1834, Lord

Brougham, a lord chancellor of England, was turned away because of an outbreak of cholera. He landed at Cannes and liked it so much he decided to build a villa there. Returning every winter until his death in 1868, he proselytized it in London, drawing a long line of British visitors. In the 1890s, Cannes became popular with Russian grand dukes (it is said more caviar was consumed there than in all of Moscow). One French writer claimed that when the Russians returned as refugees in the 1920s, they were given the garbage-collection franchise.

A port of call for cruise liners, the seafront of Cannes is lined with hotels, apartment houses, and chic boutiques. Many of the bigger hotels, some dating from the 19th century, claim part of the beaches for the private use of their guests. But there are public areas.

Above the harbor, the **old town** of Cannes sits on the hill of Suquet. There rises the high **Lords' Tower,** dating from the 12th century. Nearby is the **Musée de Cannes,** housing an ethnography section (Peruvian and Mayan pottery, objects of daily use from the Pacific islands, sculptures and ceramics from Southeast Asia), as well as a gallery of ancient civilizations of the Mediterranean, ranging from Roman to Egyptian to Greek to Etruscan to Cypriot artifacts. Charging 3F (68¢) for admission, the museum is open in July, August, and September from 10 a.m. to noon and from 3 to 7 p.m. From October to June, hours are from 10 a.m. to noon and from 3 to 5 p.m. On Sundays, entrance is free. The museum is closed in November and on Mondays.

THE LÉRINS ISLANDS: Floodlit at night, the Lérins Islands stare across the bay at Cannes, forming the most interesting excursion from the port. From the harbor at Cannes a boat leaves frequently, taking 15 minutes to reach Île Ste.-Marguerite, 30 minutes to Île St.-Honorat. Round-trip fare between Cannes and Île Ste.-Marguerite costs 10F ($2.28), increasing to 12F ($2.74) between Cannes and Île St.-Honorat.

The first island is named after St. Honorat's sister, St. Marguerite, who once lived there with a group of nuns in the fifth century. Today the island is a youth center, whose members are dedicated to the restoration of the fort when they aren't practicing sailing and diving. From the dock where the boat lands, you can stroll along the island (signs point the way) to the **Fort de l'Île,** built by Spanish troops from 1635 to 1637 above a Roman town from the first century B.C., where *The Man in the Iron Mask* was held prisoner.

One of the perplexing mysteries of French history concerns the identity of the man who wore the *masque du fer.* A prisoner of Louis XIV, he arrived at Ste.-Marguerite in 1698. Dumas fanned the legend that he was a brother of Louis XIV, and it has even been suggested that his son (by a mysterious woman) went to Corsica and "founded" the Bonaparte family. However, it is most often ventured that the prisoner was a manservant of the superintendent, Fouquet, named Eustache Dauger. At any rate, he died at the Bastille in Paris in 1703.

You can visit his cell at Ste.-Marguerite, in which every visitor seemingly has written his or her name. As you stand (hopefully without a crowd) listening to the sound of the sea, you realize what a forlorn outpost this was. The entrance fee is 4F (91¢). From June to September a son-et-lumière spectacle is staged on the island at 9 p.m. on Thursday, Saturdays, and Sundays. The return is at 11:15 p.m. The round-trip ticket costs 18F ($4.11).

The **Musée de la Mer** traces the history of the island, displaying artifacts of Ligurian, Roman, and Arab civilizations, plus the remains discovered by excavations. These include paintings, mosaics, and ceramics. The museum is

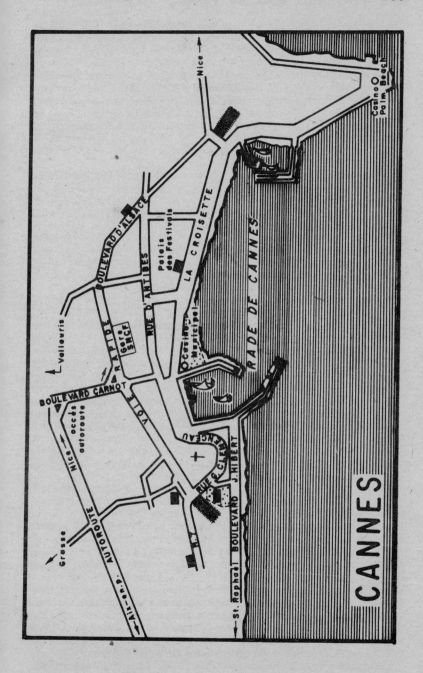

open from June to September—10 a.m. to noon and 2 to 6 p.m. Off-season its hours are 10 a.m. to noon and 2 to 5 p.m. It is closed in November and December, and charges an admission of 3F (68¢).

Note: hours can vary, depending on the arrival of the boats.

Île St.-Honorat, only a mile long, is even lonelier. St. Honorat founded a monastery there in the fifth century. Since the 1860s the Cistercians have owned the ecclesiastical complex, consisting of both an old fortified monastery and a contemporary one. You can spend the entire day wandering through the pine forests on the west side of the island, the other part being reserved for prayers in silence.

HOTELS: Putting aside contemplation of such accommodations as prisons and monasteries, turn your thoughts to—

The Leading Deluxe Hotel

Majestic, Boulevard de la Croisette (tel. 68-91-00), is getting livid looks from the traditional but fading leader, the Carlton. Built many decades ago, the Majestic now reigns supreme, befitting its name. Constructed around an overscale front patio with a lush swimming pool, the hotel opens directly upon the esplanade and the sea. Under tall palms and flowering orange and fig trees, it welcomes a cult of some of the chicest suntans in Europe. Inside, the setting is one of glistening marble, clusters of "dripping" crystal chandeliers, tapestries, seasoned antiques and reproductions, salons with Oriental carpets, Louis XV silk furniture, potted palms, a bar with an equestrian theme, and attentive service. Dining is special in the formal hall, with Louis XVI-style chairs spaciously placed around circular tables, against a backdrop of tall columns and draperies opening onto the courtyard greenery.

The bedrooms are all furnished with a blending of antiques and reproductions, offset by Oriental rugs, marble tables, high-fashion covers and bolsters to the beds, and (in many) black-marble baths with gold fixtures. Renovated deluxe bedrooms for two persons peak at 850F ($194.06), facing the sea, with air conditioning. Singles go from 340F ($77.62). Underground parking is available. The director, Jacques Bardet, is to be congratulated for turning the Majestic into one of the showplaces of the Côte d'Azur. It is closed from mid-October to mid-November.

Upper Bracket Living

Le Grand Hôtel, 45 Boulevard la Croisette (tel. 38-15-45), has a garden with tall date palms and a lawn sweeping right down to the waterfront esplanade. A splendid structure of glass and marble, it is part of a complex of adjoining apartment-house wings and encircling boutiques. Eleven floors of bedrooms—each with wall-to-wall picture windows—open onto tiled terraces, extending the living space. Vibrant colors are used throughout: sea-blue, olive, sunburst-red, and banana-gold. The baths are lined with colored checkerboard tiles, with matching towels and rows of decorative bottles.

Le Grand charges its highest tariffs from March 15 to October 15. A double with a sea view costs 700F ($159.81), 480F ($109.58) otherwise. Singles cost 270F ($61.64). Half pension is an extra 120F ($27.40) per person daily. The main lounge sets the style level, with "island" clusters of white plastic chairs and tables and sofas and armchairs against a backdrop of an antique Oriental folding paneled screen.

Martinez-Concorde, 67 Boulevard de la Croisette (tel. 68-91-91), tops all contenders in sheer size: 400 rooms, 700 beds. It, too, enjoys precious space on the Mediterranean. The hotel has deserted the tradition of antiques and a classic decor for a vibrant modern in primary colors. The bedrooms also use bold colors, although the furnishings are "tame." The baths—one to each room—are successful, pearl-gray and white with pink accents, for the most part.

The highest rates are charged from March 30 to October, with two persons paying 600F ($136.98) for the most expensive accommodations fronting the sea. Singles range from 220F ($50.23). At lunch, you can take your meal on an open-air terrace restaurant. Perhaps the most popular "living room" for the Martinez is the beach in front, where cabins, showers, and a water-skiing school await you.

The hotel's restaurant, L'Orangerie, is excellent, supervised by the famous Roger Vergé of Mougins. His specialties include a soup of mussels flavored with saffron, and turbot in an orange sauce. Set meals are featured at 120F ($27.40). The hotel is closed from October to mid-December.

The Moderate and Upper Range

Sofitel Méditerranée, 1 Boulevard Jean-Hibert (tel. 99-22-75), is the prime favorite of the international yachting set. It stands directly on the harbor, sun-bleached in white stucco, with surrounding balconies and an open-air rooftop swimming pool. It's a remake of an older hotel, and much ingenuity went into bringing a sense of lightness and brightness to its interior. Against the muted tone inside, color was added to give warmth, including marigold lampshades, olive carpeting, and goldenrod bedspreads. From July 1 through August, a single room costs anywhere from 280F ($63.92) to 360F ($82.19); doubles are 315F ($71.92) to 420F ($95.89) for a room with breakfast and service included. The more expensive rooms contain balconies fronting the sea and yacht harbor. Good food is served in the dining room in a setting of wood paneling and frosted globe lamps.

Victoria, Rond-Point Duboys-d'Angers (tel. 99-36-36), is a stylish modern hotel, built right in the heart of Cannes. Completely air-conditioned, it offers accommodations with baths and refrigerators. Nearly half its bedrooms have balconies overlooking the small park and the hotel's swimming pool. Despite the name, the rooms are more French than English, with coordinated colors and a judicious use of period reproductions. Bedspreads of silk (most often pink) and padded headboards evoke a boudoir quality. The lodgings facing the park cost a little more and are well worth it: 190F ($43.38) to 250F ($57.08), single; 260F ($59.36) to 280F ($63.92), double. Rooms facing the shopping street are tabbed at 210F ($47.94) for couples. Included in these prices are taxes, service, and a continental breakfast; no other meals are served. After a day on the beach, guests congregate in the paneled bar, sinking comfortably into the leather couches and armchairs. From this vantage point, it's easy to imagine you're back in Buckinghamshire, England.

Canberra, Rond-Point Duboys-d'Angers (tel. 38-20-70), shares ownership with its sister, the Victoria across the way. However, the atmosphere at the Canberra is mellower, as it's a remake of an older hotel. The overall effect is a mixture of modern and traditional. Limited parking is available in the hotel's small garden. All the air-conditioned rooms come equipped with bath or shower. Doubles start as low as 160F ($36.53) if facing the shopping street, and peak at 250F ($57.08) if fronting the park. Singles range in price from 135F ($30.82) to 200F ($45.66). Rates quoted include service, taxes, and a continental breakfast, which guests enjoy on a canopy-covered front veranda. There is also a modest reception bar and lounge.

Suisse, rue Bertrand-Lepine (tel. 38-53-67), proves once again that the Swiss are good innkeepers. Under the management of Monsieur Bode, this substantial hotel is surrounded by its own private garden, with a path leading to the seafront. It is decidedly old-fashioned, with seaview balconies and tall shuttered windows. Inside, there are many reminders of the past: antiques and family-style furnishings placing the emphasis on comfort. The service is quiet and impeccable. The highest rates are charged from July 10 to September 15, when, for demi-pension, singles pay 235F ($53.65) to 270F ($61.64); couples, 340F ($77.62) to 370F ($84.47), including taxes and service. The most expensive tariffs are for accommodations with private bath. Every room is polished and immaculately kept. The hotel closes from October 20 till January 15.

The Budget Range

Le Saint-Yves, 49 Boulevard d'Alsace (tel. 38-65-29), is a genuine old villa, set back from the busy coastal boulevard by a front garden and a grove of palm trees. It's only a five-minute stroll from the seafront, although the garden of the villa is so enjoyable that many guests spend a good part of their day there. For more than 22 years, English-speaking Madame Yvette Geolle has owned the villa. Even though there are bedrooms upstairs, the house is her home, bearing her personal stamp. For two persons in a room with private bath, she charges 220F ($50.23), including breakfast (fresh croissants, country butter, good jam). Doubles with less plumbing range in price from 140F ($31.96) without bath to 200F ($45.66) with shower. The bedrooms differ in size and are pleasantly furnished, mainly with odds and ends. Parking is free. Breakfast is the only meal served.

Westminster, 55 Boulevard d'Alsace (tel. 38-56-47), is a converted villa that vaguely suggests the New Orleans style of architecture, with vibrant shutters and wrought-iron balconies gracing its creamy façade. The garden has a central graveled area with large shade trees, and outdoor furniture placed under the date palms, a haven from the summer sun. Beds of pink geraniums and begonias give splashes of color. Off a busy boulevard, it is quiet. About a seven-minute stroll from the waterfront esplanade, it offers 41 bedrooms available year round. The highest rates are charged from April 1 through September, when full pension costs 200F ($45.66) to 235F ($53.65) per person in a double, 230F ($52.51) in a single. The bedrooms are freshly decorated, comfortable, and clean, some with a sitting area. Parking is free.

Wagram, 140 rue d'Antibes (tel. 38-55-53), is a friendly oasis. It's owned by Monsieur Biscarre, who is assisted by an English-speaking daughter, a brother, and a sister-in-law. Like a string quartet, they provide a harmonious setting for a successful stay at Cannes. The Wagram is on a busy coastal boulevard, about a five-minute walk from the seafront. Away from the traffic, breakfast in the rear garden is an ideal way to start your day. The interior is most comfortable although no style-setter, with lots of plastic-covered furniture. Open all year, the hotel requires that you take all your meals here in July and August, when two persons in a room with bath are charged 456F ($104.11) for full board. Off-season, the pension complète costs 388F ($88.58) for two.

Athénée, 6 rue Lecerf (tel. 38-69-54), is a five-story hotel with 16 bedrooms, most with private baths. It's geared for travelers who seek comfortable, inexpensive bedrooms and don't require lounges (there's only a pocketwatch reception lobby). On a quiet business street about four short blocks from the seafront, it provides only breakfast. An American film distributor who stays there at least once a year writes of the courtesy and good treatment he's always received, maintaining that the Athénée gives what "some of its competitors only claim: very good breakfast and clean, comfortable rooms." For the most expensive double with twin beds, expect to pay 200F ($45.66), although with a toilet (but no shower) that rate is reduced to 160F ($36.53). Singles range from 145F ($33.10).

Mondial, 77 rue d'Antibes (tel. 39-28-70), is a moderately modern six-floor hotel on a business street, with stores on its lower floor. The hotel is about a three-minute walk from the beach, and three-quarters of its rooms have a view of the water, the others overlooking the mountains and an avenue. Its soft Devonshire-cream façade is studded with a few small balconies. The attractive bedrooms are the draw here, with matching fabric on the beds and at the windows, sliding mirror doors for wardrobes, and compact tiled baths. The highest rates are charged in July and August, when the most expensive doubles, with breakfast, rent for 220F ($50.23). However, during the rest of the year, two persons pay anywhere from 125F ($28.54) to 162F ($36.99), a good bargain for Cannes. Closed in November.

De La Poste, 31 rue Bivouac-Napoléon (tel. 39-22-58), in the very heart of Cannes, is a modernized but modest little hotel opposite the post office. For its low rates, it offers many conveniences. There is no lobby, only a reception desk with an open staircase. The bedrooms are plain and uncluttered, often with colored candlewick bedspreads set against knotty-pine dado. Spidery modern chairs and flowery cretonne draperies complete the decor. In high season, doubles with shower baths cost 160F ($36.53); the tab is only 130F ($29.68) in a double with a shower (no toilet). It is open all year.

Hôtel de France, 85 rue d'Antibes (tel. 39-23-34), only two blocks from the sea, is right in the center of town. The rooms are large and clean, and although the furnishings generate little enthusiasm, the welcome is hearty. Doubles range from 195F ($44.52), singles from 145F ($33.10). Tariffs include a continental breakfast, service, and taxes. Rates are reduced off-season. On top of the hotel is an open-air terrace for sunbathing.

Toboso, allée des Oliviers (tel. 38-20-05), is a little away from the center, but it's a nice, homelike residence offering tranquility. Formerly a private family villa, it has been slowly and carefully transformed into a small but comfortable hotel. The former family salon is now the main lounge. If you feel romantic, you can use the concert piano to play Chopin. Dancers at the neighboring Rosella Hightower School often frequent the establishment. The 14 rooms have a personal touch. Singles cost 65F ($14.84) to 80F ($18.26); doubles, 90F ($20.55) to 115F ($26.25) with hot and cold running water, 130F ($29.68) to 150F ($34.26) with private showers or complete baths. Breakfast is included. Most of the rooms have windows facing the gardens, and some have terraces on which you can sunbathe.

READER'S HOTEL SELECTION: "I stayed at the **Hotel Bristol,** 14 rue Hoche (tel. 39-10-66), and I want to recommend it to you. Its new owners, Jean-Jacques Sedykh and Jean-Pierre Lenseigne, took great personal care in furnishing the hotel comfortably and tastefully. The lobby, with fine antiques and furnishings, has the feeling of a living room. There are 20 rooms in the hotel, and mine was light, roomy, well-heated, spotlessly clean, and comfortably furnished. Most rooms have bath or shower, and doubles range in price from 55F ($12.56) to 120F ($27.40). I liked the location as well—one block from the railroad station and two blocks from the sea. The owners themselves are the real charm of the hotel, however. Both men are warm, gracious, and personable. They speak fluent English cheerfully, and they hold breakfast for late sleepers, a kindness I appreciated" (Robin McClellan, New York, N.Y.).

RESTAURANTS: Cannes seems to have no end of excellent restaurants in all price ranges. First—

Upper-Bracket Dining

Festival, 55 Boulevard de la Croisette (tel. 38-04-81), is generally credited with having the best food. Against the South of Pago-Pago decor, many of the "beautiful people" go here to drink and dine, the former taking place outside at the sidewalk tables, the latter inside. Whatever your sexual persuasion, you'll meet some interesting people and some characters you'd rather not ("I can't abide the idea of going to Switzerland, really"). It isn't cheap. Specialties include bouillabaisse with lobster, pepper steak, and loup (bass) au golfe flambé au fenouil (fennel). The traditional opener is soupe de poissons (fish) with rouille, and the smoothest finish is a peach Melba—invented by Escoffier. Set meals are offered for 125F ($28.54) and 155F ($35.39). Most à la carte dinners cost from 110F ($25.11) to 160F ($36.53). Closed from mid-October to December 20.

La Reine Pédauque, 4 rue Maréchal-Joffre (tel. 39-40-91), serves the best food in Cannes. Set back from the water on a somewhat commercial street, it becomes divorced from its surroundings once you step inside. Within is a rustic setting and a staff devoted to the preparation and serving of quality cuisine. Two set meals are offered, one at 95F ($21.69), another at 110F ($25.11), the latter containing many specialties. First, a selection of hot canapés is set before you. From the hors d'oeuvres cart you can have, among other tidbits, the Niçois version of caviar (black olives ground into a delicious appetizer). On the à la carte menu, it is recommended that you try the light, delicate mousseline de bécasse (woodcock) Robert-Dorange, as well as le terrine et la galantine de canard (duck) en croûte. Try also the filet d'agneau (lamb) aux aromates de Provence. The cherries jubilee make for a spectacular finish. Expect to spend from 160F ($36.53) and up if you order à la carte. Closed Mondays and from July 1 to 21 and December 8 to 17.

La Voile au Vent, 17 Quai St.-Pierre (tel. 39-27-84). Right on the port, this restaurant enjoys one of the most romantic situations in Cannes. Under the sharp eye and firm hand of Monsieur Ducrot, the chef specializes in a classic French cuisine, with an emphasis on seafood dishes. You can dine inside or outside at sidewalk tables. The classic fisherman's bouillabaisse costs 140F ($31.96) for two persons. Especially good main courses are carré d'agneau (lamb) à la moutarde for two, and vol-au-vent with "fruits of the sea." Desserts include crêpes suzette. An average meal here will cost from 150F ($34.26). The restaurant is closed on Thursdays and in November.

Blue Bar, Palais des Festivals, Boulevard de la Croisette (tel. 39-03-04). On any given night in season, you're likely to spot at least four young women who look like BB in days of yore. Small and intimate, this restaurant attracts a chic crowd, mostly young people. While you can dine indoors, the sidewalk tables under umbrellas are infinitely preferred if the weather is right (which it is most of the time). The chef generally sticks to the classic French dishes, with Provençal overtones. Although the repertoire appears limited, it is exceedingly good. The fish soup is a favorite opener at 26F ($5.94), but many French diners begin their meal with a salade Niçoise, also 26F. The steak with freshly crushed peppercorns at 52F ($11.87) is a recommendable meat course, and the filets de sole bonne femme should please fish fanciers, 75F ($17.12). To end your meal, try the rich but light chocolate mousse at 18F ($4.11). A 15% service charge is added. Closed in June.

La Mère Besson, 13 rue des Frères-Pradignac (tel. 39-59-24), is owned and operated by Mother Besson, who is as French as a croissant. She's hearty, plump, and has strong culinary convictions,which she expects her staff to carry out with meticulous detail. She has a particular flair for herbs. At no place in Cannes can you get such a wonderful and typical Provençal cuisine. All the recommendable specialties are prepared here with consummate skill, plus a high degree of culinary imagination. A different Provençal dish is prepared for every day of the week. On our most recent stopover, the delectable offering was estouffade à la Provençale—beef braised with red wine and a rich country stock flavored with garlic, onions, herbs, and mushrooms. Specialties include soupe au pistou and soupe de poissons. Every Wednesday you can order Lou Piech. This is a Niçois name for a veal brisket which has been stuffed with white-stemmed vegetables, peas, ham, eggs, rice, grated cheese, and herbs. The meat is cooked in salted water with vinegar, carrots, and onions, like a stockpot, then served with a thick tomato sauce known as *coulis.* Your tab is likely to be anywhere from 100F ($22.83) to 150F ($34.26). Closed Sundays and in June.

The Medium-Priced Range

At **Laurent,** 12 rue Macé (tel. 39-32-56), the proprietors have installed a museum of antique cutlery (Le Petit Musée de la Table). Mme. Allainmat and Monsieur Laurent are the collectors who operate this prestigious little restaurant just off the promenade. A charming friend of ours from Florida, who (at the age of 72) still has herself photographed riding a camel in North Africa or going on a pilgrimage to Pakistan, writes, "Whenever I'm in Cannes, I head straight for Laurent and place myself entirely at their mercy, even though I'm charged for pension at the Carlton." Two set dinners are offered, one for 65F ($14.84), another for 100F ($22.83). The latter features Russian specialties such as smoked salmon, white herrings with cream, and beef Stroganoff. On the à la carte menu, you can order coquelet (cockerel) Mère Michèle, flambéed veal kidneys, and cheese from Auvergne. The dessert specialty of the house is tarte à Pancienne. Ordering à la carte will bring your bill up to 120F ($27.40). The restaurant is closed in November.

Romanens "La Grande aux Belles," 5 rue Notre-Dame (tel. 39-35-16). The atmosphere of this theatricalized restaurant threatens to overshadow the cuisine, but the chef manages to triumph. From hay (just plain hay) to cowbells to drippy candles to carved wooden animals to stirrups to red tablecloths, the cozy ambience goes crazy. A set dinner is offered for 60F ($13.70), another for 80F ($18.26), and a most elaborate one at 130F ($29.68). The most expensive fixed-price meal includes, for example, a medallion de langouste thermidor, canard (duckling) with olives, pommes soufflées, followed by cheese and a parfait. Some of the cooking is over an open hearth. Closed from mid-November to mid-December.

Budget Restaurants

Au Mal Assis, 15 Quai St.-Pierre (tel. 39-13-38), is our unqualified economy dining choice at the port, enjoying the same vantage point as its more expensive rivals. It is especially recommendable for its 50F ($11.42) set dinner (offered weekdays), which includes some of the chef's specialties. For that price, you're likely to get moules (mussels) Provençales, followed by a bouchée aux fruits de mer with freshly done French fries, and finally a selection of fruit or cheese. The chef's specialty is bourride Provençale (a fish stew with slices of bread), 70F ($15.98). A service charge is added. Meals are served from noon to 1:45 p.m. and from 7 to 9:30 p.m. If you go early, you can grab one of the sidewalk tables. Closed in November until mid-December.

Au Bec Fin, 12 rue du 24-Août (tel. 38-35-86), is a simple bistro-style restaurant offering especially good bargain meals. On a street halfway between the railway station and the beach, it has little in the way of decor, relying on wainscoting and nautical wallpaper. Sometimes red carnations are brought in from the nearby fields to brighten your table. In the warmer months, the place is kept humming with revolving fans overhead. Most popular is the 45F ($10.27) fixed-price luncheon or dinner, which gives you a wide selection. A first course might include salade Niçoise, the house specialty; then caneton (duckling) with cèpes (flap mushrooms), plus a choice of vegetables and dessert. Other set meals begin at 60F ($13.70) and include more elaborate selections. The restaurant is closed on Friday nights, Saturdays, and from December 20 to January 20.

La Coquille, 65 rue Félix-Faure (tel. 39-26-33), in the old town, set back from the port, is the best in a string of budget restaurants on this street. In fact, it's among the best for the budget in Cannes, if you're seeking good and inexpensive seafood such as sea bream, red snapper, sole, or bouillabaisse. La Coquille also offers a good choice of veal, beef, and lamb dishes. The restaurant has won acclaim for its 42F ($9.59) set menu, which might comprise soupe de poissons aux croûtons à rouille, followed by dorade (sea bream) du golfe grillée au fenouil (fennel), as well as spaghetti or a salad. Service is included, and your drink is extra, of course. The quality is always very good, and the fish is always fresh.

Restaurant du Lyonnais Provenial, 8 bis rue des Frères-Pradignac (tel. 39-26-65), blends two cuisines, that of Lyon and that of Provence. Run by Monsieur Gobet, it's a country-style auberge with colored cloths and terrazzo floors, offering good-quality meals at low prices. A complete four-plate dinner is only 24F ($5.48); more elaborate repasts are 30F ($6.85) and 35F ($7.99). The cooking is very tasty. For the lowest tab you're given a large selection, such as soupe au pistou (vegetable soup flavored with basil, a Côte d'Azur specialty), steak tartare, or Neapolitan spaghetti, plus cheese and dessert. This economy restaurant is only a short walk from the Promenade de la Croisette.

19. La Napoule-Plage

On the Golfe de la Napoule with its sandy beaches stands this secluded resort, once an obscure fishing village. In 1919 it was Shangri-La to an eccentric American sculptor, the son of a New York banker, and his architect wife. Fleeing from the "charlatans" of America, who he felt had profiteered in World War I, Henry Clews emphasized the fairytale existence of his new home—now the **Henry Clews Museum**—by inscribing over the entrance, "Once upon a time."

Taking over the ruins of a medieval château, the Clewses set about the mammoth task of rebuilding. The sculptor, who has been described as "the greatest America has ever produced," covered the capitals and lintels with the grotesque menagerie of his own private world, revealing a tortured (some have said perverse) mind. Scorpions, pelicans, gnomes, monkeys, lizards—no subject seemingly was taboo to him. Striking back at the critics who "didn't understand my work," he pictured them as blind. His women were often distorted and shrunken by age—his *Cat Woman* in particular, with drooping breasts revealing "feminine vice." This sculpture depicts a suffragette as he saw her marching on Fifth Avenue and expresses his view of feminism. The artist was preoccupied with old age in both men and women, and greatly admired chivalry and dignity in man as represented by Don Quixote—whom he likened to himself.

Clews died in Switzerland in 1937, and his body was returned to La Napoule-Plage for burial. Before her death in 1959, Mrs. Clews opened their château to the public ("Castle of weird images opens!" hailed the press). In summer you can arrive for guided tours at 4 and 5 p.m. (in winter, between 2:30 and 5:30 p.m.), paying an admission of 6F ($1.37). Students are admitted for 3F (68¢).

DINING: **L'Oasis,** rue de Riou (tel. 38-95-52), is the domain of the Outhier family, who have turned it into one of the greatest restaurants along the Riviera. It is a true oasis of gourmet food, attracting many visitors from Cannes (reservations are imperative). Set back from the waterfront behind the Hôtel Beau Rivage, it is not easy to find but worth the search, even if you have to drive all the way over from Nice. Louis Outhier, a fast-rising chef in his 40s, makes ordering easy. He lists set meals, each containing specialties. À la carte specialties include loup en croûte (bass in a pastry shell) for a minimum of three diners, and turbot braisé au champagne, requiring a minimum of two. Another excellent dish is foie de canard (duck liver). Expect to pay from 220F ($50.23) if you order à la carte. The restaurant is housed in a small villa with a palm garden. Everything is in exquisite taste. The inn is closed from October to December 20 and on Tuesdays.

20. St.-Tropez

Lasciviousness is rampant in this carnival town, but a true Tropezian resents the fact that the port has such a bad reputation. "We can be classy, too," insisted one native.

Creative people in the lively arts along with ordinary folk create a volatile mixture. One observer said that St.-Tropez "has replaced Naples for those who accept the principle of dying after seeing it. It is a unique fate for a place to have made its reputation on the certainty of happiness."

St.-Tropez was greatly popularized by Bardot in *And God Created Woman,* but it's been known for a long time. Colette lived here for many years. Even the diarist Anaïs Nin, confidante of Henry Miller, posed for a little cheesecake on the beach there in 1939 in a Dorothy Lamour bathing suit. Composer Ned Rorem bought a canary-yellow shirt at Vachon, to go, as related in his famous diary, with "my golden legs in khaki shorts, my tan sandals, and my orange hair." Earlier, St.-Tropez was known to Guy de Maupassant, Signac, Matisse, and Bonnard.

Artists, composers, novelists, and the film colony are attracted to St.-Tropez in summer. Trailing them is a line of humanity unmatched anywhere else on the Riviera for sheer flamboyance. Some of the most fashionable yachts bringing the chicest people anchor here in summer, disappearing long before the dreaded mistral of winter.

Near the harbor is the **Musée de l'Annonciade,** at the Place Georges-Grammont, installed in the former chapel of the Annonciade. It is open daily except Mondays from 10 a.m. to noon and from 3 to 7 p.m. (the afternoon hours are from 2 to 6 p.m. in winter), charging an admission of 6F ($1.37). As a legacy from the artists who loved St.-Tropez, the museum shelters one of the finest modern-art collections on the Riviera. Many of the artists, including Paul Signac, depicted the port of St.-Tropez itself. Opened in 1955, the collection includes such works as Kees Van Dongen's yellow-faced *Woman of the Balus-*

trade, and paintings and sculpture by Bonnard, Matisse, Rouault, Braque, Vuillard, Dufy, Utrillo, Seurat, Dunoyer de Segonzac, Vlaminck, Derain, Despiau, and Maillol. Closed in November.

On the outskirts of St.-Tropez, at a distance of two miles, **Port Grimaud** makes for an interesting outing. If you approach the village at dusk when it is softly bathed in Riviera pastels (much like Portofino, Italy), it will look like some old hamlet, perhaps from the 16th century. But this is a mirage. Port Grimaud is the dream-fulfillment of its promoter, François Spoerry, who carved it out of marshland and dug canals. Flanking these canals, fingers of land extend from the main square to the sea. The homes are Provençal-style, many with Italianate window arches. The owners of boats can anchor right at their doorsteps. One newspaper called the port "the most magnificent fake since Disneyland." One of its promoters has described it as "a village as it would have been if architects did not exist."

HOTELS: For such a famous resort, St.-Tropez has a shocking lack of hotel rooms. If you're arriving in July and August without a reservation, you'd better not entertain hopes of spending the night—unless, of course, you're good at meeting countesses.

Deluxe Living and Dining

Byblos, Avenue Paul-Signac (tel. 97-00-04). Its builder spent $3 million to create what he told the press was "an antihotel, a place like home." In that he succeeded—providing "home" has salons removed intact from Beirut palaces and 3000-B.C. Phoenician gold statues valued at $50,000! Set apart from the other hotels, up on a hill from the harbor, this deluxe establishment resembles a village complex from a bird's-eye view—complete with intimate patios and courtyards, plus a "high-fashion" swimming pool. Inside, the hotel's decorator has created a seductive retreat, filling salon after salon with antiques and rare decorative objects, many brought from Lebanon, including polychrome carved woodwork on the walls, marquetry floors, a Persian-rug ceiling, and nooks for objects of art.

Every bedroom and suite—59 in all—maintains a unique character. In one, for example, there is a fireplace with a raised hearth, paneled blue-and-gold doors, rustic beams, and a bed recess on a dais. Prices vary according to the season, the highest tariffs being charged from June 26 to mid-September. Singles cost 460F ($105.02) to 520F ($118.72); doubles, 500F ($114.15) to 680F ($155.24), plus 15% for service. Every room has a fashionably styled private bath. Your bedroom window may have a balcony overlooking the inner courtyard or else open onto a stepped-down terrace of flowers. Four bars provide varied and dramatic settings for drinks; and dining is still another treat. La Nouvelle Cuisine is prepared by the hotel's chef, Jean-Louis Simonet, who lists as his specialties suprême de saumon frais et de truffes aux poireaux (truffles and leeks); blancs de volaille (chicken) à la moutarde (mustard) de Meaux; pavé de Charolais (high-quality beef from the Charolais region of Burgundy) au vin de Provence, and a soup of mussels flavored with saffron. Expect to pay about 170F ($38.81) for an average meal in the Restaurant des Arcades. Later in the evening, you can dance on a circular floor surrounded by bas-relief columns in the hotel's new nightclub. The hotel is closed from November 5 to mid-December.

Résidence de la Pinède, Plage de la Bouillabaisse (tel. 97-04-21). In 1952, Jean Michel set out to form a holiday retreat for "house guests" right on the water on the fringe of St.-Tropez. An original building with a tower to store olives was renovated and a new house designed to provide greater comfort. In time, celebrities made their way to its door, Audrey Hepburn preferring the tower, Raquel Welch the main building, as did William Holden and Pierre Salinger. The new wing imitated the tower in a way, with its series of miniature "pepper-pot" turrets connected by balconies.

The bedrooms have a formal country look to them, with provincial furnishings. You can have breakfast on your own balcony with a view of the bay, watching the yachts go by. Open from April 30 to October 23, the hotel charges its highest rates from June through September. For demi-pension (required), one person pays from 280F ($63.92) to 420F ($95.89), with service included.

The main living room looks like that of a country home, not at all institutional. Antique furnishings, paintings, and Oriental rugs are used throughout. Most guests prefer to dine at the ornate white garden tables set under the pines.

The Upper Bracket

Le Ya Ca, Boulevard d'Aumale (tel. 97-12-79). For a sophisticated crowd seeking an intimate, informal, and stylish accommodation, Le Ya Ca is it. Set on a quiet and narrow street a good walk from the harbor, it is a great old hillside villa completely remodeled, the restoration project the inspiration of Monsieur Gormier and his son-in-law, Gerard. The terraced garden seems almost Andalusian, with subtropical trees, plants, flowers, ceramic statues, bird cages, and garden furniture. On a lower level is an outdoor barbecue, where guests dine festively on moonlit nights.

Winding, twisting stairs lead to private rooms of every shape and size, each with a private bath. Each has its own personality, some lofty with high-beamed ceilings and fireplaces as well as windows overlooking a fountain and orange trees. The decorations consist of well-chosen antiques or reproductions, interesting prints, old light fixtures, and oil paintings. Some of the rooms have a terrace, a few contain balconies, all are imbued with style and charm. The tariffs include taxes and service. In high season, the small doubles rent for 375F ($85.61), the larger ones peaking at 490F ($111.86). Breakfast is an extra 28F ($6.39).

The Middle Bracket

La Ponche, Place du Rèvelin (tel. 97-02-53), is a cluster of remodeled fishermen's houses, opening on one side onto a little plaza fronting a tiny sandy beach where a club atmosphere prevails. In a secluded and relatively unknown but central part of St.-Tropez, it attracts many interesting clients.

Most of the accommodations are small but charmingly furnished. Doubles overlooking the sea cost 180F ($41.09); doubles with terrace go for as much as 320F ($73.06). A single with shower rents for 87F ($19.86). Across the little plaza (which in the evening becomes a social center) are a few highly individualized apartments fronting the little beach.

A central glassed-in lounge in the main building is furnished with antiques and original paintings. Two dining rooms have been furnished with 18th-century antiques and original paintings. The food is rather "new cuisine," although grilled fish from the Mediterranean has always been featured. Specialties are stuffed fish at 120F ($27.40) per person and savory bouillabaisse, 130F ($29.68) per person. The hotel is open from February 15 to October 15.

Sube, 15 Quai Suffren (tel. 97-00-02), could be your first choice if you want to be dead center, right on the port. Directly over a popular coffeehouse, it is entered through an arcade of shops. The reception area is a vaulted corridor, with carpets and glass display boxes. There's a two-story-high beamed lounge with an all-glass front, letting you enjoy your morning coffee while watching the harbor activity. A 10-foot-high fireplace, a wall torchère, and provincial chairs drawn together provide the decorations. The bedrooms are overly small and decorated in a provincial style (the skill of navigating in the closed quarters of a yacht will be invaluable here). The beds are soft, and the maids keep everything neat and tidy. Two persons in a room with a patio pay 225F ($51.38), the rate rising to 350F ($79.91) for two or three guests occupying a room with private bath overlooking the port. These tariffs include a continental breakfast, service, and taxes. The restaurant on the second floor is handsomely decorated and serves good food.

The Budget Range

Coste, Port du Pilon (tel. 97-00-64), is on the outskirts of St.-Tropez, across the coastal road from the sea. Ignore the severe motel-like façade. Behind it is a large courtyard with an old garden of orange trees, palms laden with ivy, flowering oleander, terra-cotta pots of cacti and geraniums, and, of course, olive trees. Garden furniture is scattered informally, and guests can relax with a view of the sea. At the front, two tiers of bedrooms with iron-railing balconies—almost New Orleans style—are balanced on strong, square pilings. The older building (circa 1950) at the rear was once the private villa of the owner, Monsieur Coste. Between June 15 and September 15, he rents double rooms with bath for 125F ($28.54), charging only 95F ($21.69) for bathless doubles in the older villa. Served in the garden, breakfast is an additional 12F ($2.74). Open March 15 to November 1.

Le Colombier, Impasse des Conquettes (tel. 97-05-31), is a simple village home where paying guests are accepted. The emphasis is on quiet, cleanliness, and the enjoyment of the little garden studded with pines and lemon trees. You get tranquil sleep, although you're a long haul from the milling crowd along the harbor. Le Colombier isn't easily found, down a lane of dull garages. Prices here are all-inclusive (tax, service, and breakfast in the miniature garden). In high season (July through September and on holidays), expect to pay a peak of 165F ($37.68) for double rooms with shower. This tab descends to as little as 135F ($30.82) for some doubles. A single with shower goes for 120F ($27.40). Welcoming guests all year, Madame Delansorne has done a good job of making her little rooms attractive and comfortable.

Lou Cagnard, Avenue Paul-Roussel, route de Ramatuelle (tel. 97-04-24), is a pleasant place at which to stay, tranquil enough if you get a rear room overlooking the garden. A remake of an old house on a village road, it's somewhat like a roadside inn, with a tiled roof and green shutters. Madame Rul doesn't speak a word of English, but somehow she manages to cope with her North American guests. The tariffs include taxes and service, but a continental breakfast is an additional 11F ($2.51). A double-bedded room without bath goes for 92F ($21), the tariffs increasing to anywhere from 130F ($29.68) to 150F ($34.26) in a double with complete bath.

RESTAURANTS: The range is from *très chic* to affordable.

Upper-Bracket Dining

Le Mouscardins, sur le Port (tel. 97-01-53), has been loaded with culinary honors. There's almost universal agreement that it serves the best food in

St.-Tropez. At the extreme end of the port, it is an upstairs restaurant with picture windows allowing for harbor views. Inside, there's a formal Provençal atmosphere. A sun room under a canopy adjoins the restaurant. You make your dining selections—a Mediterranean classic repertoire—from the à la carte menu. If you're willing to pay for it, you can enjoy really superb viands. An excellent dish—just to get you started—is the moules (mussels) marinière, 30F ($6.85). The two celebrated fish stews of the Côte d'Azur are offered here: a bourride Provençale and a bouillabaisse, each at 115F ($26.25). The fish dishes are especially good, particularly the loup (sea bass) at 115F also. If you're not in a fishy mood, try the grilled, tender entrecôte at 60F ($13.70). The chef prepares two dessert specialties, a soufflé au Grand Marnier or with Cointreau, each costing 50F ($11.42). The restaurant is open from February to the end of October.

L'Auberge des Maures ("The Inn of the Moors"), 4 rue du Dr.-Broutin (tel. 97-01-50), is an offbeat choice. A short walk from the port, it is entered through gypsy-like curtains. You can have your meal either inside or alfresco under an arbor. On any given night you're likely to run into a table of rock singers with their groupies, a filmmaker with his starlet of the moment, a conservatively dressed judge from the U.S. midlands, or a honeymooning couple from Paris. The menu is gilt-edged, and so are the tabs—but the cuisine is really good. The fish soup is made with rouille, a "combustible" sauce of garlic and red peppers. Other specialties are mullet cooked with fennel hearts and lobster with port. The dessert specialty is sabayon. Service is an extra 15%. Savory fish specialties will mean a bill in the 110F ($25.11) to 160F ($36.53) price range. The restaurant is closed Wednesdays, and its season lasts from Easter to September 30.

The Medium-Priced Range

L'Escale ("Port of Call"), sur le Port (tel. 97-00-63). One of the most compelling reasons for dining here—other than the good cuisine—is to be seen. The setting is hard not to like: outside tables in light brown under a canopy, with portside views. On the à la carte menu, specialties include sea bass (loup), 115F ($26.25); a bourride Provençale (a savory fish stew), also 115F; and escalope à la crême, which is veal with fresh cream, costing 55F ($12.56). The restaurant is open from March 20 to October 22 and for the Christmas holidays.

Le Girelier, sur le Port (tel. 97-03-87), is right in the mainstream of social activity. The food is excellent, and there are two price levels for dinners. Pierre Rouet, the patron and chef de cuisine, charges 42F ($9.59) for his least expensive meal, which might include soupe de poisson (fish soup), followed by pipérade (a chef's specialty, an omelet with pimiento, garlic, and tomatoes) or côte de porc, with freshly fried potatoes or a salad, plus a choice of cheese or dessert. À la carte, an escalope à la crême is recommended, as are stuffed mussels. If you order à la carte, expect to pay from 65F ($14.84) to 175F ($39.95), the latter tab including lobster. A casually dressed crowd seems to gravitate here, freely eating off each other's plates. If you get a table under the canopy, you'll have an orchestra seat to examine the life on the yachts anchored in front of you. The restaurant is closed from January 1 to March 15.

21. The Riviera After Dark

For many, the Riviera comes alive only after dark. You can resort-hop your way from Menton in the east to St.-Tropez in the west, leaving the last disco as dawn breaks. Along the way, you can lose a fortune at the spin of a wheel in the gambling casinos.

MONTE CARLO: The Russian grand dukes came here at the turn of the century to break the bank at Monte Carlo. However, that legendary honor went to Charley Wells from London's East End, "The Man Who Broke the Bank at Monte Carlo," winning $200,000 in one night. He didn't really have a "system," however, and he died in poverty. A speculator, François Blanc, made the **Monte Carlo Casino** the most famous in the world, attracting in time Sarah Bernhardt, Mata Hari, Farouk, and Aly Khan (Onassis used to own a part-interest). The architect of the Paris Opéra, Charles Garnier, built the oldest part of the casino, and it remains a fascinating, extravagant example of period architecture. The nostalgia for the past has faded. The new grand dukes are fast-moving international businessmen on short-term vacations. Baccarat, roulette, and chemin-de-fer are the most popular games, although you can play "le craps" and blackjack as well. The gambling rooms are open daily from 10 a.m., charging 15F ($3.42) admission. You must carry your passport with you and be at least 21 years of age. The private rooms—for serious gamblers only—charge no admission.

The foremost winter establishment, under the same ownership, is the **Cabaret** in the **Casino Gardéns** (tel. 50-80-80). Its mode of decoration is self-styled as "Georges Reinhard 1880." You can dance to the sounds of a smooth orchestra. A good cabaret is featured, sometimes with ballet numbers. It is open from September 12 to June 20.

If you're a Princess Grace watcher and are interested in culture, you might fulfill two fantasies by attending a concert in the **Salle Garnier** of the casino. The princess appears quite regularly, usually with her children, although, of course, she is not able to attend every concert. These are held periodically, and full information about them is available at the Tourist Office. The music is usually classical, featuring the Orchèstre National de l'Opéra de Monte-Carlo; the price of seats is in the 50F ($11.42) to 120F ($27.40) range. For theatrical productions and the appearance of special guest artists, ticket prices are likely to be higher.

X'Club, 13 Avenue des Spéluges (tel. 30-70-55), is a disco nightclub that is open all night. It's owned by a fascinating character, Gregory Seguin, ex-singer, ex-movie star, ex-whatever. His friends call him "The Baron." Born in Kiev, son of a Russian baroness who escaped the October Revolution, he tramped around the world for a quarter of a century. First, he sang in St.-Germain-des-Prés, making enough money to cross the Atlantic to New York. He dreamed of making it to Hollywood, but ended up as a miner in the Dakotas.

Brigitte Bardot, Ursula Andress, Frank Sinatra, and Omar Sharif have all been club members. But Mr. Seguin welcomes all guests, whether they're film stars or not. A first drink costs 50F ($11.42).

Gregory's . . . After Dark . . ., Avenue Princesse-Grace, Le Bahia, Monte Carlo (tel. 30-78-56), is a chic, American-style piano bar. It's run by the famous Gregory ("The Baron"), who also owns the previously recommended X' Club. You can order a baby scotch for just 7F ($1.60). The club is open from 5 p.m. to 6 the next morning.

NICE: **Paradise Club,** 27 Promenade des Anglais, is a club with a prewar atmosphere, on the lower level of the belle époque Westminster Hotel. The decor is cozy and comfortable, with soft lighting and soft music for dancing. An orchestra plays, and the clientele spans a wide age spectrum. The first drink costs 35F ($7.99) in the afternoon, 50F ($11.42) to 65F ($14.84) at night.

ANTIBES: **La Siesta,** Pont de la Rivière "Brague" (tel. 34-31-68), is a kind of beach club with a dual personality. When entering, you'll see a sign posted giving the requirements for admission: *"L'élégance et la bonne éducation!"* Really an amusement center, La Siesta isn't very sleepy. In the daytime, you can spend many sunny hours lounging on the graveled beach or going for a dip in the pool. Meals are available under adjustable umbrellas set around a large reflection pool with overscale lily-pad floats. The use of the beach club facilities costs 45F ($10.27), and snacks are available, including a salade Niçoise at 25F ($5.71), or a hamburger at 30F ($6.85). At night attention focuses on the disco (at one event, 6500 showed up) and drinking lounge. You pay 55F ($12.56) for your first drink.

JUAN-LES-PINS: The **Eden Beach Casino,** Plage du Casino, is a nightclub cabaret as well as a gambling emporium. Charging an entrance fee of 10F ($2.28)—passports required—it offers the standard baccarat and roulette. In the adjoining club, a quintet and sometimes a singer perform. You pay a minimum of 35F ($7.99) for your first drink. The casino opens nightly at 9.

For the younger crowd, the biggest club in town is **Le Voom-Voom,** Boulevard de la Pinède (tel. 61-18-71). Groups from the U.S. and England perform twice a week, although the club is open nightly from 9:30 p.m. to 5 a.m., charging an admission fee of 25F ($5.71) to 50F ($11.42), depending on the class of performers. Voom-Voom is a specialist in pop music.

An alternative choice is the **Black & White Club,** Boulevard Dr.-Dautheville. You'll hear many songs in English, intermixed with French and Italian. The doors open nightly at 9:30, and you'll pay a 22F ($5.02) minimum, including the price of your first nonalcoholic drink. Should you prefer whiskey, the tab is increased to 35F ($7.99). At the crowded Sunday matinees, the admission is 20F ($4.57), drink not included.

CANNES: The **Municipal Casino** (closed summers) lives up to its legend. In a jewel-case setting, it attracts an international crowd, which passes through its spacious reception lounge with sparkling tiered crystal chandeliers. You proceed to the check-in desk just outside the main gambling room, presenting your passport and paying a 50F ($11.42) admission, good for eight days. The **New Brummel** (tel. 39-34-66) is the casino disco, providing two live combos nightly from November to May. At the side of the casino, the disco is on a lower level. For decor, bright, sharp colors are used, with a horseshoe arrangement of tables around the dance floor and a raised bandstand. The evening begins at 10 p.m. Expect to pay 50F ($11.42) for your first drink.

The **Embassy Club** (tel. 39-34-66) here is the most glamorous dinner-dance restaurant in Cannes, decorated impressively in a neoclassic style, with a dramatic view through arched windows to the Mediterranean. You can order a *menu complet* at 100F ($22.83). An à la carte menu is offered as well. Cabaret shows are presented here, sometimes with name performers. Yet another restaurant, called **Le Bistingo,** is now a gastronomic restaurant and offers a complete luncheon at 130F ($29.68).

In summer, from June 1 to October 31, when the Municipal Casino closes, the **Palm Beach Casino** handles the heaviest gambling volume in France.

Handsomely positioned at the Pointe de la Croisette (tel. 43-91-12), it is one of the leading French casinos and a powerful force in the Cannes summer scene. The Palm Beach is a glamorous nighttime rendezvous, charging a 55F ($12.56) admission to its air-conditioned salons, which open at 5 p.m. daily and include all French and American games. It is also a dining and entertainment complex, the major action centering around the **Terrasse du Masque de Fer** ("Iron Mask Terrace"). Here you'll pay 175F ($39.95) in June and September, 200F ($45.66) in July and August, plus the cost of drinks and service, for dinners in the open air. Two orchestras play for dancing. Toward the end of dinner, ballet and cabaret are featured. Every week, gala evenings take place, with special decorations, well-known showbusiness personalities, and fireworks. (Actually, you can arrive at the Palm Beach beginning at 10 a.m.) You can also dance from 11 p.m. till dawn at **Jackpot**, a private, air-conditioned disco.

Whisky à Go-Go, 115 Avenue de Lérins (tel. 43-20-63), is the favored spot if you're young—or think you are. Facing the Palm Beach Casino, it seems more a nightclub than a disco. You sit in comfortable armchairs in this two-level establishment, watching the action. Seating 700, Whisky is the biggest such club on the French Riviera, and guests are treated to a light show with colored lasers, smoke, and fog. From her glassed-in cage, a disc jockey spins the latest. Changing color patterns are projected on the mirrored back wall. In jeweled bolero jackets, waiters bring you your drink for 35F ($7.99) during the week, the entrance tariff rising to 50F ($11.42) on weekends.

Borrowing from the '20s, the **Speakeasy**, 22 rue Macé (tel. 39-31-31), bills itself as "*le club des jeunes.*" Catering, therefore, to young people, it charges a moderate 25F ($5.71) for admission, including the first drink, and is open every evening as well as for Sunday matinees. Customers dance either to live groups or else well-selected recorded music. You must be 18 years old (but not much more than that) to be admitted.

Finally, **Club La Chunga**, 72 La Croisette (tel 38-11-29), is a restaurant, bar, and disco with a panoramic terrace. An elegant Côte d'Azur rendezvous for showbusiness people, it offers meals beginning at 160F ($36.53). In the international piano bar, a scotch costs 40F ($9.13).

ST.-TROPEZ: At any time of the day or night, the social center of St.-Tropez is the **Sénéquier**, sur le Port (tel. 97-00-90). It is the most popular café in the port, drawing a lively crowd. Drinks range from 8F ($1.83) to 50F ($11.42). Also popular is the **Café de Paris**, sur le Port (tel. 97-00-56), which is under the Hotel Sube. Open year around, it is animated even in the dead of winter. A whiskey costs 25F ($5.71). Whatever you are looking for, you're likely to find it at either the Sénéquier or the Café de Paris.

The Money

1. Currency Conversions

The basic unit of French currency is the **franc,** worth about 23¢ in U.S. currency. One franc breaks down into 100 centimes. Coins are issued in units of 1, 5, 10, 20, and 50 centimes, plus 1, 5, and 10 francs.

The franc, like all world currencies, is fluctuating on the market. That means that the franc-to-dollar conversions appearing in parentheses throughout these chapters may or may not be exact. There is no way to predict what the rate of exchange will be when you visit France. Check with your bank to determine the up-to-date figure.

However, our dollar conversions listed below will give you a fair idea of what you'll be spending. Use them then as a gauge:

Francs	Dollars	Francs	Dollars
0.50	.11	25	5.71
1	.23	30	6.85
2	.46	35	7.99
3	.68	40	9.13
4	.91	45	10.27
5	1.14	50	11.42
6	1.37	75	17.12
7	1.60	100	22.83
8	1.83	110	25.11
9	2.05	120	27.40
10	2.28	130	29.68
11	2.51	140	31.96
12	2.74	150	34.26
13	2.97	175	39.95
14	3.20	200	45.66
15	3.43	250	57.08
20	4.57	500	114.15